CHALLENGING THE KREMLIN

CHALLENGING THE KREMLIN

The Soviet Jewish Movement for Freedom, 1967–1990

EDWARD DRACHMAN

PARAGON HOUSE
New York

First edition, 1991
Published in the United States by
Paragon House
90 Fifth Avenue
New York, NY 10011

Book design by Deirdre C. Amthor

Library of Congress Cataloging-in-Publication Data

Drachman, Edward R., 1940–
Challenging the Kremlin: the Soviet Jewish movement for freedom, 1967–1990 / Edward Drachman–1st ed.
p. cm.
Includes bibliographical references and index.
ISBN 1-55778-053-6
1. Jews—Soviet Union—History—1917– 2. Jews—Soviet Union—Persecutions. 3. Refuseniks. 4. Antisemitism—Soviet Union. 5. United States—Foreign relations—Soviet Union. 6. Soviet Union—Foreign Relations—United States. 7. Soviet Union—Emigration and immigration. 8. Soviet Union—Ethnic relations. I. Title.
DC135.R92D72 1991
947'.004924—dc20 90-23707
CIP

Manufactured in the United States of America

Acknowledgments

Grateful acknowledgment is made to the following for permission to use material:

"Open Letter to the 52 Soviet Citizens of Jewish Nationality, Participants in the Moscow Press Conference on March 4, 1970," from *The Lonely Course of Lazar Liubarsky,* edited by Moshe Dector. Reprinted by permission of the National Conference on Soviet Jewry.

Selection from *It Seems I Am a Jew,* by G. Freiman, edited by Melvyn B. Nathanson. Reprinted by permission of Southern Illinois University Press.

"Free My Husband, My People," by Avital Shcharansky, from *The Wall Street Journal,* November 15, 1985. Copyright © 1987 Dow Jones and Company, Inc. All rights reserved. Reprinted with permission of *The Wall Street Journal* and Avital Shcharansky.

"Moscow Denies U.S. Trade–Emigration Link," from *Pravda,* December 19, 1974. Translation copyright © 1975 by *The Current Digest of the Soviet Press,* published weekly at Columbus, Ohio.

Table from "Jews in the 1989 USSR Census," by Professor Sidney Heitman from *Soviet-Jewish Affairs,* Vol. 20, No. 1, 1990, p. 28. Reprinted by permission of *Soviet Jewish Affairs* and Sidney Heitman.

"*The Samizdat* Journal *Evrei V SSSR,*" by Julia Wishnevsky from Radio Liberty Research. RL 321/79, October 15, 1979. Reprinted by permission of Radio Liberty.

Manifesto of the National Patriotic Front 'Pamiat.' Reprinted by permission of *Central Asia and Caucasus Chronicle,* Vol. 8, No. 3, July 1989, pp. 14–15.

Contents

Preface

This book provides a review and analysis of the Soviet Jewish movement for freedom from 1967 to 1990. The book is intended for both academic and general audiences. It should be useful for college students of Judaic, Soviet, and U.S.–Soviet affairs. It should also be valuable for synagogues, churches, religious associations, Soviet Jewry advocacy groups, human rights associations, government officials, and concerned lay people.

There are three main parts to the book, each containing selected readings preceded by an analytic essay. The approach within each part is essentially chronological, allowing the reader to see clearly the development of major subjects. Readings were selected for their importance and/or representativeness. Most of the research was conducted in the files of Action for Soviet Jewry (Waltham, Mass.) and the National Conference on Soviet Jewry (New York City); in libraries and archives of the American Jewish Historical Association at Brandeis University, the Russian Research Center at Harvard University, and Radio Free Europe/Radio Liberty in New York City and Munich.

I am indebted to many colleagues, friends, and family members who helped me in this project: Marion and the late Steve Berman, who encouraged me to visit refuseniks during my several trips to the Soviet Union in the mid-1980s; "Spike" Spiegel, Bob Fishman, and Marvin Catler of the Greater Hartford Jewish Federation, who stimulated my interest in Soviet Jewry; Jonathan Sanders, CBS News correspondent in Moscow, Attorneys Hugh Barry and Donna Arzt, formerly of the Soviet Jewry Legal Advocacy Center in Waltham, and Professors Robert O. Freedman of the Baltimore Hebrew College and Jonathan Rosenbaum of the University of Hartford, who offered helpful comments during the early planning stages of my project; Joshua Rubenstein, New England

Coordinator of Amnesty International U.S.A., who helped give shape and coherence to the book and provided useful documentary sources; Sheila Galland and Judy Patkin of Action for Soviet Jewry, and Bradley Frome, Mark Heutlinger, Myrna Sheinbaum (now of B'nai B'rith) and Martin Wenick of the National Conference on Soviet Jewry, who answered questions and provided assistance on using their files; Iwanna Rebet, Chief Librarian, and analyst Ellen Drescher of Radio Free Europe/Radio Liberty in Munich who provided important research material and assistance; Scott Weltz and David Yousha, Boston University graduate students who helped with translation and transliteration of Russian into English; Margie Moskovitz of the Greater Hartford Jewish Federation, Gideon Aronoff, formerly of Action for Soviet Jewry, Professors Don Barry of Lehigh University and Richard Saul of Boston University, who painstakingly critiqued an early draft of the manuscript; Judy and Al Lipsky, Barbara and Mike Kess, Jim Krasnoo, and Marion Gillon, good friends who made significant stylistic suggestions; and Evelyn Fazio, my editor at Paragon who gave valuable advice and encouragement. Finally, I offer a special word of thanks to my stepson Dan Sherwood who helped me understand the wonders of wordprocessing, and to my wife Barbara, whose limitless patience, understanding, assistance, and support helped me complete this undertaking. To all of you I am deeply grateful.

EDWARD DRACHMAN
Frankfurt am Main
Germany
January 1, 1991

INTRODUCTION: The Legacy of Anti-Semitism in Russia and the Soviet Union

The Soviet census of January 1989 reported 1,449,167 Jews in the Soviet Union, down approximately 362,000 (20 percent) from the 1979 census and down about 36 percent from the 1959 census. *(See Table 1.)* Unofficial estimates place the number as high as three million, depending at least partially upon the determination of "Who is a Jew?"[1] Jews are the twentieth largest and the most urbanized of the more than a hundred nationalities in the U.S.S.R. Compared to other minorities, they are the most culturally and linguistically Russified and among the most highly educated and heavily represented in the professions and Communist Party membership.

Soviet Jews comprise two geographic and cultural groups. The majority (about 95 percent) is the European or Western Jews of the Slavic heartland republics of Russia, the Ukraine, and Belorrusia ("White Russia") and those Jews living in territory taken over by the Soviet Union during World War II: the Baltic republics of Estonia, Latvia, and Lithuania; a big slice of eastern Poland; the northern half of East Prussia; Bessarabia and North Bukovina from Romania; Finnish Karelia; and the Carpatho-Ukraine region from Czechoslovakia. European Jews are mostly *Ashkenazim* (descendants of Jews from middle and eastern Europe) who have resided in a largely Christian world.

The other group, about 5 percent of the Soviet Jewish population, is the Asian or Eastern Jews of Georgia, Bukhara (mainly in the Uzbek and Tadzhik republics in Central Asia), and Daghestan ("Mountain Jews" in the northern Caucasus). These Jews, less urbanized and less highly educated (especially in the sciences) than the *Ashkenazim*, have lived for centuries in the midst of a Moslem and Christian majority. Historically, the Eastern Jews and those in the more recently incorporated European

TABLE 1

Soviet Jewish Population: 1959, 1970, 1979, 1989

Region	1959	1970	1979	1989	1959–89 Change (%)
USSR	2,267,814	2,150,707	1,807,871	1,449,167	−36.1
RSFSR	875,307	807,915	699,286	550,422	−37.1
Ukrainian SSR	840,314	777,126	632,877	484,219	−42.0
Belorussian SSR	150,084	148,011	135,416	111,789	−25.5
Moldavian SSR	95,107	98,072	80,087	65,757	−30.9
Estonian SSR	5,436	5,288	4,954	4,613	− 8.9
Latvian SSR	36,592	36,680	28,312	22,897	−37.4
Lithuanian SSR	24,672	23,564	14,644	12,312	−50.1
Armenian SSR	1,024	1,048	953	676	−34.0
Azerbaidzhan SSR	40,204	41,382	35,455	30,762	−23.5
Georgian SSR	51,582	55,382	28,121	24,669	−52.2
Kazakh SSR	28,048	27,689	23,379	19,863	−29.2
Uzbek SSR	94,344	102,855	99,863	94,659	+ 0.1
Tadzhik SSR	12,414	14,615	14,655	14,621	+17.8
Kirgiz SSR	8,610	7,680	6,814	5,950	−20.9
Turkmen SSR	4,078	3,494	2,818	2,356	−42.2

Source: Soviet census reports for 1959, 1970, 1979, and 1989.

Table source: Sidney Heitman, "Jews in the 1989 U.S.S.R. Census," *Soviet Jewish Affairs,* Vol. 20, No. 1, p. 28.

lands have tended to be more religiously observant, more Zionist, and much less culturally assimilated than Jews in the heartland.

Anti-Semitism is pervasive throughout most of the Soviet Union but varies in intensity from region to region. In the Ukraine, for example, Jews have long been victimized, whereas in Georgia they have been widely accepted. Anti-Semitism is deeply rooted in Russian history. A wide popular base of anti-Semitic sentiment has developed over centuries and was reinforced by the tsars and by Soviet leaders after the Revolution. For many Jews, this anti-Semitism was a festering irritant in their daily life and evoked their strongest response.

By the latter part of the nineteenth century, pressures that had built up on Russian Jews were forcing them to make a difficult choice: struggle to maintain their own culture, assimilate, emigrate, organize groups for economic and political reform, or join forces with other revolutionaries to overthrow the tsarist regime and establish a new order.

The *zaddikim* (righteous ones), leaders of the *Hasidic* movement that grew in Russia and Eastern Europe in the eighteenth century, stressed the maintenance, reinforcement, and even glorification of traditional Judaism. Believing that intellectual Judaism would not help most Russian Jews, they looked inside the Jewish soul and saw a joyous mysticism. For *Hasidim* (pious ones) the road to salvation was through revivalist song-and-dance prayer meetings. They advocated strengthening Yiddish as the mother tongue for all Jews. Their influence was largely with the uneducated masses in the shtetls (small towns) where most of the Jews then lived.

The *maskilim* (the enlightened), disciples of *Haskalah* (the Jewish Enlightenment movement), which gathered strength in Eastern Europe and Russia in the late eighteenth and early nineteenth centuries, maintained that Jews should look toward a more Western, modern, secular life-style. Intellect and reason, they believed, should guide their action. They held that anti-Semitism would diminish and eventually disappear if Jews tried to assimilate by looking and acting like gentiles. This meant, for instance, that Jews should discard their traditional garb, adopt local customs, stop speaking Yiddish (which the *maskilim* considered the "low" language of the uneducated, "unwashed" masses), learn their local language, and pursue a secular education. The *maskilim* also advised meek subservience to the tsar. Yizhak Ber Levinsohn, for example, a leading figure of the *Haskalah*, praised Tsar Nicholas I as a "prince of God who never ceased to act as our enlightener and benefactor, our merciful father and great savior."[2] The *Haskalah* appealed mostly to the younger and more wealthy Jewish intellectuals. Some of these Jews, however—like Chaim Weizmann (1874–1952), who became the first president of Israel—believed Russian Jews should learn Hebrew, the "high" language that would prepare them for eventual return to their homeland. These Jews focused not on assimilation, which to them seemed an undesirable, failed policy, but on the creation of a Jewish state in Palestine.[3]

Russian Zionists rejected both approaches. They argued that the *Haskalah*'s assimilationist policy would lead to the eventual demise of Russian Judaism and that the *Hasidic* movement's espousal of traditional Judaism was unlikely to succeed in Russia's hostile environment. Their recommendation was emigration to Palestine. Inspired by the Enlightenment and the success of Italian, German, and other nationalist movements in Europe, these Russian Jewish intellectuals dreamed of the realization of Jewish nationalism. But, shocked by the turn of European nationalist movements after the failed revolutions of 1848 toward what historian Hans Kohn called "aggressive exclusivism" based increasingly on blood and race, they felt an urgency to create their own state outside Europe, where they were labeled foreigners.[4] Russian Zionists, embittered by vicious pogroms and punishing restrictions imposed in the aftermath of the assassination of Tsar Alexander II in 1881, for which Jews were blamed (one of the accused conspirators was a Jewish woman, Gesia Helfman), were the first to strike out for Palestine. One small band of *Biluim* (members of the socialist BILU, from the initials of the Hebrew "House of Jacob, Come and Let Us Go") left Russia the next year to found the first agricultural settlements in Palestine, such as Rishon Le-Zion. Much of the financial support for these settlements would be provided by Baron Edmund de Rothschild, a French Jewish philanthropist.

Even though the Zionist movement in Russia was illegal (because the tsar deemed it subversive), it grew rapidly in the latter part of the nineteenth century. On November 6, 1884, about forty members of *Hovevei Zion* (Lovers of Zion) groups, most of whom were from Russia and Romania, met secretly at Katowice, in Upper Silesia. These "Palestinians" believed that the best hope for Jews to lead a free, independent life was in their biblical homeland.

Russian Zionists were heavily represented in the first Zionist Congress, which met in Basel, Switzerland, in 1897 under the leadership of Theodore Herzl, a Budapest-born Jew from Vienna. Like most Jewish movements, Russian Zionism split into factions.[5] The main Zionist parties that grew in the early part of the twentieth century were the Zionist Socialist Workers' Party, organized in 1904, which urged emigration to and establishment of a socialist state in Palestine or another suitable area (thus it was not purely Zionist); the Social Democratic Workers' Party, or *Poalei Zion,* founded in 1906, which was Zionist and Marxist and called upon Jews to build a socialist society only in Palestine; and the Jewish Socialist Workers' Party, or Sejmists (from the Polish *Sejm,* or parliament), established between 1904 and 1906. These non-Marxist populists urged establishment of national autonomy for Jews within Russia during a transitional period before Jews could emigrate to Palestine. Russian Zionists differed over strategy, tactics, and orientation toward Marxist and non-Marxist socialism. What most did agree on was that the salvation of Russian Jews was in emigration to Palestine, either right away or eventually. By the time of the Bolshevik Revolution the Zionist movement had grown to about 300,000 members, dispersed in roughly 1200 towns.[6] This explains in part why it was Russian Jews who founded the majority of Zionist settlements in Palestine before World War I.[7]

But most Russian Jews did not become Zionists. For them the appeal of Zionism was unrealistic. They believed that return to their Jewish homeland in Palestine was chimerical. These "Americans," including young workers and students from *Am Olam* (Eternal Nation), believed their "land of milk and honey" was the United States. Mired in wretched poverty, held down by increasingly onerous restrictions, numbed by odious anti-Semitic propaganda, and battered by heinous pogroms, Russian Jews fled their country. In one of the largest exoduses in history, Jews poured out of Russia in the latter part of the nineteenth and early twentieth centuries. Of about five million Russian Jews, between 1881 and 1914 about two million departed.[8] Many thousands more got out during and after World War I. During the first *Aliyah* (ascent to Palestine), between 1881 and 1903, twenty to thirty thousand Russian Jews emigrated to Palestine. During the second *Aliyah,* between 1905 and 1914, some forty thousand went to Palestine. A small number went to Canada, Australia, South Africa, and various countries of Western Europe and South America, but most (about 70 percent) landed in the United States. In 1891, for example, after Jews were expelled from

Moscow, about 111,000 Russian Jews emigrated to the United States. The figure for 1892 was 137,000. In the wake of the terrible year of pogroms between mid-1905 and mid-1906, over 200,000 Jews fled from Russia. About 3500 went to Palestine, but most (about 154,000) emigrated to the United States.

Other Russian Jews considered Zionism, which offered a national solution for Jews in Palestine, incompatible with their reformist goals or revolutionary socialist philosophy that called for the international proletariat to rise up and destroy capitalism. Some Jews who decided to stay in Russia formed various political socialist labor organizations.

The most important Jewish labor organization was the Jewish Social Democratic Union, known as the *Bund,* which was established in the Lithuanian city of Vilna in 1897. At this time more and more Jews were joining the ranks of the proletariat. The *Bund* opposed the Zionists, whom they considered "bourgeois utopians" and criticized for lack of interest in helping Jews improve their lot inside Russia. The *Bund*'s appeal was mainly to those Jewish workers who desperately wanted to improve their wages and working conditions but who rejected the Marxist approach of political organizations such as the Russian Social Democratic Labor Party (RSDLP), which preached atheism and assimilation. At first, the *Bund* was part of the RSDLP, but in 1903 it was forced to leave for its espousal of "national-cultural autonomy." Workers in the *Bund,* aiming both to improve their economic lot and to strengthen their Jewish identity, chose Yiddish as their language and the strike as their weapon. Although warned by Marxist leaders to cease their "deviationism" and join forces with the Russian proletariat, the *Bundists* steadfastly resisted. Their appeal to Jewish workers grew as they began to win concessions from employers. At the same time, the *Bund* stimulated a resurgence of Yiddish cultural activity. Yiddish literature, education, and the arts grew from the beginning of the century till the outbreak of World War I. The most famous Yiddish writer of that period was Sholom Aleichem, whose humorous folk stories about life in the shtetl helped many Jews laugh at their own poverty and social problems.

Russian Jews suffered more than ever during the early years of the First World War. Jews in the zones of German occupation felt the pain of extreme deprivation, especially economically. But those under tsarist control perhaps suffered even more, mainly because the tsar doubted their loyalty. Some Jewish leaders, when the war started, proudly proclaimed their allegiance to Russia and their determination to fight for their country despite their hardships. As one Jewish deputy stressed in a passionate speech in the Duma (the parliament established by Tsar Nicholas II after the revolution of 1905 to consult on legislative matters):

> . . . the Jews march on the battlefield, shoulder to shoulder with all the other nationalities. We, the Jews, have lived, and continue to live, under exceptionally harsh legal conditions. Nevertheless, we have always felt ourselves to be citizens of Russia, have always been loyal sons of our fatherland. No power whatsoever can tear us from our native Russia, from the soil to which we are bound by ties, centuries old. . . . In this hour of trial, we, Russian Jews, will as one man take our stand under the banners of Russia and devote all our strength to the repulsion of the enemy. The Jewish people will do their duty to the last. . . .[9]

But the tsar, keenly aware of the revolutionary sentiment and activities of some Russian Jews, accused them all of disloyalty in the face of invading German forces. He even blamed Russian army defeats on Jewish treachery. Subsequently, beginning in early 1915, he ordered Jews expelled from their homes. As the Russian council of ministers described the situation then: "Jewish refugees are driven with a whip from the neighborhood of the front. They are accused as a body, without differentiation of any kind, of spying, signaling, and in other ways helping the enemy"[10] Approximately a hundred thousand Jews—many of them weak and infirm—died during this period. Approximately 600,000 were uprooted and never could return to their homes. which were destroyed by both fighting and government-sponsored raids.[11]

It is little wonder that the spirits of Russian Jews were buoyed by the Revolution of March 1917 (February by the old Russian calendar), which overthrew the tsar. Many hoped for a democratic form of government that would ensure the civil liberties and rights of all individuals, regardless of nationality, religion, or culture. They were excited by the decree of March 20, 1917, passed by the provisional government, which read: "All the limitations on rights of Russian citizens imposed by hitherto existing laws on the basis of religion, creed, or nationality are hereby revoked."[12]

What followed was a spurt of Jewish culture. Jewish energy, pent up for years in tsarist Russia, now was released. Jews opened new synagogues, and Jewish life blossomed in all directions—especially in education, the arts, and politics. The Zionist movement became particularly alluring to Russian Jews in the fall as they learned of Britain's Balfour Declaration of November 2, which promised a Jewish homeland in Palestine. Yet this period of excitement was short-lived. The provisional government, beset from within by internal dissension and pressured from without by invading German armies, finally succumbed to Lenin's Bolshevik forces on November 7 (October 25 by the old Russian calendar).

Some Jews had been attracted to Bolshevism because revolution, however achieved, was at the top of its agenda. But of those Jews who did join the revolutionary movement, a much higher percentage linked up with the more moderate Mensheviks. Jews such as Yuli Martov (born Yuli Osipovich Tsederbaum) became leaders of this political grouping. Russian Jews, on the whole, tended to despise the Bolsheviks for their atheism and political tactics of terror and violence. Some also feared the Bolsheviks' anticapitalist ideology, which threatened elimination of their jobs as small entrepreneurs. Many were aware that as early as 1903 Lenin had opposed Zionism as "manifestly reactionary" and "in conflict with the interests of the Jewish proletariat." After 1917 Lenin denounced Zionism as "counterrevolutionary" and advocated the eventual assimilation of all Russian nationalities. Russian Jews were probably at least somewhat confused, however, and even angered by the fact that although relatively few Jews joined the Bolshevik Party, many were in important leadership positions. A significant number also joined the Cheka, the Bolshevik secret police, and through the mid-1930s, its successors (the GPU, OGPU and NKVD), which reinforced anti-Semitic sentiment. One Jew, Genrikh Yagoda, even became head of the NKVD until he was liquidated by Stalin in the purges of the 1930s. Why so many Jews entered the secret police is not clear. Perhaps some were just trying to get even with their anti-Semitic tormentors while others were power-hungry. Nevertheless, Bolshevism—contrary to the claims of some opponents of the Revolution—was not a "Jewish" movement. It gave this appearance only because so many were in visible leadership positions.[13]

Among the best-known Jewish Bolshevik leaders were Leon Trotsky (born Lev Davydóvich Bronstein), the organizer of the Red Army and a brilliant strategist and theoretician; Yakov Sverdlov, the first president of the new Soviet government; Grigory Zinoviev (born Ovsel Gershon

Aronov Radomyslsky), chairman of the Third Communist International (Comintern); Lev Kamenev (born Lev Borisovich Rozenfeld), editor of *Pravda,* chairman of the Politburo (1919–1925) and first director of the Institute of Marxism-Leninism; Maxim Litvinov, Soviet Foreign Minister in the 1930s; Karl Radek, sent by Lenin to Germany in 1918–1919 to help Communists in Germany foment a revolution there; and Lazar Kaganovich, who rose to a high party position under Stalin and after the dictator's death became first deputy premier but was expelled from the presidium in 1957 by Nikita Khrushchev, along with others of the "anti-Party" group.

These "Jewish" leaders were Jewish in name only. They were Communist revolutionaries and assimilationists who rejected their Jewish heritage. In fact, they held Judaism in contempt, ridiculed its "superstitious" and "bourgeois" characteristics, and sought to "emancipate" Jews from their religious balls and chains. This attitude is clearly seen in the following exchange in 1903 between Trotsky and Vladimir Medem, a political opponent: "When it comes to classifying yourself," Medem challenged Trotsky, "you certainly cannot ignore the fact of national allegiance. You consider yourself, I take it, to be either a Russian or a Jew." "No!" cried Trotsky, "you are mistaken! I am a Social Democrat, and that's all!"[14] Kaganovich, in June 1990, revealed much more explicit anti-Jewishness. In a newspaper interview, the ninety-six-year-old Communist chastised Jews for "constantly stirring up the waters." Kaganovich argued that Jews "are always confused. Even today, during the time of the collapse of our state, they are in the first ranks of those who instigate public disorder. Before the war, we successfully overcame the heritage of Jewish bourgeois nationalism, but after the war they forgot who saved them from destruction by Hitler." Then when asked how he, as a Jew, could express such views, Kaganovich retorted: "This is by birth only. In general, I never felt myself to be a Jew. I have a totally different mind-set. Unlike the Jews, who are prone to anarchy, I love order."[15]

Russian Jews were victimized by both sides in the Russian civil war. Elements of both the Red and White armies rampaged through Jewish townships and slaughtered thousands of innocent Jews. Some Red Army groups, bent on stamping out "counterrevolutionary" elements, used terror against all political opponents, real and imagined, and killed over 700 Jews. But leaders of the Red Army, who for the most part tried to protect and win Jews over to their side, severely criticized and disciplined these renegade groups. White armies, blaming the Jews for the Bolshevik takeover, launched much more widespread, devastating, and cruel pogroms. Pogroms were especially heinous in the Ukraine where anti-Semitism was rampant and where nationalist forces accused the Jews of thwarting their drive for independence. According to Soviet sources, between 180,000 and 200,000 Jews died from these pogroms.[16] After the civil war, thousands more Jews, especially Zionists and *Bundists,* were summarily herded off to labor camps in Siberia where they perished.

Jews under Communist rule continued to suffer from much of the same anti-Semitism that was inflicted on their forefathers in tsarist times. A two-track anti-Semitism continued: It was endemic among the people and was perpetrated by the government. Each track fed off the other. Jews were still victims of traditional Russian xenophobia and Russian ethnocentrism. In tsarist Russia, Slavophiles and other groups equated Judaism with all that was pernicious in Westernism. They saw Jews as foreigners who dragged Russia down rather than contributed to its rise. "Beat the Jews and save Russia," they cried. Other groups, like the *Narodniki* (agrarian populists), which had many Jewish leaders, accused Jews of being tools of capitalist exploiters even though restrictive laws had forced them into trade and small private businesses.

Jews were especially suspect and scorned because they were identified as non-Slavic aliens in a land that was not considered theirs and as followers of a religion whose principles were believed threatening to the Russian Orthodox Church. The tsars vowed not to let Jews "contaminate" the soil of Holy Russia. Thus, beginning with Catherine the Great in 1791 and continuing with only minor exceptions until 1917, when the tsar was overthrown, Jews were restricted to living in the Pale of Settlement (prescribed areas of the Ukraine, Belorussia, Lithuania, Poland, and Moldavia). In 1913 the highly publicized trial in Kiev of a Jewish factory worker, Mendel Beilis, accused of using Christian blood to prepare *matzoh* (unleavened bread) for Passover, stemmed from deep-seated anti-Semitic folklore in the Ukraine. It also symbolized the traditional, almost medieval anti-Semitism of Christianity expressed in Russia through the Orthodox Church. Beilis was eventually acquitted because of lack of evidence, but the case left its scars on Jews, especially in the Ukraine, and it continued to have significance. Reminiscent of the Dreyfus trial in France in 1894, it stirred the conscience of many liberals inside and outside Russia. Russians who felt revulsion from this trial were not necessarily sympathetic to Jews. Rather, they saw it as a symptom of Russia's uncivilized reactionary politics that was retarding her movement into the modern world of western Europe. Tsar Nicholas II, however, reacted by reintensifying anti-Semitic propaganda and policies that lasted until his overthrow.[17]

Russian Jews were already smarting from inflammatory concoctions in *The Protocols of the Elders of Zion.* Excerpts from this document, supposedly fabricated by the *Okhrana* (the tsarist secret police), first appeared in 1903 in the Russian newspaper *Znamya (Banner).* Then during the 1905 revolution in Russia it was published in full as an appendix to a religious pamphlet written by Serge Nilus, a tsarist official and priest in the Russian Orthodox Church. Its basic charge is that at the time of the first Zionist Congress in Basel in 1897 Jewish leaders had joined with Freemasons in a conspiracy to control the world. They would achieve dominion by pitting Christian nations against one another and subverting them politically, socially, economically, and spiritually. This forgery was translated into many languages. Although it received little popular response at the time it first came out, it deeply impressed Tsar Nicholas II, who supposedly wrote in its margins: "It is as if our year of 1905 is in the hands of the 'Learned Elders. . . .' " During the Russian civil war, according to eyewitnesses, *The Protocols* was "literally devoured" by Admiral A. V. Kolchak, a leader of the White armies whose newspapers published a number of different versions. Faced with certain defeat, Kolchak's propaganda organs published another forged document that allegedly was a continuation of *The Protocols.*[18] Kolchak's armies, undoubtedly backed by public support derived from propaganda associated with *The Protocols,* cruelly slaughtered thousands of Jews in one of the worst bloodbaths of that period. After World War I *The Protocols* became a staple of anti-Semitic propaganda. In the United States it was circulated by Henry Ford, who reprinted excerpts in his newspaper *The Dearborn Independent.* Subsequently, in Germany, Nazi leaders used it to "prove," among other things that Bolshevism was a Jewish conspiracy. In the Middle East, Arab countries used it as a weapon in their anti-Zionist crusade. And in the Soviet Union, Communist "scholars" and propagandists regularly utilized its arguments in their anti-Zionist and anti-Semitic writings and speeches.

Soviet leaders over the years, particularly Stalin, fanned the flames of folk anti-Semitism. Stalin categorized Jews as disloyal aliens. He denounced Jews for being "rootless cosmopolitans" who, in accordance with *The Protocols,* did the bidding of an international "Zionist-Masonic conspiracy" orchestrated by "Western imperialist circles." In the 1980s, extremist Russian nationalist groups, notably *Pamyat* (Memory) and *Otechestvo* (Fatherland), also relied heavily on *The Protocols.*[19] They stirred memories of the tsarist Black Hundreds, which operated mainly between 1906 and 1914. These groups, such as *Soyuz Russkogo Naroda* (League of the Russian People) and *Soyuz Mikhaila Arkhangela* (League of the Archangel Michael), were composed of an amalgam of wealthy landlords, merchants, clerics, and tsarist officials who organized gangs of thugs to stamp out revolutionaries and Jews through pogroms. In essence, they rallied around the tsar, the Russian Orthodox Church, and Russian nationalism. The modern-day Russia-first groups, unlike the Black Hundreds, do not usually resort to violence. Nor do they have the open imprimatur of the top government leaders, who officially oppose them yet for the most part still allow their activities. Like their predecessors, however, they engage in "Jew-hating" and appeal mostly to the base instincts of the lower classes, who readily accept the canard that Jews are responsible for their economic and social woes.

Soviet Jews, unlike their ancestors, were not restricted to the Pale. Yet they suffered from some of the same forms of oppression. Soviet Jews were also targeted by government propaganda, blamed as scapegoats for government failures, and shaken by government show trials aimed at intimidation. Moreover, they saw their children conscripted into the army, where they were often subjected to brutal assaults of anti-Semitism. Although they generally enjoyed and took advantage of far greater access to higher education, eventually they too bristled from quotas restricting their entry into the university. A *numerus clausus* initiated in 1887 under Tsar Alexander III allowed Jews only 3 percent of places in high schools and colleges in Moscow and St. Petersburg, and 5 percent elsewhere except for the Pale, where it was 10 percent. Tsarist "logic" was that admission of Jews to institutions of higher learning should be limited to their percentage in areas where they lived. Starting in the mid- to late-1940s unofficial, unannounced restrictions were placed on Jewish students trying to enter the university. More dramatic increases in discrimination against Jews applying for university admission began in the late 1960s, raising fears of the application of similar Communist "logic." Soviet leaders, like the tsars, also barred Jews from certain professions. Beginning with Stalin, Jews were kept from jobs, particularly in the Communist Party, state bureaucracy, diplomatic service, and armed forces.

Although Soviet Jews in many respects continued to be mistreated as in tsarist times, under Communist rule they faced new hardships caused by different domestic and international circumstances. These included totalitarian rule; perpetration of anti-Semitism despite its illegality; the internationalist orientation and atheistic drive in Marxist-Leninist ideology; the growing attraction to Soviet Jews of Hebrew and the birth of Israel as a Jewish homeland; the diplomatic pressure on the Soviet Union exerted by the United States and advocacy groups for Soviet Jews in the West; and Moscow's policy toward emigration. Through a review of these considerations we can better understand key developments in the history of the Kremlin's policies toward Soviet Jews.

Totalitarianism and Anti-Semitism

Like Soviet leaders, the tsars used various patterns of repression against the Jews.[20] Most tsars, like Nicholas I, knew only the stick. After he took power in 1825, he instigated a ruthless campaign against Jews. This included, among other cruelties, his *ukase* (edict) of August 26, 1827. All Russian youths then were conscripted into military service at age eighteen for a period of twenty-five years. According to this directive, Jewish children would be drafted at the age of twelve and spend six years of preparatory "cantonment" before serving their twenty-five years. The tsar intended to use this preliminary six-year period to force Jewish children to convert to Christianity. Tsar Alexander II (1855–1881), however, tried the carrot, at least at the outset. For example, he opened doors for Jews in universities and eased restrictions of Jewish residence inside the Pale. But, convinced by his advisers that his reforms bred dangerous revolutionary activity, Alexander turned to harsh reaction. After his assassination Jews became extra-special targets for discrimination and repression. As historian Benjamin Pinkus points out, sixty-five anti-Semitic laws were issued under Tsar Alexander III. For example, besides the *numerus clausus* of 1887, in 1889 Jews were forbidden to practice law, and in 1891 about twenty thousand Jewish artisans were expelled from Moscow. Tsar Nicholas II, after acceding to the throne in 1894, inflicted even more terrible pain on Russian Jews. He was a particularly dangerous visceral anti-Semite who engaged in almost a personal vendetta against Jews in his realm. During the late nineteenth and early twentieth centuries, it seemed that the prophecy of tsarist adviser Konstantin Pobedonostsev would come true. Pobedonostsev, chief procurator of the Holy Synod (head of the tsarist ministry that oversaw church affairs) from 1880 to 1905 and determined to forge a Russian Empire only for Russians and the Russian Orthodox Church, played upon the traditional xenophobia and religious bigotry of both. Regarding the future of Russian Jews, whom he despised, the story is told that he once remarked "A third of the Jews will be wiped out, a third will be converted, and a third will emigrate."[21]

The tsar's reach was deep into the shtetl, but government control over Jewish religious and cultural life, generally speaking, was significantly less than under Communist rule. Totalitarianism by definition cannot tolerate any independent, potentially competitive source of ideas or authority. The Communist Party of the Soviet Union (CPSU) felt it had to maintain itself as the sole repository of truth. Anti-Semitic campaigns conducted by the party—at least until the influence of Gorbachev's *glasnost* in 1987—fostered anti-Semitism through manipulation of the media, indoctrination of youth in the schools and party organizations, and subjection of adults in the workplace and social facilities to lectures sponsored by the *Znaniye* (Knowledge) Society. These efforts reached virtually every household and often reinforced the already deep-seated popular anti-Semitism.

De facto Anti-Semitism

Under Communist rule Jews no longer had to fear systematic, brutal, and widespread pogroms like those sponsored by the tsarist government. Nor were they subjected to the legal anti-Semitism of tsarist days. Thus anti-Semitism since the Bolshevik Revolution has been de facto only. Before the Revolution, Lenin frequently denounced the anti-Semitism of the tsarist era, though mainly for strategic and tactical reasons. He thought it distracted the worker from fighting capitalism and weakened the movement for proletarian internationalism and socialist solidarity. The Bolsheviks, just one week after seizing power, proclaimed a broad banning of discrimination against all minorities, which included the Jews. On November 15, 1917, they issued the Declaration of Rights and Peoples, which called for the "free development of national minorities and ethnic groups inhabiting Russian territory." Lenin soon urged the Council of People's Commissars to issue the decree of July 27, 1918, which stated "that the anti-Semitic movement and pogroms against the Jews are fatal to the interest of the workers' and peasants' revolution and calls upon the toiling people of Socialist Russia to fight this evil with all the means at their disposal."

The new Constitution of 1918 seemed to afford Jews even more protection. Article 22 stipulated that it was illegal "to oppress national minorities or impose any limitations whatsoever on their rights." This principle would be found in subsequent constitutions of the U.S.S.R. and its republics. But criminal law codes of the Soviet republics after 1922 contained no clear penalties for commission of anti-Semitic acts. "This shortcoming of the law," argues Pinkus, "apparently stemmed from a desire not to overstress the Jewish issue." A better explanation may be that the Bolsheviks were militant atheist ideologues who wanted to extirpate all religion and that some of their "Jewish" leaders had a special perverted interest in eradicating Judaism. In part, at least, this explains why the government, until the 1930s anyway, dealt so harshly with Soviet Jews.

Marxism-Leninism and Anti-Semitism

Marxist-Leninist ideology is a critically important backdrop to the Soviet regime's policy toward Jews. Should Soviet Jews be considered a nationality, a religion, or both? The Kremlin's position has been riddled with uncertainties, contradictions, and inconsistencies. Ideologically, Communist leaders generally have considered Jews a *temporary* nationality. Practically, however, they have treated them as an *unequal* nationality.

Marx anticipated the disappearance of all national differences as capitalism gave way to socialism. The bonds of proletarian internationalism, he believed, would eventually prevail over worker loyalty to nationality or country. The growing class consciousness of the proletarian, therefore, would gradually wean him from his national identity.[22] Marx spent little time writing on the nationality issue, for he was much more concerned with the bigger world picture of the collapse of capitalism and its replacement by socialism.

Lenin had more to say on the Jewish nationality question than Marx. He urged that Jews in Russia, whom he described as "the most oppressed and persecuted nation" who were being "*forcibly* kept in the status of a caste," should receive equal national rights before the law. In March, 1914, for example, he wrote a "Bill of National Equal Rights" that called for "the abolishment of all constitutional and other restrictions against Jews and other downtrodden nationalities (but especially Jews)."[23] After the Bolshevik Revolution he hinted that Jews might develop separately as a nationality. At the tenth Communist Party Congress in 1921, for example, he authorized a resolution that referred to the Jews as an example of a national minority who had "the right . . . to free national development." On the other hand, Lenin believed that Jewish separatism, particularly in the revolutionary movement, was contrary to the best interests of the Jewish masses and the revolution. Instead Lenin, targeting the *Bund* especially, railed against Jewish "bourgeois nationalism," arguing that the future of the Jews was assimilation. Eventually, he believed, they would be part of a single socialist society. In the meantime, though, they would be treated as a separate nationality.

Stalin also believed in the ultimate assimilation of the Jews. In his 1913 essay *Marxism and the National Question,* Stalin defined nationality as "a historically evolved, stable community of language, territory, economic life and psychological make-up manifested in a community of culture."[24] In essence, this definition became Soviet policy after the Revolution. According to Stalin, Jews did not constitute a distinct nationality; they were scattered across the land, divided economically and politically, and highly assimilated culturally and linguistically. Stalin agreed with Marx and Lenin that *nationality* was a temporary phenomenon of capitalism that would disappear in a socialist world. But Stalin, unsure how to handle the "Jewish question" and faced with the realities of rule, decided to preserve the fiction of the separate identity of Soviet Jews while also treating them in a distinctly separate and unequal way. This decision was reflected in two new policies: in the late 1920s establishment of a "Jewish homeland" in Birobidzhan, where Soviet Jews were expected eventually to become assimilated; and in 1932 passage of a law that required all Soviet citizens to list their nationality (Point 5) on their internal passport.

The Birobidzhan project was officially launched on March 28, 1928, when the Central Executive Committee of the U.S.S.R. (later the Presidium of the Supreme Soviet) allotted the Jewish Autonomous *Rayon* (district) for the settlement of Soviet Jews. On August 20, 1930, this *rayon* was officially created, and on May 7, 1934, it gained the status of Jewish Autonomous *Oblast* (region). Birobidzhan is part of the Khabarovsk Territory of the R.S.F.S.R. It is largely underdeveloped land, with a harsh climate, located in the extreme Far East across from Manchuria, about five thousand miles from the heartland areas of the U.S.S.R. where most Soviet Jews live.

There were several reasons for the establishment of Birobidzhan. One possibility was that Stalin aimed to induce young Jews to leave their families. Isolated in Birobidzhan, they might more readily develop into the "new Soviet man." Another reason was that Stalin may have wanted a more heavily populated buffer zone to thwart a possible Japanese invasion. The Japanese had designs on Manchuria, which they invaded in 1931, and they posed a serious security threat to the Soviet Far East. The official reason for Birobidzhan, however, was the establishment of a "homeland" for Jews within the U.S.S.R. that would be a more attractive alternative to Zionism. Stalin believed he would score propaganda points by showing off the land where Soviet Jews could supposedly develop their own culture. Thus Soviet Jews were encouraged to make *aliyah* to Birobidzhan rather than Palestine. This idea was so intriguing that it caught the attention of Jews from around the world. Reportedly, some 1400 came from the United States, Europe, South America, and even Palestine itself to settle in a land that promised to be a homeland *at that time,* not in the distant future.[25] Whatever the reasons for Birobidzhan, in reality this "homeland" has remained such only on paper. Although a very small number of Jews did go there to establish a community, most thought the idea ridiculous. According to the 1989 census, only 8887 Jews live there, comprising about 4 percent of the region's population and less than 1 percent of the entire Soviet Jewish population.[26]

The 1932 decree requiring all Soviet citizens to list their nationality on their internal passport, ostensibly instituted to control housing allocations in the cities, mandated that all Jews list *Evret* (Jewish) as their nationality, regardless of where they lived or which religion, if any, they professed. For other nationalities, this passport designation was generally innocuous. For Jews, however, it was used for discrimination. Even those Jews who, because of mixed marriages, did not have to list "Jewish" on their passport (at age sixteen one could choose the nationality of either parent) could not escape discrimination because of their heritage. For when they applied for a job or admission to a university, they usually had to fill out a form that asked the identity of their parents, which revealed their Jewishness.

Soviet Jews, moreover, could not escape discrimination through assimilation. In tsarist Russia, which considered Jews mainly a religious group, they could accept baptism and then assimilate after conversion to Christianity. In Soviet society, however, Jews could change their religion, not practice it, or even declare themselves atheists, but they still could not fully assimilate. As a young Jewish worker once remarked with frustration: "I can't assimilate. . . . I can recite Blok and Pushkin. . . . I might even go along with Lenin and believe that the way out is via assimilation. But there's a stick beating me around the feet—'Yid, yid'—to make sure I don't go far along that road. How often have I been turned away because I'm alien?"[27] The irony is that after a number of years under Communist rule most Jews have become culturally and linguistically assimilated—but as Russians. Yet though they consider themselves Russian, they have to mark down "Jewish" on their passport and thereby suffer discrimination as Jews. This passport system has continued, although under Gorbachev there have been signs of intentions to modify it.

Although Marxist-Leninist ideology gave Soviet leaders less than clear guidance on the nationality question, it clearly influenced their almost fanatic opposition to religion. Marx criticized religion as unscientific. He argued that practicing religion was like succumbing to superstition or illusion. He considered religion the "opium of the people," lulling them into a false sense of well-being while keeping their minds off serious difficulties caused by the evils of capitalism. Although Marx opposed all religions, he especially attacked Judaism, the religion of his heritage.

Marx was born in the German city of Trier in 1818, the descendant of rabbis on both sides of his family. At age six, however, young Karl was baptized as a Lutheran by his father, who had converted to Christianity before his son's birth. Karl's mother also converted, but a year after Karl's baptism. Karl's father presumably had converted earlier so he could practice law, which Jews in his region were legally forbidden to do. Karl's father hoped that baptism would keep his children from suffering anti-Semitism. Karl grew up officially Lutheran, but in a household that had abandoned its Jewishness. It is not known how much Judaism, or Christianity for that matter, Marx was exposed to at home. What was certain, however, was that Marx was torn from his religious roots and became alienated toward his heritage. Perhaps it was for this reason that by the time Marx became a young adult, he despised Judaism.

Marx's main anti-Semitic work was *On the Jewish Question,* which he published in 1844 as a response to Bruno Bauer's article *The Jewish Question.* Bauer, an Austrian Christian socialist, had severely criticized Jews and Judaism. Marx went beyond Bauer in Jew-hating. Marx's work was filled with vituperative anti-Semitism. He bitterly attacked Jews, for example, for haggling over what he called their god of money. In subsequent writings, such as *Theses on Feuerbach* (1845) and in private letters, he wrote similar characterizations of Jews and used such defamatory language as "usurers," "Jew-boy,"and "nigger-Jew." In short, Marx associated Jews with all he hated about capitalism. Marx's anti-Semitic writings later became a reference for Nazi anti-Semites. They also were cited by professional Soviet anti-Semites like Trofim Kichko, whose viciously anti-Semitic work *Judaism Without Embellishment,* published in the Ukraine in 1963, proved severe even by Soviet standards.[28]

Lenin, though somewhat more sympathetic and respectful toward Jews, also despised and castigated religion, for both ideological and tactical reasons. He believed that religion, like the nation, was a manifestation of capitalist exploitation that would wither away when the state did. Furthermore, he considered religion a potential barrier to building socialism because it represented an alternative to the party as a source of authority and allegiance.

After the Bolsheviks seized power, ignoring constitutional and legal provisions which seemingly safeguarded religious practice, as atheists they tried to wipe out all religion. With the help of groups like the Society of the Militant Godless, they closed churches and synagogues, religious schools, and all other religious institutions. Those houses of worship that remained were to be controlled by the state.

Judaism, like other religions, suffered from Soviet laws designed to reduce the societal impact of religion and eventually wipe it out. The law of April 1929 was nothing short of a wholesale onslaught against religion. This law required all religious associations (which had to consist of at least twenty persons over the age of eighteen) to register with the government. Henceforth all religious leaders would be paid officials of the state and presumably subject to its policies. This law also prohibited evangelism (which especially hurt the Baptists) and all religious doings outside officially sanctioned religious buildings. In this way the state could closely monitor remaining religious activities.

Jews were not specifically targeted by this legislation, but almost immediately after the Revolution they were singled out for special assimilationist attention. Bolshevik policy toward the Jews was part of a general campaign both to placate and indoctrinate all the nationalities. Nationalities could flourish, but as Stalin told the Sixteenth Congress of the Communist Party in 1930, only in accordance with the concept of "national in form and socialist in content." Nationalities thus could exercise their rights and develop their cultures, but only within the framework of Communist ideology and goals. The main party task was *korenizatsiya* (literally, the process of taking root): to secularize, communize, and Sovietize nationalities as rapidly as possible. Stalin's ultimate goal was "fusion" of all nationalities "into one common socialist culture, common both in form and in content, with one common tongue. . . ."[29]

The Bolsheviks began to use special tactics to pacify the Jews. In January 1918, they established the *Yevsektsiya,* Jewish sections of the Communist Party.[30] Many of its members were left-wing members of the *Bund* and/or Bolshevik sympathizers. Most were Communist ideologues who had no love for Judaism and surely none for Zionism. Accordingly, Jewish revolutionaries like Moishe Litvakov, editor-in-chief of the main Yiddish newspaper *Der Emes (The Truth),* tried to impose a *secular* Yiddish culture on the Jews.

But this approach met with opposition. Most Jews then spoke Yiddish, but they objected to attempts by the *Yevsektsiya* to use their language as a tool to quash their religion. Some Jews, moreover, considered Russian the gateway of "progress" from the backward shtetl to full integration into Soviet society. Thus, they wanted to learn and use Russian, to send their children to Russian schools, and to study from Russian texts. They saw Russian, in short, as the key to academic, economic, social, and professional advancement. Other Soviet Jews, seeking to learn more about their religion and perhaps dreaming of emigrating to Israel, wanted to study Hebrew. They recognized that official advocacy of the "proletarian language" of Yiddish was designed to serve the political interests of the state. They also saw through the Kremlin's use of "court Jews" who did its dirty work.

Yiddish thus flourished *artificially* in the 1920s. But at the hands of the *Yevsektsiya,* Judaism as a religion took a real beating. Whereas, for example, Yiddish secular schools expanded, religious primary and secondary schools were closed down. When the *Yevsektsiya* closed synagogues, in direct violation of the law, it argued that synagogue space was needed for other, more pressing needs of the communities they served. Finally, the *Yevsektsiya* shut down *kehilas* (Jewish communal councils) and replaced them with Communist Party and government organizations.

Over the years, the Kremlin's opposition to religion in general and to Judaism in particular was relentless, though it did ebb and flow in response to perceived domestic and foreign policy needs. Not until the ascension of power of Mikhail Gorbachev did this official Soviet policy change. Under Gorbachev, the Kremlin increasingly allowed religious freedom and curtailed anti-Semitic propaganda and activities. Finally, on October 1, 1990, the Supreme Soviet adopted a new U.S.S.R. Law on Freedom of Conscience and Religious Organizations that gave individuals and religious officials far greater freedom of religious practice. This "new thinking" on religion was a major factor leading to a reversal of long-standing official opposition to Hebrew teaching, Zionism, and the State of Israel.

Soviet Opposition to Hebrew, Zionism, and Israel

Hebrew was anathema to Soviet leaders from the outset. Their official justification for banning it (the only language to suffer this fate) beginning in the 1920s was twofold. First, they categorized it as a language of religious practice. Then, acting as constitutional sticklers, they argued that it could not be taught in government schools because this would violate the separation of church and state. They also opposed Hebrew as the language of Zionism, which they believed was plotting to undermine communism and the Soviet Union. Under Stalin, Hebrew was considered an "instrument of counterrevolutionary subversive activities by

Jewish religious clericals and Zionists." Those connected in any way with Hebrew were seen as enemies of the regime and dealt with accordingly. Kremlin leaders officially allowed the teaching of Hebrew only at theological seminaries of the Russian Orthodox Church and at major universities in Moscow, Leningrad, and Tbilisi. Such classes were limited to students preparing to be government officials (e.g., in the Jewish division of the KGB!), Islamic or Christian leaders, or academic Orientalists.

Some Jews who wanted to learn Hebrew for religious or cultural purposes, at least until *glasnost,* faced determined government opposition. The state required that private teachers be licensed. Although it licensed tutors to teach other foreign languages, it did not license the private teaching of Hebrew.

This policy remained until 1988–1989 when, under *glasnost,* Gorbachev agreed to allow private Hebrew teaching, though not with official recognition, which would have meant, among other things, the opening of private Hebrew schools. Then, on May 2, 1990, a Reuters dispatch quoted unidentified Soviet officials as stating that the Moscow State Institute of History and Archives, in the fall of 1991, would begin offering classes in Jewish studies. These would be taught by professors from the Jewish Theological Seminary and the Yivo Institute for Jewish Research (both in the United States) and would include both undergraduate and graduate classes in Jewish history, literature, culture, Hebrew, and Yiddish. These contemplated changes clearly are revolutionary. Also revolutionary was the Kremlin's decision under Gorbachev to allow the teaching of Hebrew throughout the country in *yeshivas* (talmudic academies), Jewish cultural associations, and a variety of other settings. Startling too was the Kremlin's reversal of its long-standing opposition to Zionism and Israel.

Zionism was attacked by the tsars and by Soviet leaders. The tsars banned Zionism because they saw it as a link with dissidents and revolutionaries. Soviet leaders, until Gorbachev, essentially maintained this position. After the Revolution, the Bolsheviks labeled Zionism a counterrevolutionary, reactionary bourgeois movement with ties to various hostile internationalist groups of Jews and Freemasons. Later the Kremlin began linking Zionism with an additional litany of evils such as imperialism, capitalist exploitation, espionage, organized crime, racism, and Nazism.

In the 1920s Communist leaders launched the first of many anti-

Zionism campaigns. In this campaign, the regime used anti-Zionist and anti-Jewish Jews of the *Yevsektsiya,* who needed no prodding from the party, to carry out their anti-Zionist activities. The *Yevsektsiya* was dissolved in 1930 and most of its leaders killed in the purges of the next few years. Many prominent Jewish Bolsheviks, like Kamenev and Zinoviev, were also liquidated in these purges. Trotsky was assassinated in Mexico on August 20, 1940, by a Spanish Communist, Ramon Mercador, presumably on Stalin's orders. Zionists too were caught up in the Stalinist web of purges. Their worst time in this decade was between 1936 and 1938 (known as the *Yezhovshchina* after NKVD chief Yezhov or as the Great Purge), when Stalin launched a massive campaign against real and imagined political enemies.

What the outside world knew or cared about Stalin's mass imprisonments and murders when they occurred is still debated. Stalin's liquidations took place with scarcely a protest. Surely his tight grip on the media and passion for secrecy went a long way toward minimizing outside knowledge of the Great Purge, as well as of widespread starvation stemming from forced collectivization and repression of the Ukrainians in the late 1920s and early 1930s. This campaign, according to research by Robert Conquest, killed approximately fourteen and a half million as punishment for their resistance to Soviet control and collectivization. The estimated number of those liquidated during the Great Purge runs also into several millions. Total dead from Stalin's terror may well have reached fifteen to twenty million, or even more.[31]

No protest was lodged about the many Jewish purge targets, even from Jewish circles. As Dr. Julius Margolin, who was imprisoned in 1940 in several camps of the Baltic-White Sea group, noted bitterly: "An entire generation of Zionists has died in Soviet prisons and in exile mainly because we did not care. I do not remember seeing a single article about them in the pre-war papers. Not the least effort was made to mobilize public opinion and alleviate their fate."[32] Conquest notes that if Zionists, who were especially well organized and politically sophisticated, received little outside attention and assistance from their brethren during the Great Purge, this was especially true of others in the West "whose only interest in the matter was, or might have been, to the common bonds of humanity."[33]

Stalin's purges were not directed solely or mainly against Zionists. Yet Stalin was extra-suspicious of potential party rivals of Jewish origin, especially from the ranks of the Old Bolsheviks. Moreover, Stalin's purges may have claimed so many other Jewish victims because they were highly visible in the intelligentsia, whom he feared as a source of opposition to his rule. The following excerpt from an unpublished manuscript, quoted by Soviet Marxist historian Roy Medvedev, gives a clear picture of how and why Soviet Jews suffered disproportionately from the Great Purge:

> The Soviet intelligentsia and also Party and government personnel were hit much harder by the repression of the 1930's than the workers. And within the intelligentsia and opposition as a whole, Communists suffered to a much greater extent than non-Party people. And finally, among Communists themselves, Party members of long standing were infinitely more vulnerable than those who had recently joined. But it was precisely among the Jews that there were more white-collar workers and intellectuals than industrial workers; the percentage of Jewish Communists was two, three, sometimes four times greater than that of other nationalities; and in terms of Party composition, an extremely large number of old Party members were Jewish. The result of all these disproportionate factors combined was that, although Jews were in no sense intended as special targets, they suffered greater injury in the rebound of the purges than any other national group, losing their most professional element, those who had been the most dedicated to the Revolution.[34]

But even if Jews had been the main object of the purges, and even if the outside world knew what was going on, they probably would not have received much assistance from the West, especially the United States government. For Washington, as shown in its distinctive lack of support for Jews persecuted and murdered by Nazi Germany, would surely not have rushed to help Jews in the Soviet Union.[35]

During World War II the U.S.S.R. grabbed new territory that contained about two million Jews. In these western regions of the U.S.S.R., especially in the Baltic states and the Ukraine, Jews were targeted for extermination by the Nazi invaders after June 1941. Many fled eastward before they could be hunted down by Nazi *Einsatzgruppen* (special action forces). Jewish refugees established communities in central Asian cities, especially Tashkent and Samarkand. But many other Jews remained. An estimated half-million Soviet Jews fought the Nazis, with 121 reportedly receiving the highest decoration, Hero of the Soviet Union.* But thousands of Jewish civilians perished at the hands of the Nazis. The *Einsatzgruppen* murdered about 500,000 Jews just in the first few months after the Nazi invasion of the U.S.S.R.[36] At the end of September, in one of the worst massacres of the war, the Nazis—with complicity of and help from Ukrainians—slaughtered upwards of 50,000 Jews and other Soviet citizens at Babi Yar, a ravine just outside Kiev.** Non-Jews also were killed there. The Soviets, many years after the war, erected a memorial on the site, but they did not specify that most of the victims were Jewish. This is typical of how the Kremlin publicly handled the Nazi destruction of Jews: Though Jews were singled out by the Nazis for extermination and suffered disproportionately, the Kremlin talked only about Nazi atrocities against the Soviet people in general. Yevgeny Yevtushenko, in his poem *Babi Yar,* published in 1961, called attention to the failure of the Soviet regime to be forthright about the anti-Semitism leading to the Babi Yar massacre.

During the "Great Patriotic War" the Kremlin maintained official silence about the Holocaust. Stalin, himself an anti-Semite, did not calculate that public outrage over Babi Yar or other anti-Jewish atrocities would help his cause because so much of the non-Jewish Soviet population tacitly or actively supported what the Nazis did. As historian Walter Laqueur concluded:

> Thus with few exceptions . . . the Soviet line was that the Hitlerite invaders behaved generally speaking like barbarians. But there was no mention of the fact that the Jews were singled out for "special treatment." What was the reason for this silence? The Soviet authorities could argue

---

* Soviet sources cite different numbers of Jewish medal winners. For example, *Pravda* (May 6, 1945) cites the figure 107, whereas Soviet historian Y. Kantor (quoted in Reuben Ainsztein, "Soviet Jewry in the Second World War, in Kochan, p. 287), uses the number 121.

** Estimates of the numbers of Jews slaughtered at Babi Yar vary widely. Salo Baron (*The Russian Jew Under Tsars and Soviets,* 2d ed. [New York: Schocken, 1987], p. 278) puts this figure at 33,771 (based on official German reports). Bernard Weinrub ("Antisemitism in Soviet Russia," in Kochan p. 184), cites the figure of 50,000. Elie Wiesel ("The Sun Rises for Soviet Jews," *New York Times,* February 26, 1989), uses the figure 80,000. The plaque at Babi Yar is dedicated to "over 100,000 citizens of Kiev."

> that even though the Nazis singled out the Jews in their campaign of murder, little would be gained if the Soviet Union publicized this fact. For the murder of the Jews may well have been quite popular in some sections of the population: Ukrainians, Lithuanians and Latvians had played a prominent part in the massacres. If the German invaders, nevertheless, rapidly became unpopular in the occupied areas also for some other considerations, the Soviet authorities played down the "final solution."[37]

To enlist the help of as many Soviet citizens as possible during the war, Stalin took steps that seemed to ease government opposition to religion. In 1943 he established councils for religious affairs for all religious groups. Although these councils held out the promise of greater religious freedom, in reality they institutionalized government control of religious life. A year earlier, in April, Stalin had set up the Jewish Anti-Fascist Committee, headed by Solomon Mikhoels, a well-known actor, and Itzik Fefer, a noted Yiddish poet. Its main purpose was to win support for the Soviet war effort in Western countries, especially among Jews there. This meant, among other things, that for the first time under both tsarist and Communist rule Jews were allowed a central organization.

After the war Stalin began to attack Jewish culture. In late summer of 1946 Andrei Zhdanov, a close associate of Stalin, launched a campaign against "cosmopolitanism," the new code word for anti-Semitism. Mikhoels was murdered by the MGB (Ministry of State Security) on January 13, 1948 (Soviet media reported he had "died in tragic circumstances," that is, presumably by accident, though in reality, he was pushed under a truck), and the Anti-Fascist Committee was disbanded in November of that year, when most of its members were arrested. Before its dissolution, Stalin directed it to announce: "No! Never and under no circumstances will Soviet Jews exchange their socialist homeland for another homeland." This declaration was one clue to Stalin's complex position on the creation of The State of Israel, determined by mixed considerations of both *realpolitik* and ideology.

Surprisingly, Stalin supported the Jewish cause in Palestine. In the latter part of 1944 and early 1945 there were indications that the Soviet leader would go along with an American and British commitment to a Jewish national home. He believed, moreover, that there should be unimpeded Jewish immigration to Palestine, though he would allow no Jewish emigration from the Soviet Union. At the decisive moment after

World War II, Stalin advocated the creation of the State of Israel. On May 15, 1947, Andrei Gromyko, Soviet deputy foreign minister and permanent representative to the United Nations, delivered a surprising speech supporting "the aspirations of the Jews to establish their own state." He referred, moreover, to the "historic links of the Jews with Palestine." He stated that his government preferred "an independent, homogeneous, democratic Arab-Jewish state," but if this could not be achieved, it would support partition between a Jewish and an Arab state. Subsequently the Soviet Union was the first country to extend de jure recognition to Israel when it was established on May 14, 1948. Then the U.S.S.R., through Czechoslovakia, supplied Israel with arms to defeat "Arab aggressors," as Gromyko termed Arab fighters against Israel in Security Council meetings during the summer. Thus in the formative period of Israeli statehood, Gromyko, in Israeli leader Abba Eban's words, had become "a Zionist hero."[38] During this time Stalin probably was annoyed by Arab support for fascism before and during the war and after the war for Britain, which was trying to keep Jewish refugees out of Palestine. Stalin also felt Israel could be used as a wedge against the military and political presence of the imperialist West in the Middle East, which would give him a freer hand there. Moreover, he saw in Israel an opportunity to infiltrate Soviet secret police operatives into the Middle East.[39]

But Stalin's support for Israel was short-lived. Already by August 1948, Stalin had started to reassess his policy toward Israel. Indicative of this change was a long article in *Pravda* on September 21, 1948, entitled "Concerning a Certain Letter," wherein the Jewish writer Ilya Ehrenburg criticized Zionists as mystics and condemned Israel as a bourgeois state controlled by British-American capital. Stalin also was chagrined at the wildly exuberant reception thousands of Soviet Jews gave Golda Meir, who headed the first Israeli delegation to the U.S.S.R., when she and other members of the Israeli legation attended Jewish High Holy Day services in the Great Choral Synagogue in Moscow.

Later that year Stalin began to back off further from his diplomatic support of Israel. Concerned with the increased influence of the United States in Israel, Soviet propaganda increasingly scorned the Jewish state as a tool of Western imperialism. Nevertheless, the U.S.S.R. did vote on May 11, 1949 for Israel's admission into the UN. Thus at least until this vote, Soviet policy hedged between support for Israel and its Arab neighbors. Inside the Soviet Union, however, Stalin used only the fist against Soviet Jews.

From late 1948 until his death on March 5, 1953, Stalin stepped up his campaign against "cosmopolitanism." Soviet media launched an anti-Semitic propaganda blitz. Paranoid then in his anti-Semitism, he decided to erase the visible remnants of Jewish culture that had survived the *Yezhovshchina.* On November 12, 1948 he closed down *Der Emes,* the Jewish book publishing house, and *Einikeit* (Unity), the newspaper of the Jewish Anti-Fascist Committee. Stalin also shut down the last few remaining Yiddish schools and cultural institutions. From November 1948 through early 1950, with only a brief respite between March 1949 and the end of that year, he began imprisoning several hundred Jewish cultural leaders whom he charged with "espionage" or "anti-Soviet activity" abroad. Once again there were no protests in the West—mainly, according to Roy Medvedev, because the imprisonment was largely done secretly and "usually carried out on oral instructions."[40]

In this way began the black years for Soviet Jewry that lasted until Stalin's death. These dark times were marked by an anti-Zionist and anti-Israel policy and punctuated by several stark anti-Semitic episodes. On August 12, 1952, twenty-four Jewish writers and public figures—including David Bergelson, Perez Markish, David Hofstein, and Itzik Fefer—were executed. This date of infamy became known as the "Night of the Murdered Poets." These Jewish intellectuals were charged with the political "crime" of advocating a secessionist state in the Crimea, where at the end of World War II some members of the Anti-Fascist Committee had asked to set up a Jewish autonomous republic. Stalin, paranoiac as he was, may have feared that the United States might try to utilize this republic as a base for espionage and subversion. But more likely this charge was just an excuse for Stalin to exterminate many Jewish intellectuals whom he either feared or simply disliked. In November 1952 came the rigged trial of Rudolf Slansky, the Czechoslovak Communist Party secretary. He and thirteen other leading Communists, ten of them "of Jewish origin," were charged with being Trotskyites, Titoists, and Zionist spies for Britain and other hostile countries. They were found guilty and were executed. As "evidence" against Slansky the prosecutor brought up his role as director of Czechoslovakia's arms shipments to Israel in 1948, which presumably Stalin himself had ordered.

The Slansky trial signaled the beginning of the spread of Stalin's anti-cosmopolitan campaign to his Eastern European satellites. It also set the stage for an intensified anti-Zionist campaign inside the Soviet Union.

In November 1952, as preparation for the campaign against Jewish doctors, the Soviet press started using *Zionists* as a code word for *Jews*. Then, on January 13, 1953, a front-page story in *Pravda* revealed a "Doctors' Plot." The article contended that certain "saboteur doctors"—in league with "Zionist spies," the CIA, British intelligence, and the American Joint Distribution Committee (labeled an "American espionage organization")*—were planning to "wipe out the leading cadres of the U.S.S.R." through poisoning. In January nine doctors, six of them Jewish, were arrested and incarcerated. Stalin included non-Jews to deflect charges of anti-Semitism. These doctors reportedly confessed to having poisoned Soviet leaders Andrei Zhdanov and Alexander Shcherbakov in 1949. Their deaths were supposedly planned by CIA–Zionist conspirators. The Soviet press played up the Jewishness of the accused doctors in both words and pictures reminiscent of Nazi propaganda. Many Jewish doctors lost their positions, and Jews throughout the country feared what was in store for them. Plans were soon readied for the liquidation of the accused doctors. There were indications that Stalin had decided to use show trials of these doctors to prepare the country for the deportation of Soviet Jews to Siberia. There he would presumably carry out his "final solution" to the Jewish Question.[41]

This exhaustive and frightening anti-Semitic campaign luckily was cut short by Stalin's death. On April 4, Moscow Radio announced that the Doctors' Plot had been a "provocation" and that the Jewish doctors had been falsely accused. On April 6, *Pravda* said that this affair had been fabricated by the members of the state security force. Moreover, diplomatic relations with Israel, which Stalin had broken off in February 1953 in the midst of a flurry of public accusations of "dirty Zionist espionage" after a bomb was planted in the Soviet legation in Tel Aviv, were resumed in July of that year by Georgi Malenkov, head of the post-

* The American Joint Distribution Committee was founded in the United States in 1915 as a welfare agency to help Jews around the world. It helped Jewish farmers in the Soviet Union (especially in the Crimea and Birobidzhan) in the 1920s and 1930s, until stopped by Stalin in 1938.

Stalin "collective leadership." Then in June 1954, the Soviet legation in Israel and the Israeli legation in the Soviet Union were elevated to embassy level.

Under Malenkov there was a general lightening of the political atmosphere. Within this liberalization the situation of Soviet Jews improved a little. Some were allowed to regain the jobs from which they were dismissed during Stalin's "anticosmopolitan" campaign. The Soviet press also ceased publication of anti-Semitic articles. Relations with Israel, while not warm, became businesslike. But Malenkov refused to help Soviet Jews resurrect their cultural and religious institutions. Nor did he react favorably to appeals from Jewish organizations in the West to free thousands of Jews, mostly intellectuals and Zionists, from prisons and the gulag. Malenkov did free some, but most stayed incarcerated.

Nikita Khrushchev, who in 1955 began to consolidate his position as the principal Soviet leader, adopted a mixed position toward Soviet Jews. In a secret speech to the Twentieth Party Congress of the CPSU in February 1956, Khrushchev launched his de-Stalinization campaign. He attacked Stalin for committing a number of "crimes" against the Soviet people but never for his most outrageous acts of anti-Semitism such as the Doctors' Plot. Under Khrushchev, Soviet Jews like other Soviet citizens, experienced an increasingly liberal political atmosphere. This thaw was felt especially in the arts and literature. Responding perhaps to Western pressure, Khrushchev did allow a minirevival of Jewish culture, but for a brief time only. In the late 1950s a few books in Yiddish were published, but not by contemporary authors; a *yeshiva* was established in Moscow's Great Synagogue, though it had few students, none of whom became rabbis; and in August 1961 the Yiddish periodical *Sovetish heimland (Soviet Homeland)* was started, though as an official organ of the Union of Soviet Writers and largely as a tool of Kremlin propaganda.

Although Khrushchev allowed some increased Jewish cultural and religious activity and in his memoirs he denied he was anti-Semitic, he nevertheless engaged in anti-Semitic actions. For example, on at least two separate occasions (December 17, 1962, and March 8, 1963) he reportedly lashed out against Yevtushenko for writing *Babi Yar* because this poem focused on the Kremlin's silence about the Holocaust and anti-Semitism in the U.S.S.R., particularly in the Ukraine—where

Khrushchev had been first secretary of the Communist Party from 1938 to 1947.[42] He also undertook a widespread antireligious campaign in which Jews suffered greatly. Khrushchev earlier had imposed a ban on baking *matzoh* in state bakeries. This ban, which began in 1957 in the rural areas, gradually spread throughout the country, reaching Moscow and other big cities by 1962. Never before, even under Stalin, had there been such a widespread ban on *matzoh* baking. Private *matzoh* baking was permitted, but this was very hard—not only because of the need for special ovens but also because the Soviet media denounced it as "illegal, speculative production." The government even arrested some Jews who had done their own baking. The authorities probably had singled out the Passover holiday because it celebrates the Exodus from Egypt to the Promised Land. They played up the link between Passover and Israel, which had become their *bête noire.* They eased the ban in 1963 and again in 1966, and in the face of increasing protests from Jews in the West, finally removed it in 1969.[43]

Khrushchev also hurt Soviet Jews by stepping up the closing of synagogues, supposedly because they were "nests for spies," "centers for black marketeering," or needed for "socially useful enterprises" (e.g., schools). Official Soviet figures, which may have been exaggerated, said that between 1958 and 1964, the number of synagogues was reduced from about four hundred and fifty to ninety-seven. Khrushchev also arranged the conviction of Jews for "economic crimes" against the state. Trials of non-Jews took place, as usual, to soften the obvious anti-Semitic thrust of the policy. The Soviet media paid extra-close attention to Jewish defendants, playing up Jewish financial stereotypes such as preoccupation with currency speculation and greed. This gave the Soviet people the impression that the economic achievements of Jews were largely ill-gotten.[44]

Khrushchev earlier had decided to intensify Soviet opposition toward Israel. In 1955, when the Kremlin undertook a new policy of courting neutral countries in the third world, Khrushchev began to actively support Egypt militarily, economically, and politically. The next year, he supported Nasser's takeover of the Suez Canal while rebuking the military actions of England, France, and Israel. Khrushchev's policy toward Israel thus took a negative turn, toward what Middle East scholar Nadav Safran called "qualified hostility." Khrushchev arrested and tried Jews who signaled their intention to emigrate to Israel, and he resumed a propaganda campaign against Zionism. The virulence of the media attacks was reminiscent of the black years under Stalin.

After Khrushchev was deposed on October 14, 1964, his successors, Leonid Brezhnev and Alexei Kosygin, eased the anti-Israel and anti-Zionist propaganda campaign. Between 1965 and 1967 Soviet–Israeli relations even improved. At the same time, however, the new Soviet leaders tightened the domestic political screws. In 1966 the conviction of liberal writers Andrei Sinyavsky and Yuli Daniel for publishing "anti-Soviet" publications abroad put human rights activists on notice that the "borscht days" of Khrushchev's cultural thaw were over.

Although Brezhnev denounced anti-Semitism, it actually intensified under his leadership, especially because of the 1967 Arab–Israeli war. On June 10 Moscow severed diplomatic relations with Israel. The Kremlin then began a fierce campaign against Zionism and Israel that became virtually indistinguishable from anti-Semitism. This campaign aroused Jewish consciousness, the spirit of Zionism, and a new activism among Soviet Jews. It also triggered a strong response from the United States government and newly formed groups in the West that would become strong advocates for the cause of Soviet Jewry.

U.S. Aid to Soviet Jews

Historically, the United States has tried to help Jews victimized by anti-Semitism in both tsarist and Soviet Russia. Beginning in the latter part of the nineteenth century, the United States tried to exert pressure on the tsar to curb anti-Semitism. In 1870, Secretary of State Hamilton Fish explained to the tsarist government that better treatment of its Jewish subjects not only "elevates the class relieved" but also "advances the common good and social organization."[45] In 1880, Secretary of State William M. Evarts argued for more religious freedom for Russian Jews, but tsarist officials were not responsive to these arguments. They maintained that treatment of Russian Jews was their own business, and they chided the United States for the poor treatment of its own minorities, particularly Orientals.

For a number of years Washington unhappily but quietly accepted the tsar's position on treatment of Russian Jews. U.S. frustration was seen in the immediate aftermath of the terrifying pogrom in Kishinev in April 1903, where forty-five Jews were murdered, over five hundred injured, thousands made homeless, and hundreds of businesses and homes ravaged and devastated. As exasperated Secretary of State John Hay remarked: "What possible advantage would it be to the United States, and what possible advantage to the Jews of Russia, if we should make a protest against these fiendish cruelties and be told it was none of our business?" But acting under pressure from incensed American Jews, President Theodore Roosevelt sent the tsar a copy of their petition. The St. Petersburg government refused to accept it, noting that "the Emperor whose will is the sole law of this land had no need of information from outside sources as to what is taking place within his dominions." Despite the fact that the tsar ignored the U.S. petition, it was still important. It marked the beginning of official U.S. protest against anti-Semitism based mainly on humanitarian grounds rather than on its possible effects on U.S. national interest.[46]

More frequent and severe pogroms against Russian Jews occurred in November 1905 in over three hundred cities, sparked by the Russo-Japanese War and the Russian Revolution. At first, Secretary of State Elihu Root and President Roosevelt hesitated to protest publicly. They claimed that not only would this be futile, like previous protests, but it might even result in further harm to Russian Jews. But American Jewish groups, led by the American Jewish Committee which was founded in the winter of 1906 in reaction to the pogroms, pressed their case. They began to lobby Congress for action. Results of their pressure were almost immediate, for on June 22, 1906, a joint resolution of Congress stated that Americans were "horrified by the report of the massacre of Hebrews in Russia." This resolution passed over the objection of Root, who believed that such actions by the Congress would only exacerbate dangers for Russian Jews. But Jewish groups kept up their lobbying efforts. Finally in 1911, after a long up-hill battle with the Taft Administration, they persuaded Congress to abrogate the Treaty of Commerce and Navigation of 1832. The official reason was Russia's refusal to honor the U.S. passport without discrimination, which technically was construed as a violation of the 1832 treaty. This was the first time that U.S. Jews and the U.S. government tried to link trade with improved treatment of Russian Jews. Although this action had little effect, since the tsar considered it unwarranted interference in Russia's internal affairs, it did have symbolic importance and set an important precedent—particularly for passage of the Jackson-Vanik Amendment in 1974.

U.S. pressure against the Soviet regime to stop discrimination against Jews and allow emigration was not consequential until the late 1960s, when the United States embarked on a policy of quiet diplomacy: Washington would work behind the scenes to influence Moscow to liberalize its policy toward Jews. It would encourage private parties and the United Nations to exert public pressure, but it would shun any highly publicized activities of its own which might embarrass Kremlin leaders. Soviet Jewish emigration would soon be a major concern for Washington.

Jewish Emigration

When thousands of Jews began to flee Russia in the late nineteenth and early twentieth centuries, Tsar Nicholas II reversed the policy of his predecessor, Alexander III, who tried to keep Jews inside Russia (at least until 1891, when he started to change his policy). Nicholas saw little advantage in keeping such a large, disaffected, poverty-stricken minority. He could continue to use Jews as whipping boys and scapegoats for policy failures, but he deemed it easier and wiser to wink at their leaving and even encouraged them to do so.

In the Soviet Union citizens have no constitutional right to emigrate. The emigration law of January 1, 1987 (the first printed for the public to see), allowed the legal right to emigrate but restricted this right to those with "first-degree" relatives (parents, spouses, children) abroad. This law was basically consistent with previous Soviet policy, which allowed Jewish emigration mainly for purposes of family reunification. Soviets still were not allowed the basic right under international law of emigration *per se.*

Historically, the Kremlin has dealt arbitrarily with Jewish emigration. It has jiggled the emigration spigot, allowing greater and lesser flows as it saw fit. Thousands were able to flee Russia during the Bolshevik Revolution and the ensuing civil war. Thousands more continued to emigrate until 1939. Between 1919 and 1939 an estimated 70,000 Jews emigrated.[47] Very few could emigrate at the close of World War II. In 1948, Stalin said *nyet* to Soviet Jews hoping to emigrate to the new State of Israel, and arrested them to boot. Malenkov let only about a hundred elderly Jews leave for Israel. Khrushchev allowed some Soviet Jews to be repatriated to Israel, but under unique circumstances. In 1957, Khrushchev realized that some Polish Jews in his country would go to Israel after being allowed to return to Poland in accordance with the Soviet–Polish repatriation agreement. In fact, most of these 30,000 Polish Jews from the U.S.S.R. emigrated to Israel through Poland.

Between 1954 and 1964 some 1,452 Soviet Jews emigrated directly to Israel, though only 224 did so between 1957 and 1960. In 1965 there were 891 Soviet Jewish emigrants to Israel, a figure that rose to 2046 in 1966.[48] Many Jews were encouraged to apply for emigration by Premier Kosygin's statement on December 3, 1966, carried in the Soviet press, that emigration visas would be granted for purposes of family reunification.[49] In the first few months of 1967, until the Kremlin cut off Jewish emigration after the 1967 Six-Day War, 1406 Jews emigrated.

Not until after this war did many Soviet Jews begin to see emigration not only as a serious possibility but as an absolute necessity. Until then, Soviet Jews, except for some Zionist activists in the Baltic states who after Stalin's death began to reassert their identity and seek emigration permits to Israel, were generally passive and silent about their lot. Israel's victory in the 1967 war, however, aroused their Jewish religious and cultural consciousness as never before. They began to feel that they *had* to emigrate. As one observer remarked, "Until June 1967, Soviet Jews had illusions about coexistence with the regime, despite the fact that it wanted to spiritually destroy the Jews. But suddenly they realized that the Soviet government identifies itself with those who wish to destroy the Jewish state, the sole hope left for the Jewish people. . . . Then we knew that we would never be able to live under such a regime."[50]

The Six-Day War gave Soviet Jews new confidence in shaping their own destiny. In this new atmosphere of hope and excitement, the Soviet Jewish freedom movement was born; now Soviet Jews would strive to emigrate. Until they received permission they would pressure the Kremlin to be allowed to live their lives freely as Jews. Soviet Jews, on the whole, did not plan a movement as such. As Leonid Slepak noted, "It didn't start as a movement. It grew into a big movement. They [Soviet Jews] just wanted to leave the country. They wanted to go to Israel."[51]

Over the years the Kremlin considered Soviet citizens seeking to emigrate either disloyal, psychologically disturbed, greedy for economic gain, or deluded by Western or Zionist propaganda. Who, it argued, would want to leave the motherland, which has been so good to them? When it let Jews and other groups (mainly Germans and Armenians) leave, Soviet media tended to stress the humanitarianism of the Soviet state, which allowed the reunification of families. The Kremlin preferred to restrict Jewish emigration severely. This explains the large pool of refuseniks that built up over the years until Gorbachev, in 1987, began to let most of them go. By 1989 Gorbachev had decided on a virtual open-door policy for Soviet Jews, allowing a record 71,196 to emigrate. By 1990 over 180,000 Soviet Jews had emigrated, mostly to Israel. *(See Table 2.)* Emigration projections for the next few years reach as high as a million.

Purpose, Focus, and Thesis of this Book

This book shows how the Soviet Jewish freedom movement challenged the Kremlin and how Soviet leaders responded to the challenge.

Part I shows how the Kremlin unwittingly stimulated the Jewish freedom movement by subjecting Soviet Jews to propaganda assaults, harassment, intimidation, and repression.

Part II examines how Soviet Jews took the initiative in breaking their silence, organizing, rallying themselves, and assuming leadership of their movement. Demonstrating extraordinary bravery, they formed groups to study Hebrew and learn about Judaism; they practiced their religion both secretly and openly; they sent petitions to Soviet authorities, asking them to abide by the Soviet Constitution and their country's laws; and they issued signed appeals to leaders in the United Nations, Israel, and the West. Furthermore, they denounced violations by the Kremlin of international law and international agreements it had signed.

Part III focuses on the critical role of the United States in the Soviet Jewish freedom movement. It shows how the fate of Soviet Jews has depended not only on their own will, determination, and courage, but also on their allied effort with the United States government to maintain pressure on the Soviet Union and keep their cause high on the U.S.–Soviet diplomatic agenda.

The central thesis of this study is that constant pressure by Soviet Jewish leaders and their supporters succeeded in forcing the Kremlin to look more closely at the Jewish Question. The Soviet Jewish freedom

Soviet Jewry Research Bureau

Jewish Emigration From the USSR Statistics

Oct. 1968–1970	4,235	1979	51,320
1971	13,022	1980	21,471
1972	31,681	1981	9,447
1973	34,733	1982	2,688
1974	20,628	1983	1,314
1975	13,221	1984	896
1976	14,261	1985	1,140
1977	16,736	1986	914
1978	28,864		

	1987	1988	1989	1990	1990 To Israel	1990 Cum. To Israel	1990 Cum. Total
January	98	687	2,796	4,713	4,585		4,713
February	146	697	2,425	5,791	5,746	10,331	10,504
March	470	951	4,240	7,298	7,235	17,566	17,802
April	717	1,020	4,557	10,648	10,641	28,207	28,450
May	877	1,061	3,779	10,212	10,212	38,419	38,662
June	796	1,394	4,354	11,197	11,015	49,434	49,677
July	819	1,371	4,537	15,553	15,283	64,717	65,412
August	787	1,734	6,756	17,907	17,484	82,201	83,319
September	724	2,003	8,442	19,323	18,725	100,926	102,642
October	912	2,068	9,450	20,614	20,324	121,250	123,256
November	910	2,327	11,191	26,136	25,186	146,436	149,392
December	899	3,652	8,690	37,170	35,070	181,759	186,815
	8,155	18,965	71,196	186,815			

Through November 1990, 514,279 Jews left the Soviet Union with Israeli visas, of whom 327,133 went to Israel.

movement posed a multipronged challenge to the Kremlin. Politically, it challenged Soviet leaders to honor their constitutional and legal obligations, domestic and international. Diplomatically, it pressured Moscow to negotiate with the United States over the plight of Soviet Jews, especially the right to emigrate. And morally, it demanded the right of Soviet Jews to learn about and practice their religion freely inside the U.S.S.R. This freedom movement, blessed with outstanding leadership, hammered away at the Kremlin on human rights and legality, winning some concessions and steadily weakening the edifice of totalitarianism.

Soviet Jews posed this successful challenge to the Kremlin based on their "uniqueness of oppression": Jews had no homeland in the U.S.S.R. (despite the fiction of Birobidzhan) and were treated as an unequal, temporary nationality; they alone were subjected to persecution both as a nationality and a religion; they alone were forbidden to study their language of choice, either Yiddish or Hebrew; they alone were not only vilified by the Kremlin's propaganda against religion but also scorned for their collaboration with Israel, Zionism, Freemasonry, capitalist exploitation, and Western imperialism; they alone were accused of collaborating with Hitler both before and during World War II in order to achieve their Zionist aims; they alone were attacked as foreigners who did not belong in the U.S.S.R.; and they alone were oppressed for receiving special assistance from Western governments, private advocacy groups, and from their co-religionists abroad.

The challenge for freedom by Soviet Jews was also unique, stemming in part from the uniqueness of their oppression. They especially turned their relationship with Western governments and advocacy groups into an exceptionally powerful lobbying effort that made its mark on the Kremlin. Soviet leadership, often divided over the Jewish Question, responded both positively and negatively to this challenge. At times it decided on oppression, denial of charges of anti-Semitism, and ridicule. At other times it chose accommodation, moderation, and liberalization. Moscow based its policies mostly on cold calculations of gains and losses in both domestic and foreign policy. Internal considerations such as economics and control over the population and external considerations such as relations with the United States and countries in the Middle East surely were important factors in Soviet decision-making. Ultimately the Kremlin adopted whatever strategy seemed most advantageous at the time. The overall result of the challenge, however, was that Moscow allowed significantly more Jewish emigration and domestic liberalization than could otherwise have been expected. Under Gorbachev, beginning in 1987, freedom for Jews to study their heritage and practice their religion reached remarkable, unprecedented heights. But Soviet Jews had a difficult time enjoying officially increased liberalization, for they also suffered from a resurgence of folk anti-Semitism. By the end of 1990, it seemed "the best of times and the worst of times" for Soviet Jews. How the Soviet Jewish freedom movement responds to these new circumstances will be its major strategic test for the 1990s.

Notes

1 According to Mikhail Chlenov, one of three co-presidents of the Congress of Soviet Jewish Organizations and Communities in the U.S.S.R., founded in December 1989, the number of Soviet Jews is around three million. This figure is reached by answering the question "Who is a Jew?" with the widest latitude. See Union of Councils for Soviet Jews, "Refusenik Update," April 13, 1990. For an excellent discussion of census results regarding Soviet Jews, see Sidney Heitman, "Jews in the 1989 U.S.S.R. Census," *Soviet Jewish Affairs,* Vol. 20, No. 1, 1990, pp. 23–30.

2 J. B. Levinsohn, *Beyt Yehudah* (Warsaw, 1878), Vol. 11, p. 146; cited by E. Cherikover, "The Jewish Masses, the Maskilim and the Government in the Days of Nicholai I, *Yehudim Be-itot Maapaykha* (Tel Aviv: Am Oved, 1957), p. 118ff; quoted by Zeev Ivianski, "Fathers and Sons: A Study of Jewish Involvement in the Revolutionary Movement and Terrorism in Tsarist Russia," *Terrorism and Political Violence,* Vol. 1, No. 2, April 1989, p. 138

3 For reminiscences on the origins and early development of Zionism in Russia, see Chaim Weizmann, *Trial and Error* (Westport, Ct.: Greenwood Press, 1972).

4 Hans Kohn, *Nationalism, Its Meaning and History* (Princeton, N.J.: D. Van Nostrand, 1955), p. 50.

5 For details on these factions see Benjamin Pinkus, *The Jews of the Soviet Union* (Cambridge: Cambridge University Press, 1988), pp. 39–47.

6 See Aryeh Leib Tsentsiper, *Eser Sh'not R'difot* (Ten Years of Persecution), Tel Aviv, 1930, p. 27; quoted by J. B. Schechtman, "The U.S.S.R., Zionism, and Israel," in Lionel Kochan (ed.), *The Jews in Soviet Russia Since 1917,* 3rd ed. (Oxford: Oxford University Press, 1978), p. 108.

7 Ibid, p. 106.

8 Cited by Pinkus, p. 33.

9 Speech by Deputy Friedman, *Arkhiv Russkoi Revolutsii,* XVIII, p. 32, in Frank A. Golder, *Documents of Russian History, 1914–1917,* translated by Emanuel Aronsberg (Gloucester, Mass.: Peter Smith, 1964), p. 181.

10 Published in *Novoe Vremia,* No. 13,783, August 9, 1914, in ibid., p. 36.

11 This figure is cited by Howard Morley Sachar, *The Course of Modern Jewish History* (New York: Delta, 1977), p. 297.

12 Quoted in S. Ettinger, "The Jews in Russia at the Outbreak of the Revolution," in Kochan, p. 15.

13 Pinkus concludes that of the approximately 23,000 members of the Bolshevik Party at the beginning of 1917, a little less than 5 percent, or about 1000, were Jews. In April 1917, three of nine members of the Central Committee were Jews, and by August of that year six of the twenty-one members of the Central Committee were Jews. See Pinkus, pp. 77–84.

14 *The Biography of Vladimir Medem,* quoted by Bertram Wolfe, *Three Who Made a Revolution* (Boston: Beacon Press, 1962), p. 169. For Wolfe's excellent discussion of Trotsky's prerevolutionary activities and attitudes, see "Lev Davidovich Bronstein," pp. 169–179.

15 Kaganovich interview with newspaper *Tushina Pulse,* reprinted in *Argumenty I Facty (Arguments and Facts);* quoted in David Remnick, "An Old Stalinist Reflects—on Jews," *Washington Post,* June 12, 1990.

16 See Joshua Rothenberg, "Jewish Religion in the Soviet Union," in Kochan, p. 310.

17 For details of the Beilis trial see M. Samuel, *Blood Accusations: The Strange History of the Beilis Case* (Philadelphia: Jewish Publication Society, 1966), and H. Rogger, "The Beilis Case: Anti-Semitism and Politics in the Reign of Nicholas II," *Slavic Review,* Vol. 25, No. 4, 1966, pp. 615–29.

18 See "Where Is Pamyat Heading?" *Izvestia,* June 3, 1987.

19 Ibid.

20 For extensive discussion of tsarist policies toward the Jews see Simon Dubnow, *History of the Jews in Russia and Poland, From the Earliest Times to the Present Day,* 3 volumes; translated by I. Friedlander (Philadelphia: The Jewish Publication Society of America, 1916–1920); Louis Greenberg, *The*

Jews in Russia: The Struggle for Emancipation, 2 volumes (New York: Schocken, 1976); Salo W. Baron, *The Russian Jew under Tsars and Soviets,* 2d ed. (New York: Schocken, 1987); and Zvi Gitelman, A *Century of Ambivalence: The Jews of Russia and the Soviet Union, 1881 to the Present* (New York: Schocken, 1988).

21 See R. Byrnes, *Pobedonostsev: His Life and Thought* (Bloomington: Indiana University Press, 1968), p. 207, and I. M. Aronson, "The Attitudes of Russian Officials in the 1880's Toward Jewish Assimilation and Emigration," *Slavic Review,* Vol. 34, No. 1, 1975, p.1.

22 Karl Marx and Frederick [sic] Engels, *Manifesto of the Communist Party* (New York: International Publishers, 1933), p.62.

23 Quoted by Thomas E. Sawyer, *The Jewish Minority in the Soviet Union* (Boulder, Co.: Westview Press, 1979), p. 124.

24 Joseph Stalin, *Marxism and the National and Colonial Question* (Moscow: Foreign Languages Publishing House, 1940), p. 7.

25 William Sexton, "No Land of Honey," *Newsday,* October 12, 1982.

26 For excellent discussion on Birobidzhan see Benton Arnovitz, "Zion in Siberia," *Survey,* Vol. 29, No. 3, Autumn 1985, pp. 129–152, and Lukasz Hirszowicz, "Birobidzhan after Forty Years," *Soviet Jewish Affairs,* Vol. 4, No. 2, 1975, pp. 38–45.

27 Conversation between Sasha, a young Jewish worker, and Grigori Svirsky in Grigori Svirsky, *Hostages: The Personal Testimony of a Soviet Jew,* translated by Gordon Clough (New York: Knopf, 1976), p. 219.

28 See Saul Padover, *On Religion, Karl Marx* (New York: McGraw-Hill, 1974).

29 Joseph Stalin, *Political Report to the Sixteenth Party Congress of the Russian Communist Party,* English trans. from the Russian, New York, 1930, p. 191; quoted by Baron, p. 173.

30 The *Yevkom,* the Jewish Commission, was set up by the government within the *Narkomnats* (Commissariat for Nationalities Affairs) on February 1, 1918. Its primary aim was the same as the *Yevsektsiya's,* sovietizing the Jewish masses. It worked closely with the *Yevsektsiya* until it was disbanded in 1923.

31 This figure is cited by Geoffrey Hosking, A *History of the Soviet Union* (London: Fontana Press/Collins, 1985), p. 203. Roy Medvedev in 1990 put the figure as high as thirty million.

32 Quoted by D. J. Dallin and B. I. Nicolaevsky, *Forced Labor in the Soviet Union*, London, 1948; cited by Robert Conquest, *The Great Terror, Stalin's Purge of the Thirties* (New York: Macmillan, 1968), p. 512.

33 Conquest, ibid.

34 Unpublished manuscript of B. D., *The Russian Jew Yesterday and Today*, quoted by Roy Medvedev, *On Stalin and Stalinism* (New York: Oxford University Press, 1979), p. 114.

35 For one of the definitive works on the position of the United States government toward Hitler's persecution of the Jews, see David S. Wyman, *The Abandonment of the Jews: America and the Holocaust, 1941–1945* (New York: Pantheon, 1985).

36 Walter Laqueur, *The Terrible Secret* (New York: Penguin, 1982), p. 19.

37 Ibid, p. 71.

38 See Abba Eban, "Eban Recalls the Time When Gromyko Was a Zionist Hero," Jerusalem Post Foreign Service (JPFS) dispatch in the *Jewish Advocate*, July 6, 1989. Gromyko himself wrote this recollection of the period: "Many Israeli statesmen told me of their gratitude to the Soviet Union for supporting the creation of the Jewish state." See Andrei Gromyko, *Memoirs* (New York: Doubleday, 1990), p. 276.

39 See Yaacov Ro'i, *Soviet Decision-Making in Practice: The USSR and Israel 1947–1954* (London: Transaction Press, 1980); Arnold Krammer, *The Forgotten Friendship: Israel and the Soviet Bloc 1947–1953* (Chicago: University of Illinois Press, 1974); and Robert O. Freedman, "Soviet Jews as a Factor in Soviet-Israeli Relations," in Robert O. Freedman (ed.), *Soviet Jewry in the 1980's* (Durham, N.C.: Duke University Press, 1989), pp. 61–65.

40 Roy Medvedev, *On Stalin and Stalinism*, p. 147, and *Let History Judge* (New York: Knopf, 1971) p. 494. Medvedev also quotes a document from the archives of Bolshevik E. P. Frolov, called "The Anti-Semitism of J. V. Stalin," that lists numerous examples of Stalin's blatant and cruel policies toward Jews. See ibid., pp. 495–497.

41 Medvedev, *Let History Judge*, p. 494.

42 This issue is discussed in *Encounter* Pamphlet No. 9, London, 1963, and Priscilla Johnson, *Khrushchev and the Arts* (Cambridge, Mass.: Harvard University Press, 1965); cited by Edward Crankshaw, *Khrushchev, A Career* (New York: Viking, 1966), p. 295.

43 For a good study of this *matzoh* ban see Moshe Decter, "Passover and *Matzoh.* A Case History of Soviet Policy," in Ronald Rubin (ed.), *The Unredeemed: Anti-Semitism in the Soviet Union* (Chicago: Quadrangle, 1968), pp. 97–111.

44 For details on these "economic crimes," see the International Commission of Jurists, "Soviet Jews as Economic Criminals," ibid., pp. 115–126.

45 Quoted by John Lewis Gaddis, *Russia, the Soviet Union, and the United States* (New York: Knopf, 1978), p. 30.

46 Ibid., p. 42.

47 Pinkus, p. 135.

48 Ibid., pp. 251–252.

49 *Izvestia,* December 5, 1966.

50 David Giladi, summarizing statement by Soviet immigrant to Israel at the World Zionist Congress, *Haaretz,* January 25, 1972, cited by Zvi Gitelman, "Modernization, Human Rights, and Jewish Nationalism," in I. Kamentesky (ed.), *Nationalism and Human Rights Processes of Modernization in the USSR* (Littleton, Co.: Association for the Study of the Nationalities, 1977), p. 223.

51 Leonid's parents, Vladimir and Maria Slepak, were leaders of the refusenik community in Moscow. Vladimir had been renounced by his father, a confirmed Communist and son of a rabbi. Leonid and his brother Alexander left the Soviet union several years before their parents, who were finally allowed to emigrate in 1987. For an interesting discussion of the Slepak family see David K. Shipler, "Vladimir Slepak, Like His Father and Sons a Russian Dissident, Now Isolated from Both," *New York Times,* November 26, 1977, and Hedrick Smith, *The Russians* (New York: Quadrangle, 1976), pp. 484–486.

PART I

The Setting for the Soviet Jewish Movement for Freedom: Official and Grass-Roots Anti-Semitism

Official Anti-Semitism: The Divergence Between Law and Practice

Traditionally, the Kremlin used law as a major weapon for controlling the Soviet people; against Soviet Jews the legal system was used in a particularly repressive manner. When pressed by charges of human rights violations against Soviet Jews, Kremlin leaders often responded that anti-Semitism is illegal in their country, and when manifested not tolerated and severely dealt with. Clearly there has been no de jure anti-Semitism in the Soviet Union since the October Revolution. There are no equivalents of the tsarist laws of discrimination and repression against the Jews or, for that matter, of the segregationist Jim Crow laws of the post–Civil War American South, the apartheid policies of South Africa, or the racial laws of Nazi Germany.[1]

The Bolshevik government, with Lenin taking the lead, condemned anti-Semitism from the outset. In August 1918, Lenin encouraged the Council of People's Commissars to declare that "the anti-Semitic movement and pogroms against the Jews are fatal to the interests of the workers and peasants' revolution" and to call upon "the toiling people of Socialist Russia to fight this evil with all the means at their disposal."[2] Incorporation of the right of freedom of religion and the pledge of equal treatment of all minorities in Soviet constitutions and laws gave Jews hope that anti-Semitism would soon become a vestige of the past. But expectations of constitutional and legal protection went unfulfilled. This was partially the result of the Kremlin's campaign against all religions, but it was also because of the Kremlin's special negative treatment of Soviet Jews.

The 1977 Soviet Constitution, like its 1936 predecessor, contains guarantees of freedom of worship for all Soviet citizens. It also reserves the right for citizens to conduct antireligious activities. Although Article 124 of the 1936 Constitution guaranteed "freedom of conscience" and "freedom of religious worship," it also provided for "freedom of antireligious propaganda." Propaganda could thus be conducted against religion, but not for it. This asymmetrical provision in effect placed religious freedom in a subordinate, defensive, and disadvantageous position before opposition forces of officially sanctioned atheism.

Article 52 of the 1977 Constitution "guarantees freedom of conscience, that is, the right to profess or not to profess any religion, and to conduct religious worship." But it changed the right to conduct "antireligious propaganda" to the right to conduct "atheistic propaganda." Soviet officials contended that this change was an improvement for "believers," pointing out that "antireligious propaganda" is potentially more negative and offensive toward religion than "atheistic propaganda." In reality, however, this change gave the state a freer rein to push atheism, especially among the young, and to institute more severe restrictions on religious practice.

Technically, Soviet citizens are shielded from abuse stemming from their religious belief or practice. Under the same Article 52, "incitement of hostility or hatred on religious grounds is prohibited." Soviet laws also seem protective. For example, Article 74 of the 1960 Criminal Code of the R.S.F.S.R., which became operational in 1961, clearly designates religious bigotry (specifically "propaganda or agitation aimed at inciting racial or national enmity or discord") a crime with stiff penalties. Yet despite frequent and flagrant violations of this article, there were no prosecutions or convictions until October 1990, when a leader of Pamyat was convicted in Moscow of inciting hatred against Jews.

The Soviet Constitution of 1977 and Soviet laws also provide for the protection of such cultural freedoms of minorities as the right to education in their own language. But in violation of Article 45 of the Constitution, the Kremlin did not allow Jews "the opportunity to attend a school where teaching is in the native language."[3] This ban, applied to both secular and religious education, also violated the provision in Soviet statutes that endorsed the right of children to be taught in their native language. In addition, the authorities violated Article 4 of the 1973 *Fundamentals of Legislation of the U.S.S.R. and the Union Republics on Public Education,* which guaranteed "freedom of choice of the language of instruction" and "instruction in the native language or other language of the peoples of the U.S.S.R." They even violated this guarantee in the 1986 Program of the Communist Party of the Soviet Union: "The equal right of all citizens of the U.S.S.R. to use their native language, and the free development of these languages will be ensured in the future as well."

There were some Yiddish language schools in the 1920s, some of which survived until World War II. But these schools, especially in the Ukraine and Belorussia, were destroyed by the Nazis and never reopened. Thus, despite constitutional and legal guarantees, after the war there were no Soviet schools that taught either Yiddish or Hebrew. No other Soviet minority suffered similarly.

Over the years, Soviet leaders offered several reasons for the absence of Jewish schools. First they argued that Yiddish was the native language of Jews in tsarist Russia and the Soviet Union. Hebrew, on the other hand, was the language of Jewish religious practice and "Zionist conspirators." Moreover, they claimed that Jewish schools would be too costly because Jews were so widely scattered across the country. This argument, however, was not applied to other minorities such as Germans, who also lived in several areas. The Kremlin also argued that there was little demand for Jewish schools because Jews were so assimilated. Not until *glasnost* were Jews permitted to hold classes in Jewish history or culture in any language, including Russian, which today almost all Soviet Jews speak or understand.[4]

Soviet Jews have looked for additional safeguards of their religion and culture in several international conventions and agreements to which the Soviet Union has pledged adherence. Among the most important are the Universal Declaration of Human Rights (1948); the UNESCO convention Against Discrimination in Education (signed by the U.S.S.R. in 1962); the International Convention on the Elimination of all Forms of Racial Discrimination (ratified by the U.S.S.R. in 1969); the International Covenant on Civil and Political Rights and the International Covenant on Economic, Social, and Cultural Rights (ratified by the U.S.S.R. in 1973); and the Helsinki Accords (signed by the U.S.S.R. in 1975) and concluding documents of follow-up conferences. The U.S.S.R. signed all but the Universal Declaration of Human Rights, when it was one of eight states to abstain in the original UN voting. Yet ratification of the International Covenant on Civil and Political Rights and the International Covenant on Economic, Social, and Cultural Rights meant acceptance of the Universal Declaration of Human Rights. Under Gorbachev, the U.S.S.R. reaffirmed its pledge to observe this declaration on the fortieth anniversary of its adoption.

These international agreements have aimed to codify a number of basic human rights in international law that are of special significance for Soviet Jews.

1. To be protected against discrimination and propaganda that promotes discrimination
2. To leave and to return to one's country
3. To reunify families
4. To maintain human contacts
5. To practice freely and enjoy one's own culture, religion, and language
6. To be educated in one's own schools and language
7. To receive equal treatment under law

Some legal loopholes in the Soviet Constitution and international agreements have given the Kremlin considerable leeway in abiding by their human rights provisions. The 1977 Constitution was designed to reflect and even consolidate the political conservatism of the Brezhnev era. Thus it was designed not to open new vistas for civil liberties but to keep them in tight check. This is the idea behind Articles 39 and 59, the so-called linkage clauses that tightly tie the enjoyment and exercise of civil rights to fulfillment of civic duties toward the state. Article 39 stipulates that the rights and freedoms of citizens "must not be to the detriment of the interests of society or the state, or infringe the rights of other citizens." And Article 59 states: "Citizens' exercise of their rights and freedoms is inseparable from the performance of their duties and obligations." Thus Soviet citizens have rights only insofar as they fulfill their duties. In case of conflict between rights and duties, at least until the revolutionary changes of 1989 and 1990, they had to look to Article 6, which recognized the Communist Party as "the leading and guiding force of Soviet Society . . . which determines all course of action in domestic and foreign policy." On March 13, 1990, the newly created Congress of People's Deputies repealed Article 6. This action opened the door to political pluralism in the U.S.S.R. and technically, at least, dramatically weakened the power of the CPSU.

In sharp contrast with Western republics, the Soviet Union did not protect the inalienable rights of its citizens. Historically, the Communist Party, which is separate from the state, was the ultimate source of authority that *granted* civil rights. A Soviet citizen who disputed the party's position could turn to the courts. In Western republics, citizens can usually rely on the courts to protect their rights against government encroachment. In the Soviet Union, however, individual rights were considered subordinate to the will of the people as determined by the party. Indeed, the Soviet court system itself was the greatest danger to individual rights involving political issues. The party, using "telephone justice," would decide the outcome of political cases even before they had been tried.[5] *(See Reading 1.)*

The 1977 Constitution obligates the Soviet government to assure that its domestic laws satisfy the requirements of international accords it has signed. Article 29 requires "fulfillment in good faith of obligations arising . . . from international treaties signed by the U.S.S.R." and stipulates that Soviet foreign policy is "based on observance" of the ten principles of the Helsinki Accords. These include "the equal rights of peoples and their right to decide their own destiny." The U.S.S.R., in fact, is the only signatory of the Helsinki Accords to have incorporated all the Helsinki principles into its constitution. Furthermore, a Soviet law of July 6, 1978, not only requires "unswerving observance of international treaties" (Article 19) but also necessitates "making changes in and additions to Soviet legislation" to ensure that it matches the treaties it has signed (Articles 20 and 24).

The Helsinki Accords, though a declaration of intentions rather than a treaty, spotlight human rights as a basic principle of interstate relations. Furthermore, the Universal Declaration of Human Rights is not a legal document; rather, signatories to this resolution pledged to strive for securing an ideal. Thus these agreements in themselves are not legally binding. Yet some of their provisions, such as freedom of emigration, are rights firmly embedded in international law that all states must respect. The Universal Declaration of Human Rights, for example, provides that "everyone has the right to leave any country including his own, and to return to his country" (Article 13-2). The International Covenant on

Civil and Political Rights has a similarly worded provision (Article 12-2). This fundamental right of emigration has been of vital importance to Soviet Jews. It has also been a subject of swirling controversy that has caused them much stress and heartache.

Emigration as a Tool of Soviet Policy

Prior to the Helsinki Accords, the U.S.S.R. argued that generally it accepted the principles of international law regarding emigration. At Helsinki, however, it was able to limit this blanket right of emigration to "family reunification," which until then had been its main basis for allowance of emigration. Furthermore, it argued that there are certain "exceptions" to this right, such as when certain individuals still hold "state secrets."[6]

The Kremlin also took advantage of loopholes in the language of international agreements to further narrow Soviet human rights provisions. One example is Article 12-3 of the International Covenant of Civil and Political Rights regarding freedom of movement and emigration, which states: "The above mentioned rights shall not be subject to any restrictions except those which are provided by law, are necessary to protect national security, public order *(ordre public)*, public health or morals or the rights and freedoms of others." In essence, this reservation of general compliance with international agreements was consonant with a widely accepted international principle of the predominance of national security considerations. Thus if the Kremlin believed that the emigration of certain individuals would legitimately harm the U.S.S.R. in the areas stipulated in Article 12-3, they could legally forbid it. The problem, though, is that the Kremlin abused this principle and restricted emigration for its own political purposes.

Perhaps the most telling explanation for the failure of constitutional and legal protection of Soviet Jews can be seen in an offhand response by Samuil Zivs, vice chairman of the Association of Soviet Lawyers and a leading "court Jew," to a question about anti-Semitism posed to him by Lev Shapiro. Shapiro was a long-standing refusenik in Leningrad who finally was allowed to emigrate to Israel in 1987. Shapiro had suffered from anti-Semitism all his life. He became especially irritated when his daughter Naomi, unlike her brother Israel, was refused permission to attend a particular school. Shapiro first took legal action through the courts, but to no avail. When he was in Moscow, he asked Zivs for a legal explanation of how such a thing could happen in a country which has outlawed anti-Semitism and signed numerous international conventions ensuring basic human rights. Zivs reportedly replied: "Yes, it is a law, but the fact that they refused to hear your case is because every law protects only good citizens. If you want to leave the country, you are a bad citizen!"[7]

Enacting human rights legislation, adopting constitutional provisions, and signing international agreements never secured the rights of Soviet citizens. The rights of Soviet Jews were especially trampled upon. Until Gorbachev's reforms in the late 1980s, the exercise of the right of emigration was especially galling to the Kremlin. Soviet authorities had nothing but disdain for those who wanted to leave the motherland, considering them ungrateful, unpatriotic, disloyal, and undesirable "traitors." They regularly vilified them and tried to make their lives more miserable. This stance was probably applauded by most Soviet people—who, besides their anti-Semitism, envied those who could leave the U.S.S.R. while they had to stay.[8]

The Kremlin considered emigration more a political issue than a question of law or human rights. Decisions on emigration, whether in general or individual cases, were made primarily on its assessment of internal and external political considerations. Until the emigration law of January 1, 1987, there were no publicly promulgated laws or constitutional provisions dealing with emigration. Emigration was a gray area. It was neither prohibited nor permitted. There were official directives on emigration, but they were usually secret, arbitrary, and changeable according to the needs of the moment. Soviet Jews and other groups allowed to emigrate, mainly Germans and Armenians, had to infer policies from experience and statements made by officials. These "rules" could be bent, tightened, stretched, or interpreted as party leaders and bureaucrats saw fit.

Beginning with Premier Alexei Kosygin's statement of December 3, 1966, at a press conference in France, carried in the Soviet press two days later, the Kremlin went on public record that it would consider applications to emigrate on the basis of family reunification. *(See Reading 2.)*[9] Yet emigration was little more than a trickle until 1971, when the Kremlin, mainly in the interest of furthering détente with the United States, decided to significantly increase Jewish emigration. Its overall strategy, however, was to suppress emigration. It utilized dissuading propaganda and an assortment of restrictive measures to make emigration seem a particularly unattractive option.

Soviet Jews seeking to emigrate had to satisfy myriad requirements and overcome numerous obstacles to obtain an exit visa, making the emigration process a virtual labyrinth.[10] For example, the application had to be filled out perfectly; it had to exactly match previous applications that had been denied; an acceptable reference was needed from an employer; consent from parents or spouses (current and former) had to be granted; and steep fees and taxes had to be paid. Jews also were subjected to the often arbitrary, hostile, and capricious handling of their cases by officials in OVIR (the Department of Visas and Registration). Refusals were handed down for noncompliance with any of the requirements. Refusals were also made on the basis of such excuses as "previous service in the army," "resides in a closed town," "not the whole family is leaving," "emigration is unadvisable," "for reasons of state," "inexpediency," and "the affidavit is fictitious." By far the most common reason for visa refusal was that the applicant knows "state secrets." Soviet leaders, at least until Gorbachev, were obsessed with secrecy. Almost any job could be classified as secret. What constituted a state secret was perhaps the biggest secret of all. In the view of the authorities, it seemed that every job held by an unsuccessful visa applicant, a refusenik, involved "state secrets."

In 1963, Judge Jose D. Ingles of the Philippines wrote a report on the right of emigration called "The Study of Discrimination in Respect of the Right of Everyone to Leave Any Country, Including His Own, and to Return to His Country." The 115-page analysis was prepared for the UN Sub-Commission on Prevention of Discrimination and Protection of Minorities. Alert to the possibility of abuse by totalitarian states of the right to emigrate for security reasons, Ingles stressed (following the argument of Oliver Wendell Holmes on the right of free speech in the United States) that states must demonstrate a "clear and present danger" for a refusal based on security. In the late 1980s, Zambian legal expert C. L. C. Mubanga-Chipoya suggested a tighter limit: a state's right to deny emigration on security grounds existed only when there was "a clear, imminent and serious danger to the State." He added that because of rapid advances in science and technology, no person should be refused a visa for security for "more than five years after the individual acquired such secrets."[11]

Soviet practice was to restrict emigration for reasons of "state secrets" to five, ten, or more years—even an indefinite period. Soviet leaders themselves gave mixed signals on this issue. Gorbachev told French television on October 1, 1986, that the U.S.S.R. would fix a ten-year limit, but Soviet spokesman Gennady Gerasimov then explained to the Western press that Gorbachev was "mistaken." Yet, at the first Conference of the Human Dimension (CHD), held in Paris in May 1989 (another follow-up of Helsinki), Yuri Kashlev, leader of the Soviet delegation, asserted that Soviet citizens with state secrets would have to wait a minimum of five years to emigrate. Kashlev did not specify how much longer the waiting period might be. In November 1989, the new Soviet legislature gave preliminary approval to a bill on emigration which stipulated refusals because of "state secrets" would be limited to five years. But critics pointed out that this provision was not clearly written. In the meantime, Soviet Jews continued to be refused capriciously on security grounds. As late as June 1989 some had been denied a visa for over fifteen years.[12]

Soviet authorities also placed numerous obstacles in the emigration process itself. The first hurdle was obtaining a *vyzov* (literally, the call or proper invitation) from a relative in Israel. Allowing emigration only on the basis of family reunification clearly was an unnecessary restriction of the international human right to emigrate. Requirement of the *vyzov* was an additional violation of international law because it imposed another arbitrary precondition for emigration.

At first, the OVIR accepted an invitation from any relative in Israel. Some Jews who were desperate to emigrate but who had no known relatives there would instantly develop larger families, finding new "cousins" to issue the invitations. But in 1979, Moscow narrowed its definition of *family* and tightened the invitation requirement. It was bad enough to require a *vyzov,* but now this would be accepted only from "first-degree relatives"—parents, children, and siblings. This change was in direct contravention both of Soviet law and the Helsinki agreement. The Soviet Fundamental Legislation (Code) on Marriage and the Family, with which OVIR supposedly complied, defined family as husband and wife, parents and children, grandparents, and "other members of a family." The 1979 restrictions also violated the provision in Helsinki which called for an *easing* of restrictions on emigration.

The new restriction, which previously had been imposed only sporadically, would now be fully implemented—beginning in May. Enforcement started in Odessa, then quickly spread to other Soviet cities. Almost immediately, this restriction had a major impact. For example, 220 applications in Kiev were refused on the basis of "insufficient kinship" in one week at the end of 1979. And of 429 applications from this city during one week in early 1980, 400 were refused on these grounds. The statistics were similar elsewhere. Of forty-eight refusals in Moscow in February 1980, forty-seven were for this reason. Thus a new alarming category of "nonapplicant" was created, with many Jews no longer able even to get into the emigration pipeline. Odious as this restriction was, the authorities applied it capriciously and malevolently.[13]

Many Soviet Jews, such as the Yevgeny Lein family of Leningrad and the Marat Osnis family of Chernovtsy, were denied visas even though they had invitations from "first-degree relatives" in Israel. Also left hanging by this new restriction were unresolved cases of "divided families" where "first-degree relatives" of Soviet Jews (and non-Jews) were living in other countries like the United States and Germany.[14]

This restriction was later inserted into the 1987 emigration law. Soviet Jews had hoped that this law would satisfy their long-standing desire for regularity, consistency, clarity, and fairness of emigration requirements, but close scrutiny revealed it as more restrictive than enabling. They estimated that the "first-degree relative" requirement would prevent almost 90 percent of Soviet Jews from even applying. Anatoly Shcharansky (changed to Natan Sharansky after he emigrated to Israel in 1986) thus called it "the legalization of arbitrariness . . . a unique balance of hypocrisy and discrimination."[15]

Beginning especially in the early 1980s, when the authorities severely cut back on emigration and clamped down on dissidents and human rights activists, the Kremlin systematically violated other key provisions of its constitution as well as the Helsinki Accords and other international agreements it had signed. Particularly noxious were its attempts to deny and even criminalize human contacts.

Signatories of the Helsinki Final Act agreed to "make it their aim to facilitate . . . contacts, individually and collectively, whether privately or officially, among persons . . . of the participating States, and to contribute to the solution of the humanitarian problems that arise in that connection." But new Soviet laws in 1984 placed severe restrictions on communication and relations between Soviet citizens and foreigners.

The Kremlin's main aim was isolation of Soviet citizens. These laws hit Soviet Jews, particularly refuseniks, especially hard because they tended to have more contact with foreigners. A new law made it a crime for Soviet citizens to reveal "work-related secrets" to foreigners. One new law, unlike its forerunner of 1926 (dropped in 1958 in the wake of Khrushchev's de-Stalinization campaign), had punished officials for revealing "official secrets." But as Professor Irwin Cotler points out, the 1984 law was "more expansive than its Stalinist counterpart in its application to individuals rather than just officials, and more restrictive in its prohibition on transfer to foreigners alone."[16] Furthermore, as could be expected, the new law left it up to the authorities to decide what was secret and what was not. Thus as one British newspaper stated wryly, "Telling a tourist or a Western correspondent about meat rationing in the provinces would . . . result in a stiff sentence."[17]

Western tourists themselves suffered from this law. Harassment in Kiev and Leningrad was especially disturbing. There were so many incidents in Leningrad that on August 16, 1984, the U.S. State Department issued a travel advisory that warned U.S. travelers about the danger of violence and arrest there. Soviet antiemigration and anti–human rights strategy obviously was to keep Soviet Jews as isolated from the West as possible. There were even reports that in some Soviet schools the teaching of English was cut back from four or five times a week to once a week.[18]

The regime applied an even wider range of illegal restriction against refuseniks. If Soviet Jews in general are second-class citizens, and if Jews who request applications to emigrate are third-class citizens, the refuseniks are almost total societal outcasts. Until *glasnost,* they were special targets of the state's wrath. One of the worst abuses by the Kremlin was disruption of their mail service, which increased their isolation. Such action directly violated the Helsinki Accords, the Universal Postal Convention, criminal legislation of all Soviet republics, and Article 56 of the Soviet Constitution, which guarantees the privacy of correspondence. Often refuseniks' mail was returned instead of being delivered; not delivered even when the authorities said it was; confiscated, and in some cases, opened and read. Letters with invitations to emigrate often disappeared, and intercepted letters, even from three or four years earlier, at times turned up as evidence in criminal proceedings.

The authorities also used telephone service as a weapon against refuseniks. They listened to and transcribed calls, interfered with audibility, and disrupted and disconnected service. They even took phones away altogether, especially after refuseniks had repeated conversations with Westerners. These practices were contrary to both the spirit and the letter of international agreements like Helsinki. But the Kremlin provided legal support for its actions, citing, for example, order number 593 of the U.S.S.R. Ministry of Communication, issued on September 7, 1972, which states: "The use of the telephone for purposes contrary to state interests and public order is forbidden."

Other measures the regime took against refuseniks included dismissal from work, conscription into the army, subjection to psychological institutionalization, occasional beatings by "hooligans" who acted in behalf of the authorities, surveillance and harassment by the KGB, and pressure by KGB informers recruited from inside and outside the Jewish community. Often the KGB promised a refusenik a visa in exchange for information, and sometimes the KGB used blackmail to induce a refusenik to inform. Such was the case, evidently, when Sanya Lipavsky informed on Shcharansky, leaving the state enough "evidence" to convict him as a "soldier of Zionism" and a "tool of the CIA." Usually, however, these KGB attempts did not succeed, attesting to the character and indomitable spirit of unity among refuseniks. *(See Reading 3.)*

Discrimination, Harassment, and Repression of Soviet Jews

Perhaps the violation of Soviet and international law that had the widest impact on Soviet Jews was denial of their cultural and religious rights and discrimination in higher education and employment. During the period 1967–1987, Soviet Jews faced increasing repression of their attempts to practice Judaism and learn about their Jewish heritage. The authorities closed more synagogues; prevented or broke up symposia on Jewish culture *(see Reading 4)*; outlawed formal religious instruction; manhandled Jews who gathered outside synagogues on Saturdays and Jewish holidays *(see Reading 5)* or at monuments such as Babi Yar; suppressed publication of Jewish *samizdat* (self-published) literature; and refused to license private teachers of Hebrew, whom they tried to intimidate by illegal searches and seizures, false accusations of anti-Soviet activities, and even imprisonment or institutionalization in psychiatric hospitals. The Kremlin did all this in direct violation of international law, the Helsinki Final Act, and their own laws and constitutional "protection" of citizens' rights. During trials of Soviet Jews, for example, the authorities assumed the accused was guilty and acted accordingly. They regularly intimidated witnesses; utilized illegally obtained evidence; engaged in prejudicial pretrial publicity; and refused an open, public trial.

Soviet authorities, in addition to denying Jewish children access to learning about their religion and culture in their native language and own schools, also kept them (indeed all Soviet children) from meaningful education about Judaism in the schools they did attend. Soviet authorities, of course, regularly denied this charge. In the late 1960s, when the charge grew louder and more frequent, they claimed simply, but erroneously, that Jewish history was "given sufficient space in the textbooks on ancient and medieval history for the general and higher schools."[19] Soviet historiography was notorious for its omissions and distortions.

The Kremlin has treated Soviet Jewish history much more unfairly than that of other minorities in the U.S.S.R. After Stalin, the basic policy was to leave "blank spots" in Jewish history.[20] For example, the Dreyfus affair, mentioned in a 1949 text, was omitted from the 1954 edition; and the Inquisition, which a 1951 text mentioned as persecuting Jews, after 1977 was supposedly directed only against "heretics." According to the official Soviet view of the Holocaust, the Nazis committed atrocities against all people but did not single out Jews for extermination. Official history also ignored participation of Soviet Jews in the war against the Nazis; even when the Kremlin finally erected a monument to those who had been massacred at Babi Yar, there was no specific mention of the thousands of Jews who were singled out for extermination. Also missing were contributions of Soviet Jews to Soviet society in general, and the anti-Semitism behind the "Night of the Murdered Poets" in August 1952 and the Doctors' Plot of January–February 1953.

After the Six-Day War, Soviet history textbooks tried to leave a more distinctly negative impression of Jewish history. The school curriculum became filled with malicious anti-Israel and anti-Zionist propaganda. Israel would be depicted, for example, as a "Zionist hell" beset by "racism" and "aggressive militarism," financed and controlled by the CIA.[21] Such distortions and omissions were reflective of the more widespread official efforts to tailor-make history. Until *glasnost,* for example, Trotsky's name could rarely be found in Soviet history books; nor could more accurate accounts of the horrors of Stalinism.

A report by Soviet Jewish activists in early 1981 summed up how extensive and devastating the Kremlin's suppression and distortion of Jewish history and culture had been:

> Soviet Jews are practically *cut off* from their *national history.* Not one book on Jewish history, except for a series of studies dealing with the ancient period, has been published in the U.S.S.R. since 1930. Books on Jewish history published overseas are not on sale in the U.S.S.R. and they are often confiscated from foreign tourists wishing to bring them into the U.S.S.R. Not one monograph dealing with the Nazi genocide of the Jews and with Jewish resistance against Nazism (including the revolt in the Warsaw Ghetto) has been published. Despite the fact that Jews settled on territory now included in the U.S.S.R. more than 2,000 years ago and that the largest Jewish community in the world lived on that territory at the end of the 19th and the beginning of the 20th century, there is not one museum dealing with Jewish history, culture or ethnography and no existing Soviet museum has a special section dealing with these subjects. Not even a paragraph devoted to Jews has been included in school textbooks, including those on ancient history. [Thus] . . . no sufficient conditions for the preservation, study, propagation and development of Jewish culture have been created in the U.S.S.R.[22]

Gorbachev realized official distortions in general were so widespread that at the end of the 1988 school year the Kremlin canceled final history exams in the schools. *Izvestia* justified this action when it asserted that Soviet textbooks were filled with "lies." *Izvestia* then continued: "The history exam can be canceled, but no one has a right to cancel history itself, no matter how painful. It continues, and everyone now living must take part in its creation. Today we are reaping the bitter fruit of our own moral compromises and are paying for those things that we mutely accepted and supported and now do not know how to explain to our children."[23]

Under Gorbachev, the Kremlin has tried to erase at least some of the blank spots in Russian and Soviet Jewish history. In 1988, Soviet publications like *Ogonyok (Little Flame)*, No. 2, condemned *The Protocols of the Elders of Zion; Moskovskie novosti (Moscow News)*, February 7, explained some details about the Doctors' Plot of 1953; and *Sovetskaya kultura (Soviet Culture)*, July 23, rejecting the official version of the death of Solomon Mikhoels in a car accident in 1948, stated simply: "Mikhoels was murdered, and this murder was sanctioned."[24]

The Kremlin not only owed an honest account of Soviet Jewish history, it also needed to explain and rectify all the officially sponsored discrimination against Jews, especially in employment and higher education. Beginning in the mid-1940s, Jews were increasingly told that with a "few notable exceptions" they could not fill jobs in the military, Communist Party leadership, the party apparatus, political journalism, industrial management, and diplomacy.

A few examples illustrate various ways of excluding Jews. Soviet defector Arkady Shevchenko recalls, for example, that the Moscow State Institute of International Relations (known by the Russian acronym MGIMO) "was closed to Jews when I was there."[25] *New York Times* reporter Hedrick Smith relates this anecdote: A former senior editor at a publishing house said that when the annual list of books was sent to the Communist Party Central Committee for review, "it would invariably be returned with several titles by Jewish authors crossed off. No explanation was needed; a Jewish 'quota' had been imposed." And as Jewish emigration began to increase in the 1970s, bureaucrats dismissed many Jews from their jobs or declined to hire Jews lest they emigrate or otherwise cause "problems."[26] And Vladimir Pozner, a leading Soviet political commentator and highly skilled public relations expert, recalls this occurrence during the midseventies:

> I witnessed this at my place of work, Gosteleradio (the U.S.S.R. State Committee for Television and Radio), where the chairman of the board instructed the personnel department not to hire Jews. When the Gosteleradio Symphony Orchestra came up for review—like most symphony orchestras around the world, it had a disproportionately high number of Jewish musicians—the chairman personally crossed out the names of virtually all the Jews. Others, working in the many departments of television and radio found themselves under pressure to leave.[27]

Restrictive quotas in education, common in tsarist Russia, were instituted by Stalin in the early 1940s and tightened after the war. Professor Geoffrey Hosking writes that as early as 1947 Moscow University reportedly had a "rigid quota" for Jewish applicants that applied even to Jewish "medal winners."[28] Jews who had endured the black years of anti-Semitism toward the end of Stalin's rule generally had learned to cope with this level of discrimination. Traditionally, academically talented Jewish youngsters could succeed in their professions through achievement in higher education. But dramatically reduced quotas began to have a much more significantly harmful effect on Soviet Jews in the late 1960s. The 1967 war and failed movements for reform in Poland and Czechoslovakia in 1968, for which Jews were blamed, were the catalysts for intensified discrimination in education against Soviet Jews. This meant that for the first time doors to professions and attendant status were being closed.

There was a rapid decline of the Soviet Jewish student population throughout the 1970s and 1980s, especially in the most prestigious institutions of Moscow and Leningrad. This drop was far greater than the decline of the Soviet Jewish population in general because of emigration. Even with an intensified "affirmative action" program that gave Russians preference in higher education, the decline of Jewish students was far greater than that of other non-Russian nationalities. This drop can therefore be attributed mainly to the invidious quotas.

Statistics clearly reflect the sharp downturn in the number of Jewish university students. By the late 1960s, Soviet Jews were much more highly educated than the rest of the population. Approximately one third of Soviet Jews were university graduates, compared to only about 4 percent of the overall population. In 1968, 111,900 Jews were reportedly enrolled in higher education, a figure that had reached its peak that year after a consistent rise the previous few years. But this number began to decline in 1969, dipping to 88,500 by 1972–1973 and 66,900 by 1979. Reportedly this decline was even more dramatic at the postgraduate level, with the number falling from 4945 in 1970 to 2841 in 1975.[29]

These quotas against Soviet Jewish students were shrouded in secrecy, making it exceedingly hard to prove discrimination. Moreover, they were imposed in different ways, so it was hard for Soviet Jews to beat the system. Sometimes, as Professor Grigory Freiman pointed out in his *samizdat* essay, the discrimination was subtle, as when Jewish degree candidates were asked absurdly hard questions by special "Jewish examiners." *(See Reading 6.)* Sometimes, as a 1979 study by Soviet mathematicians Valery Senderov and Boris Kanevsky concluded, discrimination was more blatant, such as when the work of Jewish degree applicants was dishonestly evaluated. Other times, Jews were simply denied admission to universities. There is also evidence that in the late 1970s, Jews began to be denied admission to the mathematics department of Moscow State University on racial grounds, reminiscent of the racial practices of Nazi Germany. In at least one case the examiners gave low marks to a candidate because they believed he was Jewish. But when the candidate's mother produced a family tree that showed no Jewish ancestry, the examiners raised his marks and admitted him.[30]

Once admitted to the university, Jewish students faced discrimination in other ways. Many Jews were expelled from the university after they revealed their intention to emigrate. Even after Jewish students graduated, some were stripped of their degrees. *(See Reading 7.)* The authorities stopped this practice in the early 1980s, soon after it began, after sustained, vigorous protest by the Western academic community coordinated, for the most part, by the Committee of Concerned Scientists based in New York City. *(See Reading 8.)*

The practice of discrimination against Jews in higher education continued through the 1980s. The 1979 study of discrimination against Jews in higher education was released by the Moscow Helsinki Watch group (established to monitor Soviet compliance with the Helsinki Accords) and circulated to Western journalists. It dealt with discrimination against Jewish students in admission to the Mathematics and Mechanics Program at Moscow State University. But in 1982 the authorities forced the Helsinki Watch groups to disband as part of a widespread crackdown on dissent. In February 1982 Senderov was sentenced to seven years in a labor camp to be followed by five years of internal exile for "anti-Soviet agitation and propaganda." Kanevsky, who is Jewish, had earlier received a sentence of five years in internal exile for "defaming the Soviet state and social system."

Because of the new climate of repression, the authors of a 1983 study, reportedly employed at specialized schools of mathematics, were anonymous. This study detailed discrimination against Jewish applicants from elite Moscow high schools for admission to the Moscow Physics and Technical Institute and to three very competitive departments of Moscow State University: the mechanics and mathematics, physics, and computer sciences. Anti-Jewish discrimination, seen in an analysis of one department's practices in 1979, was found in the 1983 study to be widespread.[31] In late 1987 Senderov, released early from labor camp, maintained that anti-Jewish discrimination still was extensive but that Jewish students could be coached to pass the special "Jewish questions" in mathematics.[32]

This continuing discrimination in higher education was officially condemned in early 1989. On February 9, historians Sergei Rogov and Vladimir Nosenko wrote a very important article in *Sovetskaya kultura,* a publication of the Central Committee of the CPSU, entitled "What Did A Say and What Did B Say?" They criticized a wide range of official anti-Semitic practices. "In the 1970s," they maintained, "the number of Jews admitted to higher educational institutions was cut in half. . . . Under the circumstances, some Jews preferred to hide their nationality." The historians condemned this anti-Semitic practice, explaining that it was one of the main causes of increased Jewish emigration.

This rebuke of anti-Jewish discrimination in the universities was reflective of Gorbachev's wider effort to officially atone for past human rights abuses. In 1987, Gorbachev began a bold human rights offensive. The Kremlin soon began to consider incorporating at least some of the improvements into new laws. This reversal was dramatic, but would it have staying power?

Human Rights Improvement under Glasnost

The Vienna Declaration on Human Rights, January 1989

Soviet Jews hoped that the Kremlin would honor the human rights agreement concluded in Vienna in January 1989 as part of the follow-up process of the Helsinki Accords. This agreement contained the most explicit language to date on the right of emigration and protection of religious worship and education. In May 1989, Moscow announced the formation of the nongovernmental Helsinki Process Humanitarian Commission of the Union of Soviet Societies for Friendship and Cultural Relations with Foreign Countries. As *Moscow News* reported, this "public commission" wants Soviet law to conform to Soviet international obligations, including the Helsinki Final Act and the Concluding Document of the Vienna meeting.[33] It remained to be seen whether the Kremlin would move beyond rhetorical promises to actual compliance. Yet there was growing optimism among Soviet citizens that it would comply, because at the same time the Kremlin was circulating for discussion new draft laws in several areas, including freedom of conscience, freedom of emigration, and the exercise of legal and political rights. In many cases, draft laws or actual laws passed codified ongoing activities. Benefits for Soviet Jews accrued within the broad framework of startling advances of the overall reform movement.

Draft Law on Freedom of Conscience

In an effort to enlist as many foot soldiers for *perestroika* as possible, Gorbachev embarked on a policy of liberalization and reconciliation with most religious groups. In a way, his actions were reminiscent of Stalin's appeal to church groups for help in the Soviet Union's desperate fight against Nazi Germany. Although Gorbachev is not faced with any serious danger from an external enemy, he is confronted with the possibility of his country's collapse from a failed economy, political instability, growing lawlessness, and an explosive nationality problem. Certainly these domestic perils were at least partially responsible for Gorbachev's turn to the church. He may also have genuinely felt that it was time to make amends for so many years of religious repression.

We should remember that toward the end of 1986, Gorbachev urged an *intensification* of antireligious propaganda. Then, in 1987, he began to make some overtures toward the church: releasing prisoners of conscience from incarceration, opening some churches (many of which Khrushchev had closed down in his own campaign against religion), allowing importing of Bibles, and permitting priests to operate their own parishes. In early 1988, as *perestroika* was clearly faltering, Gorbachev struck out toward more reconciliation with the church. A convenient opportunity to showcase this turnaround was the celebration of the anniversary of the millennium of the Christianization of Kievan Rus—the baptism of the Eastern Slavs, which took place in Kiev in 988. In April, Gorbachev met with Russian church leaders to discuss steps toward liberalization, including a new draft law on religion.

On January 27, 1988, Konstantin Kharchev, then chairman of the government's Council for Religious Affairs, wrote an important article in *Izvestia* on the need for religious reform. Kharchev admitted that historically the regime had mistreated religious practitioners, but he explained that this was caused by bureaucrats who deviated from Leninist principles. Thus Kharchev stopped short of blaming Lenin himself for what had happened. Under Gorbachev, the Kremlin had embarked on an intensive de-Stalinization campaign, but it was not ready then for de-Leninization. Thus Kharchev did not point out that it was Lenin who, like Marx, believed religion was the "opiate of the people"; that it was Lenin who attacked religion for its opposition to the Revolution and for posing the threat of a rival authority to the Communist Party; that it was Lenin who would not be content in just letting religion "wither away"; that it was Lenin who began the policy of militant atheism; and that it was Lenin whose policies led to cruel repression of reactionary clergy and believers.

Instead Kharchev stressed Lenin's "liberal" attitude toward religion. He pointed to the decree of 1905, which stated that "the state should have nothing to do with religion, and religious societies should not be connected with state power," that "everyone must be completely free to profess any religion he pleases or to acknowledge no religion, that is, to be an atheist," and that "there must be absolutely no discrimination between the rights of citizens on the grounds of their religious beliefs." These Leninist principles, according to Kharchev, were embodied on January 20, 1918, in the Decree on the Separation of Church and State and of School and Church. Kharchev continued that the key to subsequent developments in religion in the U.S.S.R. was how this decree was implemented. He noted that a special department was created to "monitor the observance of the law on freedom of conscience and to safeguard its constitutional guarantees." Though Kharchev went on to say how "the Party and the state, guided by Lenin's principles, have on the whole pursued a correct course in regard to religion," he added that "it would be wrong, of course, to overlook the debit side." Kharchev then blamed Stalin for "the negative phenomena of the thirties—the cult of personality, breaches of legality, tyranny, and repression." He also blamed the "years of stagnation" under Brezhnev, though without mentioning the name of Brezhnev. Finally Kharchev called for reconsideration of Lenin's decree, explaining that historical conditions are different now from when it was promulgated. It is now possible "under democratization," he indicated, to remove "a number of 'obstacles' to real freedom of conscience for all."[34]

Kharchev's article was a major signal that some time before then the party had decided to write a new draft law on the freedom of conscience. This draft law, as Gorbachev told delegates to the Nineteenth Conference of the CPSU in June 1988, was "based on Leninist principles and takes account of all present realities." Earlier in his speech Gorbachev had reminded the delegates "We do not conceal our attitude to the religious worldview as an unmaterialistic and unscientific one." But, he continued, "all believers, regardless of the religion they profess, are citizens of the U.S.S.R. with full rights. The overwhelming majority of them are participating actively in our economic and public life and in the solution of the tasks of restructuring."[35] Thus we could see significant clues to the future draft law: the party would still appeal to "Leninist principles"; it would not acknowledge Lenin's responsibility for the party's frontal assault on religion, but blame the "excesses" of Stalin and the "stagnation" of Brezhnev; it would retain its atheistic philosophy, but the needs of *perestroika* would necessitate moderation of the party's atheistic drive.

Religious practitioners and party and government officials were all involved in the drive to change laws on religion. The movement actually began in the mid-1970s, when unofficial representatives of various religious groups offered proposals. But there were no results until 1987, when official Soviet scholars became involved. In February 1989 the scientific-consultative commission of the Council for Religious Affairs (created in late 1988), which has members from both the religious and the scholarly communities, debated a draft within "the context of the restructuring program taking place in the U.S.S.R."[36]

Soon two different drafts of the new law on religion circulated throughout the country. The first draft was by Yuri Rozenbaum, identified officially as an "honored jurist" at the U.S.S.R. Academy of Sciences Institute of State and the Law. His draft first appeared in a February article called "Drafting the USSR Draft Law on Freedom of Conscience."[37] The other version was by Kharchev.

According to *The Economist,*[38] both versions provided firmer guarantees against religious discrimination and a return by religious organizations to the legal status they had before 1918. Yet *The Economist* claimed that Kharchev's draft was "more liberal than Rozenbaum's," and identified these major differences:

1. *Education.* Kharchev's draft let parents "ensure the religious and moral education" of their children "in accordance with their own convictions," whereas Rozenbaum's let parents "bring up their children in a religious spirit and to teach them religion." The implication of Kharchev's version, unlike Rozenbaum's, was that in sharp contrast to the law then on the books, parents could arrange religious education in religious schools outside the home, taught by themselves or anyone else they designated. Seemingly, this would allow Jews to set up religious and cultural schools of their own.

Both drafts would remove the constitutional provision that all citizens have the right "to perform religious worship or carry out atheistic propaganda." As already pointed out, this meant citizens could not proselytize or encourage religion; they could only propagandize against it. The party had taken advantage of this constitutional provision to preach atheism to youth, even in school, although this practice violated the constitutional separation of church and state. Under Kharchev's draft citizens could "propagate religious or atheistic views," whereas under Rozenbaum's citizens could only "carry out religious or atheist instruction."

2. *Religious services.* Kharchev's version would allow services in private homes, though it did not mention whether they had to be conducted by officially registered clerics. This had very important meaning for Jews as well as for other religious groups like Baptists and Catholics of the Ukrainian Uniate Church (banned by Stalin after World War II because he considered it a dangerous center of Ukrainian nationalism), which are not registered. Under Jewish tradition, only ten adult males are needed to hold a service. According to Article 59 of the 1975 Law of Religious Associations, special permission from the authorities was required to worship in homes. The authorities often used this law to repress worship. Under Kharchev's version, worshipers would not need permission to hold services in the home.

3. *Publication of religious books and the use of Hebrew.* Kharchev's draft allowed religious practitioners "freely to acquire and make use of 'religious books' in the language of their choice." Rozenbaum's version said nothing about religious publishing. Under Kharchev's version, Jews could publish prayer books in Hebrew; under his version of religious

education, they could receive religious instruction in Hebrew inside or outside the home, which would be a very significant change.

4. *Registration of religious groups.* Kharchev's and Rozenbaum's versions both stipulated that religious groups must still register with the government. Thus, at least technically, they would still be under the thumb of the state. This requirement obviously was distasteful to Jews and almost all other religious groups because it meant that the odious law of April 1929, which required registration, would remain on the books.

5. *Attendance of children at religious services.* Rozenbaum's draft proposed that children over ten must "consent" to their parents taking them to service. *The Economist* pointed out that this provision would allow Communist youth organizations and schools to continue pressuring children "to opt out" of religion.

6. *Relationship of the new law to international law.* Both versions stated that if a Soviet law on freedom of religion conflicts with an international treaty or international law, the latter would take precedence. Gorbachev had repeatedly underscored Soviet respect for international law, so there was reason for optimism in this regard.

On May 5, 1989, TASS reported that the Ideological Commission of the Communist Party Central Committee had decided that the new draft law would be delayed because it "needed more work." Probably this delay was caused by the inability of liberal and conservative groups to reconcile their differences over the Kharchev and Rozenbaum drafts and the failure to agree on the specificity and meaning of certain provisions. Soon Kharchev was replaced as chairman of the Council of Religious Affairs by Yuri Khristoradnov.[39] Though it is not known whether Kharchev was forced out, his removal certainly did not augur favorably for passage of his more liberal draft-law version.

The new Soviet parliament was not expected to move fast on the draft law on religion, not only because of the delicacy of the religious issues but also because of its immense work load. According to Dr. Yuri Reshetov, director of the Department of Humanitarian Affairs and International Human Rights Cooperation under the Ministry of Foreign Affairs, by the beginning of 1990 about fifty draft laws were being prepared for consideration by the Supreme Soviet.

On June 5, 1990, *Izvestia* published a draft law on religion for public review. The press also published various comments on the draft by clergy and non-clergy. Finally, after considerable debate, the Supreme Soviet passed the landmark USSR Law on Freedom of Conscience and Religious Organizations by a nearly unanimous vote (341 for, one against, and one abstention). The new law, capping the steady growth of religious freedom of the previous few years, officially marked the end of atheism and religious repression in the U.S.S.R. Its passage was a major step in the continued erosion of the ideology of Marxism-Leninism and the authority and power of the CPSU.

Highlights of the new law of importance for Soviet Jews include the following:

1. *The Right to Proselytize Religion.* Every citizen now has the right "to express and *spread* convictions associated with his attitude toward religion" [italics mine]. Previously, there was the right only to disseminate ideas of atheism. Now the state will no longer finance "activity associated with the propaganda of atheism." This means, among other things, that state funds for "museums of religion and atheism" found in many cities (e.g., on the main streets of Leningrad) will be cut off, and that the state's organizations of atheism will fold, unless they can be self-sustaining. This would be highly unlikely, given the difficult economic times in the U.S.S.R. and the probable absence of personal dedication to the cause of instructors of atheism.
2. *The End of Religious Discrimination.* Discrimination against any citizen on the basis of religion is forbidden "in all fields of civic, political, economic, social, and cultural life" (Article 4). This is a giant step forward. Disappointing, though, is the absence of any specific reference to discrimination in education. One could infer that this is covered by the above provision, but for Soviet Jews, with their history of discrimination in higher education in particular, this omission could be significant. Article 4 also stipulates that "no indication of the attitude of a citizen toward religion is permitted in official documents except in cases where the citizen himself so desires this" (Article 4). This could mean, for example, that Jews will no longer be required to put down "Evrei" on line 5 of their internal passport. Although this line asks for "nationality," for Soviet Jews this requirement could be construed as a violation of this new legal provision.

3. *The Right to Religious Education Inside and Outside the Home.* According to the new law, "Citizens may be instructed in religious doctrine and obtain a religious education in the language of their choice either individually or jointly with others" (Article 6). This law legalizes the teaching of Hebrew which had already been taking place under *glasnost.* Children are not mentioned in this article. They are mentioned, however, in the provision of Article 3: "Parents and persons acting in loco parentis have the right to mutual agreement to rear their own children in accordance with their personal attitudes toward religion." Under *glasnost,* one could probably conclude that whatever is not forbidden is allowed. Thus there can be religious instruction and services both outside and inside the home. What the Soviet parliament specifically rejected after heated debate, however, was authorization for the use of secular state school buildings for "after hours" religious instruction. This was probably a wise decision, for inclusion of such a provision in the law could have touched off battles among contending religious groups. Nevertheless, because forbidding this use of school buildings is not mentioned in the law, local communities could decide on their own on this matter. In such eventualities, the potential for conflict among religious groups remains real.
4. *Acquisition and Dissemination of Religious Materials.* Citizens now have "the right to acquire and make use of religious literature in the language of their choice, and likewise other religious articles and materials." In addition, the law stipulates that "religious organizations have the right to produce, export, import, and disseminate religious articles, religious literature, and other informational materials that are religious in content (Article 22). These provisions legalize activities, such as the teaching of Hebrew for religious purposes, which had already been taking place under *glasnost.*
5. *Communication with Co-religionists Abroad.* "Believers" and "religious organizations" now have the right to establish "international ties and contacts" (Article 24). This too had already been taking place unofficially.
6. *Supremacy of International Treaty to Domestic Law.* If there is a conflict between stipulations in an international treaty to which

> the U.S.S.R. is signatory and the new law, "such treaty will prevail" (Article 31). Thus the Kremlin has committed itself to the potential of even further liberalization of religion.

The new law swept away most of the odious provisions of the law "On Religious Associations" enacted in April 1929. The 1990 law, however, did leave some vestiges of the past. For example, the Council on Religious Affairs will still oversee religious activities. In the past, this organ played a key role in suppression of religion. Certainly this role will change, but how much power this Council will have, and what its impact will be, remains to be seen.

Another very important law, by the end of 1990 still in its draft stage, was on the right of emigration.

Draft Law on Entering and Exiting the Country

Between May 23 and May 29, 1989, a delegation from the National Conference on Soviet Jewry (NCSJ) went to Moscow to examine the situation on emigration and the prospects for Jewish religious and cultural life in the U.S.S.R. This visit, led by NCSJ Chairman Shoshana Cardin, marked the first time representatives from this advocacy organization met with Soviet officials.[40]

Regarding the status of Jewish emigration, Dr. Reshetov told the NCSJ delegation that he believed that everyone who wants to emigrate from the U.S.S.R. should be able to do so; that Jewish emigration in 1989 would approximate the 1979 figure (it actually exceeded it by about twenty thousand); that in 1989 the refusal rate had dropped to 0.5 percent compared to 1.5 percent in 1988; and that a new draft law on entering and exiting the country would be submitted soon to the Supreme Soviet for its review. He then outlined the following major provisions of this draft law, each of which, if implemented, would signify important improvements in the emigration situation:

1. Every Soviet citizen has the right to leave the country and return.
2. Each would-be emigrant would need to submit with his application an invitation from any person who is a permanent resident of a foreign state; the invitation would not have to come from a relative.

3. Regarding state secrecy, there would be a general rule of five years, with some exceptions that would be decided at the governmental level. Subsequent changes in these exceptions would have to be approved by a commission established under the Supreme Soviet, which would also deal with appeals of exit refusals based on state secrecy. The work of this commission would be a matter of public record. Individuals applying for employment in an establishment doing classified work would be advised in advance, in writing, of any state secrecy restrictions.
4. Regarding "poor relatives" (visa applicants who needed release from financial obligations from parents or spouses), there would either be an agreement on "alimony" among the parties or the matter would be submitted to a court for a ruling. The provision was expected to eliminate this problem.

Reshetov's comments were somewhat reassuring, but there was still cause for concern about the draft law. In May 1990, Senator Dennis DeConcini (D-Ariz.) and Congressman Steny Hoyer (D-Md.), co-chairmen of the U.S. Commission on Security and Cooperation in Europe (CSCE), and Pamela Cohen, president of the Union of Councils for Soviet Jews (UCSJ), raised serious concerns about Article 7, Paragraph 1, which dealt with grounds for refusal of foreign travel. The U.S. congressional leaders sent a cable to Soviet officials in the Supreme Soviet asking for clarification of this article. DeConcini contended that a refusal could be issued, in the words of the draft law, "for reasons concerning state security of the U.S.S.R. until these reasons shall cease to exist." The senator pointed out that this article does not spell out what is meant by "these reasons," nor does it place any time limit on the refusal period. Thus, according to DeConcini, "the language of Article Seven provides Soviet authorities with an open-ended avenue for denying Soviet citizens permission to emigrate and travel," and therefore it seems "to take us back to square one regarding the central issue of visa denials." Senator DeConcini noted, however, that Article 8 does state clearly that citizens with state secrets cannot be refused the right to travel abroad for more than five years.

Pamela Cohen stressed what she considered the "fatal problem" with Article 7. On May 18 she wrote to the Soviet embassy regarding problems with Article 7. She stated that this article distinguishes between refusal based on state secrets, which in her view the law covers adequately, and refusal based on state security, which "establishes separate grounds for a new brand of arbitrary, unreviewable refusal." She asked for clarification of these refusal categories and why they *both* existed. As things then stood, she concluded, Article 7, Paragraph 1 "nullifies the otherwise constructive progress represented in the balance of the law. In effect, it reverses the presumption of Article 1, that every Soviet citizen has the right to leave. Under Article 8, an applicant can freely choose to be subject to the limitation of state secrets. Article 7 offers no such choice."[41]

It was expected that the Supreme Soviet would pass the emigration law before President Gorbachev went to Washington for a summit meeting with President Bush in late spring 1990. The Supreme Soviet was supposed to have considered it on May 31, with the understanding that when it was passed Washington and Moscow would sign a new trade agreement and the Kremlin would begin to receive long-sought-after most-favored-nation-clause trade benefits. Surprisingly, though, the Supreme Soviet did not then consider the draft law. Perhaps this was because the Kremlin was burdened with so many other problems, such as what to do about the declaration of independence of Lithuania. It also may not have been as high a priority for the Soviets as Westerners thought. One public hint of its relatively low priority had come up a year earlier. During a press conference at the CSCE Conference on the Human Dimension in Paris in May 1989, Alexei Glukhov of the Soviet Foreign Ministry's Cultural Department told this conference that the draft law on entering and exiting the country "is not a priority concern to the great majority of Soviet citizens."[42] Then in December 1990, Fyodr Burlatsky, head of a parliamentary committee drafting the legislation, projected that this law would not take effect until July 1991. The reason, he stated, was because of bureaucratic and transportation problems. Evidently, because of the heavy flow of Soviet emigrants, there were not enough seats on trains and planes to accommodate all who wanted to leave, and office workers could not keep up with the considerable paperwork. Whatever the real reason this draft law was not debated as scheduled, there was no doubt as to the heavy workload of the Supreme Soviet. This body was then faced with the daunting task of considering numerous draft laws, each with the potential for creating revolutionary changes in the country. Another such draft law concerned reform of the Soviet legal system.

Gorbachev's Plan to Establish a Rule of Law

Gorbachev began to urge a "rule of law" in the middle of 1988, probably, like his other proposed changes in the Soviet system, as a prerequisite for the success of *perestroika.* As he explained to delegates at the 19th Conference of the CPSU in 1988: "It is necessary to raise the authority of the courts of law, to secure unconditional independence of judges and their subordination to the law alone, and to define concrete sanctions for interference in their activity and contempt of court."[43] A cornerstone of the Soviet legal system was the concept of "socialist legality," which placed the primacy of the state over the individual. The entire legal system was politically subservient to the goals and directives of the Communist Party, a principle consonant with the 1977 Constitution.

Gorbachev wanted a "rule of law" to replace "socialist legality," despite his early protestations that most problems were the result of violations of this principle. More specifically, it would mean an independent judiciary, stress on freedom of the individual more than duty to the state, a free press, and subordination of the government and Communist Party to the law. Thus in any future conflict between the individual and the state, according to Valery Savitsky of the Soviet Institute of State and Law, "one should show preference to the individual."[44] Changes were so great that in December 1989 the International Commission of Jurists concluded that a "major legal revolution" was occurring in the U.S.S.R.[45]

Implementation of these fundamental changes necessitated revision of the Constitution. As one fundamental change after another took place, the whole Soviet legal system began to be turned topsy-turvy. Chunk by chunk, the whole edifice of "socialist legality" started to crumble. Debates raged over changes in the criminal code of the republics that might modify or even abolish articles on anti-Soviet activity. These articles had been used extensively to prosecute and stiffly punish both Jewish and non-Jewish human rights activists. In typical Soviet legal fashion, terms were vaguely worded and subject to the broadest interpretation by the authorities. What was meant, for example, by *hooliganism,* defined by Article 206 of the R.S.F.S.R. Criminal Code as "intentional actions violating public order in a course manner and expressing a clear disrespect toward society," or, taken one step further, by *malicious hooliganism,* defined as "the same actions distinguished in their content by exceptional cynicism or special impudence"? Even more vague was the wording of Articles 70 ("Anti-Soviet Agitation and Propaganda") and 190-1 ("Circulation of deliberately false concoctions, slandering the Soviet state and social order") of the R.S.F.S.R. Criminal Code. In 1987, Soviet officials indicated possible repeal or modification of at least some of these articles, especially 70 and 190-1, which deal with the critical issue of free speech. In August, Alexander Sukharov, Soviet minister of justice, stated at the Chautauqua Conference in New York that Article 70 was under review.[46] Then, in September, Alexander Yakovlev of the Soviet Institute for State and Law, stated that Article 190-1 "contradicts the whole spirit of *glasnost.*"[47]

On April 8, 1989, *Izvestia* published the new Soviet decree of the Presidium of the Supreme Soviet that amended the 1958 law on crimes against the state. Purportedly its aim was to permit more diversity of political views and to protect the right of dissent. One amendment replaced Article 70, which forbade "anti-Soviet agitation and propaganda," with a provision that outlawed "public appeals to undermine or overthrow the state or political system, treason, subversion, and any act designed to incite hostility between races and nationalities." Another amendment indicated that Article 190-1 would be abolished.[48]

Some Jewish activists, like veteran Moscow Hebrew teacher and human rights activist Mikhail Chlenov, believed this legal revision was "dangerous, in that it was sufficiently vague to leave open prosecution for any public utterance." Chlenov was particularly worried by Article 11, which called for prison sentences of up to three years or fines of two thousand rubles for demonstrations against "public organizations and their all-Union organs constituted according to law and acting in conformity with the U.S.S.R. Constitution."[49] Given the long record of repression by the state, Chlenov's suspicion about the true aims of this Decree was surely understandable. How the regime would interpret such revisions obviously would be of enormous importance. One way of gauging the direction of change in this area was by seeing changes in others. It was becoming increasingly evident that a pattern of fundamental change was developing.

One major change occurred in late spring 1990 with adoption of the new U.S.S.R. Law on the Press. According to the text published by *Izvestia* on June 20, the new law incorporated a revolutionary "registration principle." Accordingly, virtually any state body, group of parliamentarians, public organization, political party, or private individual could publish a newspaper, journal, or whatever, within only certain limits such as revelation of state secrets. This new law means, among other things, the legalization of *samizdat* publications and the banning of prior censorship by Glavlit (the State Censorship body) whose job was to prevent publication of anything the Communist Party did not want Soviet citizens to see. Until then, Glavlit's immense policing power was broad and sweeping, supposedly protecting the public against subversive ideas.

There was strong resistance within the CPSU over surrendering its monopoly over the media. Indeed, Gorbachev himself found it hard to keep his hands off editors whose policies rubbed him the wrong way. The new law itself was certainly a "media milestone" in the U.S.S.R., but it was hard to tell just how far this new freedom would go. Shortly after its enactment, Glavlit was abolished. It was replaced, however, by a new organization called GUOT SSSR (the Main Administration for the Safeguarding of State Secrets in the Mass Media). Reportedly, GUOT would "consult" with editors and publishers to decide what constituted "state secrets." On October 9, *Izvestia* announced that the first thing GUOT had done was distribute a secret list of proscribed topics. This list reportedly went far beyond military secrets, raising suspicion that GUOT would also try to control publication of politically sensitive materials. But there was growing dissension within the CPSU, which then controlled most (about 90 percent) of the country's publication. As the authority of the Party diminished and its power weakened, it remained unclear how effective a control mechanism GUOT could be even if the party wanted it as such. Continuation of meaningful CPSU control over the media seemingly became less likely with the emergence and subsequent legalization of other political parties.

A truly historic change in the Soviet system took place when the new Law on Public Associations was passed on October 9, 1990. This law allowed political parties to form and compete on an equal footing with the Communist Party. Political pluralism thus moved from debate to reality. How did this law develop?

New draft legislation, proposed in September, 1989, allowed registration of any club, association, or party so long as it could not be proven in court that the goal of any of these groups was against the constitution. Banning a group would mean, for example, that it advocated ethnic hatred or violent overthrow of the regime. The only way to gain political power would be through general elections.

Conservative Communist Party members, led by Yegor K. Ligachev, criticized this proposal for political pluralism from the outset. The conservative Ligachev continued to be one of Gorbachev's most formidable opponents despite demotion on September 30, 1988, from his position as chief Kremlin ideologist and number-two man in the CPSU to a position as party secretary in charge of agriculture. At the 28th Congress of the CPSU in July 1990 Ligachev, the choice of party conservatives, made an unsuccessful bid to recapture the party's number-two position. He was also relieved then of his agricultural leadership post. He still, though, remained a powerful force for Gorbachev to reckon with. Almost a year earlier, on September 20, 1989, Ligachev had warned party leaders of a "bitter struggle for power" between the Soviet faithful and those who "call for turning toward capitalism and bourgeois democracy, introducing private ownership in the economy and a multiparty political system."

On September 23 an opposing faction, called the Interregional Deputies Group, met to discuss ways of implementing political pluralism and private enterprise. This group was trying to find ways to reduce the political monopoly of the Communist Party. It was led by noted physicist Andrei Sakharov and maverick Soviet politician Boris Yeltsin. In 1987 Yeltsin was demoted by Gorbachev from his Moscow party leadership position, but he bounced back the next year when he was elected to the new Congress of People's Deputies. In 1989 Yeltsin won a seat in the Russian Republic parliament, and then on May 29, 1990, he was elected chairman of the Russian Republic's Supreme Soviet. From this new position of strength Yeltsin continued to criticize what he considered Gorbachev's too-slow pace of economic and political reform, to underscore the independent-mindedness of the RSFSR, and to position himself as a major liberal political opponent of Gorbachev. Then, near the end of the 28th Congress of the CPSU, Yeltsin stunned the delegates by announcing he had quit the party—ostensibly to devote more time to his new position as chairman of the RSFSR, but (more important perhaps) also to consolidate his new power base in a future multiparty system. Yeltsin's defection was followed by that of others, most notably the reform mayors of Moscow and Leningrad, Gavriil Popov and Anatoly Sobchak. Both mayors declared that they had left the CPSU "in order to help create a multiparty system." This was new, startling evidence of the crumbling of the once all-powerful CPSU.

Soviet law at that time, as *New York Times* reporter Bill Keller pointed out, did not outlaw new political parties, but neither did it provide the legal wherewithal to create them. Despite falling precipitously in public approval ratings, despite its obvious failure to improve the Soviet economy, despite being wracked by internal squabbling and factionalism, despite challenges to and attacks on its traditional role as "the leading and guiding force of Soviet society and the nucleus of its political system," and despite the sprouting of many new political parties and informal political groups, at least by the time of its 28th Congress held in July 1990, the CPSU had held on to much of its immense power, though with a much-weakened grip. Until then, at least, the activities of these new political groups—which include nominating candidates for office, proposing laws, and publishing newspapers—had been conducted at the sufferance of local party officials—and, understandably, with a wide difference in their treatment.[50] Earlier Gorbachev himself had called a multiparty system for the U.S.S.R. "rubbish," but by early 1990 he began to accept this idea, especially when he felt this change was necessary for the success of *perestroika*—and, indeed, even for his political survival. In February, asserting in his report on the draft platform for the 28th Party Congress that "our ideal is a humane, democratic socialism," Gorbachev came to grips with the new political realities in the U.S.S.R.:

> It goes without saying that the Soviet Communist Party intends to struggle for the status of the ruling party. But it will do so strictly within the framework of the democratic process by giving up any legal and political advantages, putting forward its programme and defending it in discussions, cooperating with other social and political forces, and always working amidst the masses, according to their interests and needs. The extensive democratisation currently under way in our society is being accompanied by mounting political pluralism. Various social and political organizations and movements are emerging. This process may lead, at some stage, to the establishment of different parties. . . . At this crucial period the Soviet Communist Party is able to play a consolidating, inte-

grating role and ensure the progress of perestroika for the benefit of the entire nation.[51]

In March, the Congress of People's Deputies swept away the monopoly of power of the CPSU. On July 13, at the end of the 28th Party Congress, Gorbachev summed up his views on political pluralism when he told CBS News: "We're on the threshold of a multiparty system. I don't see anything frightening in that." Then, as noted above, Gorbachev broke the Communist Party's monopoly of the Soviet media by opening it up to other political parties. Finally, on October 9, the Soviet Parliament approved the Law on Public Associations.

The new law, published in *Izvestia* on October 16, legalized political parties and a wide range of public associations. The main limitations were that such groups could not aim at "changes of the constitutional order by force," violate "the territorial unity of the USSR or of its Union or autonomous republics by force," advocate war, or encourage hatred.

Passage of several landmark reform laws seemed to have ushered in the birth of a new era of freedom for the Soviet people. But by the end of 1990, the "Gorbachev express" toward a "rule of law" started to brake and possibly derail. At the Fourth Congress of People's Deputies held in late December, Gorbachev sought and received unprecedented presidential powers to try to save the Soviet Union from economic and political collapse. Because Gorbachev received significant support from conservative elements of the CPSU, military, and KGB, prospects increased that "Gorbachev's law" would soon reign supreme over the country, and that restoration of order would take priority over democratic reform.

What effect Gorbachev's new reliance on order would have on Soviet Jews was unclear. Until this *volte face,* the legal situation for Soviet Jews had improved significantly since Gorbachev's "new thinking" on human rights began to make an impact in late 1986 and early 1987. Previous legal commitments to human rights, however, had never protected Soviet Jews from flagrant discrimination. Nor had they deterred the Kremlin from spewing anti-Semitic propaganda.

The Kremlin's Anti-Semitic Propaganda Campaign, 1967–1987

Judaism and Zionism *(See Reading 9)* had long been subjects of government-sponsored propaganda attacks, especially in the last years of Stalin. But the anti-Semitic propaganda campaign the Kremlin unleashed almost immediately after the 1967 Six-Day War,[52] which continued virtually unabated until early 1987, was unprecedented in scope, intensity, persistence, virulence, and duration. Toward whom was this campaign directed? What propaganda techniques were utilized? What were its major themes and goals? What were the driving forces behind it? And what was its impact?

The Soviet anti-Semitic campaign had diverse audiences: Soviet Jews themselves, other Soviet citizens, Western governments and Jewish organizations in the West, Israel, Arabs, and third-world countries. This propaganda was transmitted through "scientific" books, novels, newspapers, journals, cartoons, films, radio broadcasts, television programs, and political lectures sponsored by the *Znaniye* Society.

Lectures held by the *Znaniye* Society are a very important transmission belt for Soviet propaganda. This "voluntary public organization," established in 1947 "to disseminate political and scientific knowledge," regularly organizes lectures, conferences, and seminars on a variety of subjects in education, work, recreation, and culture centers. These lectures (which, according to one Soviet source, in 1971 numbered about twenty million with audiences of about a billion people) aim to instill patriotism and party loyalty. Often they stimulate a frank and exciting interchange of views and are a genuine intellectual experience. Yet sometimes the party's political agenda predominates.

It is intended that "scientific-atheist propaganda occupies an important place in the work of the society."[53] Dr. William Korey, Director of International Policy Research of the International Council of B'nai B'rith, testified before a Congressional committee in 1981 that a secret party directive in the fall of 1974, sent to each party district committee, ordered the *Znaniye* Society to train lecturers "to give lectures on Zionist themes." Thus, Korey concluded, "the lecture hall became a powerful channel of the anti-Zionist drive." Korey also pointed out that Valery Yemelyanov, one of the most important anti-Semitic lecturers in the

Znaniye Society, presumably under orders from the Communist Party Central Committee, in a lecture in 1973 dredged up this shopworn theme from *The Protcols of the Elders of Zion:* "The Jews will go over the heads of other nations to dominate the world. It is well known that the Zionists are planning to seize power over the world by the year 2000."[54] Such anti-Semitic comments could usually also be found in the Soviet media, but because of their stridency of tone and extreme content, they tended to be considered unsuited for the domestic press and unintended for foreign audiences.

Historically, Soviet anti-Semitic propaganda, while denying the existence of anti-Semitism in the Soviet Union, blamed Jews for the U.S.S.R.'s internal and external problems. Propaganda campaigns prior to 1967 focused on traditional anti-Semitic stereotypes. Supposedly Jews were obsessed with money; they got drunk and brawled in the synagogue; they shirked hard physical labor; their religious rites such as circumcision were backward and dangerous to Christian society; they were unreliable soldiers; and they were "rootless cosmopolitans," or Zionists who, it was believed, were well connected with Jews outside the Soviet Union and planned anti-Soviet actions in conjunction with agents of Western imperialism.[55]

The anti-Semitic propaganda campaign of 1967–1987, while continuing to harp on these accusations, also broadened its attack on Soviet Jews by focusing on the following themes:

1. Judaism was reactionary and exploitative. It considered itself superior to other religions.
2. Judaism was immoral, treacherous, corrupt, and criminally linked to the Mafia.
3. Judaism was dominated by Zionism, which sought world domination through financial power and is linked with imperial forces in the West.
4. Israel worked closely with the United States, whose "ruling circles" controlled Israeli foreign policy.
5. Zionism was racist.
6. Zionists conspired with Freemasons to control the world.
7. Zionists were enemies of communism, the Soviet people, and the Soviet state (even in the satellite countries of East Europe) and were engaged in anti-Soviet espionage. Even when Zionists

are not spies, they are guilty of "dual loyalty," with their primary allegiance toward Israel.[56]

8. Zionists incited anti-Semitism for their own selfish interests.
9. Zionists justified the worst excesses of anti-Semitic practices throughout history.
10. Zionism was contrary to the interest of the national liberation movement in third-world countries, aligning itself, for example, with supporters of apartheid in South Africa.
11. Zionists collaborated with Nazis during the war.
12. Soviet Jews, for the most part, "sat out" World War II in cities and towns far away from the battlefield.
13. Soviet Jews had their own "homeland" in Birobidzhan, so there was no need for them to emigrate to Israel, where they would only find unhappiness.
14. The Soviet Union had a much better record on anti-Semitism and human rights than the United States.
15. Most Soviet Jews were living happily in the Soviet Union and had an equal opportunity with other Soviet citizens to succeed, so they rejected outside efforts to "save" them.[57]

Many of these themes were taken directly from tsarist and Nazi propaganda, particularly from *The Protocols of the Elders of Zion* and *Mein Kampf.* In some cases, anti-Semitic stereotypes and ideas were simple plagiarisms. In fact, targeting Jews as scapegoats for the failures of government policies, concocting stories about the dangerous "depravity" of Jewish religious and social practices, and associating Jews with sinister forces were traditional tsarist policies that consistently found popular support among all segments of the population.

After the 1967 Middle East war, Soviet propaganda tried to wrap its anti-Semitism in the cloak of anti-Zionism. By claiming it was targeting Zionism, not Judaism, the Kremlin could deny it was anti-Semitic and at the same time win support from Arab countries and other third-world states. To this end Soviet leaders publicly asserted, just as their predecessors had done, that "there never has been and there is no anti-Semitism in the U.S.S.R." and that people were publicly condemned and even prosecuted for committing anti-Semitic acts.

The distinction in Soviet propaganda between anti-Zionism and anti-Semitism is blurry at best, making it almost impossible to tell the two apart. Beginning in the 1930s, the struggle against "Trotskyism" was laced with anti-Semitism. For example, there were many references to "Trotsky-Bronstein," "the Jew Trotsky," or "the masked Zionist." In the late 1940s, *anticosmopolitanism* (also *rootless cosmopolitanism*) became a code term for anti-Semitism. And beginning in November 1952, Zionism became the new major code word for anti-Semitism. Yet by lambasting Zionism, Soviet propaganda was also attacking Jews. Indeed, anti-Semitism, through the guise of anti-Zionism, developed further as an instrument of official state policy.

After the 1967 war, Soviet propagandists went to work to condemn Judaism. Trofim Kichko, for instance, author of a wickedly anti-Semitic book in 1963 *(Judaism Without Embellishment)*, came out with a similarly hateful book in 1969. In *Judaism and Zionism* Kichko attacked the "anti-humanism of Judaism" and its exploitative morality. "Judaism cannot be a model for morality," he claimed, "because on one side it threatens people with divine punishment for sins, and, on the other hand, it itself sanctified sins if they are in the interests of religion and of the exploiting classes." *(See Reading 10.)* A few years later Vladimir Begun, another caustic anti-Semitic author who was a member of the Institute of Philosophy and Law at the Belorussian Academy of Science, attacked both the Jewish religion and Zionism in *Invasion Without Arms*. His book was published in two editions (1977 and 1979), totaling 200,000 copies. These two passages are indicative of his condemnation of Judaism:

> *The biblical instruction that all peoples, according to the Lord's will, will allegedly become slaves to the Jews* has frequently caused the adherents of Judaism trouble. It gave occasion to Christian obscurantists to hound and persecute not only supporters of clericalism but also ordinary believers who, unlike the rabbis and Jewish exploiters, were concerned only with their daily bread and dreamed nothing of the kind. *The religious Judaic ethics with its shamelessness and cynicism towards non-Jews* has undoubtedly played an exceptionally harmful role in the centuries-long history of the Jews.[58]

And a few pages later: "If [the Torah] is considered from the standpoint of modern civilization and communist morality, it *proves to be an unsurpassed textbook of bloodthirstiness, hypocrisy, treachery, perfidy and moral degeneracy—all the basest human qualities.* Jewish and Christian hypocrites alike keep silent over this."[59] Soviet authorities lavishly praised Begun's book. One reviewer referred the reader to *Caution: Zionism,* a book published in 1969 by Yuri Ivanov, a chief ideologist for the CPSU Central Committee. He then pointed out that Begun's book "is informative and full of new facts and interesting data; it is distinguished by its scientific logic, depth, and consistency of its conclusion."

The 1967 war gave Soviet leaders a new occasion to rail against Zionism and, indirectly, the Jews. They repeated themes from *The Protocols of the Elders of Zion* with only slightly updated references. Ivanov, for example, wrote several articles in important Soviet publications (such as *Izvestia* and *Komsomolskaya pravda*) wherein he claimed, among other things, that Zionism taught Jewish children, before age seven, the doctrine of "racial exclusivity," and that they were members of a "god-chosen people" destined to dominate others. Moreover, Ivanov stressed, Zionism was an "international Cosa Nostra" with the money, power, and influence to rule the world.[60] Then in *Caution: Zionism,* Ivanov made no distinction between the terms *Zionists* and *Jewish bourgeoisie.* In his view, both were racist, both strove for world domination, and both were engaged in "total war" against the Soviet Union. In an updated English edition of this book in 1970, Ivanov again charged that Jews were aiming for world domination. *(See Reading 11.)*

Soviet attempts to mask anti-Semitism by reference to "Zionism" proved unsuccessful in a celebrated court case in France in 1972. That year the French League Against Anti-Semitism successfully sued the Soviet embassy in Paris for perpetrating anti-Semitism. The main evidence was an anti-Semitic article published on September 22, 1972, by the French-language *U.R.S.S.*, a journal of the Soviet embassy in Paris. The Paris court convicted the journal's editor of inciting racial hatred, violence, and discrimination against the Jews. As a result of this trial, Soviet anti-Zionist propaganda became better understood within its broader context of anti-Semitism.[61]

One of the more frequent and controversial themes of Soviet propaganda after 1967 was the equation of Zionism with Nazism. Professor Michael Curtis explained the technique of this linkage: "Both ideologies were held to share a common hostility to communism and the Soviet Union; both elevated race and nation into absolutes; both insisted on racial purity and looked on mankind as composed of a hierarchy of peoples in which each was the dominant factor and the chosen people.

Judaism itself was world fascism."[62] Soviet propaganda also blamed Zionists for having collaborated with the Nazis before and during World War II in order to achieve their goal of an independent homeland in Palestine.

One of the first salvos equating Zionism and Nazism came on June 9, 1967, when Nikolai Fedorenko, Soviet ambassador to the United Nations, claimed Israeli leaders in the Six-Day War had behaved just like the Nazis in World War II. Premier Kosygin (on June 19) and General Secretary Brezhnev (on July 5) repeated this assertion. *(See Reading 12.)* Over the next few years this theme was highlighted in numerous books by Soviet "scholars," such as Ivanov's *Caution: Zionism,* and Yevgeny Yevseyev's *Fascism Under the Blue Star,* published in 1971.

An important adjunct to this theme beginning in 1968 was that Zionism was also a criminally racist ideology. Major articles stressed this idea. For example, P. Petylyakov, writing in *Krasnaya zvezda (Red Star)* on August 17, 1968, argued: "There is much in common between the Israeli extremists and the South African and Rhodesian racists in their attitudes toward all independent African states. Both Tel Aviv and Pretoria are glad to spread racist rule over all independent Africa."[63] And in January 1969, V. Rabinovich wrote: "The Jewish people was never like other peoples; it was always unique. . . . Both Zionism and Fascism are based on shameless nationalism, a bourgeois chauvinism which in its own interests affirms the special 'rights' of one nation by means of violation of the rights of other nations—their economic exploitation, political persecution and sometimes even their physical extermination (genocide)."[64] The charge of Zionist collaboration with Nazis in genocide was also made strikingly by Vladimir Bolshakov, writing in *Pravda* in February 1971:

> A dirty alliance with the Hitlerites stained the agents of the Zionist concern who operated during the war years in the countries of Western and Eastern Europe and in the occupied part of U.S.S.R. territory. A good many cases are known in which the Gestapo chose Kapos in the death camps and the special "police" who kept order in the Jewish ghettos from among the Zionists. "The tragedy of Babi Yar," Soviet citizens of Jewish origin living in the Ukraine wrote in a letter to Pravda, "will forever remain the embodiment not only of the cannibalism of the Hitlerites but also the indelible shame of their accomplices and followers—the Zionists."[65]

In September 1971, Soviet ambassador Yakov A. Malik, in an address before the UN Security Council, publicized and reinforced Bolshakov's argument:

> Mr. Tekoah [the Israeli Ambassador to the UN] was indignant at our parallel between Zionism and Fascism. But why not? It is all very simple: both are racist ideologies. The Fascists advocated the superiority of the Aryan race as the highest among all the races and peoples in the world. The Fascists considered that the ideal was the Aryan with his blue eyes and blond hair. I do not know what the external signs are with the Zionists; but their racist theory is the same. The Fascist advocated hatred toward all peoples and the Zionist does the same. The chosen people: is that not racism? What is the difference between Zionism and Fascism, if the essence of ideology is racism, hatred toward other peoples? The chosen people. The people elected by God. Where in the second half of the twentieth century does one hear anyone advocating this criminal absurd theory of the superiority of the one race and one people over others? Try to justify that from the rostrum of the United Nations. Try to prove that you are the chosen people and the others are nobodies. Nobody will support you, and you would be well advised not to try it.[66]

In 1972 a special committee of the Soviet Academy of Sciences was set up to vilify Zionism. In 1974, as noted above, a directive from the Central Committee of the CPSU called on the *Znaniye* Society to speak out more against Zionism. Thus by the mid-1970s the Kremlin had set the stage for one of its most extreme and politically explosive moves. The U.S.S.R., along with other Communist states, Arab states, and their third-world supporters, led the campaign for adoption of UN General Assembly Resolution 3379 of November 10, 1975, which stated that "Zionism is a form of racism and racial discrimination." The Soviets had unsuccessfully tried to include this equation in the UN ten years earlier in a Draft Convention for the Elimination of all forms of Racial Discrimination and had also stressed it in UN debates on the 1967 war. Adoption of the 1975 resolution gnawed at Jews everywhere.[67]

After this resolution, Soviet propaganda at home stepped up its linkage of Zionism with Nazism. Over the next few years the Kremlin arranged publication of a spate of anti-Zionist books. Among the most highly publicized were *Zionism and Apartheid* by Valery Skurlatov; *Zionism as a Form of Racial Discrimination* by Lydia Modzhorian; *Invasion Without*

Arms by Valery Begun; *De-Zionization* by Yevgeny Yemelyanov (published in France by the Free Palestine Press); and *Alarm* by Ivan Shevtsov. Illustrative was Shevtsov's writing of the "Israeli general staff picking up the torch from Hitler in its monstrous plan of world-wide hegemony. Israel's attitude toward world Jewry is akin to Hitler's policy to Germans who lived outside the boundaries of Germany."[68]

The Kremlin also used the arts to express the same views. In the winter of 1979–1980, to cite one instance, there was an exhibition of paintings in Minsk by the official Soviet painter Mikhail A. Savitsky. One painting, *Summer Theater,* reportedly "showed a pile of naked Russian corpses in a concentration camp [during World War II]. Standing over them, a helmeted Nazi officer and a prison camp trusty, a Jew wearing a star of David, grin sadistically at each other, as if in satisfaction over a job well done." Supposedly the authorities failed to withdraw this painting despite protests over its blatant anti-Semitism. Moreover, this painting was published in *Literatura i Mastatsva, (Literature and Art),* the journal of the Belorussian Ministry of Culture.[69]

Lev A. Korneyev (sometimes writing under the Jewish-sounding name Leo Korn) was perhaps the most prolific anti-Semitic writer of the early and mid-1980s. In his 1982 book *The Class Essence of Zionism,* Korneyev asserted that the Zionists deliberately magnified the number of Jewish victims of Nazism to win sympathy for creation of Israel and they ignored the deaths of millions of others. According to Korneyev, "The Zionists not only keep silent about the many millions of victims from among other peoples in the struggle against Fascism; they have also significantly exaggerated—to six million—the number of Jews who perished in the Second World War." He then argued that Zionists shared responsibility for the deaths of both Jewish and non-Jewish victims of Nazism, asserting: "The Nazi genocide of the 'inferior' Slavs, Jews, Gypsies, and other 'races' was insane. *But were it not for the Zionist–Nazi alliance, the number of victims, including Jews, in the Second World War would of course have been less*" (italics added).[70]

On January 17, 1984, Vladimir Bolshakov wrote another important article in *Pravda* wherein he linked Zionism with Nazis. He claimed, among other things, that Yitzhak Shamir had collaborated with the Gestapo in 1941 to plan joint terrorist operations in Palestine against the British.[71] A year later Korneyev charged that Jewish bankers had financed the Nazis and prevented Jews from fighting fascism, so both they and the Nazis should be held accountable for the Holocaust.[72]

The Soviets harped on the linkage between Zionism, Nazism, and racism throughout almost the entire twenty-year period of their propaganda vilification of the Jews. In 1968 they seized another opportunity to target the Jews, this time for their alleged conspiratorial role in the upheavals in Poland and Czechoslovakia. Under the Kremlin's direction, Communist Party leaders in Poland and Czechoslovakia blamed a "Zionist conspiracy" for anti-Communist uprisings in their country.

In Poland in March 1968, there was a rash of student protests against the regime. In June, Poland's chief Communist ideologist, Andrzej Werblan, wrote an important essay in *Miesięcznik Literacki (Literary Monthly)* called "On the Genesis of the Conflict." Werblan blamed the March events on Polish Jews who tried to stir up the people against communism. Werblan explained that the influence of Polish Jews was far out of proportion to their numbers in Poland (only about twenty-five thousand out of a total population of thirty million). Werblan then went into a long tirade against disproportionate concentration of Jews in higher education and publishing, which he vowed would be stopped. Soon the Polish Communist Party expelled thousands of Jews from the country, leaving only about eight to ten thousand. Polish Jews, like their brethren in other countries, were again made scapegoats for governmental failures. The Kremlin undoubtedly supported the Werblan thesis and subsequent Jewish expulsions. Moscow and Warsaw surely agreed on the propaganda theme that the "conspiratorial hand of international Zionism" was behind the uprisings. According to one Polish dissident, Werblan wrote his piece on the initiative of the Central Committee of the CPSU. Supposedly the Kremlin's plan was to have Poland become "the first laboratory of official anti-Semitism in the Eastern bloc."[73]

Soviet propaganda took a similar anti-Zionist tack in explaining the Prague Spring and the "necessity" of the subsequent Soviet invasion of Czechoslovakia in August 1968. The Kremlin charged several leading Czech Communists who were Jewish, or were labeled Jewish, with responsibility for the political unrest. Named specifically were Dr. Frantisek Kriegel, chairman of the Czech National Front and the only Jewish member of the Politburo; Professor Eduard Goldstueker, chairman of the liberal Writers' Union; and Ota Sik, deputy prime minister, who denied that he was Jewish. The Soviet press even charged Czech foreign minister Jiri Hajek with being a Jew who collaborated with the Nazis and who later tried to conceal his Jewishness by changing his name from Karpeles. The press then referred to Hajek as "Karpeles-Hajek," as it had referred to "Trotsky-Bronstein." This charge was a fabrication designed to find Jewish scapegoats. These men and their liberal "accomplices" were called "agents of the international Zionist organization 'Joint.' " Soviet propaganda hammered away on the theme that Zionists were a "fifth column" in Czechoslovakia and Poland, scheming and acting to undermine socialism in these countries. So it urged the people to be extra-vigilant and to assist in uprooting these dangerous "counterrevolutionaries."[74]

Charges of Zionist plots in Czechoslovakia continued into the 1970s. Yevseyev's *Fascism under the Blue Star* charged Zionist subversion in concert with Western imperialism. And Bolshakov, writing in *Pravda* in February 1971, made this incredible charge: "The Zionists sought to seize leading posts in all the mass information media of the C.S.R. in order to conduct frantic propaganda against the socialist system in Czechoslovakia, against the Czechoslovak Communist Party, the Soviet Union, the C.P.S.U. and the Communist Parties of the fraternal socialist countries." Moreover, he accused Zionists of conniving with "imperialist intelligence services to gather espionage information." Bolshakov then proceeded to give detailed "evidence" for these charges.[75]

Much of the anti-Zionist propaganda at this time had another purpose. By the early 1970s a new domestic challenge of burgeoning Jewish activism confronted the Kremlin. Soviet Jews, inspired by the swift, decisive Israeli victory in the 1967 war, decided they no longer would remain silent.[76] They began to take bold action against anti-Semitism, to practice Judaism more freely, and to demand their right to emigrate to Israel. In December 1970 several Soviet Jews (and two non-Jews) planned to hijack a plane in Leningrad and fly to Israel. The authorities learned of the plan and brought the accused to trial. The punishment of death and long prison terms shocked observers both inside and outside the U.S.S.R., whose pressure soon forced the Kremlin to moderate these harsh sentences.

Moscow was also faced with the new foreign-policy challenge posed by the beginning of detente with the United States. Kremlin leaders felt the necessity of giving some signal to Washington of liberalization on the

Jewish Question. The Kremlin had allowed small numbers of Soviet Jews to emigrate from 1967 to 1971. In 1971, Soviet leaders decided to let 13,122 leave. That year marked the beginning of what was to become a major Jewish emigration movement neither Soviet Jewish activists nor Soviet leaders expected.[77]

Coincidentally, the Soviet human rights movement began to grow at this time. Soon some Jewish activists, like Anatoly Shcharansky, linked up with this movement. This linkage reached its height just after the signing of the Helsinki Accords in 1975. Generally, however, Soviet Jewish activists focused on emigration and did not join with other human rights advocates who had to remain in the U.S.S.R. and whose agenda and priorities were different.

Moscow tried to satisfy the growing thirst for emigration by allowing some of the most notable Jewish activists, such as professors Alexander Voronel and Mark Azbel, to leave, but usually only after incarceration or excessive harassment, or both. The Kremlin even forced some Jews to emigrate, among them Leningrad poet and future Nobel Prize laureate Joseph Brodsky. Brodsky's poems, published in the West in 1965 because of Soviet censorship, contained only two works with Jewish themes: *Isaac and Abraham* and *A Jewish Cemetery near Leningrad.* In a trial tinged by anti-Semitism in 1964, Brodsky was convicted of parasitism and sentenced to exile and forced labor. In 1973 the authorities forced him to emigrate.

During this same period the Kremlin also exiled non-Jewish human rights activists such as Valentin Turchin, head of the Moscow group of Amnesty International, and non-Jewish literary dissidents such as Alexander Solzhenitsyn and Andrei Amalrik. In 1974, Solzhenitsyn was exiled mainly for his publication abroad of *The Gulag Archipelago.*[78] In 1976 Amalrik, who in 1969 had written the provocative essay *Will the Soviet Union Survive Until 1984?,* was deported. Jewish dissidents like Brodsky and non-Jewish activists like Turchin and Amalrik were forced to leave the U.S.S.R. *with visas to Israel.* In this way Moscow wanted to create the impression that a Jewish-Zionist conspiracy was the driving force behind the entire Soviet human rights and emigration movements. By the late 1970s the Kremlin decided to crush the human rights groups, many of which had sprung up after the signing of the Helsinki Accords in August 1975. By the early 1980s, they were essentially defunct.

Soviet propaganda tried to blame Soviet Jews for the "harm" Soviet human rights groups had caused Soviet society. Soviet leaders charged that Soviet Jews (like Shcharansky), egged on and supported by their Central Intelligence and Zionist "benefactors," were behind this "anti-Soviet" movement. They also charged that Soviet Jews had no real reason to emigrate or to fight for equal rights since they already had them. *(See Readings 13 and 14.)* It was Zionist propaganda, they complained, that had spread lies about the true situation of Soviet Jews in the U.S.S.R., had duped many into leaving, and had given ammunition to those who wanted to intensify the cold war.

Soviet propaganda painted a picture of an idyllic life of Jews in the U.S.S.R. It advertised glowing accounts of their happiness, contentment, and cultural and religious freedom. In contrast, it depicted life for Soviet Jewish emigres, especially those in the United States and Israel, as tragically disappointing. Several examples over the years are revealing.

In 1970, a Novosti publication, *Soviet Jews: Fact and Fiction*, stated: "Lacking evidence of official anti-Semitism in the U.S.S.R., bourgeois propaganda resorts to outright distortion and garbled facts." This publication admitted that "there still are isolated instances of anti-Semitism and prejudice towards an "alien" nation." But it added: "As a rule it is people who are culturally backward, mainly the older people, who still have such prejudices."[79] Obviously the Kremlin wanted the outside world to think that any manifestations of anti-Semitism in the U.S.S.R. were vestiges of tsarist days that would soon disappear under the Soviet system of equal rights for all.

A TASS broadcast in 1975 aimed to show the disillusionment of Soviet Jewish emigres in the United States. It quoted this comment by Grigory Melamed, who had spoken to a correspondent of *Vechernaya Moskva (Moscow Evening [News])*: "I have returned home because I couldn't breathe, as if without air. . . . It is all eyewash that we Jews, emigrants from the Soviet Union, are so eagerly expected there. Nobody wants us there, and nobody, even the American Jews, needs us there. . . . I have been to the labor exchange and employment office. . . . Every day one sees the same faces begging for any kind of work, every day the same talk of smashed hopes."[80]

Publication of the two white books was perhaps the most widely advertised example of Soviet anti-Semitic propaganda. Both books portrayed Israel as a wicked and uninviting place from which many Soviet

Jews wanted to escape; they described terrible experiences of Soviet Jews who have been "lured" to Israel by Zionist propaganda; they condemned the "subversive" actions of Zionism in the U.S.S.R.; and they charged Zionists with collaborating with the Nazis.

The first white book, appearing in Russian in 1979 and republished in English in 1981, clearly aimed at stemming the tide of Soviet Jewish emigration, which in 1979 had reached its peak. It received wide publicity in the U.S.S.R., with about 150,000 copies printed. Contributing to this volume were two of the most highly skilled and scholarly Soviet anti-Semitic propagandists: international lawyer Lydia Modzhoryan of the Soviet Academy of Sciences' Institute of Oriental Studies and E. D. Modrzhinskaya of the Soviet Academy of Sciences' Institute of Philosophy. In 1985, a second updated and beefed-up white book appeared that contained some of the same themes as the 1979 volume. It too portrayed terrible experiences of Soviet Jews who had been "lured" by Zionist propaganda to Israel; condemned the "subversive" actions of Zionism in the U.S.S.R.; and again charged Zionists with collaborating with the Nazis. It added such themes as condemnation of Israeli "aggression" in Lebanon and ridicule of anti-Semitism in the United States. In the main, this book tried to explain why Soviet Jewish emigration had come to a virtual standstill.

The first white book came out under the auspices of the Association of Soviet Lawyers (ASL). The second white book was put out by the Yuridischeskaya Literatura publishing house in Moscow and appeared under the auspices of both the ASL and the newly formed Anti-Zionist Committee of the Soviet Public. This meant, probably, that prominent court Jews had a more prominent role in its writing.[81]

The Kremlin's Utilization of Court Jews for Propaganda

Over the years the Kremlin has skillfully used court Jews to support particular domestic and foreign policy goals. The most prominent are Zivs of the Association of Soviet Lawyers; Lieutenant-General David Dragunsky, who had participated in the forced collectivization campaign of the early 1930s and was a highly decorated Hero of the Soviet Union for his exploits during the Great Patriotic War; Aaron Vergelis, editor of *Sovetish heimland,* who is identified by the Kremlin as a "well-known Soviet poet and publicist"; and assorted academics and rabbis. The

Kremlin has used these highly visible figures to reduce the desire of Soviet Jews to emigrate, to promote foreign policy goals, and to project a positive human rights image internationally. Accordingly, these Jews wrote letters and articles for newspapers and magazines, hosted groups of Western Jews visiting the U.S.S.R., went on tours to the West, and gave interviews and press conferences that were broadcast and published at home and abroad. They explained how thankful they were for the "blessings" of the Soviet system, which had made it possible for them to live a good life; how patriotic most Soviet Jews are; how, unlike in the Western capitalist countries such as the United States, anti-Semitism is illegal and strictly dealt with in the U.S.S.R.; and how they could get along very well without "uninvited defenders" from the West.

The first significant Kremlin use of court Jews was during the 1920s when "non-Jewish Jews" in the *Yevsektsiya* tried to Sovietize and communize their Jewish brethren. Then during World War II Stalin used the Jewish Anti-Fascist Committee to enlist support of Western Jews for his country's war effort against Nazi Germany. In the early 1950s Stalin, just before he died, reportedly was organizing a group of prominent Soviet Jews, led by General Dragunsky, to sign an appeal supporting his plan to deport Soviet Jews to Siberia. In 1956, Khrushchev directed a group of Soviet Jews from Bukhara to sign a declaration, "Hands off Egypt," which indicated their "profound indignation" at Israel's invasion of the Sinai and argued that it violated biblical and religious principles.[82]

The Kremlin renewed its extensive use of court Jews, mostly on an ad hoc basis, in the early 1970s. On February 27, 1970, Dragunsky wrote a scathing attack on Zionism in *Pravda.* *(See Reading 15.)* The next day, *Vechernaya Moskva* carried an interview with Leib Levin, chief rabbi of the Moscow Synagogue. Levin proposed that Western Jews who thought there was anti-Semitism in the Soviet Union should visit Moscow to learn that all the stories (about anti-Semitism in the U.S.S.R.) they had been regaled with by Zionist propaganda were vile lies."

In March 1970, the Kremlin arranged press conferences to utilize court Jews for propaganda. Particularly newsworthy was the one on March 4, staged in Moscow at the House of Friendship with the Peoples of Foreign Countries. These court Jews, along with several non-Jews to make the conference look more representative of the Soviet people as a whole, condemned the "crimes" of the Israeli military, which they equated with

Nazi atrocities, and boasted that Jews had equal rights with all other nationalities "in the 240 million Soviet family." *(See Reading 16.)* Additional press conferences were staged the following week in other cities. For example, there was one on the Middle East sponsored by the Union of Journalists of the Latvian Republic in Riga. There "citizens of the U.S.S.R. of Jewish nationality" said they wanted to "express our protest against the crimes of the military clique of the ruling extremist circles of the State of Israel," adding: "It is quite obvious that the war now waged by Israel, as well as statements made in connection with it, are the product of a conspiracy of Zionists and imperialists, the product of the policies of international Zionism, which was, still is and will continue to be a tool of the most reactionary aggressive circles. . . ."[83]

The Leningrad trial in December 1970 led to the first world conference on Soviet Jewry, held in Brussels in late February 1971. Known as Brussels 1, the Conference demanded that the Kremlin honor international law and allow Soviet Jews to emigrate to Israel. Soviet propaganda was cranked up to criticize this conference as an "anti-Soviet provocation."[84]

To offset bad publicity from Brussels 1, the Kremlin sent six court Jews to the Belgian capital. These emissaries, who included Dragunsky, Zivs, and Vladimir Peller (a Jewish chairman of a collective farm), held a press conference under the auspices of the Belgian-Soviet Friendship Society in which they denounced charges of anti-Semitism in the U.S.S.R. as fabrications and provocations.

Finally, on March 23, Kremlin leaders, after scouring the Soviet Union, convened in Moscow some sixty "leaders of the Rabbinate and Judaic Religious Congregations in the U.S.S.R." Their assigned task was to assail Israel and to assert there was no anti-Semitism in the Soviet Union. Their declaration dutifully asserted:

> We decisively reject any attempts made by international Zionist circles and by the government of Israel to speak in our name and to protect us from the non-existent injustice and oppression. . . . As citizens of our Fatherland, we hereby declare that all the allegations made by the government of Israel and by international Zionist circles concerning the purported inequality of the Jews in the Soviet Union are vicious fabrications intended for anti-Soviet purposes.[85]

The Kremlin also used court Jews to counter adverse publicity they expected from the second Brussels World Conference on Soviet Jewry held in February 1976, known as Brussels II. On January 22 a group of Jews from Odessa issued this statement to the embassies of six Western countries (Belgium, the United States, Canada, Italy, France, and the United Kingdom):

> We . . . voice our protest against the impudent intentions of the Zionists to convoke their next provocative meeting in Brussels. We understand full well what inclinations are motivating the Zionist leaders. They are not inspired by any concern for the fate of Jews but by their hatred of our Fatherland, their efforts to slander the Country of the Soviets, where for the first time in the world the national problem has been truly resolved, where all nations enjoy equal rights and are building a good life together. . . . We appeal to the sensibilities of your governments, requesting you to condemn the provocations committed by world Zionism and to ban its meeting.[86]

The Kremlin then turned to Vergelis, editor of *Sovetish heimland* to counter charges from the Brussels meeting. In February Vergelis was interviewed in *New Times*, a Soviet public affairs journal published in many languages and distributed to many countries around the world. He claimed that Jewish culture was strong in the U.S.S.R. and that accusations of its repression were unsubstantiated. Only those who wanted to destroy détente, he concluded, complained about lack of cultural freedom for Soviet Jews.[87] Then in an interview published in *Vechernaya Moskva* on December 7, 1976, designed primarily for domestic consumption, Vergelis asserted: "The Soviet Jewish literature is an inalienable, integral part of the great multinational Soviet culture." He then repeated the familiar theme that Zionists and other anti-Soviet elements were perpetrating the lie in the West regarding the true status of Soviet Jewish culture.

Vergelis was also used to try to stem the growing number of defections and the tide of Jewish emigration in 1979. He expounded on the Kremlin's argument that the prospect of a happy life outside the U.S.S.R. was a cruel illusion for Soviet Jewish emigrants. As he said in an interview with *Sovetskaya Rossiya* in September 1979, "He who abandons the land where he was born comes, as a rule, to a sorry end. Trying to get more somewhere else, he finishes up with nothing. Finally, he is overcome by despair. He dreams of the motherland. . . . I have met them in Soviet consulates in Rome, Vienna, and other capitals of the Western world—people with anguish in their eyes, pleading to be allowed to go home."[88]

Another tack used by the Kremlin in 1979 to curtail Jewish emigration was renewed publicity of happy, successful Jews who lived in Birobidzhan, their true "homeland" inside the Soviet Union. *(See Reading 17.)* In one publication by Vladimir Kostikov, *The People and Land of Birobidzhan,* published by Novosti and thus principally for foreign audiences, appeared an interview with Lev B. Shapiro, first secretary of the Communist Party regional committee in Birobidzhan. In response to an inquiry whether Birobidzhan had realized its promise for Soviet Jews, Shapiro replied: "We have in the U.S.S.R. a national home in which, over the past forty-five years, we have built everything—plants, factories, housing, schools, and theaters." Contrary to the reality of Birobidzhan as a remote, forbidding land, this book contained several pictures of its supposedly idyllic setting. The caption underneath a picture of what Kostikov described as Birobidzhan's beautiful natural setting reads "Nature is bountiful in the Jewish Autonomous Region, and there is rich diversity of animal and plant life. Roe, tiger, fox and squirrel are found in the forest, and lotuses are found in some lakes."[89] Here, then, is a picture of the U.S.S.R.'s own garden of Eden. What more could Soviet Jews ask for? Surely they do not have to look anywhere else for fulfillment of their dream of a national homeland!

In the spring of 1983 the Kremlin embarked on a new scheme to utilize court Jews in its propaganda campaign against Soviet Jews, Zionism, and the State of Israel. On April 1, eight made an appeal through the Soviet press to create an Anti-Zionist Committee of the Soviet Public, which was officially launched on April 21.[90]

Thirty-seven persons were named to the committee, with a presidium of thirteen. Dragunsky was named chairman and Zivs first deputy chairman. Chosen as regular deputy chairmen were Yuri Kolesnikov, a signer of the April 1 appeal who is a professional propagandist and author of two anti-Semitic novels on World War II (*The Promised Land,* 1973, and *The Raised Curtain,* 1977); Mark Krupkin, deputy director of Novosti Press Agency Publishing House; and Igor Belayev, a non-Jewish journalist who had specialized on Middle Eastern affairs for *Pravda* and who then headed the foreign affairs section of *Literaturnaya gazeta.* Four other notable court Jews on the committee are Grigory Bondarevsky, a professor and historian who was also a KGB officer and journalist specializing on Jewish affairs in the United Kingdom; Genrikas Zimanas, a Lithuanian Jew who, as editor of *Kommunistas* (the Lithuanian ideological journal) and deputy to the Lithuanian Supreme Soviet, had often expressed the view that Zionism was anti-Semitic; Martin Kabachnik, a chemist and member of the Academy of Sciences who had previously signed anti-Zionist statements; and Genrikh Gofman, a novelist on World War II and lecturer on military affairs who also had previously endorsed anti-Zionist activities. The rest of the committee was a mixture of Jews and non-Jews form a variety of walks of life. This was typical of Soviet efforts to show that established committees are broadly representative of the people.[91]

The Anti-Zionist Committee had several purposes. Its major stated goal was to mobilize a public campaign against Zionism through all the propaganda resources at its disposal. It also was intended, like similar campaigns against Brussels I and Brussels II, to counter adverse publicity emanating from the Third World Conference on Soviet Jewry that had just concluded in Jerusalem. The committee also went on the offensive. It lashed out against Israeli "aggression" in Lebanon, and it urged resistance against all "Zionist crimes," in the Middle East and elsewhere, which were aided by "antagonistic and imperialist activities" of the United States. It was not by chance, therefore, that the day of the committee's major press conference for Soviet and foreign journalists was June 6, just one year after Israel had invaded Lebanon. *(See Reading 18.)*

At this press conference Zivs made a pronouncement that revealed what may have been the committee's actual main goal: explanation and justification of "the considerable decrease" in Jewish emigration. Zivs asserted that essentially no more Soviet Jews would be emigrating but that this was not the Kremlin's doing. The real reason, he claimed, was that emigration for purposes of family reunification after World War II had been "basically completed" and that very few Soviet Jews (no longer "citizens of the U.S.S.R. of Jewish nationality"), now realizing the advantages of living inside the U.S.S.R., were succumbing to Zionist propaganda. This statement obviously ran counter to what was really the case then in the Soviet Union. Many thousands of Jews had already taken the initial risky step of asking for an invitation from a relative in Israel, but they were being denied visas to emigrate. Zivs probably was right when he said the number of visa applications was way down. Yet this was largely because Soviet Jews saw that very few were being approved and they wanted to avoid being cast into the status of refusenik.

The Anti-Zionist Committee is officially public, trying to create the illusion that the Kremlin did not order its formation and does not control its activities. The committee announced that local branches would be established all over the U.S.S.R., but this goal was never realized. In the provinces, however, where anti-Semitism can be practiced more vigorously because of the absence of the scrutiny of the foreign media and the difficulty of central control, local branches tended to work extra zealously for the goals of the committee.

Adolph Shayevich, chief rabbi of the Moscow Synagogue, is a member of this committee. His predecessor, Rabbi Yakov Fishman, had also joined—but he died just before the committee's press conference on June 6. On April 28, Rabbi Fishman had stated, in a Moscow Radio Peace and Progress broadcast in Hebrew to Israel, that "as a Soviet citizen . . . I do my duty by joining the Soviet Public Anti-Zionist Committee." He then attacked "Jewish capitalists" who "use others, boys and girls, whom they lure into their nets. So-called Zionists are rich persons who do not go to live in Israel but rather build factories to exploit the 'poor Jews.' "[92]

The Kremlin also used Shayevich, like other Soviet rabbis, to propagandize anti-Zionist policies and to tell Western Jews how misinformed they were about the freedom and quality of life of Soviet Jews. In his visit to New York City in 1984, for example (the first time a Soviet Jewish religious leader had visited the United States since 1976), Rabbi Shayevich insisted that reports of persecution and harassment of Soviet Jews were simply "not true." He then criticized a Fifth Avenue parade protesting anti-Semitism in the Soviet Union as an anti-Soviet demonstration.[93]

Then in an interview with TASS on May 21, 1986, Shayevich was highly critical of a report by the Parliamentary Committee on Soviet Jewry that had just been published in London. The rabbi chastised the representatives of the group that visited the U.S.S.R. for being "very much biased." "How else," he wondered, "can one view their groundless assertions that religious Jews are discriminated against in employment, that the Soviet authorities intend to eliminate Judaism. . . . The Soviet constitution guarantees the freedom of creed to all citizens." Shayevich then refuted the report's conclusion that "the learning of Hebrew is prohibited in the U.S.S.R.," arguing:

> it is not prohibited in the U.S.S.R. to learn any language, Hebrew naturally included. By the way, Hebrew is taught in three higher educational establishments—in Moscow, Tbilisi, Leningrad. . . . A Hebrew-Russian dictionary has been brought out. We publish religious literature in Hebrew. For instance, *the Pentecost According to Moses* came off the press recently. No one interferes with the study of Hebrew in groups. But there are such groups that are engaged in anti-Soviet activity under the cover of studying Hebrew. And they, naturally, are persecuted for this. Anti-state activity is punished in every country, including Britain and the United States.

Rabbi Shayevich's flat denial of discrimination against Soviet Jews defied reality. He was correct when he stated that Hebrew was taught and published legally only within strict guidelines—for academic and government purposes. What he did not say is that Hebrew could not be taught legally for religious or cultural education of Soviet Jews. *(See Readings 19, 20, 21.)* Moreover, his justification of persecution of Hebrew study groups as anti-Soviet showed that the rabbi had to reflect the positions of the Council of Religious Affairs, which oversaw and controlled his activities.

On May 14, 1984, Zivs held a press conference where he repeated the theme that Soviet Jewish emigration was just about over. According to Zivs, "the process of the reunification of divided families is practically complete. This had led to a sharp reduction in the number of people emigrating to Israel." Then Zivs added that even among "the relatively small number of people" who were duped by Zionist propaganda to emigrate, "the number of those who have realized the perniciousness of their intentions and changed their minds has risen in the last year." Several Jewish speakers were then introduced who gave personal testimonies to support Zivs's contention.[94]

The Anti-Zionist Committee, despite several reports of its imminent or actual demise, proved quite resilient. It continued to operate through 1990 and into 1991, though with diminished influence and effectiveness. During the Washington summit in December 1987, Zivs indicated that there were plans to dismantle the committee because it had outlived its usefulness.[95] This reflected the principle that the Soviet relationship with the United States has always been the most important external consideration in the Kremlin's policy toward Soviet Jews. It also indicated that changed circumstances inside the U.S.S.R., particularly Gorbachev's policy of *perestroika,* necessitated a less confrontational approach.

But in the summer of 1988 the Soviet monthly journal *Agitator* published an article by V. Makarov, entitled rhetorically "Are There Zionists in Our Country?" Makarov asserted that the continued existence of the Anti-Zionist Committee was justified "in order to counter Zionist propaganda and to expose its nationalistic essence."[96] During this summer, moreover, a new anti-Zionist committee was formed, called the Committee of the Soviet Public Against the Establishment of Diplomatic Relations with Israel. Its head is none other than the anti-Semitic author Yevgeny Yevseyev.[97]

Then, in January 1989 there was a report by Rabbi Shayevich that the Anti-Zionist Committee had been disbanded. This too proved premature. As a sign that it was still very much alive, in the summer of 1989 it issued a statement, released by TASS on August 8, that denounced "attempts by some individuals in the U.S.S.R. to create a certain sociopolitical organization, the Zionists' Union." This action, according to the committee, is "warlike Zionism" and "a deliberate stoking up of tension in interethnic relations." The committee then claimed that Zionism "is used against the interests of the Jewish working people and in practice joins ranks with rabid anti-Semites." It also blamed Zionists for "wooing away part of Soviet Jews from involvement in *perestroika.*"[98]

The Zionist Union that the Anti-Zionist Committee criticized was founded in Moscow under the leadership of Lev Gorodetsky, chairman of the Hebrew Teachers Association. According to Gorodetsky, the main aims of the union were to teach Hebrew and generally prepare Soviet Jews for life in Israel, to combat anti-Semitism, and to protect Soviet Jews at a time of increasing popularly based anti-Semitism. A week earlier, the Socialist Zionist youth movement had founded a chapter in Moscow, but deliberately without publicity.[99]

Zigzags of Anti-Semitic Propaganda

The harshness and stridency of the Anti-Zionist Committee's attack on the founding of the Zionist Union seemed to run counter to a general softening of the Kremlin's anti-Zionist and anti-Semitic propaganda. This change was first evidenced in early 1987 and generally continued through 1990. Perhaps one reason was that Soviet propaganda was continuing its swings from harshness to softness, both in content and tone. Over the years Soviet Jews were attacked viciously for "sitting out" World War II and even collaborating with the Nazis, yet they also were depicted as loyal citizens who bravely fought the Nazis; they were informed that they could leave to rejoin their families in Israel but were told repeatedly that Israel was a "Zionist hell hole" where they would not find happiness *(see Reading 22)* and that they already had their Soviet homeland in the garden spot of Birobidzhan; they were shown as happy Soviet citizens who like other nationalities were building socialism, yet they were also attacked for comprising a "fifth column" that conspired with sinister Zionist, CIA, Masonic, and Mafia forces to weaken the U.S.S.R. and destroy communism. The tone of the propaganda was at times vituperative but at other times much softer. What accounted for the inconsistencies of position and expression in Soviet anti-Semitic propaganda?

One possible explanation for these zigzags is that the propaganda had different goals for different audiences. Thus, for example, what was intended for American Jews and third-world states would most likely differ. *(See Reading 23.)* Another reason is that anti-Semitic campaigns, orchestrated from Moscow, often play out differently in the various republics and provinces. Anti-Semitism is very strong in the Ukraine, which may account for publication there of some of the most virulent anti-Semitic tracts. It is much weaker in Georgia and Uzbekistan, where comparatively little anti-Semitic literature is published.

Another explanation for propaganda inconsistency is division within the Soviet leadership itself over the Jewish Question. Arkady Shevchenko claims that Soviet leaders not only shared different views on this issue but that they also often changed their positions according to their perception of the interplay between the domestic and international situations.[100] Thus at times, such as in the early 1970s, the Kremlin publicized its approval of emigration for reunification to enhance chances that détente would succeed. But at other times, such as the early 1980s, it announced emigration was virtually over because it felt too many Jews were leaving, a more liberalized emigration policy had not won them the diplomatic gains they had sought (like substantially more credits and a most-favored-nation award from the United States, and closer cooperation with the United States regarding the People's Republic of China), and dissident activities had grown too strong and potentially dangerous.

Still another explanation is that the Kremlin wanted to hedge on anti-Semitism. This hedging was reflected in the division of professional anti-Semitic propagandists into hard-liners such as Lev Korneyev and Alexander Romanenko and soft-liners like Lionel Dadiani and A. Kislov. Soft-liners were not necessarily the more favorably disposed toward Soviet Jews. They may even have been more dangerous, for they engaged in more subtle attacks Moscow could show as evidence of opposition to anti-Semitism.

A final explanation is that Soviet propaganda had gone through a basic change under *glasnost* that signaled a long-term shift to soft-pedaling and even outright official rejection of anti-Semitic and anti-Zionist propaganda.

The Change in Soviet Anti-Semitic Propaganda Under Glasnost

The hedging hypothesis may provide some insight into the major shift in official publications that began in early 1987. At that time more Jewish names began to appear as writers in the Soviet media. The general practice until then was for Jews to use Russian-sounding pseudonyms. The media also began to cover more items of Jewish interest. *Sovetskaya Moldavia,* for example, on March 13 carried an announcement of a forthcoming Yiddish-language instruction publication. Perhaps a stronger signal of a policy shift was given two days earlier. On March 11 *Literaturnaya gazeta* carried an article by Nina Yelekhova on the Jewish Studio Theater in Moscow. Yelekhova argued that Soviet citizens "should not be isolated from one another" by the section of their internal passport that designates nationality. Until then the Kremlin had never admitted publicly that this nationality line on the passport, which especially hurts Soviet Jews, had ever caused divisiveness.[101]

At this time there was also a noticeable drop in the volume of anti-Semitic and anti-Zionist propaganda. Certain publications like *Nedelya,* the weekly supplement to *Izvestia,* began to criticize anti-Semitism in the U.S.S.R. Until then these publications had regularly printed anti-Semitic diatribes. The major newspapers, *Pravda* and *Izvestia,* also began to oppose anti-Semitism in early 1987. At the same time, however, anti-Semitic articles increased in frequency and intensity in some local newspapers, such as *Leningradskaya pravda.* Perhaps the softening of anti-Semitism in the major Moscow papers was designed to give the West the impression that under *glasnost* Soviet Jews were much better off than before.

Soviet Jews surely could take solace from evidence of a new, softer official approach to Zionism. In January 1987 an article in *Questions of the History of the CPSU,* the authoritative journal published by the party central committee's Institute of Marxism-Leninism, severely criticized the traditional hard line on Zionism. Three authors signed the article, which usually signals an important directional change in ideology. The article questioned the claim that Zionists sought "supremacy over the world," pointing out that this argument "relieves imperialism of responsibility for its global aspirations." The article then condemned Romanenko's caustically anti-Semitic book *The Class Essence of Zionism,* published in 1986. The authors accused Romanenko of "manipulating" Marxism-Leninism and argued that his analysis of Zionism lacked "the necessary tactfulness and discretion with regard to everything that impinges on nationalities policy and national relations in the U.S.S.R."[102]

The new softer line on Zionism was also shown in media attacks on other traditional hard-liners. *Sovetskaya kultura,* which until *glasnost* had propagated the traditional conspiratorial theory of Zionism, by the middle of 1987 began to reverse itself and attack the messengers of this hard-line approach. They singled out three major hardliners (Romanenko, Yevseyev, and Begun) who then turned around and sued this paper for defamation. Begun especially was criticized for his association with *Pamyat.*[103] *(See Reading 24.)*

The Growth of Grassroots Anti-Semitism

Pamyat is one of an estimated two to three thousand "informal" (not officially sanctioned) groups, clubs, and associations that have sprung up in the Soviet Union under *glasnost.* It is perhaps the largest political activist group in the Soviet Union, and surely the largest of those groups characterizing themselves as "Russian-patriotic." This group of "Russia-firsters," founded in the early 1980s under the U.S.S.R. Ministry of Aviation, supposedly to protect and restore historical monuments, has grown rapidly to more than twenty thousand members in Moscow and branches in forty other Soviet cities. *Pamyat* is comprised of numerous associations that include, among others: the Pamyat Russian National-Patriotic Front, the People's Patriotic Front of Pamyat (led by Dmitri Vassilyev), the Pamyat World Anti-Semitic and Anti-Masonic Front, the Russian Patriotic Union in Moscow and the Russian National-Patriotic Center in Leningrad, the Novosibirsk Pamyat Historic-Patriotic Association, and the Vernost Patriotic Association in Irkutsk.[104]

Sprouting up along with *Pamyat* have been smaller groups such as *Otechestvo* (Fatherland), *Spasenie* (Salvation), *Spravedlivost* (Fairness), and the *Lyubery.* This last group first came to public attention in March 1987, when the Soviet press published several articles about its activities.[105] It consists largely of physical-fitness devotees from Moscow's working-class suburb of Lyuberets whose professed aim is to clear Moscow of punk-rockers, heavy-metal enthusiasts, and the like, who they claim are undermining the social fabric of Russian society. Using roughhouse tactics generally ignored by the police, they have also targeted Jews for "special attention."

The burgeoning activities of these groups is a major sign of the growth of popularly based anti-Semitism under Gorbachev. Among other things, they are raising all the canards of anti-Semitism found in *The Protocols of the Elders of Zion.*[106] *Pamyat* groups especially use this forgery to "prove" that Soviet Jews are conspiring to overthrow the Soviet regime and, worse, to destroy Russian culture. Vassilyev in particular, who does not hide his fascist sympathies (especially for Mussolini; Zionism, he claims, was embraced by Nazism as an ideology of a chosen race), regularly quotes from *The Protocols.* He knows that Western historians have concluded that *The Protocols* are a forgery by the *Okhrana.* But even if they are, he contends that its essence is true. According to Vassilyev, *The Protocols* reveals a "satanic conspiracy of Freemasons and Zionists" bent on destroying Russia—physically, spiritually, economically, politically, and socially. According to Vassilyev, Jews are a Trojan horse and the main villains who engage in a conspiracy to undermine Russia. He singles out Zionist Bolshevik leaders, especially Trotsky, as primary strategists of the October Revolution that devastated his country. After refraining from attacking Lenin between 1985 and 1987, Vassilyev began attacking him as a "half Jew" who led the "dark forces" against Russia. Trotsky and Kaganovich, along with Masonic architects, Vassilyev claims, were responsible for building the Moscow underground subway (which runs under the Kremlin) so that when the time was right it could be blown up and destroy the capital. This issue is stressed in *Pamyat* literature and the public meetings it sponsors. "When I read these 'Protocols,' " Vassilyev told one such meeting, "I suddenly gazed in horror at a map of the Moscow Metro system. . . . All the principal junctions are right below Party and government institutions!"[107] Supposedly other Russian monuments also face the same danger of destruction, so *Pamyat* leaders shout that the people must be ever-vigilant to preserve the symbolic edifices of their heritage.

In an interview that appeared on February 26, 1988, in the Rome daily *La Repubblica,* Vassilyev expanded his views on Zionism and Soviet Jews. At the outset he stated that there were "evil forces that would like to build their power on the ruins of the world's loftiest cultures." He added that "a terrible force" of "Zionism and Freemasonry" was "trying to destroy our culture." When asked "When you say 'Zionists,' do you mean the Jews?" Vassilyev responded:

> Yes, always these Jews, as though there were nobody else in the world. The Jews live everywhere, own the capital, live like parasites throughout the world, emigrate freely from country to country, and are always depicted as the most unfortunate nation. Nobody is concerned about the Russian people, who now [are] the worst off and most unfortunate of all peoples. It is enough to read the "Protocols of the Elders of Zion" to realize who created this situation. However, not all Zionists are Jews and not all Jews are Zionists. This is why we are not anti-Semitic. Tell me,

> who invented the gas chambers? The Jews. The Free Masons, on the other hand, are the material executors of the Zionists' plans. It is a very serious matter."

Then when asked "What exactly is your attitude toward the Jewish population in the U.S.S.R. and Moscow?" Vassilyev gave this detailed response:

> The ideologue of the destruction of our monuments and our culture was Yaroslavsky,* whose real name was Gubelman. He was a Jew. Who carried out this destruction? Kaganovich—a Jew. Moreover, Trotsky, Zinoviev, and Kamenev were all Jews. . . . We have nothing against the Jews: There are some decent people among them. However, our analysis of the facts always confronts us with the Jewish nationality. Were Beria and Yagoda not Jews? Were the administrators of many of the Stalinist prison camps not Jews? We are not anti-Semitic, but the truth must be told. Now 20 percent of the state's leadership posts are held by Jews, who represent only 0.69 percent of the population. This actually goes against the constitution. No less than 50 percent of Doctors of Science and Candidates are Jews too. The majority of members of professional unions—composers, writers, movie makers, jurists, medics, and so forth—are also Jews, and they are supposed to be persecuted. There is never any mention of the persecuted Russians. In any case all Jews who have wanted to do so have emigrated with their pockets full of money, while the Russians have always been, and remain poor. Nobody is concerned about them.

Pamyat leaders stress that all the enemies of Russia must be wiped out before it is too late. In addition to Jews, Zionists, and Freemasons (all used as code words for everything they despise), these include homosexuals, historians who oppose Stalin, pro-Americans and pro-Westerners, liberal writers, proponents of *perestroika,* and other "satanic forces" whose aim is to destroy Russia through rock music, alcoholism, drugs,

* The reference is to Yemelyan Yaroslavsky (born Minei Gubelman), a political journalist who headed the Society of the Militant Godless. Through many publications, most notably *The Bible for Believers and Non-Believers, 1923–1924,* he sought to undermine the influence of religion.

AIDS, liberalism, and internationalism. Many members of *Pamyat* reportedly truly believe in Satan and that they are combating those who serve the Devil.[108]

Though there are some significant divisions of opinion within *Pamyat*, this "Russian party," in the view of Walter Laqueur, is united by three main planks: its populism, the feeling that the Russian republic has been the most discriminated against, and its crusade against "Russophobia."[109] Most members are xenophobic and, to a certain extent, intellectual and emotional descendants of the Slavophils. Many tend to idealize and romanticize the tsarist state and Tsar Nicholas II, who they claim was a victim of "ritual murder" by "you-know-who."

Pamyat's main slogans are "Patriots of the world, unite!," "No to Rootless Cosmopolitanism!," and "Yes to National Patriotism!" Another slogan that reflects *Pamyat's* agenda is "Order to the Soul—Order in the Motherland." This is the slogan of Valentin Rasputin, a talented Russian nationalist novelist from Irkutsk. Rasputin and Venyamin Yarin of the reactionary blue collar United Workers' Front, were two anti-Semites named to Gorbachev's Presidential Council. Still another anti-Semite, A. J. Suchariev, co-author of the anti-Zionist white book of 1985, was named prosecutor general of the Soviet Union. Rasputin, who was chosen to serve in the Congress of People's Deputies, told *New York Times* reporter Bill Keller in November 1989 that he blames the Jews not only "for the sin of having carried out the Revolution," but also "for the shape that it took." According to Rasputin, Jews "should feel responsible for the terror that existed during the Revolution and especially after the Revolution. They played a large role, and their guilt is great. Both for the killing of God, and for that." Rasputin concluded:

> Many Jewish leaders took part in the terror, in the repression of the kulaks, of the peasants, and so on. The ideology was produced by Jews. But to make them answer for it and to say that we won't be able to coexist, is the wrong approach. We can't make all Jews emigrate, and it's not necessary, either, because they are the brains we need. And I think the two nations, Russians and Jews, have merged to such an extent that separation would be painful—painful for the Russian nation, too. With all their faults and merits, they need each other, because on the one hand it makes for a kind of spiritual competition, and on the other hand it spurs the Russian people out of their lethargy.[110]

The appeal of *Pamyat* thus goes well beyond downtrodden workers and peasants to various writers and other intellectuals. Besides Rasputin, among the most notable are Yuri Bondarev, Viktor Astafyev, Vasily Belov, and Igor Shafarevich.

Shafarevich, a Russian mathematician and member of the Soviet Academy of Sciences, and one of the leaders of the Russian nationalist movement, uses Russophobia as his codeword for Jews. According to Shafarevich, Jews inside Russia, aided by Jews in league with other dangerous enemies in the West, are Russophobes who are conspiring to weaken and ultimately destroy the spiritual, moral, and political principles of Russia. Shafarevich urges Russians to ferret out and destroy Jewish conspirators or face their own destruction. His argument is a modern-day version of the call by Slavophils for vigilance against pernicious Westernism and by Soviet leaders over the years, especially Stalin, for vigilance against a wide assortment of domestic and foreign enemies, including "rootless cosmopolitans." Shafarevich directs his attack against those Jewish "Russophobes," such as historian Vasily Grossman, who he believes deliberately portray Russians and their history in a bad light. In an essay in the politically middle of the road journal *Novy mir (New World)* in July 1989, Shafarevich revealed more fully his anti-Americanism, anti-liberalism, and anti-socialist credo.

Shafarevich's Russophobia, the title of an essay he wrote first in *samizdat,* was republished in Russia by the conservative literary monthly *Nash sovremennik (Our Contemporary).* This, along with several other conservative publications such as *Moskva (Moscow)* and *Molodaya gvardia (Young Guard)*, regularly print pro-*Pamyat* writings and anti-Semitic articles. For example, Vyacheslav Gorbachev (no relation to Mikhail Gorbachev), deputy chief editor of *Molodaya gvardiya,* wrote an article in the March 1987 issue warning of a conspiracy between Zionists and Freemasons who were serving the Devil. Supposedly this conspiracy explains why the Russian people "does not compose or sing its own songs," and why the Russian family is being destroyed and corrupted "by sex, alcohol, and drugs."[111]

Pamyat activities have found some receptive audiences, reportedly even in the top echelons of the Communist Party. On May 6, 1987, *Pamyat* leaders were received by Boris Yeltsin, then first secretary of the Moscow City Party Committee and a candidate member of the CPSU

Politburo. They complained about the forces they believed were destroying Russia through rock music, drugs, alcohol, and the like, and they asked to be officially registered. Reportedly Yeltsin did not seek this meeting, but it was thrust upon him by circumstances surrounding *Pamyat* demonstrations in the area. He supposedly told the *Pamyat* leaders that they would not be registered because of their "virtually anti-Soviet statements." *Pamyat*'s association with Yegor Ligachev has been much more warm and cordial. When Ligachev was chief party ideologist under Gorbachev, he was an ideological ally of the conservative wing of the R.S.F.S.R. Writers' Union. Despite this intellectual camaraderie, there are no reports of Ligachev's ever making any anti-Semitic statements, at least publicly.[112]

For the most part, the Soviet media have sharply criticized *Pamyat*'s philosophy and leaders. *(See Reading 25.)* In 1987 *Pravda, Izvestia,* and *Moscow News* all began to denounce *Pamyat* and Vassilyev. In one important article *Izvestia* correspondent Pavel Gutionov warned Soviet citizens of the dangers of *Pamyat.* He compared the "witch hunt" for "Zionist-Mason conspirators" conducted by members of *Pamyat* to ominous searches for the "enemies of the people" that led to millions of deaths in the Great Purge under Stalin. Gutionov also revealed that experts who were asked to testify at the trial of Yevseyev, Begun, and Romanenko asserted that some passages from Begun's publications exactly matched *Mein Kampf,* "that Bible of German fascism." Finally, Gutionov blamed the extreme "anti-Zionism" of the Brezhnev era for *Pamyat*'s anti-Semitism.[113] *Moscow News* was especially critical of *Pamyat,* and it published letters from Soviet citizens calling *Pamyat* racist and fascist. *Izvestia* even called for legal action against *Pamyat.* But *Leningradskaya pravda,* reflecting a long standing reputation as anti-Semitic, gave at least indirect support to *Pamyat.* In an announcement on August 28, 1988, it said it would allow readers to judge for themselves whether *Pamyat* is anti-Semitic when it published *Pamyat*'s "Appeal to the Public." This Appeal referred to Jews as "guests who have remained too long" in Russia and must stop being "parasites."[114]

Until mid-1990, at least, Gorbachev allowed *Pamyat,* officially a public group, to organize, demonstrate, and disseminate anti-Semitic propaganda. *Pamyat* leaders generally are politically savvy and know how to "play the system." *(See Reading 26.)* As Boris Bochstein noted: "Their actions are carefully crafted with an eye towards what is possible and what is still not permitted under the country's current leadership. Also, being great specialists in the areas of terminology and demagogy . . . they know how to wrap themselves in the correct phrases and slogans, which has to please the people 'upstairs.' "[115]

On February 9, 1989, Rogov's and Nosenko's article in *Sovetskaya kultura* lambasted the extremity of the anti-Zionist campaign of the Brezhnev era, compared it with Nazi practices, and admitted there was extensive anti-Semitism in the Soviet Union. These were surely major reasons, the authors argued, "why tens of thousands of Jews relinquished their Soviet citizenship and emigrated to other countries, including Israel in the past twenty years." The authors cited an anti-Semitic article by V. Begun that had appeared a few months earlier in the journal *Nash sovremennik* to support their contention that Soviet anti-Semitism remained an acute problem. The main goal of this article, written just before the opening of the Mikhoels Jewish Cultural Center in Moscow, clearly was to influence Soviet Jews not to emigrate through sweet-talk rather than by the stick of previous years.[116]

Some Jewish activists, like Yuri I. Sokol, who started a private Jewish library in Moscow in early 1988, ironically argued that they were glad such anti-Semitic groups were operating in the open. "I would say thank you to *Pamyat,*" Sokol said, for "they uncovered this disease, this cancer. They wear no mask in words or acts. They stand for the hidden part of the iceberg."[117]

Official criticism of past anti-Zionist extremism which was now out in the open, the recognition of the necessity to eliminate noxious anti-Semitism, and the effort to make amends for decades of officially sponsored anti-Semitism continued throughout 1989 and into 1990. In January 1989 the Kremlin allowed a historic visit to Israel by several Jewish leaders, including Rabbi Shayevich of Moscow, Rabbi Haim Levitis of Leningrad, and Aharon Litvan, head of the Jewish community in Odessa. Until then Israel probably would have considered such a visit a Soviet propaganda stunt. But these Soviet Jewish leaders talked openly with their counterparts in Israel about rebuilding Jewish religious and cultural life in the Soviet Union, battered by over seventy years of repressive Communist rule. An arrangement was also made for a reciprocal visit to the U.S.S.R. between May 1 and 9 by Chief Rabbis Yisrael Lau of Tel Aviv, Shear Yashuv Cohen of Tel Aviv, and Simcha Kook of Rehovot.[118]

On February 12, 1989, soon after signing the Vienna Human Rights Document, the Kremlin sanctioned the opening in Moscow of the first Jewish cultural center in the U.S.S.R., named after Solomon Mikhoels. Plans for this center included classrooms for teaching Hebrew and Yiddish, a Judaica library, an exhibition gallery, audiovisual equipment, and a café. At the opening ceremonies Nobel laureate Elie Wiesel praised Gorbachev for his reforms, pointing out that the opening of this center would have been only a dream earlier. He added in amazement: "A few years ago, if you had said that a Jewish cultural center was to open in Moscow, I would not have believed it."[119] Ten days later a *yeshiva* opened in Moscow, designed to train rabbis and religious scholars. This is a project of Rabbi Adin Steinsaltz of Israel and the Soviet Academy of Sciences. Reportedly this *yeshiva* will have eighty students and its faculty will be five rabbis, three from Israel and two from the United States.

The change toward curtailment of official anti-Semitism, as explained above, has not been matched by a decrease in popular anti-Semitism. In fact, anti-Semitic groups like *Pamyat* have been growing stronger, causing widespread anxiety and fear among Soviet Jews. This discrepancy between increased folk anti-Semitism that has been allowed to manifest itself under *glasnost* and decreased official anti-Semitism posed a difficult new dilemma for Soviet Jewish activists. They realized that the Kremlin's apparent change in policy toward them did not necessarily mean a change in heart or belief. They recognized quite clearly that such changes had occurred mainly for practical purposes of helping Gorbachev succeed with *perestroika,* not for humanitarian reasons. They remembered that a major reason thus far for the Kremlin's concessions on emigration and domestic liberalization was not only support they received from the West but also their own brave, often heroic actions. To understand better what strategy and tactics Soviet Jewish activists might adopt in the 1990s and to put the current situation in perspective, it is important to examine the history of the Soviet Jewish freedom movement since its inception in 1967.

Notes

1 For an excellent discussion of this issue, see Menachem Z. Rosensaft, "The Legal Status of Soviet Jews: De Jure Equality and De Facto Discrimination," *Columbia Human Rights Law Review,* Vol. 10, 1978–1979, pp. 575–604.

2 "Decree of the Council of People's Commissars on the Uprooting of the Anti-Semitic Movement," August 9, 1918, in V. I. Lenin, *On The Jewish Question* (New York: International Publishers, 1934), pp. 22–23.

3 Soviet Jews have more than one "native language." Historically, the main language of Russian Jews was Yiddish. Oriental Jews in Georgia, Bukhara, and Daghestan tend to speak their own local language; Georgian, Tadzhik, and Tat respectively. Hebrew has been spoken to a limited extent in most Jewish communities since its revival in the nineteenth century. For more on this point, see Institute of Jewish Affairs, Research Report, "Jewish Culture in the USSR Today," No. 10, December 1985, p. 3, and William Korey, "The Legal Position of Soviet Jewry," in Kochan, op. cit., pp. 82–88.

4 For an analysis of the suppression of Jewish culture in the U.S.S.R., see Zvi Gitelman, "The Abridgement of the Rights of Jews in the Fields of Nationality, Culture, and Religion," *Soviet Jewish Affairs,* Vol. 15, No. 1, 1985, pp. 79–87.

5 Particularly informative on the subject of "Soviet justice" is Telford Taylor, *Courts of Terror* (New York: Vintage, 1976).

6 For an analysis of the relationship of international law to the right of emigration, see Yoram Dinstein, "Freedom of Emigration and Soviet Jewry," *Soviet Jewish Affairs,* Vol. 4, No. 2, 1974, pp. 17–23.

7 Quoted by Susan Birnbaum, "Now in Israel, Refusenik Warns of Drop-out Rate," *Jewish Advocate,* August 28, 1988.

8 See testimony by Yuri Orlov in Union of Councils of Soviet Jews, *Commission of Inquiry on Soviet Human Rights Violations,* Public Hearing, January 23, 1987, p. 12. Hereafter *Soviet Human Rights Violations.*

9 In July 1960, Khrushchev approved the right of Soviet citizens to emigrate based on voluntary family reunification. This approval, however, had little impact on Soviet Jews. The more important signal for Jews was Premier Kosygin's statement, which was more specifically directed toward them. See Boris Smolar, *Soviet Jewry Today and Tomorrow* (New York: Macmillan, 1971). pp. 181–82.

10 "The labyrinth," a letter sent by Soviet Jewish activists from Moscow just after Brussels II and translated by Michael Sherbourne on March 1, 1976, described the bureaucratic maze through which Soviet Jews must find their way to be eligible for emigration. This letter concludes with a compilation of "repressions" against those who applied for an exit visa. For the complete text see *Congressional Record,* July 2, 1976. The Union of Councils of Soviet Jews and the National Conference on Soviet Jews had furnished Congresswoman Bella Abzug (D., New York) with a copy.

11 See William Korey, "The Persistent Plight of Refuseniks," *Wall Street Journal,* European Edition, February 8, 1989, and Korey, "The Critical Human Right," B'nai B'rith International, undated (approximately 1987).

12 Letter to editor by Paul Summerfield of the Student and Academic Campaign for Soviet Jews, London, *The Guardian,* June 6, 1989.

13 This new regulation was applied unevenly in different regions. For example, in Chernovtsy, Odessa, Riga, and Tbilisi, in 1981–1982 *vyzovs* for siblings were not accepted, whereas they were in Leningrad. And in Lvov and other cities in Moldavia, no *vyzov* was accepted from anyone who had left before 1940, no matter what the family relationship was. See Institute for Jewish Affairs, *The Position of Soviet Jewry, 1983–1986,* Report of the Implementation of the Helsinki Final Act since the Madrid Follow-up Conference, London, 1986, p. 29.

14 For an excellent analysis of the 1979 Emigration Requirement, see Donna Arzt, Rachel M. Stone, and Harry Sinoff, "The USSR's 'First Degree Relative' Requirement For Soviet Jewish Emigration Contravention of International and Soviet Law," Soviet Jewry Legal Advocacy Center, Waltham, Mass., November 1980.

15 Testimony by Natan Sharansky, *Soviet Human Rights Violations,* p. 20.

16 For an analysis of the new "chilling" legislation of 1984, see Irwin Cotler's Exhibit P-1, ibid., p. 24.

17 *London Times,* March 31, 1984, quoted in Cotler, p. 25.

18 Conversations by author with several refusenik families in visits to the Soviet Union, 1984–1986.

19 *Soviet Jews: Fact and Fiction* (Moscow: Novosti Press Agency Publishing House, 1970), p. 46.

20 William Korey, "A Soviet 'Blank Spot' Still Unmentioned," *The Star,* August–September 1988, p. 5.

21 For a detailed treatment of how Soviet school history books "covered" Jewish History, see Daniel Fish, "The Jews in Syllabuses of World and Russian History: What Soviet School Children Read About Jewish History," *Soviet Jewish Affairs,* Vol. 8, No. 1, 1978, pp. 3–25; J. Schlesinger, *Jews as Non-Persons—A Study of Soviet History Textbooks in Elementary and Secondary Schools* (New York: B'nai B'rith, 1968); and Louise Shelley, *History Without Jews: The Vanishing Jew in Soviet History Textbooks* (Washington, D.C.: B'nai B'rith, 1977).

22 Letter of 100 Jews to 20th Congress of the CPSU on "The Situation of Soviet Jews," February 1981, in *A Chronicle of Human Rights in the USSR,* No. 41, January–March 1981, p. 47.

23 Quoted in Anthony Lewis, "When Memory Comes," *New York Times,* June 19, 1988. History exams returned in 1989, but new textbooks were not yet available. See "There Will Be An Exam, But There Still Are No Textbooks," *Izvestia,* February 8, 1989.

24 See Roman Solchanyk, "Perestroika for Soviet Jews?" *Soviet Analyst,* Vol. 17, No. 19, September 28, 1988, pp. 5–6.

25 Arkady N. Shevchenko, *Breaking With Moscow* (New York: Ballantine, 1985), p. 87.

26 Hedrick Smith, *The Russians* (New York: Quadrangle, 1976), p. 479.

27 Vladimir Pozner, *Parting with Illusions* (New York: Atlantic Monthly Press, 1990), p. 172.

28 Hosking, op. cit., p. 258.

29 See William Korey, "The Future of Soviet Jewry: Emigration and Assimi-

lation," *Foreign Affairs,* Vol. 51, No. 1, Fall 1979, pp. 71–72. In the decade of the 1970s, the number of Jewish students in higher education dropped by fifty percent. See Lukasz Hirszowicz, "Jewish Students in Moscow and the USSR," Institute for Jewish Affairs Research Reports, No. 5, June 1982; and Hirszowicz, "Anti-Jewish Discrimination in Education and Employment," *Soviet Jewish Affairs,* Vol. 15, No. 1, February 1985, pp. 25–30.

30 The Moscow Group, Document 112: Discrimination Against Jews Enrolling at Moscow University, 1979, in *Basket III: Implementation of the Helsinki Accords, Hearings before the Commission on Security and Cooperation in Europe,* 2d Sess., Vol. XIII, "Soviet Treatment of Ethnic Groups," April 29, 1980, pp. 45–49. See also Reuters dispatch, "Activist Charges Discrimination," November 21, 1979. Professor Naum Meiman was the Soviet Jewish academic who made the charges of racism.

31 See Donald Kimelman, "Fewer Jews Get in Top Soviet Schools," *Philadelphia Inquirer,* December 14, 1983.

32 See Correspondent Interview with Y. A. Senderov, *Glasnost,* Issues 7, 8, 9, November 1987, pp. 36–37.

33 "People's Democracy and Vienna Agreements," *Moscow News,* May 21, 1989.

34 Konstantin Kharchev, "Establishing Freedom of Conscience: 70th Anniversary of the Adoption of the RSFSR Soviet of People's Commissars of the Decree on the Separation of Church and State and of School and Church," *Izvestia,* January 27, 1988.

35 *19th All-Union Conference of the CPSU, Documents and Materials, Report by Mikhail Gorbachev* (Moscow: Novosti Press Agency Publishing House, 1988), p. 45. Hereafter *Documents of the 19th Party Conference.* For a good general discussion of the role of religion in Societ society, see Serge Schmemann, "Why God and Marxism Can't Mix," *New York Times,* June 19, 1988.

36 See *Izvestia,* December 8, 1988; TASS, February 15 and February 17, 1989.

37 TASS, February 2, 1989; *Sovetskoe gosudarstvo i. pravo (Soviet State and Law),* No. 2, 1989.

38 *The Economist,* Foreign Report, March 9, 1989, pp. 1–2. See also Oxana Antic, "Draft Law on Freedom of Religion," Radio Liberty Report, March 21, 1989.

39 See Oxana Antic, "Konstantin Kharchev Replaced as Chairman of the Council on Religious Affairs," Radio Liberty Report, July 10, 1989.

40 National Conference on Soviet Jewry, NEWSBREAK, June 8, 1989.

41 See "B-Wire" report, "Concerns Raised About Soviet Emigration Law," May 19, 1990; in files of Radio Free Europe/Radio Liberty, Munich.

42 Quoted in NEWSBREAK, June 8, 1989.

43 *Documents of the 19th Party Conference*, p. 158.

44 Quoted by Paul Quinn-Judge, "Rule of Law in USSR: A 180 Degree Turn?" *Christian Science Monitor*, January 18, 1989.

45 International Commission of Jurists, *The Review*, No. 43, December 1989, pp. 53–56. In early 1990, young Soviet lawyers started nine-month internships with legal firms and district attorneys' offices in the United States, and a group of U.S. lawyers planned a trip to study the Soviet legal system. See Yevgeny Pozdnyakov, "Soviet Lawyers Study American Law," *Soviet Life*, No. 6, June 1990, p. 23.

46 Quoted in *CSCE Digest*, October 1987. (This is the bulletin of the Conference on Security and Cooperation in Europe.)

47 Quoted in *Washington Post*, September 22, 1987.

48 For details on this decree see Helsinki Watch, *News from the USSR*, May 1989, pp. 3–4.

49 Quoted in NEWSBREAK, May 3, 1989.

50 See Bill Keller, "Soviets Propose Parties to Rival the Communists," *New York Times*, September 24, 1989.

51 Report by Mikhail Gorbachev, "Toward a Humane and Democratic Socialist Society." Submitted with "The Platform of the CPSU Central Committee. A Draft for the 28th Party Congress" (Moscow: Novosti Press Agency Publishing House, 1990), pp. 5–6.

52 For the first few months of this new propaganda campaign see Zev Katz, "The Aftermath of the June War. Soviet Propaganda Offensive Against Israel and World Jewry, *Bulletin on Soviet Jewish Affairs*, No. 1, January 1968, pp. 7–27.

53 For a detailed explanation of the *Znaniye* Society, see *A Dictionary for Believers and Nonbelievers* (Moscow: Progress Publishers, 1989), pp. 49–50. It is also noteworthy that the *Znaniye* Society is included in this dictionary.

54 Testimony by Dr. William Korey, "Hearings on Soviet Anti-Semitism," *Congressional Record,* First Session, October 6, 1981; and Julia Wishnevsky, "All-Union 'Znaniye' Society Steps up Anti-Zionist Propaganda," Radio Liberty Report, July 14, 1976.

55 See Moshe Decter, "The Status of the Jews in the Soviet Union," *Foreign Affairs,* Vol. 41, No. 2, January 1963, pp. 420–30.

56 See, for example, this statement on "dual loyalty" of Soviet Jews: "The Zionists stubbornly strive to make all Jews, independently of their citizenship or their class appurtenance, partners in the Israeli aggression and in the dirty actions of the large Jewish bourgeoisie and the international imperialism directed against the cause of peace and socialism. With this purpose they profess the false idea of 'dual citizenship' of the Jews: one, the 'accessory' one—of the country where they factually reside and the other, the 'fundamental' one—of Israel. Similar tricks had once been used by the Hitlerites in order to form their 'fifth columns' in various countries. . . . The concept of 'two Homelands' considerably facilitates the operations of Israel's intelligence, which, in turn, is tied with the Central Intelligence Agency of the USA and with the West German espionage service." See P. Petylyakov, "Zionism: Its Essence, Aims, and Methods." *Krasnaya zvezda,* August 17, 1968, translated in *Bulletin on Soviet and East European Jewish Affairs,* No. 3, January 1969, p. 48.

57 For more citations of anti-Semitic themes, see Institute of Jewish Affairs, *Soviet Anti-Semitic Propaganda,* London, 1978, and Allan Kagedan, "Soviet Anti-Jewish Publications 1979–1984," The American Jewish Committee, 1984.

58 Vladimir Begun, *Invasion Without Arms* (Moscow: Molodaya gvardiya, 1977), p. 35.

59 Ibid., p. 40.

60 Quoted by Emanuel Litvinoff, *Soviet Anti-Semitism: The Paris Trial* (London: Wildwood House, 1974), p. 5.

61 For a transcript and analysis of this trial, see ibid.

62 See Michael Curtis, "The United Nations, Zionism, and Racism," monograph (Quebec: Dawn Publishing Company, September 1987). Reprinted from *Global Affairs,* Vol. 1, No. 2, Spring 1986.

63 Petylyakov, op cit., p. 50.

64 *Sovetskaya Rossiya,* January 24, 1969, quoted in Zev Katz, "After the Six Day War," Kochan, op. cit., p. 347.

65 See Vladimir Bolshakov, "Anti-Sovietism is the Zionists' Profession," *Pravda,* February 18, 19, 1971, in the *Current Digest of the Soviet Press,* Vol. XXIII, No. 7, p. 3.

66 Excerpts from Malik's speech in UN Security Council, Provisional Verbatim Record, A/PV 1582 (September 25, 1971), pp. 128–30; quoted in William Korey, *The Soviet Cage* (New York: Viking, 1973), p. 160.

67 See William Korey, "The Kremlin and the UN 'Zionism Equals Racism' Resolution," *World Reports,* International Council of B'nai B'rith, 1984.

68 Quoted in Curtis, op. cit., p. 10.

69 See Craig Whitney, "Many in Soviet Concerned Over a Surge of Anti-Semitism," *New York Times,* June 27, 1979.

70 Lev Korneyev, *The Class Essence of Zionism,* Kiev, 1982, p. 135; quoted in H. Spier, "An Ominous Development in Soviet Anti-Semitic Propaganda," Radio Liberty Report, September 15, 1983.

71 Vladimir Bolshakov, "Zionism and Fascism Have Kindred Roots," *Pravda,* January 17, 1984.

72 TASS in Russian for abroad and in English, January 17, 1985. Excerpted from Reuters report of the TASS release in the *Times,* January 19, 1985, *The Daily Telegraph,* January 19, 1985; and *Le Monde,* January 20–21, 1985. Cited by David Greenberg, "Zionist 'Collaboration' with Nazis Stressed in Soviet Commemoration of World War II Anniversary," Radio Liberty Report, January 29, 1985.

73 Korey, "The Future of Soviet Jewry: Emigration and Assimilation," *Foreign Affairs,* loc. cit., p. 70.

74 Litvinoff, op. cit., pp. 6–8.

75 Bolshakov, "Anti-Sovietism is the Zionists' Profession," p. 4.

76 See Elie Wiesel, *The Jews of Silence* (New York: Holt, Rinehart, and Winston, 1966), and Joel Cang, *The Silent Millions* (New York: Taplinger, 1969).

77 Sharansky testimony, *Soviet Human Rights Violations,* p. 38.

78 Under *glasnost* there was speculation that the Kremlin would publish Solzhenitsyn's banned works. But as late as the fall of 1988 Vadim Medvedev,

Gorbachev's new chief ideologist, said that *The Gulag Archipelago* and *Lenin in Zurich* would not be published in the U.S.S.R. "because in these works [Solzhenitsyn] takes a position which is in fundamental contradiction to our social and political order, to our ideology, to our attitude toward our history, our revolution, and Lenin." Medvedev then denounced Solzhenitsyn as "anti-social and anti-socialist." Quoted in Felicity Barringer, "Kremlin Keeping Solzhenitsyn on Blacklist," *New York Times,* November 30, 1988. Then in the summer of 1989, the Soviet Writers Union voted to reinstate Solzhenitsyn (he was ousted in 1969), and *Novy mir* began publishing *The Gulag Archipelago* in serialized form. See *Wall Street Journal,* European edition, July 5, 1989.

79 *Soviet Jews: Fact and Fiction,* p. 37.

80 "Jewish Emigrant Explains Reasons for Returning to Moscow," TASS in English, March 28, 1975.

81 See David Greenberg, "Anti-Zionist 'White Book' Given Wide Publicity," Radio Liberty Report, September 30, 1985.

82 Discussed by John Gunther, *Inside Russia Today* (New York: Harper, 1958), p. 371. The authorities also required Bukharan Jews to denounce Israel for its role in the Six-Day War in 1967 and the Yom Kippur War in 1973. See James Chitchlow, "A Better Break for The Bukharan Jews?," Radio Liberty Report, August 30, 1989.

83 *Sovetskaya Latvia,* March 13, 1970.

84 TASS release, February 15, 1971; quoted in Martin Gilbert, *Shcharansky: Hero of Our Time* (New York: Viking, 1986), p. 19.

85 Quoted in G. L. Bakanursky, "Judaism and Contemporary Era," *Nauchny atheism (Scientific Atheism),* No. 1, 1978, Moscow, *Znaniye* Publishing House. Translated by Olga S. Hruby.

86 Quoted in ibid.

87 "In Cold War Trenches," *New Times,* February 1976, No. 7, pp. 12–14.

88 Quoted in Anthony Austin, *New York Times,* October 1, 1979.

89 See Vladimir Kostikov, *The People and Land of Birobidzhan* (Moscow: Novosti Press Agency Publishing House, 1979).

90 Julia Wishnevsky, " 'Anti-Zionist Committee' Formed in Soviet Union," Radio Liberty Report, April 26, 1983.

91 For a detailed, insightful analysis of the Anti-Zionist Committee, see Professor Betsy Gidwitz, "The Anti-Zionist Committee in the USSR," paper presented to the Union of Councils of Soviet Jews, San Francisco, January 29, 1984.

92 Quoted in Anthony Barbieri, Jr., "Rabbi Who Tried to Serve Both Jews and Soviet State Is Buried," *Baltimore Sun,* June 8, 1983. For an overview of Moscow Hebrew radio broadcasts to Israel since they began in 1964, see Carl Alpert, "Soviet Hebrew Radio Softens," Jewish *Advocate,* June 16, 1989. The Russian section of *Kol Yisrael* (the Voice of Israel) was not established until 1968. Broadcasts increased significantly in the early 1970s, when the Kremlin allowed much more Jewish emigration. In those years most Soviet Jewish emigrants went to Israel, so these broadcasts into the Soviet Union helped them significantly, both psychologically and practically. See Pinkus, op. cit., p. 321.

93 Kevin Freeman, "Moscow Rabbi Assails New York Rally for Soviet Jews," *Jewish Advocate,* May 10, 1984.

94 Howard Spier, "Soviet Authorities Exclude Emigration as Option for Jews," Radio Liberty Report, June 14, 1984.

95 Andrew Rosenthal, "Soviet Might Break Up Anti-Zionist Committee," *New York Times,* December 8, 1987.

96 NEWSBREAK, August 30, 1988.

97 Ibid., October 28, 1988.

98 Quoted in ibid., August 18, 1989.

99 Jewish Telegraphic Agency (JTA) report, "Zionism in the USSR," *Jewish Advocate,* August 10, 1989.

100 Shevchenko, op. cit., pp. 346–49.

101 Julia Wishnevsky, "Some Good News for Soviet Jews," Radio Liberty Report, March 23, 1987.

102 See Roman Solchanyk, "In the Soviet Press, Evidence of a Softer Line on Zionism," *International Herald Tribune,* March 14–15, 1987.

103 David Greenberg, "New Thinking on Zionism," Radio Liberty Report, January 22, 1988 and "Vladimir Begun—A Doughty Fighter Against 'The Zionist Conspiracy,' " Radio Liberty Report, November 18, 1987.

104 See "Public Movements in the USSR: Who? Where? How Many?" *Moscow News,* February 18, 1990.

105 See *Komsomolskaya pravda,* December 6, 1986, and Vera Tolz, "Controversy in Soviet Press over Unofficial Youth Groups," Radio Liberty Report, March 11, 1987.

106 See Howard Spier, "Soviet Anti-Semitism Unchained: The Rise of the 'Historical and Patriotic Association Pamyat,' " IJA Research Report No. 3, July 1987; and "Russian Chauvinists and the Thesis of a Jewish World Conspiracy: Three Case Studies," IJA Research Report No. 6, August 1987. One of the main charges of *Pamyat* leaders is that there is a Zionist-Masonic conspiracy to achieve world domination. This theme first was publicized in anti-Zionist propaganda in the 1970s. It first came to the attention of Western analysts in V. I. Skurlatov's book, *Sionism i aparteid (Zionism and Apartheid),* published in Kiev in 1975. For a discussion of the early development of this propaganda theme in the U.S.S.R. see Howard Spier, "Zionist-Masonic Theme Fashionable in Soviet Publications," Radio Liberty Report, February 15, 1984.

107 See "Where Is Pamyat Heading?" *Izvestia,* June 3, 1987.

108 See *Komsomolskaya pravda,* May 22, 1987. Cited by Julia Wishnevsky, "The Origins of Pamyat," *Survey,* Vol. 30, No. 7, October 1988, p. 86.

109 See Walter Laqueur, "From Russia with Hate," *New Republic,* Vol. 202, No. 6, February 5, 1990, pp. 21–25.

110 Quoted in Bill Keller, "Russian Nationalists: Yearning for an Iron Hand," *New York Times Magazine,* January 28, 1990, p. 48.

111 *Molodaya gvardiya,* March 1987, pp. 250–77, cited by Wishnevsky, pp. 87–88.

112 See Wishnevsky, "Ligachev, "Pamyat," and Conservative Writers," Radio Liberty Report, February 28, 1989.

113 *Izvestia,* February 27, 1988; analyzed by Julia Wishnevsky, "A Little More Glasnost for Soviet Jews," Radio Liberty Report, March 14, 1988.

114 For a discussion of *Pamyat*'s activities in Leningrad, see Andrew Katell, "Dissident Group Raises Soviet Concern," *Christian Science Monitor,* August 19, 1988.

115 Boris Bochstein, "A Spring of Fascism," *Novoye russkoye slovo (New Russian Word),* New York, July 2, 1987. Translated by Scott Weltz.

116 See Julia Wishnevsky, "Soviet Newspapers Sound Alarm over Anti-Semitism," Radio Liberty Report, February 13, 1989.

117 Quoted in Scott Shane, "The Jewish Museum Packs Them In," *Baltimore Sun,* August 30, 1988.

118 See "Soviet Rabbis in Israel," editorial, *Jewish Advocate,* January 5, 1989. The Israeli rabbis were part of an international delegation of rabbis headed by Romanian Chief Rabbi Moshe Rosen. This delegation also included French Chief Rabbi Joseph Sitruk and Rabbi Arthur Schneier, senior rabbi of New York's Park East Synagogue and president of the Appeal of Conscience Foundation. See JTA report, "Rabbis to Visit the USSR," ibid., April 27, 1989. See also "Lubavitch Growing in Soviet Union," *Jewish Chronicle,* January 6, 1989; Haim Shapiro, "Moscow, Leningrad Rabbis Arrive," *The Jerusalem Post* International Edition, January 7, 1989; "Rabbis Say There's Hope for Soviet Jews," ibid., January 14, 1989; and "Rabbis Fortify Russian Ties," *Jewish Chronicle,* May 12, 1989.

119 Quoted in UPI dispatch, "Jewish Center Opens in Moscow," *Stars and Stripes,* February 14, 1989. See also "First Jewish Center Opens in Moscow," *International Herald Tribune,* February 14, 1989.

Reading 1

Testimony of Reyza Palatnik, *USSR Labor Camps*, Hearings before the Subcommittee to Investigate the Administration of the Internal Security Act and Other Internal Security laws of the Committee of the Judiciary, U.S. Senate, 93rd Cong., 1st Sess., Part 2, February 1 and 2, 1973, pp. 108–109

Reyza Palatnik, a librarian from Riga, was convicted in one of several trials associated with the Leningrad hijacking episode of 1970. She was allowed to go to Israel in December 1972, after having served a two-year sentence in a prison and corrective labor camp. Her testimony reveals the crude attempts by the authorities to intimidate Soviet Jews from applying to emigrate. Her description of life in prison camp shows how Jews were treated especially badly compared to other prisoners.

Reyza Palatnik, born 1936, librarian, arrived in Israel on 21 December 1972, after serving a two-year sentence both in a prison and a corrective labor camp.

Reyza Palatnik tells the following story:
It all began on 14 October 1970 when my apartment was raided under the pretext that the authorities were looking for stolen goods. . . . They found three folders of Samizdat materials. Before the arrest, which took place on 1 December 1970, I was called three times to the KGB. They tried to associate me with one of the Zionist groups in Leningrad, Riga or Kishinev, but since I categorically refused to support their lies, I was arrested and accused of distributing slanderous information on the Soviet state and particularly the Soviet legal system. Witnesses were called: these were my friends, who had been threatened that if they didn't testify

against me, they would be arrested. Seven months after my arrest, on 24 June 1971, I was tried and sentenced to two years in a standard regime corrective labor colony.

The trial itself was a mockery. The verdict was decided upon in advance. Even the defending attorney refused to carry on the defense in view of the obviously prejudiced attitude of the court.

As of 11 October 1971 I was in the Dneprodzerzhinsk camp in the Dnepropetrovskaya oblast. This was a women's camp for criminals, and I was the only political prisoner.

The camp was located in a swamp (indicative of the special "care and concern" for women . . .). The buildings were damp. . . . A continuously semi-cold and hungry existence. No medical service. Grippe and quinsy were not considered illnesses. . . . One had to lose consciousness to be allowed off for a day. . . . Only the prison uniform was allowed: in summer, a cotton dress, in winter, the same dress and a padded jacket, which provided no warmth. . . . The camp had approximately 1100 persons, despite the fact that it was designed for only 700. The result—terribly crowded conditions. I was intentionally placed in the venereal diseases ward. . . . Hot water for laundry and bathing was available only once in ten days. The food—garbage. . . . Pigs are fed better by good masters!

Despite the fact that the camp was called a corrective-educational labor colony, only four of the entire staff had any higher education. When, and who could ever conduct this educational work remains a mystery. . . . I was specially treated to endless instructive talks praising socialism and denigrating Zionism and Israel's aggressive policies. Attempts were made to induce me to participate in the "social life" of the camp's "society.". . .

Even before my arrival at the camp, people were warned that no one was to help me because I had connections with enemy Zionist organizations, that I was a dangerous criminal, and any assistance rendered me would be strictly punished.

At the camp, people worked twelve hours a day instead of eight, and often on holidays too. From the start I refused to work more than eight hours a day and thereby provoked the anger of the camp administration.

But the main thing that struck me from the very start was the prisoner's complete lack of any rights in the camp and prisons. The duties of the procurator were purely fictitious: he completely supported the administration. For instance, upon arrest, I asked for the Criminal Code of the Ukrainian SSR and a book on criminal law—a request which was refused! I wonder how many people know that in the Soviet Union, an arrested person may not meet with his lawyer until the case is over with! This means that a person is entirely at the mercy of the authorities conducting the investigations; ignorant of the law and his rights, not equipped to defend himself, the prisoner is often himself instrumental in getting himself into prison.

Insults to human dignity are infinite. For example, since last year (1971) identification insignia on the chest became mandatory; family name, father's name, unit and brigade numbers. If the identification was not worn, the prisoner was punished severely: permission was withdrawn to use the camp store, receive visitors or parcels.

A widely used method for controlling prisoners is to instigate them against each other. . . . There are also so-called activists who carry out the camp administration's orders and create the desired atmosphere. Jews, of course, are the principal and primary objects of persecution. An attempt was made to provoke me [against the administration] so that I could be given a beating, but it did not succeed. . . .

It must be emphasized that the morale of the prisoners, particularly the Jews, is severely undermined. Human rights are infringed upon at every step. For instance, I was deprived of more than half the letters sent me. Letters from my parents were more or less allowed through, but only a fourth of even my sister's letters were ever delivered. (I checked the number after my release.)

To achieve anything, the prisoner needs contact with the outside world: this is his only opportunity of alleviating his condition, and the only one that the administration has any regard for, both the prison and camp authorities. . . .

It is not only a matter of the Jewish prisoners, fighting for their right to leave for their native land: these people are the defenders and representatives of the Jewish masses, deprived of their national social organizations. To a great extent the all important question of the prospects of the Jews in Russia for mass EXODUS depends on world opinion, and particularly on Jewish world opinion and *on their active support.* The Soviet government not only does not observe its own laws, but doesn't even observe the basic principles of the Declaration of Human Rights, signed by its own representatives. Thus, this is more than just an internal Soviet problem, it is a violation of an international Declaration of Human Rights, which concerns all the peoples of the world. It is therefore a moral obligation of the free world to react to this situation.

Reyza Palatnik,
Jerusalem, Katamon Tet,
Merkaz Klita.

Reading 2

Statement by Premier Alexei Kosygin on Reunification of Families, December 3, 1966, from "To Live in Peace, To Develop Cooperation," *Pravda*, December 5, 1966

At a press conference in Paris, Premier Kosygin was asked whether it was possible to reunite Soviet Jews with family members from whom they were separated during World War II. Kosygin's positive reply excited Jews and non-Jews alike, who had thought they would never see their separated family members. Kosygin's statement, published in Pravda *and* Izvestia, *inspired some Soviet Jews to apply for emigration to Israel.*

R. *Eli Maissi* (UPI, USA): The calamities of the war separated many Jewish families; some members of these families are in the USSR while some are abroad. Can you give these families hope for reunion, as was done for many Greek and Armenian families?

A. N. *Kosygnin:* Some persons raise this question from time to time. Some even allege that anti-Semitism exists in the Soviet Union. There is nothing of the kind in our country and cannot be. It is the fruit of the imagination of those who are trying to present this question in a certain way, resorting to quite cheap means and working on a public that is attuned, as it were, in a certain manner. The posing of this question, of course, cannot be taken seriously.

As for reunifying families, if some families want to meet or want to leave the Soviet Union, the road is open to them, and no problem exists here.

. . . The nationalities question in the Soviet Union is not acute, because no nationality in our country is subjected to any discrimination whatever; each feels like part of a family of equal peoples. I emphasize that all nationalities, absolutely all the nations, in our country are equal. . . . In our country, each nationality feels it is the complete master of the situation. This accords with our Leninist policy, which we have steadfastly implemented and shall continue to implement. Everything I have said applies wholly and completely to citizens of the Jewish nationality as well.

Reading 3

"Jewish Emigration from the USSR and the Policy of the Soviet Authorities, A survey: June 1975–January 1976," in *A Chronicle of Human Rights in the USSR*, No. 19, January–March 1976, pp. 38–52.

This survey chronicles the repressive measures by the Soviet regime to harass Soviet Jews hoping to emigrate. Soviet Jewish activists felt it was crucial to publicize their plight in the West. The Chronicle *was started by Khronika Press in New York in 1973. Its main editor was Valery Chalidze.*

. . . To be refused permission to leave the country, and to end up in the unenviable position of a "refusenik" is a serious danger facing anyone who wants to emigrate. Thus the use of unfounded refusals to create a situation in which virtually anybody can become a refusenik is one of the most effective means by which the regime can reduce emigration.

A sharp increase in the number of refusals accompanied the decrease in the number of emigration permits issued. We know of thirty Jewish families in Moscow who received refusals in the period September–

November (1975) alone. This represents about 20 percent of all refusenik families known to us in Moscow. Here it should be noted that we learn of only half the refuseniks at the very most. Many persons, even after having been refused, are afraid to furnish information about themselves to Jewish activists, since they don't want to jeopardize relations with the authorities. Recently the number of such persons has certainly increased, which is one result of the constant pressure and threats on the part of authorities. In the past few months about thirty families in Leningrad have been denied permission to emigrate, so that the number of refuseniks known to us in Leningrad was increased by almost 30 percent. In December, the simultaneous refusal—in November 1975—of permits to twenty-two families of Jews from the hill country (these families average six to eight persons) quadrupled the number of refuseniks known to us.

The "geography" of the refuseniks is expanding. In certain places—e.g., in Dushanbe (Tadzhikistan) and Shakhrisabze (Uzbekistan)—refuseniks have been reported for the first time. . . .

For a long time (roughly from March 1975), not a single well-known Jewish activist received permission to emigrate. It may be assumed that this demonstration of the "harm of activism" was a form of pressuring the activists and also intended to isolate them from other Jews who wanted to emigrate. In January 1976, on the eve of the Twenty-Fifth Party Congress, a few refuseniks in Moscow, Leningrad, Kiev, and Kishinev have received permission to leave for Israel. In the past there has been more than one occasion when on the eve of some big event in Moscow—a party congress or an important visit—the authorities have let out a certain number of refuseniks so as to reduce criticism of themselves. Unfortunately, experience shows that this does not improve the situation of the remaining refuseniks, or signify a liberalization of the emigrating process as a whole.

The Induction of Potential Emigrants

The military call-up of persons expressing a desire to emigrate, or the threat of induction into the armed forces became in 1975 one of the commonest ways of checking emigration. From the preceding examples of refusals based on past service in the armed forces one can gather what military induction means for a person who wants to emigrate. (It is important to note that this method has most often affected persons who were exempt from military service before they applied for permission to emigrate.) . . .

It is easy to understand why the authorities are following such a harsh policy in this matter. Using official statistics, one can calculate that no less than 35 percent of all adult males can be inducted into the armed forces after applying for permission to emigrate, or can be refused emigration visas because of past service. (This is based on loss of eligibility for emigration for a seven year period after discharge which is by no means the limit, as the experience of many refuseniks shows.) Thus this danger threatens the majority of families who want to emigrate.

Prosecutions of Potential Emigrants

As was mentioned above, four of the eight trials of Jewish activists held in 1975 involved refusals to serve in the armed forces.

Anatoly Malkin was tried in Moscow in late August 1975. In June 1974, Malkin, a student of seventeen, passed his exams at the Moscow Steel Institute and was admitted to the next class. According to Soviet law, he was not subject to military induction. On July 7, 1974, he announced his wish to go to Israel, and asked the administration of the institute to issue him a reference required when applying for an exit visa. Immediately afterward he was expelled from the institute "for behavior unbecoming a Soviet student," and hence became liable for induction. For several months, Malkin received no reply to his request for an exit visa, "owing to the absence of permission from his parents"; and in October he received an induction notice. Malkin regarded this as a reprisal by the authorities for his wish to emigrate to Israel. And since he considered himself a citizen of Israel (he had been granted Israeli citizenship at his own request, and had been sent an Israeli passport), he refused to serve in the armed forces.

At the trial, defense counsel demanded Malkin's acquittal. He had found no criminality in his client's actions, since the element of intent was lacking. But the court gave Malkin the longest possible sentence under the article in question: three years in corrective labor camps. The verdict stated that "attempting to emigrate was a way of avoiding military service." . . .

The most crudely trumped-up case has been that of Lev Roitburd, of Odessa, charged with resisting the authorities when he attempted to fly to Moscow on July 2 during the visit by a group of American Senators. This case hardly differs from the famous Feldman case, either in technique or in its conception. On the eve of his arrest, Roitburd was warned by the KGB that if he tried to leave the city, he would be arrested. They told him: You won't be a political prisoner; you'll be put in prison for an ordinary crime." And that is what happened.

Roitburd's wife, other eyewitnesses, and Roitburd himself testified that he did not resist when he was detained at the airport; that he was taken from the waiting room on orders from three men in plain clothes who accompanied him and headed for the administration building. But right in court—with the help of testimony from policemen—the "scene of the crime" was shifted to the closed area of the airport's "Red Corner." It was there, it seems, that Roitburd resisted. But this left unanswered why he had been removed from the waiting room, since according to the prosecution's witnesses his resistance began later. Before the opening of this strange trial, held at the airport, a maliciously anti-Semitic lecture on Zionism was delivered to the airport employees. Roitburd's friends were not allowed in the room where the trial was held, and the airport employees assembled there were prevented by force from leaving. Tape recorders were confiscated from those friends of Roitburd who chanced to get in; and the judge prohibited any recording of the proceedings. Arkady Polishchuk, who was returning to Moscow after Roitburd's appellate hearing, was searched on the train, and all his tapes were seized.

Lev Roitburd was sentenced to two years' deprivation of freedom, and is now in a corrective labor camp.

The Situation of the Prisoners of Zion

There is very little information about Jews who are being held in prisons and labor camps because of their wish to emigrate to Israel. Here are some recent incidents.

Yakov Vinarov has been beaten by prisoners in a labor camp, and on one occasion was beaten by an employee of the camp administration. In December 1975, on the basis of a false charge, Lev Roitburd was deprived of the right to buy food items at the camp canteen, and of a scheduled visit with his wife, Yury Vudka. The administration of Vladimir Prison has systematically confiscated letters sent to him by friends abroad. . . .

How the Regime Combats Jewish Activists

While several dozen Jews struggled for the right to emigrate are being kept in prisons and labor camps, many other Jewish activists are being subjected to various kinds of threats and persecution.

On November 6, in Odessa, some policemen visited the apartment of refusenik Abram Yutsis, while a Hebrew lesson was in progress. Yutsis was arrested the next day, and detained for ten days with no explanation. As a result of his arrest, Yutsis was expelled from the Institute from which he had been taking correspondence courses. . . .

On December 24, the Day of Solidarity with Prisoners of Zion, dozens of Jews went to the USSR Supreme Soviet for a silent protest demonstration. But not all of them got there. Eight persons (Ilya Rubin, Leonid Koshevoi, Anatoly Sharansky, Alexander Lunts, Yuly Kosharovsky, Mark Azbel, and Victor Brailovsky) were picked up by KGB agents as they left their homes, and searches were conducted at homes of four persons (Iosif Begun, Pavel Abramovich, Vladimir Prestin, and Ilya Essas). . . .

To the many instances in which the telephone service of Jewish refuseniks in Moscow and other cities has been cut off because of conversations with people abroad, we can now add the case of Mark Nashpits, exiled to the settlement of Tupik, 6,500 kilometers from Moscow. (Nashpits had used his telephone on a few occasions to talk with friends and relatives in Moscow.) This would appear to be the most easterly point in the USSR where a telephone has been disconnected. . . .

How the KGB Recruits Informers

Sometimes, of course, instead of hampering contacts with refuseniks the KGB encourages them. In recent months we have learned of many cases when KGB agents demanded of Jews who maintained contacts with refuseniks that they become informers. Unfortunately, we cannot name those persons here, since we do not want to complicate their situation.

We shall mention only Vladimir Kuravsky, a teacher of Modern Hebrew. It was his teaching of Hebrew (in the USSR a teacher of Hebrew cannot register officially) that was exploited by the KGB agents as a pretext for threatening and pressuring Vladimir with a view to inducing him to collaborate. Of course it can be assumed that the KGB has always recruited informers from among the circles associated with Jewish emigration. But the fact that recently we have learned of such attempts more frequently indicates that the KGB is stepping up its efforts.

Here is an example of an attempt to recruit a Jew who had applied for an exit visa. In March 1975, Candidate of Mathematical Sciences Evgeny Veklerov and his family (a wife and daughter who are seriously ill) applied for permission to emigrate to Israel. In June he was summoned to OVIR, where some KGB agents proposed that he become an informer. They led him to understand that the response to his application would depend upon his readiness to collaborate with them, and that such collaboration could be useful for him both now and in the future. Veklerov declined the proposal, with the result that in August his application was rejected without any explanation. But this case has a happy ending. After the rejection, Veklerov appealed to various authorities for help, not concealing the fact that the KGB had tried to recruit him. And in November he and his family received permission to leave for Israel.

The Anti-Semitic and Anti-Zionist Campaign in the Press

The so-called anti-Zionist campaign in the Soviet press has not let up for a single day. In addition to the many trashy and genuinely anti-Semitic books, the newspapers and magazines publish articles attacking everything in any way connected with Israel and Judaism. And the same sort of thing is said in regular lectures and meetings. The argument runs roughly as follows: Zionism is fascism, as is demonstrated by the fact that the Zionists have always been the chief allies of the Nazis, from the burning of the Reichstag to the present time. Consequently, Israel is a fascist state and everyone who wants to go there is a renegade and traitor. As for Jewish culture, it is a bourgeois nationalist culture associated with a fascist state, and thus not necessary for Soviet Jews. We quote from a few articles published in recent months.

"From the very first years after the fascists seized power in Germany, they (the Zionists) began heart and soul to serve the Nazi cannibals" (Hitler's Mercenaries," *Vechernyaya Odessa,* June 23, 1975).

"Now it has been proved that all those Ben-Gurions, Eshkols, Kastners, and many other prominent Zionists collaborated with the Nazis just as successfully as did Nossig" ("The Career of Simon Wiesenthal," in the newspaper *Sotsialisticheskaya industriya*—an organ of the Communist Party Central Committee—January 10, 1976). In this article the fact that Simon Wiesenthal ran Eichmann to earth is attributed to the necessity to kill off an embarrassing witness to deals between the fascists and the Jews.

"It would appear that in terms of the racial hatred with which it is loaded, Zionism exceeds any other form of racial discrimination" (from an article by V. Simonov, political commentator for the Novosti Press Agency).

"Only a negligible number of renegades have been caught in the trap of Zionist propaganda and have chosen mankind's yesterday, capitalist Israel, over the great socialist fatherland" ("Zionism on Trial" in the newspaper *Znamya,* Odessa).

Attacks on individual Jewish activists have become another important feature of these articles. On September 11, in Kishinev, the republic newspaper *Sovetskaya Moldaviya* published an article titled "Servants of the Big Lie" in which the Jewish activist Mark Abramovich was directly charged with obtaining funds for the gathering and dissemination of libelous information. (We note that a few months after the publication of an article containing similar—though formally less severe—charges against Lev Roitburd in Odessa, he was arrested and convicted of . . . hooliganism.) On September 23 in Kharkov the paper *Krasnoye znamya* published a mendacious article, "Visa to Nowhere," about the Jewish refusenik Gerder and the Vainman brothers, prisoners of Zion. . . .

One important theme of all these articles is a threat directed toward foreign tourists who contact Jewish refuseniks. The authors let it be plainly understood that such contacts are regarded as a violation of Soviet laws. . . .

The regime's policy—examples of which we have given in this survey—is intended primarily to frighten potential emigrants. We are convinced that this is the real cause of the drop in Jewish emigration from the USSR.

—Dina Beilina, Alexander Lerner, Alexander Lunts,
Ida Nudel, Vitaly Rubin, Vladimir Slepak,
Anatoly Sharansky, Eitan Finkelshtein
Moscow, February 2, 1976.

Reading 4

The Public Group to Promote Observance of the Helsinki Agreements in the USSR, Document #19, "The Soviet Authorities Break up the International Symposium on Jewish Culture," January 10, 1977, Appendix H-VII, in *Commission on Security and Cooperation in Europe*, 99th Cong., 2d Sess., Documents of the Helsinki Monitoring Groups in the USSR and Lithuania (1976–1986), Vol. 1, pp. 99–101

In December 1976 Soviet Jewish activists tried to hold a symposium on Jewish culture in Moscow to help Soviet Jews learn more about their heritage. They also invited foreign guests to participate. The authorities prevented the holding of this seminar and prevented the foreign guests from coming. This detailed account was provided by the Moscow group set up in 1976 to monitor Soviet compliance with the human rights provisions of the Helsinki Accords.

Concerned by the prospects of the destruction of the culture of an entire people, an initiative group headed by Professor Veniamin Fain set itself the goal of holding in Moscow an international symposium on Jewish culture—a committee for the symposium was set up and sent out invitations to a group of well known scholars and cultural leaders abroad and to the corresponding official Soviet organizations. The symposium was supposed to open on December 21, 1976, and to last three days. Its schedule included fifty-five reports, of which fourteen were to have been given by foreign guests.

Despite the fact that the preparations for the symposium were conducted completely in the open, the authorities reacted to it as a "dangerous," "provocative" enterprise. An avalanche of prohibitions and direct repressions descended on the organizing committee and the prospective participants:

1. All foreign scholars who had been invited to the symposium were refused entrance visas. Even tourists who were suspected of being interested in the symposium received refusals. At least three citizens of the USA (lawyers Frederick Stant and Charles Hofheimer and Dr. Larry Goldman from Norfolk, Virginia) who informed the authorities about their interest in the symposium were expelled from the Soviet Union.
2. The members of the organizing committee and people connected with it were subjected to house searches and questioning which lasted for many hours. During the searches, all literature in Hebrew and Yiddish—including dictionaries—the text of reports for the symposium and all preparatory materials for them were confiscated.
3. Nineteen Jews who had any relation at all to the symposium had their phones cut off.
4. On December 21, the members of the organizing committee and most of the people who were supposed to give papers were arrested in Moscow. As a result, over the next three days these people were either under house arrest or held for questioning in the Moscow city procurate, the usual post-search investigative agency.
5. In Riga, Kishinev, Tallin, Tbilisi, Minsk, Leningrad, Vinnitsa, and Odessa, people were held when they attempted to go to Moscow to attend the symposium. Some of these people were subjected to lengthy questioning (for example, P. Reitberg in Kishinev was held for questioning for ten days). In Vilnius, criminal proceedings were begun against a member of the organizing committee, Professor N. Salansky.

All this repression was aimed not only at breaking up the symposium, but also at frightening its possible participants. Despite this, on December 21, in Grigory Rozenshtein's apartment sixty people got together to listen to seven papers which had been saved from confiscation. In this way, the symposium which was supposed to have been broadly based, became a purely symbolic one-day seminar, but the authorities wanted to break up even this: from time to time KGB workers tried to force their way into the apartment.

By breaking up the symposium on Jewish culture, the authorities violated the Soviet Constitution and Soviet laws. All their actions took place in clear contradiction to both the spirit and letter of the Final Act of the Conference on Security and Cooperation in Europe. (See Principles VII and VIII of the section "Declaration on Principles Guiding Relations between Participating States" and Section I, Paragraphs 2–4 of "Cooperation in Humanitarian and Other Fields.")

Reading 5

"Outside the Moscow Synagogue, 29 March 1972," in *A Chronicle of Current Events*, No. 25, May 20, 1972, pp. 199–200

This reading shows how the authorities tried to intimidate Moscow Jews from congregating outside the Choral Synagogue and celebrating on the eve of Passover. The Chronicle of Current Events *was the first and major* samizdat *journal covering the Soviet human rights movement. It began publication in 1968, and continued until 1982 when the regime forced it to shut down.*

Outside the Moscow Synagogue, 29 March 1972

On 29 March 1972 Jews who had gathered outside the Moscow synagogue were dispersed by police and *druzhinniki.* That evening, the eve of Passover, there were several bus- and carloads of policemen in the vicinity of the synagogue building. For half a day a fence was erected opposite the synagogue, and passages to the street between houses were closed. Persons who gathered were either herded off the road and onto the pavement, or forbidden to walk on the pavements. Toward seven o'clock that evening the police began clearing the pavements and driving everyone on to the steps of the synagogue. Some individuals were dragged out of the crowd and taken away by the police. The assembled persons sang in chorus: "Chevenu shalom aleichem"—"We have brought you peace." Then the *druzhinniki* started elbowing their way up the steps through the crowd and chased everybody down off the steps. Linking arms, they split the crowd into two parts, formed a barrier across the entire street, and forming two chains, in this way began to clear the Jews out of Arkhipov Street, one chain moving up the street, the other down. A large group of young Jewish people (about 200) had assembled in the square near the memorial to the heroes of Plevna. They were singing Jewish songs and dancing. At about nine o'clock in the evening large numbers of policemen and plain-clothes men appeared there and began to disperse the young people. Someone in plain clothes shouted: "Damned Yids, at last we've shown you what's what!" Someone was grabbed and dragged into a bus. One girl had her face battered, and as they dragged another into the bus they shouted: "Take this Jewish girl!" Then all the persons detained (about twenty) were driven off to police station No. 26 where they were kept until midnight. They were told that if they were ever detained again at the synagogue, criminal proceedings would be instituted against them.

Reading 6

Grigory Freiman, *It Seems I Am a Jew* (Carbondale: Southern Illinois University Press, 1979), pp. 95–97.

Discrimination against Jews in higher education was one of the most important spurs to Jewish emigration. Discrimination against Jews aspiring to enter advanced study programs in mathematics became especially acute in the late 1970s. A copy of the essay written by Freiman, then professor of mathematics in Kalinin, was brought to the U.S. in 1978 by an American tourist. In the appendix to his essay, Freiman included a sample of special questions for Jewish mathematics students, followed by a commentary on them by Andrei Sakharov.

"Jewish Problems" in Mathematics
By Melvyn B. Nathanson

To enter *Mekhmat,* the Faculty of Mechanics and Mathematics of Moscow State University, a student must take four examinations: written and oral examinations in mathematics, an oral examination in physics, and a written examination in Russian composition. The admissions procedure has been distorted to exclude Jewish students. At the oral mathematics examination, the student draws by lot a ticket with two questions. After he answers these questions, the examiner asks him several more questions. For Jewish applicants, there are special problems, called "Jewish problems," whose solution requires knowledge far beyond that contained in the secondary school curriculum in the USSR. The problems are often difficult variants of those given in the Moscow Mathematical Olympiad or the International Mathematical Olympiad. In the Olympiads, students have about one hour to solve each problem. The oral examiners for *Mekhmat* give a student only from ten to twenty minutes. Even when a particularly brilliant student manages to solve some of these "Jewish problems," he still gets a failing grade. There is no hope.

Below is a list of special "Jewish problems" used in the oral examination for *Mekhmat* in 1978:

1. Which is larger: $\sqrt[3]{413}$ or $6 + \sqrt[3]{3}$?
2. Solve the equation $x^y = y^x$ in positive integers.
3. Prove that a convex polygon of area 1 contains a triangle of area $1/4$.
4. Show that the following statement is false:

   A convex polyhedron of volume 1 contains a tetrahedron of volume $1/8$.

   A natural estimate is not $(1/2)^3 = 1/8$ but $(1/3)^3 = 1/27$. Obtain this estimate and try to improve it.
5. Does there exist an infinite family of pairwise noncongruent right triangles such that the lengths of the sides are natural numbers and the lengths of the two short sides differ by 1?
6. A function of two variables $f(x, y)$ takes on at least 3 values. For some fixed numbers a and b we have $f(a, y) \neq$ constant and $f(x, b)$

$\neq$ constant. Prove that there exist numbers p, q, r, s such that $f(p,q)$, $f(r,q)$, $f(p,s)$ are three pairwise-distinct values of the function $f(x,y)$.

7. Let ABC be a triangle. Construct a straight line that divides into two equal parts both its area and its perimeter.
8. Let $ab = 4$ and $c^2 + 4d^2 = 4$. Prove the inequality $(a - c)^2 + (b - d)^2 \geqslant 1.6$.
9. Prove the inequality $((\sin x)/x)^3 \geqslant \cos x$ for $x \in (0,\pi/2]$.
10. Prove the inequality $(\sin x)^{-2} \geqslant x^{-2} + 1 - (4/\pi^2)$ for $x \in (0,\pi/2]$.
11. Let $ABCDE$ be a convex pentagon with the property that each of the five triangles ABC, BCD, CDE, DEA, and EAB has area 1. Find the area of the pentagon $ABCDE$.
12. Solve the following equation in rational numbers:
$$(x + y\sqrt{2})^2 + (z + t\sqrt{2})^2 = 5 + 4\sqrt{2}.$$
13. On the edges of a tetrahedron of volume 1 there are given 6 points, none of which are vertices. Consider the four tetrahedrons constructed as follows: Choose one vertex of the original tetrahedron and let the remaining vertices be the three points given on the three edges incident to the chosen vertex. Prove that at least one of these four tetrahedrons has volume not exceeding ⅛.

Remarks on " 'Jewish Problems' in Mathematics"
by Andrei Sakharov
Translated by Melvyn B. Nathanson

These problems affect me deeply. I believe that to give such problems on an entrance examination is absolutely intolerable. The problems are exceedingly complicated and require extraordinary concentration and precision in carrying out lengthy computations. They presuppose knowledge and experience that far exceed what even the most gifted student could possibly possess. It is particularly inexcusable to give these problems on the *oral* examination, where the student is in a tense psychological situation and has only twenty minutes to find a solution.

I chose one of the problems on the list. Of course, the student taking the examination is not allowed to choose the particular problem he wishes to solve. I found a very pretty solution to my problem, but it required a nontrivial and ingenious argument, and it took me much more than one hour. Moreover, I was able to work quietly at home. I needed to use my considerable experience in solving these difficult mathematical problems as well as my large store of mathematical knowledge. I tried to imagine the feelings of a boy or girl who comes to take this examination, on which his future depends, who gets such a problem, and who must try to solve it while sitting directly across from him an openly hostile examiner glances impatiently at his watch. The student must feel the evil and the cruelty in an examination that has been designed to destroy him, and we, too, cannot avoid the same feelings.

Compare the problems on this list with the problems given to other applicants who are not being discriminated against. The prejudice of the examiners is obvious.

This organized discrimination on the entrance examinations is used not only against Jews, but also against others, in particular, the children of dissidents. Moreover, to be admitted to Moscow State University, students who are not residents of Moscow must obtain a higher score on the entrance examinations than Moscow residents, and this is another form of discrimination.

12 June 1979

Reading 7

"From the Stenographic Transcript of the Scientific Council of the Faculty of Geology of Moscow State University, 20 January, 1982," *Scientists Committee of the Israel Council for Soviet Jewry*, No. 221/222, June 30, 1982, p. 1

In 1976 new regulations governing VAK (the Higher Attestation Committee), which is responsible for conferring advanced degrees, required examination of the political attitude of academic degree candidates. In the early 1980s Soviet authorities began to apply this regulation retroactively and started to strip some refuseniks of their degrees. Here is an excerpted account of a hearing prior to the stripping of V. G. Melamed of his degree.

Chairman (Professor Adonis G. Gayanov): Members of the board already know the agenda for today's session: inter alia the stripping of Vladimir Grigorevich Melamed of his academic titles due to his anti-patriotic dealings, unworthy of a Soviet scientist . . .

A. G. *Lyubimov:* Allow me to read the material from the special committee of the board, set up to investigate the activities of V. G. Melamed, who expressed the desire to emigrate to the state of Israel:

Melamed has been working at Moscow State University for approximately thirty years. Latterly he was in charge of one of the laboratories, and was dealing with pressure-modification of the permafrost process. He distinguished himself by his energetic attitude and was therefore admitted to the Party. In 1975, he received the degree of DSc, specializing in geophysics. In November, 1980 he submitted a request to emigrate to the State of Israel, which is known to be capitalistic and no friend of the Soviet Union. In view of the increasing severity of the international situation and all that has been stated previously, we find that the decision of Melamed is an anti-patriotic act unworthy of a Soviet scientist. We are of the opinion that Article 104 of the VAK on the stripping of scientific titles can be applied to him. Dated 18 December 1981. Signed by all members of the committee . . .

Kalinin: . . . Academic titles in the Soviet Union are conferred not only on the grounds of scientific criteria. . . . We consider the function of an academic title to be more important than in the capitalist world. It confers not only the right to a function, but a salary. If Melamed remained a doctor, he would continue to do things to which he no longer has a right. . . . His titles should be taken away from him.

Reading 8

Letter of the Soviet Higher Attestation Commission (VAK), December 3, 1982, to Dr. Leonid D. Stonov, *Science*, Vol. 216, April 25, 1982, p. 360

In a letter to Science *by several members of the Committee of Concerned Scientists in New York, the writers included a letter to Stonov explaining the stripping of his academic degree.*

To: L.D. Stonov

The VAK of the USSR informs you that following the request of the Scientific-Technical Council at the All-Union Research Institute on Chemical Means of Plant Protection addressed to the VAK of the USSR on the 28th of January 1981 (Protocol No. 6-1), it deprives you of the academic degree of Candidate of Agricultural Sciences and the academic title of senior scientific worker. The diploma of the Candidate of Agricultural Sciences No. MSKh 003289 and the certificate of senior scientific worker No. MSN 027299 are declared to be invalid and should be returned to the office of the VAK of the USSR at the following address: Moscow, No. 12, Griboyedova St.

Deputy Chief Academic Secretary,
(Signed) V. V. Davydov

Reading 9

Official Soviet Definition of Zionism, from A *Dictionary for Believers and Nonbelievers* (Moscow: Progress Publishers, 1989), p. 619

This definition reveals the political attitude of the Kremlin toward Zionism and indicates, at least in part, why Soviet leaders over the years have been so hostile to this movement.

ZIONISM (derived from the name for Mount Zion in the outskirts of Jerusalem), ideology, policy, and system for the organizations of the powerful Jewish middle class, which became closely allied with business and political circles in the West, particularly in the United States. The Zionist movement has an openly anti-Communist and anti-Soviet thrust. The emergence of a political programme for Zionism is linked with the appearance of the brochure, "Judenstaat" (The Jewish State, 1896), by the Austrian journalist of Jewish origin, Theodore Herzl. In 1897 the first Zionist Congress was held in Basle, Switzerland, at which Zionism took shape as a political movement. The Congress set up the World Zionist Organization, to which at the present time political parties from more than 50 countries belong. The Zionists upheld the racialist idea of the "exclusiveness" of the "universalist Jewish nation," which was allegedly having to withstand the "innate" anti-semitism of all other peoples. Starting out from these reactionary principles, Zionism came to link the appeal for an "exodus" of Jews from the countries, where they were actually living, with the idea of national unification within their own state. In an attempt to conceal its reactionary essence, Zionism presents itself as the national-liberation movement of the Jews that is allegedly putting into practice the programme of "social justice" as advocated by the Old Testament prophets. In this way Zionists attempt to identify the concepts "Jew" and "Zionist," as well as concepts of ethnic Jew and Jew by religion. Using *Judaism* to further its own ends, Zionism still possesses undeniable political overtones. The links between Zionism and Judaism assumed a definitive shape back in the 1930s. The reactionary implications of this union come particularly clearly to the fore in the annexationist policy of the ruling Zionist circles in Israel.

Reading 10

T. K. Kichko, *Judaism and Zionism* (Kiev: Society Znannia of the Ukrainian SSR, 1969), in Academic Committee on Soviet Jewry, *Soviet Jewry 1969*, pp. 55–60

Kichko's previous anti-Semitic book, Judaism Without Embellishment, *was published in 1963. Soviet authorities were pressured into withdrawing it from circulation because of the tremendous outcry from all over the world, including Western Communist parties. In 1953,* Literaturnaya gazeta *revealed Kichko's past as a Nazi collaborator in the Ukraine. Despite this past and the wave of criticism against his book, by 1969 Kichko again was in the good graces of the Kremlin. He became a lecturer for the* Znaniye Society *and was awarded a Certificate of Honor for his service to education. (See* Pravda Ukrainy, *January 20, 1968). In* Judaism and Zionism, *Kichko attacked the Jewish religion and Zionism in his familiar crude manner. This book, published only in Ukrainian, was "intended for a wide circle of readers," i.e., as propaganda for the masses.*

Covering themselves by the teachings of Judaism, propagating the creation of one above-class Jewish State, the leaders of Zionism are trying to prove that the Jews of all the countries are allegedly "one Jewish nation," are propagating class cooperation and are distracting the attention of working Jews from a joint class struggle with the peoples of the countries in which they live against their own and foreign oppressors, and from the struggle for democratic freedom and peace.

By slanderous fabrications about the persecution of the Jews and of the Jewish religion in the Soviet Union and in other socialist countries, the Zionists, together with the ideologists of imperialism, are trying to becloud the consciousness of the working Jews and to paralyze their will for fighting for socialism and communism, and are conducting propaganda directed at undermining the unity of the peoples of socialist countries.

In their struggle against the ideas of communism, the Zionists have taken up as their arms not only the ideology of the Jewish bourgeois nationalism, but also cosmopolitanism and even antisemitism—masking all this by the teachings of Judaism.

Not the least role in the imperialist and racist plans of the Zionists is played by the reactionist dogmas of the Judaist teaching about the "God-chosenness" of the Jewish people, its superiority over other peoples of the world, about the "promised land," the future coming of the mythical Messiah and others.

The morality of Judaism is not connected with the real needs and interests of the people. Moreover, it is contrary to their interests, is a certain manifestation of individualism and of egoism which are characteristic of antagonistic society. Judaism cannot be a model of morality because on one side it threatens people with "divine punishment" for sins and, on the other hand, it itself sanctifies sins if they are in the interests of religion and of the exploiting classes.

Isn't the antihumanism of Judaism best illustrated by the morality of the prophet Moses himself? About this "most meek and holy man" it is said in the Torah that by his deeds he had brought about the loss of thousands of Egyptians, while the Jews had been brought by him into the desert where they were on the edge of death: "As soon as they begin rebelling against his instructions, he commits the most cruel deeds against them in the name of God. He kills them by thousands: by mass killings he brings them to subjugation; he binds them hand and foot and gives them to be preys to tyranny and victims of the extortion of the priests; that is, of his own family and tribe. Under the banner of religion he inculcates the Israelites with poisonous hatred for all other peoples; he obliges them to be inhuman, haters of man and blood-thirsty; he teaches them thievery, betrayal and perfidy; he orders them to usurp the land of the Canaanites, persuading them that God had promised these lands to their forefathers."

In the Torah it is also told that while Moses was talking with God on the Mount of Sinai, his brother, the Levite Aaron, submitted to the demands of the Israelites and made them an idol, which the Jews began to adore. When he descended from the Mountain, Moses became angry. He rebuked his brother for the "sin" committed, while, as concerns the people, this prophet ordered the Levites to annihilate a thousand Israelites in order to atone by their blood for the evil.

Judaism calls on man to reconcile himself with difficult conditions of life, because "God's ways are inscrutable." It accustoms man to the idea that on earth there is not and there cannot be justice, that misfortunes, evil, wars and the killing of millions of people occur at the wall of Yahve himself. There is a direct connection between this morality of Judaism and what the Israeli Zionists are doing in practice. Wasn't it according to the Torah that the Israeli extremists acted during the latest aggression against the Arab countries? Aren't they directed by religious teachings when they commit new provocations in the Near East?

Reading 11

Yuri Ivanov, *Caution: Zionism* (Moscow: Progress Publishers, 1970), pp. 6–9

Yuri Ivanov was the chief expert on Jewish affairs for the Central Committee of the Communist Party of the Soviet Union (CPSU). In this book (which was published originally in Russian by Moscow's Political Literature Publishing House in 1969), Ivanov attacks Zionism as a dangerous, aggressive, bellicose, anti-Communist movement controlled by U.S. imperialism. Soviet media gave Ivanov's book rave reviews, Pravda *(March 9, 1969), for example, stated: "From the pages of Yu. Ivanov's book emerge the true and evil image of Zionism and this institutes the undoubted importance of the book."*

Modern Zionism is the ideology, a ramified system of organisations and the practical politics of the wealthy Jewish bourgeoisie which has closely allied itself with monopoly circles in the USA and other imperialist countries. The main content of Zionism is bellicose chauvinism and anticommunism.

Attacking the socialist community, the international communist and working-class movement, Zionism is also opposing the national liberation movement. Practical proof of this is the aggression of the Israeli militarists against the Arab states which began in June 1967. . . .

Like the US monopolies, the Zionist concern has an extensive and long-standing range of "business interests" in the Middle East. This being the case, its role in that part of the world has been far more than that of "messenger boy." The Zionist concern acted as "employer" with regard to Israeli ruling circles, while in its dealings with the US monopolies it was by no means a minor participant in the criminal scramble for spoils in the finance jungle.

The "Six Day War" was not the first and probably not the last venture of International Zionism, whose range of interests and plans is not limited to the area of the Suez Canal. But the aggression of June 1967 was one of the rare occasions on which international Zionism, breaking the old and firmly established rules of its game, slightly lifted the veil shrouding its activity. Israel's Prime Minister Levi Eshkol let the cat out of the bag when he mentioned the sum which Zionist organisations freely granted Israeli ruling circles shortly after the outbreak of the war; an international conference of Jewish millionaires was held in Israel; and to the amazement of millions of their fellow countrymen, Zionists in a number of countries widely celebrated the success of the Israeli armed forces. However, it must be stressed that this was a rare episode in the history of the international Zionist association, which prefers more covert forms of activity. . . .

Zionism is a reactionary system of views and a system of reactionary organisations serving imperialism. In other words, Zionism is a class phenomenon. *And Zionism, like the whole imperialist system, is indeed in a state of profound crisis.* Nevertheless, on the basis of facts that shed light on the ruses of Zionist propaganda-makers, the only conclusion to be drawn is that the *potentialities, freedom of manoeuvre, the destiny and ultimate doom of Zionism are directly contingent to the possibilities, destiny and ultimate doom of the exploiter class, on the destiny and doom of imperialism.*

Zionism naturally finds it more and more difficult to operate in our day and age. But it is still a highly experienced, cunning enemy of internationalism, the friendship and fraternity of all nations, a dangerous instrument in the hands of imperialist reaction.

People who know little or nothing about Zionism tend to associate it either with the State of Israel as a whole, or with the Jews in general. It is these erroneous notions that best of all suit the leaders of international Zionism and are cultivated by Zionist propaganda.

Since a considerable number of Jewish working people in different countries, including Israel, forthrightly reject Zionist views, the leaders of Zionism are vitally concerned that all Jews, wherever they are and whatever their views, should be classed as Zionists, so that the "waverers" are pushed into serving Zionism's criminal aims.

Reading 12

Selected statements of Soviet leaders in the 1967 Arab–Israeli Six-Day War in Moshe Decter (ed.), *Israel and the Jews in the Soviet Mirror* (New York: Conferences on the Status of Soviet Jews, 1967), p. 43

These statements by Soviet leaders equate "atrocities" and "crimes" in the Six-Day War with those of Nazi Germany. This theme became a staple in the Kremlin's propaganda offensive launched against the Jews.

Ambassador Fedorenko at the United Nations, June 9, 1967

They [the Israelis] take their arguments from the same garbage heap of history and from the arsenal of the most famous criminals in history. They follow the bloody footsteps of Hitler's executioners, who always accused the victims of their aggression. . . . Even the very tactics of the blitzkrieg have shown that the leaders of Israel are repeating the tragic experience of Fascist aggression. . . . With full justification it is proper to say at this time that those who now direct the Israeli aggression should be put in the dock as the accused in an international tribunal similar to that which, twenty years ago, condemned the crimes of the main culprits of the war, the criminals against humanity.

Premier Kosygin at the United Nations, June 19, 1967

More and more reports are coming in of atrocities and violence committed by the Israeli invaders on the territories they have seized. What is going on in the Sinai Peninsula and in the Gaza Strip, in the western part of Jordan and on the Syrian soil occupied by the Israeli troops, brings to mind the heinous crimes perpetrated by the Fascists during World War II.

> . . . In the same way as Hitler's Germany used to appoint Gauleiters in the occupied regions, the Israeli government is establishing an occupation administration on the seized territories and appointing its military governors there.
>
> *Party General Secretary Brezhnev in Moscow, July 5, 1967*
>
> In the atrocities against the peaceful Arab populations, it seems they try to copy the crimes of the Nazi invaders. . . . The aggressors conduct themselves like the worst of bandits and commit atrocities in the Hitlerite style.

Reading 13

Avtandil Rukhadze, *Jews in the USSR* (Moscow: Novosti Publishing House, 1982), pp. 49–50

In this excerpt the author explains that Soviet Jews are free to study Hebrew, though most choose a broader Soviet education. This book was sent to many politicians and intellectuals in the West, who responded with disbelief at the crude propaganda.

The facts refute the lies about discrimination against Soviet Jews in education and science. Soviet Jews, exercising their free will, have deliberately chosen not a "Jewish education" but the path of diversified knowledge which the Soviet state has opened for all citizens regardless of nationality.

Like members of [any] other nationality they are free to study, and do in fact study, Hebrew history, culture and philology. It is worth noting that the level of knowledge achieved in these fields in the USSR refutes another Zionist accusation that the Soviet Union "discriminates" against the study of Hebrew history, philology and culture.

Soviet scholars are doing extensive research in ancient Hebrew history, culture and philology. Such research is being undertaken at the Institute of Oriental Studies, the USSR Academy of Sciences and the

Palestinian Society of Russia which is attached to the USSR Academy of Sciences and is one of the oldest in Europe—it celebrated its centenary in 1982. Institutes of Oriental studies and leading universities in the various republics of the USSR also devote serious attention to these questions.

Soviet scholars engaged in Hebrew studies have inherited the fine progressive traditions of their predecessors in prerevolutionary Russia. Academician Pavel Konstantinovich Kokovtsev (1861–1942), a distinguished scholar in Semitic studies, a Hebraist and Arabist, embodied these traditions.

Reading 14

Alexander Gurevich, "An Interview at the Kiev Synagogue," *Soviet Life*, October 1986, p. 40

This article attempts to convince U.S. Jews that Soviet Jews do not face the persecution and repression portrayed by the Western media. Soviet Life *is published for U.S. readers as part of a cultural exchange agreement with the U.S.S.R.*

One of the purposes of the visit to the USSR by a group of U.S. Jewish leaders was to see a place of worship.

In Kiev's synagogue the guests had a long interview with Mikhail Katz, chairman of the city's Jewish religious community. An army surgeon, he finished World War II as a captain.

The synagogue survived the war only because the Nazis used it as stables. The building is being repaired now. "We want it decorated by Passover. We have the funds, so we have hired a team of decorators," Katz said.

The guests asked questions about the freedom to profess the Jewish faith, particularly about having matzoh for Passover. Those are naive questions, of course, but, being a kindly and mild person, Katz gave a detailed a account of the community's life. He showed the guests copies of the Talmud published in the USSR and Torah scrolls. They visited the bakery in the synagogue court, which was busy baking matzoh for the holiday—nearly 40 tons will be available for Passover.

Another question was whether the authorities hamper Jewish emigration. The guests also wanted to know who emigrated, and why.

"Those who were willing to go, go all right," Katz answered. "Some go to join their families from whom they were separated during the war. As to the others—if you want my opinion, I think that some people naively believe that wealth is just raining down on people abroad like divine manna. But they soon see it is not so, and then they know the bitter truth. I think the matter is not material well-being alone. If it is so good there, in the strange land, why do the people who have gone write me letters asking me to help them return?"

"Please convey our shalom to American Jews and wish them peace and happiness," Katz went on to say. "Let them rest assured. We are OK. Let anyone who has any doubts about that come and look at our life with open eyes. We are free in faith, free in our rights and wishes, and what is more important, we have forgotten there is any such thing as anti-Semitism."

Reading 15

Lieutenant-General David Dragunsky, "The Criminal Hand of Zionism," *Pravda*, February 27, 1970, in *Bulletin on Soviet and East European Jewish Affairs*, No. 5, 1970, pp. 18–20

The author, a World-War-II Hero of the Soviet Union, is one of the most prominent Soviet "court Jews." He regularly attacked Israel, Zionism, and Western efforts to help Soviet Jews.

The deeds of the Israeli invaders revive the memory of the hard Hitlerite times. . . .

Israel, as a result of the policy of the Zionist rulers, has become a police bludgeon of the trans-Atlantic magnates. She appears in the unseemly role of a stranger of people's liberation and invader in the Middle East. The reactionary forces of Israel do not shun any means of attaining their aggressive purposes.

One trembles to see how yesterday's hangmen of the European peoples are received with honours in Tel Aviv. Franz-Josef Strauss, revanchist Number One, proclaiming at every street corner that the old times of the Hitler Reich should be brought back, is at present the best friend of Golda Meir and Moshe Dayan. Is this not blasphemy to the memory of the millions who perished? German weapons, the same that sowed the death in the West and the Middle East, now modernized, are at present flowing in a steady stream to Israel. And Israeli Foreign Minister Abba Eban makes a trip to Bonn, in order to obtain new weapons and financial assistance for strangling the freedom and independence of the Arab nations. What cynicism! What a shameful mission for the Minister!

Soviet people, irrespective of nationality, cannot help being disgusted by the inexcusable lying declarations of Premier Golda Meir and other Zionist ringleaders, about the "difficult" situation of the Jews in the Soviet Union.

Recently I got to know that Zionist elements attempted to make application to the UN, allegedly for the "defence" of Human Rights, in order to inflate the insinuations of Golda Meir. The demagogy of the imperialist ringleaders is more than obvious. They must divert public opinion from the Israeli aggression in the Middle East, the "dirty" American War in Vietnam and the negro problem in the USA herself.

I ask: Who gave this legal and moral right to people who have on their conscience so many ruined Arab families, hundreds of thousands of homeless Arab refugees driven out of their homes and forced to wander under the merciless sun, to starve, to die . . . to talk about humanism at all?

In the Soviet Union, the national problem has been solved once and for all. It was solved by the Great October Revolution which has put an end to inequality of people deprived of their rights, including the Jews. The Pale of Settlement pogroms and the lack of rights—all have passed into oblivion.

Reading 16

Excerpt from press conference by Jewish Personalities, *Pravda*, March 5, 1970, in *Bulletin on Soviet and East European Jewish Affairs*, No. 5, 1970, pp. 24–28

This conference, held by "court Jews," drew the ire of many other Soviet Jews who unsuccessfully sought equal time with the Western press. These opposing Soviet Jews did manage, however, to make their views known to the West. (See Part II, Reading 4.)

Mr. Y. F. Dymshitz spoke again when the curtailment of the rights of Soviet Jews was raised:

"This is an example of the ideological attacks made by the Western press. Today's press conference gives a full reply to such insinuations. While I was preparing for this press conference, I decided to find out how the question of the status of Jews in the USSR arose. If we consider this question carefully, we see clearly that it is our ideological enemies who try to foist the so-called Jewish question onto us. This is equivalent to raising the 'Kazak,' the 'Ukrainian,' the 'Uzbek' question; in other words, the 'question' of any of the hundred nationalities living in the USSR. There is no such question; it is an invention, pure and simple.

"V. I. Lenin wrote, 'The enemies of the workers are the capitalists of all countries.' There are workers among the Jews in all countries. They are the majority, they are our brothers, our comrades. Imperialists are trying to create and further an enmity between workers of different nationalities, between peoples.

"There are highly educated people among Jews: There are 843,000 Jews with a higher education in the Soviet Union. Is there any other country which could boast of a similar achievement?

"You have heard the words of Lieutenant-General Dragunsky. He became a general not because he was a Jew, but because he was a gifted man. He has deserved this high distinction. In our country, a man who works and who is useful to society cannot fail to find recognition whatever his nationality. The so-called question about the status of Jews in the Soviet Union is a provocation and an invention from beginning to end.

"Our country is now engaged in the peaceful building of communism, workers of all nationalities are striving for new achievements. We have no national strife. This is precisely what Zionist circles are against; their sabotage activities are aimed at disproving the unity of the Soviet people. But they will never succeed in doing this.

"The Soviet people have the right to ask the question: Where were you, Zionist gentlemen, when a war was going on? Where were you when millions of people in all countries were dying? We don't seem to be able to remember any Zionist activities in those days. Zionists forget that the Red Army saved millions of people, including people of the Jewish nationality, from Fascist slavery.

"We will not allow anybody to discredit our Soviet regime and our Leninist policies towards the different nationalities. Speaking on behalf of all those who signed our statement, on behalf of all Soviet citizens of Jewish nationality, let us state that we support our Leninist policies, our Soviet state, the policy of peaceful coexistence of states in the whole world. We are a against Israeli aggression; we are for the peace and security of all states and peoples, for peace in the Middle East."

Reading 17:

"Leadership Bodies Message to Jewish Oblast," *Moscow Pravda,* June 23, 1984

The Soviet leadership congratulates the inhabitants of Birobidzhan on the fiftieth anniversary of its formation. The party describes the supposed success of Birobidzhan as a "triumph" of its "wise nationality policy, and the indissoluble friendship and fraternity of the peoples of the great Soviet land."

The CPSU Central Committee, USSR Supreme Soviet Presidium, and USSR Council of Ministers warmly greet and congratulate the workers, Kolkhoz members, intelligentsia, and all working people of the Jewish autonomous oblast on the 50th anniversary of its formation.

The great October Socialist Revolution brought Jewish working people deliverance from social oppression and discrimination and opened up broad opportunities for their all-around development. The formation of the Jewish autonomous oblast was the real embodiment of Lenin's nationalities policy, and met with a wide international response. Jewish working people, being equal members of the united family of the Soviet union's peoples, acquired their own statehood with the formation of the autonomous oblast.

In the course of its existence, thanks to the constant concern of the Communist Party and the Soviet state, the oblast has become a developed economic region of the far east, with large-scale industry and mechanized agriculture. During the great patriotic war years the oblast's working people, together with all the Soviet people, selflessly defended the socialist motherland. In the postwar years the oblast created and further developed enterprises in agricultural machine building, the electrical equipment industry, mining, light industry, and other sectors of industry whose output is well known in many countries. The oblast is making a substantial contribution to the construction of the Baykal-Amur railroad. A multisector agriculture is developing successfully. Radical transformations have taken place in the sphere of culture, education, and health care. The working people's well-being is increasing steadily.

All this serves as vivid evidence of the great vitality of the Soviet state and social system, the triumph of the CPSU's wise nationalities policy, and the indissoluble friendship and fraternity of the peoples of the great Soviet land.

Reading 18

Press conference of the Anti-Zionist Committee of the Soviet Public, *New Times*, June 1983, No. 25, pp. 28–31

In this press conference, the Anti-Zionist Committee makes the main point that Soviet Jewish emigration is essentially over.

Dragunsky: Comrades, ladies and gentlemen.

About one and a half months have passed since the founding meeting of the Anti-Zionist Committee of Soviet Public Opinion, at which this body was elected. It is, indeed, a brief period. But the Soviet public and mass media have already shown great interest in our work and in the fact that such a committee was founded. The establishment of the Anti-Zionist Committee has also evoked interest abroad.

In this past period we have received more than 500 letters from Soviet citizens, expressing warm support for the initiative. A good many letters had come from abroad. Soviet and foreign journalists have addressed inquiries to the committee. This prompted us to hold a press conference to explain why and how our organization was set up, to outline the aims and tasks of its activity, and to answer any questions that might be put.

How did it all begin? Late in March and early in April Soviet newspapers published an appeal by a group of public leaders calling for active political unmasking of Zionism, for a more vigorous rebuff to the Zionists' anti-Soviet propaganda, for raising the effectiveness of our actions, and for sponsoring a voluntary public organization for this purpose.

The appeal was addressed to workers, collective farmers, intellectuals, scientists, writers, art workers, journalists, to all members of the various nationalities. Telegrams and letters began to arrive almost the day after the appeal was published. Our appeal met with warm, I would say, genuinely enthusiastic support. This gave us grounds for holding the inaugural meeting. We had every justification to say that we had been given a public mandate, that this broad support was an expression of public opinion. This entitled us to call ourselves the Committee of Soviet Public Opinion and to speak on behalf of the broad Soviet public.

You may ask why we decided to form the Anti-Zionist Committee at this particular moment. The struggle against Zionism as a dangerous variety of capitalist ideology was waged by Lenin as far back as the beginning of the century. The Soviet people have always regarded Zionism as an ideology which is the embodiment of the advocacy of national exclusiveness, of being the "chosen people," and hence as a chauvinistic and racist ideology.

Today imperialism, mainly U.S. reactionary circles, are using international Zionism ever more actively and widely in pursuance of aims endangering peace. As we know, the international situation has seriously deteriorated. On the initiative of Washington the latter-day crusaders are mounting ever-new attacks on communism, and no small role in this global offensive on the positions of peace and progress is assigned to international Zionism and the political adventurism of the Israeli ruling circles. The false propaganda and obviously slanderous actions of the ideological and political adventurers of international Zionism are part of the West's psychological war against the Soviet Union.

The past year has shown with particular clarity that in its development Zionism, its misanthropic ideology and practice, increasingly reproduces the ideas and methods of the defeated Hitler fascism. The events in Lebanon (Israel's bloody aggression against that country began exactly a year ago) demonstrated to the whole world that the crimes of Begin and his cutthroats differ but little from the atrocities committed by the nazis. All this impelled us to announce that the time has come when international Zionism must be combated and its anti-Soviet propaganda rebutted in a more organized way. . . .

Correspondent of Golos Rodiny (Voice of the Homeland): What could you say about the decline in emigration from the Soviet Union?

The Los Angeles *Times* correspondent asked whether the desire of Soviet Jews to emigrate to Israel or any other country is regarded in the Soviet Union as a betrayal and if so, why.

Zivs: I shall try to answer both questions at once. You see, juggling with figures is something that has long been widely practised by Zionist propaganda. It is said that now 50,000, now 700,000 Jews want to emigrate from the Soviet Union. In a book I read recently I saw the figure of 383,528 Jews mentioned as wishing to leave. I remembered that figure. From where, it may be asked, are these figures taken? It is not the actual number of people who have applied for a permission to emigrate that is counted but the numbers planned by the Zionist demographers, if one may call them so. For instance, 100,000 invitations are sent, and it is immediately announced that 100,000 people want to emigrate. How is this done? On the pretext of "reuniting families" invitations of this kind are mailed to people who have never had relatives in Israel. Sometimes invitations are sent even to nonexistent Soviet citizens, or several invitation are sent to one and the same person. In the few weeks since the establishment of the committee it has received indignant letters from Soviet citizens enclosing "official" invitations of this kind, official in the sense that they bear the red seal of a notary public and an accompanying letter from the Israel Foreign Ministry asking for a humanitarian attitude to family reunion and naming relatives who do not in fact exist. This is one aspect of the matter.

Here is another. We are indeed aware that in 1982 and this year the number of persons who emigrated from the Soviet Union has considerably decreased, which, I emphasize, means a decrease in the number of persons who apply for permission to leave.

For a number of years after the war reunification was the chief motive prompting Soviet citizens of Jewish nationality to emigrate. You know that during the war many Jewish families were separated, and this served as grounds for applications to emigrate. By now, however, reunification has in the main been completed, and the number of those who leave is naturally diminishing.

Besides, I believe, fewer people now fall for the Zionist bait, become victims of Zionist propaganda and leave our country.

This is enough for pro-Zionist propaganda in the West to start spreading the slanderous allegation that the Soviet authorities now limit emigration and now halt it altogether. Some even tried to link the substantial drop in emigration with the formation of our committee. I must add that permission to leave is given by competent government bodies. Our committee can only explain and help Soviet citizens to understand the false and poisonous character of Zionist propaganda and try to protect them against it.

I especially stress this point because our committee is already receiving letters full of anxiety, grief and despair from former Soviet citizens now living abroad.

I think it is worth quoting from some of these letters. Here is one from Soviet citizen Lubov Vinkler, now residing in West Berlin. "Dear comrades, sponsors of a voluntary organization, the Anti-Zionist Committee," she writes, "I have read with great satisfaction your appeal published in the newspaper Pravda. I congratulate you in the establishment of the committee and wish you success in your work . . . I am a victim of Zionist propaganda. For 11 years I have been suffering outside my beloved Soviet homeland . . . I am 59 years now, a physician by profession. I have seen enough and suffered enough both in Israel and here . . . I have seen the bestial essence of Zionism . . . Grief, fears, hardship, humiliation, complete isolation and loneliness in an alien and disgusting world is my lot. What has happened to me is the result of subtle Zionist propaganda. The Zionists meddled in my life and ruined it." . . .

Correspondent of the Peace and Progress radio station: One of the main themes of the provocative assembly "in defence of the Soviet Jews," held in Jerusalem in March this year, was the allegation that Soviet Jews are discriminated in the field of education and science. Will you comment on this?

[Academician Martin] Kabachnik: Zionist propaganda has always been noted for brazenness and has never stopped at juggling with facts. Let me say, to begin with, that in the Soviet Union there is universal secondary education compulsory for all children irrespective of their nationality, sex or property status. All children, Jewish included, receive an education, and this means that there is no nor can there be any discrimination in this field. Neither is there any discrimination at the next stages of education (secondary technical and higher), since in the level of education the Soviet Jews hold one of the first places among other nationalities of the Soviet Union. Furthermore, it may be confidently asserted that in educational level Soviet Jews occupy the first place in the world in comparison with the educational level of Jews in all other countries. . . .

The *Daily World* correspondent asked General Dragunsky what role the Soviet Jews played in the Great Patriotic War against fascism and what role the Soviet Army played in saving millions of Jews from death in gas chambers.

Dragunsky: Jews fought against the Nazi hordes side by side with the soldiers and officers of other nationalities. About 200,000 Jews were killed in battle, valiantly fighting in the front lines. Many thousands of Jewish servicemen were decorated for their valour in action. More than 120 Jews were awarded the title of Hero of the Soviet Union. The Soviet Union pays homage to the heroism of its fighting men in the Great Patriotic War.

I was in the Osowiec fortress when the war began. For 1,418 days and sleepless nights I fought on many battle fronts. The brigade I commanded at the end of the war included representatives of some 30 nationalities, and all of them fought for our homeland. They did not ask what your nationality was—Russian, Kazakh, Jewish or Lettish. They shared a common aim—to defeat racism and fascism as quickly as possible and win freedom for our homeland. Victory in the war was won by the single multinational family of the Soviet peoples.

I would like to mention one more thing. Every year on May 9 we all celebrate Victory Day. That day is officially observed in many countries, but not in Israel.

The historic victory over Nazi Germany, the defeat of fascism, is not observed in Israel as an official holiday. The Zionist leaders' pathological hatred of the Soviet Union does not allow them to recognize its historic contribution to the achievement of the victory that foiled the barbarous Nazi plans of exterminating all "inferior races," the Jews included. . . .

Neues Leben correspondent: The Western press often alleges that the teaching of Hebrew is banned in the Soviet Union. More, Hebrew is called the national language of the Soviet Jews. What is the real state of affairs?

Zimanas: Hebrew has never been the national language of Jews either in tsarist Russia or in the Soviet Union. Yiddish has been. At present about 14 percent of the Soviet Jews consider Yiddish their mother tongue.

As for the Hebrew language revived and adapted to the present-day conditions in Israel, it is taught in Soviet colleges which train philologists and orientalists, for instance, at the Institute of Asian and African Countries of Moscow University, and in the Tbilisi and Leningrad universities.

I shall now dwell on the fact that the Zionist leaders lay special emphasis on the introduction of Hebrew. They would like Hebrew to be studied and adopted as the common language of their widely advertised single "world Jewish nation." Hebrew is also seen by the Zionist leaders as an instrument that would help to spread Zionist ideology.

But to return to Yiddish. It can be stated with all responsibility that the Zionist self-styled "champions of Jewish Soviet culture" are absolutely indifferent to Yiddish, the national language of the Soviet Jews. Do you know of any Western publishing house which would be prepared to reprint the books of Soviet Jewish authors writing in Yiddish or at least to bring out an anthology of works in Yiddish published in the Moscow journal Sovietish Heimland? Do you know of a single Western firm that would be prepared to put out records of songs sung in Yiddish by Iosif Kobzon or Galina Kareva? Would any leading Western newspaper—from *Le Monde* to the *New York Times*—report on this handsomely got up Yiddish Primer, approved by the public education department of the Jewish autonomous region and published in Khabarovsk last year?

Why is all this hushed up? Because if it were made public, the true purpose of the "defence of Jewish culture in the Soviet Union" would become clear to everyone in the west.

Reading 19:

B. Kravtsov, "Caution: Zionism!" *Leningradskaya pravda,* April 19, 20, 1983

The author attacks private Hebrew teaching circles as subversive. This was the first time that private and unofficial Hebrew and Jewish history groups, sporadically harassed over the previous few years, were formally declared in violation of Soviet law. Kravtsov assaults the Torah, Talmud, and the overall Jewish heritage. Jews are seen as power-hungry schemers and fifth-columnists.

The article was published shortly after the formation of the Anti-Zionist Committee and is related to its goals. Leningradskaya pravda, *one of the major papers in the U.S.S.R., was then under the control of Leningrad party boss Grigory Romanov, a vicious anti-Semite who, among other things, played a major role in setting up the Leningrad hijacking trial (and related trials) of 1970–1971.*

. . . Let's be frank. The appeal to Hebrew for today's practical Zionism has an importance that is far from cultural, but is strictly political. This Hebrew is first of all the language of the "sacred" Jewish books—the Torah and the Talmud. And this is extreme religious fanaticism, chauvinism, the striving to force on Jews the idea of the exclusivity, their having been selected as the "chosen people," their superiority over other nations, and consequently, to force upon them racial intolerance toward other "inferior" nations. It is not accidental that Zionism equates itself to Judaism, politically adapting religion to the practical implementation of its geopolitical tasks. And the leaders of Zionism have never concealed the fact that these tasks are precisely geopolitical. "The Jewish nation," the same Ben-Gurion asserted in the book *Before and After the Sinai Campaign*, "at the present time is dispersed throughout the world, and the sphere in which Israel now lives includes all five continents and the islands on the oceans of the entire earth." How does one extend tentacles to these "five continents" and the "islands on the oceans of the entire earth"? First of all, with the aid of religion, Hebrew, the propagandizing of the "cultural" and "spiritual commonality" of all Jews. Those are the plans, that is the practice of Zionists.

Reading 20

Charges of Anti-Semitism in USSR Rebutted, Moscow radio in English to North America, December 12, 1984

Just one month after the stingingly anti-Semitic television documentary Hirelings and Accomplices, shown on Leningrad Television on November 12, Moscow Radio tried to rebut Western charges of Soviet anti-Semitism.

Charges of Anti-Semitism in USSR Rebutted
LD130320 Moscow in English to North America 2300 GMT
12 Dec 84
(Interview granted by commentator Alexander Yegorov to unidentified announcer-live or recorded)

(Announcer) We have been getting many letters asking about the life of Jews in the Soviet Union. Quite a few of the letters are critical. It is apparent that their authors have drawn their ideas about Soviet Jews from the American news media. But how true are the statements the media makes? What opportunities do Soviet Jews really have to, say, study their language, preserve their culture, and practice Judaism? Let us listen to Radio Moscow commentator Aleksander Yegorov: Now first, what does he think of the claim that in the Soviet Union anti-Semitism is official policy?

(Yegorov) If this claim were true it would be hard to understand how it happens that hundreds of Jews stand at the head of Soviet industrial enterprises, supervise ministries and administrations, and hold high positions in the Armed Forces. Or how it happens that six Jews are elected members of the parliaments of the various Soviet republics and the local governments.

(Announcer) Perhaps Soviet Jews are able to reach these positions despite official policy, exclusively owing to their outstanding abilities.

(Yegorov) There is no denying that the Jewish nation has many gifted people in it, just as any nation has. But what were the Jews in Russia of the tsars able to achieve? They were restricted to certain places of residence. They faced quotas in trying to enter institutions of learning. Their culture and religion were persecuted and they were barred from government positions. It was only after the victory of the socialist revolution in Russia that Jews received the same rights as all other ethnic groups and could give full expression to their talents. Soviet Government abolished all restrictions and privileges based on nationality. This gave all the ethnic groups in the country equal opportunities to develop. The Soviet Constitution makes it punishable by law to directly or indirectly restrict the rights of citizens or give citizens direct or indirect privileges because of their race or nationality. Soviet law also punishes any attempt to advocate racial or ethnic exclusiveness, enmity or contempt. Under the Criminal Code anyone found guilty is liable to imprisonment of six months to three years or internal exile of two to five years.

(Announcer) So there is no infringement on the rights of Soviet Jews. Then why is it no institution of learning in the Soviet Union gives instruction in Hebrew?

(Yegorov) Hebrew has never been the language of the Jewish community in this country. It wasn't before the revolution and hasn't been since. The language of the Jewish community has always been Yiddish, but Hebrew is studied in our institutions of higher learning that prepare philologists and specialists in eastern cultures. For example, it is taught in the Institute of Asian and African Studies at Moscow University and in the Universities of Leningrad and Tbilisi.

(Announcer) If Yiddish is the traditional language of the Jewish community in this country, why is it that the number of schools with instruc-

tion in Yiddish has declined in Soviet times? At least Western news media say this is so.

(Yegorov) And indeed it is. Let me explain why. In the first years of Soviet Government, many regions where there were fairly large Jewish communities set up general and vocational schools with instruction in Yiddish. There was a need for this because the Jews in those areas had kept to themselves and had a poor knowledge of Russian or the other language of those localities. Sometimes they didn't know them at all. But in the twenties and especially in the thirties, hundreds of thousands of Jews left these areas because now they could live wherever they wished. Soviet Government did not restrict their place of residence as the tsarist governments had done. So, gradually the schools with instruction in Yiddish closed down for lack of students. In addition many Jewish families began sending their children to Russian, Ukrainian, Belorussian, and other schools where instruction was in the local language, and not only because they wanted to take advantage of the equality of ethnic groups that Soviet Government had introduced. They realized that knowing one of the mainstream languages would make it easier for their children to communicate with people of other Soviet ethnic groups and give them more opportunities for education and jobs. Today only about 14 percent of the Jews in the Soviet Union name Yiddish as their native language. The rest consider Russian, Ukrainian, Belorussian, and other mainstream languages their native tongue. But the Soviet Union does have schools with instruction in Yiddish. These are situated in the Jewish autonomous region in the east, known as Birobidzhan. Two years ago, incidentally, the region put out a new primer in Yiddish in a large edition.

(Announcer) And what about other publications in Yiddish? Many listeners say they have heard there are none, and they want to know why.

(Yegorov) There are such publications. But before I go into details, let me say that not a single Western publisher has shown a readiness to put out the books of Soviet writers who write in Yiddish or to issue an anthology of the stories and poetry that have appeared in the Moscow-based Yiddish-language monthly *Sovietish Heimland*. . . . Now about publications in Yiddish in the Soviet Union: In just the past seventeen years we have issued 271 books by Jewish authors in a total edition of

nearly two million copies. What is more, many of the books of Jewish authors are translated into Russian and other Soviet languages, and in this way enter the mainstream of Soviet culture.

(Announcer) Some American listeners seem to think, judging by their letters, that our colleges and universities have quotas for Jews.

(Yegorov) The best proofs that this is nonsense is that the Soviet Union is ahead of all the Western nations, including the United States and even Israel, for the number of Jewish college graduates in proportion to the Jewish population. Between 1959 and 1978 the number of Soviet Jews with a higher education rose from 277,000 to 395,000.

Reading 21

Israel Government to UNESCO, "The Denial by the Soviet Government of the Right of Soviet Jews to Study the Hebrew language," April 1985

This selection decries the inability of Soviet Jews to study and teach Hebrew, arguing that the Soviet government has violated both its own laws and provisions of international pacts it has signed.

The Soviet government had long pursued a policy aimed at suppressing Jewish culture in the Soviet Union and at severing Soviet Jewry from its cultural heritage. A key element of that policy was the effort to deny Jews the right to study the Hebrew language.

Hebrew, the language of the Bible and of the Jewish people in the State of Israel, is the only language which for five thousand years has been the common property of all Jews everywhere. Knowledge of Hebrew is an integral and essential part not only of the practice of Judaism—the liturgy and sacred texts of which are in Hebrew—but also of secular Jewish culture. Nevertheless, the Jewish language has been rendered virtually inaccessible to Soviet Jews through a ban, the existence of which is not acknowledged, but which is rigorously enforced.

In the USSR, courses in the Hebrew language exist for certain narrow state purposes as a part of the curriculum of three universities. Jews, as a rule, are excluded from these courses. Officially approved Hebrew instruction is available elsewhere only in a few Christian religious seminaries. Soviet Jewry is thus denied the opportunity to study Hebrew. No textbooks of the Hebrew language are produced in the USSR and, with the sole exception of a limited edition of Shapiro's Hebrew-Russian dictionary which appeared in 1963, no books of any kind in Hebrew have been published there for over fifty years. There are no Hebrew newspapers or periodicals. Moreover, throughout the entire length and breadth of the Soviet Union there is not a single school of course for Jews with Hebrew as its language of instruction. Jews are denied the possibility of training and qualifying as teachers of Hebrew. The Jews, who according to official Soviet statistics number about 1,800,000 (a figure regarded as a substantial understatement by non-Soviet demographers) and who represent the sixteenth largest among over one hundred officially recognized Soviet nationalities, are the only such nationality whose national language is subjected to such disabilities.

Deprived of any other possibility to study the Hebrew language (their applications to emigrate to Israel have been refused by the authorities), an increasing number of Soviet Jews have been studying and teaching Hebrew privately in recent years. The authorities simultaneously sought effective means to suppress such private Hebrew instruction while falsely maintaining to the world that no prohibition exists on the study of Hebrew by Soviet Jews. They decided that the private teaching of Hebrew, in contrast to the private teaching of non-Jewish languages in the USSR, was not to be regarded as legitimate employment. Police measures figured prominently among the means employed to extirpate Hebrew among Jews. In October 1983, Yosif BEGUN of Moscow was sentenced to seven years imprisonment and five additional years of exile (his third conviction), essentially for his attempts to legitimize the teaching of Hebrew and other Jewish cultural activity. Other teachers were also subjected to arbitrary arrests, searches and seizures, summoned to interrogations, slandered in the official press and threatened with prosecution on all manner of trumped-up charges. During the past three years police harassment of Hebrew teachers greatly intensified. In a number of Soviet cities Hebrew teachers, among them KHOLMIANSKY, EDELSHTEIN and LEVIN, were warned by the KGB and the police that they must cease teaching Hebrew or else they would be tried on various pretexts and subjected to severe punishments. The police regularly raided the homes of Hebrew teachers and confiscated all Hebrew language material, including textbooks, dictionaries and other teaching aids. They also broke into the apartments where Hebrew lessons were in progress and demanded identification from those present, warning them of grave consequences if they continued their Hebrew studies.

The wave of arrests over the preceding six months represents the culmination of earlier Soviet efforts at repression and is aimed at finally liquidating the study of Hebrew among Soviet Jews.

The behavior of the Soviet authorities with regard to Hebrew language instruction for Jews and Jewish Hebrew teachers gravely infringes the individual rights of the teachers and students concerned. Quite apart from basic human rights associated with due process of law and freedom from arbitrary police harassment (rights guaranteed under numerous international human rights conventions to which the Soviet Union is a party as well as under Soviet law) the suppression of knowledge of Hebrew among Jews is also a blatant violation of the collective cultural rights of the Jewish minority to use and study its own language as expressed in the 1966 International Covenant on Civil and Political Rights (Art. 27) and the 1960 UNESCO Convention Against Discrimination in Education (Article 5(1) (c)), to which treaties the Soviet Union is a party. It is also totally at odds with the pledges made by the Soviet government in signing the Helsinki Final Act to encourage the development of minority cultures. Finally, the discriminatory suppression of the Jewish national language violates the Soviet Union's own constitution and laws which prohibit any form of discrimination on the basis of nationality, as well as any preference or limitation regarding the national language of the peoples of the USSR. It is therefore fully understandable why the measures adopted in the current wave of trials against the Hebrew teachers have evoked protests from hundreds of Soviet Jews to the Soviet authorities.

Reading 22

B. Bakanov, *Zionist Falsehoods* (Moscow: Novosti Press Agency Publishing House, 1974), pp. 35–37 (excerpts). See also Part II, Reading 3.

The Kremlin often printed excerpts from letters sent by disgruntled Soviet Jews who were disillusioned with life in Israel. Several such letters are in this publication.

Here is a letter from a former Soviet citizen, Boris Bravshtein, now living with his family in Shikun Hei, Hazvi 45 Beersheba, Israel: "I received an invitation from Israel. I was sure I was going there to build 'a Jewish state.' Soon after I arrived here I realized that I and my family had been lured here to be slaves. I have destroyed my family's happiness. I have deprived my children of their childhood, I have seen for myself the truth of all that I heard in the Soviet Union about Israel and Zionism. We find ourselves in a country where the whole of life is a mercenary undertaking and everything is based on mutual hatred and deceit. . . ."

In an effort to lure Soviet Jews to Israel the Israeli Zionists resort to deception and falsehoods. But Soviet citizens expose those who send them counterfeit invitations to come to the "Promised Land." Soviet Jews have exposed the counterfeit appeal circulated by the Israeli representative in the United Nations. They declared that they had not signed that appeal which requested that they be given the opportunity to leave for Israel. They stated in their denial that circulation of such "documents" only served to mislead world public opinion. They indignantly demanded to be safeguarded from such provocations in the future; Israel hopes to keep its immigrants in the country by using legal and economic fetters or such ruses as the one just described. But the efforts of the Zionists to hold on to those who have been deceived by their propaganda, as well as their attempts to attract immigrants to Israel with counterfeit invitations and false promises, are in vain. They are just as futile as the Zionist's attempts to deceive the people of the world by their pretended "anxiety" for the fate of Soviet Jews.

Reading 23

Gorbachev's Interview in *L'Humanité,* translated in *Moscow News,* February 23–March 2, 1986

In this excerpt Gorbachev denies the existence of a "Jewish Problem" in the U.S.S.R. He gives statistics to leave the false impression that Soviet Jews were far better off than they actually were.

Question: There is talk about persecution of Jews in the USSR, political prisoners and censorship. Some names, such as Sakharov, are mentioned. What can you say on this score?

Answer: To begin with, on Soviet Jews. This matter has become a part of a vociferous anti-Soviet campaign, a veritable act of psychological warfare against the USSR. Propaganda of anti-Semitism, as of other forms of racial discrimination, is prohibited by law in the Soviet Union and constitutes a crime. What is commonplace in the USA, and also in France and other Western countries—desecration of Jewish graves and the activities of neo-Nazi organizations preaching hatred for Jews in newspapers and radio programmes—is impossible in the USSR. Jews in our country are free and have equal rights, as do all the other nationalities. They are active in the public life and state affairs of the country. We publish books, magazines and newspapers in Yiddish, and synagogues are open. I think that the insistent "attention" of anticommunist and Zionist propaganda to the fate of Jews in the USSR is nothing short of hypocrisy which pursues far-reaching political goals—goals, moreover, which have nothing to do with the genuine interests of Soviet Jews.

I believe that in a civilized society there must be no room at all for anti-Semitism, Zionism or any other manifestation of nationalism, chauvinism or racism. And the problem of eradicating these evils on a global scale is very urgent. In South Africa the racists have launched gory repressions against the black majority. Pogroms and acts of violence against African blacks, Indians, Turks and immigrants from other Asian countries have become more frequent in West European countries. Racism has obviously launched a counteroffensive in the United States in the past few years. And the Arab people of Palestine have been locked out of their lands for many years—for commonly known reasons.

As for political prisoners, we have none, just as we do not have persecution of people for their convictions. We do not put people on trial for their convictions.

But any state must protect itself against those who try to subvert it, who call for undermining or destroying it, who, lastly, spy for foreign intelligence services. These actions are qualified by our laws as crimes against the state. In the recent period, according to my information, a little more than 200 people have been serving sentences for all crimes of such a kind in the USSR.

Reading 24

Manifesto of the National Patriotic Front *Pamiat*, printed in the *Central Asia and Caucasus Chronicle*, Vol. 8, No. 3, July 1989, pp. 14–15

These excerpts are from one of several manifestos circulated by various Pamyat associations. This manifesto has been selected for its representation of the overall Pamyat *philosophy and program.*

The national-patriotic front "Pamiat"is not a political organization. Our programme demands are not based on considerations of "politics," "economics," "ecology," "demography" and so on. We have in mind the interests of the people and common sense. Our aim is the spiritual renaissance of the people of the fatherland, which has suffered and was robbed by aggressive Zionism, Talmudic atheism and cosmopolitan usury.

1. We demand that our state ceases to be a colony, a raw material annex of the world wide Zionist financial oligarchy, and that the centuries-old spiritual, political and economic values of our ancestors be restored.
2. Great Russia is eternal.
3. We demand to know the entire truth about the perpetrators of the genocide against the Russian people and other peoples of our country.

4. We demand the entire truth about the cruel ritual murder of the Russian Tsar.
5. We desire the resurgence of religious life in the country. We demand a true separation of church and state.
6. We demand the real implementation of the constitutional guarantee of freedom of worship for all religions, and first of all for Orthodox Christianity, which was the most persecuted victim.
9. We demand the publication of the lists of all destroyed churches.
10. We demand the publication of the names of those who destroyed them and that they be brought to justice.
11. We demand the entire truth be revealed about religious persecutions.
12. We demand an end to the desecration of churches.
17. We demand economic autonomy for all the republics.
25. We demand an end to the alcoholization of the people.
28. We demand the creation of national organs of mass propaganda. The organizations of mass propaganda which do not have adequate Russian representation among their staff cannot be considered Russian, but only as Russian-speaking. This should be reflected in their name.
29. We demand legislation against tendencies in art and literature that pervert our people, and the liquidation of publishing houses that engage in such activities.
31. We demand legislation against all actions that lead to the disappearance of our land, waterways, and forests.
34. We demand legislation against the falsification of the history of our fatherland.
35. Who invented such a despicable rule, that forbids speaking about God to children? We demand that the school curriculum include the study of religion.
40. Honest people cannot come to any compromise with the Zionist state, created and existing on the basis of Jewish fascism. We categorically disagree with the establishing of diplomatic ties with Israel.
44. We demand legislation against Russophobic protectionism.
48. We demand an end to artificial assimilation and mechanical mixing of nations, since it leads to the loss of feeling towards the native land and home and, ultimately, to the creation of

rootless, soulless masses, the source of crime, prostitution, drug addition and alcoholism.

50. We believe that all manifestations of separatism and inter-ethnic conflict in the country are the result of dirty Zionist-Masonic provocation and demand publication of the names of the real instigators and their punishment.
53. We demand the adoption of a law on foreigners which would guarantee priority treatment for citizens of our country in all aspects of life. Our condition as second class people in our own land is unacceptable.
56. We demand an end to the senseless plunder of our land, forests and waterways by international Zionist capital.
58. Our people are able to use their wealth on their own. We demand an end to the plunder of the country, through leasing our land to Zionist-Masonic capital.
60. We demand the opening of the archives and the revelation of the levers of secret power that crippled our country during the times of "red terror," "military communism," "cult of personality," "voluntarism" and "stagnation," which allowed the plunder and ruin of our country, and condemned her to spiritual poverty and the genocide of all the peoples of our state, first of all the Russian people. During the period of Zionist genocide more people were exterminated in our country than in all the wars of mankind.
61. We believe that each person can develop normally only in the bosom of his native culture and native people. Only by knowing, loving, and respecting one's own people is it possible to respect another nation. Consequently, we believe that cosmopolitanism is a crime against the people, against the nation and against mankind. We are convinced that the spiritual reawakening of our people can happen only from within, on the basis of the principle that common good is higher than personal profit.

We will win—our strength is in unity. We will not sell our birthright for a lentil soup to the Zionist bastards. There is no power in the world that could break the backbone of this viper, except our spirit, except our state, except our unity—THE UNITY OF THE PEOPLE.

Reading 25

Lieutenant-General David D. Dragunsky, "What are the 'Pamyat' Pseudopatriots Seeking?," *Literaturnaya gazeta,* August 17, 1988

This criticism of Pamyat *by a "court Jew" shows the broad base of the official opposition of this ultranationalist Russian group.*

In front of me are the August issues of newspapers with articles on the rallies in Leningrad organized by the association calling itself the "Pamyat" Russian National Patriotic Front.

Alongside is the appeal to the Russian people and patriots of all countries and nations signed by the "Pamyat" leaders. Even its external format—not to mention its content—automatically puts me on my guard. At the top of the front page is the appeal: "Patriots of the world, unite!" You read it and think that either the "Pamyat" leaders are not all there, or they have deliberately distorted the immortal proletarian slogan. But that is not all. Each page of the appeal bears the imprint "Pamyat" and the signature of "D. Vasilyev," which makes it smack more of an examination paper than of a text with pretensions to a political document.

I spotted the following words: "We want to particularly stress that the 'Pamyat' Patriotic Association is profoundly international in its essence and has nothing to do with chauvinism, anti-Semitism, or any other form of racial discrimination!" Those are the words. A pretty cover for unseemly actions.

At rallies the "Pamyat" pseudopatriots demanded a ban on Russians marrying non-Russians. They called for the immediate deportation of Jews and other non-Russians to "their historical motherland." One of the speakers proposed the announcement of a hard-line campaign against those who "hide their ethnic essence behind a Russian surname." . . .

All those who are not indifferent to the fate of the fatherland should close ranks and resolutely rebuff those dark forces which bear a grave responsibility for their anticonstitutional and, quite frankly, criminal actions.

Reading 26

Alexander Kabakov, "Free-Style Wrestling with Zionism," *Moscow News*, May 21, 1989

This is an account of a rally held in Moscow by the Committee of Soviets Against the Restoration of Diplomatic Relations with Israel. It shows how a public anti-Semitic rally, in this case under the guise of a show of support for Palestinian Arabs, can be held with the permission, if not blessing, of local authorities. It is unclear whether such rallies are authorized or ordered by top Communist Party authorities.

A meeting permitted by the Leninsky District Soviet Executive Committee of Moscow was held near the Luzhniki Sports Complex. In their application, the organizers declared that they wished to offer support to the struggle being waged by Arab Palestinians. But the greater part of their posters—instead of condemning the world Zionism in the Middle East, were against Zionism in our country. There was a poster showing St. George killing a sort of reptile with the inscription "Tel-Avidenye" —a poster known by many Muscovites because it is used at Pamyat meetings.

The meeting was opened by Yevgeny Yevseyev, research associate at the Philosophy Institute of the USSR Academy of Sciences. His name is always appearing on the bulletins published by the "committee of Soviets against the restoration of diplomatic relations with Israel." At the meeting Yevseyev's speech mainly repeated the provisions being spread in the printed appeal of this unofficial committee. It noted the internal enemies infiltrating our society, counted the percentage of Jews in Moscow and declared that it was simple to build up a network of spies enabling them to work for Israel. The representatives of the Palestinian community in Moscow, who took part in the meeting, held posters which supported the aim of the meeting stated in the application. But the speakers continued to deal mainly with Russia's internal problems. The historical-enlightening society "Memorial" and the April Writers' Committee were called sources of Zionism and the magazines *Ogonyok* and *Znamya*—mouthpieces for Zionism. It was possible to buy in the crowd, for 5 roubles, literature, which contained all the information about the all-penetrating Zionists, who can easily be determined by their Jewish surnames hidden behind aliases. The manifesto of the Pamyat national-patriotic front was also available for reading.

By the way, to hold an "anti-Zionist" meeting, the trolley bus traffic had to be stopped for ninety minutes. But this was done. It is absolutely impossible to understand what guides the district Soviet executive committees when they permit or forbid variant meetings.

PART II

Origins and Development of the Soviet Jewish Movement for Freedom

Soviet Jews developed diverse strategies in their quest for freedom to emigrate and practice their religion. What they used depended on their assessment of the interplay among their own needs and goals, Soviet domestic and foreign policies, and certain international relations, particularly U.S.–Soviet and Israeli–Arab affairs. The freedom movement has therefore shifted gears several times in the face of changing circumstances both at home and abroad.

Division of any major historical movement into periods is surely artificial. Such division, however, may better illuminate the various complexities, dilemmas, continuities, and twists and turns that characterized the Soviet Jewish freedom movement over its first twenty-four years, 1967–1990.

Period 1: Jewish Revival (1967–1970)

Until the Arab-Israeli Six-Day War in 1967, Soviet Jews were essentially the "Jews of Silence." For a number of years earlier, Zionist activists in the Baltic states had initiated Jewish cultural activities and a small underground movement, and increasingly Jews in the big cities had gathered outside synagogues for comradeship and song on the Jewish holiday of Simkhat Torah. But like most Soviet citizens, Soviet Jews did not dare to criticize the regime, at least openly. In general, especially in the "heartland" republics, they tended to accept their lot and to make the best of their situation. Yet because of anti-Semitism, both popularly based and government-sponsored, they suffered more.

Premier Kosygin's public statement on December 3, 1966, which implied that Moscow might allow Soviet Jews to reunite with their families in Israel, aroused many Soviet Jews to serious thoughts of emigration. Israel's swift and decisive military victory in the 1967 War, however, was the major spur to emigration. Propaganda from the Kremlin, which had heavily armed Arab states, especially Egypt, at the outset of the war made Israel look like a pushover for the Arabs. Imagine, then, the dismay inside the Kremlin when the reverse occurred. Imagine, also, the elation of Soviet Jews at the outcome of this war. Israel's success instilled confidence and pride in Soviet Jews. Increasing numbers, sensing new dignity and awareness of their Jewishness and homeland, began trying to emigrate and to learn more about their roots.

It was not easy for Soviet Jews to determine how best to deal with Soviet authorities. They had neither precedent to follow nor any clear, open laws to scrutinize. Moreover, they had no reason to be confident of a positive response from the new triumvirate of Soviet leaders, Brezhnev, Kosygin, and Podgorny, who had deposed Khrushchev in 1964 at least partially because of his "liberal" domestic policies. But maybe the new leadership might allow some Jewish emigration, even if grudgingly.

Some Soviet Jews felt it best to maintain a very low profile. They believed the less noise the better—for themselves, their families, and friends. Others took the opposite tack of high visibility and activism. They wanted to publicize their demand to emigrate, both inside and outside the Soviet Union. A group of twenty Lithuanian Jews sent the first significant collective petition on February 15, 1968.[1] *(See Reading 1.)* It was publicized in the West on October 30, 1968, when the *Washington Post* and the *New York Times* published excerpts. This petition contained no signatures because its authors feared reprisal. Beginning with a petition by eighteen Georgian Jews in August 1969, Soviet Jews did sign their names and addresses. *(See Reading 2.)* They sent their petitions and appeals to Soviet officials, the governments of Israel and the United States, the United Nations and other international organizations,[2] Communist parties in the West, and various civic and professional groups throughout the world. Between February 1968 and October 1970, Soviet Jews reportedly sent 220 appeals.

These appeals came from all over the U.S.S.R.[3] They were designed to publicize human rights problems of Soviet Jews. They protested anti-Semitism, the absence of Jewish cultural and communal institutions, and the lack of opportunity to practice Judaism freely. They also were intended to counter highly publicized letters from supposedly disgruntled

Jewish emigrants *(see Reading 3)* and one-sided statements at press conferences by "court Jews." *(See Readings 4 and 5.)* All these appeals had the same basic plea: Let Soviet Jews emigrate (or "repatriate," the term most activists preferred then) in accordance with their rights under international law, which many activists had gotten to know quite well. Many appeals cited specific international agreements signed by the U.S.S.R. that called for the right to emigrate, such as the Universal Declaration of Human Rights, the International Covenant on Civil and Political Rights, and the International Convention on Elimination of All Forms of Racial Discrimination. Soviet ratification of this last agreement on January 22, 1969, further emboldened Soviet Jews to try to emigrate.

During the "revival" period, there was limited Jewish emigration. From June 1967 to September 1968, no Jews were allowed out. But from October 1968 to the end of 1970, 4235 Jews emigrated. Almost all went to Israel, which at the time attracted Jews who were more Zionistically inclined. More than two-thirds of these emigrants came from Georgia, which had a more liberal religious atmosphere, and the Baltic states, which the Soviet Union had annexed during World War II. All told, through wartime annexations, the Soviet Union incorporated about two million Jews. About 265,00 Jews were added from the Baltic states. Unlike the Jewish brethren inside the Soviet Union, Jews in these states, especially Latvia and Lithuania, had developed a rich cultural and religious heritage uninterrupted by years of harsh Communist rule. Thus by the time of the 1967 Six-Day War these Jews had faced a much shorter period of antireligious and anti-Semitic repression, had a much deeper sense of their Jewish identity, and were much more Zionist-oriented than Jews from the heartland, from which only about 15 percent of these early emigrants came.

Jewish activist Viktor Yakhot explained the paradox of this early period: most Soviet Jews who sought to emigrate led easier lives as Jews than those who decided to stay:

> The fact of the matter is that this is primarily a movement of Jews to Israel, not from the U.S.S.R. From this alone it follows that the movement is in no way based on anti-Sovietism. . . .
>
> Georgian Jews have no serious visible reasons for wishing to be repatriated other than national feeling. The Georgian and Baltic Jews have a

> deep sense of Jewish identity. They have never forgotten their Jewishness. They have never aspired to contribute to the cultures of other peoples at the expense of their own national identity. . . .
>
> On the other hand, the Jews of Russia and the Ukraine, having escaped from the Pale, built themselves an idol—education. They achieved this, and stopped being Jews and feeling like Jews. . . .
>
> Jewish intellectuals who understand the laws of nature, world history, and the psychology of other peoples did not understand themselves. They wanted to believe that they belonged to the world. The Georgian Jews, on the other hand, who definitely lagged behind in education, knew only that they belonged to the Jewish community, felt they were part of something that belonged to them. The intellectuals turned out to be spiritually empty despite their high cultural level.

Soon, however, according to Yakhot, these highly educated Jews strove to make up for lost time and thus began, in the words of activist Alexander Voronel, "the humanization of the scientific and technological elite."[4] Although there was a discernible pattern as to which Jews wanted to leave in this period, there was no corresponding one regarding whom the regime allowed to leave. Moreover, there were no published laws or regulations which would-be emigrants could follow. This uncertainty of selection soon became a prickly thorn in the side of the Jewish emigration movement.

Although the 1967 war was the major spark of emigration, other events, both internal and external, also had a significant effect on Soviet Jews. First, during the months right after this war when there was no emigration, the regime launched a major anti-Zionist propaganda campaign. Soviet Jews had been scarred by previous campaigns, but they were stung more by this one, which coincided with a disturbing increase of anti-Semitic discrimination in employment and admission into institutes of higher education.

Second, many Jewish activists who had admired the fledgling Soviet human rights movement and the more mature civil rights movement in the United States became attracted to the newborn human rights movement in the U.S.S.R. The beginning of this Soviet movement is usually considered to be December 5 (Soviet Constitution Day), 1965, when the first "Respect the Constitution" demonstration took place in Moscow's Pushkin Square. One reason for this demonstration was the arrest in September of writers Yuli Daniel and Andrei Sinyavsky. In January

1966, Daniel and Sinyavsky were convicted of "anti-Soviet agitation and propaganda" (under Article 70 of the R.S.F.S.R. Criminal Code). This was the first time the regime had brought criminal charges against anyone for literary criticism of the Soviet system.[5] The New Soviet leaders evidently were determined to reverse the trend of cultural liberalism and de-Stalinization which had developed under Khrushchev. The court cited as evidence the writers' publications, published illegally outside the country *(tamizdat)*. These literary dissidents, aware of the Kremlin's condemnation of Boris Pasternak for illegally publishing *Doctor Zhivago* abroad,[6] had hoped to remain anonymous by using pseudonyms. Daniel, who is Jewish, adopted the pen name Nikolai Arzhak. Sinyavsky, a non-Jew, chose the pen name Abram Tertz, who was a Jewish hero of an old Odessa song, because "I was educated in the period of the struggle against cosmopolitanism. I understood and adopted Marina Tsvetayeva's aphorism: 'In this most Christian of worlds, the poets are Jews.' A poet is an outcast evoking indignation and jeers and, in the broad sense of the term, a writer, as I understood him, is an alien."[7]

The pen-name ruse failed to save Daniel and Sinyavsky from receiving harsh prison camp sentences. Daniel got five years and Sinyavsky seven. The Kremlin's bullying tactics to stifle dissent, however, had only a limited effect on intellectuals. In May 1969 the first Soviet human rights association, the Initiative Group to Defend Human Rights in the U.S.S.R., was formed in Moscow. On November 4, 1970 the Committee for Human Rights in the U.S.S.R. was founded.

Developments in Poland and Czechoslovakia in 1968 led many Soviet Jews to consider emigration rather than hope for democratic reform of the Soviet system. The Polish Communist Party under Wladyslaw Gomulka had blamed Polish Jews for its policy failures and the disquieting "March events." It then expelled most of the remaining Polish Jews. Many left on Israeli visas.[8] According to Gomulka's speech on March 22, which was printed in full by *Pravda,* there were many "Polish citizens" not "tied to Poland by feeling and reason but to the State of Israel. . . . I suppose that this category of Jews is going to leave our country sooner or later . . . so we are ready to give emigration passports [to Jews who consider Israel their homeland]." Some Soviet Jews, aroused by what they called "the Gomulka variant," hoped that the Kremlin might decide to get rid of its "troublesome Jews" in the same manner.[9] After seeing Soviet troops invade Czechoslovakia and quash the liberalization movement, some Soviet Jews still were determined to work for liberalization in the U.S.S.R., but most became disillusioned with this approach and decided on emigration as their best alternative.

Two separate abortive attempts by Jews to leave the Soviet Union had a major impact during this period of "Jewish revival." In the summer of 1968, Boris Kochubievsky, an engineer from Kiev, and his new Russian wife, Larisa, applied to emigrate to Israel. *(See Reading 6.)* They received visas in November, but in a matter of weeks they were charged with "anti-Soviet slander." Larisa remained faithful to Boris. Although Larisa was not tried, she was expelled from the Pedagogical Institute and Komsomol. Moreover, her parents rejected her. Boris's trial was held on May 13, 1969, ironically in the same courtroom where Mendel Beilis had been acquitted in 1913 on the charge of ritualistic murder of a Christian child. Boris was found guilty and was sentenced to three years in forced labor camp. Proceedings of his trial, published in the newly founded *samizdat* journal *Chronicle of Current Events,* sent shock waves through the budding Jewish freedom movement and the West.

A foiled hijacking plan in 1970 caused an even greater furor. Nine Soviet Jews, along with two non-Jews, despairing of their lives inside the U.S.S.R., planned to hijack a plane in Leningrad and fly to Israel. They were caught on June 15, as they waited to board their plane. Concurrently, the KGB arrested approximately two hundred persons in Riga, Odessa, Kharkov, Kishinev, and Kiev.

The Leningrad hijacking trial opened on December 15.[10] At the same time, Soviet propagandists tried to whip up the populace into an anti-Semitic frenzy. Meetings held in Soviet factories clamored that "the bandits [must] receive exemplary punishment." The defendants were even told that "the people threatened to invade the prison where they were being held and lynch them." The prosecutor was Ivan Solovyov, the same man who had orchestrated the sentencing to death of five Jews in 1960 for their "economic crimes." This time the government's charge was "treason," which under Article 64-A of the R.S.F.S.R. Criminal Code is punishable by death. After a ten-day trial two of the defendants, Eduard Kuznetsov and Mark Dymshits, received the death sentence. *(See Reading 7.)* This was an incredibly harsh sentence considering their "crime" of wanting to go to Israel and its circumstances. In fact, this was the first death sentence for a political crime in the post-Stalin era. The other defendants were sentenced to long, strict-regimen terms in labor camps.[11]

The Leningrad trial alarmed the Soviet Jewish movement for freedom. *(See Reading 8.)* Reaction inside the Soviet Union by Jewish and non-Jewish activists (notably Valery Chalidze and Andrei Sakharov) was very sharp. The trial also received unprecedented international attention. Western governments, the Vatican, and even Western Communist parties expressed their indignation. *L'Humanité* (the organ of the French Communist Party), for example, issued this hard-hitting criticism: "We don't believe that an abortive attempt should be penalized by a death sentence which we hope—and we say it again—will not be applied. It is almost unnecessary to say that French Communists, who respect a German Jew named Karl Marx, are resolutely against anti-Semitism which is stupidity and a degradation."[12]

The Kremlin finally had to back off. In January 1971, after reviewing the case, the authorities commuted the two death sentences to fifteen years in a labor camp and reduced the sentences of three others as well. Yet in the spring, similar trials of Jewish *aliyah* activists (those who wanted to emigrate to Israel) in Leningrad and other Soviet cities (mainly Moscow, Riga, Vilnius, Kharkov, Kiev, and Tbilisi), caused further dismay among Jews in the U.S.S.R. and the West. Activists like Hebrew teacher Hillel Butman of Leningrad were charged with treason and dealt harsh sentences in a strict-regimen labor camp. Others, like Ruth Alexandrovich of Riga, were given lighter sentences. Her "crime" was handing out copies of her brochures "For the Return of Soviet Jews to their Homeland" and "Your Native Tongue" (in Hebrew). All these trials further galvanized Soviet Jewish activists whose protests were at least partially responsible for the Kremlin's new policy shift on emigration.

Period II: Hope and Despair (1971–1979)

In the spring of 1971 Soviet authorities decided to allow significantly large numbers of Soviet Jews to emigrate. A major domestic reason was to deflate the impact of growing internal dissent. So in addition to increasing opportunities for emigration, the Kremlin also shipped some leading activists (Jewish and non-Jewish) out of the country. This decision also gave the U.S.S.R. some unique espionage activities. As dissident Zhores Medvedev observed about a decade later: "This method of dealing with dissidents not only cleared the Soviet Union of active dissent—it also gave the KGB excellent opportunities of infiltrating various emigre organizations, anti-Soviet propaganda centers, and academic institutions."[13] The other reason lay in foreign policy: The Kremlin wanted to win some "propaganda points" with the United States in a period of budding détente.

Scholars of Soviet Jewry are divided over whether fluctuations in the rate of Jewish emigration are related more to foreign or domestic policies.[14] Evidence suggests that their interplay determines decisions on emigration. These decisions seem to be made on a year-to-year, month-to-month, and even an individual basis in high-profile cases.

During the period of hope and despair, Soviet Jewish activists faced three key dilemmas over strategy and tactics, both in dealing with the Kremlin and their own ranks:

1. Should they work with and utilize the strategies and tactics of the growing Soviet human rights movement?
2. Should they decrease, maintain, or increase the level of "noise" for publicity, at home and abroad?
3. Should they focus primarily on emigration or on freedom to practice Judaism?

Soviet human rights groups gathered strength and momentum in the early and mid-1970s. In addition to the groups already organized, Amnesty International formed a Moscow chapter in 1973. Most important, however, in terms of size and scope of action, were the Helsinki Watch Groups, which originated in Moscow on May 12, 1976, almost a year after the signing of the Helsinki Accords. Soon other watch groups sprang up in Lithuania, the Ukraine, Armenia, and Georgia. Members of these groups were acting on a centrally important right guaranteed for the first time in history by the Helsinki Accords. According to Principle VII (Respect for Human Rights and Fundamental Freedoms, including the Freedom of Thought, Conscience, Religion or Belief), the signatory states "confirm the right of the individual to know and act upon his rights and duties in this field." The main goal of these groups was to document and publicize Soviet human rights abuses to the West, which they hoped would pressure the U.S.S.R. to abide by the international human rights pacts to which it was a party. Eventually more than a hundred persons joined these groups, which included leading activists in the Soviet Jewish emigration movement. This would ensure a broad base of human rights participation. These groups operated until 1982, when they were forced to disband by Soviet authorities.

Soviet specialist Peter Reddaway suggests that the authorities allowed these organizations to develop because they were concerned about their negative international image after their invasion of Czechoslovakia in 1968. They also felt the KGB could contain any serious threat to control. Yet the Kremlin underestimated their strength. Surely Moscow did not expect the Soviet Jewish freedom movement to become such a powerful force both domestically and internationally.[15] Indeed, as noted previously, Soviet Jews themselves were surprised at how fast their movement grew.

Starting in the late 1960s, Soviet Jewish activists tended to copy methods of both American and Soviet human rights advocates. They urged the regime to abide by the Soviet Constitution, domestic laws, and international agreements it had signed; they staged demonstrations and sit-ins while categorically rejecting violence; and through *samizdat* and *tamizdat* they communicated ideas, information, and materials among themselves and to the West.

Samizdat publications were especially important to the Soviet Jewish freedom movement in the 1970s. This material was designed to inform Soviet Jews and their friends of significant developments in the movement, such as new regulations, trials, and so on. It also provided a forum for learning about Judaism and served as an outlet for various individuals to express their views.

Literary *samizdat* predated Jewish *samizdat*. Hand-copied and individually typed reproductions of officially banned manuscripts, such as Pasternak's *Doctor Zhivago,* circulated in the late 1950s. The first *samizdat* journal, *Syntax,* a collection of poetry compiled by Alexander Ginsburg, began in 1960. Jewish *samizdat* traces its origins to the publication in the U.S.S.R. in the early 1960s of Leon Uris's *Exodus,* which had a powerful effect.[16] The first human rights journal, the *Chronicle of Current Events,* began in 1968. This journal, *samizdat* by necessity, carried significant amounts of material on Jewish activists. It was published every year until

1983, when pressure from the regime forced it to stop. In 1973, Khronika Press in New York began a companion journal, a *Chronicle of Human Rights in the USSR.* Its editor was Valery Chalidze. Chalidze believed in the unity of the human rights and Jewish freedom movements, and he was a leader in both.

In 1969, Hillel Butman organized the All-Union Coordinating Committee in Leningrad to plan Jewish *samizdat.*[17] *Samizdat* began in earnest in 1970 with the publication in Riga of *Iton Aleph* and *Iton Bet* (Hebrew: *Journal 1* and 2). These journals contained articles on Jewish subjects, translations of Israeli authors, and other items of interest to the Jewish freedom movement. More *samizdat* publications soon appeared. *Iskhod (Exodus),* edited by Viktor Fedoseyev and patterned after the *Chronicle of Current Events,* was published in Moscow in 1970 and 1971. Four issues, dealing largely with emigration, carried messages, appeals, petitions, statements, accounts of house searches, and texts of relevant laws. Issue number 4, published in February 1971, contained the transcript of proceedings of the Leningrad hijacking trial of December 1970. Three issues of *Vestnik Iskhoda (Herald of the Exodus),* edited by Boris Orlov and others, came out in 1971 and 1972, providing information on various activities of Jewish activists such as demonstrations and hunger strikes. *Belaya Kniga Iskhoda (The White Book of the Exodus),* edited by Roman Rutman and others, was published twice in Moscow in 1972. The first edition carried articles with advice to those Jews who had applied for an exit visa or were contemplating applying for one; the second carried appeals for aid from President Nixon just prior to his visit to Moscow in the spring of 1972. *Evrei v SSSR (Jews in the USSR),* edited by Voronel and Yakhot, began in December 1972 and was published sporadically until the authorities shut it down in June 1979. This series of essays discussed Jewish culture and identity. The Hebrew language *Tarbut (Culture),* begun in 1975 in Moscow as a supplement to *Jews in the USSR,* generally covered the same ground. Soon it too was forced to cease publication.

By the early 1970s, Soviet Jewish activists began to use more bold, militant, and dangerous techniques of protest. They challenged the authorities in a very daring way and went beyond what the Soviet human rights movement was doing.[18] They communicated to the West by phone and smuggled tape-recorded documents out of the country. They issued mass petitions, signed by large numbers of Jews from cities throughout the country. They staged demonstrations at memorials such as Babi Yar in Kiev,[19] outside synagogues on Saturdays and Jewish holidays, at the doors of OVIR offices, and in front of the Lenin Library in Moscow. Angered by the Leningrad hijacking trial and follow-up trials designed to intimidate the Jewish movement, Jewish activists began hunger strikes and sit-ins, tactics they later used regularly. On March 10–11, 1971, for example, fifty-six Jews from Riga staged a hunger demonstration in the reception room of the Presidium of the U.S.S.R. Supreme Soviet, near the Kremlin and Red Square. The strikers conveyed their sorrowful stories to Western reporters. Western short-wave radio broadcasted the blow-by-blow account of this demonstration. Police finally cleared the room. The demonstrators shocked the authorities, who soon gave all of them exit visas. *(See Reading 9.)* In the aftermath of this hunger strike and demonstration, the Kremlin's policy toward refuseniks toughened. Yet this change did not deter other Jewish activists, some of whom renounced their Soviet citizenship, and in some cases proclaimed they were Israeli citizens.

Jewish activists generally operated within their constitutional rights and Soviet law. They tried to bring attention to their demands, both inside and outside the U.S.S.R., to encourage wider Jewish participation in the movement, and to informally communicate news of the movement to Soviet Jews and the West (who was allowed to emigrate, who was refused and why, when Congressional delegations would be visiting). During this period the "internationalization" of the movement grew dramatically.

The Kremlin, meanwhile, rejected the call of Jewish activists for a clear, consistent, rational, fair, and publicly announced procedure on emigration. The authorities continued to keep the movement off balance by acting in a seemingly whimsical, arbitrary, and inconsistent manner. Witness this testy, frustrating encounter on October 26, 1972, between a group of about one hundred would-be Jewish emigrants and Boris Shumilin, acting Minister of the Interior:

> *A. Voronel:* You spoke about some sort of limitations. It is still not clear what limitations precisely and on what persons they are imposed. This has not been published anywhere.

Minister Shumilin: And this will not be published; this will be decided in every individual case by our organs on the spot, the organs of the OVIR.

Voronel: But the thing is that not only we, but the inspectors of the OVIR do not know either what places of work are advantageous for us, and which are not. . . . There should be at least a single instruction under the guidance of which this matter should be discussed. And it should not be decided by an OVIR inspector who knows nothing.

Minister Shumilin: . . . Each of you has been given an answer [to a request for a visa].

Voices from the hall: No answer has been given!

Minister Shumilin: You are not satisfied with the contents of the answer?

Voices from the hall: There were no contents and no explanations!

Minister Shumilin: But you have been told "No." This is the answer. A good, comprehensible laconic answer.

Voronel: As a lawyer you should understand that any explanatory answer means that it would be before us and we could appeal against it. Only that would be a document. But none of us has such a document. We cannot appeal against anything.

Slepak: Yesterday I talked with the Head of the OVIR of the U.S.S.R., Verein. The only thing he told me was that my emigration was not in the interest of the state. Without any explanation. And he also added that I am a traitor.

Voronel: You demand from us that we should rely on your kindness or on the kindness of some other official. But we want to rely on the law.

Minister Shumilin: In this matter there exists one main and basic law: We decided for what term a person should be detained if his departure will cause detriment to the interest of the state.

Voices from the hall: This is arbitrary rule![20]

Arbitrary decisions on emigration and dissident activities continued. Soviet authorities allowed some leading activists, like Professor Vitaly

Rubin to leave, but prevented others, like Professor Alexander Lerner. They ignored some protest activities but cracked down hard on others.

The decade of the 1970s saw surprisingly high figures of Jewish emigration. Soviet leaders sought to release some steam, rid themselves of "troublesome" activists, silence critics in the West, present a better international image, further detente, and obtain trade concessions from the United States. Although many Soviet Jews emigrated, an increasing number became refuseniks. Never before in any country had there developed such a large, identifiable group of citizens denied the right to emigrate and forced to suffer for their efforts. Never before had a government created such a group of outcasts in their own country, whose only "crime" was their quest for freedom.

In the early 1970s, Soviet leaders imposed punishing new restraints on emigration by raising its cost. At the end of 1970, the Kremlin increased the price of a passport from forty to four hundred rubles. Soviet citizens had to pay an additional five hundred rubles if they renounced their citizenship. And on August 3, 1972, the state imposed a "diploma tax" that required payment of a fee, on a sliding scale in accordance with one's academic degree. The Kremlin felt compelled to drop this requirement on March 19, 1973, after intensive pressure from the United States, although it still kept it on the books.

Soviet Jewish activists never fully or clearly resolved the issue of whether to work with the human rights movement or go it alone. In general, human rights advocates supported the Jewish emigration movement, as emigration was a basic human right. Non-Jewish human rights leaders like Sakharov, Chalidze, and Viktor Fedoseyev were especially vocal in support of Jewish activists, issuing appeals in their behalf. Soviet Jewish leaders, however, only partially reciprocated support for the human rights movement.

At one extreme, some Jewish activists, like David Drabkin, a Zionist from Moscow, sought to avoid all contact with the human rights movement. They argued their main goal was to leave the U.S.S.R., not to reform the Soviet system. Furthermore, they felt that the situation of Soviet Jews was distinctive for a unique blend of reasons: Jews were discriminated against much more than other religious or nationality minorities; they had their homeland outside the U.S.S.R.; and they could receive significant, sharply focused support from Jewish advocacy groups, Western tourists, Israel, and Western governments, especially the United States. Finally, this group of Jewish activists did not want to give the authorities real ammunition to charge them with collaboration with dissidents and thereby provoke more serious attacks by the state.

Other Jewish activists like Mikhail Zand, however, decided to cooperate with the human rights movement. They believed that the Jewish struggle for freedom was intrinsically part of the broader struggle. But they were unsure whether publicity about their activities would help or harm their cause. Some joined the various Helsinki Watch groups. The most influential was the Moscow group, the first association to have both human rights and Jewish activist members in significant numbers. The Helsinki Act, which included reaffirmation of the right to reunification of families, became a rallying cry for several distinguished Jewish leaders. Activists like Vladimir Slepak, Vitaly Rubin, and Viktor Yelistratov from Moscow, and the Goldstein brothers, Isai and Grigory, from Tbilisi, joined non-Jewish activists like Yuri Orlov, chairman of the Moscow group, and General Pyotr Grigorenko, a longtime opponent of the Kremlin dictatorship.

One of the most important Jewish members of the Moscow group was Anatoly Shcharansky. He insisted that he was always for human rights and never against the Soviet government. Shcharansky was seen as the main link between the Jewish freedom and human rights movements and the major communicator between both movements and the West. It was Shcharansky who translated into English for Sakharov and other activists during conferences with Western newspeople, government officials, and tourists. Shcharansky also piqued the authorities by his particularly sharp, barbed, and irritating manner. So when they decided to lash out at the watch groups, Shcharansky was an obvious target.

Early in 1977, Soviet authorities arrested key Jewish activists, including Shcharansky, Lerner, Slepak, Iosif Begun, and Ida Nudel. *(See Reading 10.)* They also arrested non-Jewish human rights leaders, among them Orlov and Ginsburg. Ginsburg was Jewish on his mother's side but he was a believer in the Russian Orthodox Church. All had been very active in the watch groups. At a meeting in Belgrade in the fall of 1977, organized to review compliance with the Helsinki Accords, representatives from the United States and other Western governments besieged the Soviet delegation with questions about the detained human rights activists. A couple of months after the close of this conference, in March

1978, the Kremlin put these activists on trial. Their conviction on trumped-up charges and subsequent imprisonment shocked the human rights and Jewish freedom movements. Shcharansky, perhaps, became the best-known "prisoner of Zion" (a Soviet Jew imprisoned for activities related to emigration, religious practice, or cultural observance). Shcharansky's final statement at his trial reflected his defiance of the regime, his courage, and determination to continue fighting for his cause. *(See Reading 11.)* His name, kept in the diplomatic spotlight by his wife Avital *(see Reading 12)* and others, became a rallying cry for advocates of Soviet Jews.

The plight of the convicted Jewish leaders triggered the involvement of new Jewish activists. In June, a group of women refuseniks in Moscow, dismayed by the horrendous treatment of their fathers, husbands, and sons, stood up to Soviet authorities by demonstrating at the Kremlin Wall. *(See Reading 13.)* They were also supporting Ida Nudel, the "guardian angel" of "prisoners of Zion," who was convicted on charges of "malicious hooliganism." Nudel's "crime" was hanging a banner outside her Moscow apartment which carried a yellow star of David and her plea: "KGB, give me a visa for Israel." *(See Readings 14 and 15.)* These demonstrations were put down, but they sent an important message to Soviet leaders that woman refuseniks would no longer remain silent. They too had to be reckoned with.

Moscow seemed impervious to internal and external pressure from human rights activists. The Kremlin seemed bent on sending a signal that it would not countenance cooperation between the human rights and Jewish freedom movements. By the end of the 1970s, pressure by the state had led most Jewish activists to withdraw from the human rights movement because of the danger involved. Some refuseniks, however, did join a new organization. The Group to Establish Trust Between the U.S.S.R. and the U.S.A., which originated on June 4, 1982, in Moscow and other major cities, was an unofficial independent peace group that, unlike all other Soviet human rights groups, by and large escaped repression by the state. Survival was achieved partially by downplaying political issues and partially by aligning with Western peace groups, especially in Western Europe.[21] The Moscow Trust group included refuseniks from its inception, but it never became as influential as the Moscow Helsinki group, which from 1976 to 1982 was essentially "the only game in town."

Priority of Emigration or Cultural Revival

During the 1970s, the Jewish freedom movement was divided not only over cooperation with the human rights movement but also over its focus. Its leaders were unsure whether to concentrate more on Jewish cultural revival or on emigration. *(See Reading 16.)* The major disagreement seemed more over timing than either-or goals. Proponents of "cultural revival first" felt that Soviet Jews had to know their heritage before they could decide whether to emigrate. This group, led by Viktor Brailovsky, Mark Azbel, Iosif Begun, and Viktor Yakhot, wrote deeply spiritual, often hortatory essays in *Jews in the USSR* and *Tarbut*, and they held seminars and symposia on Jewish culture and formed groups to study Hebrew. The authorities continued their capricious handling of these activities. Sometimes they ignored them but at other times, such as with the cultural seminar planned for December 1976, they suppressed them.

A major aim of this "cultural revival first" group was to develop a sense of Jewish consciousness and provide a Jewish education to both adults and children. To this end, for instance, they set up a Jewish kindergarten in Moscow. They expected that once Soviet Jews learned about their Jewish identity, they would be more eager to emigrate. Some Jews, like mathematician Ilya Essas, believed that cultural seminars alone were not enough to overcome years of cultural and religious deprivation. They felt that Soviet Jews could not sufficiently learn about their religion and traditions without learning Hebrew. As Essas explained in 1979: "The spiritual life in the Soviet Union is non-existent. We have only one ideology. You can believe it or not. For a young Jew, it is natural for him to turn to his own background, to find out about his own religion. And a Jew cannot know his background without knowing Hebrew. It is the principle [sic] thing in Judaism. No translation can give you the knowledge. It can only give you the smell."[22] Thus he and others, like Begun, Leonid Volvosky, and Yuli Kosharovsky, learned Hebrew by themselves or in underground classes and then taught others, who in turn taught still others. They succeeded, despite harassment and imprisonment by the authorities, who were determined to stop their activities. When these Hebrew teachers tried to earn their livelihood through teaching Hebrew, the authorities told them they could not because teaching Hebrew was not a legitimate profession. Not able to teach Hebrew legally and denied the chance to find work in their chosen field, a right granted by the Constitution, they were forced to take menial jobs such as stoker of a furnace.[23] Without a job they faced charges of "parasitism," for which they could be imprisoned.

The "cultural revival first" group felt that the destination of Soviet Jews should be Israel. This group was very concerned about the growing number of Soviet Jewish *noshrim* (dropouts) who were starting to emigrate elsewhere, especially the U.S.A. They hoped, unrealistically, that cultural seminars and the study of Hebrew would reverse this trend.

During the 1970s and continuing through the 1980s, the percentage of dropouts became a sensitive, divisive issue among Soviet Jews and Soviet Jewish advocacy groups in the West and between the United States and Israel. In the period of "Jewish revival" (1967–1970), *noshrim* accounted for only about 5 percent of Jewish emigration. By 1976 this figure had shot up to about 49 percent, and by 1978 it was over 58 percent. By 1981 *noshrim* had soared to 81.4 percent. By the late 1980s about 90 percent of Jews who left the Soviet Union were *noshrim.*

There are several explanations for the dropout phenomenon. First, there was an initial euphoria and a spurt of Zionist feeling among Soviet Jews after the 1967 war that inspired many to leave for Israel. As already noted, most of these Jews, who came from the Baltic states and Georgia, where Judaism was comparatively strong, were highly disposed toward Zionism. Jews who emigrated in the mid- to late 1970s and the 1980s came more from the heartland cities. They were much less knowledgeable about their Jewish heritage, much more assimilated, and much less imbued with Zionist feelings.

Second, the 1973 Yom Kippur war revealed Israeli military, political, and societal weaknesses. Visions of living in an Israeli utopia disappeared. Soviet Jews began to see real problems with living in Israel that were accentuated and greatly exaggerated by Soviet propaganda. They also read letters from Soviet Jewish emigres in Israel who talked of serious problems there, such as absorption, which was never easy. As the years went by, the absorption problem worsened considerably. In the words of Paula Gorodetsky, a well-educated middle-class Jew who emigrated to Israel in 1985 and who was still in the overcrowded Gilo absorption center in September 1989, when increasingly large numbers of Soviet Jews were arriving monthly: "We were Zionist Jews in Leningrad. We recently wanted to come here, and in my opinion all Jews should come.

But now I don't think this is possible. This is a small state and it can't solve the problem of housing and unemployment. It's very difficult here. It's not really for everyone."[24] Thus many Soviet Jews (especially before 1989), realizing the difficulties of life in Israel, had looked first to countries in the West, particularly the United States.

Third, the Soviet anti-Semitic campaign and discriminatory policies intensified in the 1970s. Increasing numbers of Jews, who believed they could no longer make a successful career in the Soviet Union, began to see emigration as a necessity. The United States, the historic haven for Russian Jews, seemed once again "the land of opportunity" where they could fulfill their dream of financial success and lead a Jewish life as well, should they wish to do so. As more Soviet Jews went to the United States, they paved the way for relatives and friends to join them later. This initial increased emigration thus had a snowball or suctioning effect.

Fourth, the number of Soviet Jews who left Israel *(yordim)* began to grow. A very small number returned to the Soviet Union, but most went to countries in the West. Again, the Soviet media seized on and dramatized this development, always reminding Soviet Jews how bad life was in Israel. News about the *yordim* also reached Soviet Jews from Israeli and Western news sources as well as from relatives abroad. This further dampened enthusiasm for emigration to Israel.

Fifth, Soviet Jews realized that if they went directly to the United States (via way stations in Vienna and Rome), they could enter as refugees, which for economic and political reasons was a more desirable status than immigrant. They also knew they could always go to Israel from the United States. But if they went to Israel first and then decided to go to the United States, they would have to enter the United States as immigrants. This whole situation changed in the fall of 1989, however, with the introduction by the United States of new immigration regulations that made it harder for Soviet Jews to go to the United States.[25]

Finally, when seeking support for their freedom movement, Soviet Jews found Israeli efforts lacking. Some also were annoyed at Israel's insistence on being their only destination. They thus began to lean heavily on the diplomatic help of the United States. They had growing awareness that Jewish emigration was being tied more closely to U.S.–Soviet relations, to increased activities and effectiveness of Soviet Jewry advocacy groups in the West, and to public pronouncements by American presidents urging Moscow to curb its human rights abuses.

The "emigration first" group focused on emigration to any country Soviet Jews wished, although it hoped their choice would be Israel. This group, led by Shcharansky, the Slepaks, and Professors Lerner and Rubin, was larger and more influential among Soviet Jews than the group that concentrated on cultural revival. Generally speaking, the "emigration first" group believed it was not the best use of time and energy to teach Soviet Jews how to practice their religion. It felt Soviet society and the state were too hostile to Jews for any meaningful religious or cultural practice. Tactically, this group concentrated on contacting Western governments and advocacy groups; lobbying for the passage and continuation of the Jackson–Vanik Amendment, which it felt effectively put pressure on Moscow to liberalize its emigration policy; and meeting with official and unofficial Western visitors.

Soviet Jews from both major groups hoped that the large numbers of Jewish emigrants would continue and even increase in the 1980s. They were to be bitterly disappointed, however; the years 1980 to 1986 saw both sharply reduced emigration and markedly increased repression against Jewish activists.

Period III: Reversal of Large-Scale Emigration (1980–1986)

Soviet Jewish emigration peaked in 1979, with more than 51,000 leaving. This figure dropped precipitously over the next few years, reaching a low of 896 in 1984. The numbers for the next two years, 1140 in 1985 and 914 in 1986, were not much better. Why did this dramatic drop occur? Once again we must look at a mixture of international and domestic factors.

International Events Affecting Emigration

The Soviet invasion of Afghanistan in December 1979 set off a chain of events that led to the demise of detente and a growing chill in U.S.–Soviet relations. The U.S. Senate decided not to ratify SALT II, signed earlier that year in Vienna by General Secretary Leonid Brezhnev and

President Jimmy Carter, and not to waive the Jackson–Vanik Amendment. President Carter, moreover, led the Western boycott of the summer Olympics held in Moscow in 1980. Washington also set severe limits on U.S. technology transfer and placed an embargo on grain sales to the U.S.S.R. When Ronald Reagan became President, the United States sent a further message to the Kremlin that the U.S. would maintain a harder line toward the "evil empire." And when the Soviets shot down KAL 007 in 1983, Washington expressed public outrage over the incident, even after it realized that Soviet pilots probably mistook this plane for a U.S. military aircraft. Indeed, it seemed that the days of the cold war had returned.

The Israeli invasion of Lebanon in 1982 also influenced Moscow's policy toward the Jews. U.S. military intervention in Lebanon soon followed Israel's, and in Moscow's eyes the United States was actually calling the shots there.[26] The U.S.S.R. felt it had to show its major clients in the Middle East, Syria and the PLO, some sign of support. A virtual shutdown of Soviet Jewish emigration, already sharply curtailed the preceding two years, could be seen as an acceptable diplomatic response.

During the early 1980s Soviet government spokespersons conveyed the impression that the temperature of U.S.–Soviet relations had a major effect on the flow of Jewish emigration. In November 1980, for example, Sergei Kondrashin, Soviet spokesman at a closed session of the Madrid Conference—which, like the Belgrade Conference a couple of years before, was a follow-up to the Helsinki Accords—suggested that Soviet Jews wanting to emigrate were hostages to changing conditions of détente. And the next day he said: "the level of détente determines the pace of 'Basket Three' implementation."[27]

Domestic Determinants of the Scale of Emigration

Despite Kondrashin's contention, designed largely for Western consumption, Soviet domestic considerations were probably more important in formulating policy on restriction of Jewish emigration. There is evidence that well before the Soviet invasion of Afghanistan the Kremlin had decided to curtail emigration drastically and to crack down on "troublesome" Jews because of internal political and economic factors. In a report completed in December 1979 *(See Reading 17)*, several leading refuseniks predicted an increase in the number of Jews wanting to emigrate. Yet they also pointed to a number of developments threatening to reduce emigration. These included a more ominous intensification of hostile propaganda against Jewish activists in the wake of the trials of 1978, a more blatant increase in discrimination barring Jewish applicants from the most prestigious institutes of higher education, and harsher barriers to the emigration process.

The OVIR, in fact, began instituting new requirements on emigration in May 1979. Furthermore, two months earlier Alexander Lerner pointed out in an interview that news of the softening of Soviet emigration policy was "a deep illusion" that did "not correspond to reality at all." To buttress his observation he pointed out that in the previous year the number of refusals had grown more quickly than the number of successful applicants. Reacting negatively to U.S. spokesman Hodding Carter's comment that Soviet Jewish emigration had significantly improved the past year, Lerner concluded: "a substantial improvement would be if 1000 people asked to leave and 1000 people were allowed to leave." Andrei Sakharov also chastised Carter, pointing out that "such disinformation of the public is extremely harmful."[28] Still other human rights activists were cognizant of the complaint in January 1979 by Helsinki Watch groups that the Kremlin had stepped up arrests and harassment of visa applicants.

Peter Reddaway suggests that this crackdown was actually the result of a decision by the Politburo as early as 1977 to repress dissent in general.[29] Supposedly by the end of 1976, the Kremlin had decided "to show strength and not pay attention to the West." But according to Reddaway, the trials of Shcharansky et al. notwithstanding, the Soviets "beat a retreat" in the wake of "an unprecedented outcry of world condemnation," especially by newly elected President Carter, who made human rights a cornerstone of his foreign policy. In 1979, Kremlin leaders decided to try to milk détente for an agreement on SALT II and an award of most-favored-nation (MFN) treatment in trade. Furthermore, in April of that year, on the day he was named president of the U.S.S.R., Brezhnev released several political prisoners, including some from the Leningrad hijacking trial of December 1970.

But when the U.S. Senate did not reward Moscow with MFN by a waiver of the Jackson–Vanik Amendment (to the Kremlin's chagrin, the U.S. gave MFN status to the Chinese People's Republic) and looked like it was foot-dragging on ratification of SALT II, the Kremlin decided that it was time to limit the flood of Jewish emigrants, which it felt could threaten its grip over Soviet society, and to repress dissent in general. The Kremlin wanted (among other things) to reduce the possibility of disruption of the Moscow Olympics. The KGB, evidently, would finally gets its way: The regime would try to break the back of Soviet dissidents by stark repression. On January 22, 1980, the regime exiled Sakharov to Gorky after his protests about the invasion of Afghanistan. Over the next two years the authorities suppressed almost all human rights groups and publications. In this period, Jewish activists and other human rights leaders suffered almost alike.

This period of reversal of large-scale emigration saw an upsurge in internal security measures aimed at increasing control over the people. One can argue that reinforced internal security could have led either to increased emigration (get rid of problems and soften Western criticism), or to reduced emigration (make dissidents realize they must toe the line or face imprisonment). During this period, Soviet authorities opted to choke off emigration and even the desire to emigrate. They realized the former goal but not the latter.

Soviet leaders chose the emigration-restriction option partially, perhaps, because they faced serious economic problems, especially a very serious shortage of manpower and technical expertise. This problem may have been behind the pronouncement Brezhnev made in his speech to the 26th Congress of the CPSU in February 1981: "In our country, the national feeling and worth of every individual are respected. The CPSU has fought—and will always fight—decisively against such phenomena, which are alien to socialism, as chauvinism or nationalism, against any kind of nationalistic dislocations such, for example, as anti-Semitism and Zionism."[30] With this statement, intended to counteract anti-Semitism in the Soviet media, Brezhnev lamely tried to create the illusion that Jews would have equal opportunity and equal protection of the law and that henceforth they could lead normal lives as Soviet citizens and labor for Mother Russia.

After Brezhnev died in 1982, the new Soviet leadership under Yuri Andropov also stressed the need for improvement of the economy. Andropov called for higher productivity through hard work and less alcohol consumption and corruption. By further restricting emigration, perhaps he hoped that Soviet Jews might develop a Berlin-Wall mentality: They might resign themselves to the realization they might never emigrate, or at least they would not emigrate for an indefinite period, and thus start contributing more to the Soviet economy.

Following this line of thought, Soviet leaders tried to create an anti-emigration atmosphere. Through the media they attacked the emigration movement as an anti-Soviet gambit by the United States and Israel planned by greedy Jews who wanted to line their pockets with capitalist gold.[31] In November 1984, Leningrad television showed the documentary *Hirelings and Their Accomplices.* Like a similar program in 1976, *Traders of Souls,* faces of targeted refuseniks flashed across the screen. These refuseniks, and by implication all Soviet Jews, were portrayed as enemies of the state. Both television programs had at least this deleterious effect: Many Soviet Jews became victims of extra harassment on the job, at school, in the neighborhood, and from the police. Jews shown in the 1984 program, such as Lev Shapiro and Iosif Radomsylsky, suffered even more abuse and greater isolation.[32]

At the same time the Kremlin was telling the world that almost everyone who had asked to leave had received permission, except for those who held "state secrets." This exception became a very large catchall, ensnaring many an unfortunate applicant. A commentator for Radio Moscow added a new, ominous twist: "And speaking of Jewish emigration, I should say that the majority of those who wanted to leave have left."[33] This statement indicated a new Kremlin line toward emigration that became a major theme of the Anti-Zionist Committee of the Soviet Public, formed in April 1983. Members of this committee joined the Soviet media in trying to convince Soviet Jews that, in the words of veteran Soviet newsman Victor Louis, "the last train has left" and that Soviet Jews were better off for this. At the same time, the Soviet press stepped up its attacks on Judaism as a religion.

In the early 1980s a growing number of Jews, especially refuseniks, gathered in private homes to study Judaism, Jewish culture, and the Hebrew language. Some Soviet Jews had undertaken such activities in the 1970s, but with limited success because of repression by the authorities. As the number of refuseniks grew and as their period of refusal became extended, more and more wanted to learn about their Jewish traditions. One remarkable achievement was publication of a new *samizdat* journal called *Leningradskaya evreisky almanakh (Leningrad Jewish Almanac)*, whose first copy came out in September 1982. Its purpose was to replace the recently suppressed *Jews in the USSR* and *Tarbut.* Its first section, for instance, "Who Are We?," urged the approximately 140,000 Jews in Leningrad to turn from assimilation, which would amount to "national self-destruction," and seek knowledge of their Jewish heritage.[34] Jewish activists felt the need to search for their Jewish roots not only in preparation for the day they might emigrate but also for spiritual sustenance during times of extreme deprivation and stress.

In this same period Soviet authorities, operating without constraints of détente, began an unprecedented campaign of repression against Jewish cultural activists.[35] Among the most prominent victims were Viktor Brailovsky, Alexander Paritsky, and Iosif Begun. Brailovsky, editor of *Jews in the USSR* and leader of scientific seminars for refuseniks in Moscow, was arrested in November 1980 and sentenced to five years of exile. He was charged with defaming the Soviet state through his involvement with this *samizdat* journal. *(See Reading 18.)* Paritsky, berated by the Soviet press *(See Reading 19),* was arrested in August 1981, convicted in November on charges of anti-Soviet slander, and sentenced to three years in a hard-labor camp. His "crime" was organizing a "Jewish free university" for refuseniks in Kharkov, where they could study chemistry, physics, English, advanced mathematics, Hebrew, and Jewish history. The goal of this university, according to Edith Frankel, director of Hebrew University's Soviet–East European Research Center in Jerusalem, was to prepare students for the level of instruction they would experience in Israel once they emigrated there.[36] At this time, remember, Jews were increasingly discriminated against in admission to institutes of higher education and awarding of degrees. Refuseniks were even being stripped of their degrees and prevented from continuing their professional activities. Begun, a Moscow mathematician who was consistently denied permission to teach Hebrew after he was refused a visa in 1971, was arrested for the third time in November 1982. In June 1977 he was sentenced to two years in exile in Siberia for "parasitism," and soon after his release a year later he was sentenced to three years in Siberia for violating residency requirements. In October 1983, Begun was tried for "anti-Soviet agitation and propaganda." He was sentenced to seven years' hard labor and five years' internal exile. This was an unusually harsh sentence. It was the most severe since Shcharansky's in 1978 and was clearly intended as a warning to the Jewish emigration movement.

By late 1984, as part of a general assault against Jewish activists, the crackdown against unofficial Hebrew teachers and other cultural activists took an even more chilling turn. More and more activists were arrested. Some faced familiar charges of parasitism, draft evasion, malicious hooliganism, and anti-Soviet agitation and propaganda. For example, Zachar Zunsheine was convicted on June 28, 1984, in Riga of "defaming the Soviet state." His "crime" was demonstrating for a visa in front of the statue of Karl Marx on Revolution Square in Moscow with a placard that read WE DEMAND TO GIVE UP OUR SOVIET CITIZENSHIP. In July, Alexander Kholmyansky, a Moscow computer engineer, was charged first with hooliganism, and then in August falsely accused for possession of firearms. On August 10, Yakov Levin of Odessa was arrested and later found guilty under Article 187 of the Ukrainian Criminal code (equivalent to Article 190-1 of the R.S.F.S.R. Criminal Code) of "circulation of deliberately false fabrications slandering the Soviet state and social system."

Other Jewish activists were victims of new, trumped-up charges. On September 4 Yuli Edelstein was arrested and falsely accused of possession of drugs. In preparation for their arrest in October, on June 14 three Hebrew teachers from Odessa were vilified in an article by A. Svidnitsky in the Kiev paper *Rabochaya gazeta (Workers' Newspaper)*: "Yakov Mesh, Mark Nepomniashchy, and V. Boguslavsky have 'special merit' for the Zionists and 'special rights' to their moral and material support. . . . In their apartments, they organized group gatherings where, under the guise of studying Hebrew and Judaism, they openly indoctrinated those present with a Zionist, pro-Israeli spirit."[37] On November 12 Iosif Berenshtein was charged with resisting the authorities. Then, in early 1985, activists Dan Shapiro (January 22) and Roald Zelichenok (June 10) were charged with "anti-Soviet slander." After Shapiro's arrest, in their search of his home (supposedly for drugs) the authorities ripped off the *mezuzah* from his lintel and confiscated his phylacteries *(tefillin)*.

Jewish cultural activists, for the most part, did not bend under this onslaught of repression. They defied the regime by continuing to study Hebrew and conducting cultural and scientific seminars. They also kept up their letters of protest against the regime's violations of Soviet law, tried to make sure their supporters in the West kept up meaningful contact with them *(see Reading 20)*, and continued to send petitions for help from the West. In November 1984 they sent a particularly desperate appeal for help. *(See Reading 21.)*

When Gorbachev became general secretary in March 1985, Soviet human rights advocates looked for a softening in the regime's policy toward dissent and emigration. The first promising breakthrough occurred at the Geneva summit in December 1985, when Gorbachev and Reagan reached final agreement on the release of Shcharansky. Shcharansky was set free in February 1986 as part of a wider exchange of prisoners. Soviet Jews were hopeful that his release would herald the beginning of warmer U.S.–Soviet relations that might favorably affect them. Soon the words *perestroika* (restructuring, especially of the economy), *glasnost* (openness), and *democratizatsiya* (allowing the people some say in determining their own affairs, particularly in the workplace and politics) would be heard around the world. Winds of change began to blow, but how would they affect Soviet Jews?

Period IV: *Perestroika, Glasnost,* and *Democratizatsiya* (1986–1990)

Gorbachev's period of reform is the Kremlin's most sweeping and dynamic attempt at liberalization. Previous liberalization policies, such as Lenin's in the 1920s and Khrushchev's in the late 1950s and early 1960s, resulted not in lasting change but in temporary modifications of the system. Lenin introduced his New Economic Policy (NEP), marked by a return to some private enterprise and a foreign policy of "peaceful coexistence" with the West, when he realized the devastation Russia had suffered from World War I and its exhaustive civil war as well as its diplomatic isolation imposed by the victorious capitalist countries. After Lenin died in 1924, the Soviet Union fell into a long period of Communist orthodoxy under the iron fist of Stalin. When Khrushchev, after a brief leadership struggle, assumed power soon after Stalin died in 1953, he launched his de-Stalinization campaign. He released thousands of political prisoners and encouraged more openness in literature and the arts. Khrushchev felt that the Soviet people had been victimized by Stalin's terror and paranoia. He also believed that the Soviet Union had to renounce Stalin's economic and political rigidity if it wanted to compete successfully as a world power. At no time, however, did Khrushchev denounce Stalin's anti-Semitism. When Khrushchev launched his own war against religion in the early 1960s, Soviet Jews were especially hard-hit. Khrushchev closed synagogues, banned *matzoh* production and distribution, and arranged conviction of a highly disproportionate number of Jews for "economic crimes."

When Khrushchev was ousted in 1964, the new Soviet leaders felt that the domestic thaw had gone too far and that Soviet military might was lagging. The Cuban missile crisis of 1962 had indicated to Kremlin conservatives that the U.S.S.R. did not have sufficient military strength to back up its diplomatic ventures. The Brezhnev era saw a determined build-up of the Soviet military and a swing back to political orthodoxy. The Soviet economy, however, languished under the heavy weight and special interests of the bureaucracy.

When Brezhnev died in November 1982, Andropov saw the stagnation that afflicted the Soviet economy, particularly in the consumer area. As noted, he sought improvements through a campaign for stricter worker discipline. However, neither Andropov nor Konstantin Chernenko, his successor who continued this policy, was in office long enough to see meaningful results. At the same time, both leaders tightened the regime's political grip over the people.

After Gorbachev assumed power he aggressively picked up the pace of economic reform. His first plan was *uskoreniye,* or acceleration of socio-economic growth and development. Propaganda slogans were everywhere, exhorting the people to work harder and drink less. Gorbachev even reduced the hours for liquor stores, giving an early indication that he meant business with his reforms. He soon realized, however, that major changes were needed to prevent further economic backsliding. Gorbachev saw that he had to take radical measures to shake his country out of its economic lethargy and doldrums. His new strategy called for *perestroika.* Gorbachev even wrote a book *(Perestroika: New Thinking for Our Country and the World* [New York: Harper, 1988]) wherein he outlined his plans for change.

The West in the meantime was almost immediately impressed by Gorbachev's high energy level and new style of leadership. Compared to previous Soviet leaders, who had to be helped to podiums to make uninspiring canned speeches and whose frumpy wives were seen only at their husbands' funerals, Gorbachev was more vigorous, better dressed, and much more skillful in public relations. Indeed, Gorbachev seemed a new breed of leader. After meeting with Gorbachev in England, Prime Minister Margaret Thatcher claimed she could "do business" with the new Soviet leader. Moreover, Gorbachev's stylish and well-educated wife Raisa became a public figure in her own right. It seemed to some Western observers that Gorbachev might finally be the Soviet leader who would try for *real* international cooperation. They also saw him as representing the potential for presiding over lasting change of the Soviet system, perhaps even the establishment of a Western-style democracy.

The Soviet media initially focused on *perestroika.* What attracted more public interest, however, both inside and outside the U.S.S.R., was Gorbachev's policy of *glasnost.* After a little over a year in power, Gorbachev saw that *perestroika* had stalled but that it might forge ahead in a more liberalized atmosphere.

Under *glasnost* actual and potential changes covered broad areas of Soviet life. Most striking was the distinct change toward openness in the cultural and political atmosphere. There was much more candor and willingness to discuss problems in Soviet society in the official media. For the first time, the Soviet press began printing stories about drugs, AIDS, the environment, worker disgruntlement, police brutality, natural disasters, manmade calamities, nationality unrest, and a host of other problems.[38]

Like Khrushchev, Gorbachev undertook an anti-Stalin campaign. Gorbachev felt that, for *perestroika* to succeed, he had to place a public spotlight on at least some of the worst excesses of Stalinism, such as the purges of the 1930s, and spell out for the people and the party a more accurate record of the past. The dreadful Stalinist record was laid bare for all to see. The resultant historic debate struck at the heart of societal beliefs and attitudes, frozen over decades. Gorbachev also took measures to rehabilitate Khrushchev and Nikolai Bukharin, whose opposition to Stalin and his rigid economic and political policies in the late 1920s and early 1930s led to his "liquidation" in 1938.[39] There was even talk of rehabilitating Leon Trotsky, which earlier would have been unthinkable.

Glasnost also affected the arts. No longer censored, for example, were such books as Pasternak's *Doctor Zhivago* and Anatoly Rybakov's *Children of the Arbat,* and movies such as *Repentance* and *This is no Way to Live.* The Georgian film *Repentance,* made in the early 1980s but not shown publicly till 1987, clearly places responsibility for the purges of the 1930s on Stalin and Lavrenti Beria, his villainous chief of the secret police. Stanislav Govorukhin's *This is no Way to Live,* released in 1990, depicts famine, deaths of millions in Stalinist camps, mass slaughter of bourgeoisie under Lenin, destruction of churches and clergy, and the economic ruination of the U.S.S.R. through bureaucratic bungling.

Gorbachev's release of most political prisoners was one of the most important developments under *glasnost.* The release of Shcharansky in February 1986 was applauded by human rights advocates around the world. So was the release of Sakharov from internal exile in Gorky in December 1986. These men had been critically important symbols of the human rights struggle in the U.S.S.R. and had been focal points of harsh Western criticism of the Kremlin. In February 1987, officially in commemoration of the seventieth anniversary of the end of tsarist autocracy, Gorbachev released 140 political prisoners. This was the largest release since thousands had been freed after Stalin's death. Gorbachev let still more political prisoners go in subsequent months. Although some political prisoners remained, Gorbachev's prisoner releases reinforced his liberal image, especially in the West.[40]

Gorbachev also decided on a startling gamble to give people more of a say in their own affairs, although within the confines of the Soviet system. He started viewing both *glasnost* and *democratizatsiya*[41] as necessary corollaries of *perestroika.* As Gorbachev said to the Central Committee in January 1987, *glasnost* and *democratizatsiya* "are needed for us to move forward, for accomplishing huge tasks. Without active participation by the people we will not accomplish these tasks." Sakharov gave a similar explanation in early February. "I don't know what Gorbachev wants personally," he stated, "but there are a number of people at the top who understand that without *democratizatsiya,* all of these goals in the economic sphere, in the international sphere, cannot succeed."[42]

Gorbachev also indicated he intended to curb abuses in psychiatry that had been used to punish religious and political activists. Psychiatric abuse for political repression was one of Stalin's favorite tactics. It was also used extensively by his successors. Khrushchev, for example, maintained that since he had released political prisoners, anyone who still criticized the Soviet system must have been mentally ill and thus needed psychiatric "care." Brezhnev continued this practice. Thus Soviet propaganda said that Sakharov was being "treated" in Gorky for his mental illness (sometimes by a doctor flown in from Moscow), evidenced by his criticism of the Soviet invasion of Afghanistan.

At times the authorities even viewed the desire to emigrate as a sign of mental illness. Such was the case with Jewish refusenik Nadezhda Fradkova. *(See Reading 22.)* In 1978 she unsuccessfully tried to emigrate. She then went on a hunger strike, but the authorities stopped her after forty-five days and force-fed her. They warned her that if she did this again she would be sent to a psychiatric hospital. She defied the authorities by fasting again, so they institutionalized her for "treatment." Reportedly the doctor who forcibly injected her with drugs called her a "Zionist whore." After her release she was sent again to a mental hospital, where she was put in with very violent patients. After another release the authorities sentenced her to two years in a psychiatric prison for parasitism. Only under *glasnost* was she released and finally allowed to emigrate.[43]

Soviet leaders until Gorbachev, despite their record of human rights abuse, felt somewhat checked by laws that technically, at least, protected Soviet citizens. This is one reason, perhaps, that they found psychiatry such a useful weapon against dissidents. Once a defendant was judged insane they no longer needed "evidence" that a courtroom trial might require, at least for the record. The Kremlin thus exerted tremendous pressure on Soviet psychiatrists to come up with a diagnosis that could be used as a tool for political repression.

Soviet psychiatrists rarely confined dissenters to psychiatric hospitals because they were physically violent or dangerous, either to themselves or to society. Instead, they were usually charged with posing a "social danger." Soviet psychiatrist Andrei V. Snezhnevsky, head of the Serbsky Institute of General and Forensic Psychiatry in Moscow, devised the diagnosis of "sluggish schizophrenia." Supposedly people with this "illness" were afflicted with an "obsessive desire to seek social justice" hidden behind otherwise normal behavior.

Organized opposition to this abuse of psychiatry began in Moscow on January 5, 1977, when Alexander Podrabinek[44] and others founded the Working Commission to Investigate the Abuse of Psychiatry for Political Purposes. Podrabinek, an auxiliary doctor (somewhat equivalent to a paramedic in the United States) who was kept from advancing to a higher position because of his dissident views, had also been exiled to Siberia for almost five years for detailing Soviet psychiatric abuse in his book *Punitive Medicine* (Ann Arbor: Karona, 1980). The Working Commission was under the direction of the Moscow Helsinki Watch group.

Its members included victims of psychiatric abuse and Soviet psychiatrists who had refused to diagnose dissenters as insane.

Dr. Anatoly Koryagin was a leading member of this commission. In 1981, after having examined fifteen patients who had been confined to psychiatric hospitals for being "socially dangerous," Koryagin issued this blunt statement:

> The clinical meaning of the term "socially dangerous" is that the person is in danger of committing acts which endanger his own health or that of people around him (such as murder, suicide, and personal injury). There was no question of the people I examined being dangerous in this sense. It must be clearly stated that each time a decision was taken to put into hospital the people under discussion, the clinical meaning of "socially dangerous" was replaced (consciously or unconsciously?) by its judicial meaning—i.e., that the patient was capable of harming the social system as a whole.[45]

Koryagin was arrested in February 1981 for his opposition to psychiatric abuses and sentenced to seven years in labor camp and five years in exile. In 1986 he was given another two years of labor camp.

The Working Commission on Psychiatry was forced to stop its activities in 1981, after all its members were arrested. It publicized so many cases of psychiatric abuse, however, which led to an outcry in the West that in 1983 the All-Union Scientific Society of Psychiatrists (AUSSP) felt pressured to withdraw from the World Psychiatric Association (WPA) before it was forced out.[46] "Old guard" Soviet psychiatric leaders challenged the motive and basis for this action, arguing that their association was unjustifiably forced to withdraw by hostile Western propaganda. As Dr. Marat Vartanyan, head of the All-Union Research Center for Psychiatric Health, argued in a March 1987 interview:

> The political campaign that has been mounted in the West with respect to "violation of human rights" in the U.S.S.R. has a long history. We consider it our professional duty, and our duty to our conscience, to administer a resolute rebuff to attempts of this kind. . . . The activity of politicians hostile to our country . . . is unambiguously directed at worsening interstate relations. They use psychiatry as a propaganda element. . . . In 1983, we were indeed forced to withdraw from the World

> Psychiatric Association, since its former leadership had given in to pressure from the Washington "hawks" and could not resist all those insinuations on a professional basis.[47]

In late 1987 the Kremlin began to release dissenters from psychiatric confinement. Even Dr. Koryagin was released and allowed to emigrate. Snezhnevsky's death in early July gave the Soviet press an opportunity to begin making major attacks on Soviet psychiatric practice. An *Izvestia* article on July 11, "Without Defense," criticized what it called wrongful commitment of sane citizens and corruption among Soviet psychiatrists. On November 11 an article in *Komsomolskaya pravda* attacked the use of "sluggish schizophrenia" as a "very broad and very frequently used" technique that "can be applied to practically anyone, even someone sane by conventional definition." This article also reported practices of abusive "rehabilitation" of patients that in essence were "an assault on human dignity."[48]

In December 1987 the Kremlin announced its intention to switch control of all eighteen psychiatric hospitals from the KGB to the Ministry of Health. The new law went into effect in January 1988. Whether this shift in itself would mean reduction in psychiatric abuses was uncertain, for they could still take place under any ministry controlled by the party. As late as July 1989 the Ministry of Health was reportedly still issuing detailed regulations that blocked implementation of the proposed changes.[49]

Dr. Georgi Morozov, who replaced Snezhnevsky as head of the Serbsky Institute of General and Forensic Psychiatry (he then retired in August 1990), at first rejected Soviet press reports of psychiatric abuse as "incompetent" and "slanderous journalism." The Kremlin soon announced, however, that under the new jurisdictional regulations two million persons would be dropped from the government's registry of mental patients.[50] Throughout 1988 the Soviet press continued to reveal the sorry record of Soviet psychiatric abuse. The first major article was by Mikhail I. Buyanov, a psychiatrist and neurologist, who charged in the education newspaper *Uchitelskaya gazeta (The Teachers' Newspaper)*: "The leadership was content: In our country there were no dissidents—there were only insane people."[51]

Near the end of 1988 the Soviets agreed to an exchange of visits in 1989 between U.S. and Soviet mental health experts. In a two-week visit in February–March 1989 twenty-six U.S. mental health experts chosen by the National Institute of Mental Health visited four Soviet psychiatric hospitals of their choice, including the Special Psychiatric Hospital for the Criminally Insane. This is where human rights activists believed many political dissidents had been confined and punished. The U.S. team was able to choose which patients to interview. They found "no evidence of mental disorder" in fourteen of twenty-seven patients they talked with, but they concluded that some patients were still hospitalized for "anti-Soviet thoughts." The U.S. visitors noted some improvements—but not enough, in the opinion of Peter Reddaway, an expert on Soviet psychiatry,[52] to warrant readmission to the AUSSP to the World Psychiatric Association.[53]

In September 1989 the American Psychiatric Association voted to oppose readmission of the official AUSSP to the WPA. The U.S. group justified its stance by pointing out that there were still political prisoners being held in Soviet psychiatric hospitals and that the old-guard Soviet psychiatric leaders still predominated. Podrabinek also opposed readmission. Addressing a meeting of the International Association on the Political Abuse of Psychiatry (IAPUP) in Washington, D.C., on the eve of the opening of the October meeting of the WPA in Greece, he noted "There are real improvements, but around them a big propaganda noise is being made." He then listed three "essential conditions" the Soviets had to meet before being allowed back into the WPA:

1. Release of all political prisoners from mental hospitals
2. Official acknowledgment of abusive practices in Soviet psychiatry
3. Allowance of an international commission of Soviet and Western leaders and Soviet dissidents to monitor the mental-health hospitals[54]

In the first week of October Georgi S. Markosov, a senior counselor at the Soviet Embassy in Washington, told a U.S. congressional committee that the Kremlin had established an independent commission to "prevent the use of psychiatry for nonmedical purposes as well as to assure maximum openness in specific cases of misuse of psychiatry." Markosov said membership of this commission, which would include eight psychiatrists, lawyers, and social workers, would be "independent from the Health Ministry or any party or state organs." Markosov then added that Moscow would welcome representatives from the WPA "to visit and speak with any patient in the Soviet Union if a case occurs that cannot be solved" by the new commission.[55]

Soviet psychiatry's new international posture was persuasive for on October 27, by a vote of 291 to 45, the WPA readmitted the AUSSP, though on a one-year probation. It could be removed again if political abuses were found. The WPA also voted to admit, without conditions, the Independent Psychiatric Association (IPA) in the U.S.S.R. This new group, founded earlier in 1989 with about forty members, opposed the readmission decision of the WPA. The IPA could not be at the WPA meeting because its members were refused exit visas. But its president, Yuri Sovenko, issued this criticism of the decision: "This seems to be a very hasty decision. There still has not been real reform in Soviet psychiatry. The leaders of the profession are virtually the same people as those who misused psychiatry for political purposes in the 60s and 70s." But at the meeting itself Morozov denied that Soviet psychiatry ever was designed as a political weapon to curb Soviet dissidents, and he criticized the new IPA of diagnosing all persons as sane.[56]

There is strong likelihood that at least the worst abuses of Soviet psychiatry have stopped. The old guard has found it increasingly difficult to maintain its philosophy and practices. With Moscow preparing to hold a follow-up Helsinki Conference on human rights in 1991 and with Watch 91 (a group of Soviet human rights activists) monitoring Soviet human rights performance, the Kremlin will be very wary of resurrecting abusive psychiatric practices.

Glasnost in psychiatry has had limits, though, as it has in other areas of Soviet life. This was especially true in its early phase. In his speech to the Central Committee in January 1987 Gorbachev reminded his audience: "The Soviet people would be encouraged to know more of what's going on, but only what the Party and the controlled media tell them."

Under *glasnost* Soviet human rights groups again made themselves heard after having taken only a periscopic look at Soviet society since the repressiveness of the early 1980s. The Ukrainian Helsinki Watch group was reestablished. Journals like the Moscow-based *Glasnost*, covering a wide range of human rights issues, including problems of Soviet Jews, began publication, though now with official approval sought by its editors. *(See Reading 23.)* Human rights organizations such as the Moscow Perestroika Club and numerous other ostensibly independent political groups sprang up and were allowed to meet, though not without having to overcome government "obstacles." Human rights leaders like Sergei Grigoryants, publisher of *Glasnost,* were harassed and detained by the authorities.[57] When Press Club Glasnost organized an independent human rights seminar in Moscow in December 1987 local authorities closed the building it had rented for its meeting, supposedly for "public health" reasons. Yet the government did allow the seminar to take place in various apartments in Moscow. Some four hundred persons participated, including some Westerners. They reviewed issues such as "law and society," "human contacts," "nationality issues," "religious freedom," and "culture." Though the authorities prohibited some human rights activists from outside Moscow from participation, this meeting has to be considered "a milestone in the Soviet human rights movement."[58]

Throughout 1987 the authorities warned that they would not tolerate dissemination of anti-Soviet views. As one *Pravda* article warned: "Our course is not liberalization of the Western stripe, but the deepening and spreading of socialist democracy." The same article also opposed advocacy of anti-Semitic and anti-Zionist views. This may have been an oblique criticism of *Pamyat,* whose activities some higher-ups supported behind the scenes but publicly, for the most part, the authorities opposed. It may also have been a reflection of the continuing struggle among party leaders over how to handle the Jewish Question.[59]

Gorbachev, in the meantime, allowed political and economic reform to advance to a remarkable degree. In the summer of 1989, free elections were held for a new Soviet Parliament, which resulted in the ouster of many old-line Communists. Gorbachev also removed Communist leaders remaining from the Brezhnev era, notably V. Shcherbitsky of the Ukraine. But Gorbachev had to walk a political tightrope in carrying out *glasnost.* He had to avoid being pushed off either by conservative critics like Ligachev, who felt he had gone too far too fast, or by liberal opponents like Yeltsin and Sakharov, who felt he had not gone far enough or fast enough. These liberal critics themselves differed over economic strategy of how to achieve reform without compromising social justice, and political strategy of how much decision-making power the people should have.[60] In general, at least through the 28th Congress of the CPSU, Gorbachev artfully maneuvered through this political thicket, checking his key political opponents without getting derailed from his programs. But Gorbachev had to muster all his political and personal strength just to keep the wolves from the door. By the end of 1990, the Soviet economy had fallen into virtual free fall; the nationality problems had worsened; the power and authority of the Communist Party had begun to disintegrate; the voices for democracy had grown louder and shriller; law and order had broken down; and the entire Communist system had begun to look like a corpse. The future of both Gorbachev and the Soviet Union seemed very much in doubt.

How *glasnost* has been applied and how reforms have been carried out has had a major impact on Soviet Jews. Demonstrations of Soviet Jews in February 1987 in behalf of the release of Begun from hard labor were ruthlessly suppressed by the KGB, yet Begun was released shortly thereafter. The KGB reacted similarly to demonstrations by refuseniks during the Reagan–Gorbachev summit in December 1987. The authorities therefore did not hesitate to use the stick to stifle Jewish activists. But more and more they used the carrot. The result is that, for Soviet Jews, *glasnost* began having both positive and negative consequences.

Under *glasnost* the Kremlin released almost all prisoners of conscience. This was certainly encouraging. But these former prisoners, just like released political prisoners, received only amnesty. They were neither acquitted nor rehabilitated. Thus in the public eye they remained "pardoned criminals." Moreover, most had to promise that they would never again commit their "crimes"; and the more recalcitrant were not allowed to return to their homes. Instead, they were forced to settle elsewhere, which caused them additional hardship and suffering.

In the new liberal atmosphere the authorities started less aggressively to suppress the private teaching of Hebrew. For a short time after Gorbachev became general secretary, the arrests of Hebrew teachers continued. In January 1986, Vladimir Lifshitz was arrested in Leningrad. *(See Reading 24.)* According to Western diplomats, the authorities then were "clearly" trying "to isolate Hebrew students and teachers by particularly harsh treatment."[61] Alexei Magarik was the last Hebrew teacher to be arrested, on March 14, 1986. A specialist in Jewish music, Magarik was convicted on fabricated charges of drug possession. He was released on September 14, 1987, after having served only one and a half years of a three-year sentence in a labor camp. A month after Magarik's release, however, the regime again denied Begun the right to register as a Hebrew teacher. Thus at that time there still was no indication that the state would allow the teaching of Hebrew for religious or cultural purposes.

In the fall of 1987 there were several signs of beneficial changes for Soviet Jews. The Kremlin allowed importation from New York of five thousand prayer books in Hebrew and Russian translation. It also opened up a kosher restaurant at the main synagogue in Moscow.[62] Some doubted the true purpose of this move. As Begun commented, "It is a Potemkin village. The situation is very sad. Jewish people still have no right to Jewish schools, clubs. Now there are several generations who don't know their language, history, or culture."[63] This restaurant, at least initially, may have been opened largely for show for Western tourists, and observant Soviet Jews may have distrusted the *kashrut* (preparation of food in accordance with Jewish dietary laws) of an enterprise run by the state and not under proper rabbinical supervision. Furthermore, opening one kosher restaurant did not mean, at least at the outset, increased availability of kosher food. Yet this restaurant did indicate at least symbolic easing of restrictions against Jewish customs.

In December 1987 another hopeful sign of liberalization for Soviet Jews came when Begun and Zivs spoke on the same platform on the forty-sixth anniversary of the Babi Yar massacre to a gathering of about two hundred people at Moscow's Vostryakovskoye Cemetery. Begun said that the best way to honor the dead victims was to preserve the Jewishness of their survivors. Then Zivs disappointingly, but expectedly, reiterated the familiar Soviet position that there should be no distinction made between honoring Jewish and non-Jewish victims.[64] Yet before *glasnost* Begun might not have been allowed to speak at all on this site, and certainly not on the same platform as Zivs. Thus at least some progress was being made.

Also in December came an indication of a possible shift of policy on teaching Hebrew. A newspaper in Azerbaijan reported that more than seventy persons had signed up for a course "in the Jewish language" to be held at the Railwayman's Club in Baku. This course, organized by local young Jews, was in modern Hebrew. Some Jews who enrolled, and perhaps the Azerbaijani authorities, may have expected this would be a course in Yiddish. Nevertheless, the course in Hebrew did get started.[65] It lasted for several months until the local Communist Party canceled it, officially closing the site of classes for "redecoration."

In early 1988 the Kremlin announced another surprise. It would allow several rabbinical students to train in the United States. In February Rabbi Shayevich went to New York City to study for three months at

Yeshiva University. He was accompanied by Vladimir Pliss, his cantor at the Moscow Synagogue. Rabbi Arthur Schneier, president of the Appeal of Conscience Foundation, had arranged the study tour with Konstantin Kharchev, chairman of the Soviet Council of Religious Affairs. No matter what their additional training, however, many Soviet Jews continued to distrust Rabbi Shayevich and Cantor Pliss so long as they considered them still under the thumb of the state.[66]

In 1988 and 1989 *glasnost* continued its ebbs and flows. One setback was in the summer of 1988, when the authorities rescinded permission granted earlier to Yevgeny Voronov, a Moscow mathematician, to teach Hebrew, officially on the grounds that he did not possess the required diploma. When Voronov showed officials a diploma in English from the Hebrew Academy of Languages in Israel, a clerk refused to accept it, conceding she had received "orders from upstairs." Voronov earlier had attracted both potential students and anti-Semitic threats from an intriguing ad offering classes in modern and classical Hebrew he had placed in *Vechernaya moskva.*[67]

In the fall of 1988 the Kremlin reportedly agreed to allow the private teaching of Hebrew. This agreement was reached between Edgar Bronfman, president of the World Jewish Congress, and Soviet Foreign Minister Eduard Shevardnadze. The Soviets were also said to have agreed to Soviet Jewish participation in activities of the World Jewish Congress, marking the first time Soviet Jews could have official contacts outside the Soviet Union. These changes were milestones in Soviet Jewish history.[68] What Soviet Jews still awaited, however, was official sanctioning of these changes. Soviet Hebrew teachers would not feel free to conduct lessons without state certification and professional recognition. According to Mikhail Chlenov, a veteran Hebrew teacher, there was still some opposition in Moscow to granting this sanction by authorities who reserved the legal right to suppress Hebrew studies when they wanted.[69] One must remember that it was never Hebrew teaching per se that was long barred but its teaching for religious or cultural purposes, to which the Bronfman agreement refers.

In accordance with *glasnost* and the new governmental attitude toward the teaching of Hebrew, in the latter part of 1988 the authorities began to allow private teaching of Hebrew. In Vilnius, for example, nonrefuseniks Alex Berlovich and Grigory Alpernas enrolled 140 pupils in

Hebrew classes. Other small Hebrew classes were allowed elsewhere in the Soviet Union, in Minsk (where a Torah group began to meet), Riga, Dnepropetrovsk, and Dushanbe. And in Moscow, the Association of Hebrew Teachers set up an information center that provided names of Hebrew teachers, teaching materials on Jewish history and culture, and information regarding Jewish emigration. By 1989 Hebrew language and Jewish cultural classes had sprung up all over the country.[70] Who would have guessed, for instance, that in October 1989 author Leon Uris could have gone to a Jewish dayschool in Riga, the first in the Soviet Union, and reported this remarkable event: "The most heartwarming moment . . . was when we walked into the day school and the kids got up and sang to me in Yiddish and Hebrew. They were very happy, very open and very Jewish."[71]

What a pleasant surprise it also was to have seen a few months earlier some other startling developments. In April the first legal Jewish journal printed in the U.S.S.R. not under the control of the authorities appeared in Tallin, Estonia. *Hashachar (Dawn)* was published in Russian, with about 1700 copies.[72] A few days later, just in time for Passover, the first *matzoh* factory opened in Moscow. Then, on April 24, a four-page tabloid called *Herald of the Jewish Culture* was published in Moscow in about 20,000 copies. Its main front-page editorial, headlined SHALOM, was designed to spotlight Jewish culture and history. The lead story, "The Door to Dialogue Is Now Open," discussed the implications of the growing contact between the U.S.S.R. and Israel.[73]

The resumption of official political contact between the Soviet Union and Israel after Gorbachev came to power is certainly one of the most important developments for Soviet Jews. Official contact resumed in August 1986 when the two countries exchanged low-level diplomatic missions. One result was an agreement to allow some Soviet Jews to visit Israel and Israeli Jews to visit the Soviet Union. This agreement followed the Kremlin's permission for Soviet Jews now living in the United States to visit their relatives in the Soviet Union and vice versa. According to Jerry Goodman, former executive director of the National Conference on Soviet Jewry, this new visitation policy involving Israel gave the U.S.S.R. several advantages: improved public relations, new sources of hard currency, and a "low risk, nonpolitical way of having ties with Israel." Goodman also pointed out that allowing visits between members of divided families might result in a decrease in embarrassing requests for emigration.[74] Soviet–Israeli relations continued to warm throughout 1988, 1989, and 1990. This development enhanced prospects for a peaceful resolution of long-standing conflict between the two states.

How *glasnost* affected emigration was obviously of crucial importance to Soviet Jews. At the Iceland summit and the Vienna conference of the CSCE in the fall of 1986, Soviet officials began to express a willingness to discuss human rights, to cooperate on issues like divided families, and to be responsive to inquiries on individual cases. Previously they had tended to be very defensive and even combative on such issues. In November the Soviets went on the human rights offensive. Foreign Minister Shevardnadze launched a new public relations campaign by proposing that Moscow should host the next CSCE human rights conference. To pave the way for this conference the Kremlin had already announced that a new emigration law would go into effect on January 1, 1987.

Soviet Jewish leaders almost uniformly denounced this new law, mainly because an invitation from a first-degree relative in Israel was needed for an exit visa. But under pressure of criticism and with an eye toward improving its human rights image abroad, the Kremlin soon retreated from this requirement.

The key to this law, like any other in the U.S.S.R., was not so much how it was worded but how it was implemented. In July 1987 the Soviets announced an important modification of emigration policy. They said they would accept applications to emigrate based on invitations from relatives not only in Israel, but also in any country with which the U.S.S.R. had diplomatic relations. Moreover, they said they would apply this change to all Soviet citizens seeking to emigrate. Beginning in late 1987 the Kremlin let some Jews leave who did not satisfy the first-degree-relative requirement.[75]

In the spring of 1988 the Soviets suspended the first-degree-relative requirement and allowed increased Jewish emigration. Moscow may have taken this action to deflect Western criticism of its emigration policy prior to President Reagan's visit there in May. Soviet authorities, as explained earlier, also informed the United States that they had drafted new regulations that would officially eliminate the first-degree-relative requirement. Other changes called for judicial review of a parent's refusal to allow a child permission to emigrate and the establishment of a time limit for any citizen to be considered holding "state secrets."[76]

Although many long-standing, high-profile refuseniks were allowed to emigrate beginning in 1987, many refuseniks, like Professor Irina Voronkevich, Lev Milman, Mark Kotlyar, Anatoly Genis, and Emil Kunin, remained trapped inside the U.S.S.R. Perhaps Gorbachev decided to hold onto some refuseniks to use as bargaining chips in future negotiations with the United States. Certainly some of the released refuseniks saw themselves as pawns in superpower diplomacy. Ida Nudel, for example, explained her release on the eve of Yom Kippur in 1987 with these words: "In ancient times, the Pharaohs used to please the chiefs of neighboring countries with very exotic things. I feel that I am a white crocodile. I was used to please Mr. Reagan and Mr. Shultz before a meeting of the superpowers."[77]

Glasnost clearly presented a new challenge to the Soviet Jewish freedom movement. Should it adopt new strategies and tactics to deal with new Soviet policies? Was *glasnost* really a "window of opportunity" or "window dressing" to mask a differently styled attempt to preserve the Communist system?

When deciding what to do, Soviet Jewish activists had to come to grips with a number of concerns that had been building up in the freedom movement, especially among refuseniks who, by January 1, 1989, were estimated to number about 2656 (compared to about 11,000 in 1986).[78] One problem was the growing number of second generation refuseniks, children who had grown up living much or all of their lives in refusal. Some of these youngsters, now in their teens, became active in the movement. Alexei Lein, for example, started to write his own letters of protest in the summer of 1987 just before he turned sixteen. In an open letter, Alexei wrote

> I am nearly sixteen . . . and believe in friendship and hope for peace. In addition I wish to live and study in Israel. In 1978, my parents applied for visas to Israel, but they were refused. . . . In 1981, my father was arrested during the dispersal of a seminar on Jewish history and culture held by refuseniks. He was imprisoned and sent to do forced labour in Siberia. At school I am constantly told about the humanistic Soviet society and about the wonderful Soviet constitution which guarantee freedom of speech, the press, and assembly. Yet more than once I have witnessed how plain-clothed policemen violate these freedoms.[79]

In November Alexei joined his parents on a hunger strike. The Leins, like many other refuseniks, were a "divided family." Alexei's sister was allowed to emigrate to Israel in 1987 with her husband and newborn child. Alexei asked to emigrate by himself, without his parents if need be. If, as the Lein family feared, he had turned eighteen while still in the U.S.S.R. and he had to join the army, his family would have suffered an even greater setback. He would have been involved with "state secrets," which probably would have prolonged their stay in the U.S.S.R. The remaining Leins finally received permission to emigrate in late 1988, after a decade of hardship in refusal.

During 1987 refuseniks began to zero in on the secrecy issue as a reason for refusal. They wanted "state secrets" to be clearly defined so they would know more precisely why they were being refused. *(See Reading 25.)* Written explanations of secrecy never accompanied refusals. At a conference of about 150 refuseniks from many cities held in Moscow in November to study the secrecy refusal, participants wondered what secrets, if any, they once held, or when their knowledge of secrets would expire.[80] Refuseniks felt that the secrecy issue gave the regime a loophole to refuse emigration to anyone and for any reason. For example, Yuri and Tanya Zieman, organizers of the Moscow meeting, believed they had been refused a visa not because they knew state secrets (they were first refused in 1975), but because they had rebuffed attempts by the KGB to persuade them to be informers. The Ziemans were finally allowed to emigrate in August 1988, with their daughter Vera—for reasons only the authorities know.

Soviet regulations on emigration created other family problems for refuseniks. In the summer of 1987, groups of "poor relatives" formed. These Jews had been denied visas because their parents or other close family members would not sign a document showing they had no financial claims against them. By the late 1980s, a hundred years after Turgenev's book, we began to witness a new, artificially imposed twist to the conflict between fathers and sons. Some family members would not sign because they feared involvement with emigration issues or "Zionist" activities. Some may have been dedicated Communists who tried to convince the "infidels" to stay. Others wanted to get back at the applicant if, for instance, a divorce was involved. In such cases, uncooperative relatives exercised a virtual veto over emigration. The result was that the authorities could blame visa refusal on "family problems" and divert attention from the requirements that caused them.

All these problems put a tremendous strain on the family and individual members. *(See Reading 26.)* Life as a refusenik remained very hard. As Tanya Zieman explained after she emigrated, "support of the general population for refuseniks is nonexistent. They are afraid of us, because we meet with foreigners. Their lives depend on the system, and they can't jeopardize their position."[81]

As years of refusal dragged on there was increased emotional stress and conflict. Many elderly claimed their cases were more desperate and urgent than those of children. They wanted to see the Promised Land before they died. Some refuseniks, like cancer patient Ben Charney, had serious medical problems that needed immediate attention in the West. Charney's last refusal because of "state secrets" supposedly was to have lasted until 1995. Under *glasnost,* however, Charney was released in 1988. With medical treatment in the United States, Charney's health improved. But for other very sick refuseniks who had to remain in the U.S.S.R., continued refusal spelled death.

Refuseniks remember cases such as those of Inna Meiman and Mikhail Shirman. Meiman, whose husband Naum then was not allowed to emigrate, died of cancer in the United States in February 1987, three weeks after she arrived. She had tried unsuccessfully to emigrate for over three years. Shirman, who emigrated to Israel in 1980, died there of leukemia. He had needed bone marrow from his sister in the U.S.S.R., but she was not allowed to emigrate until January 1987. Shirman underwent the operation at that time, but it was too late. Thus, as a spokesman for the Israeli Public Council for Soviet Jewry concluded, "The fateful factor in Mr. Shirman's death was the Soviet regime."[82]

In 1987 problems of women refuseniks began to receive more public attention. Women refuseniks, who initially became active in the late 1970s, again began making their voices heard. One of the more influential groups is JEWAR (Jewish Women Against Refusal). In a meeting in Moscow in June 1987 members focused on problems of children. They sought to understand better the toll years of emotional, psychological, and financial stress during refusal had taken on their children. They wanted to learn more about problems of adjustment in the family, school, and neighborhood. JEWAR issued an appeal for help on March

8 (Women's Day) and on June 1 (International Children's Day), 1987. Some members also staged a hunger strike on June 1 in Moscow, Leningrad, and seven other Soviet cities. They continued hunger strikes and fasts throughout 1988 and 1989. They wanted to make sure the world knew that, despite the emigration of high-profile cases and others, there were still refuseniks who did not want to be forgotten. As Natasha Stonov, refused since 1979, commented after a three-day fast in March 1989: "It's easy to forget us, but we must not be cast aside. Only noise will get us out."[83]

The hunger strike became one of the more frequently used tactics of the Jewish freedom movement during the late 1980s, as refuseniks increasingly concluded that they had to draw attention to their individual cases. These strikes, however, began to cause some divisiveness in the refusenik community. Opposition came from those who felt that participants might suffer serious medical problems. The very young, old, and infirm were especially vulnerable. Some refuseniks also disliked the undue focus on hunger strikers. They argued that strikers diverted attention from the movement as a whole and from cases which may deserve priority—in terms of health, family circumstances, or length of refusal.

Besides using the hunger strike, Jewish activists during the *glasnost* period continued to write petitions, letters, and appeals. They also conducted public demonstrations. These demonstrations began to include refuseniks who previously had kept a very low profile. Long-standing refuseniks like Oscar Mendeleev started to feel that they had to embark on a course of high visibility and activism. Although roughed up during a few demonstrations in 1987, they continued to hope that under *glasnost* Soviet authorities would be more tolerant of their activities, which would also receive more attention in the Soviet and foreign press. Mendeleev's dream finally came true in 1988, when he and his family received permission to emigrate. Undoubtedly at least some credit for this visa approval had to go to the New Jersey–based Committee to Save the Mendeleevs, headed by Belle Schwartz, for its tireless, persistent prodding of the authorities and encouragement and support to the entire Mendeleev family.

Under *glasnost* refuseniks sought new methods of protest. Until 1987, Jewish activists rarely broke Soviet laws. In fact, they tried to hold Soviet authorities accountable to these laws and protested their violation. In 1987 activists started more breaking of certain laws related to their refusenik status. Some refused to register for the internal passport. Some also refused to register the birth of a child, claiming he or she was an Israeli citizen. As one angry refusenik asserted, he could now "affirmatively refuse" a visa and not have his child "identified with the Soviet slaveship."[84]

It is evident that *glasnost* presented opportunities, problems, and dangers for Soviet Jewish activists. They faced new challenges posed by Gorbachev's policy changes. They had to adjust not only to the dizzying pace of liberalization in the U.S.S.R. but also to the new, more brazenly open folk anti-Semitism *(see Reading 27)* and to prospects of working with an atheistic regime that had so long oppressed them.[85] In late December 1989 the newly formed Congress of the U.S.S.R. Jewish Organizations and Communities sent an urgent appeal to the Supreme Soviet and CPSU Central Committee to take urgent public and legal measures to combat growing popular anti-Semitism. *(See Reading 28.)*

Those outside the Soviet Union who were working to help Soviet Jews also had to adjust to new realities. Accordingly in early 1989, for example, the Student Struggle for Soviet Jewry embarked on Project Sefer (Book), designed to mail hundreds of books in Russian from Israel and the United States. They were sent both to refuseniks and to other Soviet Jews who wanted to learn about their Jewish heritage.[86] As another example, the National Conference on Soviet Jewry, in addition to helping the renaissance of Jewish religious and cultural life in the U.S.S.R., began to focus more on combating growing grass-roots Soviet anti-Semitism and on resettlement of Soviet Jews, which could duplicate the efforts of the Hebrew Immigration and Aid Society (HIAS) and the Council of Jewish Federations. By May 1990, the Combined Jewish Philanthropies (CJP) had begun to raise money for Operation Exodus, conceived as a rescue mission to save Soviet Jews from increased popular anti-Semitism and transport them to Israel. By then Soviet Jews* were pouring into Israel at the rate of about 10,000 per month. Israeli officials

* Some of the thousands of Soviet emigrants to Israel are part Jewish and, at least technically, may not qualify for Israeli citizenship under Israel's Law of Return. Others have no Jewish lineage. This situation poses serious legal, social, political, economic and diplomatic problems.

were estimating an influx of about 150,000 Soviet Jews in 1990, with up to as many as 500,000 in 1991. Under so many changed circumstances, Soviet Jewry advocacy groups had to redefine their mission and goals.

Soviet Jewish activists understand that whatever gains they have made have depended on their own resolve and help from Jewish advocacy groups and governments in Israel and the West. They also realize that help from the United States government has had special significance. Before the late 1960s the Jewish Question was on the back burner of U.S.–Soviet relations. Then, in fact, human rights in general was a rather insignificant issue between Washington and Moscow. But, spurred by advocacy groups, the United States government began to stress the Soviet Jewry issue with the Kremlin. This issue soon sprang to the forefront of the super-power relationship. Let us now see how and why this change came about and what effects it had on the Soviet Jewry freedom movement.

Notes

1 Soviet Jews had sent a few protests against state anti-Semitism earlier in the 1960s. An unsigned letter sent to Khrushchev in the spring of 1963 severely criticized the Kremlin's policies toward Soviet Jews. The author was especially upset by the conviction of a highly disproportionate number of Jews for "economic crimes" and the increased restriction of Jews from universities and government service. This letter was published in a Hebrew translation in the Israeli paper, *Ma'ariv,* on September 9, 1965. Another significant appeal, sent to Bertrand Russell in 1964, sought the British philosopher's help in inducing Khrushchev to allow more cultural freedom. This appeal was published in "Soviet Anti-Semitism: An Exchange," *Commentary,* Vol. 39, No.1 January 1965, p. 35. Russell asked Aaron Vergelis to publish both this appeal and his reply. But Vergelis refused, and instead he criticized both parties in *Sovetisch heimland,* No. 5, 1964, pp. 159–160. For an excellent discussion of appeals by Soviet Jews, see Shimon Redlich, "Jewish Appeals in the USSR: An Expression of National Revival," *Soviet Jewish Affairs,* Vol. 4, No. 2, 1974, pp. 24–37.

2 Of the 220 appeals sent to the West between 1968 and 1970, 56 were sent to The United Nations. The UN notified petitioners that it dealt only with governments, not private individuals. Soon, therefore, Soviet Jews sent fewer petitions to the UN and more to governments in the West.

3 34.3 percent came from Riga, 26.3 percent from Moscow, 7.7 percent from Minsk, 6.4 percent from Tbilisi, 5.7 percent from Vilnius, 3.6 percent from Kutaisk (in Georgia), 3.1 percent from Leningrad, and 9.8 percent from scattered other places. See William Korey, *The Soviet Cage* (New York: Viking, 1973), p. 173.

4 Viktor Yakhot, "Reflections on the Reasons for the Exodus of Jews to Israel," in *Jews in the USSR, Collection of Materials on the History, Culture and Problems of Jews in the USSR,* No. 1, October 1972, ed. by Alexander

Voronel and Viktor Yakhot. Reprinted by the Academic Committee on Soviet Jewry, *I Am A Jew,* Anti-Defamation League of B'nai B'rith, New York, 1973, pp. 39–43.

5 Article 70 supposedly required proof of intent to harm the Soviet regime. Because it was almost impossible to prove intent in the trial of Sinyavsky and Daniel, in September 1966 the regime added Articles 190-1 and 190-3 to the Criminal Code. Under Article 190-1, the regime could convict someone for "anti-Soviet agitation and propaganda" without having to prove intent. Article 190-3 aimed at preventing public demonstrations by groups. The Soviet press did not announce either of these new laws. For a lucid discussion of this and related issues, see Joshua Rubenstein, *Soviet Dissidents,* 2d ed. (Boston: Beacon Press, 1985).

6 Pasternak first submitted *Doctor Zhivago* to *Novy mir,* feeling that it might be published in the new atmosphere of the literary "thaw" created by Khrushchev. But the manuscript evidently was too critical of the Bolshevik Revolution and the censors rejected it. Pasternak then offered his book to Italian left-wing publisher Feltrinelli, who published the work in 1957. That year Pasternak received the Nobel Prize for literature. The Kremlin promptly denounced Pasternak. *Literaturnaya gazeta,* with a tinge of anti-Semitism, labeled him a "literary Judas who betrayed his people for thirty pieces of silver, the Nobel Prize." V.E. Semichastny, the KGB chief, called Pasternak "a pig who has fouled his own sty." Pasternak felt forced to reject the Prize. But the official attacks against him continued until he died in May 1960. His supporters showed their contempt for the regime by rejecting official burial arrangements and burying him instead in a nearby cemetery. For more on the Pasternak controversy, see Hosking, op. cit., pp. 411–412.

7 Quoted by Yelena Platonova from an interview with Sinyavsky in Paris, in "Emigration Is a Horrible but Instructive Experience," *Moscow News,* No. 2, 1989. See also Alan Ridig, "Sinyavsky in Exile: Russian Without Tears," *International Herald Tribune,* December 27, 1989.

8 On February 5, 1988, Polish scholar Josef Gierowsky, head of the Research Center of Jewish History at the Jagellonian University of Cracow, indicated that Poland was about to acknowledge the "political error" of expelling Polish Jews in 1967–1968. About 30,000 Polish Jews were expelled, leaving only about 10,000 in a country that before World War II contained several million Jews. See "Poles Said to Admit Error in Purge of Jews in 60's," *New York Times,* February 6, 1988.

9 Quoted in Gilbert, op. cit., p. 15.

10 For a first-hand account of this trial by a leading defendant, see Edward Kuznetsov, *Prison Diaries,* translated by Howard Spier (New York: Stein & Day, 1975).

11 For a reporter's account of this trial and its aftermath, see Leopold Unger, "Brezhnev Moves Jewish Pawns," *International Herald Tribune,* April 26, 1979.

12 The French Communist Party paper evidently misunderstood Marx's Jewishness." See *infra,* pp. 18–19.

13 Zhores Medvedev, *Andropov* (New York: Norton, 1983), p. 77.

14 For advocacy of the primacy of foreign policy determinants, see Robert O. Freedman, "Soviet Jewry and Soviet-American Relations," in Robert O. Freedman (ed.), *Soviet Jewry in the Decisive Decade, 1971–1980* (Durham, N.C.: Duke University Press, 1984), pp. 38–67. For the primacy of domestic determinants, see Robert J. Brym, "The Changing Rate of Jewish Emigration from the USSR: Some Lessons from the 1970s," *Soviet Jewish Affairs,* Vol. 15, No. 2, 1985, pp. 23–36.

15 Peter Reddaway, "Dissent in the Soviet Union," *Problems of Communism,* Vol. XXXII, November–December 1983, pp. 1–15.

16 According to Jerry Goodman, former executive director of the National Conference on Soviet Jewry, *Exodus* had a tremendous impact on Soviet Jews. "For Soviet Jewish activists," Goodman pointed out, *Exodus* "was probably more meaningful than even the Bible. . . . Most of the Jewish activists in the late 1960's and early 1970's always cited to me the importance of the book. They didn't treat it as a literary experience, it was history —the only knowledge they had of the Jewish experience." Ilya Essas, a Soviet Jewish mathematician who was allowed to emigrate to Israel in 1986 after living thirteen years in refusal, explains that *Exodus* "was our first encounter with Jewish history. It gave us inspiration, and turned almost everybody who read it into more or less convinced Zionists. . . . It was the first book to teach us about the Jewish tradition, which is very different from what the Government said it was." The dissemination of *Exodus* remained anathema to Soviet authorities throughout the 1980s. In 1985, for instance, when Soviet Jewish activist Leonid Volvosky was convicted of slander, one of the charges was circulation of *Exodus.* See Edwin McDowell, "Exodus in Samizdat: Still Popular and Still Subversive," *New York Times,* May 3, 1987. And as late as November 16, 1989, a Soviet customs official reportedly confiscated Russian-language copies of *Exodus* brought into the U.S.S.R. by a Soviet Jew returning from a visit to Israel on the grounds

that this book is "Zionist propaganda." Ironically, author Leon Uris had been allowed to tour the U.S.S.R. a few weeks earlier. See NEWSBREAK, December 15, 1989.

17 For a good discussion of Jewish *samizdat,* see Vladimir Lazaris, "The Saga of Jewish Samizdat," *Soviet Jewish Affairs,* Vol. 9, No. 1, 1979, pp. 4–19, and Joseph Kerler, "Jewish Russian Samizdat in the USSR," in David Prital (ed.), *In Search of Self* (Jerusalem: Mount Scopus Publications, 1983), pp. 241–247.

18 Peter Reddaway, "Dissent in the Soviet Union," *Dissent,* Spring 1976, pp. 136–154.

19 There were some fifty to seventy Jewish demonstrators at Babi Yar in 1968, 300 to 400 in 1969, 700 to 800 in 1970, 1000 in 1971. The authorities countered these demonstrations by holding "official" memorials the same day and by forcefully dispersing the Jewish demonstrators. The repression became so severe that only forty-four Jews demonstrated on September 29, 1979. See Alexeeva, *Dissent in the USSR,* p. 175.

20 Stenographic Transcript of Meeting between 100 Moscow Jews and U.S.S.R. Acting Minister of Interior and other Soviet Officials, November 12, 1972.

21 In 1985 this organization changed its name to Group to Establish Trust Between East and West. This name change reflects its wider platform and contacts (e.g. with West European peace groups). For an account of this group's history and activities, see *From Below: Independent Peace and Environmental Movements in Eastern Europe and the USSR,* a Helsinki Watch Report, October 1987.

22 Quoted in Anthony Barbieri, "Harried Tutors Pass on Hebrew to Soviet Jews," *Baltimore Sun,* December 31, 1979.

23 See Edward Drachman, "From Scientist to Stoker's Apprentice," *Hartford Courant,* January 29, 1984. This is an account of Yevgeny Lein's ordeal as a refusenik.

24 Quoted in Joel Brinkley, "Soviet Jews Finding Israel Short on Jobs and Housing," *New York Times,* September 17, 1989.

25 Reportedly, Israel and the Jewish Agency agreed to transport about 100,000 Soviet Jews to Israel between 1990 and 1992. The United States supposedly would help finance this operation. Whether Israel will be ready to handle this influx is uncertain. As Sharansky remarked with dismay: "Those of us

who fought to push the gates open are afraid that a real catastrophe could occur here if not enough housing and jobs are prepared." Quoted in Jackson Diehl, "Campaign Is Planned to Bring 100,000 Soviet Jews to Israel," *International Herald Tribune,* November 3, 1989.

26 See, for example, S. Vishnevskiy and V. Kobysh, "A Campaign Against Everybody," *Kommunist,* No. 4, 1983, p. 91, and commentary by Yuri Kornilov on television program "International Observers' Roundtable," *FBIS* (Federal Broadcast Information Service), Soviet Union, Vol. 3, No. 065, April 4, 1983.

27 Quoted by *Jewish Chronicle,* December 11, 1980.

28 See Roland Tyrell, UPI Dispatch from Moscow, March 21, 1979.

29 Reddaway, "Dissent in the Soviet Union," *Problems of Communism,* p. 8.

30 *Pravda,* March 24, 1981. Soviet scholar T. Friedgut points out that it is not accidental that "chauvinism, a mortal sin in the Leninist catechism, is paired with Zionism." See Friedgut, "Soviet Anti-Zionism and Anti-Semitism: Another Cycle," Hebrew University of Jerusalem, January 1984, Research Paper No. 54, p. 26.

31 In the years 1979–1981 attacks on Zionism in Soviet publications exceeded the level of attacks of the early 1970s.

32 Transcript of *Hirelings and Their Accomplices* and a commentary are available from the National Conference on Soviet Jewry. For a discussion of *Traders of Souls* see Gilbert, op. cit., pp. 161–168.

33 Radio Moscow, September 24, 1982. See also Serge Schmemann, "Soviet Says Jews Who Asked to Leave Have Largely Gone," *New York Times,* June 7, 1983. German and Armenian emigration also fell sharply in the early to mid-1980s. For a comparison of Jewish emigration with these two other main groups of emigrants, see Sidney Heitman, "Jewish, German, and Armenian Emigration from the USSR: Parallels and Differences," in Freedman (ed.), *Soviet Jewry in the 1980s,* pp. 115–138.

34 See David Greenberg, "The Leningrad Jewish Almanac," Radio Liberty Research Report, October 17, 1984.

35 For an interesting commentary on this issue, see Anthony Lewis, "A Bankruptcy Policy," *New York Times,* May 24, 1984.

36 See David Shipler, "Unofficial Study Group for Jews Is Reported Barred in Soviet City," *International Herald Tribune,* September 30, 1981. Yuri Tar-

nopolsky, who helped Paritsky found the "free university," was also arrested in 1981. The authorities then shut down this educational venture.

37 Quoted in Carolyn Burch, "Renewed Campaign Against Hebrew in the Soviet Union," *Religion in Communist Lands,* Spring 1985.

38 Under *glasnost* the Soviet press began to report clashes between various nationalities. In 1986 the Soviet people read that riots broke out in Alma Ata, capital of Kazakhstan, when Gorbachev chose a Russian to head the Kazakh Communist Party. In 1988 they read about violent clashes between Armenians and Azerbaijanis over control of Nagorno-Karabakh. This area contains a predominantly Christian Armenian majority but is located in Azerbaijan, which is mainly Muslim.

39 See Philip Taubman, "Soviet Panel Clears Bukharin, 50 Years After His Execution," *New York Times,* February 6, 1988.

40 In this book I use Helsinki Watch's definition of political prisoners as "those persons who have suffered reprisal for free expression, peaceful assembly, conscientious objection to armed service, and nonviolent attempts to move within or outside a country in defiance of a repressive passport system." The Helsinki Watch in the United States reported that by the fall of 1987, 218 political prisoners had been released that year, but that there remained "at least 500 known cases . . . in prisons, labor camps, psychiatric hospitals, and internal exile." Helsinki Watch, *News from the USSR,* September 30, 1987, p. 1. In the fall of 1988, Amnesty International cited a figure of 150 political prisoners in psychiatric hospitals and 50 prisoners confined for religious offenses. See *New York Times,* October 27, 1988. For 1989 Amnesty International estimated more than 2000 people were put for a short time in prison or psychiatric hospitals for their human rights activities. By the end of 1989, sixty people were still in prison or psychiatric hospitals. See *Washington Post,* July 13, 1990.

41 The Kremlin uses the term *democratizatsiya* when it refers to political reforms under *glasnost.* According to U.S. Ambassador Richard Schifter, Assistant Secretary for Human Rights and Humanitarian Affairs in the Reagan administration, the West should not confuse *democratizatsiya* with democratization. He explained: "*Democratizatsiya* . . . means allowing citizens some say in the operations of the lowest level of government, but most assuredly not allowing them to influence the policies adopted by the top leadership of the Party." Address before the Leadership Conference of the Washington group on October 10, 1987, *Department of State Bulletin,* Vol. 8., January 1988, p. 40.

42 Quoted in *New York Times,* February 9, 1987.

43 See George Will, "Still Stalinist, Still Anti-Semitic," *Washington Post,* December 21, 1984.

44 See Alexander Podrabinek, "Soviet Psychiatry: A Message from Moscow," *New York Review of Books,* XXXV, No. 19, December 8, 1988, pp. 40–42.

45 *The Lancet,* April 1981, quoted in Dissent and Religious Persecution in the Soviet Union, A Symposium, Harvard Law School, November 16, 1986, p. IV–4.

46 The World Psychiatric Association voted to comdemn Soviet abuse of psychiatry in August 1977. It had received substantial documentation for several years, especially from Soviet dissident Vladimir Bukovsky, who himself had been "treated" by Soviet psychiatrists. Bukovsky had been convicted in 1972 for dissident activities that included sending findings of Soviet psychiatric abuse to Western psychiatrists. He was convicted of "anti-Soviet agitation and propaganda" and sentenced to seven years in prison and five in exile. He did not complete this sentence, for in December 1976 the Kremlin exchanged him for Chilean Communist leader Luis Corvelan. See Vladimir Bukovsky, *To Build a Castle: My Life as a Dissenter* (New York: Viking, 1978).

47 "Speaking Frankly About Something Important," *Argumenty i Facty (Arguments and Facts),* March 21–27, 1987, in *Current Digest of the Soviet Press,* XXXIX, No. 15, 1987, pp. 6–7.

48 See Helsinki Watch, "Soviet Abuse of Psychiatry for Political Purposes," New York, January 1988, p. 4.

49 See Michael Dobbs, "Dissent and Soviet Psychiatry," *International Herald Tribune,* July 1–2, 1989.

50 Associated Press, "Two Million to Quit Soviet Mental-Patients Rolls," *Washington Post,* February 12, 1988.

51 Quoted by Associated Press, "Soviet Reports Misuse of Psychiatry in '70s," *Boston Globe,* November 23, 1988.

52 See, for example, Reddaway and S. Bloch, *Psychiatric Terror* (New York, Basic Books, 1977); and *Soviet Psychiatric Abuse: The Shadow Over World Psychiatry* (London: Gollancz, 1984). For an assessment of problems and changes in Soviet psychiatry under *glasnost,* see Reddaway, "Reform of Soviet Psychiatry: Is the Establishment Beginning to Panic?" *Report On The USSR,* Vol. 2, No. 44, November 2, 1990, pp. 1–14.

53 See David Ottaway and Michael Specter, "U.S. Psychiatrists to Visit Soviet Mental Hospitals," *Washington Post,* November 22, 1988.

54 See Michael R. Gordon, "Soviets Try to Return to Psychiatric Fold," *New York Times,* October 10, 1989. The IAPUP was founded in 1980 to coordinate activities of eight organizations, such as the British Working Group on the Internment of Dissenters in Psychiatric Hospitals. Its members, which include both medical personnel and laypeople, investigate reports of psychiatric abuse, publish appeals on behalf of alleged victims, and try to visit these persons. See Robert Van Voren, "Changes Expected in Soviet Psychiatry," *Glasnost,* Issue Numbers 16–18, January 1989, pp. 36–38. Van Voren is General Secretary of the IAPUP and a staff member of the Bukovsky Foundation in Amsterdam.

55 Michael R. Gordon, "Soviets Say Panel Will Check Psychiatric Abuses," *International Herald Tribune,* October 4, 1989.

56 Michael Dobbs, "Soviet Psychiatry Split on Readmission," ibid., October 21–22, 1989.

57 Bill Keller, "Publisher of Glasnost Magazine Is Arrested in Soviet Crackdown," *New York Times,* May 10, 1988.

58 See *Reform and Human Rights: The Gorbachev Record,* Report Submitted to the Congress of the United States by the Commission on Security and Cooperation in Europe (Washington, D.C.: U.S. Government Printing Office, May 1988), pp. 29–30.

59 *Pravda,* December 27, 1987.

60 See Boris Kagarlitsky, "Different Perestroikas for Different Folks," *International Herald Tribune,* September 8, 1988. Kagarlitsky is a sociologist who is a member of the organizing committee of the Popular Front for Perestroika, an alliance of independent leftist clubs.

61 Quoted by Gary Lee, "Leningrad's Jews Studying Mixed Signals from Moscow," *Washington Post,* January 24, 1986.

62 Francis X. Clines, "This Year in Moscow, a Kosher Feast," *New York Times,* November 21, 1987.

63 See wire report, "Attitude Toward Soviet Jews Seen Changing in USSR," November 13, 1987.

64 Felicity Barringer, "For Soviet Jews, Emigration Poses a Divisive Issue," *New York Times,* December 6, 1987.

65 See Charles Hoffman, "Hebrew Course in Soviet Union," *Jewish Advocate,* December 31, 1987, and "Hebrew Lessons, Baku Breaks Mold," *Jews in the USSR* (England), Vol. XVI, November 26, 1987, p. 4.

66 Ari Goldman, "Warmth and Suspicion for Cantor and Rabbi from Soviet," *New York Times,* February 3, 1988.

67 NEWSBREAK, July 15, 1988.

68 Associated Press dispatch, "Soviets OK the Study of Hebrew," *Boston Globe,* November 3, 1988.

69 See David Kanter, "Hebrew Teachers Face Dilemma," *Jewish Advocate,* November 24, 1988.

70 NEWSBREAK, July 31, 1989.

71 J. J. Goldberg, "Leon Uris Finds 'Unpleasantness' in USSR," *New York Jewish Weekly,* reprinted in *Jewish Advocate,* October 26, 1989. The "unpleasantness" Uris was referring to was the upsurge of popular anti-Semitism in the country. For a fuller explanation of the dangers of anti-Semitism Uris found during his trip to the U.S.S.R. see Leon Uris, "Leon Uris in the USSR: The Jews Must Be Evacuated," *Jewish Advocate,* March 8, 1990.

72 Ibid., April 6, 1989.

73 "Soviet Jewish Association Publishes Newspaper in Moscow," B Wire Report, April 27, 1989 (from files of Radio Free Liberty/Radio Liberty in Munich), and James Blitz, "When a Matzoh Factory Is Not Enough," *Financial Times,* May 12, 1989.

74 Quoted by Hugh Orgel and Andrew Silow Carroll, "Soviets Allowing Jews Mutual Visits Between Israel and USSR," Jewish Telegraphic Agency *Daily News Bulletin,* December 30, 1987.

75 At the same time the authorities claimed that some Jews would never leave the U.S.S.R. See Theodore Shabad, "Soviet Lists 8 Jews Who It Says Can't Leave," *New York Times,* February 22, 1987. Shabad cited publication of the names in *Vechernaya moskva.*

76 See Michael R. Gordon, "Soviets Act to Reduce Barriers to Emigration," *International Herald Tribune,* September 30, 1988.

77 Quoted by Gil Sedan, "Nudel Says Release Does Not Signal New Policy," *Jewish Advocate,* October 8, 1987.

78 "Bear Unchained," editorial, the *Jewish Chronicle* (London), February 10, 1989.

79 The Israel Public Council for Soviet Jewry, *Focus Soviet Jewry,* May 1987, p. 4. The following letter in 1987 from Naomi Shapiro (daughter of former refuseniks from Leningrad Lev and Leah Shapiro) also reflects the deep strains and anxiety of life in refusal: "My grandparents are very old . . . but I have never seen them . . . they live in Israel, but we are not allowed to go there. We are told that seventeen years ago, eight years before I was born, my father knew some state secrets. . . . Can it really be true that it is so dangerous for the U.S.S.R. if we live in Israel together? I hear that you are a very kind grandfather and love children; you also have a granddaughter and you spend a lot of time with her, while I cannot even see my grandparents." Ibid.

80 "In the Age of Glasnost, Sekretnost," editorial, *New York Times,* November 27, 1987. On November 25 the working committee of the conference on secrecy refusals issued the following preliminary requests to Soviet authorities: "To break the present deadlock the participants of the Symposium consider it necessary:

1. Soviet restrictions on emigration from the country should be in accord with international norms and practices.
2. Until the Soviet law is changed:
   (a) to limit the maximum term of regime refusals to five years from the termination of security work with possibilities of reducing the term further;
   (b) the refusals should be issued in a written form with an indication of the exact reasons and terms;
   (c) to forbid the practice of extending regime considerations to people without security clearance.
3. To publish periodically lists of people who applied for visas with a date of their first application.
4. To establish means of international monitoring of fulfillment of the above mentioned requests."

See *Jews in the USSR* (England), pp. 1–2.

81 Quoted by Jane Weingarten, "Ziemans End 11-Year Ordeal," *Jewish Advocate,* August 18, 1988.

82 Michael Shirman, Soviet Emigre Dies," *New York Times,* March 7, 1987.

83 Masha Hamilton, "Soviet Jewish Women Fast for Right to Emigrate," *Los Angeles Times,* March 10, 1989.

84 For an excellent discussion of problems facing refuseniks under *glasnost,* see Donna Arzt, "Paternalism in the Human Rights Movement: The Case of Soviet Jews," *HRI Reporter,* Vol. 11, No. 506, Winter/Spring 1987.

85 For a more detailed view of issues facing Soviet Jews in 1989 and the 1990s, see Isi Leibler, "Becoming Jewish in the USSR," *Jewish Advocate,* December 15, 1988. Leibler is president of the Executive Council of Australian Jewry, vice president of the World Jewish Congress, and chairman of the Pacific Jewish Association. See also Barbara and Stephen Rosenfield, "Soviet Jewry at the Crossroads," *Present Tense,* Vol. 16, No. 6, September/October 1989, pp. 24–31. The Rosenfields raise many critical questions for Soviet Jews, such as what would be the impact on them of a failed *perestroika* and extreme nationality unrest.

86 "Send Books to Soviet Jews," ibid., March 16, 1989.

Reading 1

Letter from twenty-six Lithuanian Jewish Intellectuals, February 15, 1968, to Comrade A. Snietskus, First Secretary of the Central Committee of the Lithuanian Communist Party, in Moshe Dector (ed.), *Redemption: Jewish Freedom Letters From Russia* (New York: American Conference on Soviet Jews, 1969), pp. 12–14

This letter from Soviet Jews criticizing Soviet anti-Semitism was the first to reach the West. It appeared in the Washington Post *and* New York Times *on October 30, 1968. The letter is unsigned, indicating that Soviet Jews had not yet become bold enough to sign their names. Most subsequent letters were signed.*

To Comrade A. Snietskus, First Secretary of the Central Committee of the Lithuanian Communist Party.

We, Communist and non-Party representatives of the Jewish intelligentsia who have discussed and signed this document, address ourselves to the Central Committee of the Lithuanian Communist Party because of our great anxiety about the rising wave of anti-Semitism in Soviet Lithuania. We draw the attention of the Central Committee to the fact that the earth has not yet grown cold in Ponar * and in the Ninth Fort † of Kaunas, the soil that had been watered with the blood of our parents, brothers and sisters; we draw the attention of the Central Committee to the fact that at the sites

---

* Site outside Vilna where Nazis massacred thousands of Jews.

† Located in suburb of Kaunas, where again Nazis slaughtered many Jews.

of mass murder, where tens of thousands of Jews lie buried, no monuments have been built thus far similar to that in Piritsiupys, which was erected to commemorate one hundred innocently murdered Lithuanians; we draw the attention of the Central Committee to the fact that 25,000 Jews living in Soviet Lithuania have not forgotten who carried out the mass murders.

We realize that the anti-Israel propaganda conducted by the Soviet press is not intended for internal consumption and is not directed at Jews who live in the Soviet Union. However, we should not ignore the fact that, despite all the stylistic nuances, the anti-Israel propaganda, and especially the cartoons in the central press, have revived anti-Semitic passions in a certain part of the Lithuanian (and not only Lithuanian) people. Therefore we can not be silent at a time when in the present tense situation new notes emerge that give a local character to the entire matter. We can not be silent when the press publishes material that nourishes local judeophobia.

The weekly newspaper *Kalba Vilnius (Vilnius Speaking:* No. 7, page 14) has published quotations depicting Jews as a traditional object of mockery, which ethnologist S. Skrodenis has painstakingly selected from the writings of Lithuanian classics. As one reads them, one gets the idea that mocking Jews is an old "tradition" of the Lithuanian people. The author Skrodenis knew what he was doing in his article, "Winter, Winter, Get Out of the Yard." In the traditional Shrovetide processions, the personages of a drunken Russian bureaucrat and "honorable" Polish landed gentry figured next to Jews, gypsies and Germans [among those mocked—Ed.], and sometimes even dominated the event. The cited writings of Zemaite, Jucevicius and Valancius are full of anti-Russian and anti-Polish statements. All one needs to do is to select them properly and present them together in one place.

However, the author Skrodenis and the editors of *Kalba Vilnius* know that it is not allowed to mock a drunken Russian bureaucrat or an "honorable" Polish landowner, while one can write about Jews now. Only in this way can one explain the painstaking ethnographic selection.

More than that. The editors of *Kalba Vilnius* express regret about the following: "Such processions of costumed people have almost completely disappeared today; and while somewhere deep in the

Zamaitija region some still do it, they are a little afraid. It is because in some regions the keepers of public order simply forbid it." The newspaper urges the "revival of beautiful popular traditions." What is this—an open invitation to stage anti-Semitic manifestations under the cover of reviving "popular traditions"?

On this occasion we would like to point out that, because of the one-sidedness of our propaganda, objective conditions have been created for the flourishing of anti-Semitism. Individual leading personalities, Communists, are quite openly promoting it and are personally willingly expressing it. Here are several facts out of many:

When the Deputy Minister of Trade, Kazbaras, was reproached for not observing the Leninist principle of selecting cadres on the basis of their political and technical qualifications, he replied publicly: "To be a Lithuanian in Soviet Lithuania is a political qualification."

The Deputy Chairman of Television, Kuolelis, openly criticized a correspondent in a meeting for his Jewish mannerisms on the screen.

The President of the Pedagogical Institute, Uogintas, bluntly told one of the instructors: "It matters little that today you excel others in the German or English languages, in physics or mathematics, chemistry or music. We will develop our own cadres so that tomorrow Lithuanians will be more qualified than you." All Uogintas did was to give public expression to a principle that has been in force for a long time in cadre (employment) policy.

Here are the facts. During the entire postwar period, not a single Jewish student living in Lithuania (except for a few children of privileged persons) was given a state scholarship to continue his studies at institutions of higher learning in Moscow and Leningrad. Not a single Jew originating from Lithuania has taken post-graduate courses in the institutes of Moscow or Leningrad. Not a single Jewish Communist has attended the Academy of Social Sciences or the Party University of the Soviet Communist Party's Central Committee (except M. Bordonaite).

And here are the facts about the distribution of cadres. Ten percent of the inhabitants of Vilnius are Jews. Until now not a single Jew has ever been elected chairman, deputy chairman or secretary of the city or of the city's four regional executive committees. Since the dismissal of Atamukas, not a single Jewish Communist has ever been elected secretary of a Party city committee or a city-region committee, nor have any been appointed department heads by the corresponding plenums.

Not a single Jew has been elected judge of a people's court. Not a single Jew has been elected to any higher position in the trade unions. During the entire postwar era, not a single representative of the Jewish youth has risen to a leading position in the state, party or trade union activity—while at the same time the mass of Lithuanian cadres has been educated and promoted during the postwar years. In fact, only a handful of meritorious Jewish revolutionaries of the older generation are still merely tolerated in higher positions, and they are now being hurriedly pushed out to pension as soon as possible.

We know that the Jewish cultural institutions in Lithuania were destroyed not at the initiative of the Central committee of the Lithuanian Communist Party, and therefore we do not think there is any need to raise this question now. Yet none of us have forgotten the summary punishment of Ceserkas—violinist, veteran Communist underground fighter, veteran of the Fatherland War—who dared (as the Lithuanian clandestine teachers had done in 1863–1905, when the press was prohibited in Lithuania) to teach a group of young Jews the alphabet of their native tongue. He was dismissed from the Party and thrown out from everywhere.

As for the protection of Jewish cultural monuments, it must be stated that not a single synagogue structure that survived the Occupation has been declared an architectural monument under state protection, whereas a considerable number of Catholic churches—architectural monuments are protected by the state and repaired at its expense. Moreover, one of the most outstanding architectural monuments of 16th-century Lithuania, the underground synagogue of the Gaon of Vilna (at the intersection of Muziejus and Rudininkai streets), was deliberately destroyed and desecrated during the doctors' trial in Moscow in 1952.

Local authorities, with the obvious connivance or even silent consent from above, are destroying Jewish cemeteries, while the cattle of the townspeople graze on those that remain. Tombstones are used as building materials even for the construction of public buildings. Even the Hitlerites had left Jewish cemeteries untouched throughout the period of their occupation of Lithuania. The Jewish cemeteries of Sovietsk (formerly Tilsit) or Cherniavski (formerly

Insterburg) in East Prussia remained untouched through all the thirteen years of Hitler rule. Only now have they been completely destroyed, and not a trace remains. Quite recently, the Jewish cemetery in Jonava was destroyed without warning (even the foreign radio commented on that). Pink marble from the old Jewish cemetery in Vilnius was used for the pedestal of the Pushkin monument, erected at the foot of the Gediminas Hill in Vilnius. This act of vandalism insults not only the Jews but everyone who respects Pushkin's genius.

We do not wish to overstate the case. By no means. We know that the situation of the Jews is considerably better in Lithuania than in other parts of the USSR; especially terrible is the discrimination against our compatriots in the Ukraine. During the entire postwar period in Lithuania there was only one bloody pogrom, in Plunge in 1958, while, according to our information, not fewer than twenty pogroms occurred in the Ukraine. (Victims were especially numerous in Shachty, Gorlovka and other towns.)

We highly value the Lithuanian Communist Party, the traditional internationalism of its Central Committee, and the national tolerance of the Lithuanian people. Nevertheless, as the chairman of the state security committee, Petkevicius, stated at the plenum of the Lithuanian Communist Party's Central Committee—emigrational tendencies are increasing among the Jewish inhabitants. It is known that if the borders would be opened for emigration today, some eighty percent of the entire Jewish populace would leave Soviet Lithuania and depart for Israel. These people would leave everything here—despite the unsettled conditions in the Near East, despite the fact that our people in this country are used to a damp climate and would find it difficult to acclimatize there, despite the fact that almost no one among the Lithuanian Jews knows Hebrew anymore or observes religious traditions, despite the fact that their present qualifications (most economically active people are employed in service occupations) would not make it easy for them to become integrated into Israel's society.

We are confronted with a paradox here. We are not wanted here, we are being completely oppressed, forcibly denationalized, and even publicly insulted in the press—while at the same time we are forcibly kept here. As the Lithuanian proverb goes, "He beats and he screams at the same time."

We are not speaking to you about the noble Communist ideals, about the equality of men and nations, about proletarian internationalism. All those slogans have been thrown into the dust-heap of demagogy long ago. They have been replaced now by one slogan: "Love for the great Russian people, and what is left from the 'love' let us divide up among ourselves." The authors of this document are appealing only to you and your colleagues' universal human, democratic convictions. Do all in your power to put down the menacingly rising wave of anti-Semitism. It is not too late yet. If that is not done now, Lithuania will again "adorn itself" with new Ponars and Ninth Forts.

It has been decided not to make public the surnames of the twenty-six signers of this document. We know well how people who had protested against flourishing anti-Semitism in the Soviet Union at one time or another were dealt with summarily. The Party has taught us to be watchful, and we have to be watchful now as we write to the Central Committee of the Lithuanian Communist Party. What painful irony.

Vilnius, February 15, 1968

Reading 2

Letter from eighteen Georgian Jews to the UN Committee on Human Rights, August 6, 1969

This letter was one of the most important early international appeals to allow Soviet Jews to emigrate to Israel.

We, eighteen religious Jewish families of Georgia ask you to help us emigrate to Israel. Each of us, summoned by a relative in Israel, had received the necessary questionnaires from the proper organs of the USSR and had filled them out. Each had received an oral assurance that there would be no obstacles to his emigration. Each of us, awaiting a permit form day to day, has sold his property and has resigned his job. However, long months have passed—and for some even years—and the emigration has not yet been permitted. We have sent hundreds of letters and telegrams—they disappeared like teardrops in the sands of a desert: we hear oral, one syllabled refusals, we see no written answers, nobody explains anything, our fate concerns nobody.

But we are waiting, because we believe.

We, eighteen religious families of Georgia, consider it necessary to explain why we want to go to Israel.

Everyone knows how justly the national policy in the USSR is carried out, the theoretical foundations for which had been formulated by the founder of the State, V. I. Lenin. For ages there have been no Jewish pogroms in the country, there is no Pale of Settlement and no numerus clausus. Jews can walk the streets without fearing their lives, they can settle wherever they like, occupy any post—even up to the post of a minister—as can be seen from the example of V. Dymshits, the Deputy Chairman of the Council of Ministers of the USSR. In the Supreme Soviet there is even a Jewish deputy—A. Chakovsky, the editor-in-chief of *Literaturnaya gazeta.*

Therefore, it is not racial discrimination that forces us to leave the country. Perhaps, then, it is religious discrimination? But, in this country, synagogues are allowed and we are not forbidden to pray at home either. However, our prayers are with Israel, because it is said: let my right hand shrivel up if I forget thee, Jerusalem. Because we, religious Jews, consider that there is no Jew without faith, as there is no faith without tradition. . . .

History has placed a great mission on the United Nations Organization—to think about people and to help them. Therefore we demand that the UN Commission for the Rights of Man should take all the measures that it can and, in the shortest possible time, should obtain from the government of the USSR the permit for our emigration. It is incomprehensible that, at the end of the XX Century, it should be possible to forbid people to live wherever they wish.

We shall wait for months and for years, if necessary for our entire life, but we shall not renounce our faith and our hope.

We believe: our prayers have reached God.

We know: our appeals will reach Him.

Because we do not ask for much—let us to go to the land of our ancestors!

Reading 3

Answer to Boris Bravshtein from the Jews of Kiev, "Open Letter to the Editorial Office of the Newspaper *Vecherni Kiiv (Evening Kiev)*," undated but approximately July 1972. See also Part I, Reading No. 22.

On June 7, 1972, Vecherni Kiiv *published a letter from Bravshtein entitled "I Accuse Zionism." Zinovyi Melamed and Yuriy Soroko, Jews who knew Bravshtein well, responded to his "conversion."*

It is the right of every person to have his own opinions and to change them for the sake of new opinions, but admit it, Boris, that such sharp changes that have occurred in you should be explained in detail. Unfortunately, your letter does not explain this metamorphosis. Were you truthful then, when you used to speak about the return to the land of the forefathers, and are you sincere at present—after all not even a year has passed since you arrived in Israel.

What has frightened you so? The pornographic literature, the American films about the war in Vietnam? What has this to do with the idea that you had expressed, the idea that "the only place where Jews can exist is the State of Israel"? Can it be that respect for the ancient religious traditions of our people, traditions thanks to which we, who are deprived of our Homeland have been able not remain Jews for the centuries of exile, now evokes such a disgust in you? Even though you do not mention this in your letter, we know that you have a modern four-room apartment in a new house, that you have a highly-paid job, that your wife was given free medical assistance at a high modern level, during her confinement and that the birth of your second son, whom you have named after one of the statesmen of Israel, was an occasion for great celebration for many of the inhabitants of Beer-Sheba. How will you explain in time to your son the origin of his name? To us, the ease with which you have renounced your convictions seems blasphemous. Why do you suddenly appeal to us "not to reproach the Soviet regime, not to slander it, but to thank it for having protected us from fascism and for having ensured us with comfort and happiness and having raised us to the heights of culture"? Haven't the fathers of many of us given their lives to create this State? Didn't our brothers stand in the first ranks of those who defended our country in the hours of darkness? Is it necessary to enumerate the names of those who have so enriched the science and so glorified the culture of this country? Who has given you the right to doubt the scientific value of such persons as Professor Lerner and Professor Barboy? After all, you have learned their names only from papers. Haven't we, by our man years of honest labour assisted the might of the State in which we are still living? And didn't we, leaving this country, take with ourselves the knowledge of the Russian culture, and of the Russian language in order to transmit it to our children? We do not reproach anyone of anything, we do not present any account to this country; we want only one thing—to be together with our own people, to live in the land of our fathers and to build with our own hands the Jewish State. In the letter signed with your name there are thoughts the appearance of which cannot be explained. You write: "They need the repatriation of Jews from the Soviet Union to Israel, in order to cast aspersions on the USSR." Since when did you start writing the word repatriation with quotation marks? Was it to please someone that you tried to get permission to go to Israel? Can your decision to make use of our right cast any aspersions on the USSR? And what about other countries? Do you really think that the return of the Armenians from France has caused moral harm to that great country? As for the alternative that you are trying to put before us, it is completely provocative: "With whom and where should you and your children go?"

We have made our choice long before your letter. We do not want any longer to be citizens of Jewish origin, we want to remain Jews, we want that our children and the children of our children should remain Jews.

We do not carry with us a list of the material boons that we intend demanding in Israel. And it is not "superfluous mouths," as you write, that we shall bring to our land, but our hands. We know that 25 years is an insignificant period of time in the life of any State, but our brethren there have already done so much. We want to plant our tree too in that land.

When you started writing this letter in your new apartment, built long before your arrival, did you think about those who had sacrificed everything to realize the everlasting dream of our people and who was unable to see it being realized. About those who did not spare their lives for the sake of the right of our people to have their own State, about those who knew how to defend it, about those who even now pay with long years of prison for their dream.

The logical conclusion to your letter is obviously an appeal to the Soviet Government with the request to permit you to return to the USSR. Many people here might sympathize with you, just as people always sympathize with failures.

For us, however, you will always be the person who has betrayed the dream of his people.

Zinovyi Melamed, Yuriy Soroko
Kiev

Reading 4

Open letter to the fifty-two Soviet Citizens of Jewish Nationality, Participants in the Moscow Press Conference on March 4, 1970, sent to the editorial office of *Pravda,* September 19, 1970, by Lazar Liubarsky and I. Pevzner, Moshe Decter (ed.), *The Lonely Course of Lazar Liubarsky* (New York: National Conference on Soviet Jewry, 1973), pp 18–21

This letter is a sharp response to the Kremlin-staged press conference in which "court Jews" trumpeted the Soviet propaganda line on the

Jewish Question. Liubarsky was tried, convicted, and sentenced to two years for anti-Soviet slander (Article 190-1). He emigrated to Israel in 1977.

I. To the Editorial Office of the Newspaper *Pravda*

Being unable to address ourselves separately to each of the participants in the press conference of a "group of Soviet citizens of Jewish nationality," which took place in Moscow on March 4, 1970, we ask you to publish this open letter in your newspaper.

OPEN LETTER

To the 52 Soviet Citizens of Jewish Nationality, Participants in the Moscow Press Conference on March 4, 1970:

More than a half a year has passed since you, 52 prominent Soviet citizens of Jewish nationality, held a press conference in the city of Moscow.

At this press conference particular mention was made of the question of the national life of Jews in the Soviet Union.

Your statements on this question provided such simple, almost "historical" generalizations and conclusions, that we are certain that they will be referred to for a long time to come.

And so, about the national cultural life of Jews in the Soviet Union.

At the conference this question was mentioned in connection with the fact that in Israel, as well as in a number of other countries, there is at present a movement to help the emigration from the Soviet Union to Israel of those Jews who wish it.

This movement is based on the internationally accepted right of everyone to choose freely his own citizenship and his country of residence; the movement is an outgrowth of the conviction that in the Soviet Union there are no longer conditions for a Jewish national life.

The task of the press conference was to refute this conviction and to prove the presence both of the conditions and of the national life itself.

What, in fact, was proved by the press conference?

That in the Soviet Union there is not one single Jewish school.

That in the Soviet Union are published in Yiddish: one central literary monthly, one regional newspaper *(Birobidzhaner Shtern)* and several books per year.

But, having shown this, you tried to prove something more.

While describing the "rich" national cultural life of the Jews in the Soviet Union, you told us that the last Jewish school had been closed down in 1949, because the "children of Jews and their parents in the Jewish Autonomous Region (Birobidzhan) has proposed the joint education of Jews and Russians (i.e., in Russian schools)" (Bokor).

From the USSR's half-century experience of revival of previously oppressed nationalities and peoples with their languages and their national cultures, you should know that a national school is inextricably connected with the language, history and culture of the nation, and that it is, in turn, the expression of the existence of the nation itself.

The Jews of Russia, quite aside from their historical ties with the Jews of other countries and with the ancient history of Israel, have their own centuries-old history, during which they created a rich national culture. This culture, toward the time of the victory of the October Revolution, had united over five million Russian Jews, and had found its expression in thousands of Jewish schools, numerous publishing houses, theatres and other national institutions (see the *Jewish Encyclopaedia* in 16 volumes published in Petrograd).

And then—"the last school had been voluntarily closed down."

From now on, the Jewish national culture as the expression of the Jewish nationality and its national life in the Soviet Union would "live out its life" only in the memory of those to whom it is near. There is nobody to transmit the banner of national culture to. In the new generation there are no people desirous of accepting it.

This statement of yours is brazenly summarized by I. Braginsky in his article "The Class Essence of Zionism," published in *Pravda* in that same March of 1970. He writes: "As historical experience shows, the great majority of the Jewish population of the USSR has chosen the path of joint labor and life with our Soviet peoples. A natural concomitant of this is the process of assimilation of considerable segments of the Jewish population. Mixed marriages, the knowledge of Russian, Ukrainian or Belorussian as their own languages, the dying out of religious and nationalistic prejudices, have made this process, under socialism, absolutely voluntary."

This is what you, "the group of Soviet citizens of Jewish nationality," as you are called in the preface to your statement, had wanted to prove at the press conference.

This is what you, persons who have voluntarily instilled in yourselves the feeling of belonging to another nation, have attributed to the remaining 2,500,000 Jews of the USSR.

This is what you tried to raise to the level of objectivity, predetermined by the entire process of historical development.

What the thousands of years of history of persecution, Crusades, Inquisition, pogroms and holocaust had been powerless to do, according to your sworn statement the Jews themselves have done voluntarily, in the space of only some 50 years, in the sight of only one generation.

Thus, according to you, under Soviet conditions the Jews have shown themselves unable to live as a nation.

From what treasury of Marxism-Leninism have you taken the inspiration and the proof of your ideas?

One must ask why—during a period of full national flowering of all the peoples of the USSR, when during these same 50 years there appeared new national cultures of a number of peoples who sometimes numbered only a few thousand persons and who before the Revolution had not even had a written language—there took place among the Jews the process . . . of an absolutely voluntary assimilation?

What, then, was the purpose of creating the Jewish Autonomous Region (of Birobidzhan)—to confirm the future incapability of Jews to national life in the USSR?

Why did you have to bury alive the 2,500,000 persons in whose passports the word Jew is still inscribed?

But enough of this!

Enough, Academician Strogovich, of calling the desire of those who wish to emigrate to Israel "Zionist racism," because it is your "personal point of view" that Jews should not be let out of the Soviet Union. To be doomed to further "voluntary," national extinction is nothing else but racism!

Enough, poet Dolmatovsky, of saying that Jews are, after all, studying in literary institutes, because henceforth those institutes will produce only poets who are "Jews" by passport, but not Jewish poets!

Enough, General Dragunsky, of exchanging Jewish national life, for which your mother of blessed memory sacrificed herself, for statements that in the Soviet Union "there are no pogroms, there is no pale of settlement"!

Enough, Kolkhoz member Egudin, of exploiting the memory of the two million Soviet Jews who perished under fascism and of prescribing, as a specific against anti-Semitism, that one should forget one's Jewish origin!

Enough, citizen Bokor, "of expressing your angry indignation in the name of all citizens of Jewish nationality," because having rejected the Jewish school, you have thereby rejected your own Jewishness!

Enough, generals, academicians and people's artists, of calling yourselves Soviet Jews! The only Jewish public figure we saw at the press conference was Vergelis, the editor of the magazine—not a Jewish magazine, only a magazine in Yiddish—which does not reflect any Jewish national life and which might just as effectively be published in Bengali, Nepalese, Chinese or even in the Tarabarsk languages!

We think your press conference has had exactly the opposite results:

(1) It has demonstrated the impossibility of living a Jewish national life in the USSR—and this is a higher form of national oppression, moral genocide; and

(2) Instead of teaching assimilation, it has sounded an alarm for those Jews who are building their future, arousing their national consciousness.

Thus, without intending it, you have rendered a great service to many Jews who until recently had subjected themselves to the "absolutely voluntary process of assimilation" and to whom you, at the price of your own shame, have restored the emotional and spiritual happiness of considering themselves Jews.

In conclusion, we can with all frankness state that we see no difference between you and those thugs with "vodka and onion" against whom the heroic units of Jewish self-defense were created in the dark years of Tsarism.

L. Liubarsky
I. Pevzner
Rostov-on-Don, September 19, 1970

Reading 5

Appeal by Professor German Branover, "Difficulties Faced By Jews in the USSR in the Observance of their Religion," in Michael Bourdeaux, "The Jewish Religion in the Soviet Union Since Khrushchev," Radio Liberty Research Report 79/75, February 21, 1975 (originally published in *Jews in Eastern Europe*, April 1972, pp. 52–54)

In February 1972, 92 Latvian Jews petitioned the authorities to be allowed to respond to various official press conferences wherein "court Jews" condemned Zionism and the emigration movement. They were refused permission, but they were allowed to submit their ideas in writing. In this excerpt, Professor Branover, a Doctor of Physics and Mathematics, explains the hardships of a practicing Jew in the U.S.S.R.

I wish to explain the problems I encounter as a religious Jew, to examine briefly what difficulties generally obstruct the observance of Jewish religious precepts in the Soviet Union, and to explain why my religious beliefs are the main motive for the fact that I am petitioning to emigrate.

As is known, constant study of the Torah and the teaching of the Torah to one's children is one of the main Jewish commandments, often equal in importance to all the other commandments combined. But what possibilities do I have to give my child a religious education and upbringing? Apart from the fact that there are no proper educational institutions, any sort of tutoring in this sphere has long been forbidden. If I should wish to withdraw my child from school and teach him myself, the law providing for the obligatory attendance of schools by children excludes this too.

At present in the USSR there is no possibility to obtain various essential articles necessary to believers. . . . The receipt of such articles from other countries is forbidden by Soviet customs regulations. The observance of the laws concerning kosher food is made extremely difficult. Sick and elderly people often do not have sufficient physical strength to make long trips to obtain live fowl and are forced to limit themselves to vegetarian food. Even so, in cases where they observe strict kosher, they have to bake their own bread and the like. Religious people who are patients in hospitals are in an especially difficult position with regard to food.

An insoluble problem faces those who find it necessary to end their marriage in accordance with religious laws. This can only be done by a rabbi and to register the documents it is also necessary to have a "shoifer." But there is neither a rabbi nor shoifer in all the Baltic republics, Belorussia and even at present in Moscow.

These examples show that despite the proclaimed freedom of religion, the strict observance of Jewish religious precepts is practically impossible in the Soviet Union. I have no desire to renounce my faith. On the contrary, I consider it my duty to explain to people in general, and to Jews in particular, that the widespread view of this so-called century of science that religion is an anachronism is a catastrophic mistake.

It is absurd, therefore, for the press to ascribe political, mercantile and various other motives for the longing of Jews to go to Israel.

Reading 6

Boris Kochubievsky, Letter to General Secretary Leonid Brezhnev, November 28, 1968, in Moshe Decter (ed.), *A Hero for Our Time, The Trial and Fate of Boris Kochubievsky* (New York: The Conference on Status of Soviet Jews and the Academic Committee on Soviet Jewry, 1970) p. 13

Kochubievsky, a radio engineer from Kiev and an assimilated Jew, began complaining about Soviet anti-Semitism after the 1967 Six-Day War. In the glow of Israel's victory in this war, he and his Russian wife applied for an exit visa to Israel. Visas were granted in 1968, after an initial refusal. But then he was refused permission to emigrate and was put on trial in 1969 for "anti-Soviet slander." His letter to Brezhnev, after he was refused a visa and charged, vividly describes why he sought to emigrate.

November 28, 1968

TO: The Secretary General of the CPSU Central Committee—Brezhnev
The First Secretary of the (Ukraine CP) Central Committee—Shelest
COPY TO: The Investigator of the Prosecutor's Office in the Shevchenko Region of the city of Kiev—V. V. Doroshenko
FROM: The Accused of Slander of Soviet reality—B. L. Kochubiyevsky, Jew

I am a Jew. I want to live in the Jewish State. This is my right, just as it is the right of a Ukrainian to live in the Ukraine, the right of a Russian to live in Russia, the right of a Georgian to live in Georgia.

I want to live in Israel.

This is my dream, this is the goal not only of my life but also of the lives of hundreds of generations which preceded me, of my ancestors who were expelled from their land.

I want my children to study in a school in the Hebrew language. I want to read Jewish papers, I want to attend a Jewish theatre. What's wrong with that? What is my crime? Most of my relatives were shot by the fascists. My father perished and his parents were killed. Were they alive now, they would be standing at my side: Let me go!

I have repeatedly turned with this request to various authorities and have achieved only this: Dismissal from my job, my wife's expulsion from her Institute; and, to crown it all, a criminal charge of slandering Soviet reality. What is this slander? Is it slander that in the multi-national Soviet State only the Jewish people can not educate its children in Jewish schools? Is it slander that there is no Jewish theatre in the USSR? Is it slander that in the USSR there are no Jewish papers? By the way, no one even denies this. Perhaps it is slander that for over a year I have not succeeded to obtain an exit permit for Israel? Or is it slander that nobody wants to speak to me, that there is nobody to complain to? Nobody reacts. But even this isn't the heart of the matter. I don't want to be involved in the national affairs of a state in which I consider myself an alien. I want to go away from here. I want to live in Israel. My wish does not contradict Soviet law.

I have an affidavit of invitation from my relatives; all the formalities have been observed. Is that why you are instituting a criminal case against me?

Is that why my home was searched?

I am not asking for mercy. Listen to the voice of reason:

Let me go!

As long as I live, as long as I am capable of feeling, I shall devote all my strength to obtain an exit permit for Israel. And even if you should find it possible to sentence me for this—I shall anyway, if I live long enough to be freed, be prepared even then to make my way even on foot to the homeland of my ancestors.

Kochubiyevsky

Reading 7

Statements at the Leningrad Hijacking Trial by Eduard Kuznetsov and his wife, Silva Zalmanson, *Chronicle of Current Events*, No. 17, April 1971, pp. 57–58

These statements reveal why the Jewish defendants felt compelled, as a last resort, to hijack a plane to fly to Israel.

Silva Zalmanson: I cannot seem to come to my senses. . . . I am stunned by the sentences demanded for us by the Procurator. He has just proposed execution for a crime that has not been committed. If the court agrees, then two such remarkable people as Dymshits and Kuznetsov will die. I consider that Soviet law should not regard someone's intention to live in another country as treason, and I am convinced that it is those who unlawfully trample on our right to live where we wish who should have been put on trial. Let the court at least take account of the fact that if we had been allowed to emigrate, there would never have been this "criminal conspiracy," which has brought such agony to us . . . and even more to our relatives. Israel is a country with which we, the Jews, are linked spiritually and historically. I hope the government of the USSR will soon resolve this question in a positive way. We shall never lose the dream of joining our ancient motherland. Several of us did not believe our enterprise would succeed, or hardly believed it. We noticed we were being followed at the Finland Station [the Leningrad railway station from which they left for the airport], but we could no longer turn back. We could not return to the past, to the waiting, to living out of suitcases. Our fear of the suffering which might be inflicted on us was nothing in comparison with our dream of living in Israel. We were doing no-one any harm by leaving. I wanted to live there as a family and to work. I would not have indulged in politics. My interest in politics extends only as far as my desire to emigrate. Even now I do not doubt for a minute that one day I shall live in Israel. This dream, sanctified by two thousand years of hope, will never leave me. *Next year in Jerusalem!* Even now I repeat:

> If I forget thee, Jerusalem,
> Let my right hand wither!

[She repeats these words in Hebrew. The Procurator cuts her off.] I have nothing more to say. . . .

Eduard Kuznetsov: The state prosecutor assumes from the outset that once abroad I would have engaged in activities hostile to the Soviet Union. He bases this on what he claims to be my anti-Soviet beliefs, which I have never in fact expressed. I had no intention of harming the Soviet Union. I wished only to live in Israel. I did not regard a possible request for political asylum as a hostile political act. Incorrect statements are made about this in the charge. I have not expressed the wish to speak at any press-conference, neither have I discussed this question with anyone. Without going into the various reasons why I had no such intentions, I shall say only that my ironical cast of mind has insured me against political speeches of any kind. I sincerely regret that I agreed to take part in this business and consider myself only partially guilty under Article 64-a (via 15) and Article 72 of the Russian Criminal Code. I ask the court to be lenient towards my wife Silva Zalmanson. I also ask for justice for myself. After all, you only live once. . . .

Reading 8

Letter from ten Leningrad Jews to the Deputies of the Session of the USSR Supreme Soviet, *Arkhiv Samizdata,* Book 6, 1973, undated (approximately summer 1970)

Soviet Jews point out the problems of the Jewish Question and demand their right to emigrate to Israel. The letter was written shortly after the arrest of planners of the Leningrad hijacking.

TO THE DEPUTIES OF THE SESSION OF THE USSR SUPREME SOVIET

Dear Deputies!

We address ourselves to you as to the supreme echelon of state power because we have exhausted all previous levels of authority. And we raised in dealing with them the very same core subject: the Jewish question about which one usually says that it doesn't exist. But although "it doesn't exist," it does make itself felt every day with such urgency that it gradually becomes an unhealing sore on the body of the Great Power which you represent.

There is not one amongst you who can feel that nothing is the matter, now that the whole Soviet press has suddenly started to offer unlimited space to solemn statements by "people of Jewish origin," "citizens of

Jewish nationality" (and towards the end, even simply—Jews!) saying that the Soviet Union is their real Motherland and Israel is a fascist state. It proved necessary to say at the same time, however, that there are some "renegades" who are ready "to leave for Israel at any moment, leaving behind all their belongings, to leave even on foot" (*Izvestiya* No. 60, 11 March 1970). Now you cannot but know about this.

How do you intend to deal with these "renegades," i.e. with the Jews who want to leave for Israel? Shall you answer that we are not numerous enough and therefore this problem cannot be examined by the supreme legislative institution? It is known, however, that the problem we raise (or rather, to be precise, the problem that arises from the very fact of our existence) is constantly under observation from the highest Party and State institutions; the same problem attracts more and more attention in the whole world.

Until recently the policies that were carried out concerning us included the following elements:

—periodically reactivated campaign in the press against Israel which again and again explained that Israel is a tool of imperialism and that there are no traitors in the Soviet Union wishing to go and live there;

—a gross disregard of almost all appeals for permission to leave for Israel and of all insistent demands at least to explain the motives of refusal;

—an agreement to a very low percentage of applications to leave (some of those who have now received permission to leave were even granted some time before a *motivated* refusal. For instance: "you will not go before fighting stops in the Middle East." Or else "we will not be able to let you go before the establishment in Israel of a progressive social order." There also was an argument that didn't refer to international affairs: "You must first pay by your work for the Russian bread which you have eaten!").

But now a new element of policy has made itself known to all and sundry, an element that is aimed at a final solution of the Jewish question:

—cruel repressions of Jews who insist on their rights.

This happened on 15 June of this year when—according to reports in Leningrad newspapers—a group of criminals intending to hijack an airplane was arrested at the airport. The report on the happenings of that day was not complete: at the same time eight Leningrad Jews were arrested who at that particular time were in very different places but certainly not at the airport and nowhere near the airport. At the beginning, obviously fabricated rumours about the motive for their arrest were circulated: It was said that they had known about the alleged preparations for a hijacking but didn't report them. However, the real motives for these arrests became obvious very soon: during the house searches (carried out in scores of Jewish homes all over the country) the authorities conducting the searches discovered and confiscated such *real* evidence as textbooks of the Jewish language, applications concerning departure for Israel, and so on. The reasons for the arrests are now evident for us, the more so because we are guilty of the same crimes.

We, just as they, are trying to leave for Israel and are striving in all sorts of ways to widen our knowledge of Israel, of its history, and its culture. Does this mean that we are aiming at "furthering racial or national disputes or hostility" (Article 74 of the Criminal Code of the RSFSR)?

We demand that the authorities keep within the law when considering our applications about leaving the country: does this mean that we will be accused of "agitation or propaganda carried out with the aim of sabotaging or weakening the Soviet regime" (Article 70)?

Lastly, we sometimes meet to decide together which other arguments we can put forward in order to persuade the government at last that it won't in any way benefit from forcibly retaining us here: would this be considered as "taking part in anti-Soviet organization" (Article 72)?

The reason we are still free is not at all that our "guilt" is not evident or is not considered to be proven. The reason is that these particular articles of the law are not amongst those articles that are applied automatically. In order to start proceedings on their basis the very existence of "the crime" is not sufficient: It is also necessary that the competent powers choose a given moment and some given people to frighten and edify others.

Well, our Leningrad comrades have already been chosen . . .

Citizens Deputies!

History now demands that you choose, and you have only two possibilities: either let us depart in peace, or enter onto the well-trodden path of mass reprisals. Because as long as we exist, we will continue to demand the freedom to depart—and we will raise our voice louder every day and our voice will become intolerable for you.

But remember that afterwards you will not succeed in justifying yourselves as you have been justifying yourselves for connivance in the crimes committed in the recent past: "We didn't know, and if we knew we didn't believe, and if we believed then we couldn't do anything."

I. Kerler
A. Kerler
B. Diskina
L. Freidin
R. Pozina
Kh. Vinokurova
L. Sheinkar
A. Dekatov
L. Rigerman
B. Tsukerman

Reading 9

Mark Azbel, *Refusenik* (New York: Paragon, 1987), p. 243

On March 10–11, 1971, fifty-six Jews from Riga staged a hunger demonstration in the Reception Room of the Presidium of the USSR Supreme Soviet, near the Kremlin and Red Square. The strikers conveyed their sorrowful stories to Western newspersons. Western shortwave radio broadcasted the blow-by-blow account of this demonstration. Police finally cleared the room. The demonstrators shocked the authorities, who soon gave all of them exit visas. The Kremlin's policy toward refuseniks hardened after this demonstration, but its effects were dramatic inside and outside the U.S.S.R.

On March 10th and 11th, 1971, something happened that changed the face of Soviet history—something so impossible that you would not have dared even to dream of it.

Fifty-six Jews from Riga who for years had been refused permission to leave for Israel arrived in Moscow and appeared in the reception room of the Presidium of the Supreme Soviet. Their leader handed the official at the reception desk a demand, addressed to Podgorny and Kosygin, in which they protested the contemptuous treatment they had received from the Visa Department; protested the fact that their refusals had been made orally, with nothing in writing and no reasons assigned for their detention; and announced that they would remain right there, in the Presidium, until they received an answer. Upon delivery of this declaration, the fifty-six petitioners sat down quietly and started to wait.

Telephones began to ring; police gathered in the hall. Plainclothesmen appeared. Behind the glass that separated the receptionist's office from the room, more police and KGBsts appeared. Finally, the secretary announced to the waiting people that they could receive the answer to their application at the Ministry of the Interior, 6 Ogaryova Street, and told them all to go there.

The Jews refused. "We've been there, and to the Visa Department, many times. We never got an answer. We won't leave the Presidium until some competent official tells us definitely whether or not we will receive our visas."

There was more milling about, more phone calls. At noon the secretary announced that the problems of each of the applicants would be dealt with separately, and asked each person present to sign his name. This was a common tactic; the officials preferred not to approach a group but to take each individual in turn, case by case. The Jews, who were wary of being split up in this way, rejected the proposal: "As all of our signatures are on this application, we want to be treated as a group." They were then urged to select representatives, who would be allowed to confer with a member of the Presidium. Again, the people from Riga declined, knowing perfectly well that their spokesman would be arrested and the whole demonstration fall apart. They were warned that unless they appointed representatives, they would be seen by nobody in the Presidium.

In answer, the Jews continued to occupy the reception room, simply sitting there in silence. After an hour, reinforcements arrived. By one p.m., there were one hundred and forty-one Jews in the hall: people from Lvov, from Vilnius, Sverdlovsk—from everywhere. They were in Moscow on separate errands, to present their individual pleas to the Visa Department. The news of the Riga contingent had spread like wildfire, and they came pouring into the Presidium to join the demonstration.

On the heels of this crowd came several foreign correspondents. Despite the appearance of a swarm of plainclothesmen, the Riga Jews were most willing to talk to the newsmen to explain the reasons for the demonstration and recount their own particular histories. The strikers managed to convey many of their agonizing stories—familiar by now to Soviet Jews, but novel and shocking to the foreigners—before the

KGBsts ordered the journalists out of the hall. At that point the demonstrators delivered a document to the officials at the reception desk, announcing that they were starting a hunger strike, in which again, the Jews from other cities joined them.

The Western short-wave radio picked up the story by midafternoon and began to deliver bulletins on the siege every hour. People with other business at the Presidium were absolutely astounded when they came in and saw a crowd of two hundred sitting—many of them on the floor—in the reception hall. They were rapidly ushered out, and, of course, they spread the word about the demonstration.

The Presidium is situated in the heart of Moscow, right near the Kremlin and Red Square. The authorities were obviously reluctant to conduct mass arrests in such a public place, and there was a long interval of confusion and inaction. Not until seven-thirty did a platoon of police march in to disperse the Jews. It was the eve of Purim, and the strikers were still assembled, in the dark, listening to one of their number, who was reading and translating from Esther. The police cleared them out, but they continued their strike and demonstration at the Central Telegraph Office and returned to the Presidium the next day.

All of Moscow was spellbound by this impossible event. Eventually, no less a personage than General Sholokov, Minister of the Interior, surrounded by his officers, came in to address the demonstrators. He could not force the group to choose a spokesman, so he finally had to address all of them.

"Zionism is Fascism!" he thundered. "No one can try to prevent the Soviets from building Communism and go unpunished." He concluded with an ominous warning: "You should not forget what we did with the Tatars!" But the people from Riga, with their reinforcements, remained silent and obdurate. And with international attention focused upon the demonstration, the authorities felt themselves prevented from using force. In the end, they had to back down. They finally offered to reconsider the entire list, as a unit, and only then did the refuseniks* leave. The majority of them got out of the country within two weeks.

---

* Those whose exit visas have been denied.

Reading 10

Appeal by 250 Soviet Jewish Activists to the Knesset and All Jewish Communities Throughout the World, "Anti-Jewish Hate Ready to Erupt in USSR," March 1977.

These activists reacted to charges of CIA espionage by the state against prominent refuseniks. They claimed that the anti-Semitic atmosphere was so redolent with hate that all *Soviet Jews were in danger.*

To: The Knesset and All Jewish Communities Throughout the World

Brothers in arms throughout many centuries of battle for our existence and of much suffering—

We appeal to you at one of the most dramatic moments, perhaps one of the major turning points in the history of the Jews in Russia. Our history is one never-ending web of humiliation, oppression and pogrom. Across the lives of our grandparents the infamous Beilis trial was smeared like a black thundercloud. Across the days of our fathers was the awful nightmare of the notorious arrests of the so-called "Doctors' Plot." And now in our times there has been upon us the preparations for a new trial, the trial of Jewish "spies," recalling the notorious trial of the so-called "spy and traitor" Dreyfus.

During the last few months, we have seen an escalation in the growing stream of harassments against Jews: beatings in the woods outside Moscow, mass arrests for 15 days, the suppression of the planned symposium on Jewish culture, the renewal of the threat of trial against the editors of the magazine Jews in the USSR, intimidation in all provincial towns, the trial and sentence to three years of Amner Zavurov in Uzbekistan, the arrest of Dr. Yosef Begun in Moscow, the case in preparation against Dr. Naum Salansky in Vilnius, and now the monstrous accusation in the columns of the newspaper *Izvestia.*

On the surface, only a small part of the erupting volcano can yet be seen. All the rest is inside, hidden, concealed from view. What is being cooked up down there in the depths is as yet unknown to us, but we shall no doubt very soon feel it, and experience the full effects of the depth of the anti-Jewish prejudice being stirred up to vomit forth from the mouth of the volcano.

Today, it is an accusation of spying and treason in the newspaper. From there, it is not far to a dreadful trial. Already, all around us, we can hear the echoes and murmurs of this anti-Jewish feeling in the streets, the shops, the buses, the metro, the schools where our children are pupils. Yesterday, it was only the refuseniks under threat. Today, it is every Jew in the Soviet Union who is a potential victim for sacrifice.

At this serious and dangerous moment in our lives we want you to know that no treachery, threat, slander or libel can intimidate us. We shall continue with the fight for our freedom because we know that you are with us. We shall do everything in our power to restore and maintain the honor and dignity of our people. *Am Yisroel Chai!*—The Jewish People live!

Reading 11

The final speech of Anatoly Shcharansky at his trial in 1978, in A *Chronicle of Current Events*, No. 50, November 1978, p. 67

Shcharansky, an active and vocal member of the Moscow Helsinki Watch Group and a leader of the Jewish emancipation movement, was charged with espionage for the United States. He was arrested in March 1977 and held in prison for over one year until his trial in July 1978. This speech, made on July 14, reflects the fearlessness, outspokenness, and frankness for which Shcharansky was well known.

During questioning from March to April 1977 the chief investigators warned me that because of the position I was maintaining under investigation—the same position I have kept to at this trial—I was threatened with the death penalty or a minimum of 15 years' imprisonment. They told me that if I agreed to cooperate with the security organs in their task of destroying the Jewish emigration movement I would be given only a short sentence, would be quickly released and could even have a meeting with my wife.

Five years ago I handed in an application to emigrate to Israel. Now I am further than ever from my dream. One might think that I ought to regret what has happened, but not at all—I am glad.

I am glad that I have lived honestly, at peace with my conscience, and have not acted against it, even when threatened with death. I am glad that I have helped people. I am glad that I have come to know, and have worked with, such honest and brave people as Sakharov, Orlov and Ginzburg—people who are carrying on the traditions of the Russian intelligentsia. I am glad that I am a witness to the rebirth of the Jews of the USSR. I hope that the absurd charges against me and the whole Jewish emigration movement will not hinder the liberation of my people.

My family and friends know that I wanted to exchange my work as an emigration activist for life in Israel with my wife.

My people have been scattered for more than 2,000 years, but wherever Jews have wandered they have always repeated the words: "Next year in Jerusalem!" Now that I am further than ever from my people and from my Avital, and many hard years in prison stretch ahead of me, I say to my people and to my Avital: "Next year in Jerusalem!"

To the court, which can but confirm the sentence proposed earlier, I have nothing to say.

Reading 12

Avital Shcharansky, "Free My Husband, My People," *Wall Street Journal*, November 15, 1985

This letter is an excellent example of how Avital Shcharansky tried to help her husband and all other Soviet Jews who sought freedom.

As the world wonders what the new faces and changed style of the Soviet leadership will mean at the summit meeting in Geneva, we should recall the one occasion on which Mikhail Gorbachev lost his temper during his recent state visit to France. Responding to a news conference question about the treatment of Jews and dissidents in the Soviet Union, the usually unflappable Mr. Gorbachev suddenly lost his composure and, pounding the table, shouted that no one had the right to interfere in the Soviet Union's internal affairs.

Unfortunately, none of the journalists followed up by asking how Mr. Gorbachev could reconcile his position with the fact that in 1975 his government signed the Helsinki accords, whose human-rights provisions stipulate that "everyone has a right to leave any country, including his own" and that "participating states will deal in a positive and humanitarian spirit with the applications of persons who wish to be reunited with their family."

Like millions of freedom-loving people, my husband Anatoly saw in these accords a ray of hope. If indeed the Soviet Union, in exchange for the West's recognition of its hegemony in Eastern Europe, would allow the liberalization of contact and movement, perhaps "detente" would become not just another diplomatic cliche but truly a new era of hope and promise.

So Anatoly joined a Helsinki watch committee, one of the many that sprung up throughout the world to monitor compliance with the accords. Within months he was arrested, charged with espionage for the Central Intelligence Agency, and sentenced to three years in prison and 10 years of hard labor. After transfer to a work camp, he was placed in solitary confinement for 90 days as punishment for lighting Hanukkah candles and reciting the Hebrew Psalms. While there, he was kept alive on a diet of bread and water, the bread only every other day. A year ago, he was again put in isolation.

My husband's health has deteriorated dangerously. He suffers from severe pains in his chest and eyes. Months pass when he is not heard from, when no one is allowed to visit him. In his last letter he says, "I would like to dream of our reuniting in Jerusalem but I need all my energies just to survive as a human being."

Since the signing of the accords, Soviet policy on Jewish emigration has been a roller coaster: from a peak of 50,000 visas in 1979, the year before the Moscow Olympics, to a trickle of a few hundred a year now. But there has been no inconsistency about suppressing any activity on behalf of the Helsinki accords. It is as if the Soviet Union recognizes what we too must understand—that there is more here than just a question of human rights. The Helsinki accords are an international contract that the Soviet government solemnly signed and that it has never shown the slightest intention of honoring. Living up to the Helsinki obligations, it should be noted, would entail no political or strategic risk for the U.S.S.R. One wonders how it would honor a treaty in which military and political compromises are involved.

Many hoped that the new leadership would bring change. If anything, the change has been for the worse. The treatment of dissidents is more brutal—beatings and solitary confinement are commonplace—and the charges ever more spurious and outlandish. Within the past week Roald Zelichonok of Leningrad, after corresponding with public officials in the West, was convicted of "defaming the Soviet state" and sentenced to three years in labor camp. After applying for permission to emigrate, cardiologist Vladimir Brodsky of Moscow was convicted of "hooliganism" and sentenced to three years in prison.

For appealing her husband's conviction on trumped up drug and weapon charges, Lydia Koifman was ordered confined to a mental hospital. For distributing Leon Uris's *Exodus,* Leonid Volvovsky was convicted for slander and sentenced to three years in prison.

Shirley Williams, a leader in Britain's Social Democratic Party, recently asserted that, like most reasonable people, she was fully aware of the public-relations aspects of the Soviets' summit proposals, but that it was imperative they be given a chance to prove their sincerity. I can see no better way for them to do so than to live up to an accord they signed 10 years ago, and to let my husband and 400,000 other Jews who have expressed their desire to leave the U.S.S.R. to join their families abroad.

Ms. Shcharansky, who left the Soviet Union in 1974, now lives in Israel. This week she took up a vigil in front of the Soviet Embassy in Washington.

Reading 13

Galina Nizhnikov, "Against the Kremlin Wall," undated (approximately 1980)

In 1978, Galina Nizhnikov, along with Ida Nudel and other Soviet Jewish women, demonstrated at the Kremlin for the right to emigrate. Here is her moving story of the dangerous days of June 1978.

Against the Kremlin Wall

. . .It was my privilege to participate with Ida (Nudel) in four exclusively female demonstrations in 1978. She was my partner, and a constant source of inspiration and strength. Unique in the history of Soviet women, our activities were included, with all of our names, in the Voice of America broadcasts. Only our faith—that the free world knew about, and supported us—gave us the courage to go on risking our lives. It is critical that the West insists on release of the refuseniks, and the "Prisoners of Conscience." Pressure on the Soviet government is absolutely necessary for preserving the lives of those who wait, and ultimately freedom for those who ask.

Our exit from that situation was an incredible stroke of luck. Senator Edward Kennedy arrived in Moscow with a request for the release of over a dozen refuseniks. Our names were on that list. My tears then were born of joy, relief, and wonder—why were we chosen? I tell my story for all those others, that the knowledge thus passed on may serve the spirit of freedom, the ideal which links us all.

Enroute to America, our oldest son, Alexander, then sixteen, was asked why he left the USSR. He replied, without prompting, "I want to be a Jew. In Russia they preach only Marxism-Leninism. . . ."

Moscow lost our family, really, in 1975 when we applied to emigrate. The status of "refusenik" cost my husband, Edward, his job, as is standard procedure, though many are also denied their academic credentials and all professional contact. Michael was four years old then, and the next four years were lived in an atmosphere of impending terror. He still cannot erase from his memory the horror of being followed by the KGB. Whenever I left the house my children feared never seeing me again, for there was no assurance of my safe return since I had become an activist. . . .

Women in the Soviet Union enjoy a certain amount of equality with men especially in the areas of education and employment. Day care exists for all children by age two, though not for the convenience of the mothers, but to maximize their service to the state, equality as an expedient rather than individual choice. Although women are less likely than men to be imprisoned for their protests (which was why we chose to fight this way) they are just as susceptible to short imprisonments, and to physical abuse. Small children are harassed for their parents' actions. "Bugging" and "shadowing" of individuals is expected. Even if it meant living on the razor's edge, action became our only option.

Three and one half years had passed since we applied to emigrate to Israel (the only country deemed "acceptable" to Soviet authorities). Applications for emigration are an insult to the state, and are continually rejected. Common criminals are informed how long a sentence they must serve, but we occupied an even lower strata [sic]. Denials were repeatedly issued without explanation even though we painstakingly followed all proper legal procedures. Within this time we had ample opportunity to meet at the synagogue with others in the same situation. Saturdays became our day to get to know other refuseniks, for it was very important to know each other quite well.

Ida and I joined thirty desperate women in moving just outside the law, when on the morning of May 10, 1978, we entered the Presidium of the Supreme Soviet in Moscow. We presented a secretary with a letter in which we detailed our complaints regarding the application review process as well as our demand to know when exit visas would be issued. The entire day passed without any response to our letter or our presence.

The momentum of our activities picked up on Friday when we repeated the process. Only this time the secretary directed us to the Ministry of the Interior on Herzen Street where, after two hours an official sent us to the Department of Visas and Registration, known in Russian as OVIR, which is run, as all Soviet civilian agencies, by military personnel. We were guaranteed that we would be met by Yelisov, the Deputy Minister of Internal Affairs, and head of the Visa and Registry office. Instead, we saw his second in command, General Zotov, who informed us that Yelisov was busy. We had seen Zotov so many times that he knew our first names, and we knew that all we would receive from him was abuse. Thus, we refused his offer of a metting with representatives only, insisting that General Yelisov talk with us as a group.

We were prepared to wait for this small advantage. All the time we were in the waiting room, KGB personnel watched us. As evening approached, Natasha Rosenstein wanted to lead us in prayer, it being the

Jewish Sabbath. The KGB men refused her request that they leave us alone. Still, she prayed quietly, and we felt strengthened spiritually in spite of the cynical observations of the KGB. Meanwhile, our nerves were further reduced as photographers came, and without authorization, began gathering shots of each of us. Ida, as always, unhesitatingly bolstered our morale. When the cameras were pointed at Olya Serova, Ida shouted to her "Keep your head up, Olya! We are not criminals. We have nothing to fear." The other women took courage and began to shout too, "You have no right to do this to us," and demanded to see the documents which authorized these men to photograph us. The photographing stopped for the moment, though later, when the police arrived and led us out single file, it began again.

The police were telling each of us that we were going to jail for 15 days. These "divide and conquer" tactics were well known to us, clumsily executed, and quite ineffective. Instead, we were taken in a van to a deserted part of the city and parked outside of a detoxification center for close to an hour without any explanation. The plan was, of course, to scare us into thinking we would be placed in with those drunks. The orders and behavior of the authorities were at once inexplicable and cleverly patterned to keep pressure on. We had not a clue as to why, or what was being done to, or asked of us, but this episode proved to be a critical test. Our reactions were observed, our behavior under pressure —strength or weakness—would prove to be our basis for selection, crystallization of the core group that would dare to continue. . . .

Alexander Garden was the meeting place that we chose to gather on May 15, and we sent a telegram to President Brezhnev. Of course, KGB men followed us, and at the Kremlin wall there were even movie cameras trained on us by agents in civilian dress, plainclothes men whose job it was to do this filming. Officers in uniform trailed us interminably, from the moment we left the central telegraph office—even to the rest room!

In the telegram, we protested our previous treatment, stated our intention to meet with Yelisov that day, and were bold enough to warn that if we were not received within two hours of our arrival at the Ministry, we would then proceed to the Presidium of the Supreme Soviet and stage a sit-down strike. Our telegram was, of course, ignored, so after waiting the specified two hours, we went from the Ministry to the lobby of the Presidium and sat.

It was after six in the evening when a police detail appeared, and their chief greeted us in a curiously affable way: "Ah, my old friends! How much longer are you going to break rules and make trouble for us?" He then threatened us with 15 days in jail, and loudly ordered us to remove the Stars of David from our clothes. As if this command had been a signal, police surrounded us and began shouting, "You're not allowed to wear those things. Take them off. You should be hung by your heels!" We were not intimidated, and tempers flared: Hannah Aronovna branded them fascists, and Guzelle Khait called them bandits. The police grabbed us, tore off our stars, and then led us out to the street through a back way, while all the time we were photographed again and agian. They had vented their wrath especially on Lyuda Cherkasska by simultaneously kicking her from behind and punching her stomach. She was then dragged to a police van and flung onto the front seat. Lyuda was a nursing mother, and this abuse confined her to bed for three days. When she later filed a complaint, the prosecutor, Mr. Rodenko, noted that his investigation had found no use of force against her!

Once again we were driven away in a police van, but we were lucky in that this evening an important soccer game was to be televised, and our guards simply dumped us on a quiet street, near the Udarnik theater; a hasty dispatch, and always out of public view.

For more than a year now we had sat in reception rooms of the Presidium of the Supreme Soviet and the Central Committee of the Communist Party. These rooms were filled with refuseniks—veterans of waiting, some sixty, even seventy years old. In fact, my father-in-law led a refusenik group of more than 20 World War II veterans. (Thankfully, he and my mother-in-law were allowed to emigrate with us.) Observing these people made us realize that we, too, could easily age in reception rooms—following the bureaucracy, living from one application to the next—until one day our children would be adults and we would be the veterans who were swallowed up by time. Our struggle for freedom would be trivialized—only a memory. It became obvious that since the authorities refused to take our previous attempts seriously, we would have to take a drastic course. Our only option was public demonstration. This was a critical decision. To fight for our rights as individuals took strength and courage, but those of us who were mothers bore the additional responsibility of deciding for our children. Rather than being a weak link, our perspective was that it was definitely worth taking the chance.

Gender was a part of the strategem. Six women out of the original thirty were able to bring themselves to take this unheard-of step: Natalya Khasina, Elena Chernobilskaya, Faina Kogan, Natalya Katz, Ida Nudel, and myself. Ida warned of the risks involved in these situations. We would be turning ourselves over to a beastly crowd whose actions were totally unpredictable. The civilians mixed in with KGB plainclothes men, and physical abuse was a real possibility, not to mention verbal attacks. At any rate, we had to be emotionally prepared to hide our fear, as one must from an animal so that it will not bite.

The place chosen for our demonstration was near the Borovitsky Gate of the Kremlin Wall. In addition to the obvious dramatic effect this site was ideal. Being atop a sharp incline, we would be clearly visible but not easily accessible. The particular uniqueness of our act, as previously stated, was compounded by the fact that this type of demonstration was one of the few of its kind to be attempted at all in our generation. A Saturday was picked because not only could our husbands be near to us and watch the children, but also there would be fewer KGB agents in town. One of the privileges of the job was ownership of vacation homes in the country, and naturally the agents used them whenever possible.

The day itself was bright and clear, one we would ordinarily take full advantage of with picnics or walks in the park, but that day we were not in tune with nature—just our mission. While decisions can have an invigorating effect, strengthening resolve, and offering hope, so too, can the atmosphere of spring. We were nervous, but ready.

So after careful planning affording us the element of surprise, on May 23, we climbed the hill to Borovitsky Gate and precisely at 2 P.M. unfurled our banner demanding: "VISAS TO ISRAEL." Our husbands lent moral support by their presence on a nearby green, and later reported all that they had observed. At the bottom of the hill a crowd gathered, at first just a few curious onlookers, then more joined until they numbered about thirty. The KGB had done a poor job in protecting the Kremlin. "Who would have guessed? Just minutes ago there was nothing there." Comments from observers were angry—"How dare they?" "They need a good beating!"—were mingled with "patriotic" comments regarding our religion. Most passers-by quickened their pace, fearing that any attention paid us would be equated with sympathy.

At first, the KGB and Kremlin security personnel stood oblivious. When my arm got tired, I traded places with Elena and the banner turned towards a policeman stationed at the gate. When he realized what was happening, he rushed to a telephone booth, and the way he scrambled was comically reminiscent of a Charlie Chaplin film.

With no justification for their lack of vigilance, male and female agents, all in civilian clothes, furiously started up the hill. Shouting "How dare you!" between their huffing and puffing. They finally were able to back us up against the Kremlin Wall, and seize our banner. There we stood for a moment until we could slip by. As we started down the hill more agents shouted to us to stop. Ida told us to pay no attention, but we got only a bit further before this second group barred our way. Just then uniformed police appeared, grabbed us, and herded us into an office inside the Kremlin. We had remained silent throughout this demonstration, and done something that had never been done before. This was fact, and our hope was that it would effect a decision on our cases.

It must be noted that in the confusion several foreign correspondents at the scene suffered even worse physical abuse than we did, for the KGB used force in dealing with them, confiscating cameras and film. Publicity is very important in the fight for freedom, otherwise our costly efforts would disappear without record—become non-events. Frequently those present in order to cover such an episode are as open to danger as the participants. Their attention and courage are never underestimated, but truly appreciated by us all. They are our umbilical cord to the Western world.

Once inside, our constant bodyguards from the KGB arrived in an uproar, anger showing on their red, blotchy faces because our demonstration had destroyed any chance for them to receive any bonuses. The only recognition they would get, they knew, were reprimands, and their faces reflected their anticipated disappointment, anger and cruelty. The bonus that was a pittance at best had eluded them that year anyway.

An investigator appeared and began to question us one by one—it was always singly now that we were interrogated. We were asked: "First and last name?" In reply, we held out our internal passports. As the questioning continued, his tone and volume increased.

"Do you know the others?"

"Who held the banners?"

"Who instigated this demonstration?"

"Do you know you broke the law?"

Later, we discovered that we had all given more or less the same replies: "We have not broken the law. According to the Soviet Constitution, demonstrations are permitted. We do not wish to talk with you, and you can ask your witnesses who held the banners. . . ."

"Sign this report to show that you have read it and know what it says."

"We don't see why such a report should be made at all, so we will not sign it. . . ."

Reports were made out and read to us in the presence of witnesses but, again we refused to sign them. Thus, our processing ended and at nine in the evening we were again released.

The June first demonstration required more planning and coordination than any of our activities thus far. Even so, it turned out to be the most dangerous and violent of all.

UNESCO chose June 1 as its day for the recognition of children's rights. For us, it provided the perfect opportunity for a public demonstration—women and children together. This time we would be in front of the Lenin Library, at 4 P.M., when there would be many people, and we hoped, more publicity. One month prior, we sent a letter to the City Council announcing our plan, and requesting assurances of safety for our children and ourselves. Five days before the demonstration, all of us who had signed the letter received summonses to appear before the local Party Executive Committee. Guzelle Khait decided to respond. Her appearance was used by the committee as a power exercise—to threaten her directly, and to blackmail her with threats against her husband and her children. The power play backfired totally, though, because not only was Guzelle even more determined to demonstrate, but, having revealed their purpose, the committee received no more answers to their summonses.

Meantime, we were meeting regularly at my apartment for legal seminars. In order to prepare ourselves for any possible situation which might arise in dealing with the authorities, we thought it advisable to acquaint ourselves with the rights granted us, at least in theory, under Soviet law. There was a certain irony involved in our knowledge of the system—working within it and against it simultaneously—attending to details in order to facilitate our escape. The law was studied in one room; this being a legitimate learning situation, and a cover. In another room, unbeknownst to the rest of the participants, we set time schedules and meeting places. Since we really expected to be placed under house arrest on the day of the demonstration, we decided to gather in three groups at separate places, maintaining what we thought to be the strength and ability to force our way out if necessary. Natasha Rosenstein, Galina Tsirlina, and Lena Dubyanskaya all offered their apartments. For Lena this was a curious action since apartments in Moscow are government-controlled, and even though all facts were against it happening, she obtained a flat immediately. Furthermore, towards evening we learned that Lena had changed her mind about its availability, complicating the situation, and we never found out another fact relative to her or the situation.

Ida's role in the upcoming event presented a problem. She had not signed the letter to the City Council, considering it an unnecessary act of self-incrimination, thinking that the action itself was ill advised, and chose not to participate with the group. (Even though I tended to agree with Ida, I did sign the letter.) Ida had a sense of foreboding about individual protests, and subsequent events justified her apprehensions. Those who had demonstrated in groups were not arrested. Those who protested independently were: Masha Slepak, her husband, Volodya, and Ida Nudel were sentenced to exile, and Misha Kremen got 15 days in jail.

In retrospect, I feel that Ida was right in refusing to sign the letter. Rather than providing the protection the group had naively hoped for, the information we gave the authorities allowed them time to prepare, coordinate, and consolidate their reprisals against us. The day before the demonstration the KGB stationed details of plainclothes men at the homes of each of the would-be demonstrators. This was not only expected, but an ordinary fact of life for many of us, and a bit of gallows humor helped to ease the tension, such as "Here comes my lover," or "My guy is so handsome." It was ridiculously simple to pick out the KGB by the extreme rigidity of their stance, their empty hands, empty expressions and the occasional *Pravda* . . . they carried. . . .

Our husbands had agreed to be as near to us as possible. Their presence provided great moral support, but their absence really had us worried. They were nowhere in sight. As we took turns watching from the window, we were unaware that the KGB was well informed of our mates' roles, and had prevented their coming. When a familiar face appeared, at first distant, then closer, its owner waving to us, we instantly brightened. It was Semyon Abramovich Yantovsky, our good friend and a very courageous man. Several KGB men approached him and repeatedly made Semyon show them his documents. Despite being well into his sixties, Semyon spent nearly the entire day there. What a man! If he only knew how much strength and confidence he inspired in us! . . .

Determined not to let UNESCO's Children's Day pass unnoticed, we wrote signs of protest on pieces of wallpaper (which was all we had) in preparation for a window demonstration. The children had come in with a few tree branches bearing new, green leaves which waved out the window above our signs. At 3 P.M. we began demonstrating to an audience that was mostly hostile. Almost immediately after we started, KGB men appeared at the neighboring windows on both sides, below, and even hanging off the roof! It was no problem for these people to occupy neighboring apartments because the KGB never needs permission for access. In a very well-coordinated effort they attacked our signs, and nearly ourselves, with long metal hooks and bats with nails in them, hollering loudly as they did so. Agents had gathered outside, and directed the action from below.

What was evident and infuriating was the use of such force while children could be clearly seen. The detestable hypocrisy of Soviet authorities, especially on a day dedicated to children's rights is exemplified in behavior which continually contradicts its statements. The country claims to be humanitarian, wants its citizens to shed tears for the unfortunate "victims" of capitalism, yet unhesitatingly uses hooks and bats on its own. . . .

Ida Nudel's home was very near to my parents-in-law's; thus my father-in-law had witnessed her solitary protests. He recounted it to us:

"At about six this evening I went out on the balcony, and noticed a crowd of people near Ida's building. I went downstairs and outside to a scene which filled me with terror. Ida stood on her balcony guarding a banner bearing this message: 'KGB GIVE ME MY VISA.' People in civilian dress stood on neighboring balconies waving metal pipes trying to tear it down. I was afraid they would hit Ida! The crowd was allowed to remain there while a few suspicious-looking citizens shouted loudly about Jews rebelling, and getting Stalin and Hitler on them. Around 8 P.M. an agent swung a rope with a heavy object attached and broke Ida's window. As if the sound of breaking glass were a cue, all the plainclothes men left the area, and Ida went inside. Several times I tried to reach her, but the police stopped me."

Despite the hour, Edward and I rushed over to Ida's. We rang, and after checking the peephole, she opened the door to admit us. She showed us the broken glass on the kitchen floor, and we could feel the wind blowing in. Edward's father came a little later and offered to clean up, but Ida declined as she was not yet ready to erase the traces of that scene. We stayed with her, and shared events of the day. Ida completed my father-in-law's account, telling us that she had not been allowed to leave the house all day. Since she had not signed the letter pertaining to the aborted Lenin Library demonstration, she knew of no reason for her house arrest. Throughout the day plainclothes men sat, talking and smoking on an adjacent balcony, and when she went out on her balcony, they just looked at her in defiance. Incensed by their behavior, and knowing that she was surrounded, she abandoned all caution, and answered the situation with that fateful banner. Ida had tried to answer the house arrest on her own, but a bulldozer sat nearby, and the KGB turned it on to drown her out. Rights to self-defense in the USSR are interpreted arbitrarily as in this obvious comparison of an angry, shouting mob, abusive officials, and a noisy machine to one single voice defending her honor.

With the benefit of hindsight many still ask why Ida took such a risk, rather than contain herself. If the choice of danger was all that she had, at least it was hers. To understand her mental state at that time requires either direct experience or extreme empathy. Sometimes even the most negative of options will be grasped with dignity as being the only (or last) act that a person can control. Long before this episode of harassment, the Soviet authorities had created an atmosphere of terror around Ida. She was constantly followed by plainclothes men or uniformed agents, on the street, in the subway, on a stroll through the woods—they even had swimmers monitoring the pool that she used. Black Volgas were permanently stationed at her building, watching and waiting. During Soviet, but even more so, Jewish holidays, the KGB became particularly zealous. Private conversations could never take place in her flat, nor over her telephone, as it had been disconnected long ago; and mail, of course, is censored. Ida's life was bereft of any freedom, so on June 1st, at 6 P.M. she went out on her balcony and unfurled her anger.

Several days later, Ida covered her empty kitchen window with a sheet of plywood which she had decorated with a yellow Star of David. When a policeman came to remove it, she asked him if he would remove a cross from around his mother's neck. When he admitted that he could never do that, she reminded him that by removing her window star he was, in effect, committing such an act.

In a separate but related incident which occurred also on June 1st, a window demonstration took place at Galina Tsirlina's place. This time they closed the windows and hung their signs on the inside: so the KGB simply poured whitewash all over the outside of the windows.

House arrest as a form of persecution naturally had some effect, but as detention it frequently failed or backfired. June 1st turned out to be highly unusual for many people. Natasha Khasina was stranded by the KGB when her baby suddenly fell ill. Luckily, she lived on the first floor, so that she could actually drag the baby carriage through the window, and was able to get to a doctor. Still, agents followed her all the way to the doctor's office. House arrest was enforced in spite of personal tragedy, as, for example, Isold Tufeld's father lay dying in the hospital, but she and her husband were not even allowed to go there.

Many of my companions of this time suffered restraint, verbal and even physical abuse. While Galina Kremen was with us on Butler Street, her husband Misha and their youngest son were put under house arrest. Misha needed to get bread for his son, but the KGB wouldn't let him out. Upset, he turned on his tape recorder, with an amplifier, setting up the speakers to face the street, and broadcast the story of his visa refusals. He hung out a banner which read "Long Live Israel" and played Jewish songs on the tape recorder.

A woman neighbor, who was later called in as an official witness, said that she heard such songs with words like "Israel," and "Pharaoh," and "Let my people go," over and over. She was particularly upset that the songs were not in Russian! . . .

Natasha Rosenstein was not formally prosecuted for her involvement, but the day after our demonstration, directly outside her window, someone had boldly painted on the street: JEWS TO THEIR GRAVES. While her son gathered his friends, her husband put on the traditional Jewish prayer shawl. With the words "It's been a long time since Moscow has seen a Jew in a prayer shawl," he went outside, stood over the street writing, and prayed. It was a bold move, and such an unusual sight that even the KGB kept its distance.

Presently, the KGB van arrived and parked directly over the slur. Slowly and deliberately, agents painted over the letters one by one as the vehicle moved to expose them. Typical of the way in which the

Soviet system works, there was not enough paint, so work was halted until more arrived. The second batch was another color, giving the street a ridiculous circus effect. Furthermore, by evening, this hasty cover-up proved inadequate, as the letters were already showing through. So the first thing the next morning, Natasha sent a telegram to the same police chief who had come the night of the demonstration. He had warned, and the writing in the street had confirmed that the populace was approaching a "pogrom mentality." Therefore, she informed him that she was preparing measures for her own defense. Very shortly a team of workmen appeared, broke up and then resurfaced the blacktop.

June second turned out to be as busy as the day before, and Natasha's apartment was again the scene. A press conference was unexpectedly arranged. I received word of it by telephone, and since I was near Ida's home, I immediately told her about it, and together we rode to Natasha's apartment.

As we all knew, Ida was constantly followed by tails whom she tried not to notice. But I knew that you really cannot get used to them, to the unrelenting psychological stress they cause. Only once was I ever able to elude them, and what a relief it was—a few hours of simple freedom. But my tails stuck around only a month or so, while Ida had to put up with them for several years. At times when Ida and I traveled together, we were happy and more carefree. Yet even when we were in the street she would not talk about serious matters. "KGB ears are all around us," she would say. She knew this very well since microphones had been installed in her ceiling. Her thoughts could only be written down.

By the time I approached my in-law's building it was nearly 11 P.M. and very quiet. For the first time in my life I saw with my own eyes how the Soviet authorities begin a raid on someone's home. Ida's was their objective. A police van pulled up to her building, and while several agents went inside, some others actually hid in the bushes. My parents-in-law and I kept watch until the van finally left in the early hours of the morning.

The next day Ida described the extent of this search and seizure. Her books and diary were taken along with her second typewriter—her first one had been confiscated in an earlier raid. Furthermore, the prosecutor falsified the report of the search, claiming that Ida's friends had thrown rocks at her windows in order to interfere with the agents. Clearly this was KGB bravado, for one would have to be insane to act that way in the presence of the police.

We continued our struggle with a demonstration in response to the "Jews to their graves" slur. Despite the rain on Sunday, June 4, ten women protested in Trubnay Square, which, at 4 P.M. was very busy. I approached with Guzelle Khait and Galina Kremen, while Natasha Rosenstein and Natasha Khasina came together. The Katz family pushed their baby stroller slowly through, and Lena Chernobilskaya was there with Galina Tsirlina. Ida was the last to arrive, her "tails in tow," just like the rest of us; but this time they watched indifferently, except for one who went to a telephone as we made our move. Quickly, we formed a line, and held up signs proclaiming: "Let Us Leave or Lay Us in Our Graves" and "Visas to Israel." I threw down my jacket to reveal my yellow football jersey on which I had drawn a Star of David, and had written "Visas to Israel" and "Let Us Go to Israel" on the front and back. Yellow was chosen to symbolize the yellow Magen Davids which Jews were forced to wear in Nazi Germany. The implied comparison did not go unnoticed. We only had about six minutes there before police vehicles drove up and whisked us away. My husband and Misha Khait jumped into a nearby taxi, telling the driver, "You see the car ahead? It's taking our wives away—keep after it." The idea of chasing after the police terrified the driver, but he did it. Some of our friends were standing by a bus stop nearby. A man waited there with his son. When we were herded into the police van before their very eyes, the man turned to his son and said, emphatically, "Take a good look. That is OUR 'glorious democracy.' "

It was strangely quiet at the police station. People pending trial looked out at us from the detention cell. One policeman asked me to show him my jersey, which he seemed to like. A small-time hood was brought in, his pockets were turned inside out, and he was treated very rudely. Then they brought in a woman with venereal disease. The thought of being in a cell with a woman like that forced me to ask the policeman whether we would be held together.

"Don't worry," he told me, "we don't put venereal cases in here, we take them off to special detention centers, and you will be put in with the intelligentsia." I asked what he meant by intelligentsia.

He replied, "Oh, black market speculators, and people like you—

intellectuals." Knowing that if I received a 15-day sentence, I would not be sent there, I heaved a sigh of relief, and everybody laughed together.

Prison was always a possibility. As Ida had experience, she told us to bring along wool socks and a warm, short scarf. Prisoners slept on naked, metal frames, and longer scarves would be confiscated lest the prisoner attempt suicide.

I must confess that the prevailing atmosphere this Sunday was not in the least tense, most probably due to the absence of KGB supervisors. The police regarded us with a mixture of curiosity and respect, referring to us as intellectuals. Whereupon, Ida had the idea of telling them everything, that it would be interesting, as they rarely had discourse with people like us. Natasha Katz was permitted to nurse her baby in another room. Lena knitted. We were allowed to drink water, and we even ate: Galina Kremen had brought sandwiches which were gratefully shared. Our husbands were visible from the window, and we smiled to them. No one chased them away.

Finally things began to stir, and we were taken to the second floor for questioning. The investigator was quite friendly.

"I don't know why you're all so hellbent on getting out of the country. My wife is Jewish."

When one woman asked, "Then why haven't you applied to emigrate?", everyone laughed, easing the tension. When we told him that having a Jewish wife was a way to go places, he smiled. (In the USSR only Armenians and Jews have the right to apply for emigration; so others often take a Jewish spouse, for instance, so that they, too, as part of a Jewish family, can apply. Marriage to a foreigner is another variation on this exit theme.) The investigator continued, though now clearly annoyed:

"I have a lot of friends who visit the West on business. Of course, they earned a lot of money, but not in an easy way, and they would never agree to stay there forever. Do you know the expression: 'The grass is always greener in the other fellow's yard'? Couldn't you find something else to do? I was sitting at home, in my warm, cozy apartment, drinking tea, watching television, when suddenly I got the call to come in here —out in the pouring rain."

Finally the investigator called in a policeman and said, "Let these women go."

In answer to a question about the police report, the investigator replied, "No, it is ridiculous. We don't need that." So we were released in the same way as the last time—separated from the group, and dropped off near our homes.

Anxiety was normal for us, and the next few days offered little relief. . . . Masha Slepak had been released on her own recognizance while her husband, Volodya, was being held pending trial. Ida's case also was pending, and she was as determined to win as the authorities were. She set out to familiarize herself with the law, but specifically the accumulated evidence and charges against her.

We were so distressed by the graffiti and the barbarism of the KGB that some of us thought we should protest directly in front of the KGB headquarters. Not everyone agreed. Some were simply afraid of the place, and several of the women had become disenchanted with the group's demonstrations.

"Don't you see? We march and protest and the government couldn't care less."

Conversely, we felt that the authorities would not tolerate much more protest, so we would have to make a decisive move. At that point we were each prepared to sacrifice ourselves for the freedom of even one refusenik. Naturally, we hoped to avoid the almost certain 15-day jail sentence that a demonstration at the KGB building would bring. Ida was generally democratic, allowing for individual opinions, but this time, fearing for our safety, she was adamant that our posters show nothing anti-Soviet . . . only "Let Us Go to Israel."

On June 9th we arrived at KGB headquarters to find the area was literally overrun with agents—obviously they had received advance knowledge (we later learned how, and it will be related further on)—giving them the opportunity to plan and prepare every last detail of this scene. Each individual action had been arranged, from the seemingly genuine provocateurs to the manner in which we were eventually taken away. They had personality profiles—and mine, judging from the June 1st demonstration, must have led the authorities to believe that I could be easily made to fight, thereby giving them the excuse they needed to really deal with me harshly. They were wrong. We had been set up.

We aligned ourselves at the predetermined spot: I in my yellow shirt, and Natasha Rosenstein in a blue skirt on which she wrote "Let Us, Citizens of Israel, Go!" Galina Kremen had brought her son, Sasha, who held a photo of his younger brother and a poster reading, "Let My Father out of prison." All of us held "VISAS TO ISRAEL" signs. We had barely taken our positions when a KGB agent in civilian clothes came up to us and poked at our placards, saying:

"What's all this you've written up? Come on, now, go somewhere else or I'll call the police."

We told him to go away, that the police could figure it out without him. Opposite us, photographers busily recorded the scene as our provocateur pulled off my poster, leaving me with only a dowel in my hand. This little stick was to become a piece of evidence against me, for I was accused of attacking this man with it. Instead, I fell victim to a woman who appeared in front of me alone, a professional agent, provocative and restrained; she grabbed me by the front of my jersey, thereby tearing my mezuzah, my talisman. Daring me to fight back, with an evil look and the same professional skill, she shoved her clenched fist forward, stopping only millimeters from my face. Instinctively I froze; knowing that the slightest move would have done me in, I just looked at her derisively. In front of me in the crowd, I caught the eye of Victor Yelistratov. Seeing only this—his eyes actually commanded me.

"Don't move!" How wise he is! I got his message in my most critical moment. This attempt to provoke a fight had failed.

The crowd grew larger and more unruly as the verbal abuse deteriorated: "To the gas chambers with them! Hitler did it! They've eaten their fill here, and now they are acting up!" They shouted for the police.

The police arrived and demanded to see our identification, whereupon I demanded to see theirs. Although they were the same ones who dealt with us on June 4th, their behavior was entirely different, for today the KGB was in charge, and the atmosphere was absolutely electric. My papers were in my purse, which now lay somewhere on the pavement amongst the crowd. One agent, Colonel Markov, sarcastically complied with my demand for identification, but would not allow me to go after my own.

"Let me get my purse," I shouted. "That's where my documents are. Where are you taking me? I can walk by myself?" I was dragged through the underpass leading to the opposite side of the street, and there my husband caught up with me and put my purse in my hands. It calmed me to see Edward, and to have in my possession my passport as well as the items I had brought to carry me through a fifteen-day imprisonment.

At the KGB building I was seated in a Volga with policemen at each side, taken to the same station as the last time, and waited alone. After a while the rest of the group arrived. They had been transported in a special bus which the authorities dramatically drove against the flow of traffic, using a loudspeaker to warn oncoming vehicles, and blaring a siren all the way. . . .

I was booked for malicious hooliganism, and for disobeying authority. Everyone else avoided the second charge, and even though the police tried every means possible, we all refused to sign their reports. Our names were recorded in several different files; each time required the taking of our internal passports. When they were returned, Galina and Sasha were allowed to go home. Natasha Katz and Natasha Rosenstein were next to be released, but the rest of us were required to continue what had become a morbid sort of game. One KGB agent asked a policeman which one of us had worn the yellow shirt, now invisible under my jacket. The agent pointed an accusing finger at Ida, but the officer was unsure. Pursuing the question, the agent then asked loudly for "Nizhnikov," and when I answered, he stared at me directly, trying to size me up. He then concluded that as an adversary I was not to be feared, and pronounced me a nobody, a worthless cipher, a zero. Ida was afraid that I was insulted, and told me not to pay attention to him. . . .

Meanwhile, Natasha and I set about composing telegrams to President Brezhnev. We described the illegal actions of the authorities, protested current emigration policy, declared ourselves hostages of the Soviet Union, and announced our intentions to continue our struggle. I also drafted a telegram to the police demanding the return of my passport. We went for tea when Edward returned, and when Natasha left our apartment, half the agents outside went with her.

Since I lived near the telegraph office, I offered to send them all, and despite my early departure the next morning, my "companions" were not only with me at the office, but actually straining to see what I was writing. Because there was so much to write, I took the forms back home to fill in. My father-in-law stopped by and then returned with me to the telegraph office. Waiting in line with us were "civilians" holding forms, but still trying to get a look at my messages. After dispatching the telegrams by registered mail, my father-in-law and I left.

We went to Ida's to offer help and moral support. She had a summons to appear in court the next day, but knew nothing about her case, or even if the trial date was set. As it was, she was granted permission to familiarize herself with the charges pending against her, to read and copy out the depositions, and thus to prepare her defense. Since no one else was allowed to see these documents, Ida spent the entire day in solitary labor. There were positive results in this work, though, as Ida's detailed knowledge of the law resulted in the dropping of two charges. First was the June 4th demonstration at Trubnay Square. Ida requested that the other participants be called as witnesses, correctly assuming the authorities had no desire for corroborating testimony from nine refusenik women. Second, the investigator who had searched Ida's apartment made the claim that her cohorts outside had broken her kitchen window as the search progressed. This was a lie, and my father-in-law, as noted, had witnessed the entire episode. Ida filed a countercharge against this investigator, knowing that under Soviet law his participation in the search rendered him ineligible to file a deposition on the matter. Without his testimony the KGB had nothing, so the whole thing was quietly dropped.

Meanwhile, my father-in-law and I wrote out statements of all we had witnessed, including requests to be called to testify. We sent them off by registered mail so that the receipts would be proof of delivery. Nevertheless, admission of this evidence was not in our control. My father-in-law recounted all he had seen from his window and in the street on the evening of June 1st. His statement ended with a request to be called as a witness that the trial, and the comment that the cruelty displayed towards Ida that day reminded him of the pogroms led by Petlura in the Ukraine in 1918.

My statement was shorter:

"On June 1, around 11:30 P.M., I went to the home of my friend, Ida Nudel. The left pane of her kitchen window was broken, and glass was scattered everywhere. The wind was blowing through the apartment. I wish to be called as a witness at her trial. I also wish to be examined as a witness to the events of June fourth."

Five days prior to the trial, Ida was called into the court and twelve women accompanied her for moral support. As we approached the building, KGB men took the customary photographs. Boris Chernobylskaya entered a phone booth and overheard conversation from the adjacent booth. An agent was reporting:

"They're coming in couples: the Nizhnikovs, Tsirlins, Rokhlenkos,

Shvartzmans, and the Kremens. There's one in a yellow jacket whose name I've forgotten. . . ."

Boris leaned over and stuck his head in. "You mean Rosenstein," The officer was profoundly embarrassed.

There was no reason for Ida to be called in that day since she was only informed that her trial date was indefinite. In the corridor she was approached by her court-appointed attorney. She had not requested representation, and refused to speak with him. The lawyer was Jewish also, and it was painful to see his humiliation as he followed her down the hall. Firmly, but kindly, Ida explained that she had nothing against him personally, but planned to act in her own defense.

After Ida had left the judge's chambers, I went into see him. He listened at first, but when he realized that I was there in support of Ida, he became surly, "Get out. I don't have time for this!" He would not accept my deposition, and refused to call me as a witness. At home my father-in-law and I resolved to send in our depositions anyway.

The atmosphere grew more heavy over Ida, as her customary tails were replaced by older, more experienced agents. She tried to lead her life as normally as possible during those last days before her trial. Since she often swam, one night she set off for the pool, but her tails prevented her from going. Ida needed her swimming badly for relaxation, and so she agreed to sign a form promising not to leave Moscow in return for the privilege to go swimming. Still, the agents had to swim along. In another attempt at relief from the oppression, Ida and her friends the Shvartmans took a trip into the woods one day. Her agent naturally went along, and they even brought their own picnic! We had offered to take her into the woods—to disappear—but Ida refused. More than anything, she would not show her enemies any weakness. She imposed this discipline on herself, and never faltered.

Ida was not even informed of her trial date until the day before, and she spent the remaining time sending letters and telegrams to Soviet agencies, calling on them to put an end to blatant disregard of the law. Certain that she would be imprisoned, Ida asked her friends to arrange a press conference through which she could express her opinions, and describe her situation to friends in Israel, and throughout the world. Since preparations for the dissidents' trials began, the KGB had been waging a psychological attack on foreign correspondents—the goal being to divert their attention, and to silence them. We were all totally disheartened that not even one reporter showed up for the press conference or her trial. Who knows? If the press conference had taken place, maybe we wouldn't be asking ourselves why she did as she did.

En route to the court, Ida stopped at her parents' home to give them a package to deliver to some political prisoners in Riga. Many of Ida's friends, among them a few foreign guests, came to escort her to the courthouse, and we were accompanied by six agents who made a great show of flipping over the lapels on their jackets to better transmit our whereabouts every step of the way. Cameras flashed with usual diligence as we arrived.

Volodya Slepak's case was to be tried on the same day as Ida's. When we reached the courthouse, we discovered that his trial was not only set for the same day, but for the same hour, making it impossible for all of us to be present at both trials. Hence, we divided into two groups, except for Hanna Aronova, who was ill at home. But it was through her that we learned that those who had tried to get into the courthouse where Volodya was being tried had been hosed down by the KGB.

A policeman at the entrance of the courthouse where Ida was being tried blocked our way. We lacked the necessary passes, white cards that were issued only to certain people, but the visitor's area was full, or so he claimed, and the court was closed to the public on Wednesdays. When Ida refused to enter without her friends, he resorted to a little deception. We were to go inside, and up to the second floor where we would be directed to the courtroom. Suspicious of the sudden change, we entered, and a few did follow the officer's instructions only to discover that the door through which they were sent led through an emergency exit to the street. Having discovered the ruse, we were more determined to remain with our friend, so we made use of what we had, and formed a human wall around Ida. Twice a secretary tried and failed to get her inside, so a judge came and read a statement authorizing the use of force to bring Ida to the proceedings. Of course this strengthened our will, and we tightened the ring. The fracas began with the appearance of a dozen policemen who indeed used physical force to break through our arms, spirit Ida away, and eject all of us from the building. Galina Tsirlina and Arik Rokhlenko, Ida's best friends, had to be literally carried outside. Principle prevented the participation of class enemies in official processes.

When my father-in-law showed his postal receipt to an officer and explained that he expected to be called to testify, he was allowed back in. This was just another trick, however, as they held him in a small room for several hours without food, or water, or any outside contact. When the authorities released him, claiming that his testimony was not required, he unhesitatingly expressed his contempt for this system as a mockery of justice. Desperate for information, we asked a cleaning lady who came out of the building whether she knew anything about the trial. By her position, she could see and hear everything, going completely unnoticed by the authorities, and not being an official of any kind, she would talk with us. We asked if the trial had ended yet, or if she heard any verdict. She just laughed, and said, "Are you serious? In THIS country the verdict is always known before the trial begins!"

Thus Ida was tried in a closed session; all attempts at access by friends and witnesses were denied. We waited. Our only contact with her was during a dinner break when she opened a window to tell us that the charges relative to the June 4th demonstration had been dropped. She was eating a sandwich, and seemed in good spirits. Then someone came and ordered her away from the window and closed it.

We continued to wait. Finally people began to leave the building and to mix with the crowd outside. Some of them formed a barricade around the car parked at the back entrance to the courthouse. Then Ida was led out. We glimpsed her smile and the wave of her hand.

"Ida, we're with you!" we shouted, and then the car sped off—carried Ida away to imprisonment. Someone tried to pursue a taxi driver to follow the car so we would know where she was being taken, but the taxi was stopped by KGB agents.

My father-in-law had words with one of the people who had been "invited" to attend the trial. The spectator was clearly impressed:

The proper procedures had been followed, even a lawyer for the defense and witnesses. If only you could have heard the speech that the prosecutor made," he exclaimed. "From the proceedings I gathered that these acts had been committed by a well-organized and centrally controlled group!" The authorities had obviously succeeded in convincing their audience.

Why was it necessary to create this impression? The authorities, who think only within the Marxist-Leninist framework, in terms of groups, collectives and the Party, knew the situation. The actions of the individual are of no great importance. Dealing with a single person is rather dull. It is much more productive to uncover a group, an anti-Soviet organization. That kind of thing could make one's career and, moreover, it's something the masses can "understand": they have been saturated with enough Communist Party history to "know" that the enemies of the Soviet Union, whether foreign or domestic, have always banded together in groups. Furthermore, this accused is Jewish. What could be more simple than to link this group to those reactionary Zionists they had heard about since grade school? Pure Socialist class orientation.

The invited spectator was pleased with the trial, perhaps even moved. There had been an investigation, a judge, jurors, lawyers—everything looked fine. What was missing was any support for the defense, though court records make no note of this—only that the trial had observed all rules of Socialist law.

What kind of justice can there be without the right to a fair trial? Without that all other rights are worthless. Not only do we need the right to demonstrate freely, but also the right to remain at liberty after the demonstration.

Ida was no stranger to the Soviet judicial system. She had been supportive of its victims by all possible means. She corresponded with political prisoners, traveled to prisons for visits, and fought with prison bureaucracy. She had been present at many trials similar to her own, and her opinion of the system was as clear and simple as the statement she delivered that day, "I do not wish to take part in this spectacle. This is not a trial, it's a reprisal. I ask only that I be allowed to make a final statement." Her thinking was influenced by, and her position is best explained through, the words of the Jewish journalist Vladimir Zhabotinsky.

"Once again we have become the accused. How long can this go on? Tell me, my friends, are you not weary of these long, drawn-out proceedings? Is not now the time to respond to these and all future accusations, reproaches, suspicions, slandering, and denunciations; to cross our arms over our chests and in a loud, clear, cold and calm voice utter the only statement that this public can hear and understand: Go to hell all of you! What sense is there in all these farces called trials where the outcome is predetermined? What kind of joy do we get out of voluntarily participating in this farce, in sanctifying these infamous proceedings, with speeches in which we defend ourselves? Our enemies will not believe us, the indifferent will not be listening. . . ."

Reading 14

Ida Nudel, "The Protocol of the Interrogation of Ida Nudel," translated from Russian, November 1977, from files of the National Conference on Soviet Jewry.

Ida Nudel first applied to emigrate in 1972. After repeated refusals, she was arrested in 1978 for "malicious hooliganism" and sentenced to four years of internal exile. Her "crime" was hanging a banner outside her apartment window that read "KGB Give Me a Visa to Israel." She became known as the Guardian Angel for her help to Soviet Jewish prisoners of conscience. She was finally allowed to emigrate to Israel in 1987. In November 1977, the KGB interrogated Nudel to learn details about who had helped Shcharansky "spy" against the USSR. Her account of this interrogation sheds much light on KGB methods and goals in dealing with Soviet Jewish activists during the mid- to late 1970s.

Protocol of the Interrogation of Ida Nudel
(written from memory)

The questioning took place at the Lefortovo prison on the 25th of November 1977. It was conducted by the KGB investigator, Sherudilo, and lasted from 9:30 in the morning until 17:30 in the afternoon.

After filling out a form with my personal data, the investigator wrote in the protocol, following my request, that I have been a citizen of Israel since 1972. He then explained to me what the responsibility would be for giving false testimony and for refusing to give testimony. Then the investigator, Sherudilo, said something like the following: "You were called for questioning as a witness in the case of A. Shcharansky who is accused of treason to motherland in accordance with Art. 64 'a.' However, I have no right to tell you what exactly are the charges presented against Shcharansky as this is the secret of the investigation. The accused himself knows his charge and it will be read at the trial. Any discussions about the subject of the charge would be senseless."

Then we discussed the procedure of the questioning for about an hour. I insisted on my right to write down my answer in the protocol myself. The investigator insisted that he will be writing down my answers. In the end he promised that after my answers would be read to him he would let me write them down by myself. This agreement was not stated in a categoric terms, but in rather freely interpreted sentences.

Q. Are you acquainted with A. B. Shcharansky and if so, when and under what circumstances had you met?

A. First of all, I must state my views on the so-called "Shcharansky case." You are the first official—and, I think, the only one—who wanted to talk to me about this so-called "case." My appeals to the Soviet leaders remained unanswered and therefore I would like to use this meeting with an official and to state the following:

Accusing Shcharansky of treason to motherland, his arrest, the long investigation during which about a hundred people in different Soviet cities were questioned, the detention and interrogation of the US correspondent Robert Toth in Moscow—all these are, in my opinion, a tactical step by the Soviet Union in its relations with the USA. The aim of this step is to arouse the public opinion in the US by the threat to the life of a popular Jewish refusenik, A. Shcharansky, and thus make the US government give up its policy of defending human rights in all countries, including the USSR.

The charge of spying could have been presented with the same degree of probability to any Jew. A. B. Shcharansky was chosen from a large number of Jews because he was young and was a popular among the supporters of the struggle for human rights.

This is not the first time when a government, including a Russian one, used the Jewish people and individual Jews for solving its internal and external problems. It is well known that the pogroms in Russia were initiated and encouraged by the government. The background of the 'case' of the Jew, Dreyfus, in France and the 'case' of Beilis in Russia is well known."

The investigator said that I am evading an answer to the question asked. He again cited the law about criminal responsibility for giving false testimony or refusing to give testimony. I then added the following phrase to my answer: "I am today a witness in a so-called 'case' with the hero of which I am acquainted, but I do not remember the exact time and circumstance of our first acquaintance."

This was followed by a discussion about my right to write my answer, by my accusing the investigator or depriving me of my right to answer the questions in writing. All this was not included in the protocol. For four hours I tried to gain the opportunity to write down my answers in the protocol. The investigator wrote down his own version of my answers in the protocol, but his formulations were so vague that it was impossible to understand what were they all about and what I did make my statement about.

Investigator Sherudilo then said that my sincere and truthful answers could help the just solution of the Shcharansky case. To this I answered that the procedural laws forbid the blackmailing of witnesses during interrogation and I was therefore surprised that investigator Sherudilo has been trying to use this method on me.

Q. What can you tell about Shcharansky's activities concerning his contacts with people who applied for emigration to Israel?

A. The policy of the emigration authorities had lead [sic] to the gathering in Moscow and many other Soviet cities of a number of Jews who have been waiting for years for emigration permits. Being placed outside the society, they are desperately trying to find some solution to their problem. Shcharansky was one of them and he, same as the others, was thrown out of the society and persecuted by the authorities for his desire to find out the term of validity of the restrictions to his emigration and the reason for the refusal to his application for emigration.

The answer to this question was stated by me, but investigator Sherudilo refused to let me write it down in the protocol. He hurried to write down my answer in his own words, having completely covered up the essence of my answer.

At 17:00 the investigator offered me the protocol for reading and signing. I made the following inscription: "the protocol was read by me personally."

I also wrote the following remark: "The investigator Sherudilo V. A.

had rejected my request to write down my answers by myself in the protocol, but had written down his own interpretation of my answers."

I signed this remark and also the first page of the protocol of the questioning, where my biographic data was given.

Reading 15

"Nudel's Final Plea," in *A Chronicle of Human Rights in the USSR*, No. 30, April–June 1978, p. 26

These are the last words to the court spoken by Ida Nudel after she was convicted of "malicious hooliganism." She expresses the pride of a woman confident in the rightness of her beliefs and actions.

Now I should assess my actions. A final plea—it sounds so solemn, as if from beyond the grave. A final plea—after it, there can be no other pleas and words lose all their significance.

On June 1st, I committed an act of desperation. I asserted my right to public protest. But I am not really being tried for that act although the formal charges are the June 1st demonstration on my terrace and the June 4th demonstration on Trubnaya Square. I am being tried in fact for the last seven years, the most wonderful years of my life. If I should ever find myself obliged to deliver another final plea, I am absolutely convinced that I shall affirm once again that the seven years which are the cause of this trial were the most difficult but also the most wonderful of my life. During the seven years I learned to walk with my head high, as a human being and as a Jew. The seven years have been full of daily struggle on behalf of myself and others. Every time that I was able to keep a victim alive, I experienced a rare and intense emotion comparable, perhaps, to the joy of a woman who has given birth. Even if the remainder of my life should turn out to be gray and uneventful, the memory of those seven years will warm my heart and reassure me that I have not lived my life in vain.

You, my judges, cannot conjure up a punishment which will even the score for the joy and triumph of these last seven years.

Reading 16

Alexander Lerner, "Emigration or Culture? Which Is More Important?" September 25, 1976. Furnished by the Union of Councils for Soviet Jews

Professor Lerner was an important scientist in the U.S.S.R. until 1971 when he applied to emigrate. He was refused for "state secrets" and was dismissed from his job. In this essay, Lerner argues that "the emigration movement has been and will continue to be a basic stimulant to the resurgence of national awareness among all Soviet Jews." Lerner was allowed to emigrate in 1987. This article was written on the eve of the Jewish New Year, 5737, received in London, England, December 1, 1976, translated by Michael Sherbourne of London, England, while in Israel at Kibbutz Neve Eitan on January 5, 1977.

Repatriation and Assimilation

After the October Revolution of 1917, the policy adopted in relation to the national cultures of all the peoples inhabiting this multi-national country, fitted very closely to the principle formulated by Stalin: "For a culture which will be national in form, and socialist in content." Therefore, Jewish culture in the Soviet Union was replaced by a Soviet culture in the Yiddish language. Moreover, the "socialist content" of Soviet culture means one thing and one thing only—unqualified praise for the existing regime, its leaders, and its political aims and objectives. However, even in such a form, "Jewish" culture was not destined to last long, and at the end of the 1940's it was liquidated and its leading protagonists—writers, actors, producers, artists—were all, almost entirely annihilated.

The majority of the Soviet Jews were compelled at that time to accept meekly and without protest the liquidation of every aspect of a Jewish cultural life in the USSR. They came to regard Russian as their mother tongue, and Soviet "culture" as their own culture, which they assimilated and spread and to which they brought their own special contribution. Jewish religious life was suppressed and its remains were farmed out to people who were ready to submit meekly and to quietly obey whatever instructions were given by governmental authority. However, in order to maintain a semblance of respectability in the eyes of the world, the Soviet authorities preserved (of course under their complete control) a sort of "facade" of "Jewish" institutions in the form of a few synagogues and prayer-houses, the "newspaper" *Sovietische Heimland* and a few singers of the Jewish folksongs. The poverty of this "ersatz" so-called Jewish culture can be judged by the fact that in Moscow, for a population of approaching a half a million Jews, there is just *one* synagogue and the only organs in the Yiddish language in the entire country with a population of more than two million Jews, is published in only a few thousand copies. And even that number is not sold out, as most Jews are quite sickened by the open sale of this paper.

An interest in Jewish culture has been reawakened only in recent years and then only among those Jews who have decided to be repatriated to their homeland—Israel. Although the movement for repatriation has attracted some hundreds of thousands of people, the majority of Soviet Jews for one reason or another have not yet taken the decision to emigrate. Some, as a result of mixed marriages, have become very closely knitted into the general population; others have not yet decided to attempt to emigrate because of the risk of repression; yet others fear that they may find professional difficulties. There are also those who are convinced that the USSR is their real homeland, the discrimination against the Jews is a passing phenomenon and who believe that they themselves, in spite of being registered in their passports as Jews are, in fact, not really Jews, but completely assimilated Soviet citizens. This latter condition can be characterized as "subjective" assimilation. But "objective" assimilation has no place, inasmuch as both the authorities and the indigenous population continue to consider such people as Jews with all the consequences that flow from this condition. One way or another the fact is that the major part of the Jewish population of the

USSR is not yet ready to emigrate, and is obliged to arrange its life so as to conform to existing conditions and to suffer as little as possible from discrimination. Let us call such people "assimilationists."

In order to safeguard themselves from persecution, these people have to be seen as especially loyal in relation to the existing regime—they have to try to look as little as possible like Jews and, God grant they should not have the slightest connection with anything Jewish. Among the assimilationists there are also those whom we shall call "super-assimilationists"—who are particularly assiduous in showing their zealous efforts to break away from Jewishness. They declare with pride that they do not know even a single word of a Jewish language; they give their children such emphatically un-Jewish names as Vassili and Andrei, Marfa, and Oxana; they do not miss any opportunity either publicly or in private conversations with Party members to condemn the State of Israel and those Soviet Jews who have left the USSR; they will eagerly tell an anti-Semitic anecdote and if it depends on them they will refuse to grant a Jew an interview for employment or for admission to an institute. The numbers of such "super-assimilationists" are not great, but the fact of the existence of such a streak among Soviet Jews cannot be ignored.

The question naturally arises: What will become of the assimilationists? Do we have to reconcile ourselves to their break with Jewish heritage, culture, religious customs, from a Jewish national consciousness? NO! We cannot wash our hands of these people even if their ostentatious break with Jewishness causes us dismay and indignation and their social position seems to us entirely reprehensible.

The history of 1800 years of dispersion has shown that even in the darkest periods of Jewish history, when the fire of our people's national feeling has seemed to be finally and irrevocably extinguished, it has transpired that under the ashes a few sparks of the fire have kept alive and warm, and sooner of later from these sparks there has flared up afresh the flame of immortal Judaism and the Jewish people have once more arisen like a Phoenix from the ashes and have lived and struggled for the revival of their national aspirations.

This, of course, does not mean that the rebirth has always and everywhere attracted all Jews! Some of the nation have become lost—assimilated. But side by side with this, it has been possible to observe flashes of heroic patriotism and devotion to their people in individuals who would seem to have long been lost and to have forsaken every semblance of Jewishness. Therefore, although a revival of Jewish culture in the USSR and an emergency of an attachment to it among the broad masses of Soviet Jews would seem to be unlikely, we must make an effort to preserve every single Soviet Jew as a member of the Jewish people and we do not have the right to bury all hope of the success of this mission while there remains even one Jew in the USSR.

There can be no doubt that World Jewry (outside the Soviet Union) can and must take part in this awakening of a national consciousness and of Jewish culture among Soviet Jews, and can and must declare its concern not only for those repatriates who leave the Soviet Union, but also for the assimilationists. And this must be done notwithstanding the fact that such efforts will encounter opposition—passive from the assimilationists (out of fear of persecution)—active from the super-assimilationists (out of a desire to gain some benefit from a demonstration of their opposition to "Zionist agitation").

In fact, if we take into account the situation in the USSR where there is no possibility of acquiring independence from the authorities, where every aspect of individual undertaking is strictly forbidden, where it is even illegal under the law of parasitism to live on one's own savings, and if we also bear in mind that the life of every Soviet person and especially a Soviet Jew, is under constant surveillance of the party and governmental organs, then it will not be difficult to understand what caution a Soviet Jew must employ, not only in public, but also in his private life. Thus if, for example, it became known in the Party organization or in the administration of some institute or other that a certain employee had acquired 5 kgs. of matzos, or that he had his son circumcised, then it is quite probable that at the very first opportunity this individual would be dismissed under some specious pretext or even publicly accused of Zionism and expelled from the "healthy collective" of the institute. And it will then be extremely difficult or well-nigh impossible to find work in another institute and he will be glad if eventually he manages to find a badly paid job of a much lower category in an organization of the lowest category. There is no doubt that for a Jew to be noticed as having some attachment to Judaism, even in such innocent matters as listening to Hebrew songs, following traditional observances, attending Synagogue during festivals, etc., this will mean his being seriously compromised and calls for great courage on his part to ignore the dangers inherent in this situation. But in regard to such "seditious" acts as the reading of an "illegal" Jewish magazine, or the study of Ivrit (Modern Hebrew) or even more so, the study of the Torah, then it can be said that very few dare. It is only the "refuseniks" who can afford the luxury of complete disregard of these prohibitions as in respect of their reputations vis-à-vis the authorities, they have definitely nothing to lose.

Why Are Jews Leaving?

A noticeable departure from the urge towards assimilation by a significant section of Soviet Jews, and a rebirth among them of a national awareness in recent years, have been made possible mainly by the following:

a) The creation of the State of Israel and its successful growth;
b) The flow of emigration from the USSR to Israel;
c) Discrimination against Jews in the USSR; and
d) The ever increasing growth of anti-Semitism in the USSR.

The establishment of the State of Israel, its heroic fight for existence against hostile neighboring countries and the victory of the people of this young state over its enemies, with a population ten times as great, have found an echo in the heart of every Jew.

The favorable attitude adopted by the Soviet Union towards the creation of an independent Jewish state on the territory of what had been Palestine, was regarded by Soviet Jews as an acknowledgement of the tolerance of the authorities of expressions of sympathy towards this State. Moreover, the fight of the Soviet government and people against fascism was still fresh in the memory of the Jews and valued very highly by them. It is therefore not surprising that Golda Meir was met with enthusiasm on her arrival in Moscow by thousands of Jews, as the symbol of the renaissance of the nation, the realization of the centuries-old dream of the Jews to have a home of their own, a home which they could themselves build and defend. At that moment, the Jews of the USSR for the first time in many years felt that they belonged to the Jewish people and felt close to its State which had risen anew. But this took place while Stalin was still alive when it was not possible even to mention the idea of emigrating. Moreover, very shortly after this the authorities set in motion the complete destruction of every Jewish institution and the annihilation of the Jewish elite. Thus, they showed the true attitude of the Soviet authorities towards everything Jewish.

But a wildly enthusiastic burst of Jewish patriotism was produced as a result of the legendary victory of Israel in the Six-Day War. This victory made the greatest impression on the younger generation who, because of the strength of the prejudices ruling the country, had until now been afraid of admitting their allegiance to the Jewish nation, but who now welcomed with pride the opportunity to declare themselves as Jews. The most constant abuse hurled at the Jews was the accusation of cowardice, of an inability and a reluctance to fight, of always hiding behind the backs of others when danger threatened. This, in spite of the fact that Jews fought heroically in the ranks of the Soviet, American and British armies against the Nazis and exhibited exceptional activity and bravery among the partisans in their fight against the fascists. After the Six-Day War, the slanderers of Jewish heroism were compelled to bite their tongues.

At the end of the 1960's, recollection of the "thaw" which set in after Stalin's death were still fresh. Conditions were such that the thought of emigration, although still somewhat dangerous, was no longer considered as preposterous, and did not lead to a quick and inevitable death. Therefore, influenced by the revival of feelings of nationalism, the first post-war Zionists risked making the attempt to obtain from the Soviet government permission to emigrate to Israel. One other favorable circumstance was to influence the resurgent Jewish emigration. Just at this time, the Soviet leadership decided to take steps towards a broad expansion of commercial, economic and scientific/technical connections with the West and to obtain from the West credits, equipment and technology, the shortage of which was limiting the possibility of the USSR to rapidly expand its heavy—and most important—its armaments industry [sic].

Therefore, Soviet leaders considered it unsuitable in the face of Western opinion, to encounter with open and cruel repressions the demands of a few score Jewish families asking for permission to emigrate to Israel. They made concessions to these demands also because they considered this to be a purely local, passing and entirely small-scale phenomenon. In fact who, at that time, could have foreseen that the emigration movement of Soviet Jewry would encompass some hundreds of thousands of people? When, however, it became obvious that the success of the first daring few was inspiring thousands of Jews, dreaming of repatriation, the authorities began taking steps. They attempted to intimidate prospective emigrants by criminal trials against groups of Zionist-minded people—trials which finished with monstrously cruel sentences. But this unexpectedly brought about a contrary result for, feeling that they were being threatened, Jews in the thousands streamed to OVIR asking for permission to emigrate. And world public opinion, indignant at the wave of repressions brought down upon people solely for their attachment to their historic homeland, afforded them active support.

Faced for the first time in fifty years with open protests in the form of demonstrations, hunger strikes and fiery appeals to world public opinion, and with public demands to implement Soviet laws and international undertakings which gave formal approval to emigration, the Soviet government was thrown into confusion and lost control of the situation. The numbers of those wishing to be repatriated, who openly made declarations of this desire, snowballed rapidly and the authorities replied to this avalanche with a flood of various kinds of persecutions which fell not only on the heads of those who were applying for permission to leave, but also on their relatives who were intending to stay behind in the USSR. Harsh measures of discrimination against Jews were increased; there was a greater reduction in the quotas for acceptance of Jews into institutes of higher education, and for work in scientific research establishments; the entry of Jews into party and governmental organs and into military institutions was almost completely closed; the anti-Zionist (in reality anti-Semitic) campaign in the press, radio and television was increased to an unprecedented scale. A flood of lies about Israel came pouring out.

All this brought about a situation where those who were striving to get to Israel because of the strength of their national or religious convictions were joined by people humiliated by the discriminatory measures taken against them or their children, and who were afraid that the Black Hundred* books and pamphlets, speeches and articles in the newspapers would be followed by Black Hundred deeds. Such people were striving not so much to get to Israel as to get away from the USSR.

Those who had decided on repatriation to Israel naturally developed

* Translator's note. The Black Hundreds was a society in Tsarist times devoted to violent anti-Jewish pogrom activity.

an interest in the study of Modern Hebrew, Jewish history, and Bible studies. In those families trying to emigrate to Israel, the young people started singing Hebrew songs; Jewish traditions were again observed, Jewish festivals celebrated. By the beginning of the 1970's, the number of "refuseniks" in Moscow, Leningrad, Minsk, Vilnius, Kiev, and several other towns had increased significantly. These "refuseniks" as their number is growing, are spontaneously forming something like Jewish communities of people who are linked by their common aim towards repatriation, mutual aid, solidarity and common suffering. The formation of these groups is a result of the renaissance of Jewish culture in the Soviet Union. An important role in this respect was played by Israeli radio broadcasts in Russian and Yiddish which effectively gave information about events in the exodus movement from the USSR and acted as a main source in the liquidation of the ignorance of Soviet Jews in regard to Jewish history, religion and sacred writings, and the basic specialities of the State of Israel. Unfortunately, during the last few years the quality of these broadcasts has worsened and the standard has dropped considerably. Thus, it can be seen that the renaissance of Jewish culture in the USSR began because of the emigration movement and remains closely linked to it, although gradually it is spreading also onto a certain number of Jews previously infected with the assimilationary frame of mind.

Repatriation First—Then Culture

The question as to whether it is necessary to attempt to bring about a rebirth of Jewish consciousness for all Jews does not give rise to any doubt. The question is really only how best to bring this about without causing any detriment to other problems, in particular that of emigration —and to what extent we must orient ourselves so as to bring outside pressure on the Soviet government in order to create some legally recognized Jewish institutes. Efforts for the attainment of this aim and the struggle for the legal dissemination of Judaism, Jewish culture and art, do not have the slightest prospect of success in this country, based, as it is, on a government monopoly of ideology. The Soviet system is categorically opposed to the penetration of "foreign" ideology into the consciousness of any of the nationalities of the USSR. It is quite unthinkable, therefore, that on this question they should make an exception for the Jews, and that the Jews should be placed ideologically in an exceptionally privileged position. And, in fact, when reference is made to concrete plans for the shaping of a renewal of Jewish institutions in the USSR, then we can only express our surprise at the naivete of certain people who imagine that they can obtain the consent of the authorities for the official recognition of the *Ulpanim* (Hebrew classes) or for the creation of an independent Jewish publishing house, or for the establishment in the USSR of Jewish socio-cultural centers, etc.

But let us assume that by some miracle the impossible did really happen and that by the use of powerful pressure and by the granting of considerable concessions to the Soviet Union, on what she considers to be matters of vital importance, the West managed to obtain agreement for the functioning of a few Jewish institutes. Our experience of many years of life in the USSR and an analysis of the behavior of the Soviet government in similar situations (e.g., after the signing of the Final Act of the Helsinki Agreement) permits us with absolute certainty to forecast just how matters would develop in this situation:

Officially recognized schools for the teaching of Modern Hebrew would be turned into government-controlled institutions and the *ulpanim* which at present exist and are functioning very successfully would be strictly forbidden. Permission to teach in the official schools would be granted only to persons holding officially recognized appropriate diplomas, which are not held by any of those who are at present teaching Hebrew privately, although some of them have acquired a very deep knowledge of the language and its literature by "teach yourself" methods. All those who attended such courses would have to present documents and complete inquiry forms; so that the only one who could dare to be bold enough to apply would be the refuseniks. Whereupon Soviet propaganda would declare that in the USSR there were neither (qualified) teachers of Hebrew, nor candidates to study it. So that as a result of a very dearly bought "victory" we should be deprived of the possibility that we do have at present of studying Hebrew, and we should not have acquired any possibilities!

An "independent" Jewish publishing house, as the experience of all publications on Jewish themes in recent years shows quite convincingly, would publish anti-Israel and anti-Zionist literature in "Jewish language," i.e. Yiddish, and also in Hebrew. As an example of such hypocritical publication we need only point to the notorious so-called "news" paper *Sovietische Heimland,* which specializes in abusing Israel, Zionists and the Jewish activists who are fighting for the rights of Soviet Jews. So that it is clear that the only result of the "victory" on the publishing front would be a strengthening of the anti-Semitic propaganda campaign.

Jewish socio-cultural centers—if indeed the miracle occurred and the authorities agreed to these being set up—would be controlled and directed in exactly the way the synagogues are at present controlled; that is, they would be entirely under the control and authority of agents of government security organs and they would serve quite simply only for the purpose of acting as listening posts to indicate the mood of the Jews and to expose individuals with nationalistic inclinations, whose activity causes scrutiny on the part of the authorities. At the same time, these centers would be exploited for propaganda purposes to be paraded before foreign visitors interested in the Jewish question. There would constantly be on duty a "Jew" ready and willing to feed fables to the unsuspecting well-fed foreigners who would consider unthinkable the possibility of such a hoax being perpetrated on them. It would be difficult to overestimate the harm that would be caused to Soviet Jewry by such a "victory."

From all that has been set forth here, it has in no way been implied that nothing needs to be done for the renewal of Jewish culture in the USSR and for the renaissance of a national consciousness among Soviet Jews. What has been said merely indicates that the fundamental means of attaining this objective is not and cannot be by an appeal to the Soviet government, inasmuch as firstly in a number of questions this could turn out to be counterproductive; secondly, it could create in the West the illusion of a speedy solution to the Jewish question in the USSR and thereby cause harm to the true interests of Soviet Jews—and thirdly, it could divert energy and resources away from the vitally important struggle for free emigration of Jews from the Soviet Union. A misapplied orientation in regard to priorities of aims and objectives could result in the Soviet Union receiving from the West a series of important privileges (preferential credits, technology, the status of most favored nation, etc.) in exchange for ephemeral steps in the direction of liberalization in the attitude of the authorities towards dissemination of Jewish culture in the USSR, while the problems of freedom and free emigration for those who have linked their fate with that of their people, will remain unsolved.

The fact that in the USSR there are more than two million Jews, while the prisoners and refuseniks number "only" a few thousand, does not signify that the dissemination of Jewish culture for the purpose of a renaissance of a national spirit among the broad mass of Jews should be given a higher degree of priority than freedom of emigration. This would be a fundamental mistake first of all because freedom of emigration is not by any means limited to the present-day repatriation aspirants. The emigration movement has been and will continue to be a basic stimulant to the resurgence of national awareness among all Soviet Jews. Each family which succeeds in obtaining release from the dramatic situation of refuseniks, and even more so, every former Prisoner of Conscience who departs the country, gives encouragement to people to a far greater extent and much more convincingly than even the best of hundreds of books or speeches. Moreover, proceeding from the Judaic principle of the eternal value of human life, the value for the Jewish people of even some hundreds of thousands of present-day Soviet Jews cannot outweigh the value of a few thousand prisoners and refuseniks, especially as many of today's assimilationists might very well, in the near future, become repatriationists and experience for themselves the "joy" of limitations on freedom of exit from this country.

What Can Be Done?

What measures must then be taken in order to save Soviet Jews, both for themselves and for our people? How can help be given to those who have already linked their fate with that of their people and are fighting with the strength of despair to escape to the freedom of Israel, the one country in the world where Jews can, with complete confidence, feel that they are at home—and at the same time not let slip the slightest opportunity of being able to awaken the consciousness of those who cannot hear the ashes of their fathers beating in their hearts?

In our opinion, the following are necessary:

a) The fight must be carried on for freedom of emigration as the main stimulus for a resurgence of Jewish self-awareness and as a radical solution of the Jewish problem in the USSR.
b) The study of Modern Hebrew must be made possible and Soviet Jews must be made aware of their Jewish cultural heritage. One

of the main ways for this to be done is via news broadcasts from Israel radio and other broadcasting stations giving news in Russian; the magazines *America* and *Britain;* quite an important role can be played by the unofficial journals *Jews in the USSR* and *Tarbut,* seminars on Judaism and the celebration of the traditional Jewish festivals.

c) To expose before the whole world the facts of the violation by the USSR of human rights, in regard to discrimination against Jews, the violations of the principle of freedom of emigration and the suppression of freedom of a religious and cultural life.

What Must Be Demanded From the Soviet Government?

a) Freedom for the Jewish Prisoners of Conscience and the release of the refuseniks;
b) Liberalization of the emigration policy;
c) An end to jamming of Israel radio broadcasts;
d) An end to discrimination against Jews;
e) An end to the anti-Semitic campaign which is conducted (by the Soviet government) through the mass communications media; and
f) An easing of the ban on the import into the USSR of non-political books and periodicals on Jewish themes.

With the hope that by next year we shall be in Jerusalem.*

(Signed) Professor Alexander Lerner
Moscow
September 25, 1976

---

* The traditional pious hope expressed annually at the conclusion of the Passover celebration, the Jewish Festival of Freedom.

Reading 17

Message From Moscow V, The Jewish Emigration Movement in the Soviet Union, Survey: 1978–79, compiled by Alexander Lerner, Arkady Mai, et al, December 1979, pp. 3–7, 10–13 (published by the Student Struggle for Soviet Jewry and the Union of Councils for Soviet Jews (received in the U.S. in June 1980)

This is a comprehensive, detailed account of events and circumstances involving Soviet Jews. One of the main points of this message is that Soviet emigration policy in 1979 was becoming increasingly complex and harsh.

The Emigration Movement in the USSR

Recently, the number of people allowed to leave has decreased. (The total number of those who emigrated in 1979 exceeds 50,000). This fact is widely known and though it should be welcomed, its significance is not clear. Is the increase in the number of exit visas granted in 1979 a result of a softening of the Soviet emigration policy? Is this increase a guarantee for the coming years that the number of exit visas will not diminish? The facts do not support this supposition. Actually, judging the 1979 emigration quantitatively, one notes that at the beginning of 1979 those wishing to emigrate fluctuated between 150,000 and 220,000. (According to data in Israel, 220,000 invitations were issued.) Thus only a third or a quarter received exit visas in 1979.

It is disturbing that the emigration process became significantly more complex in 1979. There has been an increase in the number of new obstacles in the path of would-be emigrants. The sharp rise in the number of these people worries officials very much. As a result, Soviet emigration policy has recently become harsher. The procedure of completing forms is more difficult, there is a hardening of repression of activists, and the retention of long-time refuseniks has exceeded ten years in some cases. It seems as though these measures have been taken to frighten off potential emigrants. The authorities use a wide range of actions to this end:

1. A harsher campaign in the press against emigration and potential emigrants.
2. Confiscation or withholding of invitations.
3. Serving of invitations through OVIR after interrogating the addressee and only in the event of the establishment of "true" (Jewish) parentage.
4. Limitation as far as possible on the issue of forms for the formal application.
5. Limitation of the quantity of accepted applications leading to long waiting lists. Moreover, the provincial OVIR offices designate the waiting list term (often one to two years) and this requires presentation of the forms certified at the place of work. In this way, those who wish to emigrate often lack work or else are subjected to every kind of pressure.
6. Refusal of an application in cases where the whole family did not decide to emigrate.
7. Refusal of an application from persons of draft age.
8. OVIR takes a very long time to examine applications, sometimes as long as two years. On the average, the examination period in Moscow is ten to twelve months, sometimes as long as two years.
9. When the forms have to be verified at the place of work, the applicant is usually dismissed following this. He is then placed on a waiting list for two to three years.
10. A warning to the applicant that people who admit indirect Jewish family ties receive refusals.
11. Refusals of their applications for reasons of "distant Jewish ancestry."
12. Repression of the activists of the Jewish emigration movement, especially in the Ukraine, where they undergo interrogation, pressures, provocations, arrests, and condemnations on absurd charges of "hooliganism."
13. Pressure on "long-time refuseniks" on various pretexts, and—with frank cynicism—no pretext whatsoever. Also, the trials of these people, like those of the Prisoners of Zion, are frightening examples for many thousands of Jews.
14. In the past months the authorities have imposed exorbitant duties (about 100 percent) on objects of value taken abroad by the

emigrant—musical instruments, furniture, numerous souvenirs, etc.)

15. During recent years the authorities have made the departure of emigrants more complex. Permission to emigrate from other republics have been completely suspended and therefore the whole stream has changed direction through the border points of Brest, Chop and Urdgheny, where huge numbers of emigrants congregate. Local customs intentionally make the procedures even more difficult—artfully creating waiting lists, accepting luggage on certain days only. They have sharply curtailed the sale of tickets for direct trains to Vienna, so that the emigrants are compelled to stop in Warsaw, where they sit at the station for days, waiting for tickets.

As to refusals in granting exit visas, we observe that the number of refusals has grown in proportion to the general growth in the number of emigrants. Motives such as "lack of advisability" and "regime considerations" had their place in 1979 as they have had before. However, something new is the appearance of a highly significant group of refuseniks in various cities in the Soviet Union. Many of them have waited for the notorious "five years" to pass and others have been waiting for ten to twelve years. Pressure on Igor Guberman, an activist, was high. He was arrested in Moscow in August 1979 on a false charge of speculation. He was one of the publishers of the *samizdat* magazine *Jews in the USSR*. . . .

Searches, interrogations, threats and scare tactics have had and continue to have their place in the treatment of activists. The innovation this year has been the use of the press. Slanderous, pogrom-like articles have appeared in Minsk, Odessa and Vilnius. The main "heroes" have been the Jewish activists, Col. Lev Ovsischer, Lev Roitburd, Vladimir Raiz, Alexander Lerner, Gennady Khassin and others. On the whole, the situation of the refuseniks in the course of the year has worsened even more, not only the precariousness and gravity of their situation, but also the possibility that their status might change from refusenik to prisoner. The problem of the refuseniks has become threatening; the institution of a refusal potentially is the basic obstacle in the way of future emigration. . . .

Despite the freeing of certain Prisoners of Zion this year, the optimism aroused by this was soon dashed. At this time the Soviet authorities would sooner demonstrate harshness and inflexibility than the desire to continue the process of freeing innocent people.

In 1979, only a third of those who received exit visas went to Israel. We think this is the reason: Real difficulties and artificial barriers in the way of new immigrants to Israel give rise to a flow of letters to the USSR which express discontent and disappointment. A significant number of Soviet emigres have left Israel for other countries. Many of these people are highly trained specialists, teachers, members of the liberal professions —people who struggled actively for the right to emigrate from the Soviet Union. However, the negative information coming from Israel, strengthened by years of Soviet propaganda, as well as a weak national self-consciousness, have led to a negative attitude toward immigration to Israel among Jews. We emphasize that Israeli propaganda is totally ineffective and does not promote the creation of pro-Israel mood among Soviet Jews. The "Kol Israel" radio station in no way helps to dispel the doubts about emigration to Israel. It is clear that an increase of immigration to Israel depends on improving the absorption process.

This is what happened in 1979. One can definitely state the number of Jews wishing to emigrate next year will increase. It is also possible that the pressure on and stream of information about the emigration situation will weaken. This will be connected with the 1980 Olympic Games and the attendant increased repressions. Moscow will be closed to *aliya* activists and possibly for the refuseniks and applicants. . . .

The fate of Prisoner of Zion Anatoly Sharansky calls for a special comment. According to his sentence, he will remain in prison for ten years. The inhuman and severe sentence he received despite his innocence plus his heroic behavior at the trial were the basis for the widespread international campaign on his behalf and made him the symbol of the honesty and integrity of those struggling for the right of Soviet Jews to emigrate. Right now, Sharansky's health is seriously undermined. He is struggling with a serious optic disease which threatens his sight. He has lost weight beyond recognition, becoming skin and bones. Despite the insistent requests of his relatives, the authorities refuse him intensive medical care in a hospital. He has been denied meetings with relatives which are permitted only twice a year, for very minor offenses in prison. The majority of letters sent to him are confiscated by prison officials; three-quarters of the letters he receives are censored heavily.

He is only allowed to send out one letter a month and these are always censored too. . . .

The Movement of Jewish Women for the Freedom to Emigrate

The movement of Jewish women in the USSR struggling for the foremost right of a citizen, to emigrate, came to life over two years ago. It was born of desperation and the poverty-stricken plight of their families caught in the tragic blind alley of the so-called "endless refusal" status. All the conditions of this blind alley—maimed souls, the crippled fate of our husbands, children and parents—bring upon us the worst suffering and put an impossible burden, naturally, on us women—mothers, wives, and daughters.

A refusenik who is denied a normal life loses his work qualifications, gets sick, ages and loses his individuality and often his personality is destroyed. Especially tragic in these families is the fate of the children. They grow with damaged souls which are forced to spend their early childhood in an atmosphere of fear, cut off from their schoolmates and teachers by their devotion to their Jewish identity and intention to live in Israel, living in secrecy so as to avoid prejudice and hostility.

From young children they grow to adulthood. Young men are faced with the dilemma of either serving in the army, then receiving exit refusals for the next ten years, or refusing to be drafted and then going to prison for draft evasion. During these years, the girls become young women, lacking opportunity of creating their own lives according to their interests and inclinations.

Many refusenik families are artificially divided: the older parents emigrate without their children who are refused, or the opposite—the parents send off their children, who leave hoping to free them and tear them out of this horrible dead end. There have even been cases of refusals to grant visas to Israel to attend funerals of parents or children, to visit their graves, or to help a sole or aged ill parent. This another cruel breach of the Helsinki Accords.

In the search for a way out from the vicious circle, seeking to put an end to all the suffering, the "endless refusal" which has uselessly and unjustifiably doomed our families, Jewish women have attempted to join forces and initiate a dialogue with officials in the Soviet government apparatus at the level of OVIR chief, and responsible members of the

Central Committee and the Ministry of Internal Affairs. We have systematically turned, for the past two years, to responsible people who, by our refusals and save our families. But our struggle seems futile. They usually promise us a meeting a day before a high-level conference or other important political event of international significance. But when these events arrive, they unfailingly refuse us this meeting.

The number of participants in the Jewish women's movement has grown from a dozen to a present seventy-three. This attests absolutely to its vitality. In contrast to previous years when up to twenty refusenik families would be released, this number has recently dropped to a minimum: three to five families yearly.

Intellectual Life—Scientific Seminars

The dismissal of Jewish scholars from direct participation in scientific work results in refuseniks being completely isolated from the mainstream of intellectual life in the country and in the world. There is a danger of their falling behind in their scientific field and social milieu. In order to prevent this danger, scientific seminars have been organized by refuseniks in many cities. They currently operate in Moscow, Leningrad, Kiev, Riga and Kishinev.

A seminar on applied mathematical methods in biology and medicine, begun in 1972 by Prof. Alexander Lerner, continues to function. The focus of the seminar has been the problem of the creation of an artificial heart, the problems of managing systems of medical service, and genetic problems. Foreign participants came to observe and speak. In 1978–79 lectures were given by Dr. Edwin Alderman (Univ. of California); Dr. Simon Levin (Cornell); Dr. Lawrence Cohen (Yale); Dr. Gerald Aaronson (U.S. National Institutes of Health); Dr. David Spin (New York Univ.); Dr. Edwin Rosen (Univ. of Massachusetts); Prof. Anatole Beck (Univ. of Wisconsin); and Dr. Michael Maxus (Northwestern Univ.).

On August 17, 1979, a seminar was attended by many scholars who had arrived in Moscow for the 11th International Congress on Political Science. Prof. Lerner lectured on "Cybernetics: Real and Imaginary Dangers." This was in commemoration of the 100th anniversary of Einstein's birth—three seminars were dedicated to his works.

In 1979 seminar members Alexander Lerner and Eitan Finkelstein were nominated to the New York Academy of Sciences.

The Moscow seminar in physics was also successful. It began under Prof. Alexander Voronel in 1972. It was run by highly qualified scholars who were singled out in 1979 for membership in the New York Academy of Sciences. Many foreign scholars participated in this seminar.

The Jewish humanities seminar, which had been under Arkady Mai's leadership since September 1976, continued its usual bi-weekly meetings in 1978–79.* The seminar's purpose is to let the Jewish scholar learn more about Jewish history and culture. For some time, the seminar dealt with a systematic history of the Jews from ancient times on. In 1979 the course began with the Second Temple period and the awakening of Talmudic Judaism. This course is considered the leading seminar of Arkady Mai and Mikhail Chlenov. . . .

The Return to the Jewish Tradition

Increasingly, Jews in the Soviet Union are returning to their tradition and heritage. They observe the holidays in their homes. On the Festivals, such as Rosh Hashana and Yom Kippur, they read the Torah and they go to the synagogue. In Moscow the number of Jews observing the holidays and gathering at the synagogue has visibly increased in 1978–79. In many cities, instruction on the emigration process and preparation for life in Israel continues, and Hebrew is taught, among other subjects. In addition, there are dedicated, serious groups studying the Bible and Talmud. Hebrew is spoken there.

Journals are published, such as *Jews in the USSR*, despite the high risk involved. Its editor-in-chief, Victor Brailovsky, had his home searched, and a member of the editorial board, Igor Guberman, was arrested, accused of a common crime.

A new tradition has begun. Large numbers of Jews meet on the outskirts of town. Since 1976, Jews have gathered and observed their holidays on the outskirts of Moscow. Since 1978 the tradition has been established to gather every two weeks from April through May and right into October. Everyone attends: young, parents with small children, and

* The seminar was begun by Vitaly Rubin in 1973. In Vilnius a continuing seminar is entitled "Hebrew Language and Civilization." The seminar was conducted weekly, every Sunday. Three topics were instituted at the seminar: Hebrew study, a talk on Jewish culture, history and philosophy. Eitan Finkelstein is in charge.

the old. Teenagers play volleyball or badminton or chess. Others hike in the woods, talk or gather mushrooms or berries. Since there is always a tape recorder with two amplifiers, those who wish can dance and hear favorite Jewish melodies. On Lag Be'Omer, the children have an archery contest. At midday there is a meal.

Everyone brings food, wine and thermoses full of tea and cakes. There is an established tradition that whoever wants to perform must tell a short story or anecdote dealing with any one of the following themes: the religious or historic significance of the holiday, or the Torah reading for these days. There have also been displays of photographs and posters such as "Cities and Suburbs of Israel"; "Jerusalem the Golden"; "Our Children in the Year of the Child"; "Refusenik Children," a photo exhibit by Mikhail Kremen; and "Jewish Heroes in the Soviet Union," a photo exhibit by S. A. Yantovsky.

Especially noteworthy were the Jewish folksong festivals in the woods. In 1978–79 they were held with great enthusiasm and attracted a great many participants, about 250, in addition to performers. Performances were in Hebrew, with one in Yiddish. And even though the audience knew many beautiful melodies, the sound of the language made an enormous impression—no one remained unmoved.

Since it is difficult for Jews in the USSR to rent their own building for their own activities, these nationalist activities hold a special meaning for those of all ages! The outdoor meetings make the circles of our friends and acquaintances larger, a "circle within a circle." This includes their children and young students.

The content and emotional consciousness of the atmosphere created by these gatherings cannot be duplicated. Jewish music, songs, dances and sporting events are a fabulous combination. And all this takes place in the open, in communion with nature, in surroundings where no one feels pressured. What else could give one such spiritual strength? Meeting beyond the city limits is the only possible way for the diverse social elements within the Jewish community to get involved with Jewish culture in a vivid, emotional way. According to long-term observers, these meetings outside the city represent the first taste, for many Jewish families, of their national reawakening.

Reading 18

Julia Wishnevsky, "The Samizdat Journal *Evrei v SSSR*," Radio Liberty Research, October 25, 1979.

This is a sophisticated, detailed analysis of a very important samizdat journal. Soviet authorities forced this journal to stop publication by the end of 1979.

The Samizdat *Journal* Evrei v SSSR

Julia Wishnevsky

Summary: The Soviet authorities have recently renewed attempts to prevent further publication of the *samizdat* journal *Evrei v SSSR*. The following is a short account of the aims pursued by the compilers of the journal and a description of the kind of materials that have been published in it. Apart from giving a place in its pages to materials on the history, culture, and religion of Jews in Russia, Israel, and the rest of the world, the journal has served as a platform for the most divergent opinions on a variety of issues. Such differences in opinion are characteristic not only of the Soviet Jews' national awareness but also of attitudes towards them on the part of the people among whom they live.

According to foreign correspondents in Moscow, on September 25 of this year a search was made in the apartment of Viktor Brailovsky, an activist in the Soviet Jewish campaign to emigrate who is also at present editor of the *samizdat* journal *Evrei v SSSR* (Jews in the USSR). The search of Brailovsky's apartment and also the arrest on August 15 of this year of another contributor to the journal, Igor Guberman, suggest that the Soviet authorities are eager to prevent further publication of *Evrei v SSSR*.[1]

Evrei v SSSR is to date the oldest of the so-called "thick journals" that are circulated by means of *samizdat*. The first issue, compiled by Aleksandr Voronel and Viktor Yakhot, was dated October 1972.[2]

The campaign against *Evrei v SSSR* began with the trial of the writer Vladimir Maramzin, whose stories were published in the fourth and sixth issues of the journal. During Maramzin's trial, which took place from February 19 to 21, 1975, the journal was described as an "illegal" and "anti-Soviet" publication.[3] On May 25, 1975, KGB operatives carried out simultaneous searches in the apartments of four individuals who all had some connections with the journal. Following this, various people were summoned to the procurator's office, and it was there that the current editors of the journal, Il'ya Rubin and Rafail Nudel'man, learned that criminal case No. 41035/3875, based on charges of "slanderous anti-Soviet propaganda," had been opened against the journal *Evrei v SSSR.*[4] Finally, at the end of December 1978, a further series of searches was carried out in the cities of Moscow, Leningrad, and Riga. In the course of these searches, materials intended for publication in *Evrei v SSSR* were confiscated. One of the people whose homes were searched was the present editor of the journal, Viktor Brailovsky. On December 22, 1978, he and his wife Irina were summoned for interrogation by the KGB and questioned about the journal.[5]

The case for branding the journal as "anti-Soviet" and "slanderous" seems an unconvincing one, particularly since the foreword "From the Editors" in each edition of *Evrei v SSSR* sets out the criteria and conditions for the acceptance of materials for publication. Articles submitted must be of a standard that demonstrates competence on the questions with which they deal, must not pursue any political goals, and must not contain any deliberate falsehood or any offensive attacks. As the foreword in each issue of the journal also states, the aim of the publication is to provide "a systematic study . . . of various views of the history, culture, and social problems of Jews in the USSR," including the views of those "whose attitude towards the role of the Jews in Russian history is a critical or even an outright negative one." According to the compilers, the need for a *samizdat* publication of this type is justified by the Soviet Jews' "natural striving for self-awareness" and also by "the unusual paucity of literature on this problem. . . ."

Production of *Evrei v SSSR* continues, now as before, to be the work of Jews who are keen to emigrate to Israel. But it would be a mistake to regard the journal as a Zionist publication. Under the rubric *Kto ya?* (Whom am I?) ethnic Jews writing about themselves in answer to this question show that they may still have an ambivalent view of their own nationality, such as Larisa Bogoraz, whose response to *Kto ya?* appeared in the journal's first issue. Other, later contributions have come from Jews who consider themselves as Russian, like the poet Pavel Kogan, who fell in World War II (No. 3); christianized Jews like Aleksandr

Galich (No. 3); those of mixed ancestry like Vladislav Khodasevich, the Russian emigre poet who was of Polish-Jewish origin (No. 5); or the Leningrad prose writer Vladimir Maramzin (No. 4). As in other sections of the journal, the heading "Who Am I?" is also often used not just for publicistic statements but also for stories, verse, and even for a play—Ninel Voronel's *Zmei educhii* (Voracious serpent) (No. 4). On the other hand, the publication of works by christianized Jews and "cosmopolitans" is not confined to the section headed "Kto ya?" In five issues of the journal, for instance, Lev Kopelev's book on Heinrich Heine was serialized (Nos. 13–18); in Nos. 7–10 and 14, there have been verse and prose by the great Russian poet Osip Mandel'shtam, who was a Christian-Jew; while under the heading of "Views from Outside," issue No. 11 published an interview with an Orthodox priest of Jewish origins, Father Aleksandr Men. . . .'

Of special interest to students of the dissident movement are the journal's interviews with two members of the Human Rights Movement in the Soviet Union—with Evgenii Barabanov in No. 14; and the Nobel Prize winner Academician Andrei Dmitrievich Sakharov in No. 11. Of similar interest is an article in issue No. 12 entitled "Evrei i Litovtsy" (Jews and Lithuanians), written by Tomas Venclova, a prominent Lithuanian poet who was to become head of the Lithuanian Helsinki monitoring group and is now in the United States. Another item worth mentioning is the well-known dissident Marxist Roy Medvedev's article in No. 7 on "Blizhnevostochnyi konflikt i evreiskii vopros v SSSR" (The Middle-East Conflict and the Jewish Question in the USSR). Among the non-Jewish authors represented in *Evrei v SSSR* are some whose attitudes towards the role of the Jews in Russian history is a critical or even an outright negative one. Thus, for instance, the thirteenth issue of the journal carries an interview with a Russian Orthodox nationalist, Gennadii Shimanov, while in No. 14 there is an article by an atheist Russian nationalist, M. Skuratov (pseudonym of A. M. Ivanov).

Among the materials printed in the journal are some blatantly anti-Semitic texts. For instance, the eighth issue alone contains: an article by V. Almazov, the prerevolutionary leader of the Russian anti-Semites, that was first published in 1912; a long poem by Sergei Vasil'ev, written as part of the Stalinist "campaign against cosmopolitanism' in the late 1940s and early 1950s; some modern anti-Semitic pro-government samizdat in the form of A. Markov's poem "Mezhelaitisu" (To Mezhelaitis); and a lecture with the title "Iudaizm i sionizm" (Judaism and Zionism) (about a supposed conspiracy of Jews and Masons with the aim of establishing world domination by the year A.D. 2000) by V. Emel'yanov, who is a lecturer at the All-Union "Znanie" Society and a teacher at the Moscow Institute of Foreign Languages. Appended to the above, there also appears the text of a directive of the Central Committee of the CPSU entitled "A Project for Measures to Reinforce Anti-Zionist Propaganda and Improve the Patriotic and National Education of Workers and Young People." On the basis of this text, the compilers of *Evrei v SSSR* are inclined to believe that the present anti-Semitic campaign in both the Soviet press and in public propaganda lectures is not inspired by the authorities but comes "from below," from the authors and lecturers themselves who are exploiting the Communist Party's campaign against Zionism as a cover for their own personal aims and views. . . .

The fact that such a process of change is bound to be extremely slow and complicated is confirmed by the latest publication of material in this theme in *Evrei v SSSR*. This is an article by a doctor of physical and mathematical sciences, Professor G. A. Freiman, on the subject of anti-Semitism in Soviet mathematics—on entering university, on starting postgraduate work or a job, on defending one's dissertation, on attempting to publish books and articles, and on taking part in scientific conferences abroad (issue No. 18). It is clear from Professor Freiman's article that certain prominent Soviet mathematicians show genuine enthusiasm in their efforts to keep anyone out of the field who has Jewish blood or even pure-blooded Russians who have "sullied" themselves through friendships with Jews. . . .

The journal *Evrei v SSSR* is published by assimilated Jews and by the children of Jews already fully integrated in the Soviet population. These are people who in most cases know no other language than Russian; if they do know others, it is only because they have been taught them in Soviet schools. Perhaps this is why the journal devotes a lot of space to translations. . . .

Thus, the interest that the editors and contributors to *Evrei v SSSR* show in the history and culture of their own people arises largely from their disappointment with assimilation as a means of counteracting anti-Semitism. . . .

The impression is left that the tragedy of Soviet Jews is rooted not in their forcible assimilation—for they have already fully integrated—but in their awareness that neither they nor their children and grandchildren (even of mixed marriages) will ever succeed in integrating to such an extent that those around them forget their Jewish origins.

1 See *Reuters* and *AP* of September 25, 1979. *The Washington Post* of October 23, 1979, reports that the editors of *Evrei v SSSR* continue to be harassed in a campaign to suppress the journal.

2 *Evrei v SSSR*, Nos. 1–15, has been published in the series "Evreisky *samizdat*" (Jewish *Samizdat*) by the Hebrew University of Jerusalem's Center for the Research and Documentation of East European Jewry. The various issues have appeared as follows: Nos. 1–2, in *Evreisky samizdat*, Vol. 4, Jerusalem, 1974; Nos. 3–4, *ibid*,; Vol. 6, 1974; Nos. 5–6, *ibid.*, Vol. 7, 1975; Nos. 7–8, *ibid.*, Vol. 10, 1976; No. 9, *ibid.*, Vol. 11, 1976; Nos. 10–11, *ibid.*, Vol. 12, 1977; Nos. 12–13, *ibid.*, Vol. 13, 1977; Nos. 14–15, *ibid.*, Vol. 16, 1978. No further reprints are available to date. The contents of issues No. 18 and 19 have so far been available in manuscript form only.

3 See AS 2095.

4 *Evrei v SSSR*, No. 10, p. 2.

5 David Shipler, "Soviet Police Said to Raid Homes of Dissident Jews in Three Cities," *New York Times*, December 23, 1978.

Reading 19

K. Arsentyev, "A Sclerosis of the Conscience," ***Leninska zmina*****, August 21, 1979, translated in** ***Basket III: Implementation of the Helsinki Accords*****, Hearings before the Commission on Security and Cooperation in Europe, 96th Congress, 2d Session, Vol. XIII, "Soviet Treatment of Ethnic Groups," April 29, 1980, pp. 136–138**

This article is an example of how the Soviet press tried to vilify refuseniks who turned into human rights activists. Alexander Paritsky of Khar-

kov is ridiculed as an ungrateful anti-Soviet dissident. Paritsky and his family were allowed to emigrate in 1988.

It is reliably known that A. S. *Paritsky,** formerly a scientific worker, who is now working as an engineer-adjuster in the "SPETSREMMONTAZHASU" department, is not used to remain in the shadows for a long time. Not so long ago his conduct, incompatible with the title of a Soviet citizen, had been discussed at the gathering of the collective of the department. It would seem that it would not be worthwhile to reap this. However, not so long ago his colleagues at work were forced to come back to this subject. A comrades' court examined a recent hooliganistic act and an almost one-and-a-half month's unauthorized absence from work by Paritsky. Why then does this man so openly disdain the norms of conduct in the collective? Where does he get his certainty that he can do anything?

For some time Paritsky's name has been included in the list of the Zionist "saints." Even though it is written in small letters and somewhere at the very end of the list, but the modest "pseudo-Dr. Alex" has been given this honour. . . .

Even though some time ago Aleksandr Solomonovich Paritsky had really had some relation to science and had even defended a dissertation for the degree of a candidate. The newly baked candidate had, as they say, rather good prospects. However, soon after this moving occurrence, Paritsky decided that to be busy near laboratory equipment was an occupation that was unfulfilling and of small interest and, what was most important, it was not profitable in accordance with his "professorial" standards. Already at that time his colleagues in the institute noted that he was overly ambitious, and since that time this trait of his, as attested

* Dr. Alexander Paritsky was dismissed from his position as Senior Scientist at the Kharkov Research Institute of Meteorology after applying to emigrate in September, 1976. Since his refusal in January 1977 he has been unable to secure work in his field and he has been forced to accept menial jobs.

The entire Paritsky family has been subjected to harassment and intimidation by neighbors, anonymous vandals and the KGB. Paritsky has been the object of a vilification campaign in the local press. His daughters have been threatened with expulsion from school.

This case typifies the anti-Semitic treatment accorded to many refuseniks.

by his present comrades at work as well, was unceasingly expanding. However, up to the day when the expected affidavit came from Israel, the pseudo-doctor kept to the shadow. From that time on, however, Paritsky, forgetting restraint, swam away from the shore once and for all.

From that day on "Doctor Alex" had no more time for science. Paritsky, who for a long time had made shameless use of the rights which are standard for a Soviet person—higher education, work in his profession, an apartment, etc.—suddenly turned into a "fighter for human rights," a "dissident."

Paritsky began to receive from his foreign "friends" parcels with imported trash and re-sold it at three times its price. And, in a sign of gratitude regularly telephoned New York, Tel Aviv and other, less well-known Zionist centers, and he told them tearfully and at length about the hard life of a "dissident." It is doubtful that these fairy tales were taken seriously. However, they became interested in him and soon Paritsky began to welcome Zionist emissaries (officially—American tourists)—Jack Lewis and Ann Elisabeth Molleyn, who naturally did not come with empty hands. The guests brought Zionist literary produce and some articles of clothing; they brought several tightly packed bags. The joy caused by the moving meeting was spoiled somewhat, it is true, by an unexpected appearance of the regional inspector of the militia, who confiscated the contraband literature.

The English tourists Anthony Cohen and Laurence Redley also intended to visit Paritsky. The workers of the Kiev customs office found in their possession "Dr. Alex's" address and a pile of Zionist reading material. And Alex still regrets this there, too, there must have been something that could have brought some money. . . .

The Kharkov newspapers have already written about this activity of the Candidate of Sciences that is far removed from science. The working collective of the "SPETSREMMONTAZHASU" severely condemned the demonstrative bows made by Paritsky to our ideological enemies, but it still decided to give him an opportunity to continue working in that organization. Especially as at the general meeting of the department, he did not at all look as sure of himself as usual, he tried to justify himself and he fervently promised to keep himself within bounds.

Time has shown what his promises are worth. On June 10 of this year Paritsky went to the post office for telephone talks with New York. It was necessary to send urgently another portion of anti-Soviet false information and also to remind his friends that they were delaying too long with the sending of imported dry goods. Citizens who were present at the conversation point and who by chance heard the contents of the conversation, expressed their indignation at what was happening. After all, both the tone and the character of the talks were frankly insulting for our state—Paritsky, without choosing his expressions, poured verbal dirt on the socialist way of life. Then, the "dissident," becoming absolutely impudent, made a hooliganistic scene in the postal department and, even after a militiaman was called, he continued to behave insolently and insulted those present. The impression was that the intensified attention towards him was merely tickling his nerves pleasantly. . . .

Reading 20

Victor Yelistratov, "An Open Letter of All Refusenik Adopters," undated, but approximately early 1982, from Chicago Action for Soviet Jewry

Yelistratov wrote a very passionate letter to those in the West who "adopt" refuseniks, i.e., who take the responsibility to help specific refuseniks emigrate and, until then, communicate with them by letter, phone, and visits.

An open letter to all Refusenik adopters
From: Victor Yelistratov, Moscow, USSR
Refused since 1973

"Our life is measured by intervals between your letters. We are waiting for another letter from you like a human being in the night is waiting for the sun to rise."

". . . A letter from abroad can encourage a prisoner in his jail, labor camp or exile and even protect him from locally initiated persecutions. But for a hard-core Refusenik in Moscow, Riga or Leningrad, letters about children, weather and landscape might only inspire vain hopes that the sender will establish long-term correspondence and will try his best to help the Refusenik out or at least to make the Refusenik's life easier. The majority of such senders are ready to self-censor, i.e., simplify their letters into small talk. People sometimes send their letters unregistered and without return receipt requested (an *unjustifiable* and saddening fact). *Many Refuseniks find out that their pen pals abroad disappear after a few letters, carelessly unaware that it might hurt and discourage their adoptant much more than the very letters had encouraged him.* On the other hand, when writing to a Refusenik, you expect to receive letters from us that would give you at least a partially true picture of personality, of the Refusenik's life and actual needs. Instead, you receive often from us either meaningless letters (just small talk) or nothing at all because when we write in our letters anything meaningful for us, our letters disappear.

Endeavoring to maintain the subtlest possible contact with you, many Refuseniks also write "weather letters' thus unintentionally creating a contorted picture of their actual life. Lust for sharing with you most painful problems, most vital thoughts, we nevertheless write you often small talk letters instead, hoping it would cater the letter-robbers and they would let that meaningful stuff through to you. Many times during the last decade we asked people in the USA, Europe and Israel to make the World Postal Union provide us with the freedom of correspondence under the provisions of the Universal Postal Convention. In response, *we have been receiving even more over-simplified letters as if people lived in countries where a person insisting upon his rights exposes himself to persecution. We ask you to send your letters insured and each time when you do not get back your return receipts with our signature always make the robbers pay you your indemnity.* Naturally, to send a letter insured with return requested costs more than just registered. It takes much time and energy to make the Postal Administration find out where a letter was lost and then to pay you the indemnity. I know, however, that many Refuseniks would prefer to receive less frequent but more meaningful letters. Better to send one costly and time-taking detailed and straight-forward letter than several small talk letters. *In order to do that ourselves, we need you to help us have copies of what your Postal*

Administration replies officially to the USSR Administration when we here put in a claim. To sum it up, I suggest that you organize yourselves into individual groups, each group working on a particular Refusenik's case. People from different countries writing now oversimplified letters to a particular Refusenik could write detailed meaningful letters to each other on how to arrange such a committee, i.e. self-organize as a working group able to *establish a reliable life-line to the adopted Refusenik.* Keeping in touch with each other, you could share every bit of news from your adoptant and provide him with all the news of your activity on his behalf.

Rules for Posting a Letter

1. A letter should be insured or at least registered and have a pink card or a return receipt requested.
2. On the envelope and on the pink card there should be the indication: "A Remettre en main propre" ("For delivery to the addressee in person").
3. The letter should bear a number and date. I usually write down the number on the return receipt as well as on the posting certificate to make it easier for myself to identify them.
4. Please begin your letters with acknowledgements: which of our letters or your own pink cards with our signature you've received.
5. When writing to me, don't make your letter just small talk, don't try to appease or cater to those who illegally interfere with our correspondence.
6. If a person writes in order to help rather than just for fun he should read once more my latest message to him and answer each of my requests especially if he considers them unimportant or impossible (e.g., "Victor, we cannot do that because we consider that's impractical," etc.). Time and again, I've got to repeat to everyone: "Nobody is in debt to me to do what I ask, but I need your frank answers. Otherwise, I sound like a voice in the wilderness." Time and again, even those who are really trying to help me simply ignore my particular questions.
7. Whatever in my message is not purely personal but deals with my plight should be shared by all of my pen pals; i.e., all those concerned about my plight should maintain regular corre-

spondence between themselves. This applies to all adopted Refuseniks.

Reading 21

Appeal for Urgent Action by Distraught Refuseniks, December 23, 1984, in *Jewish Advocate,* January 17, 1985

This is one of the most passionate appeals to the West for assistance. The signatories argue that "the time has come to sound the alarm," and that "the hour has come for some practical action."

To the Jews of the West:

We address to you our words of accusation and trust. We are those who have demanded, in an atmosphere of anathema, their right to live in their own home, in Israel. We are those who want to see joy in the eyes of their dear ones and not the bitterness of separation. We are those who are not considered model citizens in the land of victorious socialism only because each one of us has declared: "I have a dream!" We are also those who, while trying to combine loyalty to our country of residence with the unity of Jewish fate, have been using our last bit of strength to keep silent.

We call on you, the Jews of the West, those who spend their efforts on the paperwork of endless conferences and "races" and "picnics on the grass" in defence of Soviet Jewry, and those who are still full of illusions and see solidarity in philantropy expressed in gifts of jeans—we call on you to show your solidarity by your deeds. And we say: "Enough, brothers and sisters, of chewing over our despair while lunching at 'Lindy's.' Enough of flaming cocktail party declarations and touching 'twin-Bar-Mitzva' shows. There have been enough warning statements. The time has come to sound the alarm. There have been enough expressions of concern—the hour has come for some practical action."

Has not past experience been sufficient for you? Remember:

". . . in Rome, in Spain, in France, in Poland and in Russia they gave you fleshpots as fits . . ." Remember also: ". . . half of my childhood is soaked in blood . . ." Remember always: the accusation, the prophecies and the appeals of the pre-war period never found a receptive ear until the Holocaust swept everything away. Beware of demagoguery: one-third of our nation was murdered while the speeches, the marches, the strikes, the carnivals and the performances went on and on.

Do you need facts? But how can we show you the bloody larynx of Anatoly Shcharansky after his hunger-strike in prison? Is it possible to let you touch Zakhar Zunshain's ribs broken in the Siberian GULAG, or the blindness of the resident of Kiev, Yosif Berenshtein, whose eyes were gouged out in prison? Who could go through the walls of psychiatric clinics, courtrooms and prison cells and the barbed wire of labor camps to show you the pain and the anguish of Nadezhda Fradkova, Yosif Begun, Yan Mesh, Yuly Tarnopolsky, Aleksander Kholmyansky, Yakov Levin, Mark Nepomnyashchy, and Yuly Edelshtein? How can we convey to you that squeamish politeness thrown into our faces at the KGB and the OVIR offices? You, people who discuss "terrorism" at a leisurely pace, in what kind of framework would you place us?

Turn on your television sets, open your papers and ask yourselves where and how much space you have devoted to our plight in your programs and publications. Would it be too much for you to scrape together some dollars, pounds, shekels or francs and publish on the front pages of leading newspapers and magazines the lists of those who have been unable for years to see their near and dear ones?

Is it really necessary to ask you to collect drop by drop the tears of all the Jewish mothers separated from their children and to place this vat of tears in front of the Soviet Embassy? Or, perhaps, you should send it to Moscow so that they understand there that process of reunification started not in the 1970s, but 2,000 years ago. . . . It is of course very nice and it comes from the heart when you speak of solidarity with Soviet Jews. But when and where and what political problem has ever been solved by mere statements of solidarity?

The above is not an expression of base ingratitude or a reproach against your passivity, but a call for concrete action, since Russia has always understood only concrete deeds and a practical approach. Let the experience of Disraeli and Montefiore, of Rothschild and Kissinger be of help to you. It is to you, political, public and religious leaders, to you, businessmen and bankers, doctors and teachers, scientists, engineers and workers, to you, the Jews of Europe and America, those who believe in God and those who believe only in themselves, that we, Soviet Jews, are appealing now!

We appeal to all those who, in their new surroundings, have not forgotten the ancient links with Abraham, Isaac and Jacob, and to those who have turned to national nihilism: after all, Jewishness is not a club which one can leave. We in the East and those in the West have the same roots, no matter how different are the currents of the river which come together and move apart—the river keeps flowing, this river of Jewish blood. The brotherhood of Jewish martyrdom is eternal: it is not "in the blood that flows in the veins, but in the blood that flows out of the veins."

You, the sons and daughters of a nation which has suffered the most terrible blows that human madness can inflict, take the truth of the Messiah out of the sheaths of your souls and beat it into the iron will of deeds. Who, if not you, can help us remove the stone from the mouth of the well."

Yaakov Gorodetsky,
Leningrad
Evgeny Lein,
Leningrad
Tatyana Zunshain,
Riga
(35 other signatories included)

Reading 22

Letter by Nadezhda Fradkova, January–February 1984, published by Chicago Action for Soviet Jewry, pp. 6–7, 9, 11. Letter translated by Sergei Zaks and Simon Levin.

Origins and Development of the Soviet Jewish Movement for Freedom

This letter reveals how Soviet authorities used psychiatry to control Jewish activists. In 1978 Nadezhda Fradkova applied to emigrate to Israel. When she was refused permission, she began a hunger strike. In 1984 she was forced into confinement in a Leningrad psychiatric hospital, where in January she wrote this letter.

The first eleven days of my hunger strike I stayed at home. On January 4, I decided to get out to get some seltzer, mineral water. In the stairway, I was grabbed by several KGB who pretended to be doctors. This has happened to me before, so I knew what to do. I started shouting "Help me, bandits." However, I was very weak and I couldn't yell loud enough, so they dragged me to the car and we took off.

They brought me to Hospital No. 9 of the Petrograd Region. Dr. Udalov and Dr. Morazov were present. Then, in the Psychiatric Intensive Care Unit, Dr. Lazarev came in. I asked them, "Who called for you," and they answered "Your relatives." I said, "Well, that means that you called Israel because I only have relatives in Israel." They said that they had to give me a medical examination. I answered, "You cannot examine me against my will, you can only do that under court order." Udalov said, "I can hire you to move corpses around in this hospital." I told him, "Well, I worked as a cleaner in the bathhouse, it's very similar."

Much later, like forty days later, when they began injecting me with drugs in order to force-feed me, there was an incident. I started struggling with Udalov, I even bit him when he was trying to inject drugs into me. He shouted "Oh you bitch, you have two diplomas of higher education and work as a cleaner in a bathhouse." Of course, he added that he would send all Jews to the timber wharfs in Siberia; but that's beside the point, these two higher education diplomas of mine, that's what was bothering him. . . .

It's interesting that many of these people pride themselves in their own high education so much that they hate everybody else. I think that this proves one of the theories of the social roots of fascism about which I read in one very old issue of *New World* (*New World* is a Russian literary magazine). In this article, the writer states that fascism escalates when the simple people become semiliterate. You know everything is very new for them, all these ideas so to speak. They started operating with some ideas and they feel such a reverence between them, that they can be inspired on anything you want. You know, a simple religious person cannot be inspired on such things. However, I really believe that when people become semieducated and their religious system of beliefs is ruined, another belief, and very often a Fascist system of beliefs, takes its place. And, very often, they cannot go beyond that level. Well, you probably know that I don't like it when people are for consumption, but still it's much better than when people are for the State. Also, in the article in the New World, the writer goes on to say that in Communist countries, boys and girls are born for the State and in capitalist countries for consumption. And here, in this hospital, I have all these people for the State and in their brains and in their lives, this State is represented by its higher power, the KGB. Well, you probably know that Aldous Huxley didn't like both types of people, but I think that these people for the State would really like to become people for the consumption but there is nothing to consume here, so that's probably just their revenge against the State.

Well, this happened later, but at that moment, Udalov grabbed me and someone else helped him to move me onto the wheeled bed. After that, they moved me into the emergency room and gave me some injections. There were several other people there and they gave me another three injections. I remember that Udalov was saying "4 centigrams of Galoperidol." Then they also gave me some other injections. I was fighting them. Udalov and another person, Orabin, another lady and someone else were grabbing me. I tried to kick them with my legs, I tried to bite them, and it was very painful; but at the same time, it was real strange because I could say anything I wanted about these people. Well, they took my temperature, and took my blood for analysis and then they tied me up to the bed. Then, after a while, they untied me, but at that moment, the drugs were taking over. After that, everything started—24 hours a day there was a person in my room doing whatever they wanted to. When I wanted to go to the restroom, someone would go with me. They were watching me all the time. They are such bastards!

On January 26 they decided to force-feed me. They gave me an injection and said it was vitamins. Udalov, another doctor and a nurse were there and in some minutes I knew that they had given me an injection of drugs. Taking advantage of my drugged state, Udalov started asking questions like "Would I like to have something to eat, or to make love?"

I'm sitting there with my eyes half-closed and I cannot really understand what's going on around me, half-real, half hallucinations. I tell him, "No, I don't want to make love, I don't need a man, I'm too weak" or something like that. He says, "The sign says that you want to make love. Do you want anything at all?" I tell him, "Yes." He says, "What do you want?" And I tell him, "I want to leave the Soviet Union and go to Israel." "Well," he says, "then you need something more," and proceeded to give me another injection and then another two or three, I don't remember exactly. I knew at that time I was totally under this drug. I had the worst type of hallucinations, worse than I have ever experienced in my whole life. I found out that it was something called Ketalar . . . you can't understand what's happening around you. You try to ask, "What is going on?" but you can't pronounce the words because there are no words any more. It is like you have become some animal and you try to do something but you cannot. Well, I don't think that you understood anything from my explanation, but it's just HELL, total HELL, and no time at all, well how do you like that?

Miriam, they still force-feed me three or four times. Right now I cannot write you any more. They say that if I don't stop my hunger strike they will send me to the chronically ill people and from there they say "You will never return, ever, only your relatives can get you out of that department, but you don't have any relatives." They force-feed me using something like a probe directly into my stomach and they put the drugs in it. After that, I always sleep for four or five hours and sometimes I throw everything up. Almost every time after that I have convulsions.

[The letter continued on February 17, 1984.]

Udalov still says that he will send me to the chronically ill people from where I will never get out because only your relatives can get you out of there. He then added, "It's worse there than it is in our department." He also suggested injecting insulin for my appetite.

The last three days I've eaten. I ate to get my notebook. They gave me my notebook but they took the phone from the Intensive Care Unit before they gave it to me. Today I did not eat again. Udalov said that he won't force-feed me with the probe but will just send me to the chronically ill. Sometimes I feel that I'm ready to give up and start eating, but then I look at the KGB people and feel that I cannot give up. When I go to the bathroom, they follow me, of course, and it's very tiresome. My brains don't work anymore and my nerves are in a horrible state.

Yesterday, the KGB brought my father. This was probably, I think, the sixth time in my life that I have seen him. He said everything that the KGB wanted him to. He said things like, "These people around you are trying to save your life" and "You're just a toy in the wrong hands. Everybody else is free and you are here, why are you suffering here?" He couldn't, of course, say that it was unlawful for them to keep me here in the hospital. . . .

Oh yes, I didn't add something about my file; the file regarding my sickness in this hospital. I saw it and there is no mention of Galoperidol or Ketalar in my file. They didn't mention anything that affects your brains, no real strong drugs. There was also a number of an ambulance that brought me here. I would like to check that because they brought me here on January 4, 1984 at 11:10 and I'd like to check the number of the car that brought me in, because when they grabbed me at my place I tried to get the number of the car but the KGB wouldn't let me.

Sometimes I don't think that I can hold on for much longer. I need books, I need them very much. You know I read very fast. You could bring me any book on data processing, any manual, or a manual on the LISP language or something like that. I am going crazy because there is nothing to do. If you could bring me some paper and a pen, that would be very useful. Bring me anything, even something like *Karamazov Brothers* or something in English. The thicker the book, the better, or any American data processing books that are published by Muir Publishing House. Something like a translation of programming languages using interpreting automats. Anything of that nature.

I'm sorry to bother you for all these requests and really thank you for your help.

Signed:
Nadezhda Fradkova

Reading 23

Michael Beizer, " 'Yid' is a Bona Fide Literary Term." Review of book by A. Z. Romanenko, *On the Class Essence of Zionism: A Historographical Selection of the Literature*, Leningrad: Lenizdat, 1986, in *Glasnost*, Issues No. 7, 8, and 9, November 1987, pp. 43–44.

Until glasnost *it was not possible for Soviet Jews to speak out against anti-Semitic propaganda. With the magazine* Glasnost *they had a vehicle to strike back. In this review, Beizer reveals the background of the book, then analyzes its content, significance, and the circumstances surrounding its distribution.*

Actually, this book is not an appropriate subject for a review, just as it is not appropriate to use words such as research, argument, scholarly debate, historical source, document and so on, in reference to it. However, it cannot be ignored, since it is not the only one of its kind. This book is a brief survey of the achievements in Soviet scholarship on Zionism over the past two decades. From this book, one can see the qualitative leap this scholarship has made. Therefore, by the way, the quotations given here will be frequently second- and third-hand (that is, from other works quoted by the author). Furthermore, this book did not appear out of thin air: it was printed by a major publishing house of a big city in a huge edition, and got a green light from Ph.D's at Leningrad University: One, P. F. Metelnikov, is the scholarly editor; the other three, A. K. Belykh, A. N. Shmelev and V. F. Ryabova are commentators. The book is meant for practical use, to be introduced into the consciousness of the masses; it "will help propagandists," the scholarly editor believes to "thoroughly comprehend the essence of the ideological and theoretical battle against Zionism" (page 11). Therefore, we must also read this book and prepare ourselves in advance for that moment when the theory is thoroughly comprehended by the nation and they begin to put it into practice.

A brief review in *Leningradskaya Pravda* said that "the book gives a Marxist-Leninist analysis of the literature containing criticism of the reactionary essence of Zionism" (*see Leningradskaya Pravda,* "Bookshelf," September 24, 1986). Actually, the book belongs in the category of racist, pogrom literature, and in some aspects of its "scholarly findings" it even outdoes works of the same kind by authors already well known: Korneev, Begun, Yevseev, Malashko and others. Thus the very fact that this work was published in a mass-market edition is significant in the context of internal national politics today.

Using falsifications and forgeries, playing on the complete ignorance of the reader who simply has no way of knowing anything about Jewish culture, history or religion, the author fills the book with all kinds of anti-Jewish slander, from medieval to the very latest, to denigrate the Jewish people to the utmost. To this effect, the reader is offered the following themes:

1. Denial of the reality of such a concept as "the Jewish people" or "Jewish nationality." Jews are not a people or a nationality since "they don't have the common economy, territory, culture, common language or common customs, that is they don't have any of the characteristics of a nation" (page 72).

Trying to "catch fish in murky water," Zionists have brought incredible confusion into scholarly terminology in order to give a scientific veneer to the idea of a "world-wide Jewish nation" or "a single Jewish nation," also world-wide (page 71).

The author speaks of the "dangerously disguised but persistent efforts of Zionists to displace the clear and concise Marxist-Leninist theory of nationality and replace it with a perverted, anti-Communist theory" passed off as "the latest achievements of scholarship" (page 71).

Contemporary Jews cannot even take pride in a common origin, since "there is the fact of the complete disappearance" of the descendants of ancient Hebrews (multi-ethnic "ibri," the author takes note), who have "dissolved" in the mass of nations. "Soviet researchers have proved that the contemporary Jewish populations living in my countries of the world are not descendants of ancient Hebrews" (page 78).

And yet such clearly illegitimate terms as "Jewish people" and even "Jewish nation" keep popping up in our literature, either due to carelessness or some other reason (page 80).

And really—what kind of a people is this, when "a promissory note is the real god of a Jew. His god is only an imaginary promissory note (page 17)." "What is the earthly business of Jewishness? Practical needs and self-interest. What is the earthly cult of the Jew? Mercantilism. Who is his earthly god? Money" (page 15).

The Jews, therefore, are not a nationality but rather a class, a class of exploiters from which society must be liberated, and the sooner, the better. "The emancipation of the Jews is, in the end, the emancipation of humanity from Jewishness" (page 15).

2. There never was and there is not now a single Jewish language. Moreover, not one of the languages traditionally designated as Jewish is, or has ever been, a national language. "Yiddish is corrupted German." Yiddish is not a national language, but a dialect." Concerning Hebrew, "in ancient Hebrew slave-owning states, Hebrew was only the language of the religious cult and religious services," and although it is now considered the official state language of Israel, all the same, the population speaks other languages in daily life. "Thus Hebrew is actually not even common to the Judaic population of the Zionist state" (pages 72–73).

3. There is no Jewish culture, but if there were one, then it shouldn't exist, since "anyone who directly or indirectly flies the banner of Jewish 'national culture' is (however benevolent his intentions) the enemy of the proletariat, a supporter of the traditions and the caste system of Judaism, an accomplice of the Rabbis and the bourgeoisie" (page 35).

4. The Jews do not have any characteristics of a nationality but they do have their own religion. The religion, however, is such that it would be better if they didn't have one at all. Besides a lack of spirituality and mercantilism (see No. 1), the author finds "ever more clearly visible characteristics of the Judaic religious complex such as misanthropy, the propagation of genocide and the celebration of criminal methods of attaining power" (page 244). That is not surprising, because at the time Judaism was born, "the customs and morals of people were crude and barbaric. Even cannibalism existed, mostly as a part of religious ritual. In those distant times, people believed in a cannibalistic god and brought him bloody offerings including human sacrifice. We find direct evidence of this in the Bible." This is how, for example, the essence of the Judaic component in the Jehovah's Witnesses cult is viewed (page 242).

Even in antiquity the racist and class essence of Judaism was obvious, since "while there was a social hierarchy within the Jewish population," the population as a whole acted as "conquerors and oppressors of the ancient Palestinians" (note that there was no concept of Palestine at that time, but there was already a Palestinian people!—pp. 241–242). The state that emerged as a result had the character of "ancient Judaic apartheid" (p. 242).

In order to prove the anti-human nature of Judaism, there is even an attempt to revive "the blood libel," calling into doubt the innocence of Mendel Beilis. That is achieved by the following means. Knowing that the intended audience has never heard anything about the Beilis case (in fact, even many Soviet Jews know nothing about it), and reminding the readers that Alexander Kerensky was the worst enemy of Soviet power and the top counter-revolutionary, he writes, "Kerensky became widely known in connection with the Beilis case (Beilis was a Jew who went on trial in Kiev in 1913 on charges of the ritual murder of a Christian boy named Yushchinsky, and was acquitted in the trial). In 1913, Kerensky, who was then a lawyer, was very active in the defense of Beilis, about which a great deal was reported in the "press" (p. 228).

The reader is supposed to infer for himself that surely Kerensky could not defend a just cause, and surely a trial in a Tsarist court could not have been fair.

5. In addition to the revival of "the blood libel," the author also attempts (perhaps for the first time in 70 years) to legitimize the word "yid" (zhid in Russian—trans.), giving it a noteworthy explanation: "The past and present use of the term 'yid' in literary Polish is entirely legitimate and accepted, similar to analogous words formed from the same roots that are used in German, English, Spanish, and other languages: 'Jude,' 'Jewish,' 'Judeo,' and so on. The word 'yid', borrowed by Russian literature from the Polish language during the years of mass emigration of Jews from Poland to Russia, was used, for example, by great Russian writers as a bona fide literary term. Subsequently, in colloquial usage this word came to be seen by philistines as offensive to Jews" (pp. 45–46).

6. The author constantly attempts to plant in the mind of his reader the following chain of logic:

a) the majority of Jews have always belonged to the top strata of society, that is, to the parasitical, exploitative class—the bourgeoisie;

b) Zionism is the ideology of the Jewish bourgeoisie, therefore all (or the majority of) Jews are Zionists;

c) since Zionism is associated with everything dark and terrible that there is in the world, the same extends to all things Jewish.

Moving along this chain, the author constantly uses the term "Jewish" in the meaning of "Zionist" and vice versa, making these concepts identical. Thus, all Jewish parties, organizations, and activists are Zionist.

"The Bund was an organization mostly made up of petty bourgeoisie with a clearly pro-Zionist ideology" (p. 22). The pro-autonomy Jewish historian S. M. Dubnov is described as "a Zionist ideologue and organizer (p. 42).

The party founded by Moscow police chief Zubatov in 1901 in order to undermine the Bund from within the Independent Workers' Party, held "a special place" among "socialist" Zionist parties in Russia (p. 90).

In the 1920's, the international Zionist organization, Joint, operated in the USSR through its branch LEKPZhV (the Leningrad Jewish Committee to Aid the Victims of War) (page 101).

The "Prague Spring" of 1968 was hidden behind false slogans of the creation of 'national benefits' for Jews in Palestine, then the creation of a Jewish state on that territory, and then the defense of the interests of the present state" (p. 126). However, all this was said and is being said in order to pull the wool over the eyes of gullible simpletons. The true goal of Zionism is world domination.

"Indeed, long before Israel was founded, international Zionism formulated its 'optimum program,' expressed in pronouncements like 'The State of Israel must subsume within itself all the countries of the Earth,' 'the Jews are superior to other people and are destined to rule over all of humanity,' and so on" (p. 127). "Zionism has now developed its tactics for achieving world domination and is persistently working towards that goal which is entirely identical to Hitler's plans of world domination" (p. 128). "Zionists believe that Zionism has reached a crucial stage in the achievement of world domination" (p. 129).

The author admits that "it is difficult to establish the exact number of members of Zionist organizations and the number of organizations themselves, which carefully guard their secrets" (p. 193). But he has nevertheless learned that "in the United States today, there are more than 500 Zionist organizations, operating both nationally and locally" (p. 204). The largest of them, the World Jewish Congress, unites eight to ten million Jews living outside the countries of Eastern Europe (p. 197). Moreover, all "Jewish organizations are interventionist" (p. 201).

"The Jewish community of the USA is under near-totalitarian control, almost as great as in the medieval ghettos of Europe" (p. 208).

8. A special chapter is devoted to an expose of the cooperation between Zionism and Nazism (pp. 112–120). "With every passing year

the world learns more and more about the secret cooperation between the Zionists and fascism" (p. 114).

"Zionists made efforts to create a single anti-Soviet front of Nazism and Western European and American capitalism at the end of the Second World War" (p. 114). "Zionist ringleaders entered into a pact with the fascist leaders—a pact that was a crime against all humanity. By their actions they strengthened the Nazi machine of destruction and thus prolonged the death throes of the bloody regime" (p. 116).

"In their assessment of the struggle between the German and the Jewish bourgeoisie, Soviet authors maintain a rigorously class-based position. In its essence, this violent clash between Zionism and Nazism was an internal bourgeois conflict. With genuine objectivity, Soviet scholarship has pointed out the reactionary nature of both sides in this conflict" (p. 119).

Indeed, the author regards Zionism as the more dangerous phenomenon, since, first of all, "Zionists were the first, to don the masks of national socialism, before the Nazis did" (p. 119). Secondly, they are stronger, since they defeated Nazism and then fleeced the Federal Republic of Germany using blackmail and threats to force it to pay reparations for the victimization the Jews suffered at the hands of the Nazis (p. 121).

9. Israel, of course, takes a lashing in the book. Certainly, you can hang anything on Israel without risking criticism. And here are just a few samples of new discoveries in this field:

"The Israelis who slaughtered the peaceful population in Palestinian camps in Sabra and Shatila were dressed in the uniforms of the Lebanese militia" (p. 133).

There exists the opinion that Israel attacked the Arabs immediately after the Zionist state was declared. Actually, "the Zionist armed forces continued the war" begun long before that moment (p. 135). The military forces were unequal: in November 1947 the Jews had 120,000 soldiers armed with the newest weapons and tanks while the armies of Egypt, Syria and Iraq amounted to only 45,000 poorly armed soldiers and the Jordanian army "was represented only by camel-mounted troops" (p. 137). What happened to the famous Arab legion armed and trained by the British, which entered East Jerusalem during the war?

"In 1950 Israel joined the aggressors attacking the Korean People's Democratic Republic" (p. 138).

Israeli Jews are fighting in Namibia in the vile role of occupation forces (p. 183).

"Israel re-exports American technology to African countries, changing its appearance and giving it characteristics of Israeli manufacture in order to hide from the Africans the fact the Zionists are acting as agents of the neo-colonial policies of the US" (p. 186).

The freeing of Israeli hostages in Uganda in 1976 is treated as an act of direct armed aggression against Uganda (p. 192). The Israeli secret service is so strong that it feels at home even in the US. It is the Israeli secret service for example, that arranged and carried out the indecent provocation against Andrew Young, the American representative to the UN (a reference to the meeting of Young with PLO spokesmen) (p. 163).

10. The Zionists have achieved impressive economic and political success worldwide. For example, over 95 percent of the major military-industrial concerns in the US and in all the capitalist countries belong to the Jewish bourgeoisie and its allies (p. 166).

The same kind of nightmare is going on in Latin America. "In the post-war years, the US has drained more than $70 billion worth of profits from Latin American countries. Of these, about $50 billion have gone to Zionist businessmen" (p. 170).

"Zionists make up the ruling elite in the Republic of South Africa, dominating its financial system, its economy, its political life, and creating another 'model' of a racist state similar to Israel" (p. 178).

11. Although Judaism and Zionism are not exactly the same thing, they act hand in hand. "The purposeful, conscious dissemination of Judaism in Jewish communities that has increased in recent years is a somewhat disguised form of Zionist expansion carrying the banner of 'freedom of conscience.' " "Zionists use Judaism in a utilitarian way." "They resort to the services of synagogues and the Rabbinate in places where Zionist political organizations cannot exist legally—in the socialist countries, for example—for their subversive activities and recruitment among the believers" (p. 243).

12. Of particular interest is the chapter on the connection between Masons and Zionists, an old tune that has been around for a long time. This chapter is filled with such fantastic nonsense that it's hard to summarize.

It turns out that the Masons have existed for three thousand years, since the time of King Solomon (p. 223). Their leaders were "a sect of Levites which exists to this day" (p. 224). The Masons, too, are running the world. Their symbols are "the star of David, the star of Solomon (whatever that is), the Menorah, the scrolls of the Torah, and so on" (p. 225). The original name of Masonic Lodge P-2 in Italy is "the Politics of Zionism-2" or "Propaganda of Zionism-2" (p. 226). All in all, Freemasonry is "a reactionary theory coinciding in content and goals with the ideals of Nietzscheanism, neo-Malthusianism, Nazism, Zionism, apartheid, and other varieties of racism" (p. 21).

There could be many more quotations. It is worth noting that the bibliography in the appendix does not list the Jewish authors of anti-Zionist literature: Solodar, Mintz, Berenshtein, Brodsky, Shulmeister, Schreiberg, Goldenberg, Shakhnovich, Belenky and others—not even those whom Romanenko quotes in the book.

Of course, Jews are not to be trusted no matter what they do. When they go to Palestine, they are Zionists; if they go to America, it's to create new footholds of International Zionism abroad; if they stay in the USSR, it is to preserve a Zionist underground. And if Jews take part in revolutions, convert to Christianity, write books against Zionism—it's perfectly clear that Zionists are changing colors like chameleons to plant their agents in key positions in the world economy and politics.

It is interesting how the book is being distributed. It cannot be found in central bookstores where foreigners sometimes shop. It can only be bought on the outskirts of the city and out in the country. It looks like the book is needed for internal use but publicity abroad is undesirable.

But why, really? There are so many neo-Nazis all over the world who helplessly flounder on the shaky theoretical foundations left by Hitler and Goebbels, ignorant of the latest Soviet achievements. It's time to extend them a helping hand.

Mikhail Beizer

Reading 24

Testimony of Vladimir Lifshitz, formerly of Leningrad, for the Helsinki Commission, December 4, 1987, in Hearing before the Commission on Security and Cooperation to Europe, One Hundredth Congress, First Session, "Soviet Jewry Struggle," December 4, 1987, Appendix A, pp. 57–58. Supplied by Union of Councils for Soviet Jews.

Lifshitz, a former refusenik, was allowed to leave the USSR with his family in 1987 and has settled in Israel. In this testimony he does not believe that glasnost *and* perestroika *signal better times for Soviet Jews. Instead, he feels that Gorbachev is using new methods of anti-Semitism, such as allowing the proliferation of chapters of* Pamyat.

Testimony of Vladimir Lifshitz, formerly of Leningrad, for the Helsinki Commission December 4, 1987:

1. Do you think that Soviet officials will be sensitive to human rights after the summit?

Soviet officials will try to bargain with the United States in different areas and only to this end will they address human rights. They are not now, nor will they be, sensitive to human rights issues without linkage to trade and arms control.

2. To what extent do you suppose the Gorbachev's glasnost was instituted because of the Soviet economy?

I am sure that the Soviet economy, which is, in my opinion worsening now, is the decisive factor in the Soviet policy on human rights. Even some Soviet economists have stated that there cannot be any real improvement in the economy without changing the role of the Communist Party in its management. If this is so, it presents a test for Gorbachev who is a party man and cannot lessen the privileges of Party workers which are based on the Party's total control in the management of the economy (the prime source of their power).

Two years ago, people on the street in the Soviet Union believed in Gorbachev. They expected changes in their living standards but now they are deeply disappointed with the realities. Moreover, there is growing anger and dissatisfaction among the people and in a short time the Soviet leaders will need a scapegoat to channel this anger.

Since the time of the Czars, the traditional scapegoat on the Russian scene has been the Jews. Not only I, but my friends as well, see it coming. Some leaders on the highest levels have begun to prepare public opinion to place the blame on the Jews for all the mistakes and misfortunes coming down upon them. Gorbachev laid the groundwork long ago for a scapegoat in the event of his failures. The campaign includes a growing number of anti-Semitic publications in the official press, in books, on TV and the public media—much more than two years ago.

Anti-Semitic publications are a traditional tool of Soviet officials. There are some new methods. Officially not under the control of the State, nationalistic organizations, like PAMYAT, have proliferated. PAMYAT has some 12,000 members, most of them highly educated people, scientists, professors. They blame all the difficulties of life in the Soviet Union on the Jews. For example, they blame Jews for the problem of alcoholism in Russia. In a book by Professor Ugelov, a famous Soviet surgeon, it is alleged that there were a high percentage of Jewish merchants who sold alcohol. The number was taken for an anti-Semitic book published at the turn of the century. Even in this book, there was a much lower percentage number because Jews were permitted to live in only a very small part of the country where they were not permitted to engage in agriculture or industry. In Ugelov's books, areas were out of proportion to numbers.

Only a year ago, a publication appeared alleging that Jewish doctors make Russian babies ingest alcohol to make alcoholics out of them. They based their allegation on the contention that Jewish doctors prescribed "hafir" [sic], which, according to published articles, contains alcohol.

PAMYAT is an anti-Semitic society for the upper intelligentsia. But there are Hitlerist and Fascist groups for your illiterate people. This very year, around Hitler's birthday, these groups vandalized Jewish cemeteries in Leningrad on four separate occasions. The existence of these societies would have been impossible without support from the highest echelons.

PAMYAT is still allowed to meet in official halls. None of its leaders have been dismissed from their positions. At the same time, any attempt to protest against anti-Semitic propaganda is suppressed immediately. For example, recent attempts by Jews of Leningrad and Moscow to demonstrate against such anti-Semitic activities were suppressed before they started. The few who did show up at the demonstration sites were detained immediately by the militia. Some of the organizers were held by the militia from three to ten hours.

Reading 25

Complaint by Vladimir Slepak to the Presidium of the Supreme Soviet of the USSR, March 25, 1987. Translated from Russian.

Slepak asks for an explanation for his continued visa refusal based on "secrecy." Slepak was allowed to emigrate later in 1987.

My wife and I have been denied the right to leave for Israel for the last 17 years. According to what we have been told at the OVIR office, the reason for this was my "regime"; i.e. my knowledge of classified information.

Until April 1969 I worked in the Moscow Television Research Institute (affiliated with the Ministry of Radio Industry), where I served as head of a laboratory and had access to "closed" information.

Eighteen years have passed since then, but I am still being told that I know some sort of secrets. I shall try to show here the absurdity of such statements.

There can be two aspects of the "secrecy" applied in my case:

a) the technical aspect; i.e. information about equipment, its construction and the parameters involved;
b) information on the location of the closed sites which I visited.

The equipment which I helped to develop consisted of discrete elements (transistors, diodes, resistors, condensers, etc.). Electronics have progressed so much during this period that not only special equipment, but even home appliances are being constructed on the basis of solid-body integral schemes. Thus, all the parameters of the equipment have changed accordingly and, therefore, to speak of the classified nature of the equipment which I helped to develop would be equivalent to speaking of the classified nature of a stone axe.

Regarding the question of location: in view of the availability of modern space satellites, which can photograph (by optical, infrared and other beams) tiniest details on the surface of the earth, as well as under its surface, the location of closed states which I visited (one testing ground and one functioning site), is hardly a secret by now and is known to all the countries which have such satellites.

In addition, the testing ground where we tested our equipment was visited by Felix Kandel (who both visited it and worked there), who left for Israel after receiving official permission to do so in Moscow in 1977.

As far as the functioning site is concerned, Solomon Rozin, a former resident of Leningrad, worked there together with me. He also received official permission to leave and left for Israel in 1975 or 1976 (the exact date can be obtained in the Leningrad OVIR office).

In view of the above, it becomes clear that the secrecy restrictions have been used in my case for many years as merely an artificial pretext to prevent our family from leaving the Soviet Union.

Reading 26

The Problem of Being Refused Permission to Emigrate for Women and Children, March 8, 1988, by V. Gorelikova-Khassina and M. Balashinskaya-Abramovich.

This paper, prepared for the Women's Group's Symposium held in Moscow in March 1988, is an emotional discussion of how hard it is for all members of a family to live in refusal. This document was brought out of the U.S.S.R. by Michael and Caryl Kligfield, Woodbridge, Ct., on March 31, 1988.

In the conditions of Soviet reality, a Jewish family's decision to go to Israel means setting out on a road of psychological conflict with Soviet society. Distorted, one-sided facts about Israel appearing regularly in periodicals, branding Zionism as fascism; as well as outright assertions that leaving the USSR for permanent residence in Israel is unpatriotic, brainwash the population into seeing the category of refusenik citizens as disloyal to the State and ready to collaborate with a class enemy.

Often enough, a decision to participate in the affairs of one's people, to contribute one's bit to the buildup of the Jewish State, is received with fear and condemnation in one's own family. In the eyes of relatives, we become a source of danger and a threat to their welfare, since they fear that the powers that be will suspect them of endorsing our decision and sharing our views. Arguments and threats flare up within families; there are accusations and quarrels, often leading to a total break between relatives. Fathers and sons, brothers and sisters become alien to each other, harboring feelings of hostility.

Friends are wary of people who take the decision. Though no one asks them for notarized documents, they read the press, hear the radio and see television. Well-versed in the sad lessons of Soviet history, they prefer to break with us, just in case. . . . And certainly, any manager of a workplace will be enthusiastic about an employee's asking for his civil rights to go to Israel. The management's possible response to such a request may range from persuasion "not to take such a step," to advice that you "quit your job," to outright dismissal for fabricated reasons.

There has been an increase the instances lately, when a place of employment has given an authorized affidavit for emigration. But even in the best of instances, there is a sharp change in the attitude of the management and personnel toward an applicant to leave. We are usually demoted to work at lower pay, stripped of our academic degrees, and deprived of all hope of advancing in our careers or earning bonuses and privileges. Most of our fellow employees became wary of us, some even become hostile. It is not considered rude when they voice their opinion on a problem of our deep personal concern. They brand us as traitors to our country. Those who oppose us see themselves and are seen by others as true patriots.

As a result, many of us have been deprived of the possibility of working in our specialty. Former scientists and specialists work as watchmen, elevator operators, scrubwomen. This is quite common among refuseniks. The hostility of our relatives and colleagues, the loss of friendships, and professional deterioration, all breed discomfort and psychological tension. When a family is refused permission to leave, stress becomes chronic, lasting years, even decades. An area of scorched earth spreads around the refusenik, and few risk entering it. Cooperation between people disappears and one feels estranged from them, ties are broken. Social attitudes alter as situations alienate one and form new dependencies between people.

Due to the disruption of the old way of life and the break with old ties, things that used to be satisfactory become the opposite. Often emotions become deficient, the spectrum of life narrows, and a tendency appears to see the world as black and white. A new style of living must be formed.

Some people, especially the introverts, are able to overcome the barriers. For most extroverts, overcoming the barriers is extremely difficult. The authorities draw the refusenik into a psychological war. They deliberately heat up the lengthy tension of waiting. Illogical reasons are given for a refusal; there is no explanation of those reasons, and the impossibility of complaining through due process of law frustrates one into helplessness. When a refusenik grows active in his fight for his rights (by demonstrations or hunger strikes), the statement machine attacks him through mass media with false charges of hooliganism, parasitism, fraud, and the carrying out of instructions of American and Israeli "special services." The newspaper *Sovietskaya Rossiya* carried an article entitled "Magnanimity and a Break-In" last April 3, calling the departure of Jews from the USSR" a large-scale spy operation. As a result, America pumps $1,000 worth of Soviet military and other secrets out of refuseniks for every dollar invested in the operation." The newspapers have never printed a single one of the countless letters they receive refuting their routine slanderous inventions and attacks on refuseniks.

Dependence on unforeseeable international events, of whose mechanisms we have only sparse information at best, and the constant cat-and-mouse fight, rouses hopelessness and uncertainty. A constant, endless psychological burden traumatizes our personality; it makes the refusenik's condition a highly risky one.

Refuseniks constitute a relatively new stratum of Soviet society. We are people in whom national feelings have awakened, feelings which have repeatedly saved the Jewish people from destruction and extinction. These people, who feel themselves to be part of their nation, have managed throughout the ages to appreciate in full their rich, though tragic history during centuries of exile. Now they want to go home to their own land, to their brothers and sisters, to wipe out forever the bitter taste of classification as aliens.

We are refuseniks, those who are prevented from realizing our dream of joining our own people in our own land.

Is it we who are to blame for the fact that we are so prevented? Perhaps thinking too long of well-being and careers, accepting alien cultures and loving alien landscapes has dampened in us what should have awakened long ago. Perhaps. If so, we are paying dearly for it. We are paying with what is dearest to us: our children, whose future is now being crippled before our eyes while we can do nothing to help them.

Most of us have been refused permission to go to Israel for many years. Many of us applied to leave when our children were still charming and tiny tots who were thrilled by the shining buttons on the police uniforms that now and then made an appearance in our homes. How were we to explain to the tiny member of the big community in a day-care center that he must not say anything to anyone about the wonderful buttons he heard about at home, that fired his best friends? How were we to explain to the tiny member of our family why his beloved Dad, who has so many friends, was seized on the street by ruffians and carried off in a gloomy, ugly van? Where did they take him? When will he come home? Why do strangers suddenly break into our home and turn it upside down looking for something, even in his little bed?

What if the family is religious, if it observes the Jewish family laws, the Sabbath, the laws of Judaism, the very foundation of our existence? Not a single children's establishment in the USSR provides kosher food or respects the Sabbath. Every attempt to form our own Jewish children's groups where our children could be together for fun and play, to learn the history of the Jewish people and our traditions, holidays, culture, and language, is suppressed by official authority on any pretext. People who self-sacrificingly undertake the arduous work of forming such groups are threatened with dire consequences.

Now the child has passed the first stage of acquaintance with actuality. What scar has it left on the as yet unstable psychology of the little one?

Then our children, the offspring of refuseniks, go to school. What stamina the child must have to be silent when everything in his home, everything he is used to, everything he considers his own and good, is trampled upon in school, is criticized and damned by those whom he is supposed to respect and even admire?

At this moment, the little member of the Soviet society is forced into a duel with an enormous State machine. It's well if the family's aspirations are unknown to the teachers and other children, or "re-education" begins to reshape our child's soul and consciousness. For many children, especially those from religious families, the fuel is beyond their powers. What about the Sabbath, a day on which all Soviet schools function? How can he wear his skullcap without being ridiculed for it? There is constant conflict between the parents and school. The life of both children and parents is transformed into a constant struggle for dignity, for the chance to live by Judaic laws in one's own interests.

Naturally, parents try to fight for the Sabbath by any means, legal and illegal. But how is the child to understand the deceit he is forced to practice in order to celebrate his family's wonderful day of festivity? The duality persists throughout all the years of schooling, becoming more complicated in the upper grades when the time comes to join the Young Communist League.

No one can win this conflict between the little refusenik and the big school community. The school loses morally, by closing its eyes and retreating from a persistent social phenomenon instead of assessing and understanding it. The child bears, for the rest of his life, a bad school character and an unhealing moral trauma.

Our children, even before entering a life of independence, have thus experienced a psychological tragedy, that not even every adult can bear. They grow up knowing that they are ostracized. They have done everything they can. They have acquired knowledge, testified by diplomas that show their educational accomplishments. No one was able to take that away from them.

But with their increased age, new moral problems arise.

For the Jewish refusenik, direct entry into a school of higher learning is blocked. There is, however, a roundabout way. You can conceal that you are a refusenik. Again deceit, again duality. And that's still not the worst of it. There is always the army: it postpones permission to leave for an indefinitely long period, up to two years of service, followed by many years of refusal for so-called possession of state secrets. It's not for nothing that in trying to make us stop our fight to get out, the KGB doesn't threaten us with jail, as you'd expect, but with calling up our sons. They realize well that the worst tragedy for parents is to see their children's lives ruined.

That way out could be so simple. Couldn't our adult children apply to go to Israel independently? This simplest of solutions turns out to be the most complex. Their applications are blocked by any and every means, and they are not allowed to go on any pretext.

Is there any other country in the world where children must bear responsibility for the work done by their parents who may have worked at a "secret" factory ten, fifteen or twenty years ago, before they were even born?

Our children, like us, are hostages. Our fate is a target for speculation, while the life of our children is wrecked.

In this difficult situation, the lofty mission rests on us women of preserving our Jewish home, repelling evil from it, and standing up as its spiritual bulwark.

We have given life to our children. We have awakened national awareness in them. Today they cannot imagine a normal life outside Israel.

What do they have to look forward to? Will they ever be rid of their childhood experiences? How will these experiences end for them, and when? Why must we fight for their future with desperate, unnatural, abnormal steps like demonstrations and hunger strikes?

When we see no real chance for our family to go to Israel, we seek the right for our adult children to leave separately, though this poses a risk of our never seeing them again.

We Jewish women, like all human beings, thirst for peace. For the Jewish people, peace has special meaning. Throughout the centuries, our people have constantly fought for our spiritual and physical survival. We remember the lessons of history well. We will never forget the Holocaust. We therefore appeal to you and to all people of good will to support our demand for our people to be let go, to support our fight to go to Israel.

Reading 27

Refuseniks from Moscow, Letter to General Secretary Gorbachev, undated (approximately July 1987)

In this letter twenty-eight leading refuseniks complain about the aims and actions of Pamyat, *an anti-Semitic group they claim has received unofficial sanction by the state.*

To: The Secretary General of the Central Committee of the CPSU, M. S. Gorbachev.

Twenty years of anti-Zionist propaganda conducted in the mass media have not borne fruit. Anti-Semitic fires which have smoldered for a long time in the depths of Soviet society have now burst into the open in the form of the "Pamyat" ("Memory") organization.

In seeking the reasons and consequences of the destruction of traditional Russian culture and social order, "Pamyat" has found a suitable and defenseless enemy which could be blamed for all the failures and mistakes of the past years—the Jewish people.

Following the example of the anti-Semitic organizations which existed before the October Revolution, they have resurrected the "Protocols of the Elders of Zion." They have also adjusted Hitler's slogans on the "international plot of the world's financiers, Jews and Bolsheviks" to Soviet conditions and restored them in the form of an "international plot of Zionists, Masons and imperialists."

"Pamyat" has presented demands to exclude the Jews from all spheres of public life, productive work and culture. Its leaders have been overtly calling for pogroms, demanding that "they should be torn into shreds and thrown out the windows" and that "the secret meeting places of the enemies be revealed."

The organization is composed of persons of Russian nationality and headed by a member of the CPSU Andreev. All these factors could result in the members' occupation of important positions in the state and party apparatus and attempts to realize their racist programme.

None of numerous Soviet publications has contained an unequivocal and sharp rebuke against the crude charges presented against the Jews. Moreover, "Pamyat" has enjoyed the tacit support of influential personalities who have granted its members permission to use various premises for their meetings. None of the leaders of this organization has ever been charged with inciting anti-Semitism and racial hostility (under Art. 74 of the RSFSR Criminal Code).

Moreover, the meeting between "Pamyat" representatives and B. Yeltsin, Candidate Member of the Politbureau and Chairman of the Moscow Soviet, gave the organization an aura of official recognition.

The slogans used by "Pamyat" are directed against all Jews, both those wishing to leave and those wishing to remain in the USSR. However, deprived of any form of national organization and considerably smaller in number than the indigenous population, the Jews cannot repulse the attacks of their enemies within the USSR, while repatriation from the USSR has, in fact, been rendered impossible for most of them by the existing laws.

Moreover, the situation could get out of the authorities' control in conditions allowing freedom of meetings and demonstrations and verbal slogans could easily lead to physical violence. All this recalls the alarming memories of the slogans and methods used by the Nazis in the 1930's.

Therefore, before "Pamyat" has staged its first pogrom and before any Jew has become its victim we demand:

1. An immediate end to the wave of anti-Jewish propaganda and the restraining of those calling for physical violence against Jews;

2. The granting of permission to repatriate to Israel to all Jews wishing to do so and in cases, when some must delay their departure for a certain period, the granting of permission to their families.

Moscow

Reading 28

Appeal of the Delegates to the Congress of the USSR Jewish Organizations and Communities to the USSR Supreme Soviet, Soviet Government and CPSU Central Committee, adopted in Moscow on December 22, 1989. Appeal furnished by the National Conference on Soviet Jewry.

Challenging the Kremlin

This appeal calls upon the Soviet government and Communist Party to publicly condemn and combat growing grass-roots anti-Semitism in the USSR.

Anti-Semitism, a most shameful phenomenon in today's life in the Soviet Union, is acquiring more and more menacing forms. Whole social layers make attempts to identify Jews, and in particular Soviet Jews, with the "image of the enemy," laying on us the blame for all the sufferings that have befallen Russia, diverting the people's anger away from the true causes of the disastrous situation.

Such acts as mass distribution of anti-Semitic leaflets, the contents of which would make the hearts of propagandists in Nazi German beat with joy, go unpunished in cities and towns of the Soviet Union. The national dignity of Jews is being openly abused, acts of violence are being committed against them, their cemeteries are being desecrated, the danger of Jewish pogroms is becoming more and more imminent. Both local and central mass media regularly feature anti-Semitic publications. Judophobia is more and more energetically penetrating Russian literature, culture and education. The intentionally deformed concept of Zionism, one of the forms of Jewish national movement, is a target and cover for all sorts of defamation as well as propaganda of national dissent and hatred.

Anti-Semitism has many faces: It can be encountered in the notorious Pamyat movement, among Russian writers and officials who provide employment and promote people on the grounds of a person's nationality, among hooligans and Academy members—the process of anti-Semitic group formation is taking place in all those strata. The neo-Nazism is being revived unimpeded in the country though this racist movement has been repudiated and outlawed in practically all civilized states.

Neither state and party bodies, nor public organizations are engaged in any serious fight against this horrible evil, on the contrary, they are trying to play it down. There has been no reply to the appeal calling attention to the growing threat of anti-Semitism which was signed by more than 200 People's Deputies and sent to the First Congress of the USSR People's Deputies Presidium. The manifestations of anti-Semitism are becoming more and more frequent involving broader population groups. These developments cause mass panic among the Jews who now question the ability of authorities to protect them against the potential violence.

Anti-Semitism should not be looked upon as one of the national problems, it is in fact a pathological reaction of the society of its own internal crisis. No matter how a Jew may behave, he is sure to be a target of anti-Semitic attacks. We, the Jews, have got nothing to be ashamed of, every unbiased person is well aware of the great contribution made by the Soviet Jews into the life in this country. We have got the right to the guaranteed security for those who have decided to stay in the Soviet Union.

We, the representatives of 204 USSR Jewish organizations and communities assembled for our first Congress, demand that the highest Soviet authorities should immediately do the following:

- to publicly denounce anti-Semitism without any further delay;
- to take all legal actions provided for by the Soviet Law cutting short the spreading of chauvinism and neo-Nazism;
- to set up a commission of People's Deputies which will have the task of fighting anti-Semitism and ensuring the realization of national, civil and political rights of Soviet Jewry.

PART III

The Jewish Question in U.S. Relations with the Soviet Union

In the aftermath of the 1967 Six-Day War, Soviet Jews looked to Israel for leadership. They also sought her political, psychological, and emotional support. The start of *Kol Yisrael* (Voice of Israel) broadcasts into the Soviet Union in 1968, the creation in Israel of the Public Council for Soviet Jewry in 1970, and the 1971 law enacted by the Knesset that enabled the conferring of Israeli citizenship on those Soviet Jews who asked for it all gave Soviet Jews comfort and encouragement. But in general, Israel's support for Soviet Jews was lacking and its response was disappointing.

Soviet Jews sensed Israel's reticence to push hard for their cause. They felt that Israel, in an understandable but unwise reaction to the Soviet Union's breaking diplomatic relations with her after the 1967 war, was maintaining far too low a diplomatic profile and simply was not doing enough for them. They believed Israel was too hesitant to criticize the Kremlin openly and forcefully, fearing adverse diplomatic repercussions on Jewish emigration, the lives of those Soviet Jews who remained in the U.S.S.R., and chances for peace in the Middle East. In short, Soviet Jews sought far stronger support than Israel was prepared to offer. They would soon look to the United States as their main source of help.

Before the Six-Day War the United States government had offered Soviet Jews little meaningful assistance. The plight of Soviet Jews was far down on Washington's diplomatic agenda. Yet after the war Washington became increasingly absorbed with this problem. Soon it would develop into a major issue in U.S. relations with the Soviet Union.

The United States developed varied strategies toward the budding Soviet Jewish movement for freedom. Strategy was dictated by pressure from newly formed Soviet Jewry advocacy groups and Soviet human rights activists (Jewish and non-Jewish), U.S. domestic politics, perceptions of Moscow's motives and policies, and priorities within the overall U.S.–Soviet relationship. By the late 1960s circumstances in the Soviet Union, Israel, and the United States led to Washington's becoming the main governmental champion of the Soviet Jewry cause.

During the first years after the 1967 war, the Jewish political establishment in the United States took its cue from Israel in determining its policy toward Soviet Jews. It, too, made a minimal effort to help and communicate with them. The American Israel Public Affairs Committee (AIPAC), the main registered lobbying organization for American Jews in Washington, focused on helping Israel. It assumed that Israel would provide the necessary support for Soviet Jews.

There were groups in the American Jewish community, however, who decided on a more activist, interventionist course of action. The Student Struggle for Soviet Jewry (SSSJ), founded in May 1964 by Yakov Birnbaum and Glenn Richter, began protests on behalf of Soviet Jews. The Union of Councils for Soviet Jews (UCSJ), founded in 1970 by Dr. Louis Rosenblum, also assumed an activist leadership role. It soon pushed the older, more established members of the American Jewish Conference on Soviet Jewry, founded in 1964, toward more aggressive involvement. In June 1971 this group, under the leadership of Richard Maas and Jerry Goodman, changed its name to the National Conference on Soviet Jewry (NCSJ), and it too became more activist. At the same time the Jewish Defense League (JDL), founded in 1968 by Rabbi Meir Kahane, began seeking headlines. The JDL, believing militancy was needed to help Soviet Jews, staged violent protests including sit-ins at the Soviet Mission to the United Nations and disruptions of performances by Soviet artists and sports teams. Such actions angered the other Jewish organizations and Washington, which dissociated themselves from the JDL and condemned their activities.

By 1970–1971, American Jewish organizations were divided over how to help Soviet Jews. On the fringe was the rabidly anti-Soviet JDL, which almost routinely used violence; then there were the more activist SSSJ and UCSJ; and finally there was the more conservative NCSJ. In the late 1960s Jewish advocacy groups were pleased by the moral and political support for Soviet Jews given by black activists like Bayard Rustin. *(See Reading 1.)* These black leaders, convinced of the indivisibility of justice and freedom around the world, believed the drive for freedom of Soviet Jews was intrinsically linked with their own civil rights movement. They were also cognizant of many years of black-Jewish political solidarity at home. In 1972, Jewish advocacy groups welcomed the formation of the National Interreligious Task Force on Soviet Jewry spearheaded by Sister Ann Gillen. All these groups received and publicized information sent by Soviet Jews, and they began to pressure the U.S. government to assist them.[1]

The Quiet Diplomacy of Presidents Johnson, Nixon, and Ford

President Nixon inherited from Lyndon Johnson the policy of quiet diplomacy in dealing with the delicate issue of Soviet Jewry. Under Nixon, the State Department continued to "deplore," "disapprove," and express "continuing concern." It held up the Soviet Union to the scrutiny of international attention mainly in the United Nations—though only in committees, not on the floor of the General Assembly, where there would be much more publicity. The Nixon administration believed that the best way to help Soviet Jews was through appeals by private organizations and individuals. The Kremlin, it felt, would probably dismiss public U.S. governmental demands for better treatment of Soviet Jews as "cold war initiatives."

One of Washington's most important early public statements on Soviet Jews was made on November 9, 1971, by Richard Davies, Assistant Secretary for European Affairs. *(See Reading 2.)* Davies reiterated Washington's familiar position that the UN was the "best regular forum for focusing world attention on the situation of Soviet Jews."

Some American Jewish groups already were urging the United States to raise the Soviet Jewry issue at higher government levels and in other international forums. They were beginning to recognize the trend toward Soviet and third-world domination of the UN General Assembly, which since the 1967 Six-Day War had been taking a distinctly anti-Israel and anti-Jewish posture. They also felt that Davies' statement was too weak. For example, they faulted him for omitting clear-cut support for an individual's basic right to emigrate. "Since the Soviet authorities remain extremely reluctant to permit Soviet citizens to emigrate or travel abroad," Davies stated disappointingly, "we are obliged to concentrate our intervention in behalf of persons attempting to join relatives in the

United States. We cannot be of direct assistance in cases of persons seeking to emigrate to other countries."

The Nixon administration can rightly be criticized for not speaking out more forcefully for the right to emigrate. It should be credited, however, for its stance on several other issues directly affecting Soviet Jews, such as whether the Voice of America (VOA) should initiate broadcasts in Yiddish into the Soviet Union. The drive for initiating Yiddish broadcasts was led in the spring of 1971 by Congressman William Ryan. *(See Reading 3.)*

As explained earlier, in the 1920s the Kremlin, through the *Yevsektsiya,* had encouraged the use of Yiddish as a way to communize and Sovietize Jews in the U.S.S.R. During the 1930s, Moscow backed off from this aggressive approach, but it generally allowed the use of Yiddish in Jewish cultural, educational, and academic life. There were Yiddish schools, newspapers, magazines, publishing houses, theaters, and university departments and research institutes for the study of Jewish history. Stalin began to clamp down on these institutions in the late 1930s. A decade later, inspired by his perception of Hitler's "successful" Jewish policy, he completely wiped them out. There then were no cultural, religious, or educational institutions for Jews in Yiddish or any other language. There was a slight revival of official Yiddish under Khrushchev. In 1961, the Yiddish bimonthly periodical *Sovetish heimland* began publication in editions of about 25,000 copies. There was also one Yiddish newspaper, the *Birobidzhaner shtern,* published in Birobidzhan. This came out five times a week in editions of about 1000 copies. By and large, though, Khrushchev engaged in an assault on all religious groups, but particularly the Jews. This situation grew worse under Brezhnev and Kosygin.

When the Congressional proposal to initiate VOA broadcasts in Yiddish was made in 1971, already far fewer Soviet Jews than ever before spoke or understood Yiddish. In the census of 1897, 97 percent of Russian Jews cited Yiddish as their mother tongue. At the time of the Bolshevik Revolution, Yiddish was still the main language of almost all European Jews. The extent of linguistic assimilation under Communist rule is evident from these later census results: in 1926, about 70 percent of Soviet Jews named Yiddish as their first language; in 1959, only about 18 percent did so; and by 1970, this figure had dropped to about 13 percent. In the 1989 census this figure had dropped even further to 11.1

percent.* Most Soviet Jews in the 1970 census (94.3 percent) said they spoke or understood Russian. In terms of reaching the widest audience of Soviet Jews in 1971, therefore, VOA unquestionably should have chosen Russian for its broadcasts. Thus Frank Shakespeare, then head of the United States Information Agency (USIA), rightly concluded that VOA broadcasts in Yiddish would not substantially increase the number of Soviet Jewish listeners and thus would not be cost-effective. *(See Reading 4.)*

To what extent, however, could the broadcast of Yiddish programs have uplifted Soviet Jews? Could they have led to reinvigorization of Soviet Jewish culture? This argument is somewhat plausible. But by 1971, Yiddish was well on its way to becoming a dead language in the U.S.S.R., as elsewhere in the world. Soviet Jews, especially in the heartland, had become highly assimilated and they wanted to learn Russian, which they considered the key to professional and economic advancement. They were also wary of sporadic efforts by the regime, particularly the use of "court Jews," to try to resurrect Yiddish as their native tongue. The alternative of Hebrew, officially banned in 1921 as the language of "anti-Soviet" Zionism, was also a complicating factor. The more Zionist and religious-oriented Soviet Jews tended to consider the Kremlin's propping up of Yiddish as a sophisticated way of keeping them from learning and practicing Hebrew. They saw the state's publicity of Yiddish as a subtle mask of repression. Still others viewed this publicity as a propaganda stunt to show Western public opinion how Jewish culture was being allowed to flourish in the U.S.S.R. Thus many Soviet Jews in 1971 probably would have considered the beginning of VOA broadcasts in Yiddish evidence that the United States had been "taken in" by the Kremlin.[2]

In the debate over the Yiddish broadcasting issue, the White House prevailed. There was continuing controversy, however, over the wisdom of continued reliance on quiet diplomacy to help Soviet Jews. Both Nixon and Kissinger believed that quiet diplomacy was the key to the Kremlin's

* The census results on Yiddish-speaking Jews vary in Western studies because some erroneously assumed that Yiddish was the language of all Jews who considered the language of their nationality as their native language. This assumption overlooked the fact that Jews in the U.S.S.R. speak other "native languages:" Georgian for Georgian Jews; Tadzhik for Bukharan Jews in Central Asia; and Tat for Mountain Jews.

decision to start allowing significant numbers of Soviet Jews to emigrate in 1971. In 1974, Nixon told a group of Jewish leaders: "The walls of the Kremlin are very thick. If you are inside, there is a chance they will listen to you; if you are outside you are not even going to be heard."[3]

Kissinger wrote in his memoirs that beginning in 1969 he told Soviet Ambassador Anatoly Dobrynin that the United States "would take note of any voluntary regard for the moral concerns of our people with respect to Soviet emigration policy." At that time Kissinger concentrated on the release of individuals with special hardships, whose names he submitted to Soviet authorities. He told Dobrynin that Washington would not try to engage in propaganda when the U.S.S.R. released people whose names were on his lists. Kissinger took credit not only for the release of these Jews but also for greatly increased Jewish emigration in general, which grew from about 400 in 1968 to about 35,000 in 1973.[4] Kissinger downplayed other factors that probably had an influence on the Kremlin's decision to increase Jewish emigration, such as the new boldness of Soviet Jewish activists and the growing impact of American public protest and public opinion in the West. He also resisted Congressional policy initiatives toward the Soviet Union, particularly Senator Henry Jackson's linkage of U.S.–Soviet trade to a significantly higher and sustained level of Soviet Jewish emigration.

The Jackson–Vanik Amendment

In the early 1970s, the issue of stepped-up trade with the Soviet Union sparked conflict between Congress and the White House. On October 18, 1972, after long negotiations, President Nixon and Soviet Trade Minister Patolichev signed a comprehensive trade bill. The Soviets promised to pay a small portion ($722 million) of their several-billion-dollar Lend Lease debt from World War II. They would pay the balance after the U.S. granted them most favored nation (MFN) tariff status.

On October 4, 1972, Senator Henry Jackson (D-Wash.) introduced an amendment to the trade bill that linked MFN, extension of U.S. Government credits and credit or investment guarantees to liberalized Soviet emigration.[5] In January 1973, Congressman Charles Vanik (D-Ohio) introduced a similar bill in the House. The Jackson-Vanik Amendment applied to all Communist countries (officially those with a "non-market economy"), but it was aimed largely at the Soviet Union.

Furthermore, although it mentioned the right of emigration for all citizens, its main intent was to bring about greater Jewish emigration. Jackson focused on Jewish emigration rather than the broad sweep of Soviet human rights practices largely because of the political clout of American Jews in lobbying and voting. Because Jackson was contemplating a run for the presidency in 1976, he felt the Soviet Jewry issue might help propel him into the White House. For legal justification of his amendment Jackson cited Article 13(b) of the Universal Declaration of Human Rights, which codified the basic human right to leave and return to one's country.

Jackson drafted his amendment in early 1972. Supposedly he had gotten the idea of linking trade concessions with Soviet Jewish emigration from Louis Rosenblum of the Union of Councils of Soviet Jews. Jackson had also discussed this idea with Jewish senators Jacob Javits (R-N.Y.) and Abraham Ribicoff (D-Conn.). These liberal senators were initially lukewarm to Jackson's proposal, for they were proponents of easing U.S.–Soviet tensions through increased contacts and relationships. Expanded U.S.–Soviet trade, they felt, would be an important vehicle for bridging the gap between the superpowers. Soon, however, the plight of Soviet Jews became their overriding concern, and they began to strongly back the amendment drive. Another concern for Jackson was that Rosenblum and other leaders of the American Jewish community, fearing an adverse backlash, initially were hesitant to lobby Washington for the amendment. But Jackson felt otherwise, and he decided to press on with his plan. He soon received outside support from hard-line anti-Communist leaders such as George Meany, president of the AFL–CIO. Meany believed that the Soviet Union, because of its weak economy and fear of China, would benefit far more from increased trade and détente than the United States. Jackson also received the backing of several academic organizations, such as the American Psychiatric Association, which hoped to use the amendment as leverage to curb the Kremlin's utilization of psychiatry against human rights activists, and the Federation of American Scientists, which sought to pressure the Kremlin to let Jewish scientists emigrate. Support for the Jackson Amendment thus cut across an unusual coalition of liberals and conservatives that Kissinger once described as "a rare convergence, like an eclipse of the sun."

Outside the White House, opposition to the amendment was led by

U.S. business groups that saw dollar signs in the prospect of increased U.S.–Soviet trade. The most vociferous were the National Association of Manufacturers, the U.S. Chamber of Commerce, the National Foreign Trade Council, and the East-West Trade Council. They were joined by Jewish leaders such as Charlotte Jacobson, vice chair of the National Conference on Soviet Jewry; Jacob Stein, chairman of the Conference of Presidents of Major American Jewish Organizations; and Max Fisher, a political and financial supporter of President Nixon. By and large, though, the American Jewish community rallied behind Jackson–Vanik.

The major reason for this support was the Kremlin's imposition of a "diploma tax" on August 3, 1972. *(See Reading 5.)* This meant that before being allowed to leave the U.S.S.R., emigrants would have to reimburse the state for their education. The higher their degree, the higher their tax. The new policy would hit Soviet Jews especially hard, because of their comparatively high level of education. American Jews had already been disappointed by Nixon's failure to meet with Soviet Jews or press the Soviet Jewry issue during his summit meeting with Brezhnev in May 1972. Apparently Nixon did not want the problem of Soviet Jews to get in the way of an arms control agreement and possibly deter Brezhnev from helping end the Vietnam War, which then were Nixon's highest priorities. But American Jews vowed not to let Washington remain silent over this tax.

Nixon soon realized how much the "diploma tax" had galvanized American Jewish leaders and how important the Soviet Jewry issue had become to the Jewish voter. As the 1972 presidential election drew near, the president became determined to win more Jewish electoral support than he had in 1968, when he garnered only about 15 percent of the Jewish vote.

Leonard Garment, Nixon's point man with the American Jewish community, continued to preach the merits of quiet diplomacy. The Soviets would concede more, he claimed, if they were not held up to public scorn or not forced to yield to pressure from American legislation. The Jackson Amendment, however, was too alluring to American Jews, who were not convinced by Kissinger's and Garment's arguments. Nixon finally decided not to oppose the amendment before the 1972 election. This helped his Jewish strategy succeed, for he more than doubled the percentage of his 1968 Jewish vote and was overwhelmingly re-elected.[6]

After the election, Nixon tried to ignore the Jackson Amendment. But it would not fade away. Nixon clearly underestimated Jackson's tenacity. The senator, gearing up for his own run for the presidency, increasingly saw his amendment as a cornerstone for his forthcoming campaign. He could display his anti-Communist and antidétente credentials with his amendment and at the same time curry favor among organized labor, intellectuals, and the Jewish community. Richard Perle, Jackson's assistant; Mark Talisman, Vanik's assistant; and the staff of senators Javits and Ribicoff did a lot of important behind-the-scenes legwork for the amendment. Isaiah Kenen, chief lobbyist for AIPAC, also worked hard to gather support. He distributed information on the amendment to Jewish leaders all over the country, urging them to lobby Congress to back the amendment. Jerry Goodman, then executive director of the National Conference on Soviet Jewry, did his part by arranging for Jackson to speak at meetings with actual and potential supporters. These lobbying efforts were extremely effective.

The Soviets, meanwhile, believed that Nixon would prevail over the Jackson forces. They acted on the assumption that the amendment was merely temporary "static" raised during the election. Perhaps to show Americans there was no need for the amendment, the Kremlin allowed over three thousand Jews to emigrate in both November and December 1972, the highest monthly totals to date. On December 27, however, it published the Presidium's decree on the "diploma tax," which gave it more visibility and suggested more longevity. Two days later, Soviet Deputy Minister of Interior Shumilin, apparently reacting to strong Western opposition, softened the Kremlin's move. He announced that those over fifty-five years old would be exempt from the tax, which also would be lowered according to the number of years an applicant had actually worked. The Soviets even allowed some Jews to emigrate without paying any tax. This was just another indication that it was not so much the law itself that counted but how it was applied. Yet American Jews in general, were not mollified by Moscow's tempering of the "diploma tax," and they stood behind the basic thrust of the Jackson-Vanik amendment.

The Soviets, not wanting to lose out on possible trade and credits benefits, announced on March 19, 1973, that the "diploma tax" would be "suspended indefinitely."[7] Two days later Soviet journalist Victor Louis wrote in the Israeli newspaper *Yediot Achranot* that the "diploma tax will not be enforced any more," admitting that Soviet Jews who wanted to emigrate had "won a victory in the six months' war against the education tax."[8] Finally, Kissinger and Dobrynin agreed, in a letter of April 16, that the U.S.S.R. would not enforce collection of the tax. But Jackson was emboldened by the fact his amendment had achieved some success even before its passage. Thus he forged ahead with it, pointing to the capriciousness of Soviet emigration policy and seeking more concessions from Moscow.

Soviet human rights activists, both Jewish and non-Jewish, soon joined the lobbying campaign. In May, a group of recent Soviet Jewish emigrants to Israel sent a memorandum to Nixon. They warned against the value of quiet diplomacy and reliance on the U.S.S.R. for abiding by gentlemen's agreements; they explained to the President that "as long as the Tax remains a law, it acts as a stern reminder to every young Jew beginning higher education that he may be mortgaged for life"; and they urged him to support Jackson–Vanik "to ensure the fulfillment" of free emigration. *(See Reading 6.)*

Sakharov took a leading role in courageously advocating passage of Jackson–Vanik.[9] Sakharov had earlier voiced his concern for Soviet Jewry in 1968, when he criticized the Communist Party for anti-Semitism in its appointment policy. He also charged the Kremlin with "direct responsibility" for the Six-Day War by arming and exhorting Arab states to attack Israel. Subsequently he opposed Moscow's severing of diplomatic relations with Israel. Sakharov also decried discrimination against Soviet Jews in employment and higher education. One of his chief concerns, however, was the right to emigrate, evidenced, for example, by his support for defendants in the Leningrad hijacking trial when he appeared in the courtroom and spoke out on their behalf.

In September 1973, Sakharov sent an open letter to the U.S. Congress in support of Jackson–Vanik. *(See Reading 7.)* He rejected the argument that this amendment might sway the Soviets from détente. Instead he wanted Congress to see it as "simply a defense of international law, without which there can be no mutual trust," and surely no lasting peace. Sakharov also ridiculed the idea that Jackson–Vanik would cause greater anti-Semitism in the U.S.S.R. and hurt chances for Jews to emigrate. He maintained that this argument was based on "total confusion, either deliberate or based on ignorance, about the U.S.S.R." He asserted Soviet Jews could not "depend on the democratic attitudes and the humanity of OVIR" and that quiet diplomacy would be of very little help to the vast majority of Soviet Jews.

Another non-Jewish Soviet human rights activist, historian Roy Medvedev, took issue with Sakharov on Jackson–Vanik. In an essay in November 1973, Medvedev argued that "it would be unrealistic" to presume the U.S.S.R. would allow more emigration in response to pressure from the U.S. Congress. He added that passage of Jackson–Vanik "would probably not improve but only worsen prospects for resolution of the emigration problem in the near future. Soviet-American relations would also deteriorate." Medvedev then argued that the amendment might diminish chances for inclusion of the right to emigrate in the draft of a new Soviet Constitution (adopted in 1977). Thus he considered Sakharov's appeal to Congress "a mistake, both substantially and tactically." Instead, Medvedev urged creation of conditions in the U.S.S.R "such that Soviet people will not wish to leave their country." Sakharov rejected Medvedev's argument, claiming that the right to emigrate is of equal importance both to those who leave and to those who remain in the Soviet Union. *(See Readings 8 and 9.)*

At this time, Soviet Jewish activists joined in with their support of Jackson–Vanik. In one appeal in September 1973, refuseniks from Moscow and Vilnius "categorically disagreed" with claims that Soviet Jews who wanted to emigrate would suffer more from the amendment, that emigration might cease, that the amendment would mean unwarranted interference in Soviet internal affairs, and that the prospects for détente would be damaged. They denounced quiet diplomacy as unproductive, and they insisted that the reason the Kremlin suspended the "diploma tax" was because of "open and wide protests." They concluded that rejection of Jackson–Vanik "would be a deviation from the noble principles of true humanitarianism, a capitulation to unscrupulous blackmail, and a first step in the chain of further retreats."

The White House, disregarding such appeals, continued to oppose Jackson–Vanik. The Nixon administration and Jackson previously had been allies on U.S. policy toward the Soviet Union as well as on other major foreign policy issues such as Vietnam and the Middle East. They now found themselves at opposite poles regarding the best way to relieve the plight of Soviet Jews. As Kissinger notes in his memoirs, both men were now "committed to the same objective: increasing emigration from the Soviet Union. The dispute was over tactics. The administration doubted that overt pressure could succeed; Jackson insisted that no other method would work."[10]

The Jackson Amendment assumed a link between United States foreign policy and Soviet *domestic* policy. Nixon and Kissinger believed in the grand strategy of linkage to moderate Soviet *foreign* policy. They would link a whole array of foreign policy issues to create a framework for détente. Trade would be an important component of this relationship. In the early 1970s, the White House thought it could dangle before the Kremlin prospects of arms control agreements and trade benefits to entice its support in helping Nixon end the Vietnam War. As Kissinger recalled, the United States would hold out granting MFN to the Soviets until they demonstrated "a commitment to restrained international conduct and willingness to help settle concrete issues including Vietnam and Berlin."[11] Kissinger believed that linkage, if applied to domestic policy, would become too open-ended and uncontrollable. The Soviets, he felt, could start to link foreign policy commitments to U.S. progress in solving its minority problems. Pressing the Soviet Jewry issue beyond quiet diplomacy, he feared, would be totally counterproductive.

When Nixon met with Brezhnev in the United States in June 1973, the president even tried to enlist Brezhnev's support in the fight against Jackson–Vanik by warning of dire consequences of its passage. As Nixon noted in his diary: "I pointed out that if détente unravels in America, the hawks will take over, not the doves, and I urged him to make some sort of gesture on Jewish emigration if only to pull the rug out from under Jackson and some of the media critics. He proceeded to pull out from his folder the statistics and said he would give them to Dobrynin and Dobrynin would pass them on to Kissinger."[12] Nixon also believed that Jackson–Vanik might hurt the chances for Brezhnev to pursue détente. As the president observed, "the failure to produce MFN status and the agitation over Soviet Jews and emigration have made it difficult for Brezhnev to defend détente to his own conservatives."[13]

Government support for the White House came mainly from Secretary of Commerce Peter Peterson, who wanted to boost U.S.–Soviet trade. Only a few congressmen and senators supported the White House position, though one of them was Senator J. William Fulbright (D-Ark.), the influential chairman of the Foreign Relations Committee. But as 1974 rolled around, Nixon's power was being sapped almost daily by the swirling Watergate scandal. Plagued and weakened by Watergate, the

White House proved no match for Congress in the conflict over Jackson–Vanik. When Nixon visited Moscow in June 1974, Brezhnev, who till then had stuck by the president, realized he was a beaten man. Soon Nixon was forced to resign, and on August 9, 1974, Gerald Ford became president.

President Ford firmly believed in continuing Nixon's policy of quiet diplomacy on the Soviet Jewry issue. He too concluded that this is what had influenced the U.S.S.R. to liberalize its emigration policy. Ford also agreed with Nixon that extension of MFN to the U.S.S.R. would further détente and that adoption of Jackson–Vanik "would damage the good relations my Administration had achieved with the Soviets."[14]

There is no question that the Soviets were irritated by Jackson–Vanik, but seemingly they decided they could live with it. By the fall of 1974, a major stumbling block to an accommodation was the number of Soviet Jewish emigrants that would satisfy both the Kremlin and the Jackson forces. In 1973, about 35,000 Soviet Jews had emigrated, but the early monthly numbers for 1974 were only half those of the preceding year. Kissinger reportedly proposed the figure of 45,000 per year at a meeting with Gromyko in Cyprus in May 1974.[15]

In the actual exchange of letters of "understanding" *(see Readings 10 and 11)* Kissinger asserted that the Soviets had agreed to certain "criteria and practices" that would "henceforth govern emigration from the USSR." These included, for example, Moscow's supposed assurances that an applicant for an exit visa would not suffer punishment, reprisal, or recrimination and that the "diploma tax" would "remain suspended." Jackson, on his part, quoted a "benchmark" figure of 60,000 emigrants annually, which he considered "a minimum standard of initial compliance." If the Soviets met this figure, Jackson would accept a very significant modification of his amendment. He would agree to allow the president to waive credit restrictions for eighteen months, renewable annually after this initial period if the President convinced Congress that he had received "assurances" that Soviet policies would promote freer emigration. After the president waived the amendment for one more year beyond the eighteen-month waiver, the president would need approval of a concurrent resolution by Congress. If this could not be obtained, the president could issue an additional waiver on his own, but either house could veto it within a period of sixty days. Based on this "understanding" between Kissinger and Jackson, on December 20, with strong bipartisan support in both Houses, Congress passed the Trade Reform Act with the Jackson–Vanik Amendment.

Before this amendment was passed, Kissinger was invited to testify before the Senate Finance Committee, on December 3. Kissinger, asked to clarify the assurances he had received from the Kremlin on Jewish emigration, stated: "I have had many conferences on this subject with Ambassador Dobrynin and conferences with Foreign Minister Gromyko. . . . In addition, when President Ford took office he had some conferences in which the statements that I have made here were reconfirmed by the same individuals. Finally, General Secretary Brezhnev has made analogous statements to President Nixon, to myself and recently to President Ford. This is the structure of the assurances that we have." Kissinger testified that the U.S. and U.S.S.R. had not reached a "formal agreement" on emigration, for this "would immediately be repudiated by the Soviet Government." When asked by Senator Hartke whether the "assurances" were received from Brezhnev, Gromyko, and Dobrynin, Kissinger replied: "That is correct." Kissinger then stressed that the "understanding" he had received from the Kremlin could "operate only on the basis of good faith by all the parties concerned and good will among the Senators and ourselves"; that violation of the "specific assurance . . . would certainly be one that the Administration would take very seriously"; and that the president "believes that he can stand behind it."[16]

What infuriated Jackson and his supporters was that Kissinger never informed them that he had received from Gromyko on October 26 a letter that in effect seemed to reject the assurances of the October 18 letters of understanding. *(See Reading 12.)* In this letter, Gromyko referred to "elucidations" the Kremlin had made on Jewish emigration. He then reiterated what he maintained was the Kremlin's original position that "the question [of emigration] as such is entirely within the internal competence of our state." Only on December 18, on the eve of the passage of Jackson–Vanik, did the Kremlin make this letter public through a TASS news release. *Pravda* and *Izvestia* also published articles that rejected attempts by the United States at "flagrant interference in the Soviet Union's internal affairs."[17] *(See Reading 13.)*

The State Department tried to downplay the significance of the Gromyko letter, asserting that it "does not in our view change the understandings referred to in the Secretary's letter to Senator Jackson of

October 18."[18] But Jackson, incensed by what had happened, made this sharp comment: "The withholding of that crucial document must surely rank among the shabbiest deceits ever perpetrated by a Secretary of State on the Congress of the United States."[19] *(See Reading 14.)* On January 3, 1975, President Ford, fearing a certain overriding of a presidential veto, "decided reluctantly to sign the measure into law."[20] But almost immediately, in his State of the Union speech of January 14, he pledged to seek its repeal. Jackson took this as further evidence that the White House had no intention of honoring its pledge to keep the "understanding" of October 18.

There were many uncertainties, then, in both Washington and Moscow when the Jackson–Vanik Amendment was passed. Washington had not made it clear exactly what level of emigration would meet its requirements for waiver, and the White House could not guarantee waiver even if the Kremlin met a specified figure. The Kremlin did not want to appear to be pressured by Washington into changes in its emigration policy. This resultant uncertainty became an increasing irritant in U.S.–Soviet relations as the U.S.S.R. sought to win MFN status and credits.

But what seemed to anger the Soviets more than Jackson–Vanik, and what may have been more responsible for their rejection of the trade bill, was the amendment sponsored by Senator Adlai Stevenson III (D-Ill.). The Stevenson Amendment, attached to the Export-Import Bank bill, extended the Export-Import Bank (Eximbank) for four years and limited credits to the U.S.S.R. to $300 million over this period. According to this amendment, the Kremlin also faced a $40-million limit on assistance for exploration of gas and oil reserves in Siberia and the prospect of no credits for developing production of its fossil fuel resources. The president could grant additional credits, but only with Congressional approval.

Kissinger's philosophy, supported by Nixon and Ford, was that credits and loans, as well as MFN, should be granted to *spur* the Soviets toward more cooperative and less aggressive behavior. Stevenson made it clear that loans and credits would depend on more acceptable *prior demonstrations* of Soviet policy on arms control, the Middle East, and emigration.

To the Soviets at the end of 1974, MFN would have been an important but largely symbolic gesture, to be enjoyed more fully some time down the road when they had more to sell to the United States. The Soviets wanted credits at that time, however, to finance, with low interest rates, increased imports of U.S. technology. By October 1973 they had already received about half a billion dollars in credits. As a payoff for reciprocating on détente and indicating they might help the U.S. extricate itself from the Vietnam War they were banking on receiving billions more to help finance, for example, the Yakutsk/North Star Siberian energy development projects. The Soviets were shocked and insulted by the Stevenson Amendment's severe limit of credits. They were also irked by the U.S. attempt to use credits to interfere in their internal affairs.

Benefiting from an unanticipated windfall in oil revenues because of the quadrupling of oil prices in 1974, Moscow started acting with more bravado toward Washington. Thus when the Kremlin issued its statement on December 18 rejecting U.S. interference in Soviet internal affairs, Dobrynin bitterly complained to Kissinger about credit ceilings of the Stevenson Amendment. On January 10, 1975, after an intensive media attack on the Jackson–Vanik and Stevenson amendments, the Soviets unilaterally canceled the October 1972 trade agreement.[21]

It is debatable how much of an effect the Jackson–Vanik and Stevenson amendments had on Soviet Jews. What is certain is that in 1975 conditions became much tougher for them. Government-sponsored anti-Semitism intensified—evidenced, for example, by more trials of Jewish activists and increased use of military conscription to thwart Jewish emigration.

Refuseniks attributed this stepped-up repression more to the Stevenson Amendment than to Jackson–Vanik. *(See Reading 15.)* The Stevenson Amendment, argued Soviet activists Vladimir Lazaris, Vladimir Slepak, and others, had caused the Soviets to cast aside the understanding on trade they had reached with the United States in the fall of 1974. Moscow officially blamed the Jackson–Vanik Amendment, but as Slepak explained, only because "the Soviets couldn't say that $300 million was too little in exchange for the Jews."

When Jackson–Vanik passed, Soviet Jewish activists expressed their heartfelt appreciation. At a meeting with U.S. senators in Moscow on June 29, 1975, several leading refuseniks thanked all who helped it pass. Professor Alexander Lerner summed up the feelings of the group: "We are grateful to the senators, to the U.S. Congress, and the American people who have sacrificed for our plight. We are deeply moved."

Soviet Jewish emigration dropped from 20,628 in 1974 to 13,221 in

1975, most likely because of Moscow's negative reaction to the Jackson–Vanik and Stevenson amendments. It began to rise in 1976, however, and continued to rise every year to 1979, when a record 51,320 left. Thus whatever negative effects these amendments may have had on Jewish emigration were short-lived. Whether emigration would have been higher in the absence of these amendments is purely speculative. The increase in emigration after 1975 was probably a reflection of Brezhnev's hopes for reaching a SALT II agreement and receiving MFN and credits. Brezhnev also may have been trying to ease Western criticism of his crackdown against human rights activists, which intensified in 1976, ironically just one year after the signing of the Helsinki Accords.

The Helsinki Accords

After passage of Jackson–Vanik, there is no doubt that Soviet Jewish activists looked primarily to the United States for help. Although they suffered from more persecution and less emigration opportunity in the early months of 1975, their hopes were raised by the signing of the Helsinki Accords in August. Talks between the U.S.S.R., the U.S., and thirty-three other states had begun in Helsinki in November 1972. Between 1969 and 1972, within the framework of Willy Brandt's new West German policy of *Ostpolitik*, the U.S.S.R. had concluded several agreements with West Germany and Poland on Polish–German borders and Soviet territorial gains from World War II. Yet Moscow still wanted to secure *formal* Western recognition of frontiers provisionally established in 1945. Thus the Kremlin was pleased by the Helsinki document's statement that "the participating states regard as inviolable each other's frontiers as well as the frontiers of all states in Europe," and the more pro forma pledges by the signatories to observe the principles of sovereignty, territorial integrity, and noninterference in one another's internal affairs.

The chief goal of the Western states at Helsinki was Soviet acceptance of a wide range of human rights provisions. Soviet Jews, according to British historian Martin Gilbert, understood that the Helsinki talks could be of "decisive importance" for them.[22] They were impressed by the statement in "Basket One" (on security) that "the participating states will respect human rights and fundamental freedoms, including freedom of thought, conscience, religion . . . [and] they will promote and encourage the effective exercise of civil, political, economic, social, cultural and other rights . . . [which] derive from the inherent dignity of the human person." Yet it was "Basket Three" (on human rights) that caught their attention most, especially the pledge to work for reunification of families through emigration, which was to be made easier through faster and fairer emigration procedures. When Jews from around the world met in Brussels on October 10, 1975, Soviet Jews looked forward optimistically to the implementation of the accords.

Yet what many failed to realize was that the Soviet Union then had no intention of honoring its pledges toward human rights, at least as they were understood by Soviet Jews and the West. As Harvard Professor Adam Ulam observed: "To abide literally by such promises would have been strikingly in contrast with the accepted Soviet practices in such matters, and it is difficult to conceive that the Russians thought that anyone could seriously expect them to do so." The Soviets probably considered the human rights pledges in Helsinki the same way they had looked thirty years earlier upon pledges at Yalta for "free elections" in Eastern European states that fell under their control after World War II; that is, as "a harmless piece of rhetoric."[23]

President Ford confidently signed the Helsinki Accords. He pointed to what he considered Soviet concessions on the provision that national borders could be changed only by peaceful means, calling this "a real victory for our foreign policy."[24] He considered this provision, unrealistically, a virtual repudiation of the Brezhnev Doctrine, which claimed that the U.S.S.R. had the right to intervene by force, if necessary, to maintain control over states within its Communist orbit. Ford was also pleased that the Soviet Union, for the first time, had pledged to observe the human rights provisions in "Basket Three." If Moscow honored this commitment, he believed, "the cause of freedom behind the Iron Curtain would advance."[25] In a speech to the Helsinki Conference on August 1, 1975, Ford expressed his hopes for the accords. "History will judge this conference," Ford held, "not by what we say here today but what we do tomorrow—not by the promises we make but by the promises we keep."[26] The Soviets hoped the West would honor its territorial promises, but they had no intention of keeping theirs on human rights.

On March 23, 1976, Representative Millicent Fenwick (R-N.J.) introduced a bill "to establish a commission to monitor compliance with the Helsinki Accords." In her concluding statement, Fenwick foresaw that the White House might not push too hard for implementation of "Basket Three" because this might cause friction in U.S.–Soviet relations. She was worried that the United States might sacrifice human rights on the altar of détente. Fenwick's bill passed, and Congressman Dante Fascell (D-Fla.) became chairman of the Commission on Security and Cooperation in Europe (CSCE), known popularly as the Helsinki Commission. On June 3, President Ford signed the bill that officially authorized this commission. It included twelve members of Congress and three representatives of the Executive Branch, though only as "observers."

Not all segments of American society welcomed the Helsinki Accords. Conservatives criticized them for further legitimizing "mistakes" made at Yalta that paved the way for Soviet control of Eastern Europe. By accepting the postwar borders, they argued, the United States and other Western states, in effect, were dooming "captive" peoples behind the Iron Curtain to indefinite slavery. But would implementation of "Basket Three" result in the advance of freedom in East Europe and the Soviet Union? Under Nixon and Ford, human rights had taken a back seat to détente and realpolitik. It remained for the newly elected President Carter to elevate human rights to new heights in U.S.–Soviet relations, at least in the early part of his term.

Carter's Crusade

The Helsinki Accords focused unprecedented international attention on human rights. One major reason was that presidential candidate Jimmy Carter began to stress the moral dimension of U.S. foreign policy. Carter initially did not make human rights one of his most important campaign issues, but later he expressed strong concern on the matter. For example, in a speech in Washington, D.C. on September 8, 1976, he remarked: "We cannot look away when a government tortures people or jails them for their beliefs, or denies minorities fair treatment or the right to emigrate." He also lent support to the Charter 77 human rights group in Czechoslovakia and to Soviet dissident Alexander Ginsburg. On October 23, Carter even sent a telegram of support to Vladimir Slepak—who, along with other Jewish activists like Shcharansky, had been protesting arbitrary Soviet refusal of exit visas and mistreatment of several Jewish protesters. Slepak then sent Carter a telegram of thanks.[27]

In Carter's inaugural address, he indicated that human rights would be a major theme of his administration:

> The world itself is now dominated by a new spirit. People more numerous and more politically aware are craving and now demanding their place in the sun—not just for the benefit of their own physical condition, but for basic human rights . . . Because we are free we can never be indifferent to the fate of freedom elsewhere. Our moral sense dictates a clearcut preference for those societies which share with us an abiding respect for human rights.

Carter was determined to make human rights a hallmark of his foreign policy. Human rights in the Carter administration, wrote Arthur Schlesinger, Jr., seemed "the perfectly unifying principle" after the Vietnam War, Watergate, and U.S. support for dictatorships. Moreover, according to Schlesinger, "the doctrine gratified both cold warriors who wanted to indict the communist world, and idealists, who saw human rights as the only basis for lasting peace."[28]

Carter began to irritate the Kremlin with his emphasis on human rights when in late February 1977 he met in the White House with Soviet dissident Vladimir Bukovsky, who had just been released in an East-West swap of prisoners. This meeting sent an important signal to human rights activists in the Soviet Union and elsewhere because it marked a clear departure from President Ford's decision, based on advice from Kissinger (which he later acknowledged as faulty), not to meet with Alexander Solzhenitsyn in 1975 for fear of endangering détente.[29]

Carter tried to go out of his way to avoid the appearance of focusing on human rights abuses in the Soviet Union. At a press conference on February 23, 1977, for example, he said: "I have never had an inclination to single out the Soviet Union as the only place where human rights are being abridged." Nevertheless, Carter's policies irked the Soviets. At first they reacted with sarcastic rhetoric to Carter's statements on human rights. On March 12, 1977, *Pravda* maintained that dissidents the United States backed "exist only because they are supported, paid, and praised by the West." Then in an interview published in *U.S. News and World Report* on March 14, Georgi Arbatov, head of the Institute of U.S. and Canadian Studies in Moscow, criticized what he perceived as Carter's linkage of arms control and other issues with Soviet performance in human rights. He stated that the U.S.S.R. was against linkage. "What does cause apprehension here," Arbatov explained, "is the massive political campaign. . . . It is difficult for us to take the United States as a teacher who has the moral right to give us lessons all the time, and teach us how to behave in our internal affairs." He then chided the United States for its own human rights problems (e.g., treatment of blacks and Native Americans) and for its support of "the most terroristic and dictatorial regimes—in South Korea, now Chile, and many others." Arbatov hit upon a major inconsistency and weakness in Carter's human rights policy: Carter lambasted certain dictatorial regimes like those of Paraguay and Argentina, but he tiptoed over states like South Korea and the Philippines because of U.S. security arrangements there.

On March 30, the Soviet Union rejected two U.S. proposals on SALT II that Secretary of State Cyrus Vance had brought to Moscow to discuss. The next day, at a press conference in Moscow Gromyko commented on his talks with Vance. Gromyko lashed out at the Carter administration's focus on human rights, which he argued could have a negative impact on the prospects for agreement on other issues: "Everything that has recently been said in the U.S. about human rights . . . naturally poisons the atmosphere and worsens the political climate. But does this help solve other issues, including those related to strategic arms? No, it does not. On the contrary, it hinders it. . . . We shall not allow anybody to assume the pose of teachers and teach us to solve our internal affairs, and I stress—our internal affairs."[30] It was evident, therefore, that Gromyko was telling the United States to back off on its human rights criticism if it wanted a SALT II treaty.

In the fall of 1977, more tension over human rights developed in U.S.–Soviet relations. At the first Helsinki Review Conference, which opened in Belgrade on October 6, 1977, U.S. Ambassador Arthur Goldberg sharply attacked the Soviet delegation for the Kremlin's human rights abuses. He expressed Washington's indignation at the arrest a few months earlier of well-known Soviet Jewish rights activists such as Shcharansky. The Soviets replied with defensive resentment. Goldberg had struck a raw nerve, causing Soviet officials to threaten that continued assaults on their country's human rights record could ruin détente. The bland final communiqué, issued in March 1978, reflected the aim of both the U.S. and the U.S.S.R. not to derail détente. Thus it did not mention Moscow's human rights violations, nor did it call upon the Kremlin to improve its human rights policies. This was a blow to Soviet Jews and all human rights activists, who felt this omission showed a disturbing gap between what Carter said and did on human rights.

Other developments in the fall of 1977 complicated U.S.–Soviet relations. In late November the Soviets transported twenty thousand Cuban troops to Ethiopia in support of the new Marxist-Leninist military leadership, headed by Mengistu Haile Mariam. This happened soon after Somali President Ziyad Barre repudiated the Soviet–Somali Treaty of Friendship and Cooperation of 1974, which (among other provisions) allowed Moscow to use the strategic port of Berbera on the Gulf of Aden. Shipment of Cuban troops to Ethiopia alarmed Washington, coming as it did just a year after Cuban troops had landed in Angola. National Security Adviser Zbigniew Brzezinski wanted to pressure the Soviets by linking Cuban troop deployment with the SALT II talks. After much wrangling inside the administration, President Carter rejected this linkage.

Inside the Soviet Union, arrests of Jewish and non-Jewish human rights activists on charges of spying for the United States reflected increased repression of dissent. Their conviction and harsh sentencing in 1978 deeply troubled President Carter. Washington issued protests, and Carter himself guaranteed that Shcharansky, perhaps the best-known Jewish activist, was not a spy for the United States. Carter also held back on trade and other economic dealings with the U.S.S.R. In July he denied a U.S. export license for a Sperry Univac computer that was going to be shipped to Moscow for the 1980 Olympics. On August 1 he discontinued Soviet purchase of oil and gas equipment; and on August 31 he stopped a license already granted to Dresser Industries to export a drill-bit plant to the U.S.S.R. Carter then wavered and finally reversed himself by approving this license in September 1978. Carter thus showed vacillation and inconsistency, leading George Shultz to remark that he had gotten caught up in "lightswitch diplomacy."[31]

Despite Carter's economic sanctions and verbal condemnations of the U.S.S.R.'s human rights policies, détente remained very much alive. Carter had his eye on a SALT II agreement, which he placed above his concern for Soviet human rights abuses. *(See Reading 16.)* Brezhnev also was eager for a SALT pact, which, in his estimation, would not only further détente but also counterbalance the developing warmth of Sino-

American relations. Brezhnev was upset over Carter's proposal to produce the neutron bomb, but he would not let this issue interfere with détente. Brezhnev was probably more disturbed by Carter's success in mediating the Israeli-Egyptian conflict. On September 19, 1977, President Anwar Sadat of Egypt made his historic visit to Jerusalem, a move that led to the Camp David agreement in the fall of 1978 and a treaty between Egypt and Israel on March 26, 1979. The Kremlin reacted to the accords with pained indignation, calling them a "sell-out transacted behind the back of the Arab nation, one which serves the interests of Israel, American imperialism, and the Arab reactionaries." The Kremlin felt it had just "lost" Egypt and saw it was being replaced by the U.S. as the major outside diplomatic player in the Middle East.

Brezhnev, meanwhile, was receiving conflicting and confusing signals from the White House on détente. Brzezinski urged a hard line,[32] but Vance advocated moderation and conciliation.[33] Brezhnev was also puzzled by the wide split in the Carter administration over trade with the Soviet Union. The Department of Defense, for example, cautiously based plans for expansion of trade on national security considerations. The Department of Commerce, backed by private business, for the most part stressed potential economic benefits from trade. Carter himself seemed more influenced by human rights.

Brezhnev continued his crackdown on dissent. He was sending a message to Jews inside the Soviet Union that he would keep a tight lid on dissent and try to dampen enthusiasm for emigration. But he was also cognizant of the potential damage this could do to U.S.—Soviet relations. To deflect U.S. criticism of his human rights policies, he tried to send a different message to Washington. In April 1979 he pardoned five Soviet Jews sentenced at the Leningrad hijacking trial of 1970 and allowed them to go to Israel. He also exchanged several other non-Jewish dissidents for two Soviet spies caught by the United States. Perhaps the biggest gamble Brezhnev took was to significantly increase emigration. In 1978, 28,864 left, but in 1979 a record 51,320 emigrated. Brezhnev was hoping that Washington would ratify SALT II and waive Jackson–Vanik, finally allowing the U.S.S.R. to receive MFN status.

In his early years in office, President Carter seriously considered a waiver. There was also some sentiment in Congress for waiver. On February 5, 1979, Senator Adlai Stevenson III introduced legislation to amend Jackson–Vanik. Stevenson wanted to end the requirement that a Communist state must give the president "assurances" on its emigration practices. The president should decide on his own, he felt, whether emigration levels were satisfactory. Stevenson also sought a five-year waiver extension instead of one year. His goal was to remove any appearance of interference in the internal affairs of the Soviet Union, realizing its extreme sensitivity on this point.

In June, Congress held hearings on Jackson–Vanik and forceful arguments were aired on both sides. Among the proponents of waiver were C. William Verity, then chairman of the board of Armco Inc. and later secretary of commerce in the Reagan administration, and Robert Legvold, then senior fellow at the Council of Foreign Relations and later director of the Averell Harriman Institute for Advanced Study of the Soviet Union. Verity opposed using trade as a weapon in foreign policy. He argued that Jackson–Vanik would have little effect on the U.S.S.R., which could acquire technology and goods from other sources. Legvold asserted that linkage was counterproductive, and claimed emigration would probably have been much higher without it. These arguments, strong as they were, did not prevail.

Intensive lobbying efforts by Soviet Jewish activists and Soviet Jewry advocacy groups in the United States blocked efforts to change Jackson–Vanik. Soviet Jews sent statements to congressmen urging them to hold firm on Jackson–Vanik. One statement in February from sixty-eight Soviet Jews claimed that "the Jackson amendment is the only thing which stimulates the Soviets to liberalize their emigration policy." In March Professor Lerner warned Congressman Vanik, who seemed inclined toward a waiver *(see reading 17)*, that Congress should not let itself be appeased by temporary boosts in Jewish emigration. He argued that Congress should take note of the wider picture of repression of Soviet Jews. While more Jews were leaving the U.S.S.R., he wrote, even more were applying to leave. He added that Congress should realize the dark significance of the 1978 trials, the arbitrariness of exit refusals, and the overall step-up in anti-Semitism.[34] *(See Reading 18.)*

Soviet Jewry advocacy groups rallied behind Jackson–Vanik as it stood. On April 5, the UCSJ argued strongly against waiver, claiming that "the only alleged evidence of an improvement in Soviet emigration is an increase in number." *(See Reading 19.)* In July, the NCSJ also made a strong case for the status quo. It argued that while emigration was up, the percentage of refuseniks was not going down. It contended that

Congress should avoid making a waiver decision based solely on emigration figures, for this would mean a "very narrow and technical interpretation" of Jackson–Vanik. Instead, it asserted, Congress should consider the entire picture of Soviet Jewry, which was getting gloomier. The NCSJ underscored the persecution and harassment of Soviet Jews trying to emigrate, the capriciousness of Soviet emigration policy, the growing backlog of refuseniks, the increased number of prisoners of conscience, and growing anti-Semitism.

The decision in 1979 not to grant a waiver of Jackson–Vanik was a blow to the Kremlin, made even more irritating when first Romania, in 1975 (a reward for standing up to Moscow diplomatically), and then the People's Republic of China, in 1979 (the second U.S. "China card" was anti-Soviet), received MFN. The Soviets felt they had satisfied the requirements of Jackson–Vanik by allowing such a large increase in Jewish emigration in 1979. Moreover, by adding up all emigration figures, to include Armenians and Germans as well as Jews, they had satisfied the 60,000 benchmark supposedly reached in the U.S.–Soviet understanding in the fall of 1974. Jackson, however, had called for *sustained* high emigration, which arguably the Kremlin had not yet allowed.

Was failure in 1979 to waive Jackson–Vanik a missed opportunity for the United States?[35] It is possible that the Soviets would have made some concessions for Soviet Jews beyond increased emigration if Congress had waived the amendment. Whether they would have done so, and whether such concessions would have been meaningful and lasting, we will never know. We should remember, though, that in May 1979, before the Vienna summit in June, the OVIR had already put into practice new restrictions on emigration. We also know, as has been discussed, that the Soviets had already decided to crack down harder on activists. It is possible but unlikely that the Kremlin would have softened this policy if it had received MFN. In the U.S.S.R., conservative critics of the "flood" of emigration from Brezhnev's liberal exit policy were uneasy. Furthermore, they were disturbed by a number of U.S. actions. Henry Trofimenko, a Soviet academic expert on the United States, wrote in *Foreign Affairs* this summary of Moscow's assessment of U.S.–Soviet relations in late 1979:

> The refusal of the Carter Administration to carry on a constructive American-Soviet dialogue (except in the sphere of strategic armaments); the

> theoretical ranking of relationships with the USSR as almost the last among the American foreign policy priorities; the effort to remove the Soviet Union from peaceful settlement of conflict situations even in regions that lie in the immediate vicinity of its borders (recall the fate of the Joint Soviet-American Statement on the Middle East issued on October 2, 1977); the intensified buildup of the U.S. naval presence near the USSR's southern borders; the dragging on of the SALT II ratification which was accompanied by an active drive to modernize American strategic weapons and NATO armaments; and finally the use of the "China card" in an attempt to bring pressure to bear on the USSR—all these actions could not but affect Soviet assessments of the strategic situation.[36]

The Soviet invasion of Afghanistan in December 1979, followed by the internal exile of Sakharov in January 1980 after his public criticism of this act, killed any chance for a waiver of Jackson–Vanik. In 1980, as a big chill enveloped U.S.–Soviet relations, there began a significantly downward trend in Jewish emigration that continued until 1987.

President Carter reacted strongly to the Soviet invasion. Although generally he did not support linkage in U.S. relations with the Soviet Union (beyond Jackson–Vanik), he seized on it with uncharacteristic tenacity after the invasion of Afghanistan. He withdrew the SALT II treaty from the Senate; he instituted a partial embargo on grain shipments; he prohibited export of high technology; and he led a thirty-country boycott of the 1980 summer Olympics, held in Moscow. Détente was indeed dead, at least from the U.S. perspective. Its burial was arranged by the newly elected president, Ronald Reagan, who had been one of its severest critics.

The Reagan Years

Under Reagan, U.S.–Soviet relations went into a deep freeze. The new administration criticized Carter's human rights policy as naive crusading. Ambassador to the United Nations Jeane Kirkpatrick was one of Carter's harshest critics. She believed he underestimated the threat to human rights posed by Marxist-Leninist regimes. Carter would criticize non-Communist authoritarian regimes, she complained, much more than Communist states, which she argued were much more intrusive in and dangerous to the lives of their citizens. In short, according to Kirkpatrick, "the Carter administration made an operational (if inarticulate) distinction between authoritarianism and totalitarianism and preferred the latter."[37] Kirkpatrick was essentially on target regarding the first years of Carter's presidency, but not regarding his last two years, when he took strong retaliatory measures against the Soviet Union for its invasion of Afghanistan and made preparations for beefing up the U.S. military.

Reagan's human rights policy started out almost as the reverse of Carter's in the sense that he treated Communist regimes much more harshly than right-wing authoritarian dictatorships. Overall Reagan policy toward the U.S.S.R. during his first term in office was marked by verbal confrontation, breakdown of arms control talks, and intensified build-up of the U.S. military. Reagan saw U.S.–Soviet relations as "the struggle between right and wrong and good and evil," and he called the Soviet Union an "evil empire."[38]

During the last days of Brezhnev's rule and throughout the brief tenure of Andropov and Chernenko, Soviet propaganda vilified President Reagan as a second Hitler. The Soviets were especially perturbed by the placement of U.S. Cruise and Pershing missiles in Western Europe in November 1983. They were also worried about unrest in Poland, so they were angered by Reagan's support of Solidarity and his cutting of U.S. economic relations with the Polish government. Moscow felt these actions were unwarranted interference in its backyard.

In 1981 Reagan pulled back from some of Carter's hard-line retaliatory policies against the Soviet Union. He lifted the U.S. grain embargo, but this was largely a domestic political decision made to satisfy demands of American farmers. At the same time, however, he forbade the sale of surplus butter to the U.S.S.R.

During Reagan's first term as president, the U.S. and the U.S.S.R. carried on very limited quiet diplomacy. They did conduct arms control talks in Geneva and Vienna, but the Soviets walked out from both meetings in reaction to the U.S. placement of missiles in Western Europe. The only subsequent occasions for private exchange of views were when first Andropov and then Chernenko died. Vice President Bush attended both funerals and conducted some discussions with Soviet leaders. In general, however, the White House felt it could not establish sustained dialogue with the Kremlin—which then, as Strobe Talbot and Michael Mandelbaum put it, was "doubling as a geriatric ward and a funeral parlor."[39]

The Reagan administration, meanwhile, lambasted the U.S.S.R. for human rights abuses at follow-up meetings of the Helsinki process. At Madrid (November 11, 1980–September 9, 1983),[40] Ambassador Max Kampelman severely chastised the Soviet Union for "blatant government-condoned anti-Semitism." *(See Reading 20.)* The United States and other Western delegations kept up a barrage of criticism against the U.S.S.R. for its abusive human rights practices. *(See Readings 21, 22, and 23.)*

Unlike the Belgrade follow-up meeting, which issued no meaningful statement on human rights, the final communiqué from Madrid did contain some strong language in this area. It also set the stage for meetings on human rights to take place in Ottawa (May 7–June 17, 1985), Budapest (October 15–November 25, 1985), and Berne (April 15–May 27, 1986).[41]

There were more agreements at these three human rights conferences than at Belgrade and Madrid. Although they produced no meaningful documents that would have furthered the Helsinki Accords, the formal debates and informal discussions themselves were useful. At Ottawa, the Soviets were no longer hostile and defensive against charges by the West of human rights abuses. Instead, they started issuing charges of their own. Taking the offensive, they made the distinction between the U.S. concept of human rights and their own. They explained that the priority of the U.S.S.R. was economic and social rights, such as the right to shelter and health care, whereas the American priority was political rights (or civil liberties), such as those in the Bill of Rights. The Soviets insisted that in their country, where the will of the state was paramount because it supposedly represented the best interests of the people as a whole, the political rights of the individual must be subordinate to the state. They then criticized the United States (and other Western states) for failure to provide their people with adequate shelter, health care, employment, and the like. Furthermore, the Soviets claimed, racism and anti-Semitism were far more pervasive in the West than in the Soviet Union, where these practices were illegal.

The Budapest meeting focused on cultural rights and cultural cooperation. But because of their clash of perspectives, the Western states and the U.S.S.R. could not produce a final document. The West focused on deprivation of cultural rights of individuals and groups of people, such as Soviet Jews. The Soviets, however, wanted to talk only about promotion of cultural exchanges (such as orchestras and choirs) and the use of culture "to shape peaceful attitudes and behavior."

When Reagan met with Gorbachev in Geneva in December 1985, the president raised the issue of Soviet human rights abuses in general and the plight of Soviet Jews in particular. Demonstrators in behalf of Soviet Jews carried placards in downtown Geneva and put up posters in the offices of Aeroflot (the Soviet airline) and elsewhere, protesting the Kremlin's treatment of Soviet Jews. They sang refrains of "We shall overcome" and engaged in sit-ins. Avital Shcharansky was there, displaying a picture of her imprisoned husband and attracting widespread media attention. The authorities kept these demonstrators away from Gorbachev. But the new Soviet leader could not escape the penetrating questions of Jesse Jackson, who buttonholed him for an informal exchange. When Jackson twice brought up the issue of Soviet Jews, Gorbachev retorted: "We would like to say that that Jews are a part of the Soviet people. They are fine people. They contribute a lot to the development of our country. They are very talented people. Therefore, the so-called problem of Jews in the Soviet Union does not exist." If it does exist, Gorbachev added, it does so only "with those who like to mar relations."[42]

The atmosphere at the Berne conference was much more cordial than at Ottawa and Budapest. It was the first follow-up meeting on human rights held after the Geneva summit, the release of Shcharansky in February 1986, and the 27th Congress of the CPSU of February–March 1986. There was one major disturbing development at Berne, however, which directly affected Soviet Jews. For the first time, the U.S.S.R. tried to remove from discussion the issue of reunification of Soviet Jews with their relatives in Israel. The Western delegations, as expected, opposed this maneuver. The Soviets acted enraged when U.S. ambassador Michael Novak, after a passionately critical speech on Soviet emigration policy, presented them a list of Soviet citizens who wanted to be reunited with their families in Israel. The Soviets categorized this list as libelous and complained that the United States was using "McCarthyist" tactics.[43]

This bitter Soviet reaction should be understood in light of the sharp decline of Soviet Jewish emigration and the increased repression of Soviet Jews that had been occurring since 1980. By the time of the Berne meeting the Kremlin was claiming more loudly than ever before that all

Soviet Jews who wanted to leave had already done so, except for those kept in the country for possession of "state secrets." It would have been inconsistent and embarrassing for the Soviets to admit in Berne that there were cases to review of Jews who did not fall into their "secrets" category.

In 1986 the Soviets announced the creation in the foreign ministry of a Public Commission for International Cooperation on Humanitarian Issues and Human Rights, placed under the supervision of the Soviet Commission on Security and Cooperation in Europe (the Soviet CSCE).[44] The commission's chairman was public relations specialist Fyodr Burlatsky, head of the philosophy department of the Communist Party's Central Committee Institute of Social Science and former speechwriter for Khrushchev.

The formation of this commission signaled a new twist to Soviet human rights policy. The Soviets concentrated on humanitarian issues involving a relatively small number of hardship cases (such as divided spouses) rather than on human rights that involved all Soviet citizens. Furthermore, the Soviets indicated that this commission, while sanctioned by the government, was actually an unofficial agency that could deal with nongovernmental groups from the West, and possibly from inside their own country. The Kremlin, therefore, was trying to downgrade the importance of truly independent human rights monitoring groups such as Press Club Glasnost. This organization, following the tradition of the Helsinki Watch groups, which the regime forced to disband in 1982, documented cases of abuse despite harassment from the authorities.

At the Reykjavik summit on October 11–12, 1986, Reagan gave Gorbachev names and numbers of Jews who wanted to emigrate. Prior to this summit, Reagan had exchanged views on the Soviet Jewry issue with Jewish leaders from the United States and other Western countries. *(See Reading 24.)* The president had started this practice before the Geneva summit. In Reykjavik, members of the U.S. working party for negotiation of human rights questions pressed their Soviet counterparts on Soviet Jewish emigration during an all-night meeting. Throughout the summit the Soviets willingly accepted complaints from individuals and groups on treatment of Soviet Jews and tried to give the appearance of an open mind if not an open-door policy. By the conclusion of the summit the Soviets had given no ground on Soviet Jewry, particularly the issue of emigration. They did agree, however, to continue discussion of "humanitarian issues and human rights."

During the first six years of the Reagan administration, the president preached and practiced a militant hard-line policy toward Moscow. By 1986, however, in a somewhat rushed response to Gorbachev's blizzard of proposals directed at improving U.S.–Soviet relations, Reagan reversed his field. The president began to stress cooperation with the Soviets, to show serious interest in an arms control agreement, and to use quiet diplomacy to influence Soviet human rights policies. This flip-flop alarmed Reagan's conservative allies and "realistic moderates," who thought he was suddenly exhibiting astounding naivete.

But such criticism did not faze the president. By 1987, Reagan's reversal picked up momentum, evidenced by across-the-board moves toward cooperation with the Soviet Union that were unprecedented in scope and significance. Yet at the same time, Reagan continued to press for improvement in the lot of Soviet Jews. *(See Reading 25.)* In April 1987, for example, George Shultz became the first secretary of state to join refuseniks at a Passover *seder.* Shultz invited about fifty refuseniks and families to Spaso House, the residence of the U.S. ambassador in Moscow. This evening clearly made a great impression on Shultz. As David Shipler wrote:

> Shultz went slowly around the room, shaking hands and exchanging a few words with each person. He seemed in awe of these men and women who had spent many years—in some cases, more than a decade—trying to emigrate from the Soviet Union, often paying the penalty of time in labor camps or in Siberian exile. The names and pictures of many of them had been hoisted on placards during years of demonstrations in the United States: Alexander Lerner, Vladimir Slepak, Viktor Brailovsky, Iosif Begun, Ida Nudel, and Naum Meiman. And Shultz had often spoken their names in pleas to Soviet officialdom. But he had never met them before. Within a year and a half after this evening, almost all these refuseniks had emigrated.[45]

The Soviets began to receive some economic payoffs from *glasnost* and the more relaxed U.S.–Soviet relationship. In the 1970s, about two hundred U.S. companies did business with the U.S.S.R., with Pepsico and Occidental Petroleum the two largest. After the Soviet invasion of

Afghanistan, several U.S. companies stopped doing business with the Kremlin. Yet after Gorbachev took power in 1985, additional U.S. companies, notably Coca-Cola and Pizza Hut, received permission to make deals with Moscow. By the end of 1987, the Soviets had received over $5 million in loans from Western commercial banks. Over four billion of this amount (a little more than two billion from U.S. banks) was in untied loans, which meant the Soviets could use this money for any purpose they wanted. Moreover, the Soviets benefited from a far lower interest rate than was normally available to Western customers.[46]

The proposed Kemp–Roth bill authorized the president to restrict untied loans to the U.S.S.R. if he felt that they were dangerous to U.S. security or inconsistent with U.S. policy on human rights. This bill died on its own when Jack Kemp retired from the Senate to assume the position of secretary of housing and urban development in the Bush cabinet and when it was learned that the president probably already had decision-making power over untied loans.

American Jewish organizations were split over the issues of loans to the Soviet Union, especially untied ones. In statements before a congressional subcommittee in the fall of 1988, several major groups stated their positions. The UCSJ, for example, indicated that economic linkage could put pressure on Moscow to increase Jewish emigration. According to Micah Naftalin, UCSJ's national director, "without Western cash, Gorbachev's economic modernization program and the Soviet Union's global commitments will be jeopardized." Naftalin concluded, therefore, that the United States should restrict loans to the Soviet Union until Moscow more substantially increased Jewish emigration, at least to the high-water mark of 1979.

The NCSJ and the American Jewish Committee maintained a different view on loans to the Soviet Union. Morris Abram, former chairman of the NCSJ, did not take a clear stand on untied loans. "Abolishing untied loans might be the answer," he argued, or there may be other avenues that would be appropriate to pursue such as disclosure of bank loans "or imposing specific restrictions on loans to the USSR." Abram asked for a review of the policy of allowing special low lending rates for U.S. loans to the U.S.S.R., but he noted that the NCSJ did not then have a position on this issue.[47] In a statement made earlier in 1988, David Harris, the Washington representative of the AJC, advised the

U.S. not to limit or eliminate untied loans. He argued that if the United States stopped these loans, other countries like West Germany and Japan would simply "step in and replace us." But should the United States have tried to influence its allies not to provide these loans? It is unlikely these arguments could have been convincing. Moreover, no matter what stance the U.S. took, in effect loans to the U.S.S.R. provided fungible money; that is, money earmarked for use in one project could easily be used in another. Thus there was no way the U.S. could require the Soviet Union to spend loan money on specified projects.[48]

During the early period of *glasnost,* besides an increase in U.S.–Soviet economic dealings there was a major step-up in educational, cultural, and scientific exchanges. How these exchanges would impact on Soviet human rights practices was a subject of sharp debate. Especially controversial were the U.S.–Soviet sister cities program and the American Bar Association–Association of Soviet Lawyers (ABA–ASL) agreement of 1985.

There was deep concern, however, over how these might affect Soviet Jews. Most Jewish organizations did not oppose participation per se in these bilateral arrangements. Jewish groups, generally supporting the position of Ambassador Stephen Rhinesmith, who coordinated the U.S.–Soviet exchange initiative, insisted that human rights in general and Soviet Jewry in particular be part of the sister city agenda. Other Americans involved in this program, such as Rosanne Royer from Seattle (which joined with Tashkent), believed discussion of political issues got in the way of developing ties. According to Royer: "If you're trying to deal with the Soviets and all they ever hear is tiresome disrespectful haranguing, it just won't wash."[49]

The Soviets, on their part, saw the sister city program as a way of furthering their foreign policy goals. As a TASS statement of November 11, 1985, explained:

> Contacts of Soviet cities with cities in other countries demonstrate the groundlessness of the stories told by our adversaries about socialism as an allegedly "closed society" and about some kind of "isolation" of Soviet people from other countries and peoples. They confirm the truth that the Soviet Union is guided by the spirit and the letter of the Helsinki Accords.

The ABA–ASL agreement on May 2 aimed "to advance the rule of law in the world" and "to promote improvements in the system of justice." *(See Readings 26, 27, and 28.)* Soviet Jewish activists generally opposed this agreement, as did many leaders in the American Jewish community. These critics complained that the agreement conferred undeserved legitimacy on the ASL, which might be seen as equivalent to the ABA. The ASL, they argued, was government-controlled and deeply anti-Semitic. They issued reminders that the ASL had published "white books" that contained some of the most vituperative anti-Semitic propaganda. Yet supporters of the agreement maintained that a beginning had been made in U.S.–Soviet legal cooperation, that Americans had to deal with Soviets as they were, and that both sides could gain from the relationship. The United States, in the meantime, continued to push for more advanced human rights agreements at the Vienna follow-up meeting to the Helsinki Accords that began on November 4, 1986.

When the Vienna meeting opened the Soviets were giving mixed signals on human rights. Discussions on Jewish emigration at first were at a standstill. The Soviet delegates steadfastly resisted Western efforts to get them to accept the fact that international law stipulates the right of free emigration. Nevertheless, they agreed to talk about individual hardship cases and they hinted at modifying or rescinding certain laws (Articles 70 and 190-1 of the R.S.F.S.R. Criminal Code and similar laws in other Soviet republics) that had been heavily used to convict human rights activists. Moreover, they stepped up their human rights offensive by proposing to hold the next Helsinki follow-up conference on human rights in Moscow. Western states initially reacted skeptically. They might agree to a Moscow meeting, but only if the Kremlin made significant progress on human rights and allowed all human rights activists in the U.S.S.R. and elsewhere to participate.

In January 1989 the West finally agreed to the Moscow human rights parley as part of the successful conclusion of the Vienna Conference. In "Basket Three" of the Helsinki Accords of 1975 and subsequent follow-up human rights conferences, the Soviets had accepted emigration only for reunification of families. Now they accepted emigration as a basic right for all. Furthermore, for the first time, Moscow pledged adherence to Principle VII of the Helsinki Accords, stating that it "attaches paramount significance" to it. It is understandable, therefore, that Warren Zimmerman, leader of the U.S. delegation, could sum up the Vienna concluding document as "the most complete statement of human rights commitment that has ever existed in the East-West framework." He added that it established a mechanism allowing any state, at any time, to bring up human rights issues with any other state.[50] Prior to Vienna the Soviets had steadfastly resisted this idea.

The Vienna document also called for a continual review of human rights issues. Annual Conferences on the Human Dimension (CHD) would start in May 1989 in Paris, with a follow-up in June 1990 in Copenhagen, and with another follow-up in September 1991 in Moscow. Reportedly all journalists, members of nongovernmental organizations, and private individuals would have open access to the delegates at these conferences. Prior to Vienna, the Soviets had also rejected this principle.

In deciding to accept the Moscow site for a human rights meetings, the United States said it considered numerous signs of human rights progress in the U.S.S.R.:

a. The human rights atmosphere was much better.
b. There had been unprecedented openness in the Soviet media.
c. Measures had been taken to curb abuses in psychiatry, especially against dissidents.
d. More than 600 political prisoners had been released during 1987 1988, including all Helsinki monitors.
e. Emigration in 1988 was the highest in a decade for Jewish and other minorities, including Germans, Armenians, and Pentecostalists.
f. Emigration procedures had been eased. In December 1988, Gorbachev announced at the UN that the Soviet Union would institute a "strictly warranted time limitation on the secrecy rule" and a "right of appeal under the law" for all visa applicants. He then concluded that "this removes from the agenda the problem of the so-called refuseniks."
g. There had been settlement of almost all divided U.S.–Soviet family cases.
h. Moscow had announced an end to jamming of foreign radio broadcasts.

i. Moscow had announced a pullout of its troops from Afghanistan and had started the withdrawal.

Critics of the decision to hold the 1991 human rights parley in Moscow pointed out that changes had not yet been backed by legal guarantees; that emigration, while the highest it had been in the 1980s, was still far from the heights reached in the 1970s; that criminal statutes were still being used against dissidents; and that the Moscow conference might turn out to be nothing more than a giant Soviet propaganda coup. The Moscow conference thus was not considered a certainty, for it would depend on Moscow's continued progress on human rights.

At the first CHD, held in Paris from May 31–June 23, the Soviets, skillfully employing a public relations campaign, took additional giant steps toward support of human rights. In an extraordinary speech, Shevardnadze stated that the new Soviet "parliament of *perestroika*" was considering about fifty new laws to ensure the freedom of Soviet citizens. Among other things, he advocated the "long-term idea of Europe as a single legal space," and he reiterated the Soviet stress on humanitarian rights, pointing out: "Man is not free if he has no home or income necessary for a decent life. No rights will help a person to regain the health lost because of a polluted environment." *(See Reading 29.)*

U.S. Ambassador Morris Abram was clearly pleased by the new Soviet attitude and stance on human rights. In his closing statement on June 23 to the Paris CSCE conference, Abram took note of the new "spirit of collegiality and friendship" between the U.S. and Soviet delegations. He also praised "some very significant changes in the Soviet Union's conduct in the field of human rights in recent years, especially under President Gorbachev's leadership." Abram concluded, though, that "the Soviet Union clearly has not gone far enough." To fulfill its human rights pledges, Abram stressed, the Soviet parliament would have to enact those human rights bills which were on its docket.[51]

Clearly the Soviet Union was making tremendous strides toward human rights and a rule of law. As this progress continued, Moscow quite understandably began to expect trade and credit concessions from the United States, especially MFN.

Renewed Pressure for Waiver of Jackson–Vanik

In 1979, Brezhnev unsuccessfully sought MFN status and more credits, loans, and access to U.S. technology. In 1989, Gorbachev pressed hard for the same benefits. At first he seemed likely to succeed. Once again pressure mounted on Washington to waive Jackson–Vanik. As early as December 1985, less than one year after Gorbachev took power, several hundred U.S. business leaders, eager to make profits in the Soviet market, issued a statement during their visit to Moscow that the United States should abandon linkage between trade with the U.S.S.R. and Soviet human rights practices. They were encouraged by Armand Hammer, head of Occidental Petroleum and longtime acquaintance of Soviet leaders since Lenin. As Jewish emigration rose from 8149 in 1987 to 71,196 in 1989 (about 20,000 above the record figure of 1979), waiver of Jackson–Vanik seemed certain.

In 1989 arguments for waiver were basically the same as in 1979, but this time pressure was greater. There was a feeling that in 1979 the United States had missed a chance for a major breakthrough in relations with the U.S.S.R. by not extending MFN. The United States might have forestalled the Soviet invasion of Afghanistan and the subsequent return to a cold war atmosphere, the argument went, if it had granted MFN earlier in the year. With significantly increased emigration, with dramatic improvement in Soviet human rights practices, with unprecedented opening up of Soviet society under *glasnost,* with clear signs of popular political participation under *democratizatsiya,* with major economic reforms under *perestroika,* and with a startling easing of East-West tensions largely because of Gorbachev's "new thinking" in Soviet foreign policy, time for waiver seemingly had come.

More and more Americans had come to believe that a waiver of Jackson–Vanik, more than just increasing U.S.–Soviet trade, would encourage further Soviet liberalization, greater reduction of costly armaments, and more superpower cooperation across the board. In early 1989 Vanik, then a trade lawyer in Ohio, argued for a waiver. Speaking before the American Committee of U.S.–Soviet Relations, a trade group, Vanik said that "the process [of *glasnost*] under way appears to be in earnest. . . . This was precisely the kind of circumstances envisioned for the utilization of a waiver and a granting of most-favored-nation status."[52]

Until the middle of 1989, American Jewish organizations generally held fast against waiver. They maintained that whereas Jewish emigration was decidedly up under Gorbachev, it was still far below the 1979 figure. Moreover, they pointed out that the emigration figures under Gorbachev looked good only in comparison with the previous few years, when Jewish emigration had come to a virtual halt. What the United States needed before a waiver, they maintained, was evidence of much larger and *sustained* Jewish emigration. If the U.S. waived Jackson–Vanik before this evidence was in, they contended, the Soviets would receive trade benefits without having made substantial, more lasting improvements in their emigration policy.

The antiwaiver position was reinforced by the disappointing results on human rights from the Reagan–Gorbachev summit in Washington in December 1987. The American press played up the friendliness of the two leaders (Mike and Ron), the growing warmth of U.S.–Soviet relations, improved chances for economic cooperation, and the signing of the Intermediate Nuclear Forces (INF) Treaty. Americans were impressed by Gorbachev's outward pleasantness and gregariousness ("working the crowd" in Washington before television cameras, for example) and by his "new thinking" in foreign policy, which promised reduced danger of war. But the thorny issue of human rights received scant attention.[53]

With a major rise in Jewish emigration in the first few months of 1989, and with improvements in U.S.–Soviet relations coming with dramatic swiftness, major American Jewish organizations reconsidered their position on Jackson–Vanik. On June 13, the influential NCSJ voted for waiver, but only if four conditions were met:

1. President Bush must receive assurances from the Kremlin of continued, sustained high emigration.
2. Refusal of visas on the basis of "state secrets" must be much more strictly limited.
3. The "poor relatives" problem must be resolved.
4. More progress must be made on long-term refuseniks.

Shoshana Cardin, on the eve of the Malta summit in December, reiterated that the NCSJ would support waiver only after the Kremlin codified a new emigration policy and after there was sufficient evidence it was working. Cardin pointed out that although there had been "significant progress" in Soviet human rights practices, there were still 107 long-term families refused exit visas on the basis of "state secrets" and over 100 others refused because they had "poor relatives."[54]

One of the largest Jewish groups that supported conditional waiver was the National Jewish Community Relations Advisory Council. The UCSJ at this time still opposed waiver, as did several leading refuseniks such as Judith Lurie. When visiting the United States in September 1989, she argued that the U.S.S.R. should not be "rewarded" until it provided for a clear, objective standard on emigration.[55]

In the summer, the American Jewish Congress (AJC) announced support for an immediate waiver of Jackson–Vanik. In a letter of August 15 sent to Secretary of State James Baker III, the AJC said there was no need to wait for "additional Soviet assurances" of liberalized Soviet emigration policy. According to Maurice Tempelsman, chairman of the AJC Commission on International Affairs, "There is no question that during the last few months, Soviet deeds have fully merited a waiver." Noting that a "full 99.6 percent of all emigration applicants are allowed to leave," the letter concluded: "We believe that this Soviet performance, which would have been considered unimaginable just three years ago . . . ought to be rewarded now." A waiver "would constitute an appropriate reward for the dramatic improvement" and "encourage Moscow to continue its current policies in order to insure the waiver's renewal."[56] During this time President Robert Lifton of the American Jewish Congress sent a letter to President Bush that urged him to seek an immediate waiver.

The pro-waiver position was wise. The time seemed ripe to use economic inducement to encourage the Kremlin to keep the ball of liberalization rolling. It was also time to consider *repeal* of the Jackson–Vanik and Stevenson amendments as outdated relics of a bygone era.[57] In May 1989 President Bush signaled Congress that he was considering a waiver of Jackson–Vanik. In June Senator Daniel Patrick Moynihan (D-N.Y.) and Representative Thomas Downey (D-N.Y.) introduced resolutions urging Bush to act once he was assured the Soviets were "firmly on a course to sustained, high levels of emigration." Downey said: "We are witnessing very significant progress in Soviet emigration performance." He added that House and Senate leaders as well as key members of House Ways and Means and Senate Finance committees supported waiver.

Downey then added that if Bush "waits too much longer to move forward on this issue, a valuable opportunity may have been lost. This is why the President's December meeting with Mr. Gorbachev [at Malta] takes on special importance." Vanik also pressed the economic argument for waiver, noting: "While we debate and defer action on MFN . . . our trading partners are positioning themselves to feast on commerce and trade we disregard."[58]

By the fall of 1989 the Bush administration gave increasing signals it was prepared to push for waiver, but not immediately. In a letter to Shoshana Cardin, Baker maintained that the Bush administration would not seek waiver until the Soviets "codify their emigration law in accordance with international standards and implement their new law faithfully." Once this transpired, Baker added, Bush then would be "ready to work with Congress on a temporary waiver." It was significant that until then the Bush administration had given only oral assurances it was prepared to seek waiver. This was the first time the Bush administration had given *written* assurance.[59]

In October, Attorney General Richard Thornburgh reiterated the U.S. position. He told Soviet officials while in Moscow that he would support Bush's efforts to waive Jackson–Vanik if the Kremlin codified certain emigration reforms spelled out a few months earlier by Bush. At a Capitol Hill news conference in late November, Senate majority leader George Mitchell (D-Maine) issued this statement of support of a waiver: "Since May, I have urged that the dramatic improvements in Soviet emigration practices merit a temporary waiver of the Jackson–Vanik Amendment.[60]

Then, at the Malta summit at the beginning of December 1989, Bush offered Gorbachev MFN as an important component of a broader trade package to include, among other things, allowing Moscow observer status at the General Agreement of Tariffs and Trade (GATT). This would start to bring the U.S.S.R. into the Western world's economic structure. MFN was still contingent, however, on passage by the Soviet parliament of a new emigration law. Bush obviously was offering proposals that the economically strapped Gorbachev wanted to hear. Bush was cognizant of the surge of domestic political support for MFN, as well as lobbying pressure from groups like the American Corn Growers Association. Faced with a deepening financial crisis in farming, and concerned about a projected general downturn in the U.S. economy, Bush too had reason for moving fast on MFN. Still, however, he had to take notice of the opponents of MFN like the UCSJ. This Soviet Jewry advocacy group was maintaining its position that the time was still not right for waiver. The Bush administration must hold fast on Jackson–Vanik, it argued, not only until the U.S.S.R. passed a new emigration law but also until a "decent interval" had passed wherein Soviet emigration practice could be monitored to ensure good faith. By the end of 1989 this position seemed to have few supporters. By early 1990, waiver of Jackson–Vanik seemed a certainty.

But unforeseen things happened on the way to Moscow's receiving MFN. For one, MFN became embroiled in the Kremlin's conflict with Lithuania over its declaration of independence—even though Jackson–Vanik linked MFN only to Soviet emigration policy. Nevertheless, many in Congress, disturbed over Moscow's heavy-handed measures against the Baltic state, particularly its embargo on energy supplies, began to hesitate on MFN because of this new issue.[61] Another major problem was that by the time of the Gorbachev–Bush summit in Washington in early June 1990, surprisingly the Soviet parliament had not yet passed a new emigration law, which was a sine qua non for receiving MFN.

Supposedly the Supreme Soviet was to have enacted this law on May 31, but it did not. On May 24 Nikolai Fyodorov, chairman of a parliamentary subcommittee that reviews new legislation, complained that the decision to take the emigration law off the docket was made by Kremlin officials alone in an "undemocratic" and "unconstitutional" manner.[62] On June 3 Georgi Arbatov told CBS's *Face the Nation* television interview show that the emigration law had been delayed because of the back-up of laws facing the Supreme Soviet.

A more likely reason for the hold-up on the new emigration law was that the Kremlin was worried about the negative reaction of Palestinians and Arab states to the record large emigration of Soviet Jews to Israel. At a press conference the same day, Gorbachev was asked this loaded question: "Beyond words, what guarantees can you give the Palestinians that decisions you made on emigration will not result in the further usurpation of their lands?" Gorbachev responded with this warning to Israel about settlement of Soviet Jews: "Either our concern is heeded in Israel and they will make certain conclusions or else we must give further thought to it in terms of what we do in issuing permits for visas."[63]

But on June 6, at the second CHD in Copenhagen, Soviet Foreign

Minister Shevardnadze gave the Gorbachev statement on Soviet Jewish emigration to Israel a diplomatic spin to curry favor with the West. Shevardnadze wanted to do everything possible to make sure that the Soviet Union would receive MFN (and Western aid and credits), even though it might have to wait a little longer. By now it seemed clear that the Kremlin needed Western aid more than Arab support. Shevardnadze explained that Gorbachev had wanted to indicate that Moscow "would like to have certain understandings" from the Israelis that in the Soviet view "there's a problem." But Shevardnadze then added that the Soviet Union would not back off from its commitment to the new emigration law. The delay in its enactment, he said, was because the Soviet parliament was facing a full docket and it was preoccupied with Gorbachev's economic reform programs.[64]

Shevardnadze was being careful not to derail the positive Soviet human rights gambit taken under *glasnost,* as well as the overall "new thinking" in Soviet foreign policy. At Copenhagen the Soviets signed a declaration the thirty-five CSCE states "hailed as a landmark for human rights." The core of the forty-five-page document committed member states, inter alia, to multiparty democracy, free elections, an independent judiciary, and the separation of the state from political parties. The document also increased the protection of the individual's rights and recognized the rights of national minorities. Among the most important advances was section 9, paragraph 5, which further narrowed a government's right to limit emigration and return. The participating states reaffirmed that:

> They will respect the right of everyone to leave any country, including his own, and to return to his country, consistent with a state's international obligations and CSCE commitments. *Restrictions on this right will have the character of very rare exceptions, will be considered necessary only if they respond to a specific public need, pursue a legitimate aim and are proportionate to that aim, and will not be abused or applied in an arbitrary manner* [italics added].[65]

No wonder, then, that the delegates to the Copenhagen conference lavishly praised the concluding document. Canadian ambassador Edward G. Lee called the document "truly historic" and an "unparalleled achievement." And U.S. ambassador Max Kampelman said the document was "the most significant advance in the Helsinki process since the agreement itself came into being on August 1, 1975. We have now clothed our values in a political structure and framework—that of democracy and the rule of law." *(See Reading 30.)*

There is no doubt that by the time of the Copenhagen conference Gorbachev was pressing hard for the Soviet Union to move toward democracy. Without this movement, Gorbachev probably felt, there would be little chance for *perestroika* to succeed. With his strong advocacy of human rights, Gorbachev also was sending signals to audiences both at home and abroad. Most assuredly, Gorbachev saw this move at Copenhagen, as at the few previous Helsinki human rights conferences, as a highly visible central showcase for Western audiences. Gorbachev desperately needed economic assistance, which he knew would be much harder to receive without such a positive CSCE stance on human rights. Gorbachev thus had acknowledged the link between human rights, prosperity, and international security. The position on linkage of U.S. government leaders, however, still was not clear or consistent.

Linkage and Human Rights

By late 1989 the issue of linkage of human rights with emigration and issues such as arms control had seemed to have moved from the stick toward the carrot. It was unclear, however, exactly how MFN fitted into Bush's overall strategy toward the U.S.S.R. In the early 1970s, Kissinger, Nixon, and Ford envisioned granting of MFN to the U.S.S.R. as part of a grand strategy of détente in which linkage in foreign policy was a major key. They assumed that human rights in the U.S.S.R. would improve mainly within an overall improvement of U.S.–Soviet relations. Yet the thrust of the Jackson–Vanik Amendment, as we have seen, was that pressure from Washington was needed to force the Kremlin to change its human rights policies. The Soviets would finally realize, supporters of the amendment felt, that the U.S. would not give them MFN until they acted more positively on human rights, specifically the right of emigration. President Carter seemed ambivalent on MFN, but he generally supported continuation of Jackson–Vanik. In his early years as president, Reagan had accepted the idea of diplomatic linkage of arms control with human rights. Yet at the Washington summit in December 1987, despite demonstrations by more than 250,000 people for Soviet

Jews in the capital, Reagan seemed to have dropped this linkage. Secretary Shultz later made clear the administration's new position. At a speech at the Henry M. Jackson School of International Studies in Seattle (this setting was surely not coincidental), Shultz said: "It is impossible to see how we might expect to get anywhere with a policy which dictates that nothing can get solved until everything is solved." He added that linkage "deprives us of the opportunity to pursue realistic agreements that serve Western interests. It yields the initiative to the Soviets." Shultz then concluded that "most important, linkage as practiced in the past has not worked."[66]

Some proponents of linkage believe Reagan and Shultz missed its central argument. Human rights advocates such as Sakharov and Sharansky had stressed the *intrinsic* link between human rights and issues such as arms control. According to Sharansky, "arms negotiations that reduce the arsenals of the superpowers without eradicating the reasons that lead to their build-up have little chance of lasting success. At most it can achieve minor breakthroughs of limited duration that cannot serve to further the long-range goal of world peace." The Helsinki Agreement, he concluded, was a good example of a quite appropriate linkage of human rights with international security.[67]

Linkage as described by Shultz may not have succeeded. But history has shown that Western pressure on the U.S.S.R. to improve the lot of Soviet Jews has yielded positive results. Without this pressure, which was coordinated with Soviet activists, the Kremlin probably would not have softened the sentences of the Leningrad hijacking trial of 1970; would not have suspended the "diploma tax" of 1972; would not have significantly increased Jewish emigration in the late 1970s and again in the late 1980s; would not have stopped the practice in the early 1980s of stripping refuseniks of their academic degrees; would not have released virtually all political prisoners and prisoners of conscience; would not have curbed some of the worst abuses of psychiatry; and would not have initiated such extensive religious and political reforms. Other factors, like the desperate state of the Soviet economy and the vision of Gorbachev himself undoubtedly played their role, but surely they were intertwined with his perceptions of what liberalization changes the West wanted to see before responding favorably with economic aid.

Waiver of Jackson–Vanik

On December 12, 1990 President Bush announced his decision to waive some of the trade sanctions of the Jackson-Vanik Amendment until July 1991. This cleared the way for extension to the Kremlin of about $1 billion in U.S. government-guaranteed credits to buy American agricultural commodities. Bush's main intent was to alleviate the serious food shortage in the U.S.S.R. The president also wanted to pay back Gorbachev for support in the Persian Gulf crisis; to further encourage his liberal domestic reforms, especially the virtual open door policy for Soviet Jews to emigrate to Israel; to boost his leadership and thereby ward off possible chaos and danger from disintegration of the Soviet Union; and to help American farmers who expected to make good profits. Yet Bush did not extend MFN or indicate he would submit to the Senate for ratification the trade agreement he and Gorbachev had signed in Washington the previous June. According to the president, these changes would have to await passage of a Soviet emigration reform law codifying "general excellent practices of the past year."

Major Soviet Jewry advocacy groups in the U.S. generally supported Bush's decision. On December 3, the NCSJ gave public assurance that it would support the president's consideration of a one-year waiver, including granting Moscow MFN status, as this would come "against the backdrop of almost two years of sustained high levels of Jewish emigration from the Soviet Union."[68] NCSJ chairman Cardin commented that while "truly free emigration does not yet exist in the Soviet Union regarding the cases of long-term refuseniks, 'Poor Relatives,' and new refuseniks, who now number several hundred, we believe that a waiver of the Jackson-Vanik Amendment at this time will be fully consistent with the objectives of the legislation, which are to contribute to the goal of truly free emigration."[69] Cardin then praised Bush's decision which publicly recognized the Soviet Union's "move toward free emigration." The UCSJ agreed with Bush's decision to extend credits for food while holding off on MFN. According to union president Cohen, Bush had "balanced political demands and demands for improving (the) U.S.-Soviet relationship without compromising human rights." Praise for Bush's decision also came from other major Jewish groups including the Conference of Presidents of Major American Jewish Organizations and B'nai B'rith International.[70]

The occasion for Bush's action was the visit to Washington of Shevardnadze. The Soviet foreign minister was engaged in a whirlwind of meetings wherein he cooperated with the United States on resolution of the Angolan crisis, met with Prime Minister Yitzhak Shamir to further improve Soviet-Israeli relations, showed continued Kremlin solidarity with the White House position against Iraq's invasion of Kuwait on August 2, and arranged for a Bush-Gorbachev summit in Moscow in February 1991 to sign a Strategic Arms Reduction Treaty.

Bush's decision on waiver was a major step toward eliminating one of the last vestiges of the Cold War. In 1989 and 1990, emigration of Soviet Jews went far beyond requirements of Jackson-Vanik. The basic purpose of this amendment, however, was to pressure the Kremlin to recognize the right of *all* Soviet citizens to emigrate. But a new stumbling block to Soviet emigration appeared in September 1989 when Washington started to limit the number of Soviet Jewish refugees to 50,000 per annum. Furthermore, countries in Western Europe, like Germany, began to close their doors, leaving open only a crack. On December 14, 1990, Germany proposed a 1000 annual limit on Soviet Jewish immigrants. Germany reportedly was worried that large influxes of Soviet Jews would overburden its economy and social support services.[71] Soviet Jews should not fall victim to closed doors as was the case in the late 1930s when their brethren found it almost impossible to escape Nazi Germany. Thus it became imperative for the United States and countries in Europe to devise a strategy to accommodate the expected continued heavy flow of Soviet refugees, Jewish and non-Jewish alike. Israel would take in hundreds of thousands, but it faced tremendous problems of absorption.

By the end of 1990, Soviet Jews for the first time had a meaningful option of remaining inside the Soviet Union and enjoying unprecedented cultural and religious freedom. Yet the possibility of living a "normal" life there still eluded them. Those who stayed had to live in fear of a sharp rise of grass-roots anti-Semitism and of the possibility of exit gates slamming shut.

In the 1990s United States policy on the Soviet Jewish Question will require the utmost understanding, wisdom, perseverance, and patience. Soviet Jews, like the Soviet Union itself, face a very uncertain future. If the Soviet Union breaks up, and if civil war engulfs the republics, all Soviet citizens are at risk. If history is any guideline, Soviet Jews especially would be in peril as scapegoats for any number of groups and problems. The fate of the Soviet Jewish movement for freedom, perhaps as never before, will depend on how events unfold within the Soviet Union, on how successfully the United States and other Western countries influence actions of leaders both inside the Kremlin and the republics, and on how courageously and wisely its own leadership continues challenging the authorities to ensure basic human rights.

Notes

1 For more on the history of the Soviet Jewry advocacy movement in the United States, see William W. Orbach, *The American Movement to Aid Soviet Jews* (Amherst: University of Massachusetts Press, 1979).

2 In the 1980s there were increased signs of official support for Yiddish. A Russian-Yiddish dictionary was published in 1984 on the fiftieth anniversary of the founding of Birobidzhan and the 125th anniversary of Sholom Aleichem's birth. Understandably, there was not much celebrating over Birobidzhan, for only about 4 percent of this region is Jewish, but there was over Sholom Aleichem. In 1988, TASS announced the publication of a "teach yourself" Yiddish book. There was also greater allowance of Yiddish musical and theatrical groups, and by 1989, school classes in Yiddish had begun. Some of these classes in Moscow were run by Israel's Bar-Ilan University. See Charles Hoffman, "Teaching Yiddish in Moscow," *Jewish Advocate,* August 17, 1989. Moreover, by late 1989 the official All Union Society for Jewish Culture emphasized Yiddish, in order "to preserve the Jewish heritage in the Soviet Union and to further the development of the national literature and art of Soviet Jews." During these times, however, when Soviet Jews began to emigrate to Israel in increasingly large numbers, for practical reasons most preferred to learn Hebrew. See Gladys Damon, "Moscow Yiddish Editor Tells of Yiddish Cultural Revival," ibid., May 10, 1990. For an account of the genuine revival of Yiddish under *glasnost,* see David G. Roskies, "There Go Our Little Jews," *Commentary,* Vol. 89, No. 4, April 1990, pp. 49–53.

3 Richard Nixon, *RN: The Memoirs of Richard Nixon* (New York: Grosset & Dunlap, 1978), p. 876.

4 Henry Kissinger, *Years of Upheaval* (Boston: Little, Brown, 1982), p. 986.

5 One of the best accounts of the drafting and passage of the Jackson–Vanik

Amendment is Paula Stern, *At Water's Edge* (Westport, Ct.: Greenwood Press, 1979). See also William Korey, "The Critical Human Right," B'nai B'rith International, 1987.

6 See William Safire, *Before the Fall* (Garden City, NY: Doubleday, 1975), pp. 564–578.

7 The Kremlin did not officially rescind the "diploma tax."

8 Quoted in Korey, "The Critical Human Right," p. 9.

9 For an excellent account of how Sakharov helped Soviet Jews, see William Korey, "Andrey Sakharov—The Soviet Jewish Perspective," *Soviet Jewish Affairs,* Vol. 16, No. 3, 1986, pp. 17–28.

10 Kissinger, *Years of Upheaval,* p. 254.

11 Ibid., p. 985.

12 Nixon, op. cit., p. 1031.

13 Ibid., p. 1036.

14 Gerald Ford, *A Time to Heal: The Autobiography of Gerald Ford* (New York: Harper, 1979), p. 225.

15 See Raymond Garthoff, *Détente and Confrontation* (Washington, D.C.: Brookings, 1985), p. 454.

16 Quoted in Remarks by Senator Henry M. Jackson before the National Conference on Soviet Jewry, May 17, 1976.

17 *Pravda,* December 19, 1974; *Izvestia,* December 20, 1974.

18 Quoted by Richard Perle, Address before Zionist Organization of America's 78th Annual National Convention, October 1975.

19 Jackson speech, May 17, 1976.

20 Ford, op. cit.

21 See Harry Gelman, "The Rise and Fall of Détente: Causes and Consequences," in Arnold L. Horelick (ed.), *U.S.–Soviet Relations, The Next Phase* (Ithaca, N.Y.: Cornell University Press, 1986), pp. 65–66.

22 Martin Gilbert, op. cit., p. 25.

23 Adam Ulam, *Dangerous Relations, The Soviet Union in World Politics, 1970–1982* (New York: Oxford University Press, 1983), pp. 143–144.

24 Ford, op. cit., p. 299.

25 Ibid.

26 Ibid., p. 305.

27 For contents of Carter's telegram and circumstances under which he sent it, see Colin Shindler, *Exit Visa* (London: Bachman and Turner, 1978), pp. 188–199.

28 Arthur Schlesinger, Jr., "Human Rights and the American Tradition," *Foreign Affairs,* Vol. 57, No. 3, 1979, p. 514.

29 Conversation between William F. Buckley and Henry Kissinger, cited in William F. Buckley, "Human Rights and Foreign Policy: A Proposal," *Foreign Affairs,* Vol. 58, No. 4, 1980, p. 784.

30 *Pravda,* April 1, 1977, quoted in *Chronicle of Human Rights,* No. 26, April–June 1977, p. 18.

31 See Bruce Parrott (ed.), *Trade, Technology, and Soviet-American Relations* (Bloomington: Indiana University Press, 1984), pp. 250–253.

32 See Zbigniew Brzezinski, *Power and Principle* (New York: Farrar, Straus & Giroux, 1983).

33 See Cyrus Vance, *Hard Choices* (New York: Simon & Schuster, 1983).

34 Vanik then was about to travel to Moscow, where he intended to get a reading on Jackson–Vanik from refuseniks. See report by Kevin Klose, *Washington Post,* April 21, 1979.

35 For support of this position, see Marshall Goldman, "Soviet-American Trade and Soviet Jewish Emigration: Should a Policy Change Be Made by the American Jewish Community?" in Robert O. Freedman, op. cit., pp. 141–162.

36 Henry Trofimenko, "The Third World in U.S.–Soviet Competition: A Soviet View," *Foreign Affairs,* Vol. 59, No. 5, 1981, p. 1031.

37 Jeane Kirkpatrick, "Human Rights and American Foreign Policy," a symposium, *Commentary,* Vol. 72, November 1981, p. 44.

38 Speech to the National Association of Evangelicals in Orlando, Florida, March 8, 1983.

39 Michael Mandelbaum and Strobe Talbott, *Reagan and Gorbachev* (New York: Vintage, 1987), p. 27.

40 For an analysis of the Madrid meeting, see Stephen Roth, "Madrid Ends and Helsinki Continues," IJA Research Report No. 14, September 1983.

41 See Stephen Roth, "From Madrid to Vienna: What Progress in the Helsinki Process?" *Soviet Jewish Affairs,* Vol. 16, No. 3, 1986, pp. 3–16.

42 *New York Times,* November 20, 1985.

43 See William Korey, "Raising Helsinki in Vienna," *Hadassah Magazine,* November 1986, pp. 8–9.

44 For details on the Soviet CSCE, see International Helsinki Federation for Human Rights, *On Speaking Terms,* Austria, 1988.

45 David K. Shipler, "Dateline USSR: On the Human Rights Track," *Foreign Policy,* No. 75, Summer 1989, p. 166.

46 One of the largest untied loans to the U.S.S.R. was $200 million, made by First Chicago Bank. It carried a 7-percent interest rate over eight years. This is about half the rate of interest U.S. citizens were charged.

47 Quoted by Howard Rosenberg, "Soviet Jewry Groups Clash Before Congress," *Jewish Advocate,* September 29, 1988.

48 Some leaders in the American Jewish community called for divestiture of U.S. businesses in the U.S.S.R. In 1985, Glenn Richter, head of the SSSJ, asked that those companies doing business in the U.S.S.R. "not make profit over the backs of those who are oppressed." Quoted in Susan Birnbaum, "NY Group Seeks Divestiture in U.S.S.R.," ibid., August 1, 1985.

49 "Emigration Overshadows U.S.–Soviet Cities' Talks," *New York Times,* May 24, 1987.

50 Warren Zimmerman, "Vienna: Much Accomplished, Much Still to Do," *International Herald Tribune,* January 19, 1989.

51 Text of Ambassador Abram's Closing Statement to the Paris CSCE Conference on the Human Dimension, June 23, 1989; distributed by the American Embassy, Paris.

52 Quoted in Thomas Friedman, "Trade Law Author Asks Waiver for Soviets," *International Herald Tribune,* May 6–7, 1989.

53 The Joint Summit Statement of December 10, 1987 contained only these words on human rights: "The leaders held a thorough and candid discussion of human rights and humanitarian questions and their place in the U.S.–

Soviet dialogue." *Department of State Bulletin,* Vol. 88, No. 02131, February 1988, p. 15.

54 Quoted by David Friedman, "Bush May Lower Trade Barriers for Gorby," *Jewish Advocate,* November 30, 1989.

55 See Abby Morrison, "Still in Refusal," *The Jewish Monthly,* September 1989, p. 7.

56 Andrew Silow Carroll, "AJ Congress Breaks from Mainstream, Urges Waiver of Sanctions Against U.S.S.R.," *Jewish Advocate,* August 17, 1989.

57 A strong case for repeal was made by Adlai Stevenson III and Alton Frye, "Trading with the Communists," *Foreign Affairs,* Vol. 68, No. 2, 1989, pp. 53–71.

58 See Amy Kaslow, "Bush, Congress Work to Give Favored Trade Status to Soviets," *Christian Science Monitor,* November 16–22, 1989.

59 JTA dispatch, "U.S. Says No Jackson–Vanik Waiver Until the Soviets Implement Reform," *The Star,* September 1989, p. 39.

60 David Friedman, op. cit.

61 New York Times News Service, "Trade Pact: Bush Denies Any Links with Lithuania, but Congress Wants One," *International Herald Tribune,* June 4, 1990.

62 Michael Dobbs, "Soviet Emigration Delay," ibid., May 25, 1990.

63 "Gorbachev Cautions Israel," ibid., June 4, 1990.

64 "Soviets Back Off on Jews," ibid., June 7, 1990.

65 Concluding Document of the Copenhagen Meeting of the Conference on the Human Dimension of the CSCE, adopted in plenary session on June 28, 1990; distributed by the American Embassy, Paris.

66 Quoted by Fred Kaplan, "Shultz Says 'Linkage' Won't Work," *Boston Globe,* February 6, 1988.

67 Natan Sharansky, "Human Rights, Arms Talks Must Be Linked," *Wall Street Journal,* November 4, 1986. Sharansky said after this article was published that the editors of the *WSJ,* by re-wording his original title, missed his main point of *intrinsic* linkage between human rights and arms control.

68 Clifford Krauss, "Freer Trade Ties To Moscow Backed," *New York Times International,* December 4,1990.

69 NEWSBREAK, December 11, 1990, p. 2.

70 David Friedman, "Bush Lifts Some Jackson-Vanik Sanctions," *Jewish Advocate,* December 20, 1990.

71 "Bonn Proposes to Limit Immigration of Soviet Jews to 1,000 Per Year," *International Herald Tribune,* December 15–16, 1990. In December 1990, Soviet Jews began to stream into Berlin. In that month, their number increased from about a thousand to about 2,500. Most emigrated because of fear of anti-Semitism and the deteriorating economic and political situation in the Soviet Union. As 40-year old Igor Bondar, an English teacher from Leningrad explained: "I have come here because I am afraid. The situation at home gets worse by the day. There is nothing in the shops and we Jews are the people who get blamed for the situation. They say the communists are responsible for this mess and the people who started communism, such as Marx, were Jews like you. They have already started beating us up and I fear it will only get worse." See Tony Paterson, "Berlin plays host to tragic exodus of Soviet Jews," *The European,* Weekend December 28–30, 1990.

Reading 1

Bayard Rustin, "Soviet Jews and the New Abolitionists," A. Philip Randolph Institute, June 30, 1971

This is a good example of "private" pressure exerted on the Soviet government to curtail its anti-Semitic policies. Rustin explains the intrinsic relationship between the human rights struggle of American blacks and Soviet Jews.

When I asked why I, as a black American, speak out against the oppression of Soviet Jewry, my reply is that as a black person how can I not speak out, how can I not be sensitive to the oppression of a national minority.

Having experienced during slavery a brutal attempt to stamp out our freedom, our history, our language, and our identity, we can well understand the meaning of the spiritual death that accompanies oppression, and we can appreciate the overwhelming power of the rebirth of spirit that is part of the struggles against oppression. Black Americans, therefore, ought to be among the first to be concerned with the effort of the Soviet Union to destroy the identity of Soviet Jews and to crush their struggle for freedom.

It will be said, quite rightly, that there are other oppressed peoples (especially in the Soviet Union) besides Jews, and as a recent report on "Dissent in the Soviet Union" pointed out, "The problems with which Soviet Jews are faced are regarded . . . not as a question of *a* people, but rather as a question of *all* people who are deprived of their individual rights." But there is a special urgency to the problems of Soviet Jews which is the result of several factors.

One of these factors is the Soviet Union's policy in the Middle East. The Soviet Union is completely committed to the enemies of Israel. It has already made an enormous investment in military and economic aid personnel, and political prestige in the Arab world, and it now must justify that investment to the Soviet people. It does this by painting a grotesque picture of tiny Israel as a giant enemy and also by playing upon anti-Semitic prejudice in order to make Soviet Jews who want to go to Israel seem the most dangerous enemies of the Soviet Union. This is the main reason behind the massive anti-Semitic campaign which the Moscow government is now sponsoring in Russia. A second factor which makes the problems of Soviet Jews especially urgent has to do with the increasing internal instability within the Soviet Union and also in the satellite nations dominated by Moscow. We have seen signs of this instability over the past few years in the protests of Russian intellectuals, nationality groups and religious minorities and in the rebellions in Czechoslovakia and Poland which were so brutally put down. When the Soviet government branded the leaders of these rebellions "Zionists," it was not simply looking for a scapegoat on which to blame all its troubles. It was very clearly trying to direct the resentments of the people away from itself and onto a small minority which has traditionally been the object of scorn and persecution.

The greatest danger is that the anti-Semitic campaign now underway in the Soviet Union will get out of hand and the world will be confronted with a repetition of Hitler's crimes. This possibility makes more compelling than ever the desire of Soviet Jews to leave the Soviet Union.

Just as the white abolitionists fought for the liberation of black slaves before the Civil War, people in the United States, Jewish and non-Jewish, white and black, should fight for the liberation of the Jews in the Soviet Union. The Soviet Jews have their own Frederick Douglasses and Harriet Tubmans. What they need are more people like Wendell Phillips and William Lloyd Garrison—a new breed of abolitionists. The issue is not black or white, Jew or gentile, but man's responsibility to fight injustice, a fight in which blacks are in a unique position. As a result of the injustices that have been committed against us and our struggle against these injustices, we have gained a certain moral authority which can be effectively used to assist other oppressed groups in their own struggle for liberation. What we must do is to clearly and unequivocally make known our position on this issue. Far from detracting from our fight for racial equality, any efforts we make on behalf of Soviet Jewry will strengthen our movement by gracing it with a universal dimension. Nothing we could do would be more in keeping with the spirit of Martin Luther King, who raised his voice on all issues involving basic human rights.

Reading 2

Statement by Richard T. Davies, Deputy Assistant Secretary for European Affairs, Department of State, before the Subcommittee on Europe of the Committee on Foreign Affairs, House of Representatives, Hearings on Denial of Rights to Soviet Jews, November 9, 1971

Davies reviews the status of Soviet Jews and U.S. efforts to help them. He argues that world public opinion, especially through the United Nations, is "the best regular forum of focusing world attention on the situation of Soviet Jews." He adds that utilization of private diplomatic channels is also very helpful.

Mr. Chairman, my purpose here today is threefold: (1) to describe the situation of Jews in the Soviet Union as we see it; (2) to discuss what is being done in the effort to improve that situation; and (3) to offer our conclusions about the right way and the wrong way to go about this effort. Upon conclusion of my remarks, I will be glad to answer any questions you and your colleagues may wish to pose.

The Jewish Condition in the USSR

Restrictions against Jewish religious and cultural life in the Soviet Union have been amply catalogued in recent years and need no elaboration here: grossly inadequate religious facilities, pressures against synagogue attendance, lack of Yiddish or Hebrew language teaching, tokenism in the publishing and staging of Yiddish works, quota restrictions on university entrance, exclusion from careers considered sensitive or from important political jobs—these are well-documented facts. Soviet Jews deprived of the cultural ingredients needed to preserve their cultural and religious identity over the long term. And "anti-Zionism" has reached campaign proportions from time to time in connection with chronic tensions in the Middle East.

All Soviet citizens—not just Jews—suffer from the Soviet Government's policy of militant atheism and its refusal to consider emigration as a right rather than a rare privilege, as well as from other restrictions. But, the limitations on Jews have in many important respects been more stringent. This is chiefly because Jews appear to be suspect in a special way—many of them have kin abroad in Israel, the United States and Western Europe, and "Jewishness" in the Soviet Union has come to be regarded by a certain segment of Soviet officialdom as a more alien phenomenon than the fact of association with other major religious or national cultures in the USSR.

At the same time, there can be no comparison with the terrible area of the Nazi Holocaust or Stalin's blood purge of Jewish intellectuals. With respect to the majority, claims that Soviet Jews as a community are living in a state of terror seem to be overdrawn. Jews continue to be eminent in the Soviet economic, journalistic, scientific, medical, and cultural worlds, in numbers far out of proportion to their percentage of the population. They are still the best educated Soviet minority. There is still little evidence that the regime's "anti-Zionist" propaganda has spilled over into outright and widespread anti-semitism or deliberate and sustained efforts to fan a "pogrom" mentality in Soviet society at large. The line has at least officially been drawn between "loyal" Jews at home and "Zionists" abroad. The Party has generally avoided outright anti-semitism; for example, the USSR's chief anti-semite in the literary field, Ivan Shevtsov, was disavowed by *Pravda* in July 1970. It even appears that Soviet Jews have derived a peculiar kind of backhanded benefit—at least on a token basis—from the regime's sensitivity to charges of anti-semitism, for some Yiddish materials have been published, supplies of matzoh are reportedly more available—at least in large cities—and several Yiddish dramatic and variety troupes continue to tour.

The rebirth of Jewish consciousness and pride, especially among Jewish youth, has been dramatic since 1967. Jews have been in the forefront of a nascent civil rights movement that only a decade ago would have been both unthinkable and impermissible in the USSR. Under unprecedented pressure from sit-ins, petitioning, and even hunger strikes at home, and from public opinion abroad, the Kremlin has allowed an increase in emigration of Jews to Israel. The volume of emigration—more than 7000 in 1971 thus far, according to press reports—is small in absolute terms but relatively large in comparison with that of any other Soviet group. It surpasses the total of Jewish emigration for any preceding year. A small number of outspoken Jewish activists has been dealt with arbitrarily and usually harshly. A number have been sentenced to terms in forced-labor camps. Individual applicants for emigration are sometimes harassed. We deplore this. But we should note that other Soviet civil-rights activists and minority-group militants have been subjected to similar reprisals of a severity similar to or greater than that which has been given Jewish militants.

In sum, Soviet Jews remain disadvantaged compared to most other major religious and ethnic groups, but their position has not perceptibly worsened in recent years. What has changed is the new mood of militancy and expectancy among Soviet Jews and the corresponding echo evoked among Jews and men and women of good will outside the USSR by the expression of this new mood. Before, Jews practiced their religion and maintained their culture quietly, and at times furtively, or succumbed to pressures for assimilation. For some, assimilation was welcome; for others, it was a regretted necessity. Assimilated or not, they encountered subtle and at times not so subtle forms of discrimination and were subject to recurrent repressions simply because they were Jews.

But now thousands publicly demonstrate pride in their heritage and large numbers have the hope that they too, like Jews elsewhere, will not only be able to persevere as Jews, but also to occupy a place of honor in the world. Thousands of predominantly young Soviet Jews now jam the streets on Jewish holidays outside Moscow's Central Synagogue and dance the hora to the accompaniment of Israeli pop songs played on tape recorders. The "Jews of silence"—to use Elie Wiesel's apt phrase—have found their voice, so that, along with the discouraging aspects of their situation, there are also define *[sic]* grounds for hope. Those in the Soviet Union who are most determined to assert their Jewishness now tend to concentrate almost exclusively on the single issue of emigration to Israel. There is undoubtedly a much larger number of Jews in the USSR who, if not assimilated, are at least reconciled to remaining in the Russian milieu and who would welcome greater opportunities for cultural expression.

What Can Be Done to Help?

We proceed from the assumption that the Soviets are sensitive about their treatment of Jews and care about responsible public opinion abroad. We believe that the Soviets are particularly touchy about the opinion of foreign leftists and Communist parties and of prominent moral and community leaders in the West as well as in the "non-aligned" countries. That tangible progress can be made is shown by the statement on September 24 of Secretary General U Thant, who stated that more than 400 out of 800 Soviet Jews whose cases he had raised with Moscow had succeeded in reaching Israel. There are many other examples, not all of which have been equally publicized.

With this in mind, the United States Government has made clear where it stands on this issue.

On January 11, President Nixon joined leaders of the American Jewish community in urging "freedom of emigration as explicity provided in Article 13 of the Universal Declaration of Human Rights" as well as "cultural and religious freedom at home and abroad." Secretary of State Rogers, in a statement to the youth Mobilization for Soviet Jewry in October, 1970, declared:

"This Government has repeatedly expressed in public and in private its opposition to anti-humanitarian policies wherever they exist in the world. We believe that free movement is one of the basic human rights of all persons. We have expressed sympathy and support on many occasion for persons in the Soviet Union who wish to emigrate, often to rejoin their families elsewhere, but who are denied permission to do so. We shall continue to make these views known and to take every practical measure which could help to overcome the hardships suffered by such persons."

The Department of State's press spokesmen have publicly spelled out in more detail our views on the problem of Soviet Jewry, for example in a statement on February 24, 1971:

"The policy of the United States Government in accordance with the principles upon which this country was founded and in consonance with the Universal Declaration of Human Rights, supports the right of peoples everywhere to free emigration and to religious freedom. Americans of all faiths and their Government are deeply concerned by the difficulties placed in the path of citizens of the Soviet Union, including its Jewish citizens, who have applied through legal channels for emigration and who seek to preserve their cultural heritage."

World public opinion was clearly a factor in the commutation of the death sentence passed on Jews convicted of treason in Leningrad in December, 1970, for seeking to leave the USSR allegedly by plotting to commandeer an aircraft, and in general has restrained the Soviet authorities from broadening the use of quasilegal punishment against Jewish activists in the USSR.

In this connection, the Department's press spokesman, in a statement on May 27, expressed deep concern about the Soviet policy of trying people in secret and spoke for Americans of every political persuasion and religious belief in deploring the persecution of persons for actions which in most other countries would not even be offenses.

Meanwhile, the United Nations offers the best regular forum for focusing world attention on the situation of Soviet Jews, and United States officials there have repeatedly spoken out on the issue. For example, on March 17, 1970, Mrs. Rita Hauser, United States Representative on the UN Human Rights Commission, stated:

"We do not comprehend any policy which serves to preclude emigration of Soviet Jews who have families or cultural ties elsewhere. We also would hope that the conditions necessary for continued national identity of the Jews in the Soviet Union will prevail, for we are certain that the Jews of that country will add as much to Russian life as the Jews have added to the life of my country. Their distinct cultural and religious identity enhances life; suppression of this identity will diminish the spirit of all Soviet citizens."

At the United Nations General Assembly on December 9 and 10, 1970, U.S. Representative Dr. Helen G. Edmonds denounced the harassment of Jews wishing to leave the Soviet Union and declared:

"Last year before this committee we pointed out that, despite the guarantee of the Soviet Union's constitution and laws, Jews are not treated as citizens on an equal level with all other Soviet citizens. . . . In this atmosphere, it is not surprising that large numbers of Jews are seeking to leave the Soviet Union. Their hopes are supported by Article

XIII of the Universal Declaration of Human Rights which says that 'Everyone has the right to leave any country, including his own, and to return to his country.' However, the Soviet Union is allowing few Jews to emigrate."

Later, Mrs. Hauser reiterated the concern of the United States Government at a meeting of the UN Human Rights Commission on February 26, 1971:

"We hope the Soviet Government will appreciate the keen interest felt in the United States, by Jews and non-Jews alike, that the large Jewish minority group in the Soviet Union be assured the right to be free of discrimination and to practice its religion freely and fully. . . ."

The Department also had made use of private diplomatic channels to underscore the importance we attach to the right of free emigration and the reuniting of families. For example, our official representation list of Soviet residents, including many Jews, who have been refused permission to emigrate to join close relatives in the United States has regularly been presented to Soviet officials at a high level. This practice was inaugurated by the then Vice President, now President Nixon, when he visited the USSR in 1959. Most recently, the list was handed to Soviet Foreign Minister Gromyko on September 24, 1971, during his meeting with Secretary Rogers in New York, as well as to Soviet Deputy Foreign Minister Kuznetsov by Ambassador Jacob Beam in Moscow on February 19, 1971, and to Minister Gromyko by Secretary Rogers in October, 1970, in New York. This year's list contained the names of some 150 Soviet Jews as well as of other relatives of American citizens. Since the Soviet authorities remain extremely reluctant to permit Soviet citizens to emigrate or travel abroad, we are obliged to concentrate our interventions in behalf of persons attempting to join relatives in the United States. We cannot be of direct assistance in cases of persons seeking emigration to other countries.

The results of our representations in support of the right of families to reunite have not been as successful as we would like, but a small amount of emigration to the United States—averaging about 250 persons yearly—has taken place. We intend to continue this practice. This year, through October 31, our Embassy in Moscow has already issued 251 immigrant visas. Of this number, at least 134 were issued to Jews. This is a small number, but a good sign—last year only 78 Soviet Jews were permitted by the Soviet authorities to leave the USSR for the United States on immigrant visas, according to our visa records. . . .

Reading 3

Letter from Congressman William Ryan to Frank Shakespeare, Director of the USIA, May 24, 1971, in *Congressional Record,* July 7, 1971, H6438-39

Congressman Ryan makes the case for initiation of VOA broadcasts in Yiddish into the Soviet Union. Such broadcasts, he argues, would provide information, hope, and psychological support to Soviet Jews.

Hon. Frank Shakespeare
Director, U.S. Information Agency,
Washington, D.C.

Dear Mr. Shakespeare:

We are all aware of the oppression under which the Jews of the Soviet Union suffer. Their government has pursued a course of religious and cultural repression aimed at destroying the Jewish identity of the 3,000,000 Jews now living in the Soviet Union. Virtually all of those who wish to emigrate are barred from doing so.

Much has been said of the impact of world opinion in attempting to ameliorate this tragic situation. World opinion did, in fact, play a significant role in producing the reductions in sentences of the 9 Jews accused and convicted of an alleged highjacking. In this effort to muster world opinion, the House of Representatives played a significant role by its passage of House Resolution 1336 last December 31.

However, much of these effects of world opinion, and of the world support of the Soviet Jews, is unknown to them, because the Soviet press bars them from the knowledge of the world sympathy they have aroused. They need hope.

That hope and that knowledge can be provided by the Voice of America, which broadcasts into the Soviet Union. Currently, however, the Voice of America does not broadcast in Yiddish, the native tongue of many of the 3 million Soviet Jews. True, many of them can speak Russian, as well as Yiddish, and so can understand our current broadcasts. But, some of them cannot. And equally important, the very fact of broadcasting in Yiddish can be an enormously important psychological uplift for these oppressed people. . . .

We urge you to direct the Voice of America to begin broadcasts, as soon as possible, in the Yiddish language. As we have said, this action would fill a need which exists, and it would provide psychological support of enormous importance to the 3,000,000 Jews of the Soviet Union.

With best regards,
Sincerely,
William F. Ryan
(and 72 other members of the House)

Reading 4

Response to Congressman Ryan's Letter by Frank Shakespeare, June 14, 1971, in *Congressional Record,* July 7, 1971, H643

Ryan's arguments to inaugurate VOA broadcasts in Yiddish into the Soviet Union are rejected by Shakespeare, who maintains that the most cost-effective and practical broadcast language is Russian.

U.S. Information Agency
Washington, D.C.
June 14, 1971

Hon. William F. Ryan
House of Representatives

Dear Mr. Ryan:

On my return from my overseas inspection trip, I found the letter of May 24 which you and your colleagues have addressed to me regarding the situation of Jews in the Soviet Union. . . .

The problem of providing the most effective moral support to Soviet Jews—within the limits imposed by the official character of the Voice of America—has occupied our attention ever since the Leningrad trials brought the situation into the open.

We have made a thorough study of possibilities and as a result, I had from the outset instructed the Voice of America substantially to increase its coverage of news developments regarding the Jews in the USSR.

Thus, the voice has been featuring regularly the news of Jewish dissent in the Soviet Union as well as interviews with Soviet Jews who are allowed to emigrate and succeeded in reaching the free world.

The programs to which I refer have been broadcast in seven ethnic languages and especially in Russian and Ukrainian which are understood and spoken by the overwhelming majority of Soviet Jews. Unlike other ethnic groups which are concentrated in limited geographic areas and form individual Soviet republics, Soviet Jews are scattered throughout the country, and providing a service specifically directed to them would present us with technical problems of spanning eleven time zones, if we should want to reach them all.

Even assuming it were technically feasible to inaugurate a Yiddish service, we would be, in effect, increasing our costs without materially increasing our audience. Incidentally, it may be of interest that Israel's own transmitter, Kol Yisrael, beams the bulk of its programs to its coreligionists in the USSR in the Russian language.

In conclusion, I want to assure you that, although at this time we are not prepared to inaugurate the service which you propose, we shall continue, as we have in the past, to stress in our broadcasts the deep concern of the United States, its government and its elected representatives with the fate of Soviet Jewry and provide all the moral support and encouragement which is consistent with our own national interests and with the Agency's mission.

Sincerely,
Frank Shakespeare

Reading 5

"Soviet Exit Fees—The Ransom Jews" (translated from Russian) and a Discussion by the National Conference on Soviet Jewry, undated (approximately fall 1972). Document furnished by the National Conference on Soviet Jewry.

The Kremlin tried a variety of measures to make it harder for Soviet Jews to emigrate. In August, 1972, it established a schedule of fees which emigrants would have to pay as reimbursement to the State for their education. This move caused a furor in the West, resulting in the Soviet suspension of these fees.

Decree of the Presidium of the Supreme Soviet of the USSR concerning reimbursement of state expenditures on education by citizens of the USSR departing for permanent residence abroad. The presidium . . . resolves "to establish that citizens of the USSR, departing for permanent residence abroad (with the exception of those departing for socialist countries) are obliged to make reimbursement for state expenditures on education in schools of higher learning, in internships, and in military academies and for the receipt of corresponding academic degrees. The limits and conditions for the reimbursement of the indicated expenditures will be determined by the Council of Ministers."

In conjunction with the Ukaz of Presidium of Supreme Soviet of the USSR of 3 August 1972 "On Reimbursement of Government Expenses on Education by Citizens of USSR Departing for Permanent Residence Abroad," the Council of Ministers of USSR decrees:

1. To affirm the (accompanying) instruction devised by the Ministries of Finance, of Higher and Specialized Secondary Education and of Internal Affairs of USSR concerning the amounts and procedures pertaining to reimbursement by citizens of USSR departing for permanent residence abroad of government expenditures on education in institutions of higher learning, *aspirantura, ordinatura, adyunktura* and on receipt of scholastic degrees.
2. To grant to the Ministry of Finance in conjunction with the Ministry of Internal Affairs the right, in exceptional cases, given validating conditions *(V'isklyuchitel'nykh sluchayakh prinalichii uvazhitel'nykh prichin)*, partially or completely to exempt citizens departing for permanent residence abroad from reimbursement of government expenditures on education in institutions of higher learning, *aspirantura, ordinatura, adjunktura,* and on receipt of corresponding scholastic degrees.

Text of the Instruction of the Council of Ministers of the USSR of August 3, 1972 establishing the schedule of reimbursement of government expenditures on education by citizens of the USSR departing for permanent residence abroad.

1. Citizens of USSR departing for permanent residence abroad make reimbursement for government expenditures on education in institutions of higher learning of USSR in following amounts:

	(A)*	(B)	(C)	(D)	(E)	(F)
Moscow State University	12.2**	2.4	4.9	7.3	9.8	—
Other Universities	6.0	1.2	2.4	3.6	4.8	—
Engineering-technical, engineering-economic and higher military training institutions	7.7	1.5	3.1	4.6	6.1	—
Agricultural and forestry	5.6	1.1	2.3	3.4	4.5	—
Medical, pharmaceutical, dental and physeducational	8.3	1.4	2.8	4.2	5.6	7.0
Economic, law, pedagogical, historical-archival institutes and institutes of culture	4.5	0.9	1.8	2.7	3.6	—
Institutes and faculties of foreign languages	6.8	1.4	2.8	4.1	5.5	—
Institutes of art (conservatories, dramatics, art, literature)	9.6	1.9	3.8	5.7	7.7	—

* Letters in parentheses denote column headings, which are explained in full in Paragraph 7 below.
** In thousands of rubles.

2. Supplementary to the reimbursement of government expenditures envisioned by Article 1, there is to be levied on those persons completing *aspirantura, ordinatura, adyunktura,* or holding scholastic degrees.

a) On persons having completed *aspirantura, ordinatura, adyunktura,* but not having defended dissertations—1.7 for each year of study:
b) On persons awarded the degree Candidate of Sciences—5.4
c) On persons awarded the degree Doctor of Sciences [in addition to sum specified in subparagraph (b) of this article]—7.2;

3. The following citizens of USSR departing for permanent residence abroad are exempted from reimbursement specified by Articles 1 and 2 of this instruction:
a) Invalids of first and second class—(completely). Invalids of third class may be exempted from indicated reimbursement in amounts up to 50 percent;
b) Men who have attained 60 years of age and women who have attained 55 years of age—completely;
c) Men employed not less than 25, 15 and 8 years and women employed not less than 20, 12 and 6 years—75, 50 and 25 percent, respectively;
d) Persons who have completed higher educational educational institute, *aspirantura* and *adyunktura* without interruption of employment—in the amount of 50 percent;
e) Persons who have contracted marriage with citizens (subjects) of foreign governments—in amounts from 25 to 50 percent, taking into account their material circumstances, but persons married prior to 3 August 1972—completely;
f) Persons who have completed higher education institutions as non-resident students, as well as those who have received the Candidate of Science degree without passing through the course of *aspirantura, ordinatura,* and *adyunktura* —in the amount of 75 percent.

Citizens of USSR departing for permanent residence in developing countries may be exempted from reimbursement of government expenditures on education in an amount of 70 percent in addition to reductions specified in this article, and persons who have contracted marriage with citizens (subjects) of those countries in an amount up to 80 percent, and in individual cases—completely.

Partial or complete exemption from reimbursement of expenditures on education and receipt of academic degrees is determined by the Ministry of Finance of USSR in conjunction also with the Ministry of Internal Affairs of USSR and given the other validating conditions.

4. Receipt of monies indicated in Articles 1–3 of this instruction is accepted by branches of *Gosbank* for credit to the Union Government Budget.
5. Preparation and issuances of visas to persons departing for permanent residence abroad are undertaken by offices of Ministry of Internal Affairs after presentation by these persons of receipts given by branches of *Gosbank* for payment of monies in reimbursement of government expenditures on education.
6. This instruction does not apply to citizens of USSR departing for permanent residence in socialist countries.

(Signature block): Ministry of Finance/Ministry of Higher and Specialized Secondary Education/Ministry of Internal Affairs.

7. Explanation for alphabetical symbols in Paragraph 1 above.
   - A. Completion of studies at higher educational institutions or completion of the final course of instruction.
   - B. Applies to education in the duration of one year.
   - C. Applies . . . two years.
   - D. Three years.
   - E. Four years.
   - F. Five years.

Soviet Exit Fees—The Ransom of Jews

On August 3rd of this year the Soviet Union took a dramatic and, in the eyes of many, a crass and materialistic step, to halt the increasing demands of Jews to emigrate to Israel or elsewhere. These demands reflected the frustration of many Soviet Jews who have repeatedly expressed their desire to leave—to be reunited with families, or to emigrate—in order to live as Jews. A new law, number 572, was considered by the powerful Council of Ministers on that date and put into force on August 14th.

The most notorious aspect of the decree is that a schedule of fees was set up for "reimbursement for education" from Soviet citizens who leave the USSR, especially those who, as in the case of Jews, have been forced to renounce their citizenship. While the new decree has not yet been widely publicized in the Soviet Union, local OVIR (Office of Visas and Registration) officials now have a printed schedule of the fees. In addition to a fee of 5400R for high school, the lowest single fee is 4500 rubles ($5400) for a teacher's degree. The highest is 12,200R for a doctorate. The fees are incremental. Thus, a holder of the first degree (equivalent of Baccalaureate) would have to pay 5500R for that degree, plus the 5500R for high school. A candidate of Sciences, such as Dr. Benyamin Levich, would have to pay 12,200R plus 5500R (first degree) plus another 5500R (for high school) equalling 23,200R or approximately $25,000. There is also evidence that a fee of 7200R is to be charged for anyone who defended his thesis, making the total about 33,000 dollars for Levich.

It remains unclear how thorough the application of the law will be. What is apparent at the moment is that the section on high school education applies to all types of secondary education: technical, vocational and academic. There is even the possibility that the fees will be pro-rated, which would mean that a 15-year-old child would be charged for the two years or so of high school that he had already completed. The inclusion of a fee for high school thus means that the new tax is applicable to virtually every Jewish family who applied to emigrate. There are few people in the Soviet Union who are without a high school education.

First rumors of the decision, which went into effect on August 14, reached the NCSJ on that same day. But the world was appraised of the actual situation when ten Jewish scientists called a press conference on August 15. Decrying the levying of the fees, Prof. Benyamin Levich, a corresponding member of the Academy of Sciences and the only person of that rank known to have applied to emigrate, called them a form of "twentieth-century slavery." Among the others commenting at the highly unusual news conference was Vladimir Zaslavsky, who said that with this new tactic Soviet authorities were oppressing intellectual Jews and that it would deeply affect general movement.

It must be recognized that the average Soviet Jew does not have the required money which in reality represents more than several times his yearly salary. For example, a teacher would probably earn 80–100 rubles per month. An engineer might begin working at 120–140R per month and then go to 200R, with seniority, while an MD would start at 120–

130R per month and then increase with seniority. Only in the case of the scientists is there the beginning of a truly decent salary of 200–250R per month as a base. A few in the highest echelons of research could earn as much as 500R, but this is rare. To intensify the severity of the decree, the applicant cannot, under the regulations of the law, offer personal property in lieu of money. Only money will be accepted.

The apparent reasons for the move are several. It reflects in many ways the sense of despair on the part of Soviet authorities. To this date, no matter how they have tried to intimidate Jews, the movement has grown and flourished and the number who apply to emigrate continues to increase. Moreover, the number of highly skilled scientists who apply has also grown. Some observers believe that the Soviet move may well represent an attempt to stem this trend. In very subtle ways it may be an attempt to limit the number of Jews who seek higher education. Knowing that he may be charged exorbitant fees if he ever decides to leave, a Soviet Jew might opt not to continue his education at all. Finally, this tactic may be a deliberate effort on the part of the Soviet Union to obtain much-needed hard currency—if they assume that the American Jewish community will pay "ransom" for their brethren. This is especially significant in light of the need for Moscow to expand its hard currency reserves for cash purchases of Western goods, especially wheat from the United States.

The human drama of the new situation is illustrated by the fact that at this moment in Moscow there are at least 5 Jewish families with visas in hand who cannot raise the newly imposed tax, and whose exit visas will therefore expire shortly. They are: Constantin Katrov, Lev Syrkin, Yuri Putilyansky, Vladimir Elyapin and Naum Fayzik. The ultimate effect of the new law is the addition of a virtually insurmountable obstacle in the path of Jews who desire to emigrate to Israel. The drawn out, often humiliating, procedure for filing a visa application, including the necessary character references, must still be followed. Now, however, in addition to the existing fee of approximately 1100 dollars per person over 16, there is the additional schedule of fees, or "ransom" which could effectively halt what the Soviet Union has been unable to do through harassment and imprisonment.

Reading 6

Memorandum to President Richard Nixon on the Situation of Soviet Jewry, from Action Committee of Newcomers from the Soviet Union, in *News Bulletin on Soviet Jewry,* May 1973

Soviet Jewish emigrants to Israel argue forcefully against quiet diplomacy and for passage of Jackson–Vanik. They conclude that the U.S.S.R. "will relent [*on the issue of anti-Semitism*] *only under extraordinary pressure," which the United States is capable of exerting.*

Over the Jews in the Soviet Union hangs the threat of genocide—spiritual genocide from which they have suffered from the first days of the October Revolution—and physical genocide which Jews have faced all too often in recent history, in 1937, 1948, 1953 and now again in 1973. One cannot predict just what form this will take; mass arrests and deportation to camps or mass deportation to Birobidzhan. But, we assure you, Mr. President, that this interpretation of the situation is not exaggerated. The key to the rescue of our people lies now in the hands of the United States of America.

Mr. President, we have no doubt of the sincerity of your wish to help Soviet Jews, but we are deeply worried that you have chosen quiet diplomacy as the only means toward this end. The USSR is not a reliable partner for gentlemen agreements, a fact which the free world has had ample opportunity to learn, in Cuba, West Berlin, Hungary, Czechoslovakia, the Suez Canal and South Viet Nam.

We wish to point out that in May 1972, when you were in Moscow for talks in an atmosphere of mutual understanding, activist Jews were under preventive arrest, their telephones were disconnected (and have not been restored to this day), some were called up for army service, and hundreds of people who "looked Jewish" were taken off the trains, planes and buses to Moscow. After you left Russia having completed important negotiations successfully, a fact they interpreted as given *[sic]* them a free hand, the Russians intensified their campaign of persecutions designed to intimidate Jews who wish to emigrate. This campaign culminated in the imposition of the Education Tax and trials of individuals in Moscow, Kharkov, Sverdlovsk, Rostov, Leningrad and Vinnitsa, and with the preparation now for new trials in Tbilisi, Minsk and Kiev. No one knows whose turn is next. The Soviet authorities have even set a precedent by revoking under court order the parental rights of a father because of the Jewish Zionist education he gave his daughter.

We know and appreciate that during this time, you made efforts to help Soviet Jews. Some of us were included in the pre-election gift presented to you by the Soviet authorities. We know that the Soviet leaders have promised you, unofficially, not to implement the Education Tax and to maintain emigration at its present level. We leave you to judge the value of liberal promises of those who invented the doctrine of "Panzer Communism."

Permit us to summarize our position. Mass emigration of Jews to Israel is not desired by the Soviet authorities, and it affects problems other than the Jewish one. If one adds to this traditional Russian anti-Semitism, then it is quite clear that the USSR will relent only under extraordinary pressure and only if she is convinced that this is the lesser evil, or that she has no alternative. Today, the USA has all the possibilities of exerting such pressure. The help of the West, and mainly the US is, today, a matter of life and the continued existence of the Soviet Regime. The Soviet leadership that brought the national economy to the brink of catastrophy *[sic]* know this and will be ready to grant concessions if they know that the demand for such concessions is a firm and unavoidable condition for the receipt of aid. Senator Henry Jackson's amendment to the Trade Bill is an effective instrument to this end. It is hard to imagine when another such opportunity will arise, and we want to hope, Mr. President, that the American nation which you lead will not miss this one.

Mr. President, the vague promises you received from the Kremlin cover a sinister situation. The promised suspension of the Education Tax leaves Soviet Jewry in a more critical position than before its imposition. As long as the Tax remains a law, it acts as a stern reminder to every young Jew beginning higher education that he may be mortgaged to Israel, and then drafting him for military service which calls for the oath of allegiance to his tormentors from the same "traitor." There is still no protection against arrest for expression of his desire to go to Israel or his protest against his detention. He can still be charged with disturbing public order, amoral behaviour, with spying, or with anti-Soviet activity and sent to labor camp as have more than 40 Zionist prisoners. He can still be refused because of opposition of relatives, for no stated reason, or under the all-inclusive state interests or security grounds.

Only one hope impels the few, who in spite of all, dare present their documents—the hope that they will be included in the cruel quota that arouses such enthusiasm among some in the West. No one stops to think that this quota of 30,000–35,000 Jews is less than the birth rate of the Soviet Jewish population.

The Jewish people know too well what quotas mean, and have paid too dear a price for this knowledge. Even now, in the Soviet Union, the selective granting of visas occurs simultaneously with unprecedented escalation of savage anti-Jewish and anti-Zionist propaganda through all branches of the mass communication media, greatly increasing, thereby, the danger of pogroms. Highly placed Soviet officials have, themselves, openly used the threat of "popular anger."

In the name of those lucky enough to have been included in this quota, and in the name of those held in the USSR, we declare that only free emigration, only the guaranteed right to all Jews to repatriate to Israel must be the demand of the free world to the Soviet authorities. Only this will save Soviet Jews.

In order to prove the sincerity of her promises, Russia must abolish all barriers to free emigration, specifically:

- Invitations from relatives in Israel
- Character references from employers
- Permission of relatives
- Sums of money including the 9000 rubles for passport and renunciation of citizenship

- The Soviet authorities must put an end to threats, harassments, all forms of persecution and anti-Semitic propaganda.
- The Soviet authorities must immediately grant permission to all those who have been refused exit permits and must release all Jews imprisoned because of their activity for emigration, regardless of the article under which they were condemned.

Mr. President, from the above it is clear why we support Senator Jackson's amendment to the Trade Bill, which conditions granting of Most Favored Nation Status on Free Emigration, and affords the President and Congress an effective instrument to ensure the fulfillment of this condition. We wish to point out that should the Jackson amendment fail, there will be nothing to stop the Soviet authorities to take immediate vengeance on the Jews, and then, to whom will they be able to turn? . . .

Reading 7

Andrei Sakharov, Open Letter to the Congress of the United States, Moscow, September 14, 1973

The noted Soviet physicist and human rights advocate urges support for Congressional passage of the Jackson–Vanik Amendment. He argues that the Soviet Jewish emigration issue impacts on all Soviets and the overall human rights situation.

At a time when the Congress is debating fundamental issues of foreign policy, I consider it my duty to express my view on one such issue—protection of the right to freedom of residence within the country of one's choice. That right was proclaimed by the United Nations in 1948 in the UNIVERSAL DECLARATION OF HUMAN RIGHTS.

If every nation is entitled to choose the political system under which it wishes to live, this is true all the more of every individual person. A country whose citizens are deprived of this minimal right is not free even if there were not a single citizen who would want to exercise that right.

But, as you know, there are tens of thousands of citizens in the Soviet Union—Jews, Germans, Russians, Ukrainians, Lithuanians, Armenians, Estonians, Latvians, Turks and members of other ethnic groups—who want to leave the country and who have been seeking to exercise that right for years and for decades at the cost of endless difficulty and humiliation.

You know that prisons, labor camps and mental hospitals are full of people who have sought to exercise this legitimate right.

You surely know the name of the Lithuanian, Simas A. Kudirka, who was handed over to the Soviet authorities by an American vessel, as well as the names of the defendants in the tragic 1970 hijacking trial in Leningrad. You know about the victims of the Berlin Wall.

There are many more lesser known victims. Remember them, too!

For decades the Soviet Union has been developing under conditions of an intolerable isolation, bringing with it the ugliest consequences. Even a partial preservation of those conditions would be highly perilous for all mankind, for international confidence and detente.

In view of the foregoing, I am appealing to the Congress of the United States to give its support to the Jackson Amendment, which represents in my view and in the view of its sponsors an attempt to protect the right of emigration of citizens in countries that are entering into new and friendlier relations with the United States.

The Jackson Amendment is made even more significant by the fact that the world is only just entering a new course of détente and it is therefore essential that the proper direction be followed from the outset. This is a fundamental issue, extending far beyond the question of emigration.

Those who believe that the Jackson Amendment is likely to undermine anyone's personal or governmental prestige are wrong. Its provisions are minimal and not demeaning.

It should be no surprise that the democratic process can add its corrective to the actions of public figures who negotiate without admitting the possibility of such an amendment. The amendment does not represent interference in the internal affairs of socialist countries, but simply a defense of international law, without which there can be no mutual trust.

Adoption of the amendment therefore cannot be a threat to Soviet-American relations. All the more, it would not imperil international détente.

There is a particular silliness in objections to the amendment that are founded on the alleged fear that its adoption would lead to outbursts of anti-semitism in the U.S.S.R. and hinder the emigration of Jews.

Here you have total confusion, either deliberate or based on ignorance about the U.S.S.R. It is as if the emigration issue affected only Jews. As if the situation of those Jews who have vainly sought to emigrate to Israel was not already tragic enough and would become even more hopeless if it were to depend on the democratic attitudes and on the humanity of OVIR [the Soviet visa agency]. As if the techniques of "quiet diplomacy" could help anyone, beyond a few individuals in Moscow and some other cities.

The abandonment of a policy of principle would be a betrayal of the thousands of Jews and non-Jews who want to emigrate, of the hundreds in camps and mental hospitals, of the victims of the Berlin Wall.

Such a denial would lead to stronger repressions on ideological grounds. It would be tantamount to total capitulation of democratic principles in face of blackmail, deceit and violence. The consequences of such a capitulation for international confidence, détente and the entire future of mankind are difficult to predict.

I express the hope that the Congress of the United States, reflecting the will and the traditional love of freedom of the American people, will realize its historical responsibility before mankind and will find the strength to rise above temporary partisan considerations of commercialism and prestige.

I hope that the Congress will support the Jackson Amendment.

September 14, 1973 (signed) A. Sakharov

Reading 8

Roy Medvedev, "The Problem of Democratization and the Problem of Detente," excerpts in *A Chronicle of Human Rights in the USSR*, No. 5–6, November–December 1973, pp. 6–7

Reading 9

Response by Andrei Sakharov, November 20, 1973, ibid, p. 9.

Dissident Soviet historian Roy Medvedev argues that the passage of Jackson–Vanik would probably "worsen prospects for resolution of the emigration problem" . . . and that "Soviet-American relations would also deteriorate." Sahkarov disagrees, replying that "we must speak openly and loudly about our tragic problems. . . ."

Medvedev writes:

It would be a gross oversimplification, however, to presume that only with the help of outside pressure—and pressure, moreover, involving interstate relations or trade—is it possible to achieve some substantive concessions from a country such as the Soviet Union in the conduct of our domestic policy. Outside pressure can play a negative as well as a positive role: it can deter our organs of power from certain actions in some cases, and in other cases, on the contrary, it can provoke those or other undesirable actions and in that way only impede the process of democratization of Soviet society.

For example, it would be unrealistic to presume that under pressure from the American Congress the Soviet government will adopt a special law permitting unrestricted emigration from the USSR for all who so desire. And if the American Congress should adopt the Jackson Amendment . . . on this account, and should refuse most-favored-nation status to the Soviet Union, this would probably not improve but only worsen prospects for resolution of the emigration problem in the near future. Soviet-American relations would also deteriorate.

Now, as is known, major work has begun on the draft of a new USSR Constitution. This work will presumably significantly broaden the section of the Constitution on the Soviet citizen's civil and political rights, as well as the constitutional guarantees of those rights. The drafters of the Constitution cannot today ignore such an important democratic right as the right to leave one's country and to return to one's own country. No matter how formal many of the constitutional rights accorded to Soviet citizens may be, the introduction into the new Constitution of the right to free entry and exit from the USSR—even with qualifications—would have great significance. The adoption by Congress of the Jackson Amendment can only lessen the chances for introduction of this article into the new USSR Constitution. Therefore we consider Academician A.D. Sakharov's appeal to the American Congressmen to support the Jackson Amendment a mistake, both substantively and tactically.

In general the possibility of putting direct pressure on the Soviet Union by means of interstate or economic relations should not be overestimated.

And not only because the Soviet partners in the talks will reasonably protest against interference in the USSR's internal affairs. In general we strongly doubt that most leading statesmen in the West are at all seriously concerned with the problems of political or civil rights in the USSR or China. In the crunch, Nixon, Pompidou and Heath all defend the interests of their countries' ruling classes, and it is not at all axiomatic that the capitalist circles of the US, England, France or the Federal Republic of Germany are so very interested in the rapid development of socialist democracy in the USSR, or in accelerating the Soviet Union's economic, social and cultural progress.

Sakharov's Reply:

I am not in agreement with many assertions in the recent statements by Roy and Zhores Medvedev. The Medvedevs, with their pragmatism, have opposed themselves to those who today are waging a moral struggle for man's right to live and think freely. The liberation of political prisoners, freedom of emigration, freedom of conviction—these demands are strictly moral. Upon their realization depend the spiritual health of society, the economic and political living conditions of the entire people. In particular I cannot concur in any way with the Medvedevs' depreciation of the role of freedom of departure. I am convinced that this freedom is important not only for those who leave, it is no less important for those who remain. I believe that we must speak openly and loudly about our tragic problems, appealing to all honest people, whatever their political convictions may be. This is our duty to our country, and to the whole world. The position of the Medvedevs, who emphatically appeal to so-called leftist forces, seems erroneous to me.

Reading 10

Letter from Henry Kissinger to Henry Jackson, October 18, 1974

Reading 11

Letter from Jackson to Kissinger, October 18, 1974

Reading 12

Letter from Andrei Gromyko to Kissinger, October 26, 1974

These letters discuss the U.S.–Soviet negotiations over Jackson–Vanik just prior to its passage in December 1974. Kissinger and Jackson reportedly worked hard to reach a compromise on Jackson–Vanik. Gromyko claimed that the Jackson–Kissinger letters revealed a "distorted picture" of the Soviet position on Jewish emigration, which he reiterated was "entirely within the internal competence" of the U.S.S.R.

Letter from Secretary Kissinger to Senator Jackson

Dear Senator Jackson:

I am writing to you, as the sponsor of the Jackson Amendment, in regard to the Trade Bill (H.R. 10710) which is currently before the Senate and in whose early passage the administration is deeply interested. As you know, Title IV of that bill, as it emerged from the House, is not acceptable to the administration. At the same time, the administration respects the objectives with regard to emigration from the U.S.S.R. that are sought by means of the stipulations in

Title IV, even if it cannot accept the means employed. It respects in particular your own leadership in this field.

To advance the purposes we share both with regard to passage of the trade bill and to emigration from the U.S.S.R., and on the basis of discussions that have been conducted with Soviet representatives, I should like on behalf of the administration to inform you that we have been assured that the following criteria and practices will henceforth govern emigration from the U.S.S.R.

First, punitive actions against individuals seeking to emigrate from the U.S.S.R. would be violations of Soviet laws and regulations and will therefore not be permitted by the government of the U.S.S.R. In particular, this applies to various kinds of intimidation or reprisal, such as, for example, the firing of a person from his job, his demotion to tasks beneath his professional qualifications, and his subjection to public or other kinds of recrimination.

Second, no unreasonable or unlawful impediments will be placed in a way of persons desiring to make application for emigration, such as interference with travel or communications necessary to complete an application, the withholding of necessary documentation and other obstacles including kinds frequently employed in the past.

Third, applications for emigration will be processed in order of receipt, including those previously filed, and on a nondiscriminatory basis as regards the place of residence, race, religion, national origin and professional status of the applicant. Concerning professional status, we are informed that there are limitations on emigration under Soviet law in the case of individuals holding certain security clearances, but that such individuals who desire to emigrate will be informed of the date on which they may expect to become eligible for emigration.

Fourth, hardship cases will be processed sympathetically and expeditiously; persons imprisoned who, prior to imprisonment, expressed an interest in emigrating, will be given prompt consideration for emigration upon their release; and sympathetic consideration may be given to the early release of such persons.

Fifth, the collection of the so-called emigration tax on emigrants which was suspended last year will remain suspended.

Sixth, with respect to all the foregoing points, we will be in a position to bring to the attention of the Soviet leadership indications that we may have that these criteria and practices are not being applied. Our representations, which would include but not necessarily be limited to the precise matters enumerated in the foregoing points, will receive sympathetic consideration and response.

Finally, it will be our assumption that with the application of the criteria, practices, and procedures set forth in this letter, the rate of emigration from the U.S.S.R. would begin to rise promptly from the 1973 level and would continue to rise to correspond to the number of applicants.

I understand that you and your associates have, in addition, certain understandings incorporated in a letter dated today respecting the foregoing criteria and practices which will henceforth govern emigration from the U.S.S.R. which you wish the President to accept as appropriate guidelines to determine whether the purposes sought through Title IV of the trade bill and further specified in our exchange of correspondence in regard to the emigration practices of non-market economy countries are being fulfilled. You have submitted this letter to me and I wish to advise you on behalf of the President that the understanding in your letter will be among the considerations to be applied by the President in exercising the authority provided for in Sec. 402 of Title IV of the trade bill, including procedures for periodic review, so that normal trading relations may go forward for the mutual benefit of the U.S. and the U.S.S.R.

Best regards,
Henry Kissinger

Letter from Senator Jackson to Secretary Kissinger

Dear Mr. Secretary:

Thank you for your letter of October 18 which I have now had an opportunity to review. Subject to the further understandings and interpretations outlined in this letter, I agree that we have achieved a suitable basis upon which to modify Title IV by incorporation within it a provision that would enable the President to waive subsections designated (a) and (b) in Sec. 402 of Title IV as passed by the House in circumstances that would substantially promote the objectives of Title IV.

It is our understanding that the punitive actions, intimidation or reprisals that will not be permitted by the government of the U.S.S.R. include the use of punitive conscription against persons seeking to emigrate, or members of their families; and the bringing of criminal actions against persons in circumstances that suggest a relationship between their desire to emigrate and the criminal prosecution against them.

Second, we understand that among the reasonable impediments that will no longer be placed in the way of persons seeking to emigrate is the requirement that adult applicants receive the permission of their parents or other relatives.

Third, we understand that the special regulations to be applied to persons who have had access to genuinely sensitive classified information will not constitute an unreasonable impediment to emigration. In this connection we would expect such persons to become eligible for emigration within three years of the date on which they last were exposed to sensitive and classified information.

Fourth, we understand that the actual number of emigrants would rise promptly from the 1973 level and would continue to rise to correspond to the number of applicants, and may therefore exceed 60,000 per annum. We would consider a benchmark—a minimum standard of initial compliance—to be the issuance of visas at the rate of 60,000 per annum; and we understand that the President proposes to use the same benchmark as the minimum standard of initial compliance. Until such time as the actual number of emigrants corresponds to the number of applicants, the benchmark figure will not include categories of persons whose emigration has been the subject of discussion between Soviet officials and other European governments.

In agreeing to provide discretionary authority to waive the provisions of subsections designated (a) and (b) and Sec. 402 of Title IV as passed by the House, we share your anticipation of good faith in the implementation of the assurances contained in your letter of October 18 and the understandings conveyed by this letter. In particular, with respect to paragraphs 3 and 4 of your letter, we wish it to be understood that the enumeration of types of punitive action and unreasonable impediments is not and cannot be considered comprehensive or complete, and that nothing in this exchange of correspondence shall be construed as permitting types of punitive action or unreasonable impediments not enumerated therein.

Finally, in order adequately to verify compliance with the standard set forth in these letters, we understand that communication by telephone, telegraph and post will be permitted.

Sincerely yours,
Henry M. Jackson

Letter from Foreign Minister Gromyko to Secretary Kissinger

Dear Mr. Secretary of State:

I believe it necessary to draw your attention to the question concerning the publication in the United States of materials of which you are aware and which touch upon the departure from the Soviet Union of a certain category of Soviet citizens.

I must say straightforwardly that the above-mentioned materials, including the correspondence between you and Senator Jackson, create a distorted picture of our position as well as of what we told the American side on that matter.

When clarifying the actual state of affairs in response to your request, we underlined that the question as such is entirely within the internal competence of our state. We warned at the time that in this matter we had acted and shall act in strict conformity with our present legislation on that score.

But now silence is being kept precisely about this. At the same time, attempts are being made to ascribe to the elucidations that were furnished by us the nature of some assurances and, nearly, obligations on our part regarding the procedure of the departure of Soviet citizens from the U.S.S.R., and even some figures are being quoted as to the supposed number of such citizens, and there is talk about an anticipated increase of that number as compared with previous years.

We resolutely decline such an interpretation. What we said, and you, Mr. Secretary of State, know this well, concerned only and exclusively the real situation—the point was quite the contrary, namely about the present tendency toward a decrease in the number of persons wishing to leave the U.S.S.R. and seek permanent residence in other countries.

We believe it is important that in this entire matter, considering its principled significance, no ambiguities should remain as regards the position of the Soviet Union.

A. Gromyko
Minister of Foreign Affairs
of the U.S.S.R.

Reading 13:

TASS statement that denies U.S. Trade and Emigration Link, in *Pravda*, December 19, 1974, translated in *The Current Digest of the Soviet Press*, Vol. XXVI, No. 51, p. 5

The Soviets rejected any link between U.S. trade concessions and "the departure of Soviet citizens to other countries" (Jewish emigration was not specifically mentioned). Instead, they argued, a successful trade agreement between the U.S. and the U.S.S.R. had to be based on "non-interference in one another's internal affairs."

As is known, for some time now official circles in the U.S.A., including the American Congress, have been discussing bills concerning trade and economic relations between the U.S.S.R. and the U.S.A. At present, these bills have been approved separately by the House of Representatives and the Senate; after uniform texts have been worked out in the conference committee, they will be submitted to both houses for final passage.

It was intended that, in accordance with the understanding in principle that the U.S.S.R. and the U.S.A. reached in 1972, the discriminatory restrictions in the field of trade and economic relations that the U.S.A. introduced during the "cold war" years would be removed.

However, the opponents of the normalization of Soviet-American trade, who also oppose the improvement of Soviet-American relations in general, from the very outset actively obstructed this, seeking to prevent the organization of mutually advantageous economic ties between the U.S.S.R. and the U.S.A., including the reciprocal granting of most-favored-nation conditions in trade and in providing credits for trade, or, to be more precise, the removal of the discriminatory conditions applied to the Soviet Union by the U.S.A.

Matters have reached a point at which the positive resolution of these questions has been made dependent on various kinds of reservations and demands that are nothing but flagrant interference in the Soviet Union's international affairs. This is the only term that can describe the attempts to include in the bills provisions having to do with, for example, the departure of Soviet citizens to other countries, the furnishing to American institutions of economic information that is purely domestic in nature, etc.; of course, it is only as a result of a loss of any sense of reality that anyone could conceive the idea of creating in the U.S.A. some kind of agencies to supervise the Soviet Union's fulfillment of these provisions.

The adoption of reservations and restrictive conditions of this kind by the U.S. Congress would directly contradict the two sides' clear-cut commitments under the 1972 trade agreement between the U.S.S.R. and the U.S.A., which provides for the unconditional termination of discriminatory legislation against the Soviet Union.

Tass is authorized to state that the Soviet Union's leading circles categorically reject as unacceptable any attempts, from whatever source, to interfere in affairs that fall wholly within the internal jurisdiction of the Soviet state and involve no one else. The same circles believe that the artificially created complications around questions of the normalization of trade and economic ties between the U.S.S.R. and the U.S.A. do not correspond to the interests of either side. Mutually advantageous cooperation and trade are undoubtedly in the interests of both the Soviet and the American peoples.

There is only one basis on which Soviet-American relations in general and trade and economic relations in particular can be successfully built.

It has been precisely formulated in the pertinent Soviet-American documents, including the aforementioned agreement. This is the full equality of the two sides and noninterference in one another's internal affairs. It is on this basis alone that we can confidently move toward the further development of trade and economic relations between the U.S.S.R. and the U.S.A. and of relations between them as a whole.

As far as the Soviet Union is concerned, it intends to continue to adhere strictly to this principle.

Reading 14:

Remarks by Senator Henry M. Jackson before the National Conference on Soviet Jewry, Washington, D.C., May 17, 1976

Jackson reviews his negotiations with Kissinger and Washington's negotiations with Moscow prior to passage of the Jackson–Vanik Amendment, which the Senator claims has been successful. Jackson deplores, however, what he considers the "Ford administration's refusal to stand by its pledge to support the compromise of which it was a part."

Four years ago I appeared before you to ask for your support in preventing this country from walking yet another one-way street in the name of détente. I urged you to join me in turning the cul de sac of unilateral trade concessions into a highway to freedom for the thousands of brave Soviet Jews and non-Jews who demanded the right to emigrate. I called upon human rights by requiring respect for those rights, on a nondiscriminatory basis, as a condition of most-favored-nation status and access to subsidized credits.

The fight for free emigration from the Soviet Union is part of the larger struggle for human rights in all lands and for all people. We see it taking place today in Rhodesia, in Chile, in the Far East and in Latin America. We see it, in the Soviet Union, among Jews and Gentiles, in the Baltic States, in the assertion of new demands for local autonomy.

The struggle is being waged by Catholics, by Baptists, by ethnic Germans and Tartars. It has acquired a universal character to which Americans have proven themselves generous in responding.

The Jackson Amendment has been a part of this great movement. Contrary to the general impression created by the media, the Jackson amendment applies to many countries and to all the people in those countries—whether they be Jew or Gentile, without discrimination on the basis of race, religion or national origin. It is as universal as the movement of which it is a part, limited only by its application to those countries that did not enjoy the benefits of most-favored-nation status on the date that it was enacted.

The response of the American people has been overwhelming, a reaffirmation of our deepest national values. By staggering majorities in the House and Senate the Congress adopted the Jackson Amendment. And despite a massive campaign by the Soviet Union, the White House and powerful businessmen, all efforts to abandon the commitment to freedom embodied in that historic legislation have been turned aside.

I don't need to tell those of you who have been in from the beginning that we made every effort to achieve a reasonable compromise with an administration that opposed us every step of the way.

But because the history of our effort to achieve a reasonable arrangement is so widely misunderstood, I wish to take a moment to recall the flow of events.

Following the passage of the Jackson Amendment in the House in December, 1973, and with its passage in the Senate where it had 77 cosponsors virtually assured, the Soviets and the Administration began to show interest in a compromise. There followed a long negotiation extending over many months that culminated in an agreement on the texts of two letters—one from Secretary Kissinger to me and one from me to him. The exchange of letters embodying the compromise was this: the Administration would convey assurances to the Congress that the rate of emigration from the Soviet Union would increase and punitive action against persons wishing to emigrate would cease. In exchange I agreed to introduce an amendment to the trade bill that would authorize the President to waive the credit and MFN restrictions of the Jackson Amendment for 18 months with subsequent one-year waivers subject to Congressional approval.

The compromise of October 18 had been negotiated with Secretary Kissinger and approved by President Ford. Indeed, it was President Ford who invited the White House photographers into his office to record what we all regarded as a constructive compromise.

The October 18 compromise thus revolved around the assurances conveyed to Congress. As a result, the Soviet renunciation of the Trade Agreement cannot be understood unless the substance of those assurances, and the attitude of the participants toward the compromise to which they led is clear. On these issues Secretary Kissinger's testimony before the Senate Finance Committee on December 3 is especially instructive. Asked about the nature of the assurances in his October 18 letter, Secretary Kissinger went beyond what had already been made public:

> "I have had many conferences on this subject with Ambassador Dobrynin and conferences with Foreign Minister Gromyko. . . . In addition, when President Ford took office he had some conferences in which the statements that I have made here were reconfirmed by the same individuals. Finally, General Secretary Brezhnev has made analogous statements to President Nixon, to myself and recently to President Ford. This is the structure of the assurances that we have."
>
> Senator Hartke: "Are the assurances then made from Mr. Brezhnev, Mr. Gromyko and Mr. Dobrynin?"
>
> Secretary Kissinger: "That is correct."

At the same hearing, urging support for the new proposed waiver amendment, Secretary Kissinger stated:

> "I believe a satisfactory compromise was achieved on an unprecedented and extraordinarily sensitive set of issues. . . . I believe it is now essential to let the provisions and understandings of the compromise proceed in practice."

Clearly, an arrangement such as the October 18 compromise could only be negotiated on the basis of good faith on the part of all the participants, and continuing good faith was a prerequisite for its successful implementation. Secretary Kissinger and President Ford understood this well. As the Secretary put it on December 3:

> "This understanding which is reflected in these letters can operate only on the basis of good faith by all the parties concerned and good will among the Senators and ourselves. . . . This is a specific assurance which has been extended on a number of occasions, the violation of which would certainly be one that the Administration would take very seriously. The President, on a number of occasions, has told the three Senators that with respect to what is contained in our letter he believes that he can stand behind it."

It is significant that when the trade bill containing the modified Jackson Amendment was finally signed by President Ford at the White House on January 3, 1975, Stanley Lowell and Israel Miller were among the invited guests. Clearly the President regarded the October 18 compromise as a milestone in the struggle to obtain freedom for Russian Jewry.

Between the agreement of October 18 and the December 3 testimony by Secretary Kissinger that I cited, an important event took place in Moscow. On October 26, eight days after the compromise, Foreign Secretary Gromyko handed Secretary of State Kissinger a letter that had the effect of repudiating the assurances conveyed to the Congress on October 18. The Secretary of State never informed me even of the existence of such a letter, much less its contents. Nor, so far as I have been able to determine, was anyone else outside the Administration apprised of that startling development. The letter only came to light when the Soviets chose to release it on the eve of passage of the trade bill.

The withholding of that crucial document must surely rank among the shabbiest deceits ever perpetrated by a Secretary of State on the Congress of the United States. As it is, I suspect that we shall have to wait for Dr. Kissinger's memoir to discover how he intends to answer for this deplorable breach of good faith.

What is most disturbing in all of this is the Ford Administration's refusal to stand by its pledge to support the compromise of which it was a part. The facts are simple: On January 14, a mere eleven days after the President signed the trade bill into law, the Secretary of State announced the intention of the Administration to seek its repeal. The ink was hardly dry when the Secretary of State sent the Kremlin an astounding message: despite the assurances, despite the negotiations, despite the Presidential pledges, the Administration would work to wreck the law of the land by contriving to give the Soviets what they wanted. President Ford echoed this dismal message in his State of the Union speech.

We always knew that even a negotiated agreement with the Soviets could, if they so chose, be violated. We did not believe that the man who put in writing the Soviet pledge to permit freer emigration, the Secretary of State, would violate his solemn undertaking. . . .

I urge those who wish to see the Jackson Amendment modified to begin by reading the Jackson Amendment. Do they know that the President can extend most-favored-nation status and Exim credits if he certifies that doing so will lead to a significant improvement in Soviet emigration policy? Do they know—those who argue that a gesture now will free those who languish in the camps—that the Jackson Amendment gives the President all the legal authority he needs to make the gesture they are urging? The logic of the Jackson Amendment is simple: the Soviet rulers must choose between their emigration practices and trade concessions from the United States. They cannot have both. Freer emigration will bring the trade relationship they desire, and it will do so under the Jackson Amendment. Those who wish to modify the amendment must understand that they will relieve the Soviets of the necessity to choose; for their approach would enable the Soviets to receive the trade benefits they desire without changing their brutal and capricious emigration policy.

I am not prepared to let the Soviets escape the choice they now face. We have seen the results of giving the Soviets what they desire first and waiting for the promise of progress on human rights later. That is the formula to which we succumbed at Helsinki. It didn't work there and it will not work here.

What will work is patience, steadfastness and unity within the government of the United States. Nothing has been so damaging to the cause of free emigration as the Administration's ill-conceived pledge to reward the Soviets with a reversal of the Jackson Amendment in return for Moscow's refusal to honor its pledge to freer emigration. The day that the President of the United States makes it plain to the Soviet leaders that he will uphold movement toward free emigration, we will see the beginning of the change for which we have fought so long.

Let us look for that day—together.

Reading 15

"100 Jews from Eight Cities Issue Statement on Soviet Rejection of Trade Agreement," in Washington Committee for Soviet Jewry, *The Vigil*, February 1975

These Soviet Jews blame the Stevenson Amendment for Soviet abrogation of the U.S.–Soviet Trade Bill of 1972.

With regard to the rejection by the USSR of the trade agreement with the USA, we wish to make the following declaration:

In October, 1974, a compromise was reached between the governments of the USA and the USSR on an agreement concerning the Trade Bill, which was then being considered by the U.S. Senate; the agreed compromise included the points regarding the emigration from the USSR. Since that time the text of the Trade Bill has not in any way been subjected to any new conditions regarding the allocation of restrictions or obstacles in the way of the granting of credits.

So that the actual reasons for the rejection by the USSR of their agreement with the USA lie outside the text of the Trade Bill and in particular outside the conditions of Senator Jackson's amendment.

As far as we are aware, the only major event in the economic relationships between the USSR and the USA, which occurred between October, 1974 (the time of the agreement on a compromise) and January, 1975 (the time of the rejection of the USSR of the agreement) was the regulation regarding the authority of the United States Export-Import Bank. This regulation accepted by Congress in September, 1974, placed a ceiling on the credits to be authorized to the Soviet Union for the period of the next four years in the guarantee of the bank to the amount of 300 million dollars.

It is of course well known that this limitation on the amount of credits included in the authority granted to the Export-Import Bank arose purely as a result of the increase in the price of crude oil and the attempt to control the sale of it by the Arab States, and the role in this maneuvering which was played by the Soviet Union.

So that whatever may have been the reasons for the failure of a trading agreement between the USA and the USSR, it is clear that they have nothing in common with the question of the emigration of Jews from the USSR.

The refusal of the USSR to carry into effect the compromise on the Trade Bill reached in October, 1974, has brought with it an even greater uncertainty regarding the fate of those Soviet Jews who are striving to go to Israel.

However, we declare that we shall continue with even more determination to fight for our right to emigrate. We are grateful to all those who are supporting us in this fight for emigration to Israel and we are sure that this support will remain firm in the future.

The exodus of the Jews from the USSR is an historic phenomenon and it would be idle to look upon it as a chance or temporary circumstance.

Reading 16

Group for Monitoring Implementation of the Helsinki Accords in the USSR Document No. 74, January 25, 1979, U.S. Congress, Commission on Security and Cooperation in Europe, 99th Cong., 2d Sess., *Documents of the Helsinki Monitoring Groups in the USSR and Lithuania (1976–1986)*, vol. I, 1987, pp. 293–296

The Moscow Helsinki Watch Group criticizes President Carter for sending a delegation of scientists to the U.S.S.R. with the mistaken impression that repression against Soviet Jews and other human rights activists had eased. Carter's action indicates that Washington did not link Soviet progress in human rights with plans for the SALT II agreement.

As we learned from a "Voice of America" broadcast, on January 23, 1979, State Department press officer Hodding Carter gave an explanation for the decision to send an American delegation of scientists headed by President Carter's advisor on scientific affairs, Dr. Press, to Moscow in February of this year for discussions on scientific and technological contacts.

In this connection, Hodding Carter told representatives of the press that the decision to send the delegation (whose visit was postponed in the summer of 1978) was motivated by the fact that the human rights picture in the Soviet Union had improved considerably; the number of Jews who have received permission to emigrate has increased; judicial repression against dissidents has "quieted down."

Hodding Carter apparently does not know that hundreds of Jewish refuseniks continue in vain to seek permission to leave; dozens of persons, "guilty" only of persistence in pressing for their right to emigrate (Ida Nudel, the Slepaks, Begun, Nashpits, Tsitlenok, and others) continue to serve out their sentences, to say nothing of the fact that the right to leave the country and return is granted only to Jews. Hodding Carter has forgotten that all the human rights activists who were sentenced in 1978 without justification (as were hundreds of others sentenced earlier) are serving harsh sentences and that not one prisoner of conscience has been released, and that the conditions of the camps have worsened considerably.

Hodding Carter must not know that in the second half of 1978, dozens of human rights activists have been arrested, convicted, or are awaiting trial in many of the cities of the USSR. The disruption of the peaceful demonstration on December 10, 1978, in Moscow hardly points to an "improvement" in the human rights situation. . . .

Reading 17

Letter from Representative Charles Vanik to President Jimmy Carter, March 8, 1979

One of the most important issues regarding Soviet Jewry in the Carter Administration involved possible waiver of the Jackson–Vanik Amendment. In this letter, Representative Vanik discusses possible reasons for waiving this amendment. He hoped that such waiver would improve the general climate of U.S.–Soviet relations and lead to agreement in other areas such as arms control.

March 8, 1979

President Jimmy Carter
The White House
1600 Pennsylvania Avenue
Washington, D.C. 20500

Dear Mr. President:

As you may know, I am very personally concerned about the issue of Title IV of the Trade Act of 1974 and its application for possible normalized trade relations with the Soviet Union and the Peoples Republic of China. I am greatly disturbed by growing indications that most-favored-nation status might be granted to China in the very near future. It is my firm view that there must be an even-handed approach to both countries under the Trade Act emigration provisions and that if this course is followed, Congressional approval of normalized trade status could be achieved this year.

Accordingly, on Febraury 28 I met with Soviet Ambassador Anatoly Dobrynin concerning trade relations between the United States and the U.S.S.R. In the course of our discussion, I advised him that I was pleased to learn of the 31,000 exit visas granted last year and, that even more importantly, I was impressed with the reaction I received from Israeli officials who carefully monitor this issue. They advised me that the climate for emigration applications has considerably improved to a point where Soviet officials are helpful and cooperative.

In view of the improved climate, I asked him if his country would be willing to provide the emigration assurances required by the Trade Act as a condition of MFN extension. He was very quick to respond that this was not possible.

I told the Ambassador that in my opinion, it would be unlikely that the United States Congress would amend the emigration provisions of the Trade Act. If an effort were made to this end I suggested that I would have to vigorously oppose it on the basis that this principle of U.S. trade policy has become enshrined in the law. I predicted that any effort to modify this provision would result in a two-year Congressional debate with an uncertain outcome and probable loss of the opportunity to make substantial gains.

Alternately, I suggested that in view of the progress in relations with China, it might be possible that you could recommend MFN status for both countries. With respect to the Soviet Union I suggested that your recommendation could be based on a finding that the positive trend of Soviet emigration indicates the process of human rights in the U.S.S.R. is proceeding at a much improved level. Such a certification could, in my view, be accepted by the Congress as constituting the assurances of the Trade Act that emigration practices will lead to the achievement of freedom of emigration objectives under the law. I believe a finding of this nature would clear up any technical legislative defects that might be present as a prerequisite for extension of trade benefits.

I told Mr. Dobrynin that if this procedure were followed, the Soviet reaction could be limited to a continued improvement in the climate for emigration and the final decision would be an internal one made by Congress. I expressed my deep concern that the Soviet Government might react adversely to this procedure. A negative reaction demeaning, objecting to, or commenting unfavorably on the proposal would abort the effort and would be a personal embarrassment for me. I told the Ambassador that I would not want to take any initiatives if his government could not understand other political problems.

Ambassador Dobrynin reacted very warmly and understandingly to my suggested procedures stating that if an official recommendation were forthcoming from the United States, his government would read it promptly and confidentially. He seemed to have a full comprehension of the political situation in the U.S. Congress and fully understand the legislative problem when I told him we must expect approximately 160 votes against the proposal—in any form—and that any adverse reaction from his government would be fatal to the idea. With respect to action in the Senate, the Ambassador took particular note of my view that a combined Soviet-PRC request from you can be accepted by some Senators who favor MFN for the PRC but are indifferent to a Soviet relationship.

If a decision should be made by your Administration to proceed on an improvement of our trade relations with the Soviet Union as well as with the PRC, I personally believe that the opportunity would be most favorable in the immediate future. During the April Congressional recess I expect to visit the Soviet Union with the Brademas delegation and if a recommendation was made immediately after that, it would set the stage for Congressional action. It is my judgment that this legislation would have problems, but we could clear it in the House before the August recess. In my judgment, the extension of MFN should not be conditioned on any progress or lack of progress in the SALT negotiations. As a matter of fact, introduction of the trade issue would be complementary and helpful to the approval of the SALT agreement and would enhance our overall relations with both countries in the interest of world peace.

If this issue is deferred, there is no way that the Congress can take this step during the 1980 campaign year. It seems to me that progress on this issue could fulfill your promise to open doors and expand trade throughout the world. Although the waiver procedure under the law would provide for a one year review which is extremely troublesome to our trading partners, subsequent action to extend the waiver to at least two years could be handled in a later step. If our relationship between these two nations progresses in cadence with our hopes, the other issues would become moot and irrelevant.

I would be pleased to discuss this matter further with your representatives at their convenience.

Sincerely yours,
Charles A. Vanik,
Chairman

P.S. All members of the Subcommittee on Trade have read this letter and a strong majority concur with my approach.

Reading 18

An Open Letter to United States Representative Vanik, by Prof. Alexander Lerner, Moscow, March 26, 1979, dictated to Michael Sherbourne, London

Professor Lerner, reflecting the consensus of refuseniks, urges Vanik not to press for a waiver of the Jackson–Vanik Amendment. Lerner sent this letter prior to Vanik's trip to Moscow designed to study the U.S.–Soviet trade relationship.

Dear Mr. Congressman,

I had the honour of discussing with you the state of Jewish emigration from the USSR and how it is affected by the Jackson–Vanik Amendment, during your previous visit to Moscow. At that time I was deeply moved by your sympathy with people refused their legitimate right to repatriation. I was therefore all the more surprised to learn that you now intend to stand for easing or even repealing the Amendment, in view of a supposed relaxation of the Soviet emigration policy. This supposition of an improvement in the issue of emigration is based on the bare fact that the number of Jews allowed to leave the Soviet Union in 1978 was higher than the figure for the previous year. However, such an assessment, made without any comparison between the number of permissions granted and the number of people who are desirous of leaving, is absolutely incorrect. It amounts to evaluating a change in a worker's salary, without taking into account any changes in prices or the purchasing power of that salary. Imagine for instance that there would be only one thousand people wanting to emigrate in a single year and that all of them were given permission to leave without the slightest hindrance. Would that indicate a hardening in the attitude of the authorities in their emigration policy as the figure of 1,000 would be so much smaller than the previous year? If 30,000 Jews were allowed to emigrate from the Soviet Union last year, that number should be compared with the close to 200,000 (two *hundred* thousand) who, during that same year, asked for invitations without which one cannot apply to emigrate . . . signifying that something like a further 170,000 Jews had decided to leave but had not been given permission. Actually the increase in the number of Jews leaving the Soviet Union is by no means thanks to the good-will of the Soviet authorities, but is in spite of the hardening of the policy in regard to emigration and the despotism which reigns where this question is concerned. This becomes obvious when one examines several undeniable facts, of which I will submit only three:

1. The trials which took place behind closed doors of Anatoly Sharansky, Ida Nudel, Vladimir Slepak, Simon Shneerman and Iosif Begun in the summer of last year. The absurd charges and the severe sentences, show that the authorities are out to intimidate Jews who actively try to achieve their right of repatriation.
2. A White Paper just concocted and published (perhaps it would have been better to have called it a Brown Paper, as Brown is considered the colour of fascism!) officially endorsing lies and slander on Israel, on Jews wanting to go to Israel, and on Jews in general, reveals that world public opinion is being brainwashed so as to prepare it to accept new acts of repression which are being prepared.
3. The case of my son Vladimir Lerner is an example of the totally arbitrary rule employed when decisions are taken as to who shall, or shall not, be allowed to emigrate. He has been refused permission for nearly eight years though he has never had the slightest contact with any state secrets, never served in the armed forces and has no unfulfilled obligations of any kind.

The Deputy Chief of the Moscow OVIR, Colonel Zolotukhin, said in that very year, 1978, that he was being refused "for no reason whatsoever." Obviously there is no ground for seeing any liberalisation appearing in Soviet emigration policy. On the contrary, there is every reason to believe that the situation is deteriorating ominously. . . .

I naturally cannot, and do not wish to suggest how you should run your legislative activities. You may feel that the Jackson–Vanik Amendment should be relaxed or repealed altogether. That would suit businessmen like Armand Hammer, who are ready to sacrifice thousands of Soviet Jews in order to satisfy their own selfish interests! Would an easing of the Amendment serve any other American interests? There is no ground for regarding it as a humanitarian move or in the interest of Soviet Jews. There should be no talk of any non-existent relaxation in Soviet emigration policy. I have many friends in the U.S. Congress. I know that in expressing the will of their constituents and their own will, they will not retreat from their stand on human rights when it is a question of support for the right of Jews to repatriate.

I believe that when you return from your trip to Moscow after having had a better opportunity to study the situation at first hand, you will uphold your original stand on the Jackson–Vanik Amendment.

Sincerely yours,
Prof. Alexander Lerner

Reading 19

Union of Councils for Soviet Jews, The Trade Act of 1974 and Soviet Emigration, April 5, 1979

American Jewish organizations strongly supported maintenance of the Jackson–Vanik Amendment. This statement of the UCSJ reflects this position.

1) The Union of Councils for Soviet Jews is at this time strongly against any repeal or waiver of the Jackson–Vanik Amendment to the 1974 Trade Act. The very fact that the Carter Administration is willing to entertain the possibility of providing the Soviet Union with trade benefits, so soon after the anti-Semitic and anti-dissident trials in Moscow last summer, is a vivid illustration of a lack of coherence in U.S. policy vis-à-vis the USSR. Less than a year has passed since the Administration, in response to a new wave of Soviet repression, cancelled U.S.

official delegations, a computer sale to the Soviet Union, and tightened up regulations on the export of oil-drilling technology. Now, without any apparent change for the better in the Soviet treatment of people wishing to emigrate, speculations are encouraged as to the desirability of extending to the Soviet American trade benefits. Such erratic performance can only complicate efforts to develop a stable and constructive relationship with Moscow and to promote emigration opportunities for Soviet citizens.

2) The only alleged evidence of an improvement in Soviet emigration practices is an increase in numbers. It is true that more Soviet Jews were allowed to leave the country in 1978 than in any other year since 1973. But what is the meaning of the sudden jump in granted visas? There is no evidence whatsoever that the percentage of refusals is declining. If more people are allowed to leave, it is not because of a more liberal emigration policy, but rather due to the fact that far more Jews choose to apply. Their haste in submitting applications probably results from an apparent increase in anti-Semitism in general, and repression and harassment of those wishing to leave the Soviet Union in particular.

The latest statistics demonstrate a significant decline in Jewish university enrollment. There are numerous reports of growing difficulties Jews encounter in obtaining professional employment in the Soviet Union. The Soviet media has engaged in an anti-Zionist campaign with openly anti-Semitic overtones. No wonder that many Soviet Jews feel pressured to escape from what they increasingly perceive as brutal persecution. Some, as a matter of fact, are openly urged to go by the authorities for political and financial reasons. For instance, in a number of Soviet cities visa offices insist on retired parents leaving with their children, in order to save paying them their pensions. In short, to grant the USSR trade benefits on the basis of an increase in emigration figures may well mean to reward the Kremlin for an increase in anti-Semitism and repression.

3) The Union of Councils for Soviet Jews is not in principle opposed to the development of mutually beneficial trade with the Soviet Union. Generally, a growing interaction between American and Soviet societies can only be helpful to the cause of human rights in the USSR. Hermetic insulation of the Soviet Union from the rest of the world, as long as they don't comply with our interests and values, is neither realistic nor useful in creating a climate of greater political tolerance in Russia.

Nevertheless, the Union of Councils is convinced that in the long-term perspective, trade may and should be used to encourage the Soviets to be more forthcoming in relaxing their emigration practices. If and when the Soviet government, for whatever reason, will show that it is improving its performance in the emigration area, there will be ample opportunity to review the possibility of a waiver of the Amendment. After all, the intent of the Jewish community in supporting the Jackson–Vanik Amendment was not to bring the Soviets to their knees, but rather to provide better conditions for emigration from the USSR. The Jackson–Vanik Amendment is a useful political tool, but there should be no doubt that, while American humanitarian commitments are sacred, the tools we utilize in their pursuit are not.

However, it should be clear to those who advocate granting a unilateral waiver or repeal of the Jackson–Vanik Amendment that they will be confronted with strong opposition from all who care about human rights causes and do not believe that narrowly defined realpolitik adequately represents the values of our great nation. In fact, efforts to change the 1974 Trade Act provisions dealing with the emigration area without credible evidence of an improvement in Soviet performance may only lead to a replay of the bitter debate on this issue and in all probability to immobilism and the retention of the status quo.

It is vital to communicate to the Soviet government that, no matter what the individual preferences of members of the Executive and Legislative Branches are, in the current political climate of the United States, this legislation will continue to enjoy the overwhelming support of the public and the Congress, so long as there is no significant change in Soviet emigration policy. Only after it is persuasively demonstrated that there is a meaningful improvement in the Soviet emigration situation will there be any sense in discussing a waiver.

The kind of change in Soviet emigration policy that could begin this discussion is:

1. A significant release of the hard-core refusenik cases. A guideline could be the one now in practice for permission to travel abroad by Soviet citizens who had access to classified information: three years wait for those with second-form secrets, five years wait for those with first-form secrets. This would take care of the long-term refuseniks.

2. A show of leniency to the prisoners of conscience and the exiles, to reduce their sentences considerably, and to release some of them.
3. An end to punitive draft of young men who apply to emigrate.
4. Delivery of all invitations from abroad.
5. Written reasons for refusal, with a time limit stated in writing when the applicant will receive his visa to emigrate.
6. An end of harassment of Soviet Jews who apply to emigrate, including loss of jobs in most cases, disconnecting of telephones and non-delivery of mail. This should also include an end to the harassment of Hebrew teachers and those wishing to learn Jewish culture.
7. The continued rise in the numbers of those being allowed to leave.

In the final analysis, what we need from the Soviets are not, as the 1974 Trade Act requires, received assurances from the Soviet regime regarding the freedom of emigration, but rather an improvement in the Kremlin's performance. To sum up, the Union of Councils for Soviet Jews is quite flexible on the specifics of the trade legislation. Everything is negotiable, except abandoning thousands and thousands of Soviet Jews, for whom the Jackson–Vanik Amendment is a symbol of American interest in their fate.

Reading 20

Statement by Max M. Kampelman, Chairman, U.S. Delegation, Plenary Session, CSCE, Madrid, December 1, 1981

Kampelman gives a detailed account of anti-Semitism in the U.S.S.R. He spoke at the Madrid follow-up conference to the Helsinki Accords. Kampelman became the chief U.S. arms negotiator in Geneva in 1983.

Mr. Chairman:

Today is the ninth day since Dr. Andrei Sakharov and his wife, Elena Bonner, began a hunger strike in the city of Gorky, where he has been exiled by the authorities of the Soviet Union. A week ago today, the United States Senate unanimously—Republicans and Democrats, liberals and conservatives, representing all of our fifty states—adopted a resolution associating itself "fully and completely" with that protest. They joined in his condemnation of the Soviet Union for its "flagrant violation of the Helsinki Accords." I have no doubt that the Senate, in doing so, spoke for an outraged American people indignant at the harassment inflicted on Dr. Sakharov and his family. . . .

Last fall, the delegate of Belgium eloquently addressed a particularly pernicious aspect of Soviet repression: anti-Semitism. The delegate of the United Kingdom has forcefully, on a number of occasions, brought this problem to our attention as well. Last Friday he did so again. This distasteful phenomenon has grown in intensity and in ugliness.

Speaking personally for a moment, I am Jewish by ancestry and commitment. My personal stake in this subject is, therefore, clear. Wherever anti-Semitism exists, Jews elsewhere react with concern and with the thought, "There but for the grace of God go I. . . ."

The issue, Mr. Chairman, is too serious to exaggerate, and I will do my utmost not to do so. The label of anti-Semitism is too terrible to apply loosely, and I will guard against doing so. I proceed, therefore, with care to address this problem as a problem that dares not to be ignored. The evidence is overwhelming. I will refer to only a few out of the hundreds of examples:

Fact: A book published in 150,000 copies in Moscow in 1977 and republished 1979, written by Vladimir Begun and entitled *Invasion Without Arms,* characterizes the Torah, the Old Testament of the Bible, as, among other things, "an unsurpassed textbook [of] . . . hypocrisy, treachery, perfidy and moral degeneracy—all the basest human qualities." He writes: "Jewish and Christian hypocrites alike keep silent over this."

Fact: There are frequent cartoons—we have them here—representations in the official Soviet press portraying Jews with large hooked noses and evil-looking unshaven jowls. Indeed, in September 1975, after the Helsinki Final Act was signed, the *Kazakhstanskaya Pravda* reproduced a cover cartoon of the 1934 edition of the notoriously poisonous "Protocols of the Elders of Zion," depicting an evil-appearing Jewish figure under the caption, "The Jewish Peril," digging his fingers into a globe of the world and making it bleed. . . .

Fact: Anti-Jewish material has been distributed to Red Army recruits and is published in official journals of the Soviet armed forces. (Captain Y. Makulin, "Rabbis and Soldiers" in *Sovietskyvoin* November 10, 1976.)

Fact: Jewish history is deleted from Soviet elementary and secondary school textbooks. Indeed, the Russian pogroms of the late 19th century against the Jews are justified in a Soviet publication as part of the class struggle. (V. Ya Begun, ibid. pp. 55–56.)

Fact: The Soviet Union—with the third largest Jewish community in the world—is the only country with a Jewish population in which there is not a single approved Jewish school and no means for teaching Jewish history and tradition. The private teaching of Hebrew is outlawed, while the official study of the language is restricted to a very few non-Jews. In recent weeks, over eighty Jewish teachers of Hebrew, in Moscow alone, received threats of prosecution and banishment should they continue their instructions.

Mr. Chairman, all of the evidence for the above facts reflects events taking place after the signing of the Helsinki Final Act. During the past fifteen years, a total of at least 112 Soviet books and brochures with anti-Semitic overtones of various degrees have been identified, some of them printed and reprinted in editions of 150,000–200,000 copies. Anti-Semitic propaganda is also carried out through lectures, stimulated by the Communist Party and the state.

There are many more instances of blatant government-condoned anti-Semitism in the Soviet Union. These are accompanied by harassment and imprisonment of Jewish leaders, discrimination against Jews in education and employment, active and frequently violent interference with the study of Hebrew and the possession of articles of prayer, and by a drastic reduction in the number of Jews being allowed to escape this pervasive anti-Semitism through emigration. . . .

I make this plea once again. The Soviet Union is a society that is large and powerful and has existed for more than sixty years. There is no need for that society to crush human beings, small and insignificant as they may appear in the broader perspective of history. There should be no need to stimulate hatred among peoples.

It is time for that society to develop a stronger faith in itself and in the inner strength of its people. The world, and certainly my Government, would welcome a Soviet decision to mobilize its resources and its people constructively to help meet its internal problems without the use of diversionary hate tactics. This is the only way we can ever hope to achieve the spirit of understanding mandated by the Helsinki Final Act that we all seek and that eludes us.

Thank you, Mr. Chairman.

Reading 21

TASS press release on the Shcharansky case, February 4, 1983, in *Chronicle of Human Rights in the USSR*, No. 48, October 1982–April 1983, p. 26.

The Kremlin defends its conviction of Shcharansky and accuses the West of spreading false propaganda regarding his treatment in the U.S.S.R. Shcharansky was released in 1986 in a wide exchange of prisoners with the United States.

Human rights in the Soviet Union have been proclaimed and are guaranteed by the Soviet Constitution, they are protected by Soviet laws and practically ensured by the socialist system. At the same time alleged violations of human rights are among the favourite themes for Washington's slander campaigns. Why is all this being done? Merely to misrepresent the socialist system.

The so-called Shcharansky case has been chosen as the pretext for the latest slander campaign. Washington has come up with this subject and the CIA is embroidering on it. So at the present both professional misinformers and certain officials are making statements now in one NATO capital, now in another. However, all of them are deliberately withholding from the public the incontrovertible fact that we have here a criminal offense which was tried by the court in full accordance with Soviet laws.

The "case" is perfectly clear: a Soviet citizen was sentenced for one of the gravest crimes against this country, spying, in particular, supply of information about the Soviet defense industry to US intelligence services. Shcharansky's guilt was fully confirmed and proved by irrefutable evidence in an open trial. The court sentenced Shcharansky to 13 years in prison.

Of course, Soviet legislation, like the laws of many other countries, does not exclude the possibility that prison terms may be commuted in response to pleas for pardon, but the only grounds for pardon may be the conduct of the prisoner but by no means vociferous propaganda campaigns and attempts of pressure from without.

Those who are raising anew a ballyhoo over Shcharansky's name most likely understand this full well. They must be likewise aware that the rumours spread in the West about the dangerous condition of his health, caused by a hunger strike presumably called by him, do not correspond to reality in any way.

The recent "demand" of the British Foreign Secretary to release Shcharansky "out of humane considerations" sounds particularly hypocritical in this respect. One would like to hear what "humane considerations" motivated Britain's present-day conservative government when they condemned without batting an eyelid to painful death in a hunger strike ten Irish prisoners in the Long Kesh concentration camp? This fact alone shows better than any words that the present-day "concern" of the British government, like all the other Western "patrons" of Shcharansky, is nothing short of a desire to score political points by naked politicking.

Other statements of spokesmen for Washington and its allies, such as Israel, are similarly hypocritical: suppression of human rights for them has long become day-to-day practice and actually institutionalized policy.

The Soviet laws and Soviet justice were and remain the basis of decisions with regard to persons doing damage to the state and society.

Reading 22

Letter from Representative Dan Glickman (D-Kan.) to Konstantin Chernenko, June 11, 1984

Representative Glickman notes the difficulties of Viktor Brailovsky's imprisonment and urges Chernenko "to ensure Dr. Brailovsky's secure employment" after his release. He concludes that the international community understands very well Soviet violations of human rights, and he asks Chernenko "to end the repeated violations of [Brailovsky's] basic human freedoms." Brailovsky was allowed to emigrate to Israel in 1987.

Konstantin Chernenko
Chairman of the Presidium
of the Supreme Soviet
The Kremlin
Moscow
RSFSR, USSR

Dear Chairman Chernenko:

I am writing with concern for Dr. Viktor Brailovsky. I have been following Dr. Brailovsky's case for nearly five years, and the circumstances of his life have become increasingly more disturbing.

I understand that after three years of internal exile, Dr. Brailovsky has recently rejoined his family in Moscow. However, he is presently in a position of being charged with "parasitism" because he cannot find employment as no one is willing to hire him, even for menial labor. This could, through no fault of his own, lead to his arrest and subsequent trial and sentencing. Furthermore, despite the Helsinki Pact, Dr. Brailovsky and his family have been repeatedly denied permission to emigrate to Israel.

I respectfully urge you, and others in the Soviet leadership, to intervene immediately to ensure Dr. Brailovsky's secure employment, taking advantage of his expertise in the field of computer science. His situation, I can assure you, is not going unnoticed in the international community, and I urge you to end the repeated violations of his basic human freedoms.

With best regards,
Dan Glickman
Member of Congress

Reading 23

Secretary George Shultz, "Soviet Jewry and U.S.–Soviet Relations," U.S. Department of State, Bureau of Public Affairs, Current Policy No. 628, October 22, 1984

Secretary Shultz outlines the deplorable status of Soviet Jews and stresses that the United States will continue to stress the human rights issue in U.S.–Soviet relations.

I wish I could use this occasion to bring you encouraging news about the condition of Soviet Jewry, but you know, at least as well as I do, that their situation remains very grim. Soviet persecution of Jews and other minorities has not only diminished, it seems to be getting worse.

Within the past two months, four well-known Hebrew teachers have been arrested in what appears to be an intensifying campaign of repression aimed specifically at Jewish cultural activities. In the Soviet view, apparently, promoting identification with one's religious and cultural heritage constitutes "anti-Soviet agitation and propaganda."

We cannot forget Anatoly Shcharansky, courageously clinging to his principles as his health is deteriorating in Chistopol Prison. He was imprisoned on the blatantly false charge of spying for the United States, but his real "crime" was to try to escape from Soviet tyranny so that he could lead a full Jewish life with his family in Israel.

To discourage others from trying to leave, Soviet authorities are continuing to threaten many "refuseniks" with confinement in psychiatric hospitals, expulsion from their jobs, and internal exile.

While all this has been going on, there has been an alarming upsurge in officially sanctioned anti-Semitic propaganda. Scurrilous cartoons, broadcasts, and articles equate the study of Jewish culture with fanaticism and racism and compare the State of Israel to Nazi Germany.

Jews, of course, are not the only victims of Soviet persecution. Efforts to stamp out all independent thought have led to the victimization of Nobel Prize laureate Andrei Sakharov and his wife, Yelena Bonner. Within the past six months, three prominent Ukrainian human rights activists died in Soviet labor camps. All three deaths can be attributed to the brutal conditions in Soviet labor camps and prisons. The small group of Soviet idealists who tried to monitor their government's compliance with its human rights obligations under the Helsinki Final Act has been decimated by imprisonment and exile. Even foreign tourists and diplomats have been subjected to Soviet harassment.

Emigration, meanwhile, has come to a virtual standstill. Just over 1,300 Jews left the Soviet Union in 1983, approximately 2 percent of the peak year total of 51,000 in 1979. This year it looks like fewer than 1,000 Jews will leave the Soviet Union. Soviet authorities would have the world believe that almost all Soviet Jews who want to emigrate have already done so. But, clearly, this is not true. Thousands of Soviet Jews have applied for exit visas, only to have them denied. They are ready to leave on a moment's notice.

We debate the question of what to do among ourselves, as I am sure you do. We are all frustrated by the lack of progress and by the absence of any easy or ready solutions. But rather than argue inconclusively among ourselves, I am convinced that what we can and should do is to make clear to the Soviets what our own approach is and how it is related in our eyes to the U.S.–Soviet relationship as a whole.

That is what we have tried to do under this Administration. The Soviets know that we seek to put relations on a stable and constructive basis for the long term. But I think they also know that we will not stop our practice of calling them to account for their abuses of human rights. And among human rights issues, none has more urgency than the treatment of Soviet Jews.

As a government, we would prefer to deal with these issues on a confidential basis, simply because it's more effective that way. But we understand and support the efforts of public interest groups to express their concerns, and we will not be silent when the Soviets act in a way we consider dangerous or irresponsible, as they so often do in the human rights area.

The United States, therefore, continues to speak out at every opportunity against Soviet human rights violations. We have vigorously denounced Soviet anti-Semitic propaganda and practices. We have consistently condemned denial of the basic right of Soviet citizens to emigrate. In the face of blatant intimidation, our embassy in Moscow and our consulate in Leningrad have maintained contact with individual "refuseniks," and we have made numerous representations on behalf of Soviet citizens who have been denied permission to emigrate. We continue to consult with other Western nations on ways to improve human rights performance. And in all our diplomatic discussions with the Soviets—including President Reagan's recent meeting with Foreign Minister Gromyko—we have stressed human rights issues.

Soviet leaders may well be perplexed by our preoccupation with human rights. After all, they and many other governments throughout the world take the view that human rights are strictly an "internal affair." In this view, how a government treats its own citizens is not a matter of legitimate international concern or even discourse. Compassion, it seems, should stop at a country's borders.

In the aftermath and in the everlasting memory of the Nazi Holocaust, this attitude must be relentlessly exposed as a gross moral evasion. Numerous international covenants, conventions, and declaration—including the Universal Declaration of Human Rights, the Genocide Convention, and the Helsinki accords—today attest to the fact that human rights are no longer regarded as an "internal matter." On the contrary, they are intimately linked to the issues of war and peace. We recognize that governments not at peace with their own people are unlikely to be at peace with their neighbors. . . .

From the experience of World War II and its aftermath, we have learned that the issues of peace and of human rights are joined and that attempts to separate them can bring on disaster. We have learned that it is not the advocacy of human rights but rather their denial that is a source of tension in world affairs. The issue of human rights is at the top of our agenda because we have learned the great lesson of the Scriptures: We truly are our brother's keeper. . . .

Reading 24

Speech by George Shultz to the National Conference on Soviet Jewry, Press, Department of State, No. 206, October 9, 1986, pp. 5–7

Shultz gives an overview of the plight of the Soviet Jews and reiterates that the United States will always bring up the issue of human rights in negotiations with the Soviet Union. Shultz acknowledges the role of the NCSJ in preparing him for the forthcoming summit in Iceland.

. . . Our message is that the problem of human rights is right at the heart of these great global problems that we're talking about. At Reykjavik, the General Secretary and his colleagues will be hearing from the President and from me and others about Soviet Jewry and the human rights issues. [Applause]

When Morris Abram [Chairman, National Conference on Soviet Jewry] and other Jewish leaders came to see me on September 17th, which he referred to, they brought a report prepared by the National Council on Soviet Jewry, and I'm sure you're familiar with all of the tragedy it describes—been reviewing it here. The Soviets often claim that all Soviet Jews who wish to leave have already done so. In fact, there are more than 11,000, as you all know, who have applied for emigration and been refused. Many of these refuseniks have been waiting for years in difficult conditions for permission to leave the U.S.S.R.

Another, conservatively stated, 300,000 or more have taken the first step in the emigration process by requesting an invitation from abroad, and many, many more—who knows?—have not applied, because they fear harassment, loss of employment, or other forms of persecution that have been visited already on would-be emigres.

Now, the packet Morris gave me which I read carefully before my meeting with Minister Shevardnadze, included a table on just the numbers of emigration by years, and in the last three years, I think it was, by months. So I can tell you I made very good use of this material, and I held this table up and a table like that has the advantage that it doesn't need translation from English to Russian. You just look at the numbers, and the numbers tell a story. Of course, once again you see the rhythm in the numbers. It was small, and it rose, and then fell, and so he said the natural things, namely, that "Well, I guess it had that big peak period, and all the people that wanted to leave had left."

And so I had some other material from the packet which I knew—it was a very well-organized packet. It's the best little packet I've gotten, and I read it. [Laughter] And it gave the reference to the documentation. It isn't a guess; it isn't somebody's hunch. It's based on records that come out of the Israeli Foreign Ministry and have to do with actual exchanges of letters, so you can count them up. And then you have to make allowances for how many people may have died, and so on, but 300,000 is a conservative estimate, and, of course, all the people who haven't done that because of fear have to be taken into account. So the implication of the table that maybe those who have wanted to leave have left is not correct.

And that's the point I want to make. I've made it, and I'm working with Morris to see if I can't get another kind of a piece of paper that I can hold up, and it doesn't have to be translated from one language to another, but it tells a story.

It's true—a picture is better than a thousand words in some cases, and we need to keep telling this story over and over and over again. The Soviets need to know that we cannot continue to improve relations with them unless we see significant, sustained progress on human rights, including the right to emigrate.

They know that we have widespread, bipartisan support for the cause of Soviet Jewry—in fact, I don't know of any opposition. It isn't just bipartisan support; it's universal—and equally widespread outrage over the low levels of emigration, and continued persecution. They should know that there can be no lasting improvement in our relations as long as Soviet citizens are deprived in principle of the rights to speak, read, worship and live where they please. [Applause]

So our message to the Soviets is simple: Token gestures or short-term lowering of barriers will not suffice. What the American people want to see is a genuine and lasting improvement in the situation of Soviet Jews as part of a broader commitment on the part of the Soviet authorities to allow their citizens to exercise basic human rights, including freedom of movement. This goal cannot be detached from any of the others on our agenda, including bilateral issues, regional issues, and arms control.

So we come back, since we share our goal, and we struggle here together, to find the answer. What can we do that will be more effective?

None of us are here interested in beating our breasts about this issue. We're here because we'd like to see some results, and what can we do? And I think we just have to keep after it, and I think that there are the following things that we need to keep doing and doing and doing.

We need to keep making the logical arguments and presenting the facts and the statistics, as you are doing and as we do. And no doubt all of the things that I've said, you've said countless times in meetings of your own, so I haven't said anything new. But I was saying to Morris as we came down here, it is important to keep repeating the things that are true and setting out the information and the logical arguments.

Second, I think it is important to keep referring to the documents. We know that the legal aspects of these things are solemn documents—they signed them—so we need to keep reading them to them. It's an international obligation. States that respect themselves respect obligations like that.

Third, we need to keep showing that we care, we really care.

Fourth, we need to let them see that the continuation of this behavior means that they pay a price. They pay a heavy price, and they need to see that and know that, and they do.

So I stand here with you saying, as I did at the beginning, I welcome the fact that you're here. It helps us. It gives us strength. And I thank you for coming, and I pledge to you on my own behalf, and I know the President's behalf, that we will always keep after this issue; we will never give up on this issue; that it will have—right up at the top—priority in our discussions, and we will hope and pray with you that we will see a result. That's what counts.

Thank you so much for letting me be here.

Reading 25

Letter from President Reagan to the Union of Councils for Soviet Jews, September 12, 1987

In this letter Reagan reassures his readership that advancement of human rights of Soviet Jews "will remain at the forefront of our human rights policy and an integral part of our whole policy toward the Soviet Union." He also reiterates his support for "the continuation of the Jackson–Vanik and Stevenson Amendments."

I am pleased that the annual meeting of the Union of Councils for Soviet Jews gives me the opportunity to express my support for the work of your organization.

The Union of Councils has played an outstanding role in focusing the world's attention on the plight of Jews in the USSR and in bringing political pressure on the Soviet government to recognize their fundamental rights to live without discrimination, to fully practice their religion and culture, and, above all, to emigrate freely. Your efforts have helped to make concern for the rights and freedom of all people a mighty force whose power is greater than that of tyranny and arbitrary rule, clearly in retreat around the globe.

The Soviet leadership has recently taken some positive steps in the sphere of human rights. Some political prisoners have been released. Increased numbers of Jewish refuseniks, along with others, have been allowed to emigrate. We applaud these moves because they inspire hope for more progress, which we wish to encourage. But these positive steps are not only far from enough, their timing and nature suggest a quest for diplomatic effect, not justice. And they coexist with ominous indicators of possible future tightening on emigration and a growth in anti-Semitism in some Soviet quarters.

Therefore, we must maintain our witness and our efforts. Strenuous efforts to advance the human rights of Jews in the USSR, including the right of free emigration, will remain at the forefront of our human rights policy and an integral part of our whole policy toward the Soviet Union.

During Soviet Foreign Minister Shevardnadze's visit to Washington in the coming days, and in any subsequent meeting with General Secretary Gorbachev, I shall press for major improvements in the plight of Soviet Jews and for the full freedom of emigration, just as I have in previous meetings. We shall maintain constructive political pressure, the pressure of public opinion, of allied governments, and of a courageous Jewish community within the USSR, buoyed by our support. We must preserve and use the instruments of policy that advance the cause. In this connection, let me assure you that I and the whole of my administration support the continuation of the Jackson–Vanik and Stevenson Amendments and shall scrupulously abide by their provisions.

Please convey to your annual meeting my greeting and my heartfelt appreciation for your efforts. The cause of human rights for Jews in the Soviet Union is the cause of human freedom everywhere.

Sincerely,
(signed) Ronald Reagan

Reading 26

Administrative agreement between the American Bar Association and the Association of Soviet Lawyers, May 2, 1985

Reading 27

Statement on ABA/ASL Agreement by Morris Abram, chairman, National Conference on Soviet Jewry in the *Jerusalem Post* International Edition, September 27, 1986

Reading 28

The position of the Union of Councils for Soviet Jews on the American Bar Association agreement with the Association of Soviet Lawyers, December 1986

The signing of an agreement between the ABA and ASL sparked great controversy in the American Jewish community. The two major Soviet Jewry advocacy organizations, the UCSJ and the NCSJ, took differing positions. The UCSJ strongly opposed it, citing the fact that the ASL was controlled by the Soviet government and that it had published despicable anti-Semitic literature. The NCSJ, while agreeing with the charges against the ASL, felt that the ABA-ASL Declaration of Cooperation which in the summer of 1986 superseded the original Administrative Agreement, provided an opportunity "to build a model for all US-Soviet exchanges."

Administrative Agreement
between the American Bar Association and the
Association of Soviet Lawyers dated
May 2, 1985

The American Bar Association (ABA) and the Association of Soviet Lawyers (ASL), entering into this Administrative Agreement, proceed from the idea that the establishment of a cooperative arrangement between the two Associations may promote contacts between American and Soviet lawyers, may promote the development of lawyer-to-lawyer relationships between the two groups and may develop ongoing cooperation between them in the areas of mutual professional interest.

The two Associations believe that such cooperation may contribute to the development of relations between the two nations and can make an important contribution toward world peace and mutual understanding between nations.

The ABA and ASL, therefore, each acting through its principal permanent officer, enter into this Agreement in the best interest of the members of each Association guided by mutual respect. This Agreement will be performed in good faith to the best abilities of each Association.

This Agreement will encompass the following:

I. Official Delegations

a. In each odd-numbered year beginning in 1985, the ASL will send an official delegation of up to five persons to meet with the

ABA leaders in Chicago and in another city in the U.S. (at the suggestion of the receiving party) for a period of up to ten days to discuss matters of cooperation and other legal issues of mutual interest. The ABA will arrange to receive the delegation and will pay lodging, meal, internal travel, and a reasonable amount of incidental expenses of this official delegation upon arrival in the United States. An interpreter for this delegation will be provided by the ABA.

b. In each even-numbered year beginning in 1986, the ABA will send an official delegation of up to five persons to meet with the ASL leaders in Moscow and in another city in the U.S.S.R. (at the suggestion of the receiving party) for a period of up to ten days to discuss matters of cooperation and other legal issues of mutual interest. The ASL will arrange to receive the delegation and will pay lodging, meal, internal travel, and a reasonable amount of incidental expenses of this official delegation upon arrival in the Soviet Union. An interpreter for this delegation will be provided by the ASL.

c. The ABA and the ASL will be exchanging invitations to send an official delegate to attend meetings of international nature organized by the respective Associations. The expenses of such a delegate will be paid as provided for official delegations (see a. and b. above).

d. Upon reasonable notice and request, each Association will offer its good offices to assist any other officially sponsored visiting delegations or tourist groups from the ASL or the ABA, provided that such delegations or groups shall not be unreasonably burdensome in size or frequency.

II. PUBLICATIONS

a. The ABA will be sending publications of professional interest to the ASL.

b. The ASL will be sending publications of professional interest to the ABA.

III. Communication

a. In the course of cooperation the ABA and the ASL will maintain an exchange of information by correspondence, and on all matters of cooperation which require expedited resolution—by the means of telex, telegraph, or telephone. It is understood that at a future time when there are proper technical and other conditions, the ABA and the ASL shall consider possibilities to establish electronic information exchange.

IV. Cooperation in Prospect

a. The ABA and the ASL believe that this Agreement will promote mutual confidence, and the two Associations will do their best to implement this Agreement successfully.
b. The ABA and the ASL anticipate that this Agreement will be expanded in future years to encompass such concrete matters as: exchange of legal scholars; exchange of legal literature on a larger scale; exchange of legal films and photographic exhibitions; and the organization of joint seminars, symposia and other forms of joint undertakings. The scope and the essence of these matters will be the subject of future meetings between the ABA and the ASL.
c. The ABA and the ASL understand that such activities will be organized on a reciprocal basis on the condition that each party intends to commit approximately the same level of resources to such activities as does the other.

V. Conditions of the Administrative Agreement

a. The Administrative Agreement will be executed in two English and two Russian counterparts, each of which will be deemed to be an original agreement.
b. Either Association may terminate this Administrative Agreement by giving three months written notice to the other Association.

By: Thomas H. Gonser Executive Director and Chief Operating Officer American Bar Association	By: Rafael Saakov Vice President Association of Soviet Lawyers

Dated this 2nd day of May, 1985

How to Turn the ABA–ASL Agreement into a
Model for Other Cultural Exchanges
from The Jerusalem Post *International Edition,*
week ending September 27, 1986
By Morris B. Abram
Chairman, National Conference on Soviet Jewry

The resurgence of exchange programs with the Soviet Union in arts, sports, science, education and other fields should remind Americans of two complementary truths about superpower relations. First, we cannot wish our adversary away. Second, wishful thinking and wishy-washy bargaining will let the Soviets make off with the lion's share of whatever benefits the exchanges offer.

The 1985 agreement between the American Bar Association and the Association of Soviet Lawyers is a controversial case in point. An exercise in unpardonable naivete by ABA leaders, it went far beyond recognizing the undeniable reality of the Soviet state; it accorded a despicable propaganda front a completely unmerited measure of legitimacy. The ASL is in no way an independent bar. Subservient to the state, as are all institutions under a totalitarian regime, the Soviet group has been the energetic sponsor of a stream of vicious libels against the defenders of human rights broadly and of Soviet Jewish emigration specifically. Thus, some of my ABA colleagues understandably urge we should promptly cut our losses and cut off the Soviet's fraudulent claim to international status and respectability. We should terminate the agreement they say, and put the Soviet "lawyers" where they and their government belong—under the sort of interdiction medieval Popes used to pronounce against heretical nations. We should excommunicate they say, not communicate.

In fact, however, the one-sided 1985 agreement has been superseded by a somewhat better-crafted ABA–ASL Declaration of Cooperation approved two months ago. Prodded and advised by the National Conference on Soviet Jewry and other concerned groups, ABA leaders went back to Moscow this May and came away with a new accord that sets the rule of law, human rights, and improvements of justice and legal services high on the exchange's agenda. We should not scrap this admittedly small advance without putting it to a test.

The one way we can justify any ABA–ASL collaboration is by using it both to educate some prominent and influential Americans about Soviet reality—an area where the original ABA negotiations revealed woeful ignorance—and to show Soviet officials that for all Americans of all stripes human rights are a vital politic, not empty piety.

Without discourse, we cannot accomplish this aim; without contact, we can have no hope of influence on Soviet conduct. So long—and only so long—as the ABA–ASL arrangement provides a forum for substantive discussions, we should use it to build a model for all U.S.–Soviet exchanges. Instead of dropping out, American lawyers can take the lead in substituting bite and meaning for hollow formalities.

If our efforts prove fruitless, we should not hesitate to terminate the agreement on the three-months' notice it provides. But in the meantime, as skilled advocates, we should welcome this limited chance to make the case of our society's highest value. Unlike Soviet Helsinki Accord monitors who have been imprisoned, exiled, and intimidated into silence, we can be open and effective monitors of Soviet compliance with the principles of free exchange and the practice of human rights.

In sessions we should declare open to the press, we must present our detailed concerns and grievances about Soviet legal procedures. We must insist on full discussion of such issues and weigh the value of further dialogue against the evidence, if any, of Soviet reform. Our questioning and questioners should be expert and tough.

For instance:

• Why are thousands of Soviet Jews—our colleague Rachel D. Levin, a distinguished, retired Moscow defense attorney, among them—denied permission to rejoin family members abroad? Why are these refusals—lasting eight years in her case and even longer in others—open-ended and unexplained? Why can't refuseniks be represented by counsel in appealing these arbitrary administrative denials of basic rights?

• Why do Soviet prosecutors treat the study of an ancient, sacred language—Hebrew—as a crime instead of a cultural blessing? Why since Mikhail S. Gorbachev came to office, have more than a dozen more Jewish activists been imprisoned on political charges while the level of emigration has dropped to new lows in flagrant violation of the Helsinki Accords?

• Why are Moscow defense lawyers refused the travel vouchers without which they cannot represent out-of-town clients in political cases? Why are courtrooms where such cases are heard closed by subterfuge to Soviet and foreign observers when the law provides for secrecy only for trials of sex crimes and treasonous offenses?

As upholders of the rule of law, we should press such inquiries of the Soviets as vigorously as US musicians should question the censoring of recordings by Rostropovich and Vishnevskaya, as writers should protest the maltreatment of Pasternak, Aksyenov, Solzhenitsyn and others, as scientists should denounce the savagery heaped on Sakarov and Orlov, and as all Americans in all encounters with the Soviets should demand full respect for fundamental human rights.

Were all agreements reached among friends, many lawyers would be out of work. It is with confrontation and hard bargaining between hostile parties that our talents and training are most needed and most useful. We should put them to work—as convinced, knowledgeable and unshrinking advocates of human rights and the rule of law—on the Soviets. Ours is a good cause. We have nothing to fear in fighting it out in the court of public opinion.

The Position of the Union of Councils for Soviet Jews on the American Bar Association Agreement with the Association of Soviet Lawyers. Revised December 1986.

In August, 1986, the Union of Councils for Soviet Jews issued a statement urging abrogation of the "Administrative Agreement" formulated between the American Bar Association and the Association of Soviet Lawyers. Subsequently, the ABA announced that the agreement had been superceded [sic] by a "Declaration of Cooperation Between the ABA and the ASL." The UCSJ, comprised of 55,000 members and 35 affiliated councils, remains unalterably opposed to any agreement, even in a modified form. The UCSJ urges the American Bar Association to promptly abrogate the agreement with the ASL as stipulated by the Huntwork/Jejna Resolution.

Advocates of the agreement with the ASL have argued that dialogue between American and Soviet lawyers will help to promote the cause of human rights. But, in fact, any such agreement between the ABA and the ASL will simply bestow upon the ASL, and by inference the Soviet legal system, an undeserved aura of legitimacy and respectability within the international community.

As Anatoly Shcharansky has noted, the American Bar Association mistakenly views the Association of Soviet Lawyers as its counterpart in the Soviet Union. Unfortunately, he contends, the real colleagues of American lawyers, men committed to justice and due process, are in prisons throughout the USSR.

The ASL is not an independent, autonomous organization but is an arm of the Soviet government. The ASL's concerns range far beyond the matters traditionally considered to be the province of lawyers. The ASL is the most prominent official sponsor and publisher of anti-Semitic material in the USSR. Together with the Soviet Anti-Zionist Committee, the ASL is co-author and co-publisher of the infamous *White Book,* a scathing denunciation of the so-called "international Zionist conspiracy." There is not a shred of evidence to suggest that the members of an organization like the ASL, the publisher of blatantly anti-Semitic material, could have the slightest interest in fostering the development of human rights through the law.

The ASL is an integral part of the mechanism for prosecution of Soviet Jewish citizens who are tried and convicted on trumped-up charges. At the precise time the ASL was negotiating an agreement with the ABA, its members were engaged in the fabrication of evidence used to convict Soviet Jewish refusenik Vladimir Lifshitz. He is now serving three years in the Siberian gulag.

Surely there can be no more vivid example for the Soviet Union's disregard for human rights and the provisions of the Helsinki Accords.

Despite its signature on the Accords, the Soviet Union has failed to comply with any of the Accords' human rights provisions. The Soviet government has ignored provisions which allow citizens free movement between borders, respect for the religious, cultural and human rights of all citizens, and the prompt reunification of separated families.

On the contrary, there has not been the slightest indication of any relaxation of the Soviet policy of denying the right of emigration to nearly 400,000 of its Jewish citizens.

The Union of Councils believes that an agreement—either in its original or its modified form—between the American Bar Association and the Association of Soviet Lawyers serves only to enhance the image of a reprehensible arm of Soviet repression.

The Union of Councils re-emphasizes its support for the Huntworth/Jejna Resolution, which calls upon the ABA to quickly abrogate its agreement with the ASL.

Reading 29

Speech by Soviet Foreign Minister Eduard Shevardnadze at the opening session of the Conference on the Human Dimension in Paris, May 30, 1989.

Shevardnadze states that the "parliament of perestroika" will soon be enacting numerous bills which would enhance the rights of the individual, that the question of the human dimension should be considered "in the broadest possible context," that the USSR is looking forward to a "single legal space" in Europe, and that international security is tied to human rights. This speech marks another milestone in Gorbachev's policy of "new thinking" on the role of human rights in international affairs.

. . . Paris 1989 stimulates our common desire to give new properties to the human dimension. Indeed, the timing and venue of the conference encourage us in this pursuit.

We are convinced that everyone present here has the feeling of being the inheritor of the brilliant and daring minds of France who gave humanity the Declaration of the Rights of Man and Citizen.

The chamber of political weights and measures which was opened to the world by the great French Revolution holds the standard that we apply today to our times, wishing to enrich the very concept and practice of the human dimension. . . .

Reflecting on what took place two hundred years ago, the present generations ought to establish a new scale for the human dimension for at least another two hundred years.

My country is contributing to the making of that scale by the entire experience of perestroika in the country's life, by building democratic institutions which are new for it. That process is open to the world in the literal sense of the word, as exemplified by the work of the first Congress of People's Deputies of the USSR. . . .

I am becoming increasingly convinced that there is a need to raise and consider the question of human dimension in the broadest possible context. . . .

The parliament of perestroika shows, by the way things proceed there and by the content of its work, the revolutionary nature of the changes under way in our country and strengthens the guarantees that the processes of renewal will be irreversible.

The young Soviet democracy, operating in conditions of maximum openness, is immediately addressing the questions of respect for human rights, of formalizing them in legislation and of monitoring the observance of human rights in the practical activities of the state.

The new Soviet parliament has before it a number of bills on the freedom of conscience, on the press, on public organizations and on entry in an exit from the country. They are designed to consolidate equality and freedoms—social, civil, and national—in the USSR.

We are confident that our new laws will reflect the new democratic essence of our socialist society, as envisioned long before the October Revolution by Russian revolutionaries, one of whom wrote that "the socialist system is a law-based system implemented with greater consistency" and that building such a system is only possible within the framework of a state based on the rule of law. . . .

We are convinced that the process of democratization, open decision-making in foreign policy will continue to develop and that reliance on parliament in implementing decisions will help to enhance the prestige of Soviet foreign policy based on national consensus. . . .

The times are changing. Also changing are our priorities, our perceptions of problems, of the challenges we face and of possible ways to meet them.

I can state that the natural evolution of the CSCE process has also significantly changed the human dimension. It has acquired a clearly defined legal content. There now emerges a trend to bring national legislation regulating the rights and status of the individual in society into conformity with international obligations of states, the Universal Declaration of Human Rights and the International Covenant on Civil and Social Rights. . . .

We should give thought to the future of the all-European legal evolution. We find promising the long-term idea of Europe as a single legal space. . . .

It would be fruitful to conclude an all-European consular convention and a uniform visa agreement. Over time, legal norms regulating relations between participating states could be developed and codified on an all-European basis. . . .

At the same time, we must not forget that, when applied to national sovereignty, control—in this field—is an extremely sensitive sphere. The application of monitoring arrangements should not impinge on state sovereignty. What we have in mind is that when a state accepts monitoring measures, it voluntarily agrees to a certain limitation of its sovereignty.

As Mikhail Gorbachev stated addressing the United Nations General Assembly, the Soviet Union will broaden its participation in the monitoring arrangements of the United Nations and in the framework of the CSCE process.

We are preparing to accede to the Optional Protocol of the International Covenant on Civil and Political Rights. In the framework of that process, internal arrangements for the consideration of complaints involving state organs will be improved.

Early this year, the Soviet Union withdrew its reservations as regards the jurisdiction of the United Nations International Court of Justice with respect to a number of conventions. Subsequently, reservations with respect to other human rights agreements will also be withdrawn.

We applaud international and national non-governmental organizations dealing with human rights. Most of them are honestly working to promote the rights and freedoms of the individual everywhere, as sources of ideas ensuring the protection of human rights and initiators of practical action. . . .

We have sufficient reason to affirm that humanitarian problems are becoming the most advanced sphere of the CSCE process. In principle, all major substantive issues in this area can be resolved. Of course, this will take time, but it can safely be assumed that ultimately all European states will adopt a universal approach and a comparable practice in humanitarian questions. . . .

One could give the individual any rights *de Jure* but they would be worth nothing if, for example, he were not able to resist economic oppression, or if the right to education were not backed up by a sufficiently broad and accessible network of quality educational institutions. Man is not free if he has no home or income necessary for a decent life. No rights will help a person to regain the health lost because of a polluted environment.

It is absolutely impossible to determine a precise scale of the human dimension outside the actually existing level of security enjoyed by the individual, a citizen of a specific country.

If entire peoples and nations continue to be hostages of the arms race, how can man, a part of a nation and of a people, be free? . . .

It is inadmissible if the declared freedom to emigrate is not realized. It is much worse, however, when the declared readiness for arms reduction is accompanied by a refusal to negotiate. . . .

It is gratifying to see the effects of our "assertive" policy and the force of our initiatives and to realize that our peace offensive is bringing fruit. . . .

The Soviet delegation will be examining very carefully the experience that will be generated by the Paris Conference because we wish the Moscow Conference to build on it and to enrich it.

The standards have been set high. They are set by the magnificent idea of holding this conference during the bicentennial celebration of the Great French Revolution which had a profound impact on the universal perceptions of the rights of man and citizen. . . .

The first Congress of People's Deputies of the USSR, which has been called the Congress of the future, is fully consonant with the Paris Conference.

Reading 30

Speech by the Honorable Max M. Kampelman, head of the U.S. delegation to the Copenhagen meeting of the Conference on the Human Dimension, Plenary, June 29, 1990.

This speech reflects the elation felt by Kampelman over the progress made in human rights since the Helsinki Accords were signed in August 1975, stressing, among other things, the vindication of the Helsinki principle which linked international security and human rights. He is especially pleased by the continuing advances in human rights made by the Soviet Union. This speech stands in sharp contrast with the gloomy tones of his earlier speech to the Madrid Conference on Human Rights in 1980.

. . . The Conference on Security and Cooperation in Europe (CSCE) has taken an extraordinary step forward in strengthening the human dimension portion of its responsibilities. The Copenhagen Concluding Document will be regarded by our successors as a major contribution to an historic process which is moving the peoples of our countries toward a period of increased security, stability, human dignity, and peace.

. . . The Helsinki Final Act has again demonstrated its enduring qualities. What we have produced here . . . represents, I believe, the most significant advance in the Helsinki process since the agreement itself came into being. . . . We have now clothed our values in a political structure and framework—that of democracy and the rule of law.

. . . The democratic revolution we are dramatically experiencing in Europe has been a triumph of the human spirit. It is a vindication of the values that have animated this process. . . .

What we have done here is to link the human dimension of CSCE to the process of democracy-building. That is why we have emphasized the rule of law. For it is only under the rule of law and a constitutional regime of liberties that human dignity can be preserved and democratic consolidation take place.

That is why we have emphasized the importance of free elections, the role of independent political parties, and the importance of the international observers in the electoral process. An orderly, free, open and regular process of testing the people's will is essential if governments are to have legitimate and effective authority to pursue the common good.

That is why we have emphasized constitutional and legal protection for the rights of minorities. Only when those safeguards are in place can the politics of persuasion replace the politics of coercion, fear, and intolerance. . . .

A secure peace, within and among nations, can only be built on the foundation of the institutions of freedom which protect and develop the inherent dignity and individual worth of every human being. It is peace with liberty that we seek, and it is that peace which the Helsinki process has striven to attain.

The Helsinki process has entered a new phase. Democracy-building, we know, is a never-ending task. . . .

No country can be secure in isolation. We cannot achieve unilateral security by withdrawing from the world, or seeking national impregnability. Peace, freedom, and security require that we learn to accept, in each of our countries, a mutual responsibility for the security and dignity of peoples in other countries. We cannot escape from one another. We are bound together in an equation that makes the security of each of us dependent on the security of the others.

. . . We have come to understand, perhaps even more clearly than was understood by our predecessors at Helsinki in 1975, that the security dimension of CSCE and the human dimension of CSCE are mutually reinforcing. They are, in fact, two aspects of our common quest for peace-with-freedom and security.

This past year, we suffered a profound loss in the death of one of the true heroes of our century, Dr. Andrey Sakharov of the Soviet Union. In the 1975 Nobel Peace Prize speech which he was not permitted to deliver in person, Andrey Sakharov said this: "I am convinced that international trust, mutual understanding, disarmament, and international security are inconceivable without an open society with freedom of information, freedom of conscience, the right to publish, and the right to travel and choose the country in which one wishes to live."

We have, since 1975, made great strides toward realizing the kind of Europe that Andrey Sakharov envisioned. Copenhagen has added a major dimension to that forward movement, perhaps the most fundamental since 1975. There is more work to do, greater effort to make. We look ahead to our Moscow meeting in September 1991 as a waystation toward fulfilling our future responsibilities. . . .

When we are growing up . . . we are taught not be afraid of the dark. In this moment of history, so pregnant with hope and promise of a free and decent tomorrow, I respectfully suggest that we must not be afraid of the light—and of where the light can take us. . . .

Epilogue

At the beginning of 1990 widespread publicity about Gorbachev's liberalization policies fueled speculation that the Soviet Union may have turned the corner politically toward a Western-style democracy. Optimists surmised that the Jewish Question, swept up in the tide of change, was moving toward favorable resolution.

There is no doubt that *glasnost* was beneficial for many Soviet Jews, as it was for the Soviet people in general. For the first time in Soviet history, political disagreement without fear of immediate arrest or detention became possible. Furthermore, most political and religious prisoners were released; censorship in the cultural, literary, and intellectual arenas was softened; tolerance of religious practice was increased, marked, for example, by Gorbachev's eye-catching meeting with Pope John Paul II on December 1, 1989, and the establishment of official ties (called "prediplomatic relations") with the Vatican in March 1990; most restrictions on emigration and tourism abroad were removed; initial steps toward a rule of law were taken; and discussion of human rights concerns by Soviet officials in both domestic and international forums had become commonplace.

Yet *glasnost* had its limits. A Supreme Soviet decree of April 8, 1989, did not revoke the notorious Articles 70 and 190-1, but only reworded them to make it a crime to "discredit" Soviet officials or organizations. Furthermore, there were still some political prisoners; psychiatric abuse still occurred, and significant positive changes in the human rights and civil liberties areas were still tenuous because they lacked stabilization and staying power from supportive legislation.

Official anti-Semitism has eased significantly since 1987. Improvements for Soviet Jews certainly have been impressive. These include a sharp increase in Jewish emigration and permission to travel to and from

Israel and the West for visits; debate on elimination of the nationality requirement on the internal passport;[1] allowance of classes in Yiddish and Hebrew, where students learn about Jewish religion, culture, and history; proliferation of Jewish cultural associations; circulation of numerous *samizdat* publications;[2] open sale on the street of Jewish newspapers, published both by Jews themselves and the state (e.g., *Vestnik evreiskoi sovetskoi kultury (VESK)*, or *Herald of Soviet Jewish Culture*); establishment of the Rabbi Adin Steinsaltz *yeshiva* in Moscow, which by May 1990 was training twenty full-time rabbinic students; creation of the Cantorial Institute attached to the Choral Synagogue in Moscow, which started with about ten students; allowance of the *Machanaim* group, whose members emigrate to Israel, study at leading rabbinical colleges, and then return to the U.S.S.R. to train Jews as teachers, community leaders, and rabbis;[3] opening of the Solomon Mikhoels Jewish cultural center in Moscow; importation of kosher food, Bibles, and books on Judaism; the first public Judaica books exhibition, which took place in Moscow in late February 1990; establishment of troupes in the performing arts, such as the Mazel Tov Theater in Kiev in 1989; permission for Jews to learn *schechita* (kosher slaughtering of animals) and circumcision in the United States;[4] authorization for Soviet Jewish activists to lobby for their rights at the Paris Conference on the Human Dimension (CHD) in May 1989 and the next follow-up CHD in Copenhagen in June 1990;[5] progress toward elimination of "blank spots" in Soviet Jewish history; attraction of Jewish support by the Ukrainian nationalist movement *RUKH* (the People's Movement for *Perebudova,* Ukrainian for *perestroika*), which has publicly condemned anti-Semitism;[6] and approval for Soviet Jews to have contacts with their co-religionists both inside[7] and outside the Soviet Union.

On December 21, 1989, a Congress with about 700 Jews representing 204 Soviet Jewish organizations and communities from across the U.S.S.R. and an estimated hundred visitors from the West including former refusenik leaders Iosif Begun and Vladimir Slepak met in Moscow's Central Cinema. This Congress established a *Va'ad* (Hebrew "committee"). Its three elected co-presidents were Mikhail Chlenov, president of the Moscow Jewish Cultural Association; Dr. Samuel Zilberg of Riga, co-chair of the Latvian Jewish Cultural Society; and Joseph Zissek, chair of the Public Fund for Development of Jewish Culture in the Ukraine. The Congress's main organizational goal was to establish an open group that would coordinate activities of Soviet Jews. Operationally, according to Leonid Stonov, head of the Jewish Legal Seminar, the *Va'ad* would "outline a strategy for Jewish life in the Soviet Union, stimulate a revival of religious and cultural traditions, and above all, restore to Soviet Jews a sense of dignity and self-assurance."[8] Some of the most important issues the Congress discussed at its inaugural meeting were growing anti-Semitism in the U.S.S.R., new opportunities for Jewish cultural and religious practice, repatriation, and strengthening of ties with Israel.[9]

By early 1990 Gorbachev was allowing Jews to leave in record-smashing numbers. Indeed, Sharansky even was predicting that all refuseniks would emigrate by the end of the year.[10] Yet official liberalization policy toward Soviet Jews was not unbounded. For example, there were still refuseniks, such as Boris Kelman of Leningrad (refused on grounds of "secrecy"),[11] and still Jewish prisoners of conscience, such as Michael Kazachkov, who was convicted of treason in 1975 for trying to enlist the support of a U.S. consular official to emigrate and sentenced to fifteen years in prison; three more were added for "hooliganism" because Kazachkov protested by a hunger strike.[12] Moreover, the Anti-Zionist Committee of the Soviet Public was still active; the Soviets had made no effort to work for the repeal of the Zionism equals Racism UN Resolution which they sponsored in 1975; discrimination against Jews in employment and higher education was still rampant; and Soviet Jews still could not feel "at home" in the synagogues where they saw the few rabbis as tainted for their long-time collaboration with the state.[13] And when Sakharov died on December 14, 1989, the authorities denied a visa to some former Jewish activists like Sharansky who wanted to attend the funeral.

Yet Gorbachev has also tried to induce Soviet Jews to remain in the U.S.S.R. by holding out prospects of unprecedented religious freedom. His success will be determined in large part by whether he forcefully, publicly, and convincingly condemns growing anti-Semitism in the U.S.S.R., as called for by the *Va'ad.* The *Va'ad* also demanded "rehabilitation" of the word 'Zionism' which for so many years the authorities had used to vilify Soviet Jews. According to Chlenov, Kremlin leaders do not seem to understand that anti-Semitism has its own deep roots in Soviet society and that it is not, as they claim, just part of the overall tension among Soviet nationalities. This official position is reflective, for example, of the Kremlin's response to the massacre at Babi Yar during World War II, which was that all Soviet citizens alike were victims of fascism. Thus even when memorials were finally erected there (the last one inscribed in Yiddish in 1989), there was no mention of the fact that Nazi forces and Ukrainian sympathizers singled out Jews for slaughter.

By the late 1980s, Jews had become alarmed over the spurt of popular anti-Semitism. Although official anti-Semitism, on the whole, had decreased, the dramatic rise in grass-roots anti-Semitism caused ripples of fear to spread through Jewish families and institutions. How and why did this happen?

Under *glasnost*, Soviet authorities encouraged citizens to speak their minds on wide-ranging issues. One result is that grass-roots anti-Semitism, heretofore kept somewhat in check by the regime, became much more open. In the first few months of 1988, vandalism of Jewish grave sites in Moscow, Leningrad, and other cities took place; warnings to citizens of Leningrad not to rent summer houses to Jews were issued; demonstrations on Leningrad's Nevsky Prospect (the main street) demanding expulsion from the country of Soviet Jews occurred; and placards with swastikas linked with Stars of David and with an inscription reminiscent of tsarist days—"Hit the Jews to Save Russia"—were displayed in Moscow and other Soviet cities.

Soviet Jews were also fearful that opponents of *perestroika* might stage anti-Semitic incidents to make Gorbachev look bad or blame them directly for the continuing failure of the Soviet economy. On March 13, 1988, *Sovetskaya Rossiya* published a letter to the editor supposedly written by Nina Andreyeva, a teacher at the Leningrad Institute of Technology. This letter, entitled "Polemics: "I Cannot Forsake Principles," criticized *perestroika* in blunt, striking terms. It contained a sweeping indictment of a litany of "evils" in Soviet society such as "God-seeking liberal socialism" and "ideological omnivorousness." It attacked liberal intellectuals, particularly Jewish writers such as novelist Anatoly Rybakov and playwright Mikhail Shatrov, for their unbridled anti-Stalinism. It also resurrected traditional anti-Semitic canards such as Trotsky's Jewishness, "militant cosmopolitanism" and ungrateful, disloyal refuseniks who shamelessly used their benefits from the Soviet educational system to help "special services" in the West. Only three weeks later did a top party official respond to these stinging criticisms of *perestroika*. On April

5, Alexander Yakovlev wrote a long rebuttal in *Pravda,* though it skirted the anti-Semitic references.

Soviet Jewish activists felt they should publicize the anti-Semitic dimension of the anti-*perestroika* attacks. In a letter to party officials in the spring of 1988, refuseniks Yuli Kosharovsky, Roald Zelichonok, Vladimir Kislik and others warned that "the scope of recent anti-Semitism makes us suspect that anti-Semitic groups must have the support of top-level and powerful elements who are fanning the flames of Judaeophobia in order to discredit *perestroika* and to destabilize the political situation." Soviet minister of internal affairs Alexander Vlasov, referring to this possibility at a press conference in May 1988 (on the eve of the Moscow summit), stated that rumors of pogroms against Jews "were designed to cause panic and incite a revolt against the current reforms and democratization in the country."[14]

Soviet Jews nonetheless began to be blamed as scapegoats for the failures of *perestroika.* During these new times of extreme economic privation, especially food shortages, Jews, as usual, became easy marks. Complaints like "there's no butter because the kikes took it all to Israel" could be heard increasingly in long food lines where frustrated, angry consumers fell back on attacking familiar targets. Moreover, as some Soviet citizens, including Jews, succeeded in new private or "cooperative" enterprises, the less well off began calling them "profiteers" and "exploiters." This is reminiscent of the accusations in the late 1920s and early 1930s by poor farmers against the Kulaks who, largely through initiative, risk-taking, and hard work, had prospered. The Kulaks soon paid for their newly acquired wealth with the loss of their farms and even their lives. Evidently when all people are poor, suffering seems more bearable. But when some persons prosper and most do not, then the least successful blame those better off for their woes. This is what radical Soviet economic reformer Nikolai Shmelyov calls the syndrome of "equal poverty for all" and what Hedrick Smith in *The New Russians* (New York: Random House, 1990) calls "the culture of envy."

Soviet Jews also have been victims of Gorbachev's increasingly liberal emigration policy. The same arguments for discrimination in jobs and education that were heard in the 1970s, when large numbers of Soviet Jews emigrated, are being heard again. "Because you people are leaving, why should we award you places in our universities, or why do you need a promotion in work?"

By the late 1980s, Soviet Jews also began to be victimized by increased tension among Soviet nationalities. In Uzbekistan, for example, one slogan is "Tartars to Kazan, Russians to Ryazan, we'll deal with the Jews ourselves." In Moldavia, a nationalist slogan reads "We'll drown the Jews in Russian blood." In Azerbaijan, Azeri nationalists reportedly had become increasingly hostile toward Jews. Slogans seen in Baku read: "We give the Armenians one year, the Russians three years, the Jews five years." Moslem nationalists also exhorted Jews to join them in their fight against Armenians, arguing: "We gave you homes and jobs. Now it's time to repay us." Nathan V. Yeremeyev, a Jew who fled Baku in January 1990 with his family, told this incident to a reporter: "A friend of mine was approached by a gang of Azerbaijanis. He said he wasn't Armenian, and they said, 'but you are Jewish, right? So we will beat you for the Arabs.' "[15] And perhaps most frightening were calls by anti-Semitic Russian nationalist groups for "de-Zionification" of the country.

Soviet Jews have been driven to emigration by fear of rapidly growing anti-Semitic organizations, left uncurbed by the authorities. They are especially worried over the growth of right wing groups like *Pamyat*, which have conducted anti-Semitic demonstrations, distributed anti-Semitic literature, and tried to whip up old-fashioned popular anti-Semitism. *Pamyat* has blamed Jews for undermining "pure" Russian culture, for their fathering (from the pen of Marx and Trotsky) of communism, for their supposedly key role in the Bolshevik Revolution and the Stalinist terror that followed (Jews are believed by some nationalists to have manipulated Stalin for their own selfish ends); and for a slew of current problems, including the sorry state of the Soviet economy and the nuclear disaster at Chernobyl. To more readily identify Jewish targets, *Pamyat*'s leaders reportedly began requiring prospective members to furnish the names and addresses of at least four Jews.

By late 1989 and early 1990, *Pamyat* had become increasingly open and bold in its anti-Semitic slogans and activities. In the fall of 1989, they held a rally in Red Square. It was unusual then for a rally of any sort to take place there. Moreover, police did not interfere as members broadcast their inflammatory charges against the "Jewish-Freemason conspiracy" and other "dark forces" they deemed hostile to Russia. Then on January 18, a group of twenty to thirty *Pamyat* members and other "Russian patriots" interrupted a meeting of the April Committee, a liberal writers group in Moscow with Jewish and non-Jewish members.

The intruders led by Konstantin Smirnov-Ostashvili, used taunts, curses, and threats, such as "Bastards! Yid-Masons! Get the hell out of here! We declare this our own rally! Next time we'll come here with assault rifles!"[16] Soviet authorities again did nothing to prevent this incident from occurring. A few weeks later in Leningrad, members of *Pamyat* and other nationalist groups reportedly shouted anti-Semitic slogans and threats against Jews outside a Metro station, again with no interference from the authorities.

Officially the Kremlin opposed *Pamyat.* In February 1990, Soviet prosecutors even started criminal proceedings against this organization for "inciting national and racial hatred and strife."[17] Finally on October 12, 1990, a three-judge tribunal convicted Ostashvili for inciting hatred against Jews and sentenced him to two years in a labor camp. Until this landmark decision, *Pamyat*'s activities had continued unimpeded and unpunished, thus presumably with the acquiescence of at least some of the highest authorities. This verdict was a milestone, for as Abraham Foxman, U.S. national director of the Anti-Defamation League of B'nai B'rith, noted, this was the first time the Kremlin had sent a clear signal that it would not tolerate anti-Semitism.

In the winter of 1989/1990 *Pamyat* and other "patriotic" organizations began spreading rumors of an impending pogrom that would take place on May 5, 1990. This was both Karl Marx's birthday and St. George's Day, which celebrated the patron saint of the Russian Orthodox Church. Luckily this date passed without pogroms. Yet though Jews suffered no physical harm then, they became psychological victims of the crescendo of taunts, insults, and accusations. Jews began suffering from anxiety, intimidation, and fear for their safety and life. This fear soon became the driving force behind the latest surge of Jewish emigration—mostly to Israel. In general, these new emigrants are very highly assimilated. They are not Zionists, they do not speak Hebrew, and they do not practice Judaism. What they have in common is expectation of imminent danger. As *The Economist* noted, by the end of 1989 there was "a special air of urgency, almost panic, about the Jewish exodus," with many "beginning to talk not just of emigration, but of 'evacuation.' "[18] Some Jewish leaders in the West, comparing the situation in the U.S.S.R. in 1990 to that in Nazi Germany prior to World War II, even began calling for major rescue efforts to get the Jews out before time ran out.[19]

Glasnost, therefore, while presenting opportunities for improved conditions for Soviet Jews, was also fraught with danger. *Glasnost* is not a policy of humanitarianism but a tool of *perestroika.* If *perestroika* continues to falter, or if the anti-Gorbachev forces win out, even darker days for Soviet Jews could return. This feeling led many Soviet Jews to doubt that the officially sanctioned improvements they were seeing would last, and it fueled their desire to leave the country as quickly as possible—while they could.

Regardless of what happens with *perestroika,* deep-seated popular anti-Semitism will remain. How the Kremlin handles this grass-roots phenomenon, and how it deals itself with anti-Semitism, will be determined in large measure by its perception of the persistence and determination of Soviet Jewish activists, the course of Soviet–Israeli relations, and pressure by the United States government and Soviet Jewry advocacy groups in the West.

Soviet Jewish activists have pressed the limits of *glasnost* for their right to emigrate, practice Judaism, and be safe from anti-Semitism. In the 1970s, most looked to emigration for their salvation. When Soviet authorities virtually shut down emigration in the early and mid-1980s, some Soviet Jews turned toward "internal emigration." In defiance of harsh repression by the regime, they concentrated more on studying Hebrew, Jewish culture, traditions, and religion. Unlike their predecessors of the late 1960s and 1970s, who were mainly secular Jews with little knowledge of their religion, many Jewish activists of the 1980s became orthodox practitioners. A danger then arose that a cleavage might develop between these two groups.[20]

In 1987 there was a significant increase in Jewish emigration. Although many longtime refuseniks finally were allowed to go, many had to remain. In July of that year, Soviet authorities decided to let Jews emigrate to any country for purposes of family reunification. This meant disregarding provisions of the new emigration law of January 1987 and putting aside any previous objection that Soviet Jews with visas from Israel were going elsewhere, especially the United States.

Israel complicated the emigration-destination issue by trying new tactics to reduce "dropouts," who during the 1980s averaged more than 80 percent. Israel was very much concerned about "losing" so many potential immigrants. In early 1988, Israel indicated that the Dutch embassy in Moscow, which had represented her interests in the U.S.S.R. since the Kremlin severed relations with Israel after the 1967 war, would no longer issue Israeli visas. The embassy had been issuing these visas to Jews who would travel to Vienna. There they would decide whether to travel on to Israel or another country. In June 1988, Israel reportedly decided to issue visas only for direct flights to Tel Aviv through Bucharest, the capital of Romania and the only Communist state then with full diplomatic relations with Israel. The Soviet Union, in turn, supposedly had agreed to this arrangement. Though some Soviet Jews did fly to Israel through Romania, later that year Israel suspended this new approach. It pulled back, seemingly because of opposition from the Netherlands, the United States, and some Soviet Jewry advocacy groups in the West who argued strongly that Soviet Jews should have complete freedom to choose their country of destination.[21]

The proposed change in the Israeli visa policy for Soviet Jews heated up the debate over "dropouts" between Israel and the United States. At first, the U.S. State Department's Bureau of Human Rights and Humanitarian Affairs recommended that Washington modify its refugee procedures to allow Soviet Jews who go to Israel the right of early immigration into the United States. The White House, lobbied by the Bureau of Near Eastern and South Asian Affairs, blocked this plan, fearing it might further strain U.S.–Israeli relations. At that point the U.S. was continuing to grant Soviet Jews refugee status without their having to demonstrate a "well-founded fear of persecution." This exempted them from immigration quotas and other immigration restrictions or qualifications, such as showing a guarantee of financial support from relatives or friends in the U.S. before being able to obtain a visa.

In September 1988, in a surprise move that stunned Soviet Jews planning to emigrate to the United States, Washington stopped giving visas and refugee status to some Soviet emigrants, a practice that until then had been virtually automatic. Between September 1988 and September 1989, 5430 Soviet Jews (19 percent of the 28,767 who applied) were denied admission to the United States as refugees.[22] According to Philip A. Saperia, assistant executive vice president of the Hebrew Immigrant Aid Society (HIAS), this policy caused "panic" among Soviet Jews inside the U.S. and the U.S.S.R. Saperia added with exasperation: "We don't know how long the Soviet Union will have a liberal emigration policy for Soviet Jews. It could change at any time. This is a window of opportunity. We have to get them out while we have the chance."[23]

On October 1, 1989, the Bush administration put into practice a new policy on admitting Soviet emigres. For a long time Washington had chastised Moscow for restricting free emigration. Ironically, now it looked like Washington would do most of the restricting—of immigration. Before this date, it usually took several months to process Soviet Jews waiting in Vienna and then Rome. Yet after October 1, Soviet Jews wanting to go to the United States had to apply in the U.S. embassy in Moscow, where they would then be screened to see whether they qualified to enter as refugees.[24] Those who qualified could fly directly to the United States from Moscow. Moreover, the U.S. imposed a ceiling of 50,000 Soviet Jewish refugees per year, about two-fifths of Washington's entire annual immigration quota. According to the State Department, this new policy was made largely for financial reasons (the cost of each refugee is approximately $7000). It said that the U.S. could no longer absorb the cost of an unlimited influx of Soviet Jews, especially when immigration figures were increasingly swollen by applicants from other areas of the world. The cost for Soviet emigres waiting in Italy for permission to enter the United States was estimated at about $34 million in fiscal year 1988. Princeton N. Lyman, the new director of the refugee programs at the State Department, concluded simply that "We are short of money." Washington also doubted that under *glasnost* most Soviet Jews were still political or religious refugees.[25]

These policy changes presented several major problems. Under the Refugee Act of 1980, the president had the authority to decide how many refugees were admissible each year. The Bush administration also argued that this act required review of each application, to be judged on its own merits. Soviet Jewry advocates in the U.S. assailed the new policy. The NCSJ and UCSJ, for example, argued that the 1980 law did not place the burden on applicants to prove they themselves were persecuted; they just had to prove they had a "well-founded fear of persecution." All Soviet Jews, they maintained, clearly met this test. David Harris, spokesman for the American Jewish Committee, feared that the State Department's policy change would bring the country back to the situation of the 1930s when Jews from Nazi Germany faced severe restrictions on immigration to the United States. According to Harris, the United States should "keep its door open as a sort of expiation to the closed doors of 45 years earlier."[26] Some congressional opposition was also voiced. "We have a great American ideal of an open door for refugees," lamented Representative Charles E. Schumer (D-N.Y.), "but then we come up against the hard reality of cold cash."[27] Boris Levin was one Soviet emigrant of an estimated 30,000 caught in the "pipeline" during the summer of 1989. Waiting in Ladispoli (just outside Rome) as "a man without a country" for permission to enter the United States, he summed up the frustrations of Soviet Jews in a similar situation: "The American government fought for us to leave. It's very difficult for us to understand why America is now rejecting us."[28]

Israel has been the beneficiary of the new Bush policy. The Israeli government welcomed "spillovers" from the growing numbers of Soviet Jewish emigrants.[29] Many Israelis, however, became chagrined at the increasing influx of Soviet Jews who competed with them for scarce housing, jobs, and government resources. In 1989, only 16.9 percent of Soviet Jewish emigrants went to Israel. In 1990, over 186,000 Jews left the U.S.S.R. Most went to Israel because they could not go elsewhere, particularly to the United States.[30] According to a forecast made by Leonid Stonov in September 1990, by 1993 Israel could expect to receive as many as a million Soviet Jews.

By early 1990 Arab leaders were decrying the latest influx of Soviet Jews to Israel, condemning especially alleged Israeli government plans to settle many of them in the territories captured in the 1967 war. On January 27, 1990, for example, Saudi Arabia warned: "If Palestine is not turned into an inferno by escalation of the military struggle in order to deter the Russian immigrants, then the Jews in Palestine will number over 8 million by the beginning of the 21st century." Then on February 5, 1990, Radio al-Quds in Damascus blared: "Here we witness the tens of thousands of Soviet Jews descending upon our Holy Land, dressed in military uniforms in order to oppress our Arab people. . . . The Islamic Jihad is lying in wait for you. . . . We tell the Zionists in Palestine and everyone else: we will fight you, women, children, and the elderly . . . the armed struggle is our road to Palestine." Yasir Arafat, on French television, even claimed that Soviet Jews were "being kidnapped by Israel."[31] And in March, the Islamic Jihad for the Liberation of Palestine, a Muslim extremist group that claims to hold American hostages, sent a threatening statement to the *An Nahar* newspaper. It warned: "Our people will not remain idle in the face of this conspiracy. We will start taking the appropriate measures to prevent the arrival of the Soviets. . . . All airports, airlines, planes and offices which help in their transport will be a direct target for us."[32] On July 4, according to a Reuters report, the PLO warned that the emigration of Soviet Jews to Israel could spark a new Middle East war. In a statement made in Tunis but issued in Helsinki as a warning against Finland's decision to allow transit flights of Soviet Jews to Israel, the PLO complained that "organized immigration waves" were an aggression against the Palestinians and reinforced Israeli occupation of Palestinian territories.[33]

Earlier in 1990, Arab officials had warned other countries against providing transit flights of Soviet Jews to Israel. In May, Hungary's state-owned airline, Malev, bowing to Arab pressure and threats of sabotage, announced that it would suspend transit service. Yet at the same time, other former Communist states in East Europe, notably Poland and the German Democratic Republic, began to assist Soviet Jews. Poland, which in February had resumed diplomatic relations with Israel after twenty-three years, announced it would provide charter service for Soviet Jews flying to Israel. Polish officials then announced strengthening of their special anti-terrorist unit to protect their flights from Warsaw Airport. And the German Democratic Republic, then prepared to accept its share of responsibility for the Holocaust and to improve ties with Israel, began quietly welcoming several hundred Soviet Jews. The mass influx of Soviet Jews to Israel, however, remained the major international problem.

Arab states and organizations were not alone in criticizing Israel for preparing to settle some Soviet immigrants in the territories. In January 1990, Soviet deputy foreign minister Yuli Vorontsov warned that settlement of Soviet refugees in the territories could force Moscow to restrict Jewish emigration. And Grigory Olhovikov, head of a Soviet economic delegation then visiting Israel, asked for Israeli assurances that Soviet Jewish immigrants would not settle in the territories. In late April, Dr. Yuri Reshetov told an official of the Zionist Organization of America who visited the U.S.S.R. that the Kremlin might treat Soviet Jews who settled in the territories as war criminals if they returned to the U.S.S.R. as tourists.[34] Earlier, on March 1, Secretary of State James Baker had stated at a congressional hearing that any additional Israeli settlements in Gaza or the West Bank would be "an obstacle to peace." Baker also stressed that the U.S. did not want money it was sending to Israel for absorption of Soviet Jews to be used in the territories. Even some American Jewish groups, such as the National Jewish Community Relations

Advisory Council (NJCRAC) adopted a narrowly passed resolution in February stating that building homes for Soviet Jewish settlers in the West Bank and the Gaza Strip "can only increase tensions between Israelis and Palestinians living there."[35] The shaky coalition government in Israel, however, seemed determined to stick to its policy of allowing all immigrants to choose where they live. By April 1990 only about 1 percent of Soviet Jewish immigrants had chosen to live in the territories (excluding East Jerusalem and the Golan Heights). Nevertheless, by then this issue had become a serious source of controversy that threatened Israeli relations with Moscow, Washington, and the American Jewish community. Moreover, it endangered the already precarious prospects for peace between Israel and her Arab neighbors. On June 24, Israeli Housing Minister Ariel Sharon, trying to defuse this hot issue, stated that the Israeli government would not aim to settle Soviet Jews in the West Bank or the Gaza Strip.[36] Caution over settlement surely was wise.

In the past, Israel was misguided when it tried to force the issue of where Soviet Jews could emigrate. Soviet Jews, like all Soviet citizens, should be able to emigrate anywhere they please, to whatever country will accept them, because this is their fundamental right. The only legitimate restriction on otherwise free emigration is national security, but only, as we have seen, within very narrow limits.

Without official recognition of this right to emigrate, Soviet citizens can indefinitely be subject to the arbitrariness and capriciousness of Soviet authorities. One day the obstacle to emigration may be a "diploma tax" or the requirement of a "first-degree" relative in Israel, and another day it may be fear of a "brain drain" or possession of "state secrets." In early 1988, the Kremlin erected still another barrier to emigration. Families with sons between the ages of fifteen and twenty-seven were informed that they could not apply to emigrate before their sons had completed their army service. Then they would have to wait another three years. Furthermore, students who had not fulfilled their military obligation but who had already completed their university studies would have to work for three years following graduation, and then spend two years in the army and another three working for the state.

If the basic right to emigrate is not codified in Soviet law and honored, the regime, in effect, can continue to regard emigration as a privilege it grants. It will permit emigration only so long as it suits its interest. Historically, the Kremlin used emigration as a weapon of control and punishment. It did not release Jews as an act of good will; rather it released them *against* its will. Soviet Jews did not want to leave the marvelous Soviet system, Kremlin leaders maintained; rather they were pulled by family reunification or lured by Zionist propaganda.

Soviet Jews understand that the regime grants visas to a large extent because of pressure from inside and outside the Soviet Union. Soviet Jewish activists realize the necessity of maintaining their fortitude, tenacity, and indomitable spirit. Yet they also understand that they cannot achieve their goal alone. In the twenty-four year period 1967–1990, there were peaks and valleys in Soviet Jewish emigration. Soviet authorities opened and closed the spigot in response to perceived internal and external needs and interests.

By the late 1980s, Soviet Jews believed that there was an increased causal relationship between Soviet Jewish emigration and the state of Soviet–Israeli relations. They hoped that the warming of Soviet–Israeli relations that began under Gorbachev would mean increased Jewish emigration and a more liberal official attitude toward the practice of Judaism inside the U.S.S.R.

From the 1967 war until Gorbachev's assumption of power in 1985, Soviet–Israeli relations were in a deep freeze. When Gorbachev realized that Soviet influence in the Middle East was at a low point and Soviet policy there at a dead end, he decided to change it. One possibility was to improve relations with Israel.[37] In July 1985, Soviet and Israeli ambassadors to France met in a private residence to discuss the possibility of resumption of Soviet relations with Israel, Soviet Jewish emigration to Israel, and the future of land Israel acquired in the 1967 war. In 1987 the Soviet Union began to significantly soften its diplomatic posture toward Israel. Early in the year, low-level contacts were established between Israel and several East European states, including Poland, Hungary, and Bulgaria. In July a Soviet delegation spent three months in Israel, officially to inspect Russian church properties. In 1988 Moscow greatly increased the number of Soviet Jews allowed to visit their relatives in Israel. According to the Israeli newspaper *Maariv,* more than 1700 Soviet Jewish tourists visited Israel in the first five months of 1988, compared to 183 in all of 1987. Also in 1988, the Soviet Union and Israel established consulate offices. First a Soviet delegation went to Israel, and then, in May, Moscow decided to offer visas to an Israeli consular delegation to Moscow—officially to check its representation by the Dutch embassy. In July, six Israeli diplomats opened a consulate office in the Soviet capital.

During the first few months of 1988, Soviet leaders also indicated their willingness to modify preconditions for resumption of higher-level diplomatic relations with Israel. No longer did Moscow insist that Israel first give up all land seized in the 1967 war. Nor did it demand the establishment of a Palestinian state. Instead Moscow called on Israel to participate in an international peace conference where the Soviet Union presumably could play a major role and all key issues could be discussed.[38] Israel expressed willingness to talk with the Soviet Union, but not at an international conference. Israel also continued seeking a much more liberal emigration policy for Soviet Jews and diplomatic recognition by Moscow.

Soviet–Israeli relations even benefited in 1988 from chance happenings. The Kremlin thanked Israel for quickly sending back several Soviet criminals who had hijacked a plane to Israel and for the assistance team it sent to Armenia after the devastating earthquake there.[39] Yet official Kremlin praise for Israel's role in this disaster was denounced inside the U.S.S.R. by the Committee Against Restoration of Diplomatic Relations with Israel as "an immoral attempt to use tragedy for political purposes." This committee reportedly has close ties to *Pamyat* and other "public" groups such as the Soviet Anti-Zionist Committee.[40] This divergent opinion on Israel's role in the earthquake typifies how the Kremlin had offered praise of Israel with one hand but with the other condoned "unofficial" condemnation and scorn.

Soviet Jews on the whole were pleased by developing Soviet–Israeli cultural and athletic exchanges and closer connections with worldwide organizations. In January 1989, for example, an Israeli basketball team played a Soviet team inside the Soviet Union. Since the Soviet Union had severed diplomatic relations with Israel in 1967, these teams had met several times on courts outside their countries. Soviet Jews attended this game, which was televised, and felt free to show their Jewishness by wearing *yarmulkes* (skullcaps), singing Hebrew songs, and rooting hard. There were no anti-Jewish incidents or harassments, either during or after the game, as had previously been the case when Israeli athletes played in the U.S.S.R. Also in 1989, thirty-eight Jewish leaders in Moscow founded the first B'nai B'rith chapter in the Soviet Union. During negotiations for this chapter, Jewish leaders pressed Soviet authorities on such issues as the fate of Raoul Wallenberg, denials of visas to Soviet Jews for reasons of "state secrets," and relaxation of cultural restrictions against Soviet Jews, particularly the teaching of Hebrew.[41] In July 1989, Soviet–Israeli relations continued their thaw when Israel welcomed Soviet Jewish athletes to participate in its Maccabiah games[42] and when Israel and the Soviet Union announced plans to exchange press missions. In August, eight Jewish university graduates from the U.S.S.R. went to Israel to participate in the "Russian Orange" Project. They were adopted by kibbutz families, toured Israel, and attended seminars—with the supposed aim of enticing them to emigrate to Israel.[43] In September, the U.S.S.R. and Israel announced their decision to exchange trade offices for the first time since 1967.[44] Then in October 1989, the Soviet Union voted to abstain instead of to expel Israel from the United Nations. The only other time the U.S.S.R. had abstained on this voting issue was in 1982. Every other year it had sided with the Arab states (except Egypt). Ambassador Johanan Bein, Israel's acting permanent representative to the United Nations, called the Kremlin's vote "definitely a move in the right direction," though obviously he would have preferred Moscow to have voted no.[45] Then at the "saltwater" summit in Malta in December, Bush reportedly asked Gorbachev to renew diplomatic relations with Israel. Gorbachev supposedly promised to consider the idea, especially if it was linked with possible U.S. economic aid.[46]

In 1990 there was further significant warming of Soviet–Israeli relations. In January, when Israeli science minister Ezer Weizman met Soviet Foreign Minister Shevardnadze in Moscow, the Kremlin reportedly offered to raise diplomatic relations to the level of chargé d'affaires.[47] Then on September 30, Israeli Foreign Minister David Levy met with Shevardnadze at the United Nations. The ministers agreed that their countries would establish full consular relations and would conduct "an ongoing dialogue to establish peace and security in the Middle East."[48] On December 12, Shevardnadze met with Israeli Prime Minister Yitzhak Shamir in Washington. At a joint Soviet–Israeli press conference, Shamir stated his wish for establishing diplomatic relations: "We have to establish normal diplomatic relations, and we don't see any reason for not establishing them now." But the Soviets were not quite ready to take this final step, for as Shevardnadze said: "We are moving toward relations. A process is evolving in normal fashion." As evidence of warmer relations, both sides seemed to give a little on previous positions. Shamir, wanting to pay back Gorbachev for allowing record numbers of Soviet Jews to emigrate to Israel, publicly urged President Bush to waive the Jackson–Vanik Amendment and said Israel would send boxes of oranges to the Soviet Union. Shamir also said he supported in principle a Soviet proposal for a nuclear free zone in the Middle East.[49] A few days later, in a major policy shift, Vitaly Churkin, the Soviet Foreign Ministry spokesman, stated in Moscow that the Soviet Union no longer attached conditions to full diplomatic relations.[50] This meant that the Soviets would no longer insist that Israel would first have to agree to participate in an international conference on Middle East peace which Moscow wanted to co-chair. Shamir reiterated Israel's refusal to participate in such a conference.

Finally, on December 25 Alexei Tchistiakov presented his credentials as consul-general to Israel. This raised Soviet–Israeli ties to their highest level since Moscow severed diplomatic relations at the end of the Middle East war in 1967. As a condition for restoration of full diplomatic relations, Tchistiakov reiterated Moscow's support for an international conference to discuss peace in the Middle East. At the end of 1990, the confrontation between Iraq and UN coalition forces in the Persian Gulf complicated Soviet–Israeli relations. How this conflict would be resolved would surely affect, to a great degree, all major diplomatic relationships in the Middle East.

Although Soviet–Israeli relations have had some importance for Soviet Jews, Soviet–U.S. relations have had the most influence, especially on Soviet Jewish emigration. After the summit in Washington in December 1987, punctuated by the signing of the INF treaty, and the one in Moscow in May 1988, where Reagan and Gorbachev played to the crowd in Red Square, the United States and the Soviet Union seemed to have moved beyond the détente of the 1970s to a new era of entente.[51] Some observers, no doubt touched by the near-delirium over "Gorbymania" sweeping the Western world, proclaimed an end to the cold war and even history itself. President Reagan withdrew his categorization of the Soviet Union as an "evil empire," and he himself became a cheerleader for *glasnost.* In 1989, President Bush said that the United States backed *perestroika,* and Secretary of State Baker remarked that the two superpowers had moved from confrontation to dialogue to cooperation. This was especially true in the area of human rights.

Beginning in 1986, the United States and the Soviet Union began to develop a new, broader, more constructive dialogue on human rights. Human rights became a regular subject of their negotiations, along with arms control, regional conflicts, and bilateral issues. Working-level negotiations on human rights between U.S. and Soviet advisers improved in pace and tone. There was less name-calling, and both sides stressed their priorities. The Soviet side focused on social and economic rights (such as shelter, health care), which required government to take "positive human rights" action. The U.S. side held that civil liberties or political rights had to come first. Washington thus insisted on "negative human rights," which required that government not interfere, for example, with freedom of speech, religion, and assembly. U.S.–Soviet negotiators began to discuss all these human rights, with each side recognizing it could learn from the other's perspective. The Americans took notice of the Soviet charge, for example, that treatment of the homeless is a shameful violation of human rights. The Soviets, on their part, became willing to acknowledge that their history is marred by gross violations of political rights, and they began to rectify these abuses.

During the Moscow summit of May 1988, the Soviets again showed their customary sensitiveness on the political human rights issue. They called President Reagan's meeting with Soviet dissidents and refuseniks "tactless and not in good taste," and they decried what they termed the U.S.'s "sermonizing" on this issue. President Reagan, despite not wanting to embarrass Gorbachev in his own country (Reagan blamed Soviet bureaucracy for "delays" in issuing exit visas for Soviet Jews), did speak out forcefully for human rights in a speech at Moscow State University. Although the Soviet media did not carry this speech, it did carry the press conference held by the two leaders.

The extraordinary Communist Party Conference of June 1988 generated optimism and greater hopes for Soviet political liberalization. There was a call for political reform as an absolute necessity to achieve the desired results of *perestroika.* There was the sense that most party leaders, including Gorbachev, wanted to put wasteful military ventures like Afghanistan behind them so that they could concentrate on internal political and economic reform. Gorbachev submitted a dazzling blueprint for reform, though it was designed to make Communism work better, not to abolish it. With unprecedented candor and spontaneity, Gorbachev and other political leaders admitted mistakes, but they then issued a challenge for correction. The political atmosphere was charged with excitement, with conservative and liberal delegates getting complaints off their chests and letting their views "hang out." The next month, in a speech before senior foreign ministry and military officials, Foreign Minister Shevardnadze explained: "The image of a state is its attitude toward its own citizens, the respect for their rights and freedoms and recognition of the sovereignty of the individual. . . . We must do a good deal to make certain that the principles of the presumption of innocence, the openness of a court trial, and ensuring the full right to defense becomes deeply rooted."[52]

In January 1989, the successful conclusion of the CSCE Vienna Conference marked a milestone in East–West cooperation over human rights. The Soviets accepted emigration as a basic human right and agreed to the right of signatory countries to question one another's human rights policies. At the first Conference on the Human Dimension, held in Paris in June 1989, the Kremlin went even further toward a rule of law and acceptance of international norms of human rights. Despite these striking advances, President Bush continued to press the Soviets on behalf of Soviet Jews. At the Malta summit in December, once again an American president handed his Soviet counterpart a list of divided families and Jewish refuseniks. Once again, moreover, Soviet Jewry advocacy groups from the United States were on hand to publicize the Soviet Jewry issue and to keep it high on the agenda of the superpower leaders. And at the Washington summit in June 1990, Bush pressed Gorbachev to condemn grass-roots anti-Semitism inside the Soviet Union, to release long-term refuseniks, and to push the Supreme Soviet to enact the long-awaited liberal emigration law. Soviet Jewry advocacy groups were in Washington to exert additional pressure.[53]

With the euphoria associated with the new U.S.–Soviet relationship and calls for a more liberal Soviet political system, many Soviet Jews hoped that the Kremlin would further restrict and even eliminate anti-Semitic practices and policies. They realized, however, that changes they saw were not the result of changed attitudes of Soviet leaders but of changed policy needs and pressure exerted on them by Soviet Jewish activists and supporters both inside and outside the U.S.S.R.

Both before and during the period of *glasnost,* Soviet leaders felt obligated to make concessions even after having made apparently conclusive policy decisions. For example, when the authorities stopped Jewish emigration after the Six-Day War, they told those seeking exit visas that they would have to wait for them until the U.S.S.R. resumed diplomatic relations with Israel. Yet in September 1968, after fourteen months without any Jewish emigration, the Kremlin granted visas to five Soviet Jews. This droplet of Jewish emigration was to become a large wave in the 1970s. The authorities also reversed themselves on other major issues. They softened the sentences of defendants at the Leningrad hijacking trial of 1970; suspended the "diploma tax" on emigrants of 1972; stopped the practice of revocation of academic degrees of refuseniks in the early 1980s; and allowed Jewish emigration to increase substantially beginning in 1987 after having announced a few years earlier, with the formation of the Anti-Zionist Committee of the Soviet Public, that this emigration was essentially over. In 1987–1989, the Kremlin also allowed the emigration of several well-known refuseniks who earlier had been refused until the 1990s, or even told that they would never receive an exit visa. In each reversal, the Kremlin was made to realize that continuation of its policy would be counterproductive to its best interests, especially prospects for Western economic assistance.

It became hard to gauge how many Soviet Jews still wanted to leave now that *glasnost* seemingly was providing them with better opportunities to lead a Jewish life inside the U.S.S.R., at least without being vilified and persecuted by the regime. By early 1989 there was some feeling in Israel that these changes inside the U.S.S.R. would hurt the *aliyah* movement and thus should not be supported, and maybe even resisted. But as Iosif Begun pointed out then, this position was foolish. It missed the basic point, he argued, that "there is no contradiction between establishing Jewish communal life in the Soviet Union and the continuing *aliyah* of Soviet Jews." Begun concluded that "Israelis and Diaspora Jews are two organs of the same body, with the same origins and the same fate. The distinction made between "Israeli" and "Jewish" culture, which is at the root of official policy toward Jews in the U.S.S.R., displays a serious lack of understanding." He thus recommended continuing help to Soviet Jews, whether or not they want to remain in the U.S.S.R.[54]

The United States must also adapt its strategy to the new realities of Soviet Jewish life. It must continue pressing for the right of emigration, yet it must also help those Jews who choose to remain. Serious consideration should be given to adoption of the Slepak Principles of dealing with the Soviet Union. This is a seven-point human rights code written by the Slepak Foundation in Philadelphia, founded by Dr. Alexander Slepak, son of the well-known former refuseniks Maria (Masha) and Vladimir. These principles, modeled after the Sullivan Principles adopted by the United States in 1985 to help combat apartheid in South Africa, would urge U.S. companies to make a "good-faith" effort to refuse participation in joint ventures with Soviet firms which violate human rights such as engaging in racial, religious, or ethnic discrimination.

A House bill urging adoption of the Slepak Principles was introduced in the late spring of 1989 by Representatives John Miller (R-Wash.) and Lawrence Smith (D-Fla.). The Senate version was initiated by Senators John Heinz (R-Pa.) and Dennis DeConcini. Some U.S. companies objected to this bill, arguing that the Slepak Principles would unnecessarily limit investment opportunities. Secretary Baker, testifying before the Senate Foreign Relations Committee, maintained that under *glasnost* this was not the best time to be pressing the Soviets harder on human rights. The AFL–CIO actively supported the Slepak Principles, as did Soviet Jewry advocacy groups such as the UCSJ, which actively tied them to the issue of waiver of Jackson–Vanik. In the words of Micah Naftalin, UCSJ's national director, "For years we've been hearing from those parts of the private sector that we don't need Jackson–Vanik, that there are better ways for the private sector to promote human rights and emigration. . . . It is our sense that the Slepak Principles have the effect of asking the private sector to put their money where their mouth is."[55]

In the years 1987–1990 there was a profound improvement in U.S.–Soviet relations undreamed of earlier in the decade. Soviet Jewish activists should try to keep up these good relations, which over the years have been tied so closely to their fate. They should also follow a multitrack strategy of pushing for codification on the right of emigration; resolving the issues of "poor relatives" and of length of time of visa refusal based on "state secrets"; helping those Soviet Jews who choose to stay, for example by urging the Kremlin to denounce anti-Semitism and allow registration of Jewish organizations such as the *Va'ad;* and nurturing the normalization of Soviet-Israeli relations.

The Soviet Jewish movement for freedom cannot relax. It must redouble its efforts to sustain the positive momentum of the late 1980s. It must continue to press the Kremlin to make further progress on human rights by keeping the Jewish Question in the public limelight. Realistically, it must also recognize the recency, fragility, and possible transitory nature both of this "new era" in Soviet-American affairs and Gorbachev's call for political liberalization within the Soviet Union. Indeed, Gorbachev may not be able to survive in power because of a rapidly deteriorating economy, an explosive nationality crisis, and the possible disintegration of the Soviet Union itself.

The resignation of Shevardnadze on December 20, 1990 caused even more upheaval in the Soviet "political circus." Shevardnadze, an open-minded, forceful advocate of the "new thinking" in Soviet foreign policy and democratization at home, warned that the U.S.S.R. was taking a dangerous turn away from democratic principles and toward authoritarianism and dictatorship. His resignation speech was a verbal slap at Gorbachev, who in previous weeks had turned increasingly toward the KGB and other conservative forces to strengthen his control over the country. It remained to be seen how much of an effect Shevardnadze's resignation would have on all aspects of Soviet life. Surely it pointed out the growing strength of the conservatives. It was also a serious cause for concern for Soviet Jews, who are ever wary of a resurgence of reactionary forces.

By the end of 1990, events inside the Soviet Union were moving at a feverish pace, though more in a swirl than in a single direction. Soviet Jews, like all Soviet citizens, had a great stake in the outcome of the intensified struggle between liberal and conservative forces. Jewish activists could not stand above the fray, for the future of Jewish emigration and Jewish life inside the Soviet Union was in serious question.

Jewish activists must continually reassess their strategy, trying to decide how best to influence reformist elements inside the Kremlin. They probably will hedge by working also with new forces of authority in the republics. Whatever the strategy, the freedom movement must insist that any promises by the Kremlin and the republics be matched by deeds and that progress be genuine and sustained. This will be the challenge for the 1990s.

Notes

1 See "Refuseniks May Now Go," *Moscow News,* December 18, 1988; Ernest Ametisov (member of the Public Commission for International Humanitarian Cooperation and Human Rights under the Soviet Commission for European Security and Cooperation), "The Individual and the Law," ibid., December 11, 1988; and Viktor Kozlov, "My Nationality Is My Business," ibid., October 2, 1988.

2 Among the most important *samizdat* journals are *Problemi otkaza* (*Problems of Refusal*), quarterly; *Bulletin on Refusenik Activities* (including petitions and appeals), bimonthly; *Shalom* (a literary journal emphasizing Jewish cultural life in the USSR); *Leah* (a Jewish almanac published in Leningrad specializing in culture and religion); and *A Jewish Historical Almanac* (published in Moscow). See NEWSBREAK, July 15, 1988.

3 Reuters, "Jewish Teachers Emerge from Soviet Underground," January 16, 1990.

4 "Soviets Permit 2 Jews to Learn Shechita, Circumcision in U.S.," *Jewish Advocate,* September 8, 1988.

5 "Soviet Jews Lobby Abroad," *World Monitor,* Vol. 2, No. 9, September 1989, p. 10.

6 For a discussion of *RUKH,* see Henry Abramson, "Standing up for Ukrainian Jews," *Toronto Globe and Mail,* May 4, 1990, and David S. Broder, "The Sounds in Kiev Have to Do with Democracy," *International Herald Tribune,* June 19, 1990.

7 In the spring of 1989, 200 Jewish religious and cultural activists representing forty Jewish organizations met in Riga, the capital of Latvia, to discuss problems facing Soviet Jews. See "Riga Conference Scores Gains for Soviet Jews," *Jewish Advocate,* June 1, 1989. On November 2–4, Jews from about

twenty Soviet cities attended a Conference on the Problems of Religion in the U.S.S.R., also in the Latvian capital. See NEWSBREAK, October 27, 1989.

8 "Exodus, revised version," *The Economist,* Vol. 313, No. 7634/7635, December 23, 1989, p. 55.

9 See David Landau, "Soviet Jewish Va'ad in Moscow," *Jewish Advocate,* December 28, 1989; and NEWSBREAK, January 5 and 29, 1990.

10 Ruben Vis, "Shcharansky Believes All Refuseniks Can Leave This Year," *Jewish Advocate,* May 24, 1990. Sharansky predicted this in an address on May 18 before the Rotterdam Jewish Community.

11. NEWSBREAK, February 12, 1990.

12 See Helsinki Watch, *News from the USSR,* May 1989, p. 19; Eliot Lister, "A Prisoner's Mother Awaits Good News," *International Herald Tribune,* September 22, 1989; and report by two members of the U.S. Congressional Helsinki Watch Commission, Frank Wolf (R-Va.) and Chris Smith (R-N.J.), "Glasnost or Not, the Old Gulag Is Still in Business," ibid., November 30, 1989.

13 See Nicholas Daniloff, "Soviet Standards on Human Rights," *Boston Globe,* January 13, 1989.

14 NEWSBREAK, June 13, 1988.

15 See Masha Hamilton, "Fearful Jews Flee Azerbaijan, Set Sights on U.S., Israel," *Los Angeles Times,* January 20, 1990.

16 For a discussion of this incident, see Robert Rozhdestvensky, "Pogromists at the Central House of Writers," *Literaturnaya gazeta,* January 24, 1990.

17 AP, "Soviets File Charges Against Pamyat," *International Herald Tribune,* February 22, 1990.

18 *The Economist,* loc. cit.

19 In early 1990, numerous articles were written on the resurgence of popularly based anti-Semitism in the Soviet Union. See, for example, Flora Lewis, "Old Habits Surface in Russia," *International Herald Tribune,* February 28, 1990; Vitalii I. Goldanskii, "Anti-Semitism: The Return of a Russian Nightmare," *Washington Post,* February 18, 1990; William Korey, "A Fear Of Pogroms Haunts Soviet Jews," *New York Times,* January 25, 1990; Joel Brinkley, "Soviet Emigres to Israel Tell of Hate Back Home," *New York*

Times International, February 4, 1990; Karla Goldman, "Pogroms and Perestroika," *World Monitor,* Vol. 3, No. 5, May 1990, pp. 16–19; Irina Ginzburg, "We Russian Jews Fear for Our Lives," *New York Times,* May 5, 1990; and Susan Birnbaum, "Threatened Pogroms Fail to Materialize," *Jewish Advocate,* May 10, 1990.

20 For a good discussion of this issue, see Isi Leibler, "The Future of the Soviet Jewry Movement," *Midstream,* Vol.XXIV, No. 2, February–March 1988, pp. 6–9.

21 John M. Goshko, "Israel Fails to Force Entry on Soviet Jews," *International Herald Tribune,* October 24, 1988.

22 Robert Pear, "U.S. Drafting Plans to Cut Back on Admission of Soviet Jews," *New York Times,* September 3, 1989.

23 Quoted by Robert Pear, "U.S. Bars Some Soviet Jews as Refugees," ibid., December 5, 1988.

24 Soviet Jews could enter the United States under the *parole authority* of the U.S. Attorney General but, unlike refugees, they would get no financial aid and would not necessarily be eligible for U.S. citizenship. See Henrietta Boas, "New Refugee Policy Turns Influx into Trickle," *Jewish Advocate,* October 5, 1989.

25 See Robert Pear, "Why U.S. Closed the Door Halfway on Soviet Jews," *New York Times,* September 24, 1989.

26 Quoted in George Perkovich, "Refugees, Quotas," *Boston Globe,* June 26, 1989.

27 Pear, "Why U.S. Closed the Door Halfway on Soviet Jews," loc. cit.

28 Quoted in Robert Greenberger, "Now That Soviet Jews Are Free to Emigrate, U.S. Is Less Hospitable," *Wall Street Journal,* June 25, 1989.

29 See Aaron Rubinger, "Bush's New Move Is a Boon to Aliyah," *Jewish Advocate,* June 8, 1989.

30 See Joel Brinkley, "Soviet Jews Leave at a Record Pace, Many for Israel," *New York Times,* December 14, 1989, and Meron Benvenisti, "Last Tribe Out of Bondage," *Washington Post,* March 11, 1990.

31 Quoted in "How the Arab Press Views Soviet Jewish Aliyah," *Jewish Advocate,* March 29, 1990. Quotes were compiled and distributed by the Israeli Consulate of Boston, Massachusetts.

32 Quoted by Reuters, "A Jihad Threat to Soviet Jews," *International Herald Tribune,* March 16, 1990.

33 "PLO Warns Over Soviet Emigration," ibid., July 5, 1990.

34 NEWSBREAK, May 11, 1990.

35 JTA, "Settling of Soviets in Territories Decried," *Jewish Advocate,* February 22, 1990.

36 "Israel Relents on Settlement of Soviet Jews," *Washington Post,* June 26, 1990.

37 See Carol Saivetz, " 'New thinking' and Soviet Third World Policy," *Current History,* Vol. 88, No. 540, October 1989, pp. 327–328, and Robert O. Freedman, "Soviet-Israeli Relations," loc. cit.

38 For more on these developments, see Lisa Clayton, "Moscow's Climate of Change . . . and the Danger Clouds," *Jerusalem Post International Edition,* June 11, 1988.

39 See Marina Kiselyova, "Israeli Charity," *Moscow News,* July 2, 1989, and UPI, "Soviet Quake Victims to Be Treated in Israel," *Boston Globe,* June 28, 1989.

40 NEWSBREAK, May 3, 1989.

41 See Michael Parks, "Jewish Organization Opens First Soviet Chapter," *Los Angeles Times,* February 22, 1989.

42 Hugh Orgel, "Maccabiah Games Open with Cheers for First Soviet Team," *Jewish Advocate,* July 6, 1989.

43 Hugh Orgel, "Soviet Students in Israel," ibid. August 3, 1989.

44 Reuters, "Israeli–Soviet Trade Ties Planned," *International Herald Tribune,* September 28, 1989.

45 Quoted in Allison Kaplan, "USSR Abstains in Move to Oust Israel from UN," *Jewish Advocate,* October 19, 1989. See also Jeane Kirkpatrick, "Soviets Shift, so UN Ritual Takes an Interesting Turn," *Atlanta Constitution,* October 22, 1989.

46 Reuters, "Soviet–Israeli Ties: Fruit of Summit?," *International Herald Tribune,* December 6, 1989.

47 "Jewish Teachers Emerge from Soviet Underground," loc. cit.

48 See Allison Kaplan, "Israel and USSR To Establish Consular Relations," *Jewish Advocate,* October 4, 1990.

49. "Shamir Supports Nonnuclear Mideast," *International Herald Tribune,* December 13, 1990; and "Soviets Rebuff Israel on Ties," ibid., December 14, 1990.

50 "Moscow Confirms It No Longer Puts Conditions on Resuming Israeli Ties," ibid., December 17, 1990.

51 The distinction between détente and entente in U.S.–Soviet relations is made very well by Jerry Hough, *Russia and the West, Gorbachev and the Politics of Reform* (New York: Simon & Schuster, 1988), pp. 217–218, 223–224.

52 Quoted in George Shultz, "The Ecology of International Change," *Harvard International Review,* 10th anniversary issue, Fall 1989, p. 10.

53. Howard Rosenberg, "Anti-Semitism as Issue for Bush and Gorbachev," *Jewish Advocate,* May 31, 1990; and JTA, "Soviet Activists Protest at Summit," ibid., June 7, 1990.

54 Iosif Begun, "Helping Soviet Jews Who Stay," ibid., November 9, 1989.

55 See Andrew Silow Carroll, "Congress Pondering Human Rights Hurdles to Trade with the Soviets," ibid., July 27, 1989.

Glossary

Aliyah Hebrew word for emigration of Jews to Israel.

Beilis Trial In 1911, Mendel Beilis, a Jew from Kiev, was arrested and formally accused of the ritual murder of a young boy. Beilis was charged with having drained the blood from the boy while he was still alive, for use in baking *matzoh* for Passover. Despite pressure by the authorities, who produced "evidence" from witnesses who testified to Beilis' guilt, he was finally acquitted after having faced more than two years of shameful persecution. Beilis was aided by journalist Brazul Brushovsky, whose independent investigation exposed the farcical charges. This trial was reminiscent of the Dreyfus Affair in France in the mid-1890s.

Anti-Zionist Committee of the Soviet Public An "unofficial" group founded in April 1983 when eight "court Jews" appealed to the Soviet press for its creation. With branches in several Soviet cities, its main goal was to combat Zionism. Specifically, it aimed to provide the "real" Soviet perspective on Moscow's policies toward Soviet Jews, Israel, and the "CIA–Zionist conspiracy."

Babi Yar A ravine near Kiev, capital of the Ukraine, where Nazi soldiers, aided by Ukrainians, slaughtered over 50,000 Soviet citizens, mostly Jews. A monument on this site commemorates this massacre, but it contains no mention of Jewish victims. Until *glasnost,* Soviet authorities resisted efforts of Soviet Jews to hold memorial services at this site.

Basket III The section of the 1975 Helsinki Accords that deals with human contacts and basic human rights such as emigration, reunification of families, and freedom of religion and thought. Soviet Jews looked to this "basket" for international legal support for their struggle for freedom.

Birobidzhan In 1928 Stalin set aside this autonomous *Rayon* (district) as a "homeland" for Soviet Jews. In 1934 it gained the status of Jewish Autonomous

Oblast (region). It is a remote, barren area in Siberia, near the border of the People's Republic of China. This "homeland" concept has remained a fiction of Soviet propaganda. Fewer than 1 percent of the Soviet Jewish population (8897 based on the 1989 census) live there, and Jews comprise only about 4 percent of the entire population of the area.

Black Years of Soviet Jewry The last years of Stalin's rule, from 1948 through 1953, which were marked by especially virulent anti-Semitism, attempts to wipe out Jewish culture, and plans for the eventual elimination of Soviet Jews themselves through deportation to Siberia.

Brussels Conferences for the Defense of Soviet Jewry Two conferences, one in February 1971 and the other in February 1976, publicized the plight of Soviet Jews. They were attended by Jews and non-Jews from around the world. In October 1975 Western and Israeli government officials also met in Brussels to draw world attention to the Soviet Jewry problem.

Bukharan Jews Soviet Jews who live in Central Asia, especially in the Uzbek and Tadzhik republics. They are called such because when the tsar conquered this area, most of these Jews lived in the territory of the Amirate of Bukhara. Today, most live in the Uzbek cities of Samarkand, Tashkent, and Bukhara, and in several small towns. In the Tadzhik republic, almost all Bukharan Jews live in Dushanbe, the capital.

Cosmopolitans Stalin's code word for Jews. Soviet propaganda used this as a pejorative term to lash out against Soviet Jews for their alleged support of an anti-Soviet plot for world domination by international Zionism.

Democratizatsiya (democratization) Allowance by the Kremlin of a measure of popular political participation and decision-making. Not to be confused with democracy, where the people themselves are sovereign and choose all their political leaders.

Diploma tax A tax imposed in August 1972 by the Kremlin on emigrants, who were ordered to reimburse the state for their education. The higher their degree, the higher their tax. The Kremlin suspended this tax in March 1973 under pressure from the U.S. government and newly formed Soviet Jewry advocacy groups.

Dissidents Soviet citizens who try either to get the Soviet government to abide by its own laws and international commitments or to change what they consider unjust laws or applications of laws.

Dropouts Soviet Jews who emigrate with a visa to Israel but choose to go to another country. Most come from the "heartland" cities (especially Odessa,

Kiev, Moscow, and Leningrad), where Jews have been most assimilated. See also *Noshrim.*

Evrei v SSSR (Jews in the USSR) A Jewish *samizdat* journal that printed information on Soviet Jewish history, culture, and problems. It contained details on Soviet anti-Semitism and criticized distortions of Jewish history in the Soviet media and schools. It began in April 1972 and was published sporadically until 1979, when it was forced by the authorities to close down.

Glasnost The policy of "openness" fostered by President Gorbachev. Also the name of an independently published magazine on human rights in the U.S.S.R., prepared in Moscow. Its English-language edition is published by the Center for Democracy in the U.S.S.R. based in New York.

Haskalah The 17th- and 18th-century Jewish Enlightenment in Eastern Europe and Russia, that stressed assimilation for Jews as the best way for advancement and avoidance of anti-Semitism.

Hasidism The 17th- and 18th-century Jewish movement in Eastern Europe and Russia that advocated strengthening of traditional Judaism.

Heartland Jews Jews from the Soviet republics of Russia, the Ukraine, and Belorussia ("White Russia"). They comprise the majority of Soviet Jews and generally are the most assimilated.

Helsinki Accords On August 1, 1975, 35 countries, including the U.S. and the U.S.S.R., signed the Final Act of the Conference on Security and Cooperation in Europe (CSCE), also known as the Helsinki Accords. They contain three "baskets," affirming the European borders after World War II; calling for cooperation in military, economic, and technical areas as well as guidelines for cultural, educational, and human contacts; and pledging adherence to basic human rights.

Iskhod (Exodus) A Jewish *samizdat* journal dealing with Soviet Jewish emigration. It contained appeals, petitions, information on the Leningrad hijacking trial of 1970, and a variety of news items on the human rights struggle.

Iton Aleph and Iton Bet (Journal A and Journal B) The first Jewish *samizdat* publications, appearing in Riga in 1970. They contained articles on Jewish subjects, translations of Israeli authors, and other items of interest to Soviet Jews seeking their identity and freedom.

Jackson–Vanik Amendment An amendment to the Trade Reform Act of 1974, sponsored by Senator Henry Jackson and Congressman Charles Vanik. It stipulated that extension of credits and most-favored-nation benefits to the

U.S.S.R. or any other "nonmarket economy" depended on a significantly liberalized policy of emigration. The amendment did not specify Jewish emigration from the Soviet Union, though this was its main intent.

Leningrad Hijacking Trial of 1970 On June 15, 1970, Soviet authorities arrested nine Jewish activists and two non-Jews for planning to hijack an airplane from Smolny Airport in Leningrad and fly it to Israel. On December 15, the defendants stood trial for "crimes against the state." The severe sentences (two defendants received the death penalty) shocked Soviet Jews and Jews and governments around the world. After considerable pressure from Western governments and Western Soviet Jewry advocacy groups, the Soviets softened the sentences. All of the defendants were released by the early 1980s and allowed to leave the U.S.S.R.

Mountain Jews Soviet Jews who live mainly in the Daghestani Autonomous Socialist Republic and the Azerbaijani Republic. In Daghestan they live mainly in the cities of Derbent, Makhachqal'ah, and Buynaksk. In Azerbaijan they live mainly in Baku, the capital. Their native language is Tat, part of the Iranian family of languages.

Noshrim Hebrew word for dropouts who leave the U.S.S.R. with visas for Israel but go to another country.

Olim Hebrew word for those Jews who emigrate or make *aliyah* to Israel.

OVIR The Office of Visas and Registration to which Soviet citizens must apply to emigrate.

Pale of Settlement In 1794 Catherine the Great issued a ukase (edict) that confined Jews largely to those lands obtained by Russia after the partitioning of Poland. Its aim was to prevent Jews from competing economically with Russians or from "infecting" the members of the Russian Orthodox Church. Tsar Nicholas I further restricted Jewish residency and more cruelly oppressed Jews within the Pale. The Pale existed in its basic form until the revolution of February 1917, when the new Russian government removed anti-Jewish laws.

Pamyat An organization of extremist Russian nationalists, founded in the early 1980's, that blames Soviet Jews for a multitude of ills and shortcomings in Soviet society. Although ostensibly a private organization, it has received unofficial sanction from the state, which has allowed it to organize, demonstrate, and distribute anti-Semitic propaganda. *Pamyat* is comprised of numerous associations that share similar philosophy and goals.

Perestroika Restructuring the Soviet economy and society under Gorbachev's leadership. Goal is to achieve greater productivity through harder work, more competition, and some free enterprise.

Pogrom An organized physical attack on Soviet Jews, primarily in tsarist times.

Poor Relatives Group Soviet Jews unable to emigrate because their relatives will not sign affidavits acquitting them of all financial obligations.

Prisoner of Conscience Soviet citizen imprisoned for his religious practice, cultural observance, or attempts to emigrate.

Prisoner of Zion Jewish prisoner of conscience who aspires to emigrate to Israel.

Protocols of the Elders of Zion A forgery by the tsarist secret police in the late 1890s claiming that an international Jewish–Freemason conspiracy aims at world domination. Copies of *The Protocols*, or references to it, have surfaced regularly in the Soviet Union, the Middle East, and elsewhere.

Refusenik Soviet Jew whose request to emigrate has been officially refused. The "new refusenik," starting in 1989, is one who decides to reject membership and participation in the Communist Party and to take an independent political stance.

Samizdat Self-published, usually clandestine, literature dealing with freedom and human rights. Jewish *samizdat* disseminates information on Jewish culture, Jewish activism, and the emigration movement.

Shtetls Towns in the Pale of Settlement, where most Russian Jews lived under the tsars.

Sovetish heimland Official Yiddish literary monthly journal that began in 1961.

Stevenson Amendment Attached to Export-Import bill of 1974; extended Export-Import Bank for four years and limited credits to the U.S.S.R. to $300 million during this period. The president could grant additional credits only with congressional approval, which would depend on acceptable Soviet policy on arms control, the Middle East, and emigration.

Tamizdat Underground Soviet literature that is smuggled abroad, published there, and then smuggled back into the Soviet Union.

Vyzov A letter of invitation to emigrate, which until 1987 Soviet Jews needed from "first-degree" relatives in Israel in order to complete their visa applications. After July 1987, invitations could come from relatives in Israel or any country that had diplomatic relations with the U.S.S.R.

Yevrei Russian word for Jews. All Soviet Jews must list this "nationality" designation on line 5 of their internal passport.

Yordim Hebrew word for those who emigrate from Israel to other countries.

VAK The Soviet Higher Certification Commission, which confers academic degrees. VAK discriminated against Jewish degree applicants and in the early 1980s even revoked degrees held by refuseniks. In 1974, VAK was switched from the authority of the Ministry of Higher and Specialized Secondary Education to that of the Council of Ministers. Subsequently applicants for higher degrees had to "combine a profound professional knowledge with a mastery of Marxist-Leninist theory" and had to have "the convictions of an active builder of a Communist society."

Znaniye (Knowledge) Society Under aegis of the Communist party, holds meetings, conferences, seminars, and lectures on a variety of economic, political, and cultural issues. Its general aim is to educate citizens and instill party loyalty and Soviet patriotism. One of its specific aims is to disseminate "scientific-atheistic" propaganda. The society has its own reading rooms and information centers, and its publishing house puts out several journals, such as *Nauka i religiya (Science and Religion)*.

Chronology

1794
Catherine the Great decrees Jews must live only within the Pale of Settlement.

1897
First Congress of the *Bund* (the Jewish Social Democratic Union).

1903
The Kishinev pogrom in April sees about 45 Jews killed, between 400 and 600 injured, and more than 10,000 made homeless. This event sparks major protests inside the United States that influence President Theodore Roosevelt to lodge a protest to the tsarist government calling for more humane treatment of Russian Jews. Additional severe pogroms occur in 1905 and 1906.

1911
Mendel Beilis, a Jew from Kiev, is prosecuted for having committed ritual murder of a young boy. He is finally acquitted in 1913 after a journalist exposes the fabricated charges. Anti-Semitism surrounding this case is reminiscent of the Dreyfus Affair in France.

1918
Lenin establishes the *Yevsektsiya,* or Jewish section, of the Communist Party. Its main purpose is to destroy Soviet Judaism through assimilation. It is abolished in 1930, when Stalin opts for more centralized and personal control over the entire Soviet population.

1928
Stalin establishes a "homeland" for Soviet Jews in Birobidzhan, located in the Amur Basin of the Soviet Far East.

1941
In September, Nazis and Ukrainians massacre over 50,000 Jews and other Soviet citizens in Babi Yar, a ravine outside Kiev.

Chronology

1948
U.S.S.R. is first country to extend de jure diplomatic recognition to Israel, after supporting UN partition plan for creation of separate Jewish and Arab states. Stalin's support for Israel is short-lived, as he soon adopts a pro-Arab stance and resumes and intensifies campaign against Zionism.

1952
In August Stalin liquidates many outstanding Jewish writers in an episode called by historians the "Night of the Murdered Poets."

1953
In January, Stalin reveals his "Doctors' Plot." Jewish doctors are accused of various "plots" and "crimes," particularly the poisoning of Soviet leaders. The Kremlin exonerates the accused doctors in April, about one month after Stalin dies.

1961
Yevgeny Yevtushenko publishes *Babi Yar,* a poem that wonders "why there are no monuments at Babi Yar." The Kremlin finally erects a monument in 1976, with no specific mention of Jewish victims. This poem is an indirect indictment of Soviet anti-Semitism.

1966
Elie Wiesel publishes *The Jews of Silence,* which rouses and alerts the Western world to the plight of Soviet Jews.

1967
Six-Day War sparks birth of Soviet Jewish emigration movement.
Anti-Israel campaign begins in Poland; Polish Communist Party chief Gomulka calls Jews who support Israel a "fifth column."
On last day of Six-Day War, U.S.S.R. breaks diplomatic relations with Israel; rest of Communist East European states (except Romania) do same.
Kremlin cuts off Jewish emigration from June 1967 to September 1968.

1968
Soviet invasion of Czechoslovakia; Moscow blames Czech Jews for "evils" of Prague Spring; Soviet Jewish activists begin to see emigration as only solution to their ordeal.
Chronicle of Current Events, a *samizdat* monthly journal on human rights, begins publication.

1969
First appeal by Soviet Jews (from Georgia) to West.
Boris Kochubievsky, whose father and grandfather were killed at Babi Yar, tries

to emigrate but instead is tried and sentenced to three years in prison for "anti-Soviet slander."

1970

Leningrad trial of Jews who planned to hijack plane to Israel; court hands down severe sentences that are soon softened in wake of unprecedented outcry from the West.

First issue of Jewish *samizdat* newspaper *Exodus* is published.

1971

First World Jewish Conference on Soviet Jewry held in Brussels.

Soviet Jews send more petitions to West.

Beginning of large-scale Soviet Jewish emigration (13,022).

Soviet Jews start to stage demonstrations, sit-ins, and hunger strikes.

Second Leningrad trial and related trials of Jewish activists in Riga, Moscow, Vilnius, Kharkov, Kiev, and Tbilisi.

Formation of the Union of Councils for Soviet Jews (UCSJ) and National Conference on Soviet Jewry (NCSJ).

1972

Three-year $750-million grain deal between U.S. and U.S.S.R.

Nixon visits Moscow in May (first president to visit U.S.S.R. in peacetime); Jewish activists put under house arrest during visit.

Trials of Jewish activists in Moscow and other cities.

Kremlin initiates diploma tax on emigrants.

Senator Henry Jackson introduces amendment to Trade Bill linking most-favored-nation privileges to Soviet emigration policy.

99 percent of Soviet Jewish emigrants go to Israel.

1973

Yom Kippur War in Middle East.

Brezhnev visits U.S.

Soviets suspend diploma tax after pressure by Western governments and Soviet Jewry advocacy groups.

A record 34,000 Soviet Jews emigrate.

Chronicle of Human Rights in the USSR, a companion journal to the *Chronicle of Current Events*, begins publication in New York. It is published by Khronika Press and edited by Valery Chalidze.

1974

Solzhenitsyn is exiled to West.

Nixon visits Moscow.

Congress passes Jackson–Vanik and Stevenson amendments to Trade Bill and Export-Import Bill.

Chronology

1975

Thirty-five countries, including the U.S. and U.S.S.R., sign Helsinki Accords.
Andrei Sakharov receives Nobel Peace Prize but is not allowed to travel to Oslo to accept it.
Soviets, irritated over Jackson–Vanik and Stevenson amendments, cancel 1972 trade agreement with the U.S.
Kremlin institutes new tax laws on money received from abroad by Soviet citizens; law hits refuseniks hardest.

1976

Second World Conference on Soviet Jewry held in Brussels.
First Helsinki monitoring groups set up in Moscow and other Soviet cities.
Soviet authorities suppress "Symposium on Jewish Culture" scheduled to be held in Moscow.
Soviet television documentary *Traders of Souls* depicts refuseniks as "enemies of the state"; its showing marks the beginning of the Kremlin's use of TV as a weapon of anti-Semitism.

1977

Arrests of highly visible Jewish and non-Jewish activist leaders, including Shcharansky, Orlov, Slepaks, Nudel, and Begun.
First Helsinki Review Conference opens in Belgrade.
New Soviet Constitution goes into effect.
President Sadat of Egypt visits Jerusalem, leading to Camp David agreement.

1978

Conviction and sentencing of leading Jewish refuseniks and other Soviet human rights activists.
Helsinki monitoring group calls Shcharansky trial "a contemporary version of the Dreyfus trial."

1979

Peak year to date of Soviet Jewish emigration (over 51,000).
Carter–Brezhnev summit in Vienna, signing of SALT II.
Soviet invasion of Afghanistan signals end of détente.
Reversal of large-scale Jewish emigration.
New Soviet restrictions on emigration, such as institution of "first-degree" relative requirement for a visa, limitation of hours of OVIR offices, and closing of some OVIR offices.
Congress holds hearings on possible waiver of Jackson–Vanik Amendment. No change occurs.

1980
U.S. leads boycott of Summer Olympics in Moscow.
Sakharov stripped of academic honors and exiled to Gorky.
U.S. places embargo on grain exports to U.S.S.R.
Helsinki Review Conference begins in Madrid, lasts till September 1983.
Sentencing of Igor Guberman, an editor of *samizdat* journal *Jews in the USSR*, arrest of its editor-in-chief, Victor Brailovsky.

1981
U.S. lifts grain embargo against U.S.S.R., imposed earlier by Carter after Soviet invasion of Afghanistan.
Sentencing of Alexander Paritsky of Kharkov, founder of "Jewish Free University" for refuseniks.

1982
Brezhnev dies; Yuri Andropov becomes general secretary of Communist Party.
Further crackdown on Jewish intellectuals and dissidents.
Helsinki watch groups forced to disband.

1983
Formation of Anti-Zionist Committee of the Soviet Public.
Sentencing of Iosif Begun for third time.
Further drop in Jewish emigration.
New legislation makes it much riskier for Soviet citizens to have contacts with foreigners—hits refuseniks especially hard.

1984
Jewish emigration reaches nadir (896).
Increased crackdown against Jewish cultural activists.

1985
Gorbachev becomes general secretary of Communist Party after death of Chernenko, who led the Soviet Union for a short time after death of Andropov.
On state visit to France, Gorbachev says Jews refused permission to emigrate because of "state secrets" can leave after ten years. Gorbachev's deeds do not match his words, for many refuseniks cannot emigrate even after ten-year waiting period.
Helsinki Review Conference in Ottawa (May–June) and Budapest (October–November).
Agreement signed between American Bar Association and Association of Soviet Lawyers.
Reagan–Gorbachev summit in Geneva furthers thaw in U.S.–Soviet relations.

Chronology

1986

Shcharansky is released from gulag and emigrates to Israel.

Sakharov is released from internal exile in Gorky and returns to Moscow; resumes campaign for human rights.

Formation of Soviet Public Commission on International Cooperation on Humanitarian Issues and Human Rights (under Soviet CSCE).

Vienna Review Conference on Human Rights opens.

Reagan–Gorbachev summit in Rejkavik; Soviets soften stance on human rights.

1987

Release of many political prisoners and prisoners of conscience.

New emigration law goes into effect on January 1, disappoints Soviet activists.

Growth of *Pamyat,* which preaches anti-Semitism.

Many longtime refusenik leaders (e.g., Begun, Nudel, Slepaks) allowed to emigrate.

Jewish emigration up nine times over previous year.

Reagan–Gorbachev summit in Washington; signing of INF treaty.

Jackson–Vanik Amendment again under pressure for waiver, which does not occur.

Some former refuseniks allowed to visit U.S.S.R.

Formation of "Poor Relatives" group and group of "second generation" of refuseniks.

Secretary of State Shultz hosts Passover *seder* for Soviet refuseniks in Moscow.

Significant decrease in official anti-Semitic and anti-Zionist propaganda.

1988

Opening of first kosher restaurant in Moscow.

Israelis aid victims of Armenian earthquake.

Kremlin allows Bibles to be shipped to U.S.S.R.

Kremlin allows Hebrew to be taught for religious and cultural purposes.

Rabbi Shayevich and Cantor Pliss from Moscow's Choral Synagogue study for a few months at Yeshiva University in New York.

Release of most political prisoners and "prisoners of Zion."

Circulation of draft proposals for new laws on emigration, freedom of religion, and freedom of speech; Gorbachev calls for a "rule of law" with an independent judiciary.

Kremlin allows U.S. delegates from American Psychiatric Association and National Institute of Mental Health to visit Soviet psychiatric hospitals.

More than 10,000 Soviet Jews visit Israel as tourists.

Approximately 19,000 Soviet Jews emigrate.

1989

Soviet–Israeli relations warm up considerably.

Renewed pressure to waive Jackson–Vanik.

Increased grass-roots anti-Semitism in U.S.S.R.

Continuation of anti-Jewish discrimination in admission to institutes of higher education.

Opening of Jewish Cultural Center in Moscow.

38 Soviet Jewish activists found first B'nai B'rith chapter in Moscow.

Soviets reiterate claim Raoul Wallenberg died in Soviet prison (at hands of KGB).

U.S. institutes new policy on admitting Soviet Jews as refugees; Soviet Jews must now prove "well-founded fear of persecution."

Signing of most advanced human rights agreement in Vienna; first Conference of the Human Dimension in Paris; plans made for follow-up human rights conferences to be held in Copenhagen in 1990 and Moscow in 1991.

71,196 Soviet Jews emigrate, highest total since 1979.

Bush-Gorbachev summit off coast of Malta; Bush presses cases of refuseniks, declines to waive Jackson-Vanik until Kremlin codifies new policy on emigration.

First Convening of Congress of People's Deputies in U.S.S.R.

Founding of the Congress of the U.S.S.R. Jewish Organizations and Communities in Moscow.

First International Conference on Judaica ("The Historical Fates of the Jews in Russia and the USSR—The Beginning of a Dialogue") takes place in Moscow's Shalom Theater.

1990

Intensifying grass-roots anti-Semitism strikes fear among Soviet Jews.

Rumors of pogroms to occur on May 5 fail to materialize, but still cause Jews great stress and anxiety.

Record number of Soviet Jews emigrate (186,815), mostly to Israel, causing increased tension in the Middle East, in Israel's relations with the U.S. and U.S.S.R., and within Israel itself. Main diplomatic uproar is over prospects of settlement of Soviet Jews in the territories. Second Conference on the Human Dimension (CHD) in Copenhagen concludes with Soviet embrace of human rights concepts and multiparty democracy.

Bush-Gorbachev summit in Washington further promotes U.S.-Soviet good will, but Soviets fail to receive MFN because Supreme Soviet had not yet passed new emigration law.

Twenty-eighth Congress of the CPSU ends with hollow personal victory for Gorbachev.

Power of the CPSU continues to weaken; the Soviet economic crisis deepens; ethnic tensions and conflicts become more severe, political instability grows; and an increasing number of Soviet republics move toward autonomy or independence.

Soviet-Israeli diplomatic relations reach highest level since Moscow severed them at the end of the 1967 Six-Day War.

President Bush announces waiver of some restrictions of Jackson-Vanik Amendment.

Bibliography

Soviet Human Rights Activists

Alexeeva, Ludmilla. *Soviet Dissent: Contemporary Movements for National, Religious, and Human Rights.* Middleton, Ct.: Wesleyan University Press, 1985.

Azbel, Mark. *Refusenik.* New York: Paragon House, 1987.

Bukovsky, Vladimir. *To Build a Castle: My Life as a Dissenter.* Translated by Michael Scammel. New York: Viking, 1978.

Chalidze, Valery. *The Soviet Human Rights Movement: A Memoir.* New York: Jacob Blaustein Institute for the Advancement of Human Rights, 1984.

Freiman, Grigory. *It Seems I Am A Jew.* Translated and edited by Melvyn B. Nathanson. Carbondale, Ill.: Southern Illinois University Press, 1980.

Kuznetsov, Edward. *Prison Diaries.* Translated by Howard Spier. New York: Stein & Day, 1975.

Marchenko, Anatoly. *My Testimony.* Translated by Michael Scammel. New York: Dutton, 1969.

Rubin, Vitaly. "Moscow Testimony: Is There Any Hope for Those Who Choose to Stay?" *Present Tense,* Spring 1975, 55–59.

Rusinek, Alla. *Like a Song, Like a Dream.* New York: Scribner, 1973.

Sharansky, Natan. *Fear No Evil.* New York: Random House, 1988.

Stern, August. *The USSR vs. Dr. Mikhail Stern.* New York: Urizen Books, 1974.

Yakhot, Viktor, and Voronel, Alexander (eds.). *I Am a Jew.* New York: Academic Committee on Soviet Jewry, 1973.

———. *Jewishness Rediscovered.* New York: Academic Committee on Soviet Jewry, 1974.

Soviet Publications (in English)

Anti-Zionist Committee of the Soviet Public. *The White Book.* Moscow: Progress Publishers, 1981.

Dadiani, Lionel. *Zionism Through the Statements of Its Leaders.* Moscow: Novosti, 1986.

A Dictionary for Believers and Nonbelievers. Moscow: Progress Publishers, 1989.

Documents and Materials. 19th All-Union Conference of the CPSU. Moscow: Novosti, 1988.

Ivanov, Yuri. *Caution: Zionism!* Moscow: Progress Publishers, 1970.

Kostikov, Vyacheslav. *The People and Land of Birobidzhan.* Moscow: Novosti, 1979.

Kuritsyn, Vsevolod. *The Development of Rights and Freedoms in the Soviet State.* Moscow: Progress Publishers, 1987.

Lenin, V. I. *On the Jewish Question.* New York: International Publishers, 1934.

———. *Critical Remarks on the National Question.* Moscow: Progress Publishers, 1985.

Plenum of the CPSU Central Committee. *Towards a Humane and Democratic Socialist Society.* The Platform of the CPSU Central Committee. A Draft for the 28th Party Congress. Moscow: Novosti, 1990.

The Real Truth: Profiles of Soviet Jews. Moscow: Raduga Publishers, 1986.

Rokotov, S. "Zionism in the Fight Against Socialism and Détente," in *ZIONISM—Enemy of Peace and Progress,* Issue 4. Moscow: Progress Publishers, 1985, 36–80.

Rukhadze, Avtandil. *Jews in the USSR.* Moscow: Novosti, 1982.

Zivs, Samuil. *Human Rights: Continuing the Discussion.* Moscow: Progress Publishers, 1980.

United States Government Publications

U.S. Congress, Commission on Security and Cooperation in Europe, *Implementation of the Helsinki Accords, Repercussions of the Trials of the Helsinki Monitors in the USSR,* 95th Congress, 2d sess., July 11, 1978.

———. *Implementation of the Helsinki Accords, Human Rights and the CSCE Process,* 99th Congress, 1st sess., October 3, 1985.

———. *Implementation of the Helsinki Accords, Soviet and East European Emigration Policies,* 99th Congress, 2d sess., April 22, 1986.

———. *Implementation of the Helsinki Accords, Soviet Jewry Struggle,* 100th Congress, 1st sess., December 4, 1987.

———. *Reform and Human Rights, The Gorbachev Record,* 100th Congress, 2d sess., May 1988.

Western Authors: Books and Documents

Baron, Salo. *The Russian Jew under Tsars and Soviets.* 2d ed. New York: Schocken, 1987.

Cang, Joel. *The Silent Millions.* New York: Taplinger, 1969.

Cotler, Irwin. *The Shcharansky Appeal: Petition to the Procurator-General of the USSR from Avital Shcharansky, on behalf of herself and her husband, Anatoly Shcharansky, by her attorney Professor Irwin Cotler,* presented on August 30, 1978.

Decter, Moshe (ed.). *Redemption: Jewish Freedom Letters from Russia.* New York, 1974.

Freedman, Robert O. (ed.). *Soviet Jewry in the Decisive Decade, 1971–80.* Durham: Duke University Press, 1984.

———. *Soviet Jewry in the 1980s.* Durham: Duke University Press, 1989.

Gilbert, Martin, *Shcharansky, Hero of Our Time.* New York: Viking, 1986.

———. *The Jews of Hope.* New York: Viking, 1984.

Gitelman, Zvi. *A Century of Ambivalence: The Jews of Russia and the Soviet Union.* New York: Schocken, 1989.

Kochan, Lionel (ed.). *The Jews in Soviet Russia since 1917,* 3rd ed. New York: Oxford University Press, 1978.

Korey, William. *The Soviet Cage.* New York: Viking, 1973.

Levin, Nora. *The Jews in the Soviet Union Since 1917,* 2 vols. New York: New York University Press, 1988.

Low, Alfred. *Soviet Jewry and Soviet Policy*, New York: Columbia University Press, 1990.

Pinkus, Benjamin. *The Jews of the Soviet Union.* Cambridge: Cambridge University Press, 1988.

Rubenstein, Joshua. *Soviet Dissidents: Their Struggle for Human Rights,* 2d ed. Boston: Beacon, 1985.

Sawyer, Thomas. *The Jewish Minority in the Soviet Union.* Boulder, Colo.: Westview Press, 1979.

Schroeter, Leonard. *The Last Exodus,* 2d ed. Seattle: University of Washington Press, 1979.

Shindler, Colin. *Exit Visa: Détente, Human Rights and the Jewish Emigration Movement.* London: Bachin and Turner, 1978.

Smolar, Boris. *Soviet Jewry Today and Tomorrow.* New York: Macmillan, 1971.

Stern, Paula. *Water's Edge. Domestic Politics and the Making of American Foreign Policy.* Westport, Ct.: Greenwood Press, 1979.

Taylor, Telford, with Alan Dershowitz et al. *Courts of Terror: Soviet Criminal Justice and Jewish Emigration.* New York: Knopf, 1976.

Wiesel, Elie. *The Jews of Silence.* New York: Holt, 1966.

Western Authors: Articles

Albright, Joseph. "Pact of Two Henrys: Trade Bill Amendment Linked to Russian Emigration," *New York Times Magazine,* January 5, 1979, 22–27.

Boiman, Igor. "Jewish Emigration from the USSR: Some Observations," *Soviet Jewish Affairs,* Vol. 9., No. 2, 1979, 46–63.

Brovkin, Vladimir. "Revolution from Below: Informal Political Associations in Russia 1988–1989," *Soviet Studies,* Vol. 42, No. 2, April 1990, 233–257.

Dalos, Gyorgy, "What Is Pamyat?" *Across Frontiers,* Vol. 5, No. 2, Summer 1989, 7–8ff.

"Exodus, revised version," *The Economist,* Vol. 313, No. 7634/7635, 55–56.

Gitelman, Zvi. "Moscow and the Soviet Jews: A Parting of the Ways," *Problems of Communism,* Vol. XXIX, January–February 1980, 18–34.

Goldman, Karla. "Pogroms and Perestroika," *World Monitor,* Vol. 3, No. 5, May 1990, 16–19.

Jaffe, Daniel. "Refusenik Life," *Soviet Jewish Affairs,* Vol. 8, No. 2, 1978, 24–35.

Keller, Bill. "Russian Nationalists: Yearning for an Iron Hand," *New York Times Magazine,* January 28, 1990, 18–21, 46, 48, 50.

Korey, William. "International Law and the Right to Study Hebrew in the USSR," *Soviet Jewish Affairs,* Vol. 11, No. 1, 1981, 3–18.

———. "The Future of Soviet Jewry: Emigration and Assimilation," *Foreign Affairs,* Vol. 58, No. 1, Fall 1979, 67–81.

———. "Helsinki in Paris," *New Leader,* Vol. LXII, No. 11, July 10–24, 1989, 12–14.

———. "The Critical Human Right," New York: B'nai B'rith International, 1987.

Kuznetsov, Edward. "Flight from the Gulag," Translated by L. Thorne. *New York Times Magazine,* April 27, 1980, 36–41.

Laqueur, Walter. "From Russia with Hate," *The New Republic,* Vol. 202, No. 6, February 5, 1990, 21–25.

Lazaris, Vladimir. "The Saga of Jewish Samizdat," *Soviet Jewish Affairs,* Vol. 9, No. 1, 1979, 4–19.

Meeter, Stephen. "The Relation of the Helsinki Final Act to the Emigration of Soviet Jews," *Boston College International and Comparative Law Journal,* Vol. 1, No. 1, 1977, 111–147.

Paramonov, Boris. "The Culture of Soviet Anti-Semitism," *Partisan Review,* Vol. LVII, No. 2, Spring 1990, 193–201.

Reddaway, Peter. "Dissent in the Soviet Union," *Problems of Communism,* Vol. XXXII, November–December 1983, 1–15.

Rosenfield, Barbara and Stephen. "Soviet Jewry at the Crossroads," *Present Tense,* Vol. 16, No. 6, September/October 1989, 24–31.

Rosensaft, Menachem Z. "The Legal Status of Soviet Jewry: De Jure Equality and De Facto Discrimination," *Columbia Human Rights Law Review;* October 29, 1979, 575–604.

Sinyavsky, Andrei. "Russophobia," *Partisan Review,* Vol. LVII, No. 3, Summer 1990, 339–344.

Wishnevsky, Julia. "The Origins of Pamyat," *Survey,* Vol. 30, No. 3, October 1988, 79–91.

Soviet Jewry Advocacy Groups
Newsletters and Bulletins

ENGLAND

Insight: Soviet Jews (London)

Institute for Jewish Affairs Research Report (London)

Jews in the USSR (London)

Women's Campaign for Soviet Jewry, *35's Circular* (London)

ISRAEL

The Israel Public Council for Soviet Jewry, *Focus Soviet Jewry*

Scientists Committee of the Israel Public Council for Soviet Jewry, *News Bulletin*

Soviet Jewish Education and Information Center, *Bulletin*

UNITED STATES

Action for Soviet Jewry, *Soviet Jewry Report,* and *Medical Mobilization for Soviet Jewry* (Waltham, Mass.)

Chicago Action for Soviet Jewry, *Refusenik*

Coalition to Free Soviet Jews, *Lifeline* (New York)

National Conference on Soviet Jewry, *NEWSBREAK*

National Interreligious Task Force on Soviet Jewry, *The Task* (Chicago)

Student Struggle for Soviet Jewry, *Soviet Jewry Action Newsletter*

Union of Councils for Soviet Jews, *Alert*

Washington Committee for Soviet Jewry, *The Vigil*

Index